Big Book of
Winners, Losers and Honoured

Complete guide through
all Academy Awards® Ceremonies

1929 - 2022

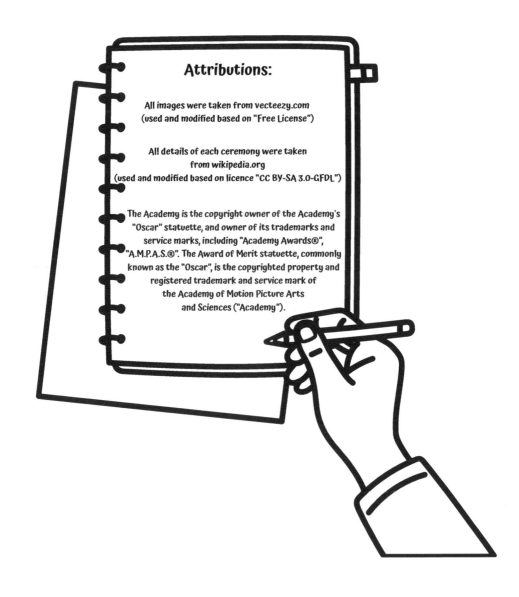

Attributions:

All images were taken from vecteezy.com
(used and modified based on "Free License")

All details of each ceremony were taken
from wikipedia.org
(used and modified based on licence "CC BY-SA 3.0-GFDL")

The Academy is the copyright owner of the Academy's
"Oscar" statuette, and owner of its trademarks and
service marks, including "Academy Awards®",
"A.M.P.A.S.®". The Award of Merit statuette, commonly
known as the "Oscar", is the copyrighted property and
registered trademark and service mark of
the Academy of Motion Picture Arts
and Sciences ("Academy").

The 1st Academy Awards® - May 16, 1929

Host: Douglas Fairbanks
Venue: Blossom Room of the Hollywood Roosevelt Hotel
Honoring movies released: August 1, 1927 - August 1, 1928

Best Actor

⚐ Emil Jannings ⚐
The Last Command (1928) role "Grand Duke Sergius Alexander",
The Way of All Flesh (1927) role "August Schilling"

Richard Barthelmess
The Noose (1928) role "Nickie Elkins",
The Patent Leather Kid (1927) role "Patent Leather Kid"

Best Actress

⚐ Janet Gaynor ⚐
7th Heaven (1927) role "Diane", Street Angel (1928) role "Angela",
Sunrise: A Song of Two Humans (1927) role "The Wife"

Louise Dresser
A Ship Comes In (1928) role "Mrs. Pleznik"

Gloria Swanson
Sadie Thompson (1928) role "Sadie Thompson"

Best Art Direction

⚐ William Cameron Menzies ⚐
The Dove (1927), Tempest (1928)

Rochus Gliese
Sunrise: A Song of Two Humans (1927)

Harry Oliver
7th Heaven (1927)

Best Engineering Effects

⚐ Roy Pomeroy ⚐
Wings (1927)

Ralph Hammeras
this nomination was not associated with any individual film title

Nugent Slaughter
this nomination was not associated with any individual film title

Best Outstanding Picture

⚐ Paramount Famous Lasky ⚐
Wings (1927)

The Caddo Company
The Racket (1928)

Fox
7th Heaven (1927)

Best Cinematography
⚱ **Charles Rosher, Karl Struss** ⚱
Sunrise: A Song of Two Humans (1927)
George Barnes
Sadie Thompson (1928), The Devil Dancer (1927), The Magic Flame (1927)

Best Directing, Comedy Picture
⚱ **Lewis Milestone** ⚱
Two Arabian Knights (1927)
Ted Wilde
Speedy (1928)

Best Directing, Dramatic Picture
⚱ **Frank Borzage** ⚱
7th Heaven (1927)
Herbert Brenon
Sorrell and Son (1927)
King Vidor
The Crowd (1928)

Best Unique and Artistic Picture
⚱ **Fox** ⚱
Sunrise: A Song of Two Humans (1927)
Metro-Goldwyn-Mayer
The Crowd (1928)
Paramount Famous Lasky
Chang: A Drama of the Wilderness (1927)

Honorary Award
⚱ **Charles Chaplin** ⚱
for acting, writing, directing and producing The Circus (1928)
⚱ **Warner Bros.** ⚱
for producing The Jazz Singer (1927) and pioneering in talking picture.

Best Writing, Adaptation
⚱ **Benjamin Glazer** ⚱
7th Heaven (1927)
Alfred A. Cohn
The Jazz Singer (1927)
Anthony Coldeway
Glorious Betsy (1928)

Best Writing, Original Story
⚱ **Ben Hecht** ⚱
Underworld (1927)
Lajos Biró
The Last Command (1928)

Best Writing, Title Writing
⚱ **Joseph Farnham** ⚱
this nomination was not associated with any individual film title
Gerald C. Duffy
(Posthumous)
The Private Life of Helen of Troy (1927)
George Marion Jr.
this nomination was not associated with any individual film title

The 2ⁿᵈ Academy Awards® - April 3, 1930
Host: William C. de Mille
Venue: Cocoanut Grove of the Ambassador Hotel
Honoring movies released: August 1, 1928 - July 31, 1929

Best Actor
⚱ **Warner Baxter** ⚱
In Old Arizona (1928) role "The Cisco Kid"
George Bancroft
Thunderbolt (1929) role "Thunderbolt Jim Lang"
Chester Morris
Alibi (1929) role "Chick Williams"
Paul Muni
The Valiant (1929) role "James Dyke"
Lewis Stone
The Patriot (1928) role "Count Pahlen"

Best Actress
⚱ **Mary Pickford** ⚱
Coquette (1929) role "Norma Besant"
Ruth Chatterton
Madame X (1929) role "Jacqueline Floriot"
Betty Compson
The Barker (1928) role "Carrie"
Jeanne Eagels
(Posthumous)
The Letter (1929) role "Leslie Crosbie"
Corinne Griffith
The Divine Lady (1928) role "Emma Hart"
Bessie Love
The Broadway Melody (1929) role "Harriet 'Hank' Mahoney"

Best Cinematography
⚱ **Clyde De Vinna** ⚱
White Shadows in the South Seas (1928)
George Barnes
Our Dancing Daughters (1928)
Arthur Edeson
In Old Arizona (1928)
Ernest Palmer
4 Devils (1928), Street Angel (1928)
John F. Seitz
The Divine Lady (1928)

Best Writing

⚱ Hanns Kräly ⚱
The Patriot (1928)

Tom Barry
In Old Arizona (1928), The Valiant (1929)

Elliott J. Clawson
Sal of Singapore (1928), Skyscraper (1928), The Cop (1928), The Leatherneck (1929)

Hanns Kräly
The Last of Mrs. Cheyney (1929)

Josephine Lovett
Our Dancing Daughters (1928)

Bess Meredyth
A Woman of Affairs (1928), Wonder of Women (1929)

Best Outstanding Picture

⚱ Metro-Goldwyn-Mayer ⚱
The Broadway Melody (1929)

Feature Productions
Alibi (1929)

Fox
In Old Arizona (1928)

Metro-Goldwyn-Mayer
The Hollywood Revue of 1929 (1929)

Paramount Famous Lasky
The Patriot (1928)

Best Art Direction

⚱ Cedric Gibbons ⚱
The Bridge of San Luis Rey (1929)

Hans Dreier
The Patriot (1928)

Mitchell Leisen
Dynamite (1929)

William Cameron Menzies
Alibi (1929), The Awakening (1928)

Harry Oliver
Street Angel (1928)

Best Directing

⚱ Frank Lloyd ⚱
The Divine Lady (1928)

Lionel Barrymore
Madame X (1929)

Harry Beaumont
The Broadway Melody (1929)

Irving Cummings
In Old Arizona (1928)

Frank Lloyd
Drag (1929), Weary River (1929)

Ernst Lubitsch
The Patriot (1928)

The 3rd Academy Awards® - November 5, 1930

Host: Conrad Nagel
Venue: Fiesta Room of the Ambassador Hotel
Honoring movies released: August 1, 1929 - July 31, 1930

Best Actress

⚊ Norma Shearer ⚊
The Divorcee (1930) role "Jerry Bernard Martin"

Nancy Carroll
The Devil's Holiday (1930) role "Hallie Hobart"

Ruth Chatterton
Sarah and Son (1930) role "Sarah Storm"

Greta Garbo
Anna Christie (1930) role "Anna Christie", Romance (1930) role "Madame Rita Cavallini"

Norma Shearer
Their Own Desire (1929) role "Lucia (Lally) Marlett"

Gloria Swanson
The Trespasser (1929) role "Marion Donnell"

Best Actor

⚊ George Arliss ⚊
Disraeli (1929) role "Benjamin Disraeli"

George Arliss
The Green Goddess (1930) role "The Raja"

Wallace Beery
The Big House (1930) role "Machine Gun 'Butch' Schmidt"

Maurice Chevalier
The Big Pond (1930) role "Pierre Mirande",
The Love Parade (1929) role "Count Alfred Renard"

Ronald Colman
Bulldog Drummond (1929) role "Captain Hugh 'Bulldog' Drummond",
Condemned! (1929) role "Michel Oman"

Lawrence Tibbett
The Rogue Song (1930) role "Yegor"

Best Sound Recording

Douglas Shearer (Sound Director),
Metro-Goldwyn-Mayer Studio Sound Department
The Big House (1930)

George Groves (Sound Director),
First National Studio Sound Department
The Song of the Flame (1930)

Franklin Hansen (Sound Director),
Paramount Famous Lasky Studio Sound Department
The Love Parade (1929)

Oscar Lagerstrom (Sound Director),
United Artists Studio Sound Department
Raffles (1930)

John E. Tribby (Sound Director),
RKO Radio Studio Sound Department
The Case of Sergeant Grischa (1930)

Best Cinematography
⚑ Joseph T. Rucker, Willard Van der Veer ⚑
With Byrd at the South Pole (1930)

William H. Daniels
Anna Christie (1930)

Arthur Edeson
All Quiet on the Western Front (1930)

Gaetano (Tony) Gaudio, Harry Perry
Hell's Angels (1930)

Victor Milner
The Love Parade (1929)

Best Outstanding Production
⚑ Universal ⚑
All Quiet on the Western Front (1930)

Cosmopolitan
The Big House (1930)

Metro-Goldwyn-Mayer
The Divorcee (1930)

Paramount Famous Lasky
The Love Parade (1929)

Warner Bros.
Disraeli (1929)

Best Writing
⚑ Frances Marion ⚑
The Big House (1930)

George Abbott, Maxwell Anderson, Del Andrews
All Quiet on the Western Front (1930)

Howard Estabrook
Street of Chance (1930)

Julien Josephson
Disraeli (1929)

John Meehan
The Divorcee (1930)

Best Directing
⚑ Lewis Milestone ⚑
All Quiet on the Western Front (1930)

Clarence Brown
Anna Christie (1930), Romance (1930)

Robert Z. Leonard
The Divorcee (1930)

Ernst Lubitsch
The Love Parade (1929)

King Vidor
Hallelujah (1929)

Best Art Direction
⬇ **Herman Rosse** ⬇
King of Jazz (1930)
Hans Dreier
The Love Parade (1929), The Vagabond King (1930)
William Cameron Menzies
Bulldog Drummond (1929)
Jack Okey
Sally (1929)

The 4ᵗʰ Academy Awards® - November 10, 1931
Host: Lawrence Grant
Venue: Sala D'Oro in the Biltmore Hotel
Honoring movies released: August 1, 1930 - July 31, 1931

Best Actor
⬇ **Lionel Barrymore** ⬇
A Free Soul (1931) role "Stephen Ashe"
Jackie Cooper
Skippy (1931) role "Skippy Skinner"
Richard Dix
Cimarron (1931) role "Yancey Cravat"
Fredric March
The Royal Family of Broadway (1930) role "Tony Cavendish"
Adolphe Menjou
The Front Page (1931) role "Walter Burns"

Best Actress
⬇ **Marie Dressler** ⬇
Min and Bill (1930) role "Min Divot"
Marlene Dietrich
Morocco (1930) role "Mademoiselle Amy Jolly"
Irene Dunne
Cimarron (1931) role "Sabra Cravat"
Ann Harding
Holiday (1930) role "Linda Seton"
Norma Shearer
A Free Soul (1931) role "Jan Ashe"

Best Art Direction
⬇ **Max Rée** ⬇
Cimarron (1931)
Richard Day
Whoopee! (1930)
Hans Dreier
Morocco (1930)
Stephen Goosson, Ralph Hammeras
Just Imagine (1930)
Anton Grot
Svengali (1931)

Best Cinematography

⚊ Floyd Crosby ⚊
Tabu: A Story of the South Seas (1931)

Edward Cronjager
Cimarron (1931)

Lee Garmes
Morocco (1930)

Charles Lang
The Right to Love (1930)

Barney McGill
Svengali (1931)

Best Writing, Original Story

⚊ John Monk Saunders ⚊
The Dawn Patrol (1930)

Harry d'Abbadie d'Arrast, Douglas Z. Doty, Donald Ogden Stewart
Laughter (1930)

John Bright, Kubec Glasmon
The Public Enemy (1931)

Rowland Brown
The Doorway to Hell (1930)

Lucien Hubbard, Joseph Jackson
Smart Money (1931)

Best Directing

⚊ Norman Taurog ⚊
Skippy (1931)

Clarence Brown
A Free Soul (1931)

Lewis Milestone
The Front Page (1931)

Wesley Ruggles
Cimarron (1931)

Josef von Sternberg
Morocco (1930)

Best Outstanding Production

⚊ RKO Radio ⚊
Cimarron (1931)

Fox
East Lynne (1931)

Metro-Goldwyn-Mayer
Trader Horn (1931)

Paramount Publix
Skippy (1931)

The Caddo Company
The Front Page (1931)

Best Writing, Adaptation
⚱ Howard Estabrook ⚱
Cimarron (1931)
Francis Edward Faragoh, Robert N. Lee
Little Caesar (1931)
Horace Jackson
Holiday (1930)
Joseph L. Mankiewicz, Sam Mintz
Skippy (1931)
Seton I. Miller, Fred Niblo Jr.
The Criminal Code (1930)

Best Sound Recording
(all nominations were not associated with any individual film title)
⚱ Paramount Publix Studio Sound Department ⚱
Metro-Goldwyn-Mayer Studio Sound Department
RKO Radio Studio Sound Department
Samuel Goldwyn - United Artists Studio Sound Department

The 5ᵗʰ Academy Awards® - November 18, 1932
Hosts: Lionel Barrymore, Conrad Nagel
Venue: Fiesta Room of the Ambassador Hotel
Honoring movies released: August 1, 1931 - July 31, 1932

Best Actor
⚱ Wallace Beery ⚱
The Champ (1931) role "Andy Purcell - The Champ"
⚱ Fredric March ⚱
Dr. Jekyll and Mr. Hyde (1931) role "Dr. Henry Jekyll / Mr. Edward Hyde"
Alfred Lunt
The Guardsman (1931) role "The Actor"

Best Actress
⚱ Helen Hayes ⚱
The Sin of Madelon Claudet (1931) role "Madelon Claudet"
Marie Dressler
Emma (1932) role "Emma Thatcher Smith"
Lynn Fontanne
The Guardsman (1931) role "The Actress"

Best Writing, Original Story
⚱ Frances Marion ⚱
The Champ (1931)
Lucien Hubbard
The Star Witness (1931)
Grover Jones, William Slavens McNutt
Lady and Gent (1932)
Jane Murfin, Adela Rogers St. Johns
What Price Hollywood? (1932)

Best Writing, Adaptation
⚊ Edwin J. Burke ⚊
Bad Girl (1931)
Percy Heath, Samuel Hoffenstein
Dr. Jekyll and Mr. Hyde (1931)
Sidney Howard
Arrowsmith (1931)

Best Outstanding Production
⚊ Metro-Goldwyn-Mayer ⚊
Grand Hotel (1932)
First National
Five Star Final (1931)
Fox
Bad Girl (1931)
Metro-Goldwyn-Mayer
The Champ (1931)
Paramount Publix
One Hour with You (1932), Shanghai Express (1932), The Smiling Lieutenant (1931)
Samuel Goldwyn Productions
Arrowsmith (1931)

Best Art Direction
⚊ Gordon Wiles ⚊
Transatlantic (1931)
Richard Day
Arrowsmith (1931)
Lazare Meerson
À nous la liberté (1931)

Best Cinematography
⚊ Lee Garmes ⚊
Shanghai Express (1932)
Ray June
Arrowsmith (1931)
Karl Struss
Dr. Jekyll and Mr. Hyde (1931)

Best Directing
⚊ Frank Borzage ⚊
Bad Girl (1931)
Josef von Sternberg
Shanghai Express (1932)
King Vidor
The Champ (1931)

Honorary Award
⚊ Walt Disney ⚊
For the creation of Mickey Mouse.

Best Short Subject, Cartoon

ǂ **Walt Disney (Producer)** ǂ
Flowers and Trees (1932)

Walt Disney (Producer)
Mickey's Orphans (1931)

Leon Schlesinger (Producer)
It's Got Me Again! (1932)

Best Short Subject, Novelty

ǂ **Mack Sennett (Producer)** ǂ
Wrestling Swordfish (1931)

Metro-Goldwyn-Mayer
Swing High (1932)

Paramount Publix
Screen Souvenirs (1932)

Best Short Subject, Comedy

ǂ **Hal Roach (Producer)** ǂ
The Music Box (1932)

Mack Sennett (Producer)
The Loud Mouth (1932)

RKO Radio
Scratch-As-Catch-Can (1931)

Masquers Club
(Film was disqualified. No reason was given for the disqualification.)
Stout Hearts and Willing Hands (1931)

Best Sound Recording

(all nominations were not associated with any individual film title)

ǂ **Paramount Publix Studio Sound Department** ǂ
Metro-Goldwyn-Mayer Studio Sound Department
RKO Radio Studio Sound Department
Warner Bros. First National Studio Sound Department

The 6ᵗʰ Academy Awards® - March 16, 1934

Host: Will Rogers

Venue: Fiesta Room of the Ambassador Hotel

Honoring movies released: August 1, 1932 - December 31, 1933

Best Actor

ǂ **Charles Laughton** ǂ
The Private Life of Henry VIII (1933) role "King Henry VIII of England"

Leslie Howard
Berkeley Square (1933) role "Captain Peter Standish"

Paul Muni
I Am a Fugitive from a Chain Gang (1932) role "James Allen"

Best Actress
⚱ Katharine Hepburn ⚱
Morning Glory (1933) role "Eva Lovelace"
May Robson
Lady for a Day (1933) role "Apple Annie"
Diana Wynyard
Cavalcade (1933) role "Jane Marryot"

Best Art Direction
⚱ William S. Darling ⚱
Cavalcade (1933)
Roland Anderson, Hans Dreier
A Farewell to Arms (1932)
Cedric Gibbons
When Ladies Meet (1933)

Best Cinematography
⚱ Charles Bryant Lang Jr. ⚱
A Farewell to Arms (1932)
George J. Folsey
Reunion in Vienna (1933)
Karl Struss
The Sign of the Cross (1932)

Best Directing
⚱ Frank Lloyd ⚱
Cavalcade (1933)
Frank Capra
Lady for a Day (1933)
George Cukor
Little Women (1933)

Best Outstanding Production
⚱ Fox ⚱
Cavalcade (1933)
Columbia
Lady for a Day (1933)
Fox
State Fair (1933)
London Films
The Private Life of Henry VIII (1933)
Metro-Goldwyn-Mayer
Smilin' Through (1932)
Paramount
A Farewell to Arms (1932), She Done Him Wrong (1933)
RKO Radio
Little Women (1933)
Warner Bros.
42nd Street (1933), I Am a Fugitive from a Chain Gang (1932)

Best Assistant Director

(all nominations were not associated with any individual film title)

⚑ Charles Barton (Paramount) ⚑
⚑ Scott Beal (Universal) ⚑
⚑ Charles Dorian (Metro-Goldwyn-Mayer) ⚑
⚑ Fred Fox (United Artists) ⚑
⚑ Gordon Hollingshead (Warner Bros.) ⚑
⚑ William Tummel (Fox) ⚑
⚑ Dewey Starkey (RKO Radio) ⚑
Al Alborn (Warner Bros.)
Sidney S. Brod (Paramount)
Orville O. Dull (Metro-Goldwyn-Mayer)
Percy Ikerd (Fox)
Arthur Jacobson (Paramount)
Eddie Killey (RKO Radio)
Joe McDonough (Universal)
W. J. Reiter (Universal)
Frank X. Shaw (Warner Bros.)
Benjamin Silvey (United Artists)
John S. Waters (Metro-Goldwyn-Mayer)

Best Short Subject, Cartoon

⚑ Walt Disney (Producer) ⚑
Three Little Pigs (1933)

Walt Disney (Producer)
Building a Building (1933)

Walter Lantz (Producer)
The Merry Old Soul (1933)

Best Short Subject, Comedy

⚑ Lou Brock (Producer) ⚑
So This Is Harris! (1933)

Lou Brock (Producer)
A Preferred List (1933)

Warren Doane (Producer)
Mister Mugg (1933)

Best Short Subject, Novelty

⚑ Joe Rock (Producer) ⚑
Krakatoa (1933)

Educational
The Sea (1933)

Pete Smith (Producer)
Menu (1933)

Best Writing, Adaptation

⚑ Victor Heerman, Sarah Y. Mason ⚑
Little Women (1933)

Paul Green, Sonya Levien
State Fair (1933)

Robert Riskin
Lady for a Day (1933)

Best Writing, Original Story
⚑ **Robert Lord** ⚑
One Way Passage (1932)
Charles MacArthur
Rasputin and the Empress (1932)
Frances Marion
The Prizefighter and the Lady (1933)

Best Sound Recording
⚑ **Franklin Hansen (Sound Director),** ⚑
Paramount Studio Sound Department
A Farewell to Arms (1932)
Nathan Levinson (Sound Director),
Warner Bros. Studio Sound Department
42nd Street (1933), Gold Diggers of 1933 (1933), I Am a Fugitive from a Chain Gang (1932)

The 7ᵗʰ Academy Awards® - February 27, 1935
Host: Irvin S. Cobb
Venue: Biltmore Bowl of the Biltmore Hotel
Honoring movies released in 1934

Best Actor
⚑ **Clark Gable** ⚑
It Happened One Night (1934) role "Peter Warne"
Frank Morgan
The Affairs of Cellini (1934) role "Alessandro, Duke of Florence"
William Powell
The Thin Man (1934) role "Nick Charles"

Best Actress
⚑ **Claudette Colbert** ⚑
It Happened One Night (1934) role "Ellie Andrews"
Bette Davis
Of Human Bondage (1934) role "Mildred Rogers"
Grace Moore
One Night of Love (1934) role "Mary Barrett"
Norma Shearer
The Barretts of Wimpole Street (1934) role "Elizabeth Barrett"

Best Music, Song
⚑ **Con Conrad (Music), Herb Magidson (Lyrics)** ⚑
for the song "The Continental"
The Gay Divorcee (1934)
Ralph Rainger (Music), Leo Robin (Lyrics) for the song "Love in Bloom"
She Loves Me Not (1934)
Vincent Youmans (Music), Edward Eliscu, Gus Kahn (Lyrics)
for the song "Carioca"
Flying Down to Rio (1933)

Best Music, Scoring

Louis Silvers (Head of Department),
Columbia Studio Music Department,
Thematic music by Victor Schertzinger, Gus Kahn
One Night of Love (1934)

Max Steiner (Head of Department), RKO Radio Studio Music Department,
Score by Kenneth S. Webb, Samuel Hoffenstein
The Gay Divorcee (1934)

Max Steiner (Head of Department),
RKO Radio Studio Music Department, Score by Max Steiner
The Lost Patrol (1934)

Best Art Direction

Cedric Gibbons, Fredric Hope
The Merry Widow (1934)

Carroll Clark, Van Nest Polglase
The Gay Divorcee (1934)

Richard Day
The Affairs of Cellini (1934)

Best Outstanding Production

Columbia
It Happened One Night (1934)

20th Century
The House of Rothschild (1934)

Columbia
One Night of Love (1934)

First National
Flirtation Walk (1934)

Jesse L. Lasky (Production Company)
The White Parade (1934)

Metro-Goldwyn-Mayer
The Barretts of Wimpole Street (1934), The Thin Man (1934), Viva Villa! (1934)

Paramount
Cleopatra (1934)

RKO Radio
The Gay Divorcee (1934)

Universal
Imitation of Life (1934)

Warner Bros.
Here Comes the Navy (1934)

Best Assistant Director

John Waters
Viva Villa! (1934)

Scott R. Beal
Imitation of Life (1934)

Cullen Tate
Cleopatra (1934)

Best Sound Recording

**John P. Livadary (Sound Director),
Columbia Studio Sound Department**
One Night of Love (1934)

Carl Dreher (Sound Director), RKO Radio Studio Sound Department
The Gay Divorcee (1934)

**Douglas Shearer (Sound Director),
Metro-Goldwyn-Mayer Studio Sound Department**
Viva Villa! (1934)

Edmund H. Hansen (Sound Director), Fox Studio Sound Department
The White Parade (1934)

Franklin Hansen (Sound Director), Paramount Studio Sound Department
Cleopatra (1934)

**Nathan Levinson (Sound Director),
Warner Bros. First National Studio Sound Department**
Flirtation Walk (1934)

Theodore Soderberg (Sound Director), Universal Studio Sound Department
Imitation of Life (1934)

**Thomas T. Moulton (Sound Director),
United Artists Studio Sound Department**
The Affairs of Cellini (1934)

Juvenile Award

Shirley Temple

for outstanding contribution to screen entertainment during the year 1934

Best Cinematography

Victor Milner
Cleopatra (1934)

George J. Folsey
Operator 13 (1934)

Charles Rosher
The Affairs of Cellini (1934)

Best Directing

Frank Capra
It Happened One Night (1934)

Victor Schertzinger
One Night of Love (1934)

W.S. Van Dyke
The Thin Man (1934)

Best Film Editing

Conrad A. Nervig
Eskimo (1933)

Anne Bauchens
Cleopatra (1934)

Gene Milford
One Night of Love (1934)

Best Short Subject, Cartoon

⬇ **Walt Disney (Producer)** ⬇
The Tortoise and the Hare (1935)

Walter Lantz (Producer)
Jolly Little Elves (1934)

Charles Mintz (Producer)
Holiday Land (1934)

Best Short Subject, Comedy

⬇ **Kenneth Macgowan (Producer)** ⬇
La Cucaracha (1934)

Warner Bros.
What, No Men? (1935)

Jules White (Producer)
Men in Black (1934)

Best Short Subject, Novelty

⬇ **Horace Woodard, Stacy Woodard (Producers)** ⬇
City of Wax (1934)

Skibo Productions
Bosom Friends (1934)

Pete Smith (Producer)
Strikes and Spares (1934)

Best Writing, Adaptation

⬇ **Robert Riskin** ⬇
It Happened One Night (1934)

Frances Goodrich, Albert Hackett
The Thin Man (1934)

Ben Hecht
Viva Villa! (1934)

Best Writing, Original Story

⬇ **Arthur Caesar** ⬇
Manhattan Melodrama (1934)

Mauri Grashin
Hide-Out (1934)

Norman Krasna
The Richest Girl in the World (1934)

The 8ᵗʰ Academy Awards® - March 5, 1936

Host: Frank Capra
Venue: Biltmore Bowl of the Biltmore Hotel
Honoring movies released in 1935

Honorary Award

⬇ **D.W. Griffith** ⬇
for creative achievements as director and producer, also for initiative and
Contributions to the progress of the motion picture

Best Actor
⚐ Victor McLaglen ⚐
The Informer (1935) role "Gypo Nolan"
Clark Gable
Mutiny on the Bounty (1935) role "Lt. Fletcher Christian"
Charles Laughton
Mutiny on the Bounty (1935) role "Captain William Bligh"
Franchot Tone
Mutiny on the Bounty (1935) role "Midshipman Roger Byam"
Paul Muni
Black Fury (1935) role "Joe Radek"

Best Actress
⚐ Bette Davis ⚐
Dangerous (1935) role "Joyce Heath"
Elisabeth Bergner
Escape Me Never (1935) role "Gemma Jones"
Claudette Colbert
Private Worlds (1935) role "Dr. Jane Everest"
Katharine Hepburn
Alice Adams (1935) role "Alice Adams"
Miriam Hopkins
Becky Sharp (1935) role "Becky Sharp"
Merle Oberon
The Dark Angel (1935) role "Kitty Vane"

Best Art Direction
⚐ Richard Day ⚐
The Dark Angel (1935)
Roland Anderson, Hans Dreier
The Lives of a Bengal Lancer (1935)
Carroll Clark, Van Nest Polglase
Top Hat (1935)

Best Assistant Director
⚐ Clem Beauchamp, Paul Wing ⚐
The Lives of a Bengal Lancer (1935)
Joseph M. Newman
David Copperfield (1935)
Sherry Shourds
A Midsummer Night's Dream (1935)
Eric Stacey
Les Misérables (1935)

Best Short Subject, Cartoon
⚐ Walt Disney (Producer) ⚐
Three Orphan Kittens (1935)
Walt Disney (Producer)
Who Killed Cock Robin? (1935)
Hugh Harman, Rudolf Ising (Producers)
The Calico Dragon (1935)

Best Short Subject, Comedy

⚊ **Jack Chertok (Producer)** ⚊
How to Sleep (1935)

Hal Roach (Producer)
Tit for Tat (1935)

Jules White (Producer)
Oh, My Nerves (1935)

Best Dance Direction

⚊ **Dave Gould for "I've Got a Feeling You're Fooling"** ⚊
Broadway Melody of 1936 (1935)

Dave Gould for "Straw Hat"
Folies Bergère de Paris (1935)

Busby Berkeley for "Lullaby of Broadway" and "The Words Are in My Heart"
Gold Diggers of 1935 (1935)

Bobby Connolly for "Latin from Manhattan"
Go Into Your Dance (1935)

Bobby Connolly for "Playboy of Paree"
Broadway Hostess (1935)

Sammy Lee for "Lovely Lady" and "Too Good to Be True"
King of Burlesque (1936)

Hermes Pan for "Piccolino" and "Top Hat, White Tie, and Tails"
Top Hat (1935)

LeRoy Prinz for "Elephant - It's the Animal in Me"
The Big Broadcast of 1936 (1935)

LeRoy Prinz for "Viennese Waltz"
All the King's Horses (1935)

Benjamin Zemach for "Hall of Kings"
She (1935)

Best Sound Recording

⚊ **Douglas Shearer (Sound Director),**
Metro-Goldwyn-Mayer Studio Sound Department ⚊
Naughty Marietta (1935)

Carl Dreher (Sound Director), RKO Radio Studio Sound Department
I Dream Too Much (1935)

Edmund H. Hansen (Sound Director),
20th Century-Fox Studio Sound Department
Thanks a Million (1935)

Franklin Hansen (Sound Director), Paramount Studio Sound Department
The Lives of a Bengal Lancer (1935)

Gilbert Kurland (Sound Director), Universal Studio Sound Department
The Bride of Frankenstein (1935)

Nathan Levinson (Sound Director),
Warner Bros. First National Studio Sound Department
Captain Blood (1935)

John P. Livadary (Sound Director), Columbia Studio Sound Department
Love Me Forever (1935)

Thomas T. Moulton (Sound Director),
United Artists Studio Sound Department
The Dark Angel (1935)

Republic Studio Sound Department
1,000 Dollars a Minute (1935)

Best Cinematography
⭣ Hal Mohr ⭣
A Midsummer Night's Dream (1935)
Ray June
Barbary Coast (1935)
Victor Milner
The Crusades (1935)
Gregg Toland
Les Misérables (1935)

Best Directing
⭣ John Ford ⭣
The Informer (1935)
Michael Curtiz
Captain Blood (1935)
Henry Hathaway
The Lives of a Bengal Lancer (1935)
Frank Lloyd
Mutiny on the Bounty (1935)

Best Outstanding Production
⭣ Metro-Goldwyn-Mayer ⭣
Mutiny on the Bounty (1935)
20th Century
Les Misérables (1935)
Cosmopolitan
Captain Blood (1935)
Metro-Goldwyn-Mayer
Broadway Melody of 1936 (1935), David Copperfield (1935), Naughty Marietta (1935)
Paramount
Ruggles of Red Gap (1935), The Lives of a Bengal Lancer (1935)
RKO Radio
Alice Adams (1935), The Informer (1935), Top Hat (1935)
Warner Bros.
A Midsummer Night's Dream (1935)

Best Film Editing
⭣ Ralph Dawson ⭣
A Midsummer Night's Dream (1935)
Margaret Booth
Mutiny on the Bounty (1935)
George Hively
The Informer (1935)
Ellsworth Hoagland
The Lives of a Bengal Lancer (1935)
Robert Kern
David Copperfield (1935)
Barbara McLean
Les Misérables (1935)

Best Music, Song

Harry Warren (Music), Al Dubin (Lyrics)
for the song "Lullaby of Broadway"
Gold Diggers of 1935 (1935)

Irving Berlin (Music & Lyrics) for the song "Cheek to Cheek"
Top Hat (1935)

Jerome Kern (Music) Dorothy Fields, Jimmy McHugh (Lyrics)
for the song "Lovely to Look at"
Roberta (1935)

Best Music, Scoring

Max Steiner (Head of Department), RKO Radio Studio
Music Department, Score by Max Steiner
The Informer (1935)

Irvin Talbot (Head of Department), Paramount Studio Music
Department, Score by Ernst Toch
Peter Ibbetson (1935)

Leo F. Forbstein (Head of Department), Warner Bros. First
National Studio Music Department, Score by Erich Wolfgang Korngold
Captain Blood (1935)

Nat W. Finston (Head of Department), Metro-Goldwyn-Mayer
Studio Music Department, Score by Herbert Stothart
Mutiny on the Bounty (1935)

Best Short Subject, Novelty

Richard Robinson (Producer), Gaumont British and Skibo Productions
Wings Over Mt. Everest (1934)

Pete Smith (Producer), Metro-Goldwyn-Mayer
Audioscopiks (1935)

Charles E. Ford (Producer), Universal
Camera Thrills (1935)

Best Writing, Screenplay

Dudley Nichols
The Informer (1935)

Achmed Abdullah, John L. Balderston, Grover Jones,
William Slavens McNutt, Waldemar Young
The Lives of a Bengal Lancer (1935)

Jules Furthman, Talbot Jennings, Carey Wilson
Mutiny on the Bounty (1935)

Casey Robinson
Captain Blood (1935)

Best Writing, Original Story

Ben Hecht, Charles MacArthur
The Scoundrel (1935)

Moss Hart
Broadway Melody of 1936 (1935)

Don Hartman, Stephen Morehouse Avery
The Gay Deception (1935)

Darryl F. Zanuck (as Gregory Rogers)
'G' Men (1935)

8th Ceremony 5/5

The 9ᵗʰ Academy Awards® - March 4, 1937

Host: George Jessel
Venue: Biltmore Bowl of the Biltmore Hotel
Honoring movies released in 1936

Best Actor

⚊ Paul Muni ⚊
The Story of Louis Pasteur (1936) role "Louis Pasteur"

Gary Cooper
Mr. Deeds Goes to Town (1936) role "Longfellow Deeds"

Walter Huston
Dodsworth (1936) role "Sam Dodsworth"

William Powell
My Man Godfrey (1936) role "Godfrey Park"

Spencer Tracy
San Francisco (1936) role "Father Tim Mullin"

Best Actor in a Supporting Role

⚊ Walter Brennan ⚊
Come and Get It (1936) role "Swan Bostrom"

Mischa Auer
My Man Godfrey (1936) role "Carlo"

Stuart Erwin
Pigskin Parade (1936) role "Amos Dodd"

Basil Rathbone
Romeo and Juliet (1936) role "Tybalt - Nephew to Lady Capulet"

Akim Tamiroff
The General Died at Dawn (1936) role "General Yang"

Best Actress

⚊ Luise Rainer ⚊
The Great Ziegfeld (1936) role "Anna Held"

Irene Dunne
Theodora Goes Wild (1936) role "Theodora Lynn / Caroline Adams"

Gladys George
Valiant Is the Word for Carrie (1936) role "Carrie Snyder"

Carole Lombard
My Man Godfrey (1936) role "Irene Bullock"

Norma Shearer
Romeo and Juliet (1936) role "Juliet - Daughter to Capulet"

Best Actress in a Supporting Role

⚊ Gale Sondergaard ⚊
Anthony Adverse (1936) role "Faith Paleologus"

Beulah Bondi
The Gorgeous Hussy (1936) role "Rachel Jackson"

Alice Brady
My Man Godfrey (1936) role "Angelica Bullock"

Bonita Granville
These Three (1936) role "Mary Tilford"

Maria Ouspenskaya
Dodsworth (1936) role "Baroness Von Obersdorf"

Best Cinematography

⚐ Gaetano (Tony) Gaudio ⚐
Anthony Adverse (1936)

George J. Folsey
The Gorgeous Hussy (1936)

Victor Milner
The General Died at Dawn (1936)

Best Assistant Director

⚐ Jack Sullivan ⚐
The Charge of the Light Brigade (1936)

Clem Beauchamp
The Last of the Mohicans (1936)

William H. Cannon
Anthony Adverse (1936)

Joseph M. Newman
San Francisco (1936)

Eric Stacey
The Garden of Allah (1936)

Best Art Direction

⚐ Richard Day ⚐
Dodsworth (1936)

Albert S. D'Agostino, Jack Otterson
The Magnificent Brute (1936)

William S. Darling
Lloyds of London (1936)

Perry Ferguson
Winterset (1936)

Cedric Gibbons, Eddie Imazu, Edwin B. Willis
The Great Ziegfeld (1936)

Cedric Gibbons, Fredric Hope, Edwin B. Willis
Romeo and Juliet (1936)

Anton Grot
Anthony Adverse (1936)

Best Dance Direction

⚐ Seymour Felix for "A Pretty Girl Is Like a Melody" ⚐
The Great Ziegfeld (1936)

Busby Berkeley for "Love and War"
Gold Diggers of 1937 (1936)

Bobby Connolly for "1000 Love Songs"
Cain and Mabel (1936)

Dave Gould for "Swingin' the Jinx"
Born to Dance (1936)

Jack Haskell for "Skating Ensemble"
One in a Million (1936)

Russell Lewis for "The Finale"
Dancing Pirate (1936)

Hermes Pan for "Bojangles of Harlem"
Swing Time (1936)

Best Directing
⚡ **Frank Capra** ⚡
Mr. Deeds Goes to Town (1936)
Gregory La Cava
My Man Godfrey (1936)
Robert Z. Leonard
The Great Ziegfeld (1936)
W.S. Van Dyke
San Francisco (1936)
William Wyler
Dodsworth (1936)

Best Outstanding Production
⚡ **Metro-Goldwyn-Mayer** ⚡
The Great Ziegfeld (1936)
Columbia
Mr. Deeds Goes to Town (1936)
Cosmopolitan
The Story of Louis Pasteur (1936)
Metro-Goldwyn-Mayer
A Tale of Two Cities (1935), Libeled Lady (1936), Romeo and Juliet (1936),
San Francisco (1936)
Samuel Goldwyn Productions
Dodsworth (1936)
Universal
Three Smart Girls (1936)
Warner Bros.
Anthony Adverse (1936)

Best Short Subject, Cartoon
⚡ **Walt Disney (Producer)** ⚡
The Country Cousin (1936)
Max Fleischer (Producer)
Popeye the Sailor Meets Sindbad the Sailor (1936)
Hugh Harman, Rudolf Ising (Producers)
The Old Mill Pond (1936)

Best Short Subject, One Reel
⚡ **Hal Roach (Producer)** ⚡
Bored of Education (1936)
Paramount
Moscow Moods (1936)
Pete Smith (Producer)
Wanted, A Master (1936)

Best Short Subject, Two Reel
⚡ **Metro-Goldwyn-Mayer** ⚡
The Public Pays (1936)
RKO Radio
Dummy Ache (1936)
Warner Bros.
Double or Nothing (1936)

Best Music, Scoring

Leo F. Forbstein (Head of Department), Warner Bros. Studio Music Department, Score by Erich Wolfgang Korngold
Anthony Adverse (1936)

Leo F. Forbstein (Head of Department), Warner Bros. Studio Music Department, Score by Max Steiner
The Charge of the Light Brigade (1936)

Boris Morros (Head of Department), Paramount Studio Music Department, Score by Werner Janssen
The General Died at Dawn (1936)

Nathaniel Shilkret (Head of Department), RKO Radio Studio Music Department, Score by Nathaniel Shilkret
Winterset (1936)

Max Steiner (Head of Department), Selznick International Pictures Music Department, Score by Max Steiner
The Garden of Allah (1936)

Best Music, Song

Jerome Kern (Music), Dorothy Fields (Lyrics) for the song "The Way You Look Tonight"
Swing Time (1936)

Louis Alter (Music), Sidney D. Mitchell (Lyrics) for the song "A Melody from the Sky"
The Trail of the Lonesome Pine (1936)

Walter Donaldson (Music), Harold Adamson (Lyrics) for the song "Did I Remember"
Suzy (1936)

Arthur Johnston (Music), Johnny Burke (Lyrics) for the song "Pennies from Heaven"
Pennies from Heaven (1936)

Cole Porter (Music & Lyrics) for the song "I've Got You Under My Skin"
Born to Dance (1936)

Richard A. Whiting (Music), Walter Bullock (Lyrics) for the song "When Did You Leave Heaven"
Sing, Baby, Sing (1936)

Best Film Editing

Ralph Dawson
Anthony Adverse (1936)

Edward Curtiss
Come and Get It (1936)

William S. Gray
The Great Ziegfeld (1936)

Barbara McLean
Lloyds of London (1936)

Otto Meyer
Theodora Goes Wild (1936)

Conrad A. Nervig
A Tale of Two Cities (1935)

Best Short Subject, Color

⚐ Warner Bros. ⚐
Give Me Liberty (1936)
Lewis Lewyn (Producer)
La Fiesta de Santa Barbara (1935)
Paramount
Popular Science J-6-2 (1935)

Best Sound Recording

Douglas Shearer (Sound Director),
⚐ **Metro-Goldwyn-Mayer Studio Sound Department** ⚐
San Francisco (1936)
J. O. Aalberg (Sound Director), RKO Radio Studio Sound Department
That Girl from Paris (1936)
E. H. Hansen (Sound Director),
20th Century-Fox Studio Sound Department
Banjo on My Knee (1936)
Franklin B. Hansen (Sound Director),
Paramount Studio Sound Department
The Texas Rangers (1936)
Nathan Levinson (Sound Director),
Warner Bros. Studio Sound Department
The Charge of the Light Brigade (1936)
John P. Livadary (Sound Director), Columbia Studio Sound Department
Mr. Deeds Goes to Town (1936)
Thomas T. Moulton (Sound Director),
United Artists Studio Sound Department
Dodsworth (1936)
Elmer A. Raguse (Sound Director), Hal Roach Studio Sound Department
General Spanky (1936)
Homer G. Tasker (Sound Director), Universal Studio Sound Department
Three Smart Girls (1936)

Honorary Award

W. Howard Greene, Harold Rosson
(plaque) for the color cinematography of the The Garden of Allah (1936)
The March of Time
for its significance to motion pictures and for having revolutionized the newsreel

Best Writing, Original Story

⚐ **Pierre Collings, Sheridan Gibney** ⚐
The Story of Louis Pasteur (1936)
Adele Comandini
Three Smart Girls (1936)
Robert E. Hopkins
San Francisco (1936)
Norman Krasna
Fury (1936)
William Anthony McGuire
The Great Ziegfeld (1936)

Best Writing, Screenplay

⚐ Pierre Collings, Sheridan Gibney ⚐
The Story of Louis Pasteur (1936)

Frances Goodrich, Albert Hackett
After the Thin Man (1936)

Eric Hatch, Morrie Ryskind
My Man Godfrey (1936)

Sidney Howard
Dodsworth (1936)

Robert Riskin
Mr. Deeds Goes to Town (1936)

The 10ᵗʰ Academy Awards® - March 10, 1938
Host: Bob Burns
Venue: Biltmore Bowl of the Biltmore Hotel
Honoring movies released in 1937

Best Actor

⚐ Spencer Tracy ⚐
Captains Courageous (1937) role "Manuel Fidello"

Charles Boyer
Conquest (1937) role "Emperor Napoleon Bonaparte"

Fredric March
A Star Is Born (1937) role "Norman Maine"

Robert Montgomery
Night Must Fall (1937) role "Danny"

Paul Muni
The Life of Emile Zola (1937) role "Emile Zola"

Best Actor in a Supporting Role

⚐ Joseph Schildkraut ⚐
The Life of Emile Zola (1937) role "Captain Alfred Dreyfus"

Ralph Bellamy
The Awful Truth (1937) role "Daniel "Dan" Leeson"

Thomas Mitchell
The Hurricane (1937) role "Dr. Kersaint"

H.B. Warner
Lost Horizon (1937) role "Chang"

Roland Young
Topper (1937) role "Cosmo Topper"

Best Actress

⚐ Luise Rainer ⚐
The Good Earth (1937) role "O-Lan"

Irene Dunne
The Awful Truth (1937) role "Lucy Warriner"

Greta Garbo
Camille (1936) role "Marguerite Gautier"

Janet Gaynor
A Star Is Born (1937) role "Esther Victoria Blodgett aka Vicki Lester"

Barbara Stanwyck
Stella Dallas (1937) role "Stella Martin 'Stell' Dallas"

Best Actress in a Supporting Role
⚊ Alice Brady ⚊
In Old Chicago (1938) role "Molly O'Leary"
Andrea Leeds
Stage Door (1937) role "Kay Hamilton"
Anne Shirley
Stella Dallas (1937) role "Laurel "Lollie" Dallas"
Claire Trevor
Dead End (1937) role "Francey"
Dame May Whitty
Night Must Fall (1937) role "Mrs. Bramson"

Best Assistant Director
⚊ Robert D. Webb ⚊
In Old Chicago (1938)
Charles C. Coleman
Lost Horizon (1937)
Russell Saunders
The Life of Emile Zola (1937)
Eric Stacey
A Star Is Born (1937)
Hal Walker
Souls at Sea (1937)

Best Art Direction
⚊ Stephen Goosson ⚊
Lost Horizon (1937)
Roland Anderson, Hans Dreier
Souls at Sea (1937)
Carroll Clark
A Damsel in Distress (1937)
William S. Darling, David S. Hall
Wee Willie Winkie (1937)
Richard Day
Dead End (1937)
Cedric Gibbons, William A. Horning
Conquest (1937)
Anton Grot
The Life of Emile Zola (1937)
Wiard Ihnen
Every Day's a Holiday (1937)
John Victor Mackay
Manhattan Merry-Go-Round (1937)
Jack Otterson
You're a Sweetheart (1937)
Alexander Toluboff
Walter Wanger's Vogues of 1938 (1937)
Lyle R. Wheeler
The Prisoner of Zenda (1937)

Best Cinematography

⚜ Karl Freund ⚜
The Good Earth (1937)

Gregg Toland
Dead End (1937)

Joseph A. Valentine
Wings Over Honolulu (1937)

Best Short Subject, Cartoon

⚜ Walt Disney (Producer) ⚜
The Old Mill (1937)

Charles Mintz (Producer)
The Little Match Girl (1937)

Paramount
Educated Fish (1937)

Best Short Subject, Color

⚜ Pete Smith (Producer) ⚜
Penny Wisdom (1937)

Paramount
Popular Science J-7-1 (1937)

Warner Bros.
The Man Without a Country (1937)

Best Directing

⚜ Leo McCarey ⚜
The Awful Truth (1937)

Gregory La Cava
Stage Door (1937)

William Dieterle
The Life of Emile Zola (1937)

Sidney Franklin
The Good Earth (1937)

William A. Wellman
A Star Is Born (1937)

Best Dance Direction

⚜ Hermes Pan for "Fun House" ⚜
A Damsel in Distress (1937)

Busby Berkeley for "The Finale"
Varsity Show (1937)

Bobby Connolly for "Too Marvelous for Words"
Ready, Willing and Able (1937)

Dave Gould for "All God's Children Got Rhythm"
A Day at the Races (1937)

Sammy Lee for "Swing Is Here to Stay"
Ali Baba Goes to Town (1937)

Harry Losee for "Prince Igor Suite"
Thin Ice (1937)

LeRoy Prinz for "Luau"
Waikiki Wedding (1937)

Best Film Editing
⚐ Gene Havlick, Gene Milford ⚐
Lost Horizon (1937)
Bernard W. Burton
One Hundred Men and a Girl (1937)
Al Clark
The Awful Truth (1937)
Elmo Veron
Captains Courageous (1937)
Basil Wrangell
The Good Earth (1937)

Best Music, Song
⚐ Harry Owens (Music & Lyrics) for the song "Sweet Leilani" ⚐
Waikiki Wedding (1937)
Sammy Fain (Music), Lew Brown (Lyrics) for the song "That Old Feeling"
Walter Wanger's Vogues of 1938 (1937)
George Gershwin (Music), Ira Gershwin (Lyrics)
for the song "They Can't Take That Away from Me"
(George Gershwin - Posthumous)
Shall We Dance (1937)
Friedrich Hollaender (Music), Leo Robin (Lyrics)
for the song "Whispers in the Dark"
Artists and Models (1937)
Harry Warren (Music), Al Dubin (Lyrics) for the song "Remember Me"
Mr. Dodd Takes the Air (1937)

Best Outstanding Production
⚐ Warner Bros. ⚐
The Life of Emile Zola (1937)
20th Century-Fox
In Old Chicago (1938)
Columbia
Lost Horizon (1937), The Awful Truth (1937)
Metro-Goldwyn-Mayer
Captains Courageous (1937), The Good Earth (1937)
RKO Radio
Stage Door (1937)
Samuel Goldwyn Productions
Dead End (1937)
Selznick International Pictures
A Star Is Born (1937)
Universal
One Hundred Men and a Girl (1937)

Best Short Subject, One Reel
⚐ Skibo Productions ⚐
The Private Life of the Gannets (1934)
Metro-Goldwyn-Mayer
A Night at the Movies (1937)
Pete Smith (Producer)
Romance of Radium (1937)

Honorary Award

⚜ **Mack Sennett** ⚜

for contribution to the comedy technique of the screen, also for being master of fun, discoverer of stars, sympathetic, kindly, understanding comedy genius

W. Howard Greene

(plaque) for the color photography of A Star Is Born (1937)

Edgar Bergen

(wooden statuette) for outstanding comedy creation, Charlie McCarthy

Museum of Modern Art Film Library

(certificate) for work in collecting films dating from 1895 and making available to the public

Best Music, Scoring

⚜ **Charles Previn (Head of Department), Universal Studio Music Department, (no composer credit)** ⚜

One Hundred Men and a Girl (1937)

C. Bakaleinikoff (Musical Director), Grand National Studio Music Department, Score by Victor Schertzinger

Something to Sing About (1937)

Alberto Colombo (Head of Department), Republic Studio Music Department, Score by Alberto Colombo

Portia on Trial (1937)

Nat W. Finston (Head of Department), Metro-Goldwyn-Mayer Studio Music Department, Score by Herbert Stothart

Maytime (1937)

Leo Forbstein (Head of Department), Warner Bros. Studio Music Department, Score by Max Steiner

The Life of Emile Zola (1937)

Leigh Harline (Head of Department), Walt Disney Studio Music Department, Score by Frank Churchill, Leigh Harline, Paul J. Smith

Snow White and the Seven Dwarfs (1937)

Marvin Hatley (Head of Department), Hal Roach Studio Music Department, Score by Marvin Hatley

Way Out West (1937)

Boris Morros (Head of Department), Paramount Studio Music Department, Score by W. Franke Harling, Milan Roder

Souls at Sea (1937)

Alfred Newman (Head of Department), Samuel Goldwyn Studio Music Department, Score by Alfred Newman

The Hurricane (1937)

Alfred Newman (Musical Director), Selznick International Pictures Music Department, Score by Alfred Newman

The Prisoner of Zenda (1937)

Dr. Hugo Riesenfeld (Musical Director), Principal Productions, Score by Dr. Hugo Riesenfeld

Make a Wish (1937)

Louis Silvers (Head of Department), 20th Century-Fox Studio Music Department, (no composer credit)

In Old Chicago (1938)

Morris Stoloff (Head of Department), Columbia Studio Music Department, Score by Dimitri Tiomkin

Lost Horizon (1937)

Roy Webb (Musical Director), RKO Radio Studio Music Department, Score by Roy Webb

Quality Street (1937)

Best Sound Recording

Thomas T. Moulton (Sound Director),
United Artists Studio Sound Department
The Hurricane (1937)

John Aalberg (Sound Director), RKO Radio Studio Sound Department
Hitting a New High (1937)

Edmund H. Hansen (Sound Director),
20th Century-Fox Studio Sound Department
In Old Chicago (1938)

A. E. Kaye (Sound Director), Grand National Studio Sound Department
The Girl Said No (1937)

Nathan Levinson (Sound Director), Warner Bros. Studio Sound Department
The Life of Emile Zola (1937)

John P. Livadary (Sound Director), Columbia Studio Sound Department
Lost Horizon (1937)

Elmer A. Raguse (Sound Director), Hal Roach Studio Sound Department
Topper (1937)

Loren L. Ryder (Sound Director), Paramount Studio Sound Department
Wells Fargo (1937)

Douglas Shearer (Sound Director),
Metro-Goldwyn-Mayer Studio Sound Department
Maytime (1937)

Homer G. Tasker (Sound Director), Universal Studio Sound Department
One Hundred Men and a Girl (1937)

Best Writing, Original Story

Robert Carson, William A. Wellman
A Star Is Born (1937)

Niven Busch
In Old Chicago (1938)

Heinz Herald, Geza Herczeg
The Life of Emile Zola (1937)

Hanns Kräly
One Hundred Men and a Girl (1937)

Robert Lord
Black Legion (1937)

Best Writing, Screenplay

Heinz Herald, Geza Herczeg, Norman Reilly Raine
The Life of Emile Zola (1937)

Alan Campbell, Robert Carson, Dorothy Parker
A Star Is Born (1937)

Marc Connelly, Dale Van Every, John Lee Mahin
Captains Courageous (1937)

Viña Delmar
The Awful Truth (1937)

Morrie Ryskind, Anthony Veiller
Stage Door (1937)

Irving G. Thalberg Memorial Award

Darryl F. Zanuck

Best Short Subject, Two Reel
⚰ Metro-Goldwyn-Mayer ⚰
Torture Money (1937)
RKO Radio
Deep South (1937), Should Wives Work? (1937)

The 11ᵗʰ Academy Awards® - February 23, 1939
Host: No official host
Venue: Biltmore Bowl of the Biltmore Hotel
Honoring movies released in 1938

Juvenile Award
⚰ Deanna Durbin, Mickey Rooney ⚰
for contribution in bringing to the screen the spirit and personification of youth

Best Actor
⚰ Spencer Tracy ⚰
Boys Town (1938) role "Father Flanagan"
Charles Boyer
Algiers (1938) role "Pepe le Moko"
James Cagney
Angels with Dirty Faces (1938) role "Rocky Sullivan"
Robert Donat
The Citadel (1938) role "Dr. Andrew Manson"
Leslie Howard
Pygmalion (1938) role "Professor Henry Higgins"

Best Actor in a Supporting Role
⚰ Walter Brennan ⚰
Kentucky (1938) role "Peter Goodwin"
John Garfield
Four Daughters (1938) role "Mickey Borden"
Gene Lockhart
Algiers (1938) role "Regis"
Robert Morley
Marie Antoinette (1938) role "King Louis XVI"
Basil Rathbone
If I Were King (1938) role "King Louis XI"

Best Actress
⚰ Bette Davis ⚰
Jezebel (1938) role "Julie Marsden"
Fay Bainter
White Banners (1938) role "Hannah Parmalee"
Wendy Hiller
Pygmalion (1938) role "Eliza Doolittle"
Norma Shearer
Marie Antoinette (1938) role "Marie Antoinette"
Margaret Sullavan
Three Comrades (1938) role "Patricia "Pat" Hollmann"

Best Actress in a Supporting Role

⇩ Fay Bainter ⇩
Jezebel (1938) role "Aunt Belle Massey"

Beulah Bondi
Of Human Hearts (1938) role "Mary Wilkins"

Billie Burke
Merrily We Live (1938) role "Emily Kilbourne"

Spring Byington
You Can't Take It with You (1938) role "Penelope "Penny" Sycamore"

Miliza Korjus
The Great Waltz (1938) role "Carla Donner"

Best Outstanding Production

⇩ Columbia ⇩
You Can't Take It with You (1938)

20th Century-Fox
Alexander's Ragtime Band (1938)

Metro-Goldwyn-Mayer
Boys Town (1938), Pygmalion (1938), Test Pilot (1938), The Citadel (1938)

Realization D'Art Cinematographique
La Grande Illusion (1937)

Warner Bros.
Jezebel (1938)

Warner Bros. - First National
Four Daughters (1938), The Adventures of Robin Hood (1938)

Best Short Subject, One Reel

⇩ Metro-Goldwyn-Mayer ⇩
That Mothers Might Live (1938)

20th Century-Fox
Timber Toppers (1938)

Metro-Goldwyn-Mayer
The Great Heart (1938)

Best Short Subject, Two Reel

⇩ Warner Bros. ⇩
The Declaration of Independence (1938)

Metro-Goldwyn-Mayer
They're Always Caught (1938)

Warner Bros.
Swingtime in the Movies (1938)

Best Directing

⇩ Frank Capra ⇩
You Can't Take It with You (1938)

Michael Curtiz
Angels with Dirty Faces (1938), Four Daughters (1938)

Norman Taurog
Boys Town (1938)

King Vidor
The Citadel (1938)

Best Art Direction

⊥ Carl Jules Weyl ⊥
The Adventures of Robin Hood (1938)

Lionel Banks, Stephen Goosson
Holiday (1938)

Richard Day
The Goldwyn Follies (1938)

Hans Dreier, John B. Goodman
If I Were King (1938)

Cedric Gibbons
Marie Antoinette (1938)

Charles D. Hall
Merrily We Live (1938)

Bernard Herzbrun, Boris Leven
Alexander's Ragtime Band (1938)

Jack Otterson
Mad About Music (1938)

Van Nest Polglase
Carefree (1938)

Alexander Toluboff
Algiers (1938)

Lyle R. Wheeler
The Adventures of Tom Sawyer (1938)

Best Writing, Original Story

⊥ Eleanore Griffin, Dore Schary ⊥
Boys Town (1938)

Irving Berlin
Alexander's Ragtime Band (1938)

Rowland Brown
Angels with Dirty Faces (1938)

Marcella Burke, Frederick Kohner
Mad About Music (1938)

John Howard Lawson
Blockade (1938)

Frank Wead
Test Pilot (1938)

Best Writing, Screenplay

⊥ Ian Dalrymple, Cecil Lewis, W. P. Lipscomb, George Bernard Shaw ⊥
Pygmalion (1938)

Lenore J. Coffee, Julius J. Epstein
Four Daughters (1938)

Ian Dalrymple, Elizabeth Hill, Frank Wead
The Citadel (1938)

John Meehan, Dore Schary
Boys Town (1938)

Robert Riskin
You Can't Take It with You (1938)

Best Cinematography
⚐ Joseph Ruttenberg ⚐
The Great Waltz (1938)
Norbert Brodine
Merrily We Live (1938)
Robert De Grasse
Vivacious Lady (1938)
Ernest Haller
Jezebel (1938)
James Wong Howe
Algiers (1938)
J. Peverell Marley
Suez (1938)
Ernest Miller, Harry J. Wild
Army Girl (1938)
Victor Milner
The Buccaneer (1938)
Leon Shamroy
The Young in Heart (1938)
Joseph A. Valentine
Mad About Music (1938)
Joseph Walker
You Can't Take It with You (1938)

Best Film Editing
⚐ Ralph Dawson ⚐
The Adventures of Robin Hood (1938)
Gene Havlick
You Can't Take It with You (1938)
Tom Held
The Great Waltz (1938), Test Pilot (1938)
Barbara McLean
Alexander's Ragtime Band (1938)

Honorary Award
⚐ Walt Disney (Producer) ⚐
(One statuette and seven miniature statuettes, representing the Seven Dwarfs)
for Snow White and the Seven Dwarfs (1937) recognized as screen innovation and great entertainment
Gordon Jennings (special effects), Jan Domela, Devereaux Jennings, Irmin Roberts, Art Smith (assistants special effects), Farciot Edouart (transparencies), Loyal Griggs (assistant transparencies), Loren L. Ryder (sound effects), Harry D. Mills, Louis Mesenkop, Walter Oberst (assistants sound effects)
(plaque) Spawn of the North (1938) for outstanding achievements in creating special effects and sound effects
Allen M. Davey, Oliver T. Marsh
(plaque) Sweethearts (1938) for the color cinematography
Arthur Ball
(certificate) for contributions to the advancement of color in movies
Harry M. Warner
(certificate) for historical short subjects

Best Music, Song

⚐ **Ralph Rainger (Music), Leo Robin (Lyrics)** ⚐
for the song "Thanks for the Memory
The Big Broadcast of 1938 (1938)

Irving Berlin (Music & Lyrics) for the song "Now It Can Be Told"
Alexander's Ragtime Band (1938)

Irving Berlin (Music & Lyrics) for the song "Change Partners"
Carefree (1938)

Phil Charig (Music), Arthur Quenzer (Lyrics) for the song "Merrily We Live"
Merrily We Live (1938)

Johnny Marvin (Music & Lyrics) for the song "Dust"
Under Western Stars (1938)

Jimmy McHugh (Music), Harold Adamson (Lyrics) for the song "My Own"
That Certain Age (1938)

Lionel Newman (Music), Arthur Quenzer (Lyrics)
for the song "The Cowboy and the Lady"
The Cowboy and the Lady (1938)

Ben Oakland (Music), Oscar Hammerstein II (Lyrics)
for the song "A Mist Over the Moon"
The Lady Objects (1938)

Edward Ward (Music), Chet Forrest, Bob Wright (Lyrics)
for the song "Always and Always"
Mannequin (1937)

Harry Warren (Music), Johnny Mercer (Lyrics) for the song "Jeepers Creepers"
Going Places (1938)

Best Music, Scoring

⚐ **Alfred Newman** ⚐
Alexander's Ragtime Band (1938)

Victor Baravalle
Carefree (1938)

Cy Feuer
Storm Over Bengal (1938)

Marvin Hatley
There Goes My Heart (1938)

Boris Morros
Tropic Holiday (1938)

Alfred Newman
The Goldwyn Follies (1938)

Charles Previn, Frank Skinner
Mad About Music (1938)

Max Steiner
Jezebel (1938)

Morris Stoloff, Gregory Stone
Girls' School (1938)

Herbert Stothart
Sweethearts (1938)

Franz Waxman
The Young in Heart (1938)

Best Sound Recording

**Thomas T. Moulton (Sound Director),
United Artists Studio Sound Department**
The Cowboy and the Lady (1938)

John O. Aalberg (Sound Director), RKO Radio Studio Sound Department
Vivacious Lady (1938)

Bernard B. Brown (Sound Director), Universal Studio Sound Department
That Certain Age (1938)

**Edmund H. Hansen (Sound Director),
20th Century-Fox Studio Sound Department**
Suez (1938)

Nathan Levinson (Sound Director), Warner Bros. Studio Sound Department
Four Daughters (1938)

John P. Livadary (Sound Director), Columbia Studio Sound Department
You Can't Take It with You (1938)

Charles L. Lootens (Sound Director), Republic Studio Sound Department
Army Girl (1938)

Elmer A. Raguse (Sound Director), Hal Roach Studio Sound Department
Merrily We Live (1938)

Loren L. Ryder (Sound Director), Paramount Studio Sound Department
If I Were King (1938)

**Douglas Shearer (Sound Director),
Metro-Goldwyn-Mayer Studio Sound Department**
Sweethearts (1938)

Best Music, Original Score

Erich Wolfgang Korngold
The Adventures of Robin Hood (1938)

Robert Russell Bennett
Pacific Liner (1939)

Richard Hageman
If I Were King (1938)

Marvin Hatley
Block-Heads (1938)

Werner Janssen
Blockade (1938)

Alfred Newman
The Cowboy and the Lady (1938)

Louis Silvers
Suez (1938)

Herbert Stothart
Marie Antoinette (1938)

Franz Waxman
The Young in Heart (1938)

Victor Young
Army Girl (1938), Breaking the Ice (1938)

Best Short Subject, Cartoon

Walt Disney (Producer)
Ferdinand the Bull (1938)

Walt Disney (Producer)
Brave Little Tailor (1938), Good Scouts (1938), Mother Goose Goes Hollywood (1938)

Paramount
Hunky and Spunky (1938)

Irving G. Thalberg Memorial Award

(The only year for which non-winning nominations were announced)

↓ Hal B. Wallis ↓
Samuel Goldwyn
Joe Pasternak
David O. Selznick
Hunt Stromberg
Walter Wanger
Darryl F. Zanuck

The 12ᵗʰ Academy Awards® - February 29, 1940
Host: Bob Hope
Venue: Coconut Grove of the Ambassador Hotel
Honoring movies released in 1939

Best Actor
↓ Robert Donat ↓
Goodbye, Mr. Chips (1939) role "Charles Edward Chipping"
Clark Gable
Gone with the Wind (1939) role "Rhett Butler - Visitor from Charleston"
Laurence Olivier
Wuthering Heights (1939) role "Heathcliff"
Mickey Rooney
Babes in Arms (1939) role "Mickey Moran"
James Stewart
Mr. Smith Goes to Washington (1939) role "Jefferson Smith"

Best Actor in a Supporting Role
↓ Thomas Mitchell ↓
Stagecoach (1939) role "Dr. Josiah Boone"
Brian Aherne
Juarez (1939) role "Emperor Maximilian von Habsburg"
Harry Carey
Mr. Smith Goes to Washington (1939) role "President of the Senate"
Brian Donlevy
Beau Geste (1939) role "Sergeant Markoff"
Claude Rains
Mr. Smith Goes to Washington (1939) role "Senator Joseph Harrison Paine"

Best Actress
↓ Vivien Leigh ↓
Gone with the Wind (1939) role "Scarlett O'Hara"
Bette Davis
Dark Victory (1939) role "Judith Traherne"
Irene Dunne
Love Affair (1939) role "Terry McKay"
Greta Garbo
Ninotchka (1939) role "Nina Yakushova "Ninotchka" Ivanoff"
Greer Garson
Goodbye, Mr. Chips (1939) role "Katherine Bridges"

Best Actress in a Supporting Role
↓ Hattie McDaniel ↓
Gone with the Wind (1939) role "Mammy"
Geraldine Fitzgerald
Wuthering Heights (1939) role "Isabella Linton"
Olivia de Havilland
Gone with the Wind (1939) role "Melanie Hamilton"
Edna May Oliver
Drums Along the Mohawk (1939) role "Sarah McKlennar"
Maria Ouspenskaya
Love Affair (1939) role "Grandmother Janou"

Juvenile Award
↓ Judy Garland ↓
for outstanding performance as a screen juvenile during 1939

Best Short Subject, Cartoon
↓ Walt Disney (Producer) ↓
Ugly Duckling (1939)
Walt Disney (Producer)
The Pointer (1939)
Metro-Goldwyn-Mayer
Peace on Earth (1939)
Warner Bros.
Detouring America (1939)

Best Cinematography, Black and White
↓ Gregg Toland ↓
Wuthering Heights (1939)
Bert Glennon
Stagecoach (1939)

Best Cinematography, Color
↓ Ernest Haller, Ray Rennahan ↓
Gone with the Wind (1939)
W. Howard Greene, Sol Polito
The Private Lives of Elizabeth and Essex (1939)

Best Directing
↓ Victor Fleming ↓
Gone with the Wind (1939)
Frank Capra
Mr. Smith Goes to Washington (1939)
John Ford
Stagecoach (1939)
Sam Wood
Goodbye, Mr. Chips (1939)
William Wyler
Wuthering Heights (1939)

Best Music, Song

Harold Arlen (Music), E.Y. Harburg (Lyrics)
for the song "Over the Rainbow"
The Wizard of Oz (1939)

Irving Berlin (Music & Lyrics) for the song "I Poured My Heart Into a Song"
Second Fiddle (1939)

Ralph Rainger (Music), Leo Robin (Lyrics) for the song "Faithful Forever"
Gulliver's Travels (1939)

Buddy G. de Sylva (Music & Lyrics) for the song "Wishing"
Love Affair (1939)

Irving G. Thalberg Memorial Award

David O. Selznick

Best Film Editing

Hal C. Kern, James E. Newcom
Gone with the Wind (1939)

Al Clark, Gene Havlick
Mr. Smith Goes to Washington (1939)

Charles Frend
Goodbye, Mr. Chips (1939)

Otho Lovering, Dorothy Spencer
Stagecoach (1939)

Barbara McLean
The Rains Came (1939)

Best Art Direction

Lyle R. Wheeler
Gone with the Wind (1939)

Lionel Banks
Mr. Smith Goes to Washington (1939)

James Basevi
Wuthering Heights (1939)

William S. Darling, George Dudley
The Rains Came (1939)

Hans Dreier, Robert Odell
Beau Geste (1939)

Cedric Gibbons, William A. Horning
The Wizard of Oz (1939)

Anton Grot
The Private Lives of Elizabeth and Essex (1939)

Charles D. Hall
Captain Fury (1939)

Alfred Herman, Van Nest Polglase
Love Affair (1939)

John Victor Mackay
Man of Conquest (1939)

Martin Obzina, Jack Otterson
First Love (1939)

Alexander Toluboff
Stagecoach (1939)

Best Short Subject, One Reel
⚊ Paramount ⚊
Busy Little Bears (1939)
Metro-Goldwyn-Mayer
Prophet Without Honor (1939)
RKO Radio
Information Please (1939)
Warner Bros.
Sword Fishing (1939)

Best Short Subject, Two Reel
⚊ Warner Bros. ⚊
Sons of Liberty (1939)
Metro-Goldwyn-Mayer
Drunk Driving (1939)
RKO Radio
Five Times Five (1939)

Best Music, Original Score
⚊ Herbert Stothart ⚊
The Wizard of Oz (1939)
Anthony Collins
Nurse Edith Cavell (1939)
Aaron Copland
Of Mice and Men (1939)
Lud Gluskin, Lucien Moraweck
The Man in the Iron Mask (1939)
Werner Janssen
Eternally Yours (1939)
Alfred Newman
The Rains Came (1939), Wuthering Heights (1939)
Max Steiner
Dark Victory (1939), Gone with the Wind (1939)
Victor Young
Golden Boy (1939), Gulliver's Travels (1939), Man of Conquest (1939)

Best Special Effects
⚊ Fred Sersen (Photographic), Edmund H. Hansen (Sound) ⚊
The Rains Came (1939)
Jack Cosgrove (Photographic), Fred Albin, Arthur Johns (Sound)
Gone with the Wind (1939)
Roy Davidson (Photographic), Edwin C. Hahn (Sound)
Only Angels Have Wings (1939)
Farciot Edouart, Gordon Jennings (Photographic), Loren L. Ryder (Sound)
Union Pacific (1939)
A. Arnold Gillespie (Photographic), Douglas Shearer (Sound)
The Wizard of Oz (1939)
Byron Haskin (Photographic), Nathan Levinson (Sound)
The Private Lives of Elizabeth and Essex (1939)
Roy Seawright (Photographic)
Topper Takes a Trip (1938)

Best Music, Scoring
⚐ **Richard Hageman, W. Franke Harling, John Leipold, Leo Shuken** ⚐
Stagecoach (1939)

Phil Boutelje, Arthur Lange
The Great Victor Herbert (1939)

Aaron Copland
Of Mice and Men (1939)

Roger Edens, George Stoll
Babes in Arms (1939)

Cy Feuer
She Married a Cop (1939)

Louis Forbes
Intermezzo (1939)

Erich Wolfgang Korngold
The Private Lives of Elizabeth and Essex (1939)

Alfred Newman
The Hunchback of Notre Dame (1939), They Shall Have Music (1939)

Charles Previn
First Love (1939)

Louis Silvers
Swanee River (1939)

Dimitri Tiomkin
Mr. Smith Goes to Washington (1939)

Victor Young
Way Down South (1939)

Best Sound Recording
⚐ **Bernard B. Brown (Sound Director),** ⚐
Universal Studio Sound Department
When Tomorrow Comes (1939)

John Aalberg (Sound Director), RKO Radio Studio Sound Department
The Hunchback of Notre Dame (1939)

Edmund H. Hansen (Sound Director),
20th Century-Fox Studio Sound Department
The Rains Came (1939)

Nathan Levinson (Sound Director), Warner Bros. Studio Sound Department
The Private Lives of Elizabeth and Essex (1939)

John P. Livadary (Sound Director), Columbia Studio Sound Department
Mr. Smith Goes to Washington (1939)

Charles L. Lootens (Sound Director), Republic Studio Sound Department
Man of Conquest (1939)

Thomas T. Moulton (Sound Director),
Samuel Goldwyn Studio Sound Department
Gone with the Wind (1939)

Elmer A. Raguse (Sound Director), Hal Roach Studio Sound Department
Of Mice and Men (1939)

Loren L. Ryder (Sound Director), Paramount Studio Sound Department
The Great Victor Herbert (1939)

Douglas Shearer (Sound Director),
Metro-Goldwyn-Mayer Studio Sound Department
Balalaika (1939)

A. W. Watkins (Sound Director), Denham Studio Sound Department
Goodbye, Mr. Chips (1939)

Best Outstanding Production

⊥ Selznick International Pictures ⊥
Gone with the Wind (1939)

Columbia
Mr. Smith Goes to Washington (1939)

Metro-Goldwyn-Mayer
Goodbye, Mr. Chips (1939), Ninotchka (1939), The Wizard of Oz (1939)

RKO Radio
Love Affair (1939)

Hal Roach (production company)
Of Mice and Men (1939)

Samuel Goldwyn Productions
Wuthering Heights (1939)

Walter Wanger (production company)
Stagecoach (1939)

Warner Bros. First National
Dark Victory (1939)

Best Writing, Original Story

⊥ Lewis R. Foster ⊥
Mr. Smith Goes to Washington (1939)

Mildred Cram, Leo McCarey
Love Affair (1939)

Felix Jackson
Bachelor Mother (1939)

Melchior Lengyel
Ninotchka (1939)

Lamar Trotti
Young Mr. Lincoln (1939)

Best Writing, Screenplay

⊥ Sidney Howard ⊥
(Posthumous)
Gone with the Wind (1939)

Charles Brackett, Walter Reisch, Billy Wilder
Ninotchka (1939)

Sidney Buchman
Mr. Smith Goes to Washington (1939)

Ben Hecht, Charles MacArthur
Wuthering Heights (1939)

Eric Maschwitz, R.C. Sherriff, Claudine West
Goodbye, Mr. Chips (1939)

Honorary Award

⊥ Douglas Fairbanks ⊥
for the contribution to the international development of the motion picture

⊥ The Technicolor Company ⊥
for contributions in bringing three-color feature production

William Cameron Menzies
(plaque) for achievement in the use of color in the Gone with the Wind (1939)

Jean Hersholt (president), Ralph Morgan (chairman of the executive committee), Ralph Block (first vice-president), Conrad Nagel
(plaque) for services to the movie industry during 1939 of the Motion Picture Relief Fund and for progressive leadership

12th Ceremony 6/6

The 13ᵗʰ Academy Awards® - February 27, 1941

Host: Bob Burns
Venue: Biltmore Bowl of the Biltmore Hotel
Honoring movies released in 1940

Best Actor

⚊ James Stewart ⚊
The Philadelphia Story (1940) role "Macaulay "Mike" Connor"
Charles Chaplin
The Great Dictator (1940) role "Adenoid Hynkel / The Barber"
Henry Fonda
The Grapes of Wrath (1940) role "Tom Joad"
Raymond Massey
Abe Lincoln in Illinois (1940) role "Abraham Lincoln"
Laurence Olivier
Rebecca (1940) role "Maximilian "Maxim" de Winter"

Best Actor in a Supporting Role

⚊ Walter Brennan ⚊
The Westerner (1940) role "Judge Roy Bean"
Albert Bassermann
Foreign Correspondent (1940) role "Van Meer"
William Gargan
They Knew What They Wanted (1940) role "Joe"
Jack Oakie
The Great Dictator (1940) role "Benzino Napaloni (Dictator of Bacteria)"
James Stephenson
The Letter (1940) role "Howard Joyce"

Best Actress

⚊ Ginger Rogers ⚊
Kitty Foyle (1940) role "Kitty Foyle"
Bette Davis
The Letter (1940) role "Leslie Crosbie"
Joan Fontaine
Rebecca (1940) role "The Second Mrs. de Winter"
Katharine Hepburn
The Philadelphia Story (1940) role "Tracy Lord"
Martha Scott
Our Town (1940) role "Emily Webb"

Best Actress in a Supporting Role

⚊ Jane Darwell ⚊
The Grapes of Wrath (1940) role "Ma Joad"
Judith Anderson
Rebecca (1940) role "Mrs. Danvers"
Ruth Hussey
The Philadelphia Story (1940) role "Elizabeth Imbrie"
Barbara O'Neil
All This, and Heaven Too (1940) role "Françoise, Duchess de Praslin"
Marjorie Rambeau
Primrose Path (1940) role "Mamie Adams"

Best Short Subject, One Reel

⚊ **Pete Smith (Producer), Metro-Goldwyn-Mayer** ⚊
Quicker 'n a Wink (1940)

Frank P. Donovan, Frederic Ullman Jr. (Producers), RKO Radio
Siege (1940)

Alfred Duff-Cooper (Producer), Warner Bros.
London Can Take It! (1940)

Carey Wilson (Producer), Metro-Goldwyn-Mayer
More About Nostradamus (1941)

Best Short Subject, Two Reel

⚊ **Warner Bros.** ⚊
Teddy the Rough Rider (1940)

Metro-Goldwyn-Mayer
Eyes of the Navy (1940)

Warner Bros.
Service with the Colors (1940)

Best Cinematography, Color

⚊ **Georges Périnal** ⚊
The Thief of Bagdad (1940)

Allen M. Davey, Oliver T. Marsh
Bitter Sweet (1940)

W. Howard Greene, Victor Milner
North West Mounted Police (1940)

Arthur C. Miller, Ray Rennahan
The Blue Bird (1940)

Ray Rennahan, Leon Shamroy
Down Argentine Way (1940)

William V. Skall, Sidney Wagner
Northwest Passage (1940)

Best Outstanding Production

⚊ **Selznick International Pictures** ⚊
Rebecca (1940)

20th Century-Fox
The Grapes of Wrath (1940)

Argosy-Wanger
The Long Voyage Home (1940)

Charles Chaplin Productions
The Great Dictator (1940)

Metro-Goldwyn-Mayer
The Philadelphia Story (1940)

RKO Radio
Kitty Foyle (1940)

Sol Lesser (production company)
Our Town (1940)

Walter Wanger (production company)
Foreign Correspondent (1940)

Warner Bros.
All This, and Heaven Too (1940), The Letter (1940)

Best Directing
⇲ John Ford ⇱
The Grapes of Wrath (1940)
George Cukor
The Philadelphia Story (1940)
Alfred Hitchcock
Rebecca (1940)
Sam Wood
Kitty Foyle (1940)
William Wyler
The Letter (1940)

Best Art Direction, Color
⇲ Vincent Korda ⇱
The Thief of Bagdad (1940)
Roland Anderson, Hans Dreier
North West Mounted Police (1940)
Richard Day, Joseph C. Wright
Down Argentine Way (1940)
John S. Detlie, Cedric Gibbons
Bitter Sweet (1940)

Best Art Direction, Black and White
⇲ Cedric Gibbons, Paul Groesse ⇱
Pride and Prejudice (1940)
Lionel Banks, Robert Peterson
Arizona (1940)
James Basevi
The Westerner (1940)
Richard Day, Joseph C. Wright
Lillian Russell (1940)
Hans Dreier, Robert Usher
Arise, My Love (1940)
Alexander Golitzen
Foreign Correspondent (1940)
Anton Grot
The Sea Hawk (1940)
Mark-Lee Kirk, Van Nest Polglase
My Favorite Wife (1940)
John Victor Mackay
Dark Command (1940)
Jack Otterson
The Boys from Syracuse (1940)
John DuCasse Schulze
My Son, My Son! (1940)
Lewis J. Rachmil
Our Town (1940)
Lyle R. Wheeler
Rebecca (1940)

Best Cinematography, Black and White

⚐ **George Barnes** ⚐
Rebecca (1940)

Gaetano (Tony) Gaudio
The Letter (1940)

Ernest Haller
All This, and Heaven Too (1940)

James Wong Howe
Abe Lincoln in Illinois (1940)

Charles B. Lang Jr.
Arise, My Love (1940)

Rudolph Maté
Foreign Correspondent (1940)

Harold Rosson
Boom Town (1940)

Joseph Ruttenberg
Waterloo Bridge (1940)

Gregg Toland
The Long Voyage Home (1940)

Joseph A. Valentine
Spring Parade (1940)

Best Music, Original Score

⚐ **Leigh Harline, Paul J. Smith, Ned Washington** ⚐
Pinocchio (1940)

Aaron Copland
Our Town (1940)

Louis Gruenberg
The Fight for Life (1940)

Richard Hageman
The Howards of Virginia (1940), The Long Voyage Home (1940)

Werner R. Heymann
One Million B.C. (1940)

Alfred Newman
The Mark of Zorro (1940)

Miklós Rózsa
The Thief of Bagdad (1940)

Frank Skinner
The House of the Seven Gables (1940)

Max Steiner
The Letter (1940)

Herbert Stothart
Waterloo Bridge (1940)

Franz Waxman
Rebecca (1940)

Roy Webb
My Favorite Wife (1940)

Meredith Willson
The Great Dictator (1940)

Victor Young
Arizona (1940), Dark Command (1940), North West Mounted Police (1940)

Best Music, Scoring

⚑ **Alfred Newman** ⚑
Tin Pan Alley (1940)

Anthony Collins
Irene (1940)

Aaron Copland
Our Town (1940)

Roger Edens, George Stoll
Strike Up the Band (1940)

Cy Feuer
Hit Parade of 1941 (1940)

Erich Wolfgang Korngold
The Sea Hawk (1940)

Charles Previn
Spring Parade (1940)

Artie Shaw
Second Chorus (1940)

Victor Young
Arise, My Love (1940)

Best Music, Song

⚑ **Leigh Harline (Music), Ned Washington (Lyrics)** ⚑
for the song "When You Wish Upon a Star"
Pinocchio (1940)

Roger Edens (Music), Arthur Freed (Lyrics) for the song "Our Love Affair"
Strike Up the Band (1940)

Chet Forrest, Bob Wright (Music & Lyrics) for the song "It's a Blue World"
Music in My Heart (1940)

Jimmy McHugh (Music), Johnny Mercer (Lyrics)
for the song "I'd Know You Anywhere"
You'll Find Out (1940)

James V. Monaco (Music), Johnny Burke (Lyrics) for the song "Only Forever"
Rhythm on the River (1940)

Artie Shaw (Music), Johnny Mercer (Lyrics) for the song "Love of My Life"
Second Chorus (1940)

Robert Stolz (Music), Gus Kahn (Lyrics) for the song "Waltzing in the Clouds"
Spring Parade (1940)

Jule Styne (Music), Walter Bullock (Lyrics) for the song "Who Am I?"
Hit Parade of 1941 (1940)

Harry Warren (Music), Mack Gordon (Lyrics)
for the song "Down Argentine Way"
Down Argentine Way (1940)

Best Writing, Screenplay

⚑ **Donald Ogden Stewart** ⚑
The Philadelphia Story (1940)

Joan Harrison, Robert E. Sherwood
Rebecca (1940)

Nunnally Johnson
The Grapes of Wrath (1940)

Dudley Nichols
The Long Voyage Home (1940)

Dalton Trumbo
Kitty Foyle (1940)

Best Sound Recording

Douglas Shearer (Sound Director),
Metro-Goldwyn-Mayer Studio Sound Department
Strike Up the Band (1940)

John Aalberg (Sound Director), RKO Radio Studio Sound Department
Kitty Foyle (1940)

Bernard B. Brown (Sound Director), Universal Studio Sound Department
Spring Parade (1940)

Edmund H. Hansen (Sound Director),
20th Century-Fox Studio Sound Department
The Grapes of Wrath (1940)

Nathan Levinson (Sound Director), Warner Bros. Studio Sound Department
The Sea Hawk (1940)

John P. Livadary (Sound Director), Columbia Studio Sound Department
Too Many Husbands (1940)

Charles L. Lootens (Sound Director), Republic Studio Sound Department
Behind the News (1940)

Thomas T. Moulton (Sound Director),
Samuel Goldwyn Studio Sound Department
Our Town (1940)

Elmer A. Raguse (Sound Director), Hal Roach Studio Sound Department
Captain Caution (1940)

Loren L. Ryder (Sound Director), Paramount Studio Sound Department
North West Mounted Police (1940)

Jack Whitney (Sound Director), General Service Sound Department
The Howards of Virginia (1940)

Best Writing, Original Screenplay

Preston Sturges
The Great McGinty (1940)

Charles Bennett, Joan Harrison
Foreign Correspondent (1940)

Norman Burnstine, Heinz Herald, John Huston
Dr. Ehrlich's Magic Bullet (1940)

Charles Chaplin
The Great Dictator (1940)

Ben Hecht
Angels Over Broadway (1940)

Best Writing, Original Story

Benjamin Glazer, Hans Székely (as John S. Toldy)
Arise, My Love (1940)

Hugo Butler, Dore Schary
Edison, the Man (1940)

Stuart N. Lake
The Westerner (1940)

Leo McCarey, Bella Spewack, Samuel Spewack
My Favorite Wife (1940)

Walter Reisch
Comrade X (1940)

Best Film Editing
↓ **Anne Bauchens** ↓
North West Mounted Police (1940)

Hal C. Kern
Rebecca (1940)

Warren Low
The Letter (1940)

Robert L. Simpson
The Grapes of Wrath (1940)

Sherman Todd
The Long Voyage Home (1940)

Best Short Subject, Cartoon
↓ **Rudolf Ising, Fred Quimby (Producers), Metro-Goldwyn-Mayer** ↓
The Milky Way (1940)

Rudolf Ising (Producer), Metro-Goldwyn-Mayer
Puss Gets the Boot (1940)

Leon Schlesinger (Producer), Warner Bros.
A Wild Hare (1940)

Best Special Effects
↓ **Lawrence W. Butler (Photographic), Jack Whitney (Sound)** ↓
The Thief of Bagdad (1940)

Ray O. Binger, R. T. Layton (Photographic), Thomas T. Moulton (Sound)
The Long Voyage Home (1940)

**William Bradford, Howard J. Lydecker, Ellis J. Thackery (Photographic),
Herbert Norsch (Sound)**
Women in War (1940)

Jack Cosgrove (Photographic), Arthur Johns (Sound)
Rebecca (1940)

Paul Eagler (Photographic), Thomas T. Moulton (Sound)
Foreign Correspondent (1940)

Farciot Edouart, Gordon Jennings (Photographic)
Dr. Cyclops (1940)

**Farciot Edouart, Gordon Jennings (Photographic),
Loren L. Ryder (Sound)**
Typhoon (1940)

John P. Fulton (Photographic), Bernard B. Brown, William Hedgecock (Sound)
The Invisible Man Returns (1940)

John P. Fulton (Photographic), Bernard B. Brown, Joseph Lapis (Sound)
The Boys from Syracuse (1940)

A. Arnold Gillespie (Photographic), Douglas Shearer (Sound)
Boom Town (1940)

Byron Haskin (Photographic), Nathan Levinson (Sound)
The Sea Hawk (1940)

Roy Seawright (Photographic), Elmer Raguse (Sound)
One Million B.C. (1940)

Fred Sersen (Photographic), Edmund H. Hansen (Sound)
The Blue Bird (1940)

Vernon L. Walker (Photographic), John O. Aalberg (Sound)
Swiss Family Robinson (1940)

Honorary Award
Bob Hope
(special silver plaque) for unselfish services to the motion picture industry
☦ **Colonel Nathan Levinson** ☦
for service to the motion picture industry and the Army

The 14ᵗʰ Academy Awards® - February 26, 1942
Host: Bob Hope
Venue: Biltmore Bowl of the Biltmore Hotel
Honoring movies released in 1941

Irving G. Thalberg Memorial Award
☦ **Walt Disney** ☦

Best Actor
☦ **Gary Cooper** ☦
Sergeant York (1941) role "Sergeant Alvin C. York"

Cary Grant
Penny Serenade (1941) role "Roger Adams"

Walter Huston
All That Money Can Buy (aka The Devil and Daniel Webster) (1941) role "Mr. Scratch"

Robert Montgomery
Here Comes Mr. Jordan (1941) role "Joe Pendleton"

Orson Welles
Citizen Kane (1941) role "Charles Foster Kane"

Best Actor in a Supporting Role
☦ **Donald Crisp** ☦
How Green Was My Valley (1941) role "Gwilym Morgan"

Walter Brennan
Sergeant York (1941) role "Pastor Rosier Pile"

Charles Coburn
The Devil and Miss Jones (1941) role "John P. Merrick"

James Gleason
Here Comes Mr. Jordan (1941) role "Max Corkle"

Sydney Greenstreet
The Maltese Falcon (1941) role "Kasper Gutman"

Best Actress
☦ **Joan Fontaine** ☦
Suspicion (1941) role "Lina McLaidlaw Aysgarth"

Bette Davis
The Little Foxes (1941) role "Regina Giddens"

Olivia de Havilland
Hold Back the Dawn (1941) role "Emmy Brown"

Greer Garson
Blossoms in the Dust (1941) role "Edna Gladney"

Barbara Stanwyck
Ball of Fire (1941) role "Katherine "Sugarpuss" O'Shea"

Best Actress in a Supporting Role
⬇ Mary Astor ⬇
The Great Lie (1941) role "Sandra Kovak"
Sara Allgood
How Green Was My Valley (1941) role "Beth Morgan"
Patricia Collinge
The Little Foxes (1941) role "Birdie Bagtry-Hubbard"
Teresa Wright
The Little Foxes (1941) role "Alexandra Giddens"
Margaret Wycherly
Sergeant York (1941) role "Mary Brooks-York"

Best Outstanding Motion Picture
⬇ 20th Century-Fox ⬇
How Green Was My Valley (1941)
Columbia
Here Comes Mr. Jordan (1941)
Mercury
Citizen Kane (1941)
Metro-Goldwyn-Mayer
Blossoms in the Dust (1941)
Paramount
Hold Back the Dawn (1941)
RKO Radio
Suspicion (1941)
Samuel Goldwyn Productions
The Little Foxes (1941)
Warner Bros.
One Foot in Heaven (1941), Sergeant York (1941), The Maltese Falcon (1941)

Best Cinematography, Black and White
⬇ Arthur C. Miller ⬇
How Green Was My Valley (1941)
Edward Cronjager
Sun Valley Serenade (1941)
Karl Freund
The Chocolate Soldier (1941)
Charles Lang
Sundown (1941)
Rudolph Maté
That Hamilton Woman (1941)
Sol Polito
Sergeant York (1941)
Joseph Ruttenberg
Dr. Jekyll and Mr. Hyde (1941)
Gregg Toland
Citizen Kane (1941)
Leo Tover
Hold Back the Dawn (1941)
Joseph Walker
Here Comes Mr. Jordan (1941)

Best Cinematography, Color

Ⱡ **Ernest Palmer, Ray Rennahan** Ⱡ
Blood and Sand (1941)

Wilfrid M. Cline, William E. Snyder, Karl Struss
Aloma of the South Seas (1941)

Karl Freund, W. Howard Greene
Blossoms in the Dust (1941)

Bert Glennon
Dive Bomber (1941)

Harry Hallenberger, Ray Rennahan
Louisiana Purchase (1941)

William V. Skall, Leonard Smith
Billy the Kid (1941)

Best Directing

Ⱡ **John Ford** Ⱡ
How Green Was My Valley (1941)

Alexander Hall
Here Comes Mr. Jordan (1941)

Howard Hawks
Sergeant York (1941)

Orson Welles
Citizen Kane (1941)

William Wyler
The Little Foxes (1941)

Best Film Editing

Ⱡ **William Holmes** Ⱡ
Sergeant York (1941)

James B. Clark
How Green Was My Valley (1941)

Harold F. Kress
Dr. Jekyll and Mr. Hyde (1941)

Daniel Mandell
The Little Foxes (1941)

Robert Wise
Citizen Kane (1941)

Honorary Award

Walt Disney, William E. Garity, John N.A. Hawkins, RCA Manufacturing Company
(certificate) for contribution to the advancement usage sound in Fantasia (1940)

Rey Scott
(certificate) for achievement in photography with 16mm camera under the difficult and dangerous conditions during producing Kukan: The Battle Cry of China (1941)

Leopold Stokowski (and his associates)
(certificate) for achievement in the creation of a new form of visualized music in Walt Disney's production Fantasia (1940)

The British Ministry of Information
(certificate) for vivid and dramatic presentation of the heroism of the RAF in the documentary film Target for Tonight (1941)

Best Art Direction, Black and White

⚱ Richard Day, Nathan Juran (Art Direction), ⚱
Thomas Little (Interior Decoration)
How Green Was My Valley (1941)

Lionel Banks (Art Direction), George Montgomery (Interior Decoration)
Ladies in Retirement (1941)

Hans Dreier, Robert Usher (Art Direction), Sam Comer (Interior Decoration)
Hold Back the Dawn (1941)

John DuCasse Schulze (Art Direction), Edward G. Boyle (Interior Decoration)
The Son of Monte Cristo (1940)

Randall Duell, Cedric Gibbons (Art Direction),
Edwin B. Willis (Interior Decoration)
When Ladies Meet (1941)

Perry Ferguson, Van Nest Polglase (Art Direction),
Al Roland Fields, Darrell Silvera (Interior Decoration)
Citizen Kane (1941)

Alexander Golitzen (Art Direction), Richard Irvine (Interior Decoration)
Sundown (1941)

Stephen Goosson (Art Direction), Howard Bristol (Interior Decoration)
The Little Foxes (1941)

John Hughes (Art Direction), Fred M. MacLean (Interior Decoration)
Sergeant York (1941)

Vincent Korda (Art Direction), Julia Heron (Interior Decoration)
That Hamilton Woman (1941)

Martin Obzina, Jack Otterson (Art Direction),
Russell A. Gausman (Interior Decoration)
The Flame of New Orleans (1941)

John Victor Mackay (Art Direction)
(nomination was withdrawn by Republic Studios is not counted as an official nomination)
Sis Hopkins (1941)

Best Art Direction, Color

⚱ Cedric Gibbons, Urie McCleary (Art Direction), ⚱
Edwin B. Willis (Interior Decoration)
Blossoms in the Dust (1941)

Raoul Pene du Bois (Art Direction), Stephen A. Seymour (Interior Decoration)
Louisiana Purchase (1941)

Richard Day, Joseph C. Wright (Art Direction),
Thomas Little (Interior Decoration)
Blood and Sand (1941)

Best Short Subject, One Reel

⚱ Metro-Goldwyn-Mayer ⚱
Of Pups and Puzzles (1941)

20th Century-Fox
Sagebrush and Silver (1941)

Paramount
Beauty and the Beach (1941), Speaking of Animals Down on the Farm (1941)

Pete Smith (Producer), Metro-Goldwyn-Mayer
Army Champions (1941)

Warner Bros.
Forty Boys and a Song (1941), Kings of the Turf (1941)

Best Short Subject, Two Reel

⚊ **Metro-Goldwyn-Mayer** ⚊
Main Street on the March! (1941)

Metro-Goldwyn-Mayer
Forbidden Passage (1941)

United States Army, Warner Bros.
The Tanks Are Coming (1941)

Warner Bros.
The Gay Parisian (1941)

Woodard Productions, Inc.
Alive in the Deep (1941)

Best Short Subject, Cartoon

⚊ **Walt Disney (Producer)** ⚊
Lend a Paw (1941)

Columbia
How War Came (1941)

Walt Disney (Producer)
Truant Officer Donald (1941)

Max Fleischer (Producer)
Superman (1941)

Walter Lantz (Producer)
Boogie Woogie Bugle Boy of Company 'B' (1941)

Metro-Goldwyn-Mayer
The Night Before Christmas (1941), The Rookie Bear (1941)

George Pal (Producer)
Rhythm in the Ranks (1941)

Leon Schlesinger (Producer)
Hiawatha's Rabbit Hunt (1941), Rhapsody in Rivets (1941)

Best Writing, Original Screenplay

⚊ **Herman J. Mankiewicz, Orson Welles** ⚊
Citizen Kane (1941)

Harry Chandlee, Abem Finkel, John Huston, Howard Koch
Sergeant York (1941)

Paul Jarrico
Tom, Dick and Harry (1941)

Norman Krasna
The Devil and Miss Jones (1941)

Karl Tunberg, Darrell Ware
Tall, Dark and Handsome (1941)

Best Writing, Original Story

⚊ **Harry Segall** ⚊
Here Comes Mr. Jordan (1941)

Richard Connell, Robert Presnell Sr.
Meet John Doe (1941)

Monckton Hoffe
The Lady Eve (1941)

Thomas Monroe, Billy Wilder
Ball of Fire (1941)

Gordon Wellesley
Night Train to Munich (1940)

Best Writing, Screenplay
⚱ Sidney Buchman, Seton I. Miller ⚱
Here Comes Mr. Jordan (1941)
Charles Brackett, Billy Wilder
Hold Back the Dawn (1941)
Philip Dunne
How Green Was My Valley (1941)
Lillian Hellman
The Little Foxes (1941)
John Huston
The Maltese Falcon (1941)

Best Documentary, Short Subject
⚱ National Film Board of Canada, United Artists ⚱
Churchill's Island (1941)
Amkino
Russian Soil (1941)
British Ministry of Information, United Artists
A Letter from Home (1941)
British Ministry of Information, Warner Bros.
Christmas Under Fire (1940)
Film Associates
Adventure in the Bronx (1941)
National Film Board of Canada, Metro-Goldwyn-Mayer
War clouds in the Pacific (1941)
Philadelphia Housing Association
A Place to Live (1941)
The March of Time, RKO Radio
Norway in Revolt (1941)
Truman Talley (Producer), 20th Century Fox
Life of a Thoroughbred (1941), Soldiers of the Sky (1941)
**United States Office for Emergency Management Film Unit,
Motion Picture Committee Cooperating for National Defense**
Bomber: A Defense Report on Film (1941)

Best Special Effects
**⚱ Farciot Edouart, Gordon Jennings (Photographic),
Louis Mesenkop (Sound) ⚱**
I Wanted Wings (1941)
Lawrence W. Butler (Photographic), William A. Wilmarth (Sound)
That Hamilton Woman (1941)
Farciot Edouart, Gordon Jennings (Photographic), Louis Mesenkop (Sound)
Aloma of the South Seas (1941)
John P. Fulton (Photographic), John D. Hall (Sound)
The Invisible Woman (1940)
A. Arnold Gillespie (Photographic), Douglas Shearer (Sound)
Flight Command (1940)
Byron Haskin (Photographic), Nathan Levinson (Sound)
The Sea Wolf (1941)
Roy Seawright (Photographic), Elmer Raguse (Sound)
Topper Returns (1941)
Fred Sersen (Photographic), Edmund H. Hansen (Sound)
A Yank in the R.A.F. (1941)

Best Music, Song

✝ Jerome Kern (Music), Oscar Hammerstein II (Lyrics) ✝
for the song "The Last Time I Saw Paris"
Lady Be Good (1941)

Louis Alter (Music), Frank Loesser (Lyrics) for the song "Dolores"
Las Vegas Nights (1941)

Harold Arlen (Music), Johnny Mercer (Lyrics)
for the song "Blues in the Night"
Blues in the Night (1941)

Gene Autry, Fred Rose (Music & Lyrics) for the song "Be Honest with Me"
Ridin' on a Rainbow (1941)

Frank Churchill (Music), Ned Washington (Lyrics) for the song "Baby Mine"
Dumbo (1941)

Lloyd B. Norlind (Music & Lyrics) for the song "Out of the Silence"
All-American Co-Ed (1941)

Cole Porter (Music & Lyrics) for the song "Since I Kissed My Baby Goodbye"
You'll Never Get Rich (1941)

Hugh Prince (Music), Don Raye (Lyrics)
for the song "Boogie Woogie Bugle Boy of Company B"
Buck Privates (1941)

Harry Warren (Music), Mack Gordon (Lyrics)
for the song "Chattanooga Choo Choo"
Sun Valley Serenade (1941)

Best Sound Recording

✝ Jack Whitney (Sound Director), General Service Sound Department ✝
That Hamilton Woman (1941)

John Aalberg (Sound Director), RKO Radio Studio Sound Department
Citizen Kane (1941)

Bernard B. Brown (Sound Director), Universal Studio Sound Department
Appointment for Love (1941)

Edmund H. Hansen (Sound Director),
20th Century-Fox Studio Sound Department
How Green Was My Valley (1941)

Nathan Levinson (Sound Director), Warner Bros. Studio Sound Department
Sergeant York (1941)

John P. Livadary (Sound Director), Columbia Studio Sound Department
The Men in Her Life (1941)

Charles L. Lootens (Sound Director), Republic Studio Sound Department
The Devil Pays Off (1941)

Thomas T. Moulton (Sound Director),
Samuel Goldwyn Studio Sound Department
Ball of Fire (1941)

Elmer Raguse (Sound Director), Hal Roach Studio Sound Department
Topper Returns (1941)

Loren L. Ryder (Sound Director), Paramount Studio Sound Department
Skylark (1941)

Douglas Shearer (Sound Director),
Metro-Goldwyn-Mayer Studio Sound Department
The Chocolate Soldier (1941)

Best Music, Music Score of a Dramatic Picture

⇊ **Bernard Herrmann** ⇊
All That Money Can Buy (aka The Devil and Daniel Webster) (1941)

Cy Feuer, Walter Scharf
Mercy Island (1941)

Louis Gruenberg
So Ends Our Night (1941)

Richard Hageman
This Woman Is Mine (1941)

Bernard Herrmann
Citizen Kane (1941)

Werner R. Heymann
That Uncertain Feeling (1941)

Edward J. Kay
King of the Zombies (1941)

Alfred Newman
Ball of Fire (1941), How Green Was My Valley (1941)

Miklós Rózsa
Lydia (1941), Sundown (1941)

Frank Skinner
Back Street (1941)

Max Steiner
Sergeant York (1941)

Morris Stoloff, Ernst Toch
Ladies in Retirement (1941)

Edward Ward
Cheers for Miss Bishop (1941), Tanks a Million (1941)

Franz Waxman
Dr. Jekyll and Mr. Hyde (1941), Suspicion (1941)

Meredith Willson
The Little Foxes (1941)

Victor Young
Hold Back the Dawn (1941)

Best Music, Scoring of a Musical Picture

⇊ **Frank Churchill, Oliver Wallace** ⇊
Dumbo (1941)

Anthony Collins
Sunny (1941)

Robert Emmett Dolan
Birth of the Blues (1941)

Cy Feuer
Ice-Capades (1941)

Bronislau Kaper, Herbert Stothart
The Chocolate Soldier (1941)

Emil Newman
Sun Valley Serenade (1941)

Charles Previn
Buck Privates (1941)

Heinz Roemheld
The Strawberry Blonde (1941)

Morris Stoloff
You'll Never Get Rich (1941)

Edward Ward
All-American Co-Ed (1941)

14th Ceremony 8/8

The 15th Academy Awards® - March 4, 1943

Host: Bob Hope
Venue: Cocoanut Grove of the Ambassador Hotel
Honoring movies released in 1942

Honorary Award

Charles Boyer
(certificate) for progressive cultural achievement in establishing the French Research Foundation in Los Angeles as a source of reference

Noël Coward
(certificate) for achievement in production of In Which We Serve (1942)

Metro-Goldwyn-Mayer
(certificate) for achievement in representing the American Way of Life in the Andy Hardy series of films

Best Actor

⚊ **James Cagney** ⚊
Yankee Doodle Dandy (1942) role "George M. Cohan"

Ronald Colman
Random Harvest (1942) role "Charles Rainier"

Gary Cooper
The Pride of the Yankees (1942) role "Lou Gehrig"

Walter Pidgeon
Mrs. Miniver (1942) role "Clem Miniver"

Monty Woolley
The Pied Piper (1942) role "John Sidney Howard"

Best Actor in a Supporting Role

⚊ **Van Heflin** ⚊
Johnny Eager (1941) role "Jeff Hartnett"

William Bendix
Wake Island (1942) role "Pvt. Aloysius K. 'Smacksie' Randall"

Walter Huston
Yankee Doodle Dandy (1942) role "Jerry Cohan"

Frank Morgan
Tortilla Flat (1942) role "The Pirate"

Henry Travers
Mrs. Miniver (1942) role "James Ballard"

Best Actress

⚊ **Greer Garson** ⚊
Mrs. Miniver (1942) role "Kay Miniver"

Bette Davis
Now, Voyager (1942) role "Charlotte Vale"

Katharine Hepburn
Woman of the Year (1942) role "Tess Harding"

Rosalind Russell
My Sister Eileen (1942) role "Ruth Sherwood"

Teresa Wright
The Pride of the Yankees (1942) role "Eleanor Twitchell Gehrig"

Best Actress in a Supporting Role
↓ **Teresa Wright** ↓
Mrs. Miniver (1942) role "Carol Beldon"

Gladys Cooper role
Now, Voyager (1942) "Mrs. Henry Vale"

Agnes Moorehead
The Magnificent Ambersons (1942) role "Fanny Minafer"

Susan Peters
Random Harvest (1942) role "Kitty Chilcet"

Dame May Whitty
Mrs. Miniver (1942) role "Lady Beldon"

Irving G. Thalberg Memorial Award
↓ **Sidney Franklin** ↓

Best Cinematography, Color
↓ **Leon Shamroy** ↓
The Black Swan (1942)

Edward Cronjager, William V. Skall
To the Shores of Tripoli (1942)

W. Howard Greene
The Jungle Book (1942)

W. Howard Greene, Milton R. Krasner, William V. Skall
Arabian Nights (1942)

Victor Milner, William V. Skall
Reap the Wild Wind (1942)

Sol Polito
Captains of the Clouds (1942)

Best Cinematography, Black and White
↓ **Joseph Ruttenberg** ↓
Mrs. Miniver (1942)

Charles G. Clarke
Moontide (1942)

Stanley Cortez
The Magnificent Ambersons (1942)

Edward Cronjager
The Pied Piper (1942)

James Wong Howe
Kings Row (1942)

Rudolph Maté
The Pride of the Yankees (1942)

John J. Mescall
Take a Letter, Darling (1942)

Arthur C. Miller
This Above All (1942)

Leon Shamroy
Ten Gentlemen from West Point (1942)

Ted Tetzlaff
The Talk of the Town (1942)

Best Art Direction, Color

⚊ Richard Day, Joseph C. Wright (Art Direction), ⚊
Thomas Little (Interior Decoration)
My Gal Sal (1942)

Roland Anderson, Hans Dreier (Art Direction),
George Sawley (Interior Decoration)
Reap the Wild Wind (1942)

Alexander Golitzen, Jack Otterson (Art Direction),
Russell A. Gausman, Ira S. Webb (Interior Decoration)
Arabian Nights (1942)

Vincent Korda (Art Direction), Julia Heron (Interior Decoration)
The Jungle Book (1942)

Ted Smith (Art Direction), Casey Roberts (Interior Decoration)
Captains of the Clouds (1942)

Best Art Direction, Black and White

⚊ Richard Day, Joseph C. Wright (Art Direction), ⚊
Thomas Little (Interior Decoration)
This Above All (1942)

Roland Anderson, Hans Dreier (Art Direction),
Sam Comer (Interior Decoration)
Take a Letter, Darling (1942)

Lionel Banks, Rudolph Sternad (Art Direction),
Fay Babcock (Interior Decoration)
The Talk of the Town (1942)

Ralph Berger (Art Direction), Emile Kuri (Interior Decoration)
Silver Queen (1942)

Albert S. D'Agostino (Art Direction),
Al Roland Fields, Darrell Silvera (Interior Decoration)
The Magnificent Ambersons (1942)

Randall Duell, Cedric Gibbons (Art Direction),
Jack D. Moore, Edwin B. Willis (Interior Decoration)
Random Harvest (1942)

Perry Ferguson (Art Direction), Howard Bristol (Interior Decoration)
The Pride of the Yankees (1942)

John B. Goodman, Jack Otterson (Art Direction),
Russell A. Gausman, Edward R. Robinson (Interior Decoration)
The Spoilers (1942)

Mark-Lee Kirk, Max Parker (Art Direction),
Casey Roberts (Interior Decoration)
George Washington Slept Here (1942)

Boris Leven (Art Direction), Boris Leven (Interior Decoration)
The Shanghai Gesture (1941)

Best Short Subject, One Reel

⚊ Paramount ⚊
Speaking of Animals and Their Families (1942)

20th Century-Fox
Desert Wonderland (1942)

Pete Smith (Producer)
Marines in the Making (1942)

Warner Bros.
The United States Marine Band (1942)

Best Short Subject, Two Reel
ꙇ **Warner Bros.** ꙇ
Beyond the Line of Duty (1942)

Metro-Goldwyn-Mayer
Don't Talk (1942)

RKO Radio
This Is America Series No. 33-101: Private Smith of the U.S.A. (1942)

Best Film Editing
ꙇ **Daniel Mandell** ꙇ
The Pride of the Yankees (1942)

George Amy
Yankee Doodle Dandy (1942)

Harold F. Kress
Mrs. Miniver (1942)

Otto Meyer
The Talk of the Town (1942)

Walter Thompson
This Above All (1942)

Best Directing
ꙇ **William Wyler** ꙇ
Mrs. Miniver (1942)

Michael Curtiz
Yankee Doodle Dandy (1942)

John Farrow
Wake Island (1942)

Mervyn LeRoy
Random Harvest (1942)

Sam Wood
Kings Row (1942)

Best Outstanding Motion Picture
ꙇ **Metro-Goldwyn-Mayer** ꙇ
Mrs. Miniver (1942)

20th Century-Fox
The Pied Piper (1942)

Columbia
The Talk of the Town (1942)

Metro-Goldwyn-Mayer
Random Harvest (1942)

Mercury
The Magnificent Ambersons (1942)

Ortus
49th Parallel (aka The Invaders) (1941)

Paramount
Wake Island (1942)

Samuel Goldwyn Productions
The Pride of the Yankees (1942)

Warner Bros.
Kings Row (1942), Yankee Doodle Dandy (1942)

Best Documentary

⚑ **Australian News, Information Bureau** ⚑
Kokoda Front Line! (1942)

⚑ **Artkino** ⚑
Razgrom nemetskikh voysk pod Moskvoy (eng. Moscow Strikes Back) (1942)

⚑ **United States Army Special Services** ⚑
Prelude to War (aka Why We Fight) (1942)

⚑ **United States Navy** ⚑
The Battle of Midway (1942)

British Ministry of Information
Klein Belgie (eng. Little Belgium) (1942), Listen to Britain (1942), Twenty-One Miles (1942)

Concanen Films
The White Eagle (1942)

Walt Disney (Producer)
The Grain That Built a Hemisphere (1943), The New Spirit (1942)

Edgar Loew, Victor Stoloff (Producers)
Little Isles of Freedom (1943)

National Film Board of Canada
High Over the Borders (1942), Inside Fighting China (1942)

William H. Pine (Producer)
Paramount Victory Short No. T2-3: The Price of Victory (1942)

The March of Time
Africa, Prelude to Victory (1943)

The Netherlands Information Bureau
High Stakes in the East (1942)

William C. Thomas (Producer)
Paramount Victory Short No. T2-2: We Refuse to Die (1942)

Frederic Ullman Jr. (Producer)
Conquer by the Clock (1942)

United States Army Air Force
Winning Your Wings (1942)

United States Army Signal Corps
Combat Report (1942)

United States Department of Agriculture
Henry Browne, Farmer (1942)

United States Merchant Marine
A Ship Is Born (1942)

United States Office of War Information
It's Everybody's War (1942), Mister Gardenia Jones (1942), Mr. Blabbermouth! (1942)

Best Short Subject, Cartoon

⚑ **Walt Disney (Producer)** ⚑
Der Fuehrer's Face (1942)

20th Century-Fox
All Out for 'V' (1942)

Walter Lantz (Producer)
Juke Box Jamboree (1942)

Metro-Goldwyn-Mayer
Blitz Wolf (1942)

George Pal (Producer)
Tulips Shall Grow (1942)

Leon Schlesinger (Producer)
Pigs in a Polka (1943)

Best Music, Music Score of a Dramatic or Comedy Picture

⚓ **Max Steiner** ⚓
Now, Voyager (1942)

Frank Churchill, Edward H. Plumb
(Frank Churchill - posthumous)
Bambi (1942)

Richard Hageman
The Shanghai Gesture (1941)

Leigh Harline
The Pride of the Yankees (1942)

Werner R. Heymann
To Be or Not to Be (1942)

Friedrich Hollaender, Morris Stoloff
The Talk of the Town (1942)

Edward J. Kay
Klondike Fury (1942)

Alfred Newman
The Black Swan (1942)

Miklós Rózsa
The Jungle Book (1942)

Frank Skinner
Arabian Nights (1942)

Herbert Stothart
Random Harvest (1942)

Max Terr
The Gold Rush (re-release) (1925)

Dimitri Tiomkin
The Corsican Brothers (1941)

Roy Webb
I Married a Witch (1942), Joan of Paris (1942)

Victor Young
Flying Tigers (1942), Silver Queen (1942), Take a Letter, Darling (1942)

Best Music, Scoring of a Musical Picture

⚓ **Ray Heindorf, Heinz Roemheld** ⚓
Yankee Doodle Dandy (1942)

Robert Emmett Dolan
Holiday Inn (1942)

Roger Edens, George Stoll
For Me and My Gal (1942)

Leigh Harline
You Were Never Lovelier (1942)

Alfred Newman
My Gal Sal (1942)

Charles Previn, Hans J. Salter
It Started with Eve (1941)

Walter Scharf
Johnny Doughboy (1942)

Edward Ward
Flying with Music (1942)

Best Music, Song

⚡ **Irving Berlin (Music & Lyrics) for the song "White Christmas"** ⚡
Holiday Inn (1942)

Frank Churchill (Music), Larry Morey (Lyrics) for the song "Love Is a Song"
(Frank Churchill - posthumous)
Bambi (1942)

Jerome Kern (Music), Johnny Mercer (Lyrics) for the song "Dearly Beloved"
You Were Never Lovelier (1942)

Burton Lane (Music), Ralph Freed (Lyrics) for the song "How About You?"
Babes on Broadway (1941)

**Ernesto Lecuona (Music), Kim Gannon (Lyrics)
for the song "Always in My Heart"**
Always in My Heart (1942)

Gene de Paul (Music), Don Raye (Lyrics) for the song "Pig Foot Pete"
Hellzapoppin' (1941)

**Harry Revel (Music), Mort Greene (Lyrics)
for the song "There's a Breeze on Lake Louise"**
The Mayor of 44th Street (1942)

**Jule Styne (Music), Sammy Cahn (Lyrics)
for the song "It Seems I Heard That Song Before"**
Youth on Parade (1942)

**Edward Ward (Music), Chet Forrest, Bob Wright (Lyrics)
for the song "Pennies for Peppino"**
Flying with Music (1942)

**Harry Warren (Music), Mack Gordon (Lyrics)
for the song "I've Got a Gal in Kalamazoo"**
Orchestra Wives (1942)

Best Special Effects

⚡ **Farciot Edouart, Gordon Jennings, William L. Pereira
(Photographic), Louis Mesenkop (Sound)** ⚡
Reap the Wild Wind (1942)

Byron Haskin (Photographic), Nathan Levinson (Sound)
Desperate Journey (1942)

Howard Lydecker (Photographic), Daniel J. Bloomberg (Sound)
Flying Tigers (1942)

John P. Fulton (Photographic), Bernard B. Brown (Sound)
Invisible Agent (1942)

**A. Arnold Gillespie, Warren Newcombe (Photographic),
Douglas Shearer (Sound)**
Mrs. Miniver (1942)

Ronald Neame (Photographic), C. C. Stevens (Sound)
One of Our Aircraft Is Missing (1942)

Fred Sersen (Photographic), Roger Heman Sr., George Leverett (Sound)
The Black Swan (1942)

Lawrence W. Butler (Photographic), William H. Wilmarth (Sound)
The Jungle Book (1942)

Vernon L. Walker (Photographic), James G. Stewart (Sound)
The Navy Comes Through (1942)

Ray Binger, Jack Cosgrove (Photographic), Thomas T. Moulton (Sound)
The Pride of the Yankees (1942)

Best Sound Recording

Nathan Levinson (Sound Director),
Warner Bros. Studio Sound Department
Yankee Doodle Dandy (1942)

Daniel J. Bloomberg (Sound Director), Republic Studio Sound Department
Flying Tigers (1942)

Bernard B. Brown (Sound Director), Universal Studio Sound Department
Arabian Nights (1942)

Steve Dunn (Sound Director), RKO Radio Studio Sound Department
Once Upon a Honeymoon (1942)

James L. Fields (Sound Director), RCA Sound
The Gold Rush (re-release) (1925)

Edmund H. Hansen (Sound Director),
20th Century-Fox Studio Sound Department
This Above All (1942)

John P. Livadary (Sound Director), Columbia Studio Sound Department
You Were Never Lovelier (1942)

Thomas T. Moulton (Sound Director),
Samuel Goldwyn Studio Sound Department
The Pride of the Yankees (1942)

Loren L. Ryder (Sound Director), Paramount Studio Sound Department
Road to Morocco (1942)

Douglas Shearer, (Sound Director),
Metro-Goldwyn-Mayer Studio Sound Department
Mrs. Miniver (1942)

Sam Slyfield (Sound Director), Walt Disney Studio Sound Department
Bambi (1942)

Jack Whitney (Sound Director), Sound Service, Inc.
Friendly Enemies (1942)

Best Writing, Screenplay

George Froeschel, James Hilton, Claudine West, Arthur Wimperis
Mrs. Miniver (1942)

Rodney Ackland, Emeric Pressburger
49th Parallel (aka The Invaders) (1941)

Sidney Buchman, Irwin Shaw
The Talk of the Town (1942)

George Froeschel, Claudine West, Arthur Wimperis
Random Harvest (1942)

Herman J. Mankiewicz, Jo Swerling
The Pride of the Yankees (1942)

Best Writing, Original Screenplay

Michael Kanin, Ring Lardner Jr.
Woman of the Year (1942)

W.R. Burnett, Frank Butler
Wake Island (1942)

Frank Butler, Don Hartman
Road to Morocco (1942)

George Oppenheimer
The War Against Mrs. Hadley (1942)

Michael Powell, Emeric Pressburger
One of Our Aircraft Is Missing (1942)

Best Writing, Original Motion Picture Story
⚑ Emeric Pressburger ⚑
49th Parallel (aka The Invaders) (1941)

Irving Berlin
Holiday Inn (1942)

Robert Buckner
Yankee Doodle Dandy (1942)

Paul Gallico
The Pride of the Yankees (1942)

Sidney Harmon
The Talk of the Town (1942)

The 16th Academy Awards® - March 2, 1944
Host: Jack Benny
Venue: Grauman's Chinese Theatre
Honoring movies released in 1943

Honorary Award
⚑ George Pal ⚑
(Plaque replaced with statuette in 1967) for the development of novel methods and
techniques in the production of short subjects known as Puppetoons

Irving G. Thalberg Memorial Award
⚑ Hal B. Wallis ⚑

Best Actor
⚑ Paul Lukas ⚑
Watch on the Rhine (1943) role "Kurt Muller"

Humphrey Bogart
Casablanca (1942) role "Rick Blaine"

Gary Cooper
For Whom the Bell Tolls (1943) role "Robert Jordan"

Walter Pidgeon
Madame Curie (1943) role "Pierre Curie"

Mickey Rooney
The Human Comedy (1943) role "Homer Macauley"

Best Actor in a Supporting Role
⚑ Charles Coburn ⚑
The More the Merrier (1943) role "Benjamin Dingle"

Charles Bickford
The Song of Bernadette (1943) rolc "Father Peyramale"

J. Carrol Naish
Sahara (1943) role "Giuseppe"

Claude Rains
Casablanca (1942) role "Captain Louis Renault"

Akim Tamiroff
For Whom the Bell Tolls (1943) role "Pablo"

Best Actress
↓ Jennifer Jones ↓
The Song of Bernadette (1943) role "Bernadette Soubirous"
Jean Arthur
The More the Merrier (1943) role "Constance "Connie" Milligan"
Ingrid Bergman
For Whom the Bell Tolls (1943) role "María"
Joan Fontaine
The Constant Nymph (1943) role "Tessa Sanger"
Greer Garson
Madame Curie (1943) role "Marie Curie"

Best Actress in a Supporting Role
↓ Katina Paxinou ↓
For Whom the Bell Tolls (1943) role "Pilar"
Gladys Cooper
The Song of Bernadette (1943) role "Sister Marie Therese Vauzous"
Paulette Goddard
So Proudly We Hail! (1943) role "Lieutenant Joan O'Doul"
Anne Revere
The Song of Bernadette (1943) role "Louise Casterot-Soubirous"
Lucile Watson
Watch on the Rhine (1943) role "Fanny Farrelly"

Best Directing
↓ Michael Curtiz ↓
Casablanca (1942)
Clarence Brown
The Human Comedy (1943)
Ernst Lubitsch
Heaven Can Wait (1943)
Henry King
The Song of Bernadette (1943)
George Stevens
The More the Merrier (1943)

Best Art Direction, Color
↓ Alexander Golitzen, John B. Goodman (Art Direction), ↓
Russell A. Gausman, Ira S. Webb (Interior Decoration)
Phantom of the Opera (1943)
James Basevi, Joseph C. Wright (Art Direction),
Thomas Little (Interior Decoration)
The Gang's All Here (1943)
Daniel B. Cathcart, Cedric Gibbons (Art Direction),
Jacques Mersereau, Edwin B. Willis (Interior Decoration)
Thousands Cheer (1943)
Haldane Douglas, Hans Dreier (Art Direction),
Bertram C. Granger (Interior Decoration)
For Whom the Bell Tolls (1943)
John Hughes, Lt. John Koenig (Art Direction),
George James Hopkins (Interior Decoration)
This Is the Army (1943)

Best Art Direction, Black and White

⚐ **James Basevi, William S. Darling (Art Direction),** ⚐
Thomas Little (Interior Decoration)
The Song of Bernadette (1943)

Carroll Clark, Albert S. D'Agostino (Art Direction),
Harley Miller, Darrell Silvera (Interior Decoration)
Flight for Freedom (1943)

Hans Dreier, Ernst Fegté (Art Direction),
Bertram C. Granger (Interior Decoration)
Five Graves to Cairo (1943)

Perry Ferguson (Art Direction), Howard Bristol (Interior Decoration)
The North Star (1943)

Cedric Gibbons, Paul Groesse (Art Direction),
Hugh Hunt, Edwin B. Willis (Interior Decoration)
Madame Curie (1943)

Carl Jules Weyl (Art Direction), George James Hopkins (Interior Decoration)
Mission to Moscow (1943)

Best Cinematography, Black and White

⚐ **Arthur C. Miller** ⚐
The Song of Bernadette (1943)

Elmer Dyer, James Wong Howe, Charles A. Marshall
Air Force (1943)

Arthur Edeson
Casablanca (1942)

Tony Gaudio
Corvette K-225 (1943)

James Wong Howe
The North Star (1943)

Charles Lang
So Proudly We Hail! (1943)

Rudolph Maté
Sahara (1943)

Joseph Ruttenberg
Madame Curie (1943)

John F. Seitz
Five Graves to Cairo (1943)

Harry Stradling Sr.
The Human Comedy (1943)

Best Cinematography, Color

⚐ **W. Howard Greene, Hal Mohr** ⚐
Phantom of the Opera (1943)

Charles G. Clarke, Allen M. Davey
Hello Frisco, Hello (1943)

Edward Cronjager
Heaven Can Wait (1943)

George J. Folsey
Thousands Cheer (1943)

Ray Rennahan
For Whom the Bell Tolls (1943)

Leonard Smith
Lassie Come Home (1943)

Best Documentary, Feature

⚰ **British Ministry of Information** ⚰
Desert Victory (1943)

United States Army
Baptism of Fire (1943)

United States Army Pictorial Service
Report from the Aleutians (1943)

United States Department of War Special Service Division
The Battle of Russia (1943)

United States Office of Strategic Services Field Photographic Bureau
War Department Report (1943)

Best Documentary, Short Subject

⚰ **United States Navy** ⚰
December 7th (1943)

Metro-Goldwyn-Mayer
Plan for Destruction (1943)

RKO Radio
Children of Mars (1943)

The March of Time
Youth in Crisis (1943)

United States Navy Bureau of Aeronautics
Tomorrow We Fly (1943)

**United States Office of War Information Overseas
Motion Picture Bureau**
Swedes in America (1943)

Walter Wanger (Producer)
To the People of the United States (1943)

Best Short Subject, Two Reel

⚰ **Jerry Bresler, Sam Coslow (Producers)** ⚰
Heavenly Music (1943)

Gordon Hollingshead (Producer)
Women at War (1943)

Walter MacEwen (Producer)
Mardi Gras (1943)

Frederic Ullman Jr. (Producer)
Letter to a Hero (1943)

Best Short Subject, One Reel

⚰ **Grantland Rice (Producer)** ⚰
Amphibious Fighters (1943)

Gordon Hollingshead (Producer)
Cavalcade of Dance (1943)

Edmund Reek (Producer)
Champions Carry on (1943)

Pete Smith (Producer)
Seeing Hands (1943)

Ralph Staub (Producer)
Screen Snapshots Series 23, No. 1: Hollywood in Uniform (1943)

Best Music, Music Score of a Dramatic or Comedy Picture

⚱ Alfred Newman ⚱
The Song of Bernadette (1943)

C. Bakaleinikoff, Roy Webb
The Fallen Sparrow (1943)

Phil Boutelje
Hi Diddle Diddle (1943)

Gerard Carbonara
The Kansan (1943)

Aaron Copland
The North Star (1943)

Hanns Eisler
Hangmen Also Die! (1943)

Louis Gruenberg, Morris Stoloff
Commandos Strike at Dawn (1942)

Hans J. Salter, Frank Skinner
The Amazing Mrs. Holliday (1943)

Leigh Harline
Johnny Come Lately (1943)

Arthur Lange
Lady of Burlesque (1943)

Edward H. Plumb, Paul J. Smith, Oliver G. Wallace
Victory Through Air Power (1943)

Walter Scharf
In Old Oklahoma (1943)

Max Steiner
Casablanca (1942)

Herbert Stothart
Madame Curie (1943)

Dimitri Tiomkin
The Moon and Sixpence (1942)

Victor Young
For Whom the Bell Tolls (1943)

Best Outstanding Motion Picture

⚱ Warner Bros. ⚱
Casablanca (1942)

20th Century-Fox
Heaven Can Wait (1943), The Ox-Bow Incident (1942), The Song of Bernadette (1943)

Columbia
The More the Merrier (1943)

Metro-Goldwyn-Mayer
Madame Curie (1943), The Human Comedy (1943)

Paramount
For Whom the Bell Tolls (1943)

Two Cities
In Which We Serve (1942)

Warner Bros.
Watch on the Rhine (1943)

Best Music, Scoring of a Musical Picture

⚊ Ray Heindorf ⚊
This Is the Army (1943)

Robert Emmett Dolan
Star Spangled Rhythm (1942)

Leigh Harline
The Sky's the Limit (1943)

Alfred Newman
Coney Island (1943)

Edward H. Plumb, Paul J. Smith, Charles Wolcott
Saludos Amigos (1942)

Frederic E. Rich
Stage Door Canteen (1943)

Walter Scharf
Hit Parade of 1943 (1943)

Morris Stoloff
Something to Shout About (1943)

Herbert Stothart
Thousands Cheer (1943)

Edward Ward
Phantom of the Opera (1943)

Best Music, Song

**Harry Warren (Music), Mack Gordon (Lyrics)
for the song "You'll Never Know"**
Hello Frisco, Hello (1943)

**Harold Arlen (Music), E.Y. Harburg (Lyrics)
for the song "Happiness Is a Thing Called Joe"**
Cabin in the Sky (1943)

Harold Arlen (Music), Johnny Mercer (Lyrics) for the song "My Shining Hour"
The Sky's the Limit (1943)

**Harold Arlen (Music), Johnny Mercer (Lyrics)
for the song "That Old Black Magic"**
Star Spangled Rhythm (1942)

**Jimmy McHugh (Music), Herb Magidson (Lyrics)
for the song "Say a Prayer for the Boys Over There"**
Hers to Hold (1943)

**James V. Monaco (Music), Al Dubin (Lyrics)
for the song "We Mustn't Say Good Bye"**
Stage Door Canteen (1943)

Cole Porter (Music & Lyrics) for the song "You'd Be So Nice to Come Home to"
Something to Shout About (1943)

**Arthur Schwartz (Music), Frank Loesser (Lyrics)
for the song "They're Either Too Young or Too Old"**
Thank Your Lucky Stars (1943)

Jule Styne (Music), Harold Adamson (Lyrics) for the song "Change of Heart"
Hit Parade of 1943 (1943)

**Charles Wolcott (Music), Ned Washington (Lyrics)
for the song "Saludos Amigos"**
Saludos Amigos (1942)

Best Short Subject, Cartoon

⚰ **Fred Quimby (Producer)** ⚰
The Yankee Doodle Mouse (1943)

Walt Disney (Producer)
Reason and Emotion (1943)

Dave Fleischer (Producer)
Imagination (1943)

Walter Lantz (Producer)
The Dizzy Acrobat (1943)

George Pal (Producer)
The 500 Hats of Bartholomew Cubbins (1943)

Leon Schlesinger (Producer)
Greetings Bait (1943)

Best Special Effects

⚰ **Fred Sersen (Photographic), Roger Heman Sr. (Sound)** ⚰
Crash Dive (1943)

Ray O. Binger, Clarence Slifer (Photographic), Thomas T. Moulton (Sound)
The North Star (1943)

Farciot Edouart, Gordon Jennings (Photographic), George Dutton (Sound)
So Proudly We Hail! (1943)

A. Arnold Gillespie, Donald Jahraus (Photographic), Michael Steinore (Sound)
Stand by for Action (1942)

Hans F. Koenekamp, Rex Wimpy (Photographic), Nathan Levinson (Sound)
Air Force (1943)

Vernon L. Walker (Photographic), Roy Granville, James G. Stewart (Sound)
Bombardier (1943)

Best Writing, Original Motion Picture Story

⚰ **William Saroyan** ⚰
The Human Comedy (1943)

Steve Fisher
Destination Tokyo (1943)

Guy Gilpatric
Action in the North Atlantic (1943)

Gordon McDonell
Shadow of a Doubt (1943)

Frank Ross, Robert Russell
The More the Merrier (1943)

Best Writing, Original Screenplay

⚰ **Norman Krasna** ⚰
Princess O'Rourke (1943)

Noël Coward
In Which We Serve (1942)

Lillian Hellman
The North Star (1943)

Dudley Nichols
Air Force (1943)

Allan Scott
So Proudly We Hail! (1943)

Best Writing, Screenplay

⚜ **Julius J. Epstein, Philip G. Epstein, Howard Koch** ⚜
Casablanca (1942)

Richard Flournoy, Lewis R. Foster, Frank Ross, Robert Russell
The More the Merrier (1943)

Dashiell Hammett
Watch on the Rhine (1943)

Nunnally Johnson
Holy Matrimony (1943)

George Seaton
The Song of Bernadette (1943)

Best Sound Recording

⚜ **Stephen Dunn (Sound Director), RKO Radio Studio Sound Department** ⚜
This Land Is Mine (1943)

Daniel J. Bloomberg (Sound Director), Republic Studio Sound Department
In Old Oklahoma (1943)

Bernard B. Brown (Sound Director), Universal Studio Sound Department
Phantom of the Opera (1943)

James L. Fields (Sound Director), RCA Sound
So This Is Washington (1943)

**Edmund H. Hansen (Sound Director),
20th Century-Fox Studio Sound Department**
The Song of Bernadette (1943)

Nathan Levinson (Sound Director), Warner Bros. Studio Sound Department
This Is the Army (1943)

John P. Livadary (Sound Director), Columbia Studio Sound Department
Sahara (1943)

**Thomas T. Moulton (Sound Director),
Samuel Goldwyn Studio Sound Department**
The North Star (1943)

Loren L. Ryder (Sound Director), Paramount Studio Sound Department
Riding High (1943)

**Douglas Shearer (Sound Director),
Metro-Goldwyn-Mayer Studio Sound Department**
Madame Curie (1943)

C. O. Slyfield (Sound Director), Walt Disney Studio Sound Department
Saludos Amigos (1942)

Jack Whitney (Sound Director), Sound Service, Inc.
Hangmen Also Die! (1943)

Best Film Editing

⚜ **George Amy** ⚜
Air Force (1943)

Doane Harrison
Five Graves to Cairo (1943)

John F. Link Sr., Sherman Todd
For Whom the Bell Tolls (1943)

Owen Marks
Casablanca (1942)

Barbara McLean
The Song of Bernadette (1943)

The 17ᵗʰ Academy Awards® - March 15, 1945

Hosts: John Cromwell, Bob Hope
Venue: Grauman's Chinese Theatre
Honoring movies released in 1944

Honorary Award

Bob Hope

(life membership in the AMPAS®) for many services to the Academy

Irving G. Thalberg Memorial Award

⚱ **Darryl F. Zanuck** ⚱

Best Actor

⚱ **Bing Crosby** ⚱

Going My Way (1944) role "Father Chuck O'Malley"

Charles Boyer

Gaslight (1944) role "Gregory Anton (Sergius Bauer)"

Barry Fitzgerald

Going My Way (1944) role "Father Fitzgibbon"

Cary Grant

None But the Lonely Heart (1944) role "Ernie Mott"

Alexander Knox

Wilson (1944) role "Woodrow Wilson"

Best Actor in a Supporting Role

⚱ **Barry Fitzgerald** ⚱

Going My Way (1944) role "Father Fitzgibbon"

Hume Cronyn

The Seventh Cross (1944) role "Paul Roeder"

Claude Rains

Mr. Skeffington (1944) role "Job Skeffington"

Clifton Webb

Laura (1944) role "Waldo Lydecker"

Monty Woolley

Since You Went Away (1944) role "Colonel William G. Smollett"

Best Actress

⚱ **Ingrid Bergman** ⚱

Gaslight (1944) role "Paula Alquist Anton"

Claudette Colbert

Since You Went Away (1944) role "Mrs. Anne Hilton"

Bette Davis

Mr. Skeffington (1944) role "Frances Beatrice "Fanny" Trellis Skeffington"

Greer Garson

Mrs. Parkington (1944) role "Susie Parkington"

Barbara Stanwyck

Double Indemnity (1944) role "Phyllis Dietrichson"

Best Actress in a Supporting Role
⚑ Ethel Barrymore ⚑
None But the Lonely Heart (1944) role "Ma Mott"
Jennifer Jones
Since You Went Away (1944) role "Jane Deborah Hilton"
Angela Lansbury
Gaslight (1944) role "Nancy Oliver"
Aline MacMahon
Dragon Seed (1944) role "Ling Tan's Wife"
Agnes Moorehead
Mrs. Parkington (1944) role "Baroness Aspasia Conti"

Best Documentary, Feature
⚑ United States Navy ⚑
The Fighting Lady (1944)
United States Army Air Force
Resisting Enemy Interrogation (1944)

Best Documentary, Short Subject
⚑ United States Marine Corps ⚑
With the Marines at Tarawa (1944)
RKO Radio
New Americans (1944)
United States Office of War Information Overseas Motion Picture Bureau
Hymn of the Nations (1944) (nominated as Arturo Toscanini)

Best Film Editing
⚑ Barbara McLean ⚑
Wilson (1944)
LeRoy Stone
Going My Way (1944)
Owen Marks
Janie (1944)
Roland Gross
None But the Lonely Heart (1944)
Hal C. Kern, James E. Newcom
Since You Went Away (1944)

Best Cinematography, Color
⚑ Leon Shamroy ⚑
Wilson (1944)
Edward Cronjager
Home in Indiana (1944)
Allen M. Davey, Rudolph Maté
Cover Girl (1944)
George J. Folsey
Meet Me in St. Louis (1944)
Ray Rennahan
Lady in the Dark (1944)
Charles Rosher
Kismet (1944)

Best Cinematography, Black and White

⭤ Joseph LaShelle ⭤
Laura (1944)

Stanley Cortez, Lee Garmes
Since You Went Away (1944)

George J. Folsey
The White Cliffs of Dover (1944)

Charles Lang
The Uninvited (1944)

Lionel Lindon
Going My Way (1944)

Glen MacWilliams
Lifeboat (1944)

Harold Rosson, Robert Surtees
Thirty Seconds Over Tokyo (1944)

Joseph Ruttenberg
Gaslight (1944)

John F. Seitz
Double Indemnity (1944)

Sidney Wagner
Dragon Seed (1944)

Best Directing

⭤ Leo McCarey ⭤
Going My Way (1944)

Alfred Hitchcock
Lifeboat (1944)

Henry King
Wilson (1944)

Otto Preminger
Laura (1944)

Billy Wilder
Double Indemnity (1944)

Best Art Direction, Color

⭤ Wiard Ihnen (Art Direction), Thomas Little (Interior Decoration) ⭤
Wilson (1944)

Lionel Banks, Cary Odell (Art Direction), Fay Babcock (Interior Decoration)
Cover Girl (1944)

**Daniel B. Cathcart, Cedric Gibbons (Art Direction),
Richard Pefferle, Edwin B. Willis (Interior Decoration)**
Kismet (1944)

**Hans Dreier, Raoul Pene Du Bois (Art Direction),
Ray Moyer (Interior Decoration)**
Lady in the Dark (1944)

Ernst Fegté (Art Direction), Howard Bristol (Interior Decoration)
The Princess and the Pirate (1944)

**Alexander Golitzen, John B. Goodman (Art Direction),
Russell A. Gausman, Ira S. Webb (Interior Decoration)**
The Climax (1944)

Charles Novi (Art Direction), Jack McConaghy (Interior Decoration)
The Desert Song (1943)

Best Art Direction, Black and White

**William Ferrari, Cedric Gibbons (Art Direction),
Paul Huldschinsky, Edwin B. Willis (Interior Decoration)**
Gaslight (1944)

**Lionel Banks, Walter Holscher (Art Direction),
Joseph Kish (Interior Decoration)**
Address Unknown (1944)

**Carroll Clark, Albert S. D'Agostino (Art Direction),
Claude E. Carpenter, Darrell Silvera (Interior Decoration)**
Step Lively (1944)

**Hans Dreier, Robert Usher (Art Direction),
Samuel M. Comer (Interior Decoration)**
No Time for Love (1943)

Perry Ferguson (Art Direction), Julia Heron (Interior Decoration)
Casanova Brown (1944)

**Leland Fuller, Lyle R. Wheeler (Art Direction),
Thomas Little (Interior Decoration)**
Laura (1944)

John J. Hughes (Art Direction), Fred M. MacLean (Interior Decoration)
The Adventures of Mark Twain (1944)

Mark-Lee Kirk (Art Direction), Victor A. Gangelin (Interior Decoration)
Since You Went Away (1944)

Bernard Herzbrun (Art Direction)
(nomination withdrawn)
Song of the Open Road (1944)

Best Motion Picture

Leo McCarey (Producer), Paramount
Going My Way (1944)

Arthur Hornblow Jr. (Producer), Metro-Goldwyn-Mayer
Gaslight (1944)

David O. Selznick (Producer), Selznick International Pictures
Since You Went Away (1944)

Joseph Sistrom (Producer), Paramount
Double Indemnity (1944)

Darryl F. Zanuck (Producer), 20th Century-Fox
Wilson (1944)

Best Short Subject, One Reel

Jerry Fairbanks (Producer)
Who's Who in Animal Land (1944)

Gordon Hollingshead (Producer)
Jammin' the Blues (1944)

Edmund Reek (Producer)
Blue-Grass Gentlemen (1944)

Pete Smith (Producer)
Movie Pests (1944)

Ralph Staub (Producer)
Screen Snapshots' 50th Anniversary of Motion Pictures (1944)

Best Short Subject, Two Reel
⚊ **Gordon Hollingshead (Producer)** ⚊
I Won't Play (1944)
Jerry Bresler (Producer), Herbert Moulton (Associate Producer)
Main Street Today (1944)
Louis Harris (Producer)
Bombalera (1945)

Juvenile Award
⚊ **Margaret O'Brien** ⚊
for outstanding child actress of 1944

Best Music, Music Score of a Dramatic or Comedy Picture
⚊ **Max Steiner** ⚊
Since You Went Away (1944)
C. Bakaleinikoff, Hanns Eisler
None But the Lonely Heart (1944)
Karl Hajos
Summer Storm (1944)
W. Franke Harling
Three Russian Girls (1943)
Arthur Lange
Casanova Brown (1944)
Michel Michelet
Voice in the Wind (1944)
Michel Michelet, Edward Paul
The Hairy Ape (1944)
Alfred Newman
Wilson (1944)
Edward Paul
Up in Mabel's Room (1944)
Frederic Efrem Rich
Jack London (1943)
David Rose
The Princess and the Pirate (1944)
Miklós Rózsa
Double Indemnity (1944), The Woman of the Town (1943)
Hans J. Salter
Christmas Holiday (1944)
Walter Scharf, Roy Webb
The Fighting Seabees (1944)
Max Steiner
The Adventures of Mark Twain (1944)
Morris Stoloff, Ernst Toch
Address Unknown (1944)
Robert Stolz
It Happened Tomorrow (1944)
Herbert Stothart
Kismet (1944)
Dimitri Tiomkin
The Bridge of San Luis Rey (1944)

Best Music, Song

Jimmy Van Heusen (Music), Johnny Burke (Lyrics)
for the song "Swinging on a Star"
Going My Way (1944)

Harold Arlen (Music), Ted Koehler (Lyrics) for the song "Now I Know"
Up in Arms (1944)

Ary Barroso (Music), Ned Washington (Lyrics) for the song "Rio de Janeiro"
Brazil (1944)

Ralph Blane, Hugh Martin (Music & Lyrics) for the song "The Trolley Song"
Meet Me in St. Louis (1944)

M.K. Jerome (Music), Ted Koehler (Lyrics)
for the song "Sweet Dreams Sweetheart"
Hollywood Canteen (1944)

Walter Kent (Music), Kim Gannon (Lyrics) for the song "Too Much in Love"
Song of the Open Road (1944)

Jerome Kern (Music), Ira Gershwin (Lyrics)
for the song "Long Ago and Far Away"
Cover Girl (1944)

Jimmy McHugh (Music), Harold Adamson (Lyrics)
for the song "I Couldn't Sleep a Wink Last Night"
Higher and Higher (1943)

James V. Monaco (Music), Mack Gordon (Lyrics)
for the song "I'm Making Believe"
Sweet and Low-Down (1944)

Lew Pollack (Music), Charles Newman (Lyrics)
for the song "Silver Shadows and Golden Dreams"
Lady, Let's Dance (1944)

Harry Revel (Music), Paul Francis Webster (Lyrics)
for the song "Remember Me to Carolina"
Minstrel Man (1944)

Jule Styne (Music), Sammy Cahn (Lyrics) for the song "I'll Walk Alone"
Follow the Boys (1944)

Best Special Effects

A. Arnold Gillespie, Warren Newcombe,
Donald Jahraus (Photographic), Douglas Shearer (Sound)
Thirty Seconds Over Tokyo (1944)

David Allen, Ray Cory, Robert Wright (Photographic),
Harry Kusnick, Russell Malmgren (Sound)
Secret Command (1944)

Jack Cosgrove (Photographic), Arthur Johns (Sound)
Since You Went Away (1944)

John Crouse, Paul Detlefsen (Photographic), Nathan Levinson (Sound)
The Adventures of Mark Twain (1944)

Farciot Edouart, Gordon Jennings (Photographic), George Dutton (Sound)
The Story of Dr. Wassell (1944)

Fred Sersen (Photographic), Roger Heman Sr. (Sound)
Wilson (1944)

Vernon L. Walker (Photographic), Roy Granville, James G. Stewart (Sound)
Days of Glory (1944)

Best Music, Scoring of a Musical Picture

⚑ **Carmen Dragon, Morris Stoloff** ⚑
Cover Girl (1944)

C. Bakaleinikoff
Higher and Higher (1943)

Robert Emmett Dolan
Lady in the Dark (1944)

Leo Erdody, Ferde Grofé Sr.
Minstrel Man (1944)

Louis Forbes, Ray Heindorf
Up in Arms (1944)

Ray Heindorf
Hollywood Canteen (1944)

Werner R. Heymann, Kurt Weill
Knickerbocker Holiday (1944)

Edward J. Kay
Lady, Let's Dance (1944)

Mahlon Merrick
Sensations of 1945 (1944)

Alfred Newman
Irish Eyes Are Smiling (1944)

Charles Previn
Song of the Open Road (1944)

Hans J. Salter
The Merry Monahans (1944)

Walter Scharf
Brazil (1944)

Georgie Stoll
Meet Me in St. Louis (1944)

Best Writing, Original Motion Picture Story

⚑ **Leo McCarey** ⚑
Going My Way (1944)

David Boehm, Chandler Sprague
A Guy Named Joe (1943)

Edward Doherty, Jules Schermer
The Fighting Sullivans (aka The Sullivans) (1944)

Alfred Neumann, Joseph Than
None Shall Escape (1944)

John Steinbeck
Lifeboat (1944)

Best Writing, Original Screenplay

⚑ **Lamar Trotti** ⚑
Wilson (1944)

Jerome Cady
Wing and a Prayer (1944)

Richard Connell, Gladys Lehman
Two Girls and a Sailor (1944)

Preston Sturges
Hail the Conquering Hero (1944),
The Miracle of Morgan's Creek (1943)

Best Writing, Screenplay

⚑ **Frank Butler, Frank Cavett** ⚑
Going My Way (1944)

John L. Balderston, John Van Drutcn, Walter Reisch
Gaslight (1944)

Irving Brecher, Fred F. Finklehoffe
Meet Me in St. Louis (1944)

Raymond Chandler, Billy Wilder
Double Indemnity (1944)

Jay Dratler, Samuel Hoffenstein, Betty Reinhardt
Laura (1944)

Best Sound Recording

⚑ **Edmund H. Hansen (Sound Director),**
20th Century-Fox Studio Sound Department ⚑
Wilson (1944)

Daniel J. Bloomberg (Sound Director), Republic Studio Sound Department
Brazil (1944)

Bernard B. Brown (Sound Director), Universal Studio Sound Department
His Butler's Sister (1943)

W. M. Dalgleish (Sound Director), RCA Sound
Voice in the Wind (1944)

Stephen Dunn (Sound Director), RKO Radio Studio Sound Department
Music in Manhattan (1944)

Nathan Levinson (Sound Director), Warner Bros. Studio Sound Department
Hollywood Canteen (1944)

John P. Livadary (Sound Director), Columbia Studio Sound Department
Cover Girl (1944)

Thomas T. Moulton (Sound Director),
Samuel Goldwyn Studio Sound Department
Casanova Brown (1944)

Loren L. Ryder (Sound Director), Paramount Studio Sound Department
Double Indemnity (1944)

Douglas Shearer (Sound Director),
Metro-Goldwyn-Mayer Studio Sound Department
Kismet (1944)

Jack Whitney (Sound Director), Sound Service, Inc.
It Happened Tomorrow (1944)

Best Short Subject, Cartoon

⚑ **Frederick C. Quimby (Producer), Loew's** ⚑
Mouse Trouble (1944)

Walt Disney (Producer), Walt Disney Productions
How to Play Football (1944)

Walter Lantz (Producer), Walter Lantz Productions
Fish Fry (1944)

George Pal (Producer), Paramount Pictures
And to Think That I Saw It on Mulberry Street (1944)

Leon Schlesinger (Producer), Warner Bros.
Swooner Crooner (1944)

Screen Gems
Dog, Cat, and Canary (1945)

Paul Terry (Producer), Terrytoons
My Boy Johnny (1944)

17th Ceremony 8/8

The 18ᵗʰ Academy Awards® - March 7, 1946

Hosts: Bob Hope, James Stewart
Venue: Grauman's Chinese Theatre
Honoring movies released in 1945

Honorary Award

**Republic Studio, Daniel J. Bloomberg and
the Republic Studio Sound Department**
(certificate) for outstanding musical scoring auditorium which provides optimum
recording conditions and combines all elements of acoustic and engineering design

Walter Wanger
(special plaque) for six years service as President of the AMPAS®

**Lewis Allan, Mervyn LeRoy, Albert Maltz, Earl Robinson,
Frank Ross, Frank Sinatra**
(certificate) for tolerance short subject; produced by Frank Ross & Mervyn LeRoy;
directed by Mervyn LeRoy; screenplay by Albert Maltz; song "The House I Live In"
music by Earl Robinson, lyrics by Lewis Allan; starring Frank Sinatra;
released by RKO Radio

Juvenile Award

♦ **Peggy Ann Garner** ♦
for the outstanding child actress of 1945

Best Actor

♦ **Ray Milland** ♦
The Lost Weekend (1945) role "Don Birnam"

Bing Crosby
The Bells of St. Mary's (1945) role "Father Chuck O'Malley"

Gene Kelly
Anchors Aweigh (1945) role "Joseph "Joe" Brady"

Gregory Peck
The Keys of the Kingdom (1944) role "Father Francis Chisholm"

Cornel Wilde
A Song to Remember (1945) role "Frédéric Chopin"

Best Actor in a Supporting Role

♦ **James Dunn** ♦
A Tree Grows in Brooklyn (1945) role "Johnny Nolan"

Michael Chekhov
Spcllbound (1945) role "Dr Alexander "Alex" Brulov"

John Dall
The Corn Is Green (1945) role "Morgan Evans"

Robert Mitchum
Story of G.I. Joe (1945) role "Lieutenant/Captain Bill Walker"

J. Carrol Naish
A Medal for Benny (1945) role "Charley Martin"

Best Actress
⚊ Joan Crawford ⚊
Mildred Pierce (1945) role "Mildred Pierce Beragon"
Ingrid Bergman
The Bells of St. Mary's (1945) role "Sister Mary Benedict"
Greer Garson
The Valley of Decision (1945) role "Mary Rafferty"
Jennifer Jones
Love Letters (1945) role "Victoria Morland aka Singleton"
Gene Tierney
Leave Her to Heaven (1945) role "Ellen Berent Harland"

Best Actress in a Supporting Role
⚊ Anne Revere ⚊
National Velvet (1944) role "Mrs. Araminty Brown"
Eve Arden
Mildred Pierce (1945) role "Ida Corwin"
Ann Blyth
Mildred Pierce (1945) role "Veda Pierce Forrester"
Angela Lansbury
The Picture of Dorian Gray (1945) role "Sibyl Vane"
Joan Lorring
The Corn Is Green (1945) role "Bessie Watty"

Best Art Direction, Black and White
⚊ Wiard Ihnen (Art Direction), A. Roland Fields (Interior Decoration) ⚊
Blood on the Sun (1945)
Albert S. D'Agostino, Jack Okey (Art Direction), Claude E. Carpenter, Darrell Silvera (Interior Decoration)
Experiment Perilous (1944)
Roland Anderson, Hans Dreier (Art Direction), Sam Comer, Ray Moyer (Interior Decoration)
Love Letters (1945)
James Basevi, William S. Darling (Art Direction), Frank E. Hughes, Thomas Little (Interior Decoration)
The Keys of the Kingdom (1944)
Cedric Gibbons, Hans Peters (Art Direction), John Bonar, Hugh Hunt, Edwin B. Willis (Interior Decoration)
The Picture of Dorian Gray (1945)

Best Cinematography, Black and White
⚊ Harry Stradling Sr. ⚊
The Picture of Dorian Gray (1945)
George Barnes
Spellbound (1945)
Ernest Haller
Mildred Pierce (1945)
Arthur C. Miller
The Keys of the Kingdom (1944)
John F. Seitz
The Lost Weekend (1945)

Best Art Direction, Color

Hans Dreier, Ernst Fegté (Art Direction), Sam Comer (Interior Decoration)
Frenchman's Creek (1944)

Cedric Gibbons, Urie McCleary (Art Direction), Mildred Griffiths, Edwin B. Willis (Interior Decoration)
National Velvet (1944)

Stephen Goosson, Rudolph Sternad (Art Direction), Frank Tuttle (Interior Decoration)
A Thousand and One Nights (1945)

Maurice Ransford, Lyle R. Wheeler (Art Direction), Thomas Little (Interior Decoration)
Leave Her to Heaven (1945)

Ted Smith (Art Direction), Jack McConaghy (Interior Decoration)
San Antonio (1945)

Best Cinematography, Color

Leon Shamroy
Leave Her to Heaven (1945)

George Barnes
The Spanish Main (1945)

Charles P. Boyle, Robert H. Planck
Anchors Aweigh (1945)

Allen M. Davey, Tony Gaudio
(Allen M. Davey - posthumous)
A Song to Remember (1945)

Leonard Smith
National Velvet (1944)

Best Directing

Billy Wilder
The Lost Weekend (1945)

Clarence Brown
National Velvet (1944)

Alfred Hitchcock
Spellbound (1945)

Leo McCarey
The Bells of St. Mary's (1945)

Jean Renoir
The Southerner (1945)

Best Film Editing

Robert J. Kern
National Velvet (1944)

George Amy
Objective, Burma! (1945)

Doane Harrison
The Lost Weekend (1945)

Harry Marker
The Bells of St. Mary's (1945)

Charles Nelson
A Song to Remember (1945)

Best Motion Picture

⚱ Paramount ⚱
The Lost Weekend (1945)

Metro-Goldwyn-Mayer
Anchors Aweigh (1945)

Rainbow Productions
The Bells of St. Mary's (1945)

Selznick International Pictures
Spellbound (1945)

Warner Bros.
Mildred Pierce (1945)

Best Documentary, Feature

⚱ The Governments of Great Britain and the United States of America ⚱
The True Glory (1945)

United States Army Air Force
The Last Bomb (1945)

Best Documentary, Short Subject

⚱ Gordon Hollingshead (Producer) ⚱
Hitler Lives (1945)

United States Marine Corps
To the Shores of Iwo Jima (1945)

United States Office of War Information Overseas Motion Picture Bureau
Library of Congress (1945)

Best Short Subject, One Reel

⚱ Herbert Moulton (Producer), Jerry Bresler (Executive Producer) ⚱
Stairway to Light (1945)

Joseph O'Brien, Thomas Mead (Producers)
(Joseph O'Brien - posthumous)
Your National Gallery (1945)

Gordon Hollingshead (Producer)
Story of a Dog (1945)

Edmund Reek (Producer)
Along the Rainbow Trail (1946)

Grantland Rice (Producer)
White Rhapsody (1945)

Ralph Staub (Producer)
Screen Snapshots Series 25, No. 1: 25th Anniversary (1945)

Best Short Subject, Two Reel

⚱ Gordon Hollingshead (Producer) ⚱
Star in the Night (1945)

Chester M. Franklin (Producer), Jerry Bresler (Executive Producer)
A Gun in His Hand (1945)

George Templeton (Producer)
The Little Witch (1945)

Jules White (Producer)
The Jury Goes Round 'n' Round (1945)

Best Music, Music Score of a Dramatic or Comedy Picture

⚔ Miklós Rózsa ⚔
Spellbound (1945)

Daniele Amfitheatrof
Guest Wife (1945)

Louis Applebaum, Ann Ronell
Story of G.I. Joe (1945)

R. Dale Butts, Morton Scott
Flame of Barbary Coast (1945)

Robert Emmett Dolan
The Bells of St. Mary's (1945)

Louis Forbes
Brewster's Millions (1945)

Hugo Friedhofer, Arthur Lange
The Woman in the Window (1944)

Karl Hajos
The Man Who Walked Alone (1945)

Werner Janssen
Captain Kidd (1945), Guest in the House (1944), The Southerner (1945)

Edward J. Kay
G.I. Honeymoon (1945)

Alfred Newman
The Keys of the Kingdom (1944)

Miklós Rózsa
The Lost Weekend (1945)

Miklós Rózsa, Morris Stoloff
A Song to Remember (1945)

Hans J. Salter
This Love of Ours (1945)

Herbert Stothart
The Valley of Decision (1945)

Alexander Tansman
Paris Underground (1945)

Franz Waxman
Objective, Burma! (1945)

Roy Webb
The Enchanted Cottage (1945)

Victor Young
Love Letters (1945)

Best Writing, Original Screenplay

⚔ Richard Schweizer ⚔
Marie-Louise (1944)

Myles Connolly
Music for Millions (1944)

Milton Holmes
Salty O'Rourke (1945)

Harry Kurnitz
What Next, Corporal Hargrove? (1945)

Philip Yordan
Dillinger (1945)

Best Special Effects

⚱ **John P. Fulton (Photographic), Arthur W. Johns (Sound)** ⚱
Wonder Man (1945)

Lawrence W. Butler (Photographic), Ray Bomba (Sound)
A Thousand and One Nights (1945)

Jack Cosgrove (Photographic)
Spellbound (1945)

**A. Arnold Gillespie, Donald Jahraus, Robert A. MacDonald (Photographic),
Michael Steinore (Sound)**
They Were Expendable (1945)

**Sol Halperin, Fred Sersen (Photographic),
Roger Heman Sr., Harry M. Leonard (Sound)**
Captain Eddie (1945)

Best Music, Song

⚱ **Richard Rodgers (Music), Oscar Hammerstein II (Lyrics)** ⚱
for the song "It Might as Well Be Spring"
State Fair (1945)

**Harold Arlen (Music), Johnny Mercer (Lyrics)
for the song "Accentuate the Positive"**
Here Come the Waves (1944)

**Ray Heindorf, M.K. Jerome (Music), Ted Koehler (Lyrics)
for the song "Some Sunday Morning"**
San Antonio (1945)

**Jimmy Van Heusen (Music), Johnny Burke (Lyrics)
for the song "Aren't You Glad You're You?"**
The Bells of St. Mary's (1945)

**Jimmy Van Heusen (Music), Johnny Burke (Lyrics)
for the song "Sleighride in July"**
Belle of the Yukon (1944)

Walter Kent (Music), Kim Gannon (Lyrics) for the song "Endlessly"
Earl Carroll Vanities (1945)

Jerome Kern (Music), E.Y. Harburg (Lyrics) for the song "More and More"
(Jerome Kern - Posthumous)
Can't Help Singing (1944)

**Jay Livingston (Music), Ray Evans (Lyrics)
for the song "The Cat and the Canary"**
Why Girls Leave Home (1945)

Ann Ronell (Music & Lyrics) for the song "Linda"
Story of G.I. Joe (1945)

David Rose (Music), Leo Robin (Lyrics) for the song "So in Love"
Wonder Man (1945)

Jule Styne (Music), Sammy Cahn (Lyrics) for the song "Anywhere"
Tonight and Every Night (1945)

**Jule Styne (Music), Sammy Cahn (Lyrics)
for the song "I Fall in Love Too Easily"**
Anchors Aweigh (1945)

**Allie Wrubel (Music), Herb Magidson (Lyrics)
for the song "I'll Buy That Dream"**
Sing Your Way Home (1945)

Victor Young (Music), Edward Heyman (Lyrics) for the song "Love Letters"
Love Letters (1945)

Best Sound Recording

⚱ **Stephen Dunn (Sound Director), RKO Radio Studio Sound Department** ⚱
The Bells of St. Mary's (1945)

Daniel J. Bloomberg (Sound Director), Republic Studio Sound Department
Flame of Barbary Coast (1945)

Bernard B. Brown (Sound Director), Universal Studio Sound Department
Lady on a Train (1945)

Nathan Levinson (Sound Director), Warner Bros. Studio Sound Department
Rhapsody in Blue (1945)

John P. Livadary (Sound Director), Columbia Studio Sound Department
A Song to Remember (1945)

**Thomas T. Moulton (Sound Director),
20th Century-Fox Studio Sound Department**
Leave Her to Heaven (1945)

Loren L. Ryder (Sound Director), Paramount Studio Sound Department
The Unseen (1945)

Gordon Sawyer (Sound Director), Samuel Goldwyn Studio Sound Department
Wonder Man (1945)

**Douglas Shearer (Sound Director),
Metro-Goldwyn-Mayer Studio Sound Department**
They Were Expendable (1945)

C. O. Slyfield (Sound Director), Walt Disney Studio Sound Department
The Three Caballeros (1944)

Jack Whitney (Sound Director), General Service
The Southerner (1945)

W. V. Wolfe (Sound Director), RCA Sound
Three Is a Family (1944)

Best Writing, Original Motion Picture Story

⚱ **Charles G. Booth** ⚱
The House on 92nd Street (1945)

Alvah Bessie
Objective, Burma! (1945)

László Görög, Thomas Monroe
The Affairs of Susan (1945)

Ernst Marischka
A Song to Remember (1945)

John Steinbeck, Jack Wagner
A Medal for Benny (1945)

Best Writing, Screenplay

⚱ **Charles Brackett, Billy Wilder** ⚱
The Lost Weekend (1945)

Frank Davis, Tess Slesinger
(Tess Slesinger - posthumous)
A Tree Grows in Brooklyn (1945)

Leopold Atlas, Guy Endore, Philip Stevenson
Story of G.I. Joe (1945)

Ranald MacDougall
Mildred Pierce (1945)

Albert Maltz
Pride of the Marines (1945)

Best Music, Scoring of a Musical Picture

⬇ **Georgie Stoll** ⬇
Anchors Aweigh (1945)

Robert Emmett Dolan
Incendiary Blonde (1945)

Louis Forbes, Ray Heindorf
Wonder Man (1945)

Walter Greene
Why Girls Leave Home (1945)

Ray Heindorf, Max Steiner
Rhapsody in Blue (1945)

Charles Henderson, Alfred Newman
State Fair (1945)

Edward J. Kay
Sunbonnet Sue (1945)

Jerome Kern, Hans J. Salter
(Jerome Kern - Posthumous)
Can't Help Singing (1944)

Arthur Lange
Belle of the Yukon (1944)

Edward H. Plumb, Paul J. Smith, Charles Wolcott
The Three Caballeros (1944)

Morton Scott
Hitchhike to Happiness (1945)

Marlin Skiles, Morris Stoloff
Tonight and Every Night (1945)

Best Short Subject, Cartoon

⬇ **Frederick Quimby (Producer)** ⬇
Quiet Please! (1945)

Walt Disney (Producer)
Donald's Crime (1945)

Screen Gems
Rippling Romance (1945)

Walter Lantz (Producer)
The Poet & Peasant (1945)

George Pal (Producer)
Jasper and the Beanstalk (1945)

Edward Selzer (Producer)
Life with Feathers (1945)

Paul Terry (Producer)
Mighty Mouse in Gypsy Life (1945)

The 19th Academy Awards® - March 13, 1947

Host: Jack Benny
Venue: Shrine Civic Auditorium
Honoring movies released in 1946

Irving G. Thalberg Memorial Award

⬇ **Samuel Goldwyn** ⬇

Best Actor
♟ Fredric March ♟
The Best Years of Our Lives (1946) role "Platoon Sergeant Al Stephenson"
Laurence Olivier
Henry V (1944) role "King Henry V of England"
Larry Parks
The Jolson Story (1946) role "Al Jolson"
Gregory Peck
The Yearling (1946) role "Ezra "Penny" Baxter"
James Stewart
It's a Wonderful Life (1946) role "George Bailey"

Best Actor in a Supporting Role
♟ Harold Russell ♟
The Best Years of Our Lives (1946) role "Petty Officer 2nd Class Homer Parrish"
Charles Coburn
The Green Years (1946) role "Alexander Gow"
William Demarest
The Jolson Story (1946) role "Steve Martin"
Claude Rains
Notorious (1946) role "Alexander Sebastian"
Clifton Webb
The Razor's Edge (1946) role "Elliott Templeton"

Best Actress
♟ Olivia de Havilland ♟
To Each His Own (1946) role "Miss Josephine "Jody" Norris"
Celia Johnson
Brief Encounter (1945) role "Laura Jesson"
Jennifer Jones
Duel in the Sun (1946) role "Pearl Chavez"
Rosalind Russell
Sister Kenny (1946) role "Elizabeth Kenny"
Jane Wyman
The Yearling (1946) role "Orry Baxter"

Best Actress in a Supporting Role
♟ Anne Baxter ♟
The Razor's Edge (1946) role "Sophie MacDonald"
Ethel Barrymore
The Spiral Staircase (1946) role "Mrs. Warren"
Lillian Gish
Duel in the Sun (1946) role "Laura Belle McCanles"
Flora Robson
Saratoga Trunk (1945) role "Angclique Buiton"
Gale Sondergaard
Anna and the King of Siam (1946) role "Lady Thiang"

Juvenile Award
♟ Claude Jarman Jr. ♟
for the outstanding child actor of 1946

Best Art Direction, Black and White
William S. Darling, Lyle R. Wheeler (Art Direction),
Frank E. Hughes, Thomas Little (Interior Decoration)
Anna and the King of Siam (1946)

Richard Day, Nathan Juran (Art Direction),
Paul S. Fox, Thomas Little (Interior Decoration)
The Razor's Edge (1946)

Hans Dreier, Walter H. Tyler (Art Direction),
Sam Comer, Ray Moyer (Interior Decoration)
Kitty (1945)

Best Art Direction, Color
Cedric Gibbons, Paul Groesse (Art Direction),
Edwin B. Willis (Interior Decoration)
The Yearling (1946)

John Bryan (Art Direction)
Caesar and Cleopatra (1945)

Carmen Dillon, Paul Sheriff (Art Direction)
Henry V (1944)

Best Cinematography, Black and White
Arthur C. Miller
Anna and the King of Siam (1946)

George J. Folsey
The Green Years (1946)

Best Cinematography, Color
Arthur E. Arling, Charles Rosher, Leonard Smith
The Yearling (1946)

Joseph Walker
The Jolson Story (1946)

Best Special Effects
Thomas Howard (Visual)
Blithe Spirit (1945)

William C. McGann (Visual), Nathan Levinson (Audible)
A Stolen Life (1946)

Best Directing
William Wyler
The Best Years of Our Lives (1946)

Clarence Brown
The Yearling (1946)

Frank Capra
It's a Wonderful Life (1946)

David Lean
Brief Encounter (1945)

Robert Siodmak
The Killers (1946)

Best Music, Music Score of a Dramatic or Comedy Picture

↓ **Hugo Friedhofer** ↓
The Best Years of Our Lives (1946)

Bernard Herrmann
Anna and the King of Siam (1946)

Miklós Rózsa
The Killers (1946)

William Walton
Henry V (1944)

Franz Waxman
Humoresque (1946)

Best Music, Scoring of a Musical Picture

↓ **Morris Stoloff** ↓
The Jolson Story (1946)

Robert Emmett Dolan
Blue Skies (1946)

Lennie Hayton
The Harvey Girls (1946)

Ray Heindorf, Max Steiner
Night and Day (1946)

Alfred Newman
Centennial Summer (1946)

Best Music, Song

↓ **Harry Warren (Music), Johnny Mercer (Lyrics)**
for the song "On the Atchison, Topeka and Santa Fe" ↓
The Harvey Girls (1946)

Irving Berlin (Music & Lyrics)
for the song "You Keep Coming Back Like a Song"
Blue Skies (1946)

Hoagy Carmichael (Music), Jack Brooks (Lyrics)
for the song "Ole Buttermilk Sky"
Canyon Passage (1946)

Jerome Kern (Music), Oscar Hammerstein II (Lyrics)
for the song "All Through the Day"
(Jerome Kern - posthumous)
Centennial Summer (1946)

James V. Monaco (Music), Mack Gordon (Lyrics)
for the song "I Can't Begin to Tell You"
(James V. Monaco - posthumous)
The Dolly Sisters (1945)

Best Sound Recording

↓ **John P. Livadary (Sound Director), Columbia Studio Sound Department** ↓
The Jolson Story (1946)

John Aalberg (Sound Director), RKO Radio Studio Sound Department
It's a Wonderful Life (1946)

Gordon Sawyer (Sound Director), Samuel Goldwyn Studio Sound Department
The Best Years of Our Lives (1946)

Best Documentary, Short Subject

⚑ **United States Department of War** ⚑
Seeds of Destiny (1946)

Artkino
Life at the Zoo (1946)

Herbert Morgan (Producer)
Traffic with the Devil (1946)

Paramount
Paramount News Issue #37 (1946)

The March of Time
Atomic Power (1946)

Best Film Editing

⚑ **Daniel Mandell** ⚑
The Best Years of Our Lives (1946)

Arthur Hilton
The Killers (1946)

William Hornbeck
It's a Wonderful Life (1946)

Harold F. Kress
The Yearling (1946)

William A. Lyon
The Jolson Story (1946)

Best Motion Picture

⚑ **Samuel Goldwyn Productions** ⚑
The Best Years of Our Lives (1946)

20th Century-Fox
The Razor's Edge (1946)

J. Arthur Rank-Two Cities Films
Henry V (1944)

Liberty Films
It's a Wonderful Life (1946)

Metro-Goldwyn-Mayer
The Yearling (1946)

Best Short Subject, Cartoon

⚑ **Frederick Quimby (Producer)** ⚑
The Cat Concerto (1947)

Walt Disney (Producer)
Squatter's Rights (1946)

Walter Lantz (Producer)
Musical Moments from Chopin (1946)

George Pal (Producer)
John Henry and the Inky-Poo (1946)

Edward Selzer (Producer)
Walky Talky Hawky (1946)

Best Writing, Original Motion Picture Story

⚘ Clemence Dane ⚘
Vacation from Marriage (1945)

Charles Brackett
To Each His Own (1946)

Jack Patrick
The Strange Love of Martha Ivers (1946)

Vladimir Pozner
The Dark Mirror (1946)

Victor Trivas
The Stranger (1946)

Best Writing, Original Screenplay

⚘ Muriel Box, Sydney Box ⚘
The Seventh Veil (1945)

Raymond Chandler
The Blue Dahlia (1946)

Melvin Frank, Norman Panama
Road to Utopia (1945)

Ben Hecht
Notorious (1946)

Jacques Prévert
Les enfants du paradis (eng. Children of Paradise) (1945)

Best Writing, Screenplay

⚘ Robert E. Sherwood ⚘
The Best Years of Our Lives (1946)

Sergio Amidei, Federico Fellini
Roma città aperta (eng. Rome, Open City) (1945)

Sally Benson, Talbot Jennings
Anna and the King of Siam (1946)

Anthony Havelock-Allan, David Lean, Ronald Neame
Brief Encounter (1945)

Anthony Veiller
The Killers (1946)

Best Short Subject, One Reel

⚘ Gordon Hollingshead (Producer) ⚘
Facing Your Danger (1946)

Jack Eaton (Producer)
Dive-Hi Champs (1946)

Gordon Hollingshead (Producer)
Smart as a Fox (1946)

Edmund Reek (Producer)
Golden Horses (1946)

Pete Smith (Producer)
Sure Cures (1946)

Best Short Subject, Two Reel
⚐ **Gordon Hollingshead (Producer)** ⚐
A Boy and His Dog (1946)
Jerry Bresler (Producer)
The Luckiest Guy in the World (1947)
George B. Templeton (Producer)
College Queen (1946)
Jules White (Producer)
Hiss and Yell (1946)

Honorary Award
⚐ **Harold Russell** ⚐
for bringing hope and courage to his fellow veterans through appearance in
The Best Years of Our Lives (1946)
⚐ **Laurence Olivier** ⚐
for outstanding achievement as actor, producer and director of Henry V (1944)
Ernst Lubitsch
(certificate) for distinguished contributions to the art of the motion picture

The 20ᵗʰ Academy Awards® - March 20, 1948
Hosts: Agnes Moorehead, Dick Powell
Venue: Shrine Civic Auditorium
Honoring movies released in 1947

Honorary Award
⚐ **Bill and Coo (1948)** ⚐
(Plaque, replaced with Statuette in 1976) for artistry and patience blended in a novel and
entertaining use of the medium of motion pictures
⚐ **Sciuscià (eng. Shoeshine) (1946)** ⚐
for high quality motion picture which brought to eloquent life in a country scarred by war,
is proof to the world that the creative spirit can triumph over adversity
⚐ **Thomas Armat, Colonel William N. Selig, Albert E. Smith,** ⚐
George Kirke Spoor
the small group of pioneers whose belief in a new medium, and whose contributions to its
development, blazed the trail along which the motion picture has progressed, in their
lifetime, rom obscurity to world-wide acclaim
⚐ **James Baskett** ⚐
for heart-warming characterization of Uncle Remus, friend and story teller to the children
of the world in Walt Disney's Song of the South (1946)

Best Actor
⚐ **Ronald Colman** ⚐
A Double Life (1947) role "Anthony John"
John Garfield
Body and Soul (1947) role "Charlie Davis"
Gregory Peck
Gentleman's Agreement (1947) role "Philip Schuyler Green"
William Powell
Life with Father (1947) role "Clarence Day Sr."
Michael Redgrave
Mourning Becomes Electra (1947) role "Orin Mannon"

Best Actor in a Supporting Role
↓ **Edmund Gwenn** ↓
Miracle on 34th Street (1947) role "Kris Kringle"
Charles Bickford
The Farmer's Daughter (1947) role "Joseph Clancy"
Thomas Gomez
Ride the Pink Horse (1947) role "Pancho"
Robert Ryan
Crossfire (1947) role "Montgomery"
Richard Widmark
Kiss of Death (1947) role "Tommy Udo"

Best Actress
↓ **Loretta Young** ↓
The Farmer's Daughter (1947) role "Katie Holstrom"
Joan Crawford
Possessed (1947) role "Louise Howell"
Susan Hayward
Smash-Up: The Story of a Woman (1947) role "Angie Evans"
Dorothy McGuire
Gentleman's Agreement (1947) role "Kathy Lacey"
Rosalind Russell
Mourning Becomes Electra (1947) role "Lavinia Mannon"

Best Actress in a Supporting Role
↓ **Celeste Holm** ↓
Gentleman's Agreement (1947) role "Anne Dettrey"
Ethel Barrymore
The Paradine Case (1947) role "Lady Sophie Horfield"
Gloria Grahame
Crossfire (1947) role "Ginny Tremaine"
Marjorie Main
The Egg and I (1947) role "Ma Kettle"
Anne Revere
Gentleman's Agreement (1947) role "Mrs. Green"

Best Cinematography, Black and White
↓ **Guy Green** ↓
Great Expectations (1946)
George J. Folsey
Green Dolphin Street (1947)
Charles Lang Jr.
The Ghost and Mrs. Muir (1947)

Best Cinematography, Color
↓ **Jack Cardiff** ↓
Black Narcissus (1947)
Harry Jackson
Mother Wore Tights (1947)
J. Peverell Marley, William V. Skall
Life with Father (1947)

Best Art Direction, Black and White

⬐ **John Bryan (Art Direction), Wilfred Shingleton (Set Decoration)** ⬐
Great Expectations (1946)

Maurice Ransford, Lyle R. Wheeler (Art Direction),
Paul S. Fox, Thomas Little (Set Decoration)
The Foxes of Harrow (1947)

Best Art Direction, Color

⬐ **Alfred Junge (Art Direction & Set Decoration)** ⬐
Black Narcissus (1947)

Robert M. Haas (Art Direction), George James Hopkins (Set Decoration)
Life with Father (1947)

Best Directing

⬐ **Elia Kazan** ⬐
Gentleman's Agreement (1947)

Edward Dmytryk
Crossfire (1947)

George Cukor
A Double Life (1947)

Henry Koster
The Bishop's Wife (1947)

David Lean
Great Expectations (1946)

Best Documentary, Feature

Sid Rogell (Executive Producer),
⬐ **Richard O. Fleischer, Theron Warth (Producers)** ⬐
Design for Death (1947)

Paul Rotha (Producer)
The World Is Rich (1947)

United States Department of State Office of Information and
Educational Exchange
Journey Into Medicine (1947)

Best Documentary, Short Subject

⬐ **United Nations Division of Films and Visual Information** ⬐
First Steps (1947)

Australian News & Information Bureau
School in the Mailbox (1947)

Frederic Ullman Jr. (Producer)
Passport to Nowhere (1947)

Best Special Effects

⬐ **A. Arnold Gillespie, Warren Newcombe (Special Visual),** ⬐
Douglas Shearer, Michael Steinore (Special Audible)
Green Dolphin Street (1947)

Farciot Edouart, Devereux Jennings, Gordon Jennings, Wallace Kelley,
Paul K. Lerpae (Special Visual), George Dutton (Special Audible)
Unconquered (1947)

Best Film Editing

⚐ **Francis D. Lyon, Robert Parrish** ⚐
Body and Soul (1947)

Monica Collingwood
The Bishop's Wife (1947)

Harmon Jones
Gentleman's Agreement (1947)

Fergus McDonell
Odd Man Out (1947)

George White
Green Dolphin Street (1947)

Best Music, Music Score of a Dramatic or Comedy Picture

⚐ **Miklós Rózsa** ⚐
A Double Life (1947)

Hugo Friedhofer
The Bishop's Wife (1947)

Alfred Newman
Captain from Castile (1947)

David Raksin
Forever Amber (1947)

Max Steiner
Life with Father (1947)

Best Music, Song

⚐ **Allie Wrubel (Music), Ray Gilbert (Lyrics)** ⚐
for the song "Zip-A-Dee-Doo-Dah"
Song of the South (1946)

Ralph Blane, Roger Edens, Hugh Martin (Music & Lyrics)
for the song "Pass That Peace Pipe"
Good News (1947)

Frank Loesser (Music & Lyrics) for the song "I Wish I Didn't Love You So"
The Perils of Pauline (1947)

Josef Myrow (Music), Mack Gordon (Lyrics) for the song "You Do"
Mother Wore Tights (1947)

Arthur Schwartz (Music), Leo Robin (Lyrics) for the song "A Gal in Calico"
The Time, the Place and the Girl (1946)

Best Music, Scoring of a Musical Picture

⚐ **Alfred Newman** ⚐
Mother Wore Tights (1947)

Daniele Amfitheatrof, Paul J. Smith, Charles Wolcott
Song of the South (1946)

Robert Emmett Dolan
Road to Rio (1947)

Johnny Green
Fiesta (1947)

Ray Heindorf, Max Steiner
My Wild Irish Rose (1947)

Best Motion Picture

↓ 20th Century-Fox ↓
Gentleman's Agreement (1947)
20th Century-Fox
Miracle on 34ᵗʰ Street (1947)
J. Arthur Rank-Cineguild
Great Expectations (1946)
RKO Radio
Crossfire (1947)
Samuel Goldwyn Productions
The Bishop's Wife (1947)

Best Short Subject, One Reel

↓ Herbert Moulton (Producer) ↓
Goodbye, Miss Turlock (1948)
Jerry Fairbanks (Producer)
Moon Rockets (1947)
Gordon Hollingshead (Producer)
So You Want to Be in Pictures (1947)
Thomas Mead (Producer)
Brooklyn, U.S.A. (1947)
Pete Smith (Producer)
Now You See It (1947)

Best Short Subject, Two Reel

↓ Irving Allen (Producer) ↓
Climbing the Matterhorn (1947)
Ben K. Blake (Producer)
A Voice Is Born: The Story of Niklos Gafni (1947)
Harry Grey (Producer)
Champagne for Two (1947)
Thomas Mead (Producer)
Fight of the Wild Stallions (1947)
Herbert Morgan (Producer)
Give Us the Earth! (1947)

Best Writing, Motion Picture Story

↓ Valentine Davies ↓
Miracle on 34ᵗʰ Street (1947)
Georges Chaperot, René Wheeler
A Cage of Nightingales (1945)
Herbert Clyde Lewis, Frederick Stephani
It Happened on Fifth Avenue (1947)
Eleazar Lipsky
Kiss of Death (1947)
Dorothy Parker, Frank Cavett
Smash-Up: The Story of a Woman (1947)

Best Writing, Original Screenplay

⬩ Sidney Sheldon ⬩
The Bachelor and the Bobby-Soxer (1947)

Sergio Amidei, Adolfo Franci, Cesare Giulio Viola, Cesare Zavattini
Sciuscià (eng. Shoeshine) (1946)

Charles Chaplin
Monsieur Verdoux (1947)

Ruth Gordon, Garson Kanin
A Double Life (1947)

Abraham Polonsky
Body and Soul (1947)

Best Writing, Screenplay

⬩ George Seaton ⬩
Miracle on 34th Street (1947)

Moss Hart
Gentleman's Agreement (1947)

Anthony Havelock-Allan, David Lean, Ronald Neame
Great Expectations (1946)

Richard Murphy
Boomerang! (1947)

John Paxton
Crossfire (1947)

Best Short Subject, Cartoon

⬩ Edward Selzer (Producer) ⬩
Tweetie Pie (1947)

Walt Disney (Producer)
Chip an' Dale (1947), Pluto's Blue Note (1947)

George Pal (Producer)
Tubby the Tuba (1947)

Frederick Quimby (Producer)
Dr. Jekyll and Mr. Mouse (1947)

Best Sound Recording

Gordon Sawyer (Sound Director),
⬩ **Samuel Goldwyn Studio Sound Department** ⬩
The Bishop's Wife (1947)

Douglas Shearer (Sound Director),
Metro-Goldwyn-Mayer Studio Sound Department
Green Dolphin Street (1947)

Jack R. Whitney (Sound Director), Sound Service, Inc.
T-Men (1947)

The 21st Academy Awards® - March 24, 1949

Host: Robert Montgomery

Venue: Academy Award Theater

Honoring movies released in 1948

Irving G. Thalberg Memorial Award
⚱ Jerry Wald ⚱

Best Actor
⚱ Laurence Olivier ⚱
Hamlet (1948) role "Hamlet, Prince of Denmark"
Lew Ayres
Johnny Belinda (1948) role "Dr. Robert Richardson"
Montgomery Clift
The Search (1948) role "Ralph "Steve" Stevenson"
Dan Dailey
When My Baby Smiles at Me (1948) role ""Skid" Johnson"
Clifton Webb
Sitting Pretty (1948) role "Lynn Aloysius Belvedere"

Best Actor in a Supporting Role
⚱ Walter Huston ⚱
The Treasure of the Sierra Madre (1948) role "Howard"
Charles Bickford
Johnny Belinda (1948) role "Black MacDonald"
José Ferrer
Joan of Arc (1948) role "The Dauphin, later Charles VII of France"
Oscar Homolka
I Remember Mama (1948) role "Uncle Chris Halvorsen"
Cecil Kellaway
The Luck of the Irish (1948) role "Horace (A Leprechaun)"

Best Actress
⚱ Jane Wyman ⚱
Johnny Belinda (1948) role "Belinda MacDonald"
Ingrid Bergman
Joan of Arc (1948) role "Jeanne d'Arc"
Olivia de Havilland
The Snake Pit (1948) role "Virginia Stuart Cunningham"
Irene Dunne
I Remember Mama (1948) role "Marta "Mama" Hanson"
Barbara Stanwyck
Sorry, Wrong Number (1948) role "Leona Stevenson"

Best Actress in a Supporting Role
⚱ Claire Trevor ⚱
Key Largo (1948) role "Gaye Dawn"
Barbara Bel Geddes
I Remember Mama (1948) role "Katrin Hanson"
Ellen Corby
I Remember Mama (1948) role "Aunt Trina"
Agnes Moorehead
Johnny Belinda (1948) role "Aggie MacDonald"
Jean Simmons
Hamlet (1948) role "Ophelia"

Best Art Direction, Black and White

⚑ Roger K. Furse (Art Direction), Carmen Dillon (Set Decoration) ⚑
Hamlet (1948)

Robert M. Haas (Art Direction), William Wallace (Set Decoration)
Johnny Belinda (1948)

Best Art Direction, Color

⚑ Hein Heckroth (Art Direction), Arthur Lawson (Set Decoration) ⚑
The Red Shoes (1948)

Richard Day (Art Direction),
Joseph Kish, Edwin Casey Roberts (Set Decoration)
Joan of Arc (1948)

Best Cinematography, Black and White

⚑ William H. Daniels ⚑
The Naked City (1948)

Joseph H. August
(Posthumous)
Portrait of Jennie (1948)

Charles B. Lang Jr.
A Foreign Affair (1948)

Ted D. McCord
Johnny Belinda (1948)

Nicholas Musuraca
I Remember Mama (1948)

Best Cinematography, Color

⚑ Winton C. Hoch, William V. Skall, Joseph A. Valentine ⚑
Joan of Arc (1948)

Charles G. Clarke
Green Grass of Wyoming (1948)

Robert H. Planck
The Three Musketeers (1948)

William E. Snyder
The Loves of Carmen (1948)

Best Directing

⚑ John Huston ⚑
The Treasure of the Sierra Madre (1948)

Anatole Litvak
The Snake Pit (1948)

Jean Negulesco
Johnny Belinda (1948)

Laurence Olivier
Hamlet (1948)

Fred Zinnemann
The Search (1948)

Juvenile Award

⚑ Ivan Jandl ⚑
for the juvenile performance of 1948, as Karel Malik in The Search (1948)

Best Costume Design, Black and White
⚜ **Roger K. Furse** ⚜
Hamlet (1948)

Irene
B.F.'s Daughter (1948)

Best Costume Design, Color
⚜ **Dorothy Jeakins, Barbara Karinska** ⚜
Joan of Arc (1948)

Edith Head, Gile Steele
The Emperor Waltz (1948)

Best Documentary, Feature
⚜ **Orville O. Dull (Producer)** ⚜
The Secret Land (1948)

Janice Loeb (Producer)
The Quiet One (1948)

Best Film Editing
⚜ **Paul Weatherwax** ⚜
The Naked City (1948)

Reginald Mills
The Red Shoes (1948)

Christian Nyby
Red River (1948)

Frank Sullivan
Joan of Arc (1948)

David Weisbart
Johnny Belinda (1948)

Best Music, Music Score of a Dramatic or Comedy Picture
⚜ **Brian Easdale** ⚜
The Red Shoes (1948)

Hugo Friedhofer
Joan of Arc (1948)

Alfred Newman
The Snake Pit (1948)

Max Steiner
Johnny Belinda (1948)

William Walton
Hamlet (1948)

Best Documentary, Short Subject
⚜ **United States Army** ⚜
Toward Independence (1948)

Herbert Morgan (Producer)
Heart to Heart (1949)

United States Army Air Force
Operation Vittles (1948)

Best Music, Scoring of a Musical Picture
⚐ Roger Edens, Johnny Green ⚐
Easter Parade (1948)
Lennie Hayton
The Pirate (1948)
Ray Heindorf
Romance on the High Seas (1948)
Alfred Newman
When My Baby Smiles at Me (1948)
Victor Young
The Emperor Waltz (1948)

Best Music, Song
**⚐ Ray Evans, Jay Livingston (Music & Lyrics) ⚐
for the song "Buttons and Bows"**
The Paleface (1948)
**Harold Arlen (Music), Leo Robin (Lyrics)
for the song "For Every Man There's a Woman"**
Casbah (1948)
**Friedrich Hollaender (Music), Leo Robin (Lyrics)
for the song "This Is the Moment"**
That Lady in Ermine (1948)
**Ramey Idriss, George Tibbles (Music & Lyrics)
for the song "The Woody Woodpecker Song"**
Wet Blanket Policy (1948)
Jule Styne (Music), Sammy Cahn (Lyrics) for the song "It's Magic"
Romance on the High Seas (1948)

Special Foreign Language Film Award
⚐ France ⚐
Monsieur Vincent (1947)

Best Motion Picture
⚐ J. Arthur Rank-Two Cities Films ⚐
Hamlet (1948)
20th Century-Fox
The Snake Pit (1948)
J. Arthur Rank-Archers
The Red Shoes (1948)
Warner Bros.
The Treasure of the Sierra Madre (1948), Johnny Belinda (1948)

Best Short Subject, Cartoon
⚐ Fred Quimby (Producer) ⚐
The Little Orphan (1948)
Walt Disney (Producer)
Mickey and the Seal (1948), Tea for Two Hundred (1948)
Edward Selzer (Producer)
Mouse Wreckers (1948)
United Productions of America
Robin Hoodlum (1948)

Best Short Subject, One Reel
ℹ **Edmund H. Reek (Producer)** ℹ
Människor i stad - En kortfilm från Stockholm (eng. Rhythm of a City) (1947)
Gordon Hollingshead (Producer)
Cinderella Horse (1948), So You Want to Be on the Radio (1948)
Herbert Moulton (Producer)
Annie Was a Wonder (1949)
Pete Smith (Producer)
You Can't Win (1948)

Best Short Subject, Two Reel
ℹ **Walt Disney (Producer)** ℹ
Seal Island (1948)
Harry Grey (Producer)
Samba-Mania (1948)
Gordon Hollingshead (Producer)
Calgary Stampede (1948)
Thomas Mead (Producer)
Snow Capers (1948)
Herbert Morgan (Producer)
Going to Blazes! (1948)

Best Sound Recording
ℹ **Thomas T. Moulton (Sound Director),** ℹ
20th Century-Fox Studio Sound Department
The Snake Pit (1948)
Daniel J. Bloomberg (Sound Director), Republic Studio Sound Department
Moonrise (1948)
Col. Nathan O. Levinson (Sound Director),
Warner Bros. Studio Sound Department
Johnny Belinda (1948)

Best Special Effects
ℹ **Paul Eagler, J. McMillan Johnson, Russell Shearman,** ℹ
Clarence Slifer (Visual), Charles L. Freeman, James G. Stewart (Audible)
Portrait of Jennie (1948)
Ralph Hammeras, Fred Sersen, Edward Snyder (Visual),
Roger Heman Sr. (Audible)
Deep Waters (1948)

Best Writing, Motion Picture Story
ℹ **Richard Schweizer, David Wechsler** ℹ
The Search (1948)
Borden Chase
Red River (1948)
Frances H. Flaherty, Robert J. Flaherty
Louisiana Story (1948)
Emeric Pressburger
The Red Shoes (1948)
Malvin Wald
The Naked City (1948)

Best Writing, Screenplay
⬇ **John Huston** ⬇
The Treasure of the Sierra Madre (1948)
Charles Brackett, Richard L. Breen, Billy Wilder
A Foreign Affair (1948)
Millen Brand, Frank Partos
The Snake Pit (1948)
Irmgard Von Cube, Allen Vincent
Johnny Belinda (1948)
Richard Schweizer, David Wechsler
The Search (1948)

Honorary Award
⬇ **Walter Wanger** ⬇
for distinguished service to the industry in adding to its moral stature in the world
community by his production of the picture Joan of Arc (1948)
⬇ **Sid Grauman** ⬇
master showman, who raised the standard of exhibition of motion pictures
⬇ **Adolph Zukor** ⬇
for services to the industry over a period of forty years,
for man who has been called the father of the feature film in America

The 22nd Academy Awards® - March 23, 1950
Host: Paul Douglas
Venue: RKO Pantages Theatre
Honoring movies released in 1949

Best Actor
⬇ **Broderick Crawford** ⬇
All the King's Men (1949) role "Willie Stark"
Kirk Douglas
Champion (1949) role "Michael "Midge" Kelly"
Gregory Peck
Twelve O'Clock High (1949) role "Brigadier General Frank Savage"
Richard Todd
The Hasty Heart (1949) role "Corporal Lachlan "Lachie" MacLachlan"
John Wayne
Sands of Iwo Jima (1949) role "Sergeant John M. Stryker"

Best Actor in a Supporting Role
⬇ **Dean Jagger** ⬇
Twelve O'Clock High (1949) role "Major Harvey Stovall"
John Ireland
All the King's Men (1949) role "Jack Burden"
Arthur Kennedy
Champion (1949) role "Connie Kelly"
Ralph Richardson
The Heiress (1949) role "Dr. Austin Sloper"
James Whitmore
Battleground (1949) role "Sergeant Kinnie"

Best Actress
⚊ **Olivia de Havilland** ⚊
The Heiress (1949) role "Catherine Sloper"

Jeanne Crain
Pinky (1949) role "Patricia "Pinky" Johnson"

Susan Hayward
My Foolish Heart (1949) role "Eloise Winters"

Deborah Kerr
Edward, My Son (1949) role "Evelyn Boult"

Loretta Young
Come to the Stable (1949) role "Sister Margaret"

Best Actress in a Supporting Role
⚊ **Mercedes McCambridge** ⚊
All the King's Men (1949) role "Sadie Burke"

Ethel Barrymore
Pinky (1949) role "Miss Em"

Celeste Holm
Come to the Stable (1949) role "Sister Scholastica"

Elsa Lanchester
Come to the Stable (1949) role "Amelia Potts"

Ethel Waters
Pinky (1949) role "Dicey Johnson"

Juvenile Award
⚊ **Bobby Driscoll** ⚊
for the outstanding juvenile actor of 1949.

Best Art Direction, Black and White
⚊ **Harry Horner, John Meehan (Art Direction), Emile Kuri (Set Decoration)** ⚊
The Heiress (1949)

**Cedric Gibbons, Jack Martin Smith (Art Direction),
Richard A. Pefferle, Edwin B. Willis (Set Decoration)**
Madame Bovary (1949)

**Lyle R. Wheeler, Joseph C. Wright (Art Direction),
Paul S. Fox, Thomas Little (Set Decoration)**
Come to the Stable (1949)

Best Art Direction, Color
⚊ **Cedric Gibbons, Paul Groesse (Art Direction),
Jack D. Moore, Edwin B. Willis (Set Decoration)** ⚊
Little Women (1949)

Edward Carrere (Art Direction), Lyle B. Reifsnider (Set Decoration)
Adventures of Don Juan (1948)

William Kellner, Jim Morahan, Michael Relph (Art Direction)
Saraband (1948)

Best Special Foreign Language Film Award
⚊ **Italy** ⚊
Ladri di biciclette (eng. Bicycle Thieves) (1948)

Best Cinematography, Black and White
⚊ Paul C. Vogel ⚊
Battleground (1949)
Joseph LaShelle
Come to the Stable (1949)
Frank Planer
Champion (1949)
Leon Shamroy
Prince of Foxes (1949)
Leo Tover
The Heiress (1949)

Best Cinematography, Color
⚊ Winton C. Hoch ⚊
She Wore a Yellow Ribbon (1949)
Charles G. Clarke
Sand (1949)
Charles Edgar Schoenbaum, Robert H. Planck
Little Women (1949)
William E. Snyder
Jolson Sings Again (1949)
Harry Stradling Sr.
The Barkleys of Broadway (1949)

Best Costume Design, Black and White
⚊ Edith Head, Gile Steele ⚊
The Heiress (1949)
Vittorio Nino Novarese
Prince of Foxes (1949)

Best Costume Design, Color
⚊ Marjorie Best, Leah Rhodes, Travilla ⚊
Adventures of Don Juan (1948)
Kay Nelson
Mother Is a Freshman (1949)

Best Documentary, Feature
⚊ Crown Film Unit ⚊
Daybreak in Udi (1949)
Paul F. Heard (Producer)
Kenji Comes Home (1949)

Best Documentary, Short Subject
⚊ Richard de Rochemont (Producer) ⚊
A Chance to Live (1949)
French Cinema General Cooperative
Eighteen Forty-Eight (1950)
Edward Selzer (Producer)
So Much for So Little (1949)
St. Francis-Xavier University, Antigonish, Nova Scotia
The Rising Tide (1949)

Best Short Subject, Cartoon

⚊ **Edward Selzer (Producer)** ⚊
For Scent-imental Reasons (1949)

Stephen Bosustow (Producer)
The Magic Fluke (1949)

Walt Disney (Producer)
Toy Tinkers (1949)

Fred Quimby (Producer)
Hatch Up Your Troubles (1949)

Edward Selzer (Producer)
(Withdrawn by the producer)
Canary Row (1950)

Best Directing

⚊ **Joseph L. Mankiewicz** ⚊
A Letter to Three Wives (1949)

Carol Reed
The Fallen Idol (1948)

Robert Rossen
All the King's Men (1949)

William A. Wellman
Battleground (1949)

William Wyler
The Heiress (1949)

Best Film Editing

⚊ **Harry Gerstad** ⚊
Champion (1949)

Al Clark, Robert Parrish
All the King's Men (1949)

John D. Dunning
Battleground (1949)

Richard L. Van Enger
Sands of Iwo Jima (1949)

Frederic Knudtson
The Window (1949)

Best Motion Picture

⚊ **Robert Rossen Productions** ⚊
All the King's Men (1949)

20th Century-Fox
A Letter to Three Wives (1949), Twelve O'Clock High (1949)

Metro-Goldwyn-Mayer
Battleground (1949)

Paramount
The Heiress (1949)

Best Special Effects

⚊ **ARKO Productions** ⚊
Mighty Joe Young (1949)

Walter Wanger Pictures
Tulsa (1949)

Best Short Subject, One Reel
⚑ **Jack Eaton (Producer)** ⚑
Aquatic House Party (1950)

Walton C. Ament (Producer)
Spills and Chills (1949)

Justin Herman (Producer)
Roller Derby Girl (1949)

Gordon Hollingshead (Producer)
So You Think You're Not Guilty (1950)

Pete Smith (Producer)
Water Trix (1949)

Best Short Subject, Two Reel
⚑ **Gaston Diehl, Robert Haessens (Producers)** ⚑
Van Gogh (1948)

Irving Allen (Producer)
Chase of Death (1949)

Gordon Hollingshead (Producer)
The Grass Is Always Greener (1950)

Gordon Hollingshead (Producer)
Snow Carnival (1949)

William Lasky (Producer)
Boy and the Eagle (1949)

Honorary Award
⚑ **Fred Astaire** ⚑
for his unique artistry and his contributions to the technique of musical pictures.

⚑ **Cecil B. DeMille** ⚑
distinguished motion picture pioneer, for 37 years of brilliant showmanship.

⚑ **Jean Hersholt** ⚑
for distinguished service to the motion picture industry.

Best Music, Scoring of a Musical Picture
⚑ **Roger Edens, Lennie Hayton** ⚑
On the Town (1949)

George Duning, Morris Stoloff
Jolson Sings Again (1949)

Ray Heindorf
Look for the Silver Lining (1949)

Best Music, Song
⚑ **Frank Loesser (Music & Lyrics) for the song "Baby, It's Cold Outside"** ⚑
Neptune's Daughter (1949)

Eliot Daniel (Music), Larry Morey (Lyrics) for the song "Lavender Blue"
So Dear to My Heart (1948)

**Alfred Newman (Music), Mack Gordon (Lyrics)
for the song "Through a Long and Sleepless Night"**
Come to the Stable (1949)

Jule Styne (Music), Sammy Cahn (Lyrics) for the song "It's a Great Feeling"
It's a Great Feeling (1949)

**Victor Young (Music), Ned Washington (Lyrics)
for the song "My Foolish Heart"**
My Foolish Heart (1949)

Best Sound Recording

Thomas T. Moulton (Sound Director),
20th Century-Fox Studio Sound Department
Twelve O'Clock High (1949)

Daniel J. Bloomberg (Sound Director), Republic Studio Sound Department
Sands of Iwo Jima (1949)

Leslie I. Carey (Sound Director),
Universal-International Studio Sound Department
Once More, My Darling (1949)

Best Writing, Motion Picture Story

Douglas Morrow
The Stratton Story (1949)

Harry Brown
Sands of Iwo Jima (1949)

Valentine Davies, Shirley W. Smith
It Happens Every Spring (1949)

Virginia Kellogg
White Heat (1949)

Clare Boothe Luce
Come to the Stable (1949)

Best Writing, Screenplay

Joseph L. Mankiewicz
A Letter to Three Wives (1949)

Carl Foreman
Champion (1949)

Graham Greene
The Fallen Idol (1948)

Robert Rossen
All the King's Men (1949)

Cesare Zavattini
Ladri di biciclette (eng. Bicycle Thieves) (1948)

Best Music, Music Score of a Dramatic or Comedy Picture

Aaron Copland
The Heiress (1949)

Max Steiner
Beyond the Forest (1949)

Dimitri Tiomkin
Champion (1949)

Best Writing, Story and Screenplay

Robert Pirosh
Battleground (1949)

Sergio Amidei, Federico Fellini, Alfred Hayes, Marcello Pagliero,
Roberto Rossellini
Paisà (eng. Paisan) (1946)

Sidney Buchman
Jolson Sings Again (1949)

T. E. B. Clarke
Passport to Pimlico (1949)

Helen Levitt, Janice Loeb, Sidney Meyers
The Quiet One (1948)

The 23rd Academy Awards® - March 29, 1951

Host: Fred Astaire
Venue: RKO Pantages Theatre
Honoring movies released in 1950

Honorary Award

⚊ George Murphy ⚊
for his services in interpreting the film industry to the country at large.

⚊ Louis B. Mayer ⚊
for distinguished service to the motion picture industry.

Irving G. Thalberg Memorial Award

⚊ Darryl F. Zanuck ⚊

Best Actor

⚊ José Ferrer ⚊
Cyrano de Bergerac (1950) role "Cyrano de Bergerac"

Louis Calhern
The Magnificent Yankee (1950) role "Oliver Wendell Holmes Jr."

William Holden
Sunset Boulevard (1950) role "Joe Gillis"

James Stewart
Harvey (1950) role "Elwood P. Dowd"

Spencer Tracy
Father of the Bride (1950) role "Stanley T. Banks"

Best Actor in a Supporting Role

⚊ George Sanders ⚊
All About Eve (1950) role "Addison DeWitt"

Jeff Chandler
Broken Arrow (1950) role "Cochise"

Edmund Gwenn
Mister 880 (1950) role ""Skipper" Miller"

Sam Jaffe
The Asphalt Jungle (1950) role ""Doc" Erwin Riedenschneider"

Erich von Stroheim
Sunset Boulevard (1950) role "Max von Mayerling"

Best Actress

⚊ Judy Holliday ⚊
Born Yesterday (1950) role "Emma "Billie" Dawn"

Anne Baxter
All About Eve (1950) role "Eve Harrington"

Bette Davis
All About Eve (1950) role "Margo Channing"

Eleanor Parker
Caged (1950) role "Marie Allen"

Gloria Swanson
Sunset Boulevard (1950) role "Norma Desmond"

Best Actress in a Supporting Role

⚊ Josephine Hull ⚊
Harvey (1950) role "Veta Louise Dowd Simmons"

Hope Emerson
Caged (1950) role "Evelyn Harper"

Celeste Holm
All About Eve (1950) role "Karen Richards"

Nancy Olson
Sunset Boulevard (1950) role "Betty Schaefer"

Thelma Ritter
All About Eve (1950) role "Birdie Coonan"

Best Art Direction, Black and White

**⚊ Hans Dreier, John Meehan (Art Direction), ⚊
Sam Comer, Ray Moyer (Set Decoration)**
Sunset Boulevard (1950)

**George W. Davis, Lyle R. Wheeler (Art Direction),
Thomas Little, Walter M. Scott (Set Decoration)**
All About Eve (1950)

**Cedric Gibbons, Hans Peters (Art Direction),
Hugh Hunt, Edwin B. Willis (Set Decoration)**
The Red Danube (1949)

Best Art Direction, Color

**⚊ Hans Drcicr, Waltcr H. Tyler (Art Direction), ⚊
Sam Comer, Ray Moyer (Set Decoration)**
Samson and Delilah (1949)

Ernst Fegté (Art Direction), George Sawley (Set Decoration)
Destination Moon (1950)

**Cedric Gibbons, Paul Groesse (Art Direction),
Richard A. Pefferle, Edwin B. Willis (Set Decoration)**
Annie Get Your Gun (1950)

Best Special Effects

⚊ George Pal Productions ⚊
Destination Moon (1950)

Cecil B. DeMille Productions
Samson and Delilah (1949)

Best Cinematography, Black and White

⚊ Robert Krasker ⚊
The Third Man (1949)

Milton R. Krasner
All About Eve (1950)

Victor Milner
The Furies (1950)

Harold Rosson
The Asphalt Jungle (1950)

John F. Seitz
Sunset Boulevard (1950)

Best Cinematography, Color
↓ Robert Surtees ↓
King Solomon's Mines (1950)

George Barnes
Samson and Delilah (1949)

Ernest Haller
The Flame and the Arrow (1950)

Ernest Palmer
Broken Arrow (1950)

Charles Rosher
Annie Get Your Gun (1950)

Best Costume Design, Color
↓ Edith Head, Dorothy Jeakins, Elois Jenssen, Gile Steele, Gwen Wakeling ↓
Samson and Delilah (1949)

Walter Plunkett, Valles
That Forsyte Woman (1949)

Michael Whittaker
The Black Rose (1950)

Best Costume Design, Black and White
↓ Edith Head, Charles Le Maire ↓
All About Eve (1950)

Jean Louis
Born Yesterday (1950)

Walter Plunkett
The Magnificent Yankee (1950)

Best Directing
↓ Joseph L. Mankiewicz ↓
All About Eve (1950)

George Cukor
Born Yesterday (1950)

John Huston
The Asphalt Jungle (1950)

Carol Reed
The Third Man (1949)

Billy Wilder
Sunset Boulevard (1950)

Best Film Editing
↓ Conrad A. Nervig, Ralph E. Winters ↓
King Solomon's Mines (1950)

Oswald Hafenrichter
The Third Man (1949)

Doane Harrison, Arthur P. Schmidt
Sunset Boulevard (1950)

Barbara McLean
All About Eve (1950)

James E. Newcom
Annie Get Your Gun (1950)

Best Documentary, Feature
ꜞ **Robert Snyder (Producer)** ꜞ
The Titan: Story of Michelangelo (1950)
Jack Arnold, Lee Goodman (Producers)
With These Hands (1950)

Best Documentary, Short Subject
ꜞ **Edmund Reek (Producer)** ꜞ
Why Korea? (1951)
Film Documents, Inc.
Steps of Age (aka The Stairs) (1950)
Guy Glover (Producer)
The Fight: Science Against Cancer (1950)

Best Music, Music Score of a Dramatic or Comedy Picture
ꜞ **Franz Waxman** ꜞ
Sunset Boulevard (1950)
George Duning
No Sad Songs for Me (1950)
Alfred Newman
All About Eve (1950)
Max Steiner
The Flame and the Arrow (1950)
Victor Young
Samson and Delilah (1949)

Best Music, Scoring of a Musical Picture
ꜞ **Adolph Deutsch, Roger Edens** ꜞ
Annie Get Your Gun (1950)
Ray Heindorf
The West Point Story (1950)
Lionel Newman
I'll Get By (1950)
André Previn
Three Little Words (1950)
Paul J. Smith, Oliver Wallace
Cinderella (1950)

Best Music, Song
ꜞ **Ray Evans, Jay Livingston (Music & Lyrics) for the song "Mona Lisa"** ꜞ
Captain Carey, U.S.A. (1949)
Nicholas Brodszky (Music), Sammy Cahn (Lyrics) for the song "Be My Love"
The Toast of New Orleans (1950)
**Mack David, Al Hoffman, Jerry Livingston (Music & Lyrics)
for the song "Bibbidi-Bobbidi-Boo"**
Cinderella (1950)
**Fred Glickman, Hy Heath, Johnny Lange (Music & Lyrics)
for the song "Mule Train"**
Singing Guns (1950)
Josef Myrow (Music), Mack Gordon (Lyrics) for the song "Wilhelmina"
Wabash Avenue (1950)

Best Motion Picture
⚱ 20th Century-Fox ⚱
All About Eve (1950)
Columbia
Born Yesterday (1950)
Metro-Goldwyn-Mayer
Father of the Bride (1950), King Solomon's Mines (1950)
Paramount
Sunset Boulevard (1950)

Best Short Subject, Cartoon
⚱ Stephen Bosustow (Producer) ⚱
Gerald McBoing-Boing (1950)
Stephen Bosustow (Producer)
Trouble Indemnity (1950)
Fred Quimby (Producer)
Jerry's Cousin (1951)

Best Short Subject, One Reel
⚱ Gordon Hollingshead (Producer) ⚱
Grandad of Races (1950)
Pete Smith (Producer)
Wrong Way Butch (1950)
Robert Youngson (Producer)
Blaze Busters (1950)

Best Short Subject, Two Reel
⚱ Walt Disney (Producer) ⚱
Beaver Valley (1950)
Falcon Films, Inc.
Grandma Moses (1950)
Gordon Hollingshead (Producer)
My Country 'Tis of Thee (1950)

Best Sound Recording
⚱ Thomas T. Moulton (Sound Director), 20th Century-Fox Studio Sound Department ⚱
All About Eve (1950)
Leslie I. Carey (Sound Director), Universal-International Studio Sound Department
Louisa (1950)
Cyril Crowhurst (Sound Director), Pinewood Studio Sound Department
Trio (1950)
Gordon Sawyer (Sound Director), Samuel Goldwyn Studio Sound Department
Our Very Own (1950)
C. O. Slyfield (Sound Director), Walt Disney Studio Sound Department
Cinderella (1950)

Honorary Foreign Language Film Award
⚱ France/Italy ⚱
Le mura di Malapaga (eng. The Walls of Malapaga) (1949)

Best Writing, Motion Picture Story
⭍ **Edna Anhalt, Edward Anhalt** ⭍
Panic in the Streets (1950)
William Bowers, André De Toth
The Gunfighter (1950)
Sy Gomberg
When Willie Comes Marching Home (1950)
Carlo Lizzani, Giuseppe De Santis
Riso amaro (eng. Bitter Rice) (1949)
Leonard Spigelgass
Mystery Street (1950)

Best Writing, Screenplay
⭍ **Joseph L. Mankiewicz** ⭍
All About Eve (1950)
Frances Goodrich, Albert Hackett
Father of the Bride (1950)
John Huston, Ben Maddow
The Asphalt Jungle (1950)
Albert Maltz
Broken Arrow (1950)
Albert Mannheimer
Born Yesterday (1950)

Best Writing, Story and Screenplay
⭍ **Charles Brackett, D. M. Marshman Jr., Billy Wilder** ⭍
Sunset Boulevard (1950)
Carl Foreman
The Men (1950)
Ruth Gordon, Garson Kanin
Adam's Rib (1949)
Virginia Kellogg, Bernard C. Schoenfeld
Caged (1950)
Joseph L. Mankiewicz, Lesser Samuel
No Way Out (1950)

The 24th Academy Awards® - March 20, 1952
Host: Danny Kaye
Venue: RKO Pantages Theatre
Honoring movies released in 1951

Best Actor
⭍ **Humphrey Bogart** ⭍
The African Queen (1951) role "Charlie Allnut"
Marlon Brando
A Streetcar Named Desire (1951) role "Stanley Kowalski"
Montgomery Clift
A Place in the Sun (1951) role "George Eastman"
Arthur Kennedy
Bright Victory (1951) role "Larry Nevins"
Fredric March
Death of a Salesman (1951) role "Willy Loman"

Best Actor in a Supporting Role
⭣ **Karl Malden** ⭣
A Streetcar Named Desire (1951) role "Harold "Mitch" Mitchell"
Leo Genn
Quo Vadis (1951) role "Petronius"
Kevin McCarthy
Death of a Salesman (1951) role "Biff Loman"
Peter Ustinov
Quo Vadis (1951) role "Nero"
Gig Young
Come Fill the Cup (1951) role "Boyd S. Copeland"

Best Actress
⭣ **Vivien Leigh** ⭣
A Streetcar Named Desire (1951) role "Blanche DuBois"
Katharine Hepburn
The African Queen (1951) role "Rose Sayer"
Eleanor Parker
Detective Story (1951) role "Mary McLeod"
Shelley Winters
A Place in the Sun (1951) role "Alice Tripp"
Jane Wyman
The Blue Veil (1951) role "Louise Mason"

Best Actress in a Supporting Role
⭣ **Kim Hunter** ⭣
A Streetcar Named Desire (1951) role "Stella Kowalski"
Joan Blondell
The Blue Veil (1951) role "Annie Rawlins"
Mildred Dunnock
Death of a Salesman (1951) role "Linda Loman"
Lee Grant
Detective Story (1951) role "Shoplifter"
Thelma Ritter
The Mating Season (1951) role "Ellen McNulty"

Best Art Direction, Color
⭣ **E. Preston Ames, Cedric Gibbons (Art Direction),
F. Keogh Gleason, Edwin B. Willis (Set Decoration)** ⭣
An American in Paris (1951)
**Edward C. Carfagno, Cedric Gibbons, William A. Horning (Art Direction),
Hugh Hunt (Set Decoration)**
Quo Vadis (1951)
**George W. Davis, Lyle R. Wheeler (Art Direction),
Paul S. Fox, Thomas Little (Set Decoration)**
David and Bathsheba (1951)
**Leland Fuller, Lyle R. Wheeler (Art Direction) Joseph C. Wright
(Musical Settings), Thomas Little, Walter M. Scott (Set Decoration)**
On the Riviera (1951)
Hein Heckroth (Art Direction)
The Tales of Hoffmann (1951)

Best Art Direction, Black and White

⚐ **Richard Day (Art Direction), George James Hopkins (Set Decoration)** ⚐
A Streetcar Named Desire (1951)

John DeCuir, Lyle R. Wheeler (Art Direction),
Paul S. Fox, Thomas Little (Set Decoration)
The House on Telegraph Hill (1951)

Jean d'Eaubonne (Art Direction)
La Ronde (1950)

Leland Fuller, Lyle R. Wheeler (Art Direction),
Thomas Little, Fred J. Rode (Set Decoration)
Fourteen Hours (1951)

Cedric Gibbons, Paul Groesse (Art Direction),
Jack D. Moore, Edwin B. Willis (Set Decoration)
Too Young to Kiss (1951)

Best Cinematography, Black and White

⚐ **William C. Mellor** ⚐
A Place in the Sun (1951)

Norbert Brodine
The Frogmen (1951)

Robert Burks
Strangers on a Train (1951)

Frank Planer
Death of a Salesman (1951)

Harry Stradling Sr.
A Streetcar Named Desire (1951)

Best Cinematography, Color

⚐ **John Alton (Ballet Photography), Alfred Gilks** ⚐
An American in Paris (1951)

W. Howard Greene, John F. Seitz
When Worlds Collide (1951)

Charles Rosher
Show Boat (1951)

Leon Shamroy
David and Bathsheba (1951)

William V. Skall, Robert Surtees
Quo Vadis (1951)

Best Costume Design, Black and White

⚐ **Edith Head** ⚐
A Place in the Sun (1951)

Lucinda Ballard
A Streetcar Named Desire (1951)

Margaret Furse, Edward Stevenson
The Mudlark (1950)

Charles Le Maire, Renié
The Model and the Marriage Broker (1951)

Walter Plunkett, Gile Steele
(Gile Steele - posthumous)
Kind Lady (1951)

Best Costume Design, Color

⬇ **Orry-Kelly, Walter Plunkett, Irene Sharaff** ⬇
An American in Paris (1951)

Hein Heckroth
The Tales of Hoffmann (1951)

Charles Le Maire, Edward Stevenson
David and Bathsheba (1951)

Herschel McCoy
Quo Vadis (1951)

Helen Rose, Gile Steele
(Gile Steele - posthumous)
The Great Caruso (1951)

Best Documentary, Feature

⬇ **Olle Nordemar (Producer)** ⬇
Kon-Tiki (1950)

Bryan Foy (Producer)
I Was a Communist for the F.B.I. (1951)

Honorary Foreign Language Film Award

⬇ **Japan** ⬇
Rashômon (eng. Rashomon) (1950)

Best Documentary, Short Subject

⬇ **Fred Zinnemann (Producer), Paramount Pictures Corporation** ⬇
for the Los Angeles Orthopaedic Hospital
Benjy (1951)

Owen Crump (Producer),
United States Department of Defense and the
Association of Motion Picture Producers for Disabled American Veterans
One Who Came Back (1951)

Gordon Hollingshead (Producer)
The Seeing Eye (1951)

Best Film Editing

⬇ **William Hornbeck** ⬇
A Place in the Sun (1951)

Adrienne Fazan
An American in Paris (1951)

Chester W. Schaeffer
The Well (1951)

Dorothy Spencer
Decision Before Dawn (1951)

Ralph E. Winters
Quo Vadis (1951)

Honorary Award

⬇ **Gene Kelly** ⬇
In appreciation of his versatility as an actor, singer, director and dancer,
and specifically for his brilliant achievements in the art of choreography
on film An American in Paris (1951).

Best Special Effects
⚊ Paramount ⚊
When Worlds Collide (1951)

Best Directing
⚊ George Stevens ⚊
A Place in the Sun (1951)
John Huston
The African Queen (1951)
Elia Kazan
A Streetcar Named Desire (1951)
Vincente Minnelli
An American in Paris (1951)
William Wyler
Detective Story (1951)

Best Music, Music Score of a Dramatic or Comedy Picture
⚊ Franz Waxman ⚊
A Place in the Sun (1951)
Alfred Newman
David and Bathsheba (1951)
Alex North
Death of a Salesman (1951), A Streetcar Named Desire (1951)
Miklós Rózsa
Quo Vadis (1951)

Best Music, Scoring of a Musical Picture
⚊ Saul Chaplin, Johnny Green ⚊
An American in Paris (1951)
Peter Herman Adler, Johnny Green
The Great Caruso (1951)
Adolph Deutsch, Conrad Salinger
Show Boat (1951)
Alfred Newman
On the Riviera (1951)
Oliver Wallace
Alice in Wonderland (1951)

Best Music, Song
⚊ Hoagy Carmichael (Music), Johnny Mercer (Lyrics) for the song "In the Cool, Cool, Cool of the Evening" ⚊
Here Comes the Groom (1951)
Nicholas Brodszky (Music), Sammy Cahn (Lyrics) for the song "Wonder Why"
Rich, Young and Pretty (1951)
Oscar Hammerstein II, Bert Kalmar, Harry Ruby (Music & Lyrics) for the song "A Kiss to Build a Dream On"
(Bert Kalmar - posthumous)
The Strip (1951)
Burton Lane (Music), Alan Jay Lerner (Lyrics) for the song "Too Late Now"
Royal Wedding (1951)
Lionel Newman (Music), Eliot Daniel (Lyrics) for the song "Never"
Golden Girl (1951)

Best Motion Picture

⚑ **Arthur Freed (Producer)** ⚑
An American in Paris (1951)

Charles K. Feldman (Producer)
A Streetcar Named Desire (1951)

Anatole Litvak, Frank McCarthy (Producers)
Decision Before Dawn (1951)

George Stevens (Producer)
A Place in the Sun (1951)

Sam Zimbalist (Producer)
Quo Vadis (1951)

Best Short Subject, Cartoon

⚑ **Fred Quimby (Producer)** ⚑
The Two Mouseketeers (1952)

Stephen Bosustow (Producer)
Rooty Toot Toot (1951)

Walt Disney (Producer)
Lambert the Sheepish Lion (1952)

Best Short Subject, One Reel

⚑ **Robert Youngson (Producer)** ⚑
World of Kids (1951)

Jack Eaton (Producer)
Ridin' the Rails (1951)

Robert G. Leffingwell (Producer)
The Story of Time (1951)

Best Short Subject, Two Reel

⚑ **Walt Disney (Producer)** ⚑
Nature's Half Acre (1951)

Les Films du Compass
Balzac (1951)

Tom Mead (Producer)
Danger Under the Sea (1951)

Best Sound Recording

⚑ **Douglas Shearer (Sound Director),**
Metro-Goldwyn-Mayer Studio Sound Department ⚑
The Great Caruso (1951)

John O. Aalberg (Sound Director), RKO Radio Studio Sound Department
Two Tickets to Broadway (1951)

Leslie I. Carey (Sound Director),
Universal-International Studio Sound Department
Bright Victory (1951)

Col. Nathan Levinson (Sound Director),
Warner Bros. Studio Sound Department
A Streetcar Named Desire (1951)

Gordon Sawyer (Sound Director), Samuel Goldwyn Studio Sound Department
I Want You (1951)

Best Writing, Motion Picture Story

⤓ **James Bernard, Paul Dehn** ⤓
Seven Days to Noon (1950)

Budd Boetticher, Ray Nazarro
Bullfighter and the Lady (1951)

Liam O'Brien, Robert Riskin
Here Comes the Groom (1951)

Alfred Hayes, Stewart Stern
Teresa (1951)

Oscar Millard
The Frogmen (1951)

Best Writing, Screenplay

⤓ **Harry Brown, Michael Wilson** ⤓
A Place in the Sun (1951)

James Agee, John Huston
The African Queen (1951)

Jacques Natanson, Max Ophüls
La Ronde (1950)

Tennessee Williams
A Streetcar Named Desire (1951)

Robert Wyler, Philip Yordan
Detective Story (1951)

Best Writing, Story and Screenplay

⤓ **Alan Jay Lerner** ⤓
An American in Paris (1951)

Philip Dunne
David and Bathsheba (1951)

Clarence Greene, Russell Rouse
The Well (1951)

Walter Newman, Lesser Samuels, Billy Wilder
Ace in the Hole (1951)

Robert Pirosh
Go for Broke! (1951)

Irving G. Thalberg Memorial Award

⤓ **Arthur Freed** ⤓

The 25th Academy Awards® - March 19, 1953

Hosts: Bob Hope, Conrad Nagel
Venue: RKO Pantages Theatre
Honoring movies released in 1952

Honorary Foreign Language Film Award

⤓ **France** ⤓
Jeux interdits (eng. Forbidden Games) (1952)

Irving G. Thalberg Memorial Award

⤓ **Cecil B. DeMille** ⤓

Best Actor
⚊ Gary Cooper ⚊
High Noon (1952) role "Marshall Will Kane"
Marlon Brando
Viva Zapata! (1952) role "Emiliano Zapata"
Kirk Douglas
The Bad and the Beautiful (1952) role "Jonathan Shields"
José Ferrer
Moulin Rouge (1952)
role "Henri de Toulouse-Lautrec / Comte Alphonse de Toulouse-Lautrec"
Alec Guinness
The Lavender Hill Mob (1951) role "Henry "Dutch" Holland"

Best Actor in a Supporting Role
⚊ Anthony Quinn ⚊
Viva Zapata! (1952) role "Eufemio Zapata"
Richard Burton
My Cousin Rachel (1952) role "Philip Ashley"
Arthur Hunnicutt
The Big Sky (1952) role "Zeb Calloway / Narrator"
Victor McLaglen
The Quiet Man (1952) role "Squire "Red" Will Danaher"
Jack Palance
Sudden Fear (1952) role "Lester Blaine"

Best Actress
⚊ Shirley Booth ⚊
Come Back, Little Sheba (1952) role "Lola Delaney"
Joan Crawford
Sudden Fear (1952) role "Myra Hudson Blaine"
Bette Davis
The Star (1952) role "Margaret "Maggie" Elliot"
Julie Harris
The Member of the Wedding (1952) role "Frances "Frankie" Addams"
Susan Hayward
With a Song in My Heart (1952) role "Jane Froman"

Best Actress in a Supporting Role
⚊ Gloria Grahame ⚊
The Bad and the Beautiful (1952) role "Rosemary Bartlow"
Jean Hagen
Singin' in the Rain (1952) role "Lina Lamont"
Colette Marchand
Moulin Rouge (1952) role "Marie Charlet"
Terry Moore
Come Back, Little Sheba (1952) role "Marie Buckholder"
Thelma Ritter
With a Song in My Heart (1952) role "Clancy"

Best Special Effects
⚊ Metro-Goldwyn-Mayer ⚊
Plymouth Adventure (1952)

Best Art Direction, Black and White

Edward C. Carfagno, Cedric Gibbons (Art Direction), F. Keogh Gleason, Edwin B. Willis (Set Decoration)
The Bad and the Beautiful (1952)

Roland Anderson, Hal Pereira (Art Direction), Emile Kuri (Set Decoration)
Carrie (1952)

John DeCuir, Lyle R. Wheeler (Art Direction), Walter M. Scott (Set Decoration)
My Cousin Rachel (1952)

Leland Fuller, Lyle R. Wheeler (Art Direction), Claude E. Carpenter, Thomas Little (Set Decoration)
Viva Zapata! (1952)

Takashi Matsuyama (Art Direction), H. Motsumoto (Set Decoration)
Rashomon (1950)

Best Art Direction, Color

Paul Sheriff (Art Direction), Marcel Vertès (Set Decoration)
Moulin Rouge (1952)

Antoni Clave, Richard Day (Art Direction), Howard Bristol (Set Decoration)
Hans Christian Andersen (1952)

John DeCuir, Lyle R. Wheeler (Art Direction), Paul S. Fox, Thomas Little (Set Decoration)
The Snows of Kilimanjaro (1952)

Cedric Gibbons, Paul Groesse (Art Direction), Arthur Krams, Edwin B. Willis (Set Decoration)
The Merry Widow (1952)

Frank Hotaling (Art Direction), John McCarthy Jr., Charles S. Thompson (Set Decoration)
The Quiet Man (1952)

Best Cinematography, Black and White

Robert Surtees
The Bad and the Beautiful (1952)

Russell Harlan
The Big Sky (1952)

Charles B. Lang Jr.
Sudden Fear (1952)

Joseph LaShelle
My Cousin Rachel (1952)

Virgil E. Miller
Navajo (1952)

Best Cinematography, Color

Winton C. Hoch, Archie Stout
The Quiet Man (1952)

George J. Folsey
Million Dollar Mermaid (1952)

Leon Shamroy
The Snows of Kilimanjaro (1952)

Harry Stradling Sr.
Hans Christian Andersen (1952)

Freddie A. Young
Ivanhoe (1952)

Best Costume Design, Black and White
⚊ **Helen Rose** ⚊
The Bad and the Beautiful (1952)

Edith Head
Carrie (1952)

Dorothy Jeakins, Charles Le Maire
My Cousin Rachel (1952)

Jean Louis
Affair in Trinidad (1952)

Sheila O'Brien
Sudden Fear (1952)

Best Costume Design, Color
⚊ **Marcel Vertès** ⚊
Moulin Rouge (1952)

Antoni Clave, Barbara Karinska, Mary Wills
Hans Christian Andersen (1952)

Edith Head, Dorothy Jeakins, Miles White
The Greatest Show on Earth (1952)

Charles Le Maire
With a Song in My Heart (1952)

Helen Rose, Gile Steele
(Gile Steele - posthumous)
The Merry Widow (1952)

Best Directing
⚊ **John Ford** ⚊
The Quiet Man (1952)

Cecil B. DeMille
The Greatest Show on Earth (1952)

John Huston
Moulin Rouge (1952)

Joseph L. Mankiewicz
5 Fingers (1952)

Fred Zinnemann
High Noon (1952)

Best Music, Song
Dimitri Tiomkin (Music), Ned Washington (Lyrics)
⚊ **for the song "High Noon (Do Not Forsake Me, Oh My Darlin')"** ⚊
High Noon (1952)

Nicholas Brodszky (Music), Sammy Cahn (Lyrics)
for the song "Because You're Mine"
Because You're Mine (1952)

Jack Brooks (Music & Lyrics) for the song "Am I in Love"
Son of Paleface (1952)

Frank Loesser (Music & Lyrics) for the song "Thumbelina"
Hans Christian Andersen (1952)

Harry Warren (Music), Leo Robin (Lyrics) for the song "Zing a Little Zong"
Just for You (1952)

Best Documentary, Feature

⚊ **Irwin Allen (Producer)** ⚊
The Sea Around Us (1953)

Hall Bartlett (Producer)
Navajo (1952)

Dore Schary (Producer)
The Hoaxters (1952)

Best Documentary, Short Subject

⚊ **Norman McLaren (Producer)** ⚊
Neighbours (1952)

Alberto Ancilotto (Producer)
Epeira Diadema (1952)

Stephen Bosustow (Executive Producer)
Man Alive! (1952)

Herbert Morgan (Producer)
Devil Take Us (1955)

Best Film Editing

⚊ **Harry Gerstad, Elmo Williams** ⚊
High Noon (1952)

William Austin
Flat Top (1952)

Anne Bauchens
The Greatest Show on Earth (1952)

Ralph Kemplen
Moulin Rouge (1952)

Warren Low
Come Back, Little Sheba (1952)

Best Motion Picture

⚊ **Cecil B. DeMille (Producer)** ⚊
The Greatest Show on Earth (1952)

Pandro S. Berman (Producer)
Ivanhoe (1952)

Merian C. Cooper, John Ford (Producers)
The Quiet Man (1952)

John Huston (Producer), Romulus Films
Moulin Rouge (1952)

Stanley Kramer (Producer)
High Noon (1952)

Best Music, Music Score of a Dramatic or Comedy Picture

⚊ **Dimitri Tiomkin** ⚊
High Noon (1952)

Herschel Burke Gilbert
The Thief (1952)

Alex North
Viva Zapata! (1952)

Miklós Rózsa
Ivanhoe (1952)

Max Steiner
The Miracle of Our Lady of Fatima (1952)

Best Music, Scoring of a Musical Picture

⚐ Alfred Newman ⚐
With a Song in My Heart (1952)

Lennie Hayton
Singin' in the Rain (1952)

Ray Heindorf, Max Steiner
The Jazz Singer (1952)

Gian Carlo Menotti
The Medium (1951)

Walter Scharf
Hans Christian Andersen (1952)

Best Sound Recording

⚐ London Film Sound Department ⚐
The Sound Barrier (1952)

Daniel J. Bloomberg (Sound Director), Republic Studio Sound Department
The Quiet Man (1952)

**Thomas T. Moulton (Sound Director),
20th Century-Fox Studio Sound Department**
With a Song in My Heart (1952)

Pinewood Studios Sound Department
The Promoter (1952)

Gordon Sawyer (Sound Director), Samuel Goldwyn Studio Sound Department
Hans Christian Andersen (1952)

Honorary Award

⚐ Merian C. Cooper ⚐
For his many innovations and contributions to the art of motion pictures.

⚐ Bob Hope ⚐
For his contribution to the laughter of the world, his service to the motion picture industry,
and his devotion to the American premise.

⚐ Harold Lloyd ⚐
Master comedian and good citizen.

⚐ George Alfred Mitchell ⚐
For the design and development of the camera which bears his name and for his continued
and dominant presence in the field of cinematography.

⚐ Joseph M. Schenck ⚐
For long and distinguished service to the motion picture industry.

Best Short Subject, One Reel

⚐ Boris Vermont (Producer) ⚐
Light in the Window: The Art of Vermeer (1952)

Crown Film Unit
Royal Scotland (1952)

Jack Eaton (Producer)
Athletes of the Saddle (1952)

Gordon Hollingshead (Producer)
(Gordon Hollingshead - posthumous)
Desert Killer (1952)

Norman McLaren (Producer)
Neighbours (1952)

Best Short Subject, Two Reel

ﾠ⚊ **Walt Disney (Producer)** ⚊ﾠ
Water Birds (1952)

Gordon Hollingshead (Producer)

(posthumous)

Thar She Blows! (1952)

London Film Production
Bridge of Time (1950)

Herbert Morgan (Producer)
Devil Take Us (1955)

Best Writing, Motion Picture Story

⚊ **Frank Cavett, Fredric M. Frank, Theodore St. John** ⚊
The Greatest Show on Earth (1952)

Edna Anhalt, Edward Anhalt
The Sniper (1952)

Martin Goldsmith, Jack Leonard
The Narrow Margin (1952)

Leo McCarey
My Son John (1952)

Guy Trosper
The Pride of St. Louis (1952)

Best Writing, Screenplay

⚊ **Charles Schnee** ⚊
The Bad and the Beautiful (1952)

John Dighton, Roger MacDougall, Alexander Mackendrick
The Man in the White Suit (1951)

Carl Foreman
High Noon (1952)

Frank S. Nugent
The Quiet Man (1952)

Michael Wilson
5 Fingers (1952)

Best Writing, Story and Screenplay

⚊ **T. E. B. Clarke** ⚊
The Lavender Hill Mob (1951)

Sydney Boehm
The Atomic City (1952)

Ruth Gordon, Garson Kanin
Pat and Mike (1952)

Terence Rattigan
The Sound Barrier (1952)

John Steinbeck
Viva Zapata! (1952)

Best Short Subject, Cartoon
⚐ Fred Quimby (Producer) ⚐
Johann Mouse (1953)

Stephen Bosustow (Executive Producer)
Madeline (1952), Pink and Blue Blues (1952)

Tom Daly (Producer)
The Romance of Transportation in Canada (1952)

Fred Quimby (Producer)
Little Johnny Jet (1953)

The 26th Academy Awards® - March 25, 1954
Hosts: Donald O'Connor, Fredric March
Venue: RKO Pantages Theatre
Honoring movies released in 1953

Best Actor
⚐ William Holden ⚐
Stalag 17 (1953) role "Sergeant J. J. Sefton"

Marlon Brando
Julius Caesar (1953) role "Mark Antony"

Richard Burton
The Robe (1953) role "Marcellus Gallio"

Montgomery Clift
From Here to Eternity (1953) role "Private Robert E. Lee "Prew" Prewitt"

Burt Lancaster
From Here to Eternity (1953) role "First Sergeant Milton Warden"

Best Actor in a Supporting Role
⚐ Frank Sinatra ⚐
From Here to Eternity (1953) role "Private Angelo Maggio"

Eddie Albert
Roman Holiday (1953) role "Irving Radovich"

Brandon deWilde
Shane (1953) role "Joey Starrett"

Jack Palance
Shane (1953) role "Jack Wilson"

Robert Strauss
Stalag 17 (1953) role "Sergeant Stanislas "Animal" Kuzawa"

Best Actress
⚐ Audrey Hepburn ⚐
Roman Holiday (1953) role "Princess Ann"

Leslie Caron
Lili (1953) role "Lili Daurier"

Ava Gardner
Mogambo (1953) role "Eloise "Honey Bear" Y. Kelly"

Deborah Kerr
From Here to Eternity (1953) role "Karen Holmes"

Maggie McNamara
The Moon Is Blue (1953) role "Patty O'Neill"

Best Actress in a Supporting Role
⚐ Donna Reed ⚐
From Here to Eternity (1953) role "Alma Burke aka Lorene"
Grace Kelly
Mogambo (1953) role "Linda Nordley"
Geraldine Page
Hondo (1953) role "Angie Lowe"
Marjorie Rambeau
Torch Song (1953) role "Mrs. Stewart"
Thelma Ritter
Pickup on South Street (1953) role "Moe Williams"

Best Cinematography, Black and White
⚐ Burnett Guffey ⚐
From Here to Eternity (1953)
Henri Alekan, Frank Planer
Roman Holiday (1953)
Joseph C. Brun
Martin Luther (1953)
Hal Mohr
The Four Poster (1952)
Joseph Ruttenberg
Julius Caesar (1953)

Best Cinematography, Color
⚐ Loyal Griggs ⚐
Shane (1953)
Edward Cronjager
Beneath the 12-Mile Reef (1953)
George J. Folsey
All the Brothers Were Valiant (1953)
Robert H. Planck
Lili (1953)
Leon Shamroy
The Robe (1953)

Best Art Direction, Color
⚐ George W. Davis, Lyle R. Wheeler (Art Direction), ⚐
Paul S. Fox, Walter M. Scott (Set Decoration)
The Robe (1953)
E. Preston Ames, Edward C. Carfagno, Cedric Gibbons,
Gabriel Scognamillo (Art Direction), F. Keogh Gleason, Arthur Krams,
Jack D. Moore, Edwin B. Willis (Set Decoration)
The Story of Three Loves (1953)
Cedric Gibbons, Paul Groesse (Art Direction),
Arthur Krams, Edwin B. Willis (Set Decoration)
Lili (1953)
Alfred Junge, Hans Peters (Art Direction), John Jarvis (Set Decoration)
Knights of the Round Table (1953)
Cedric Gibbons, Urie McCleary (Art Direction),
Jack D. Moore, Edwin B. Willis (Set Decoration)
Young Bess (1953)

Best Art Direction, Black and White

**Edward C. Carfagno, Cedric Gibbons (Art Direction),
Hugh Hunt, Edwin B. Willis (Set Decoration)**
Julius Caesar (1953)

Leland Fuller, Lyle R. Wheeler (Art Direction), Paul S. Fox (Set Decoration)
The President's Lady (1953)

Paul Markwitz, Fritz Maurischat (Art Direction)
Martin Luther (1953)

Hal Pereira, Walter H. Tyler (Art Direction)
Roman Holiday (1953)

**Maurice Ransford, Lyle R. Wheeler (Art Direction),
Stuart A. Reiss (Set Decoration)**
Titanic (1953)

Best Costume Design, Black and White

Edith Head
Roman Holiday (1953)

Jean Louis
From Here to Eternity (1953)

Charles Le Maire, Renié
The President's Lady (1953)

Herschel McCoy, Helen Rose
Dream Wife (1953)

Walter Plunkett
The Actress (1953)

Best Costume Design, Color

Charles Le Maire, Emile Santiago
The Robe (1953)

Charles Le Maire, Travilla
How to Marry a Millionaire (1953)

Mary Ann Nyberg
The Band Wagon (1953)

Walter Plunkett
Young Bess (1953)

Irene Sharaff
Call Me Madam (1953)

Best Directing

Fred Zinnemann
From Here to Eternity (1953)

George Stevens
Shane (1953)

Charles Walters
Lili (1953)

Billy Wilder
Stalag 17 (1953)

William Wyler
Roman Holiday (1953)

Irving G. Thalberg Memorial Award

George Stevens

Best Documentary, Short Subject

⚊ **Walt Disney (Producer)** ⚊
The Alaskan Eskimo (1953)

John Adams, John Healy (Producers)
The Word (1953)

John Barnes (Producer)
The Living City (1953)

James Carr (Producer)
They Planted a Stone (1953)

United States Army Signal Corps
Operation Blue Jay (1953)

Best Documentary, Feature

⚊ **Walt Disney (Producer)** ⚊
The Living Desert (1953)

Leon Clore, John Taylor, Grahame Tharp (Producers)
The Conquest of Everest (1953)

Castleton Knight (Producer)
A Queen Is Crowned (1953)

Best Film Editing

⚊ **William Lyon** ⚊
From Here to Eternity (1953)

Everett Douglas
The War of the Worlds (1953)

Otto Ludwig
Roman Holiday (1953)

Robert Swink
The Moon Is Blue (1953)

Irvine Cotton Warburton
Crazylegs (1953)

Best Special Effects

⚊ **Paramount Studio** ⚊
The War of the Worlds (1953)

Best Music, Song

⚊ **Sammy Fain (Music), Paul Francis Webster (Lyrics)** ⚊
for the song "Secret Love"
Calamity Jane (1953)

Nicholas Brodszky (Music), Leo Robin (Lyrics)
for the song "My Flaming Heart"
Small Town Girl (1953)

Herschel Burke Gilbert (Music), Sylvia Fine (Lyrics)
for the song "The Moon Is Blue"
The Moon Is Blue (1953)

Lester Lee (Music), Ned Washington (Lyrics)
for the song "Sadie Thompson's Song (Blue Pacific Blues)"
Miss Sadie Thompson (1953)

Harry Warren (Music), Jack Brooks (Lyrics) for the song "That's Amore"
The Caddy (1953)

Best Music, Music Score of a Dramatic or Comedy Picture
ꜜ **Bronislau Kaper** ꜜ
Lili (1953)

George Duning, Morris Stoloff
From Here to Eternity (1953)

Louis Forbes
This Is Cinerama (1952)

Hugo Friedhofer
Above and Beyond (1952)

Miklós Rózsa
Julius Caesar (1953)

Best Music, Scoring of a Musical Picture
ꜜ **Alfred Newman** ꜜ
Call Me Madam (1953)

Saul Chaplin, André Previn
Kiss Me Kate (1953)

Adolph Deutsch
The Band Wagon (1953)

Ray Heindorf
Calamity Jane (1953)

Frederick Hollander, Morris Stoloff
The 5,000 Fingers of Dr. T. (1953)

Best Sound Recording
ꜜ **John P. Livadary (Sound Director), Columbia Studio Sound Department** ꜜ
From Here to Eternity (1953)

**Leslie I. Carey (Sound Director),
Universal-International Studio Sound Department**
The Mississippi Gambler (1953)

William A. Mueller (Sound Director), Warner Bros. Studio Sound Department
Calamity Jane (1953)

Loren L. Ryder (Sound Director), Paramount Studio Sound Department
The War of the Worlds (1953)

**A. W. Watkins (Sound Director),
Metro-Goldwyn-Mayer Studio Sound Department**
Knights of the Round Table (1953)

Honorary Award
ꜜ **Bell and Howell Company** ꜜ
For their pioneering and basic achievements in the advancement of
the motion picture industry.

ꜜ **Joseph I. Breen** ꜜ
For his conscientious, open-minded and dignified management of
the Motion Picture Production Code.

ꜜ **Pete Smith** ꜜ
For his witty and pungent observations on the American scene in his series of
"Pete Smith Specialties".

ꜜ **Twentieth Century-Fox Film Corporation** ꜜ
In recognition of their imagination, showmanship and foresight in introducing the
revolutionary process known as CinemaScope.

Best Motion Picture

ᛞ **Buddy Adler (Producer)** ᛞ
From Here to Eternity (1953)

John Houseman (Producer)
Julius Caesar (1953)

Frank Ross (Producer)
The Robe (1953)

George Stevens (Producer)
Shane (1953)

William Wyler (Producer)
Roman Holiday (1953)

Best Short Subject, One Reel

ᛞ **Johnny Green (Producer)** ᛞ
Overture to The Merry Wives of Windsor (1953)

Jack Eaton (Producer)
Wee Water Wonders (1953)

Vincenzo Lucci-Chiarissi (Producer)
Christ Among the Primitives (1953)

National Film Board of Canada
Herring Hunt (1953)

Boris Vermont (Producer)
Joy of Living (1952)

Best Short Subject, Two Reel

ᛞ **Walt Disney (Producer)** ᛞ
Bear Country (1953)

Walt Disney (Producer)
Ben and Me (1953)

Dublin Gate Theatre Productions
Return to Glennascaul (1953)

Cedric Francis (Producer)
Winter Paradise (1953)

Otto Lang (Producer)
Vesuvius Express (1953)

Best Writing, Motion Picture Story

ᛞ **Dalton Trumbo** ᛞ
Roman Holiday (1953)

Ray Ashley, Morris Engel, Ruth Orkin
Little Fugitive (1953)

Alec Coppel
The Captain's Paradise (1953)

Beirne Lay Jr.
Above and Beyond (1952)

Louis L'Amour
(withdrawn)
Hondo (1953)

Best Writing, Screenplay
ⵊ **Daniel Taradash** ⵊ
From Here to Eternity (1953)

Eric Ambler
The Cruel Sea (1953)

Helen Deutsch
Lili (1953)

John Dighton, Ian McLellan Hunter
Roman Holiday (1953)

A. B. Guthrie Jr.
Shane (1953)

Best Writing, Story and Screenplay
ⵊ **Charles Brackett, Richard L. Breen, Walter Reisch** ⵊ
Titanic (1953)

Harold Jack Bloom, Sam Rolfe
The Naked Spur (1953)

Betty Comden, Adolph Green
The Band Wagon (1953)

Millard Kaufman
Take the High Ground! (1953)

Richard Murphy
The Desert Rats (1953)

Best Short Subject, Cartoon
ⵊ **Walt Disney (Producer)** ⵊ
Toot, Whistle, Plunk and Boom (1953)

Stephen Bosustow (Producer)
Christopher Crumpet (1953), The Tell-Tale Heart (1953)

Walt Disney (Producer)
Rugged Bear (1953)

Edward Selzer (Producer)
From A to Z-Z-Z-Z (1953)

The 27ᵗʰ Academy Awards® - March 30, 1955
Hosts: Bob Hope, Thelma Ritter
Venue: RKO Pantages Theatre
Honoring movies released in 1954

Best Actor
ⵊ **Marlon Brando** ⵊ
On the Waterfront (1954) role "Terry Malloy"

Humphrey Bogart
The Caine Mutiny (1954) role "Lieutenant Commander Philip Francis Queeg"

Bing Crosby
The Country Girl (1954) role "Frank Elgin"

James Mason
A Star Is Born (1954) role "Norman Maine"

Dan O'Herlihy
Robinson Crusoe (1954) role "Robinson Crusoe / Crusoe's father"

Best Actor in a Supporting Role
⚊ Edmond O'Brien ⚊
The Barefoot Contessa (1954) role "Oscar Muldoon"
Lee J. Cobb
On the Waterfront (1954) role "Michael J. Skelly aka Johnny Friendly"
Karl Malden
On the Waterfront (1954) role "Father Barry"
Rod Steiger
On the Waterfront (1954) role "Charley "The Gent" Malloy"
Tom Tully
The Caine Mutiny (1954) role "Lieutenant Commander William H. De Vriess"

Best Actress
⚊ Grace Kelly ⚊
The Country Girl (1954) role "Georgie Elgin"
Dorothy Dandridge
Carmen Jones (1954) role "Carmen Jones"
Judy Garland
A Star Is Born (1954) role "Esther Victoria Blodgett / Vicki Lester"
Audrey Hepburn
Sabrina (1954) role "Sabrina Fairchild"
Jane Wyman
Magnificent Obsession (1954) role "Helen Phillips"

Best Actress in a Supporting Role
⚊ Eva Marie Saint ⚊
On the Waterfront (1954) role "Edie Doyle"
Nina Foch
Executive Suite (1954) role "Erica Martin"
Katy Jurado
Broken Lance (1954) role "Señora Devereaux"
Jan Sterling
The High and the Mighty (1954) role "Sally McKee"
Claire Trevor
The High and the Mighty (1954) role "May Holst"

Best Art Direction, Color
⚊ John Meehan (Art Direction), Emile Kuri (Set Decoration) ⚊
20,000 Leagues Under the Sea (1954)

Gene Allen, Malcolm C. Bert, Irene Sharaff (Art Direction), George James Hopkins (Set Decoration)
A Star Is Born (1954)

E. Preston Ames, Cedric Gibbons (Art Direction), F. Keogh Gleason, Edwin B. Willis (Set Decoration)
Brigadoon (1954)

Roland Anderson, Hal Pereira (Art Direction), Sam Comer, Ray Moyer (Set Decoration)
Red Garters (1954)

Leland Fuller, Lyle R. Wheeler (Art Direction), Paul S. Fox, Walter M. Scott (Set Decoration)
Désirée (1954)

Best Art Direction, Black and White
↓ Richard Day (Art Direction) ↓
On the Waterfront (1954)
Roland Anderson, Hal Pereira (Art Direction),
Sam Comer, Grace Gregory (Set Decoration)
The Country Girl (1954)
Edward C. Carfagno, Cedric Gibbons (Art Direction),
Emile Kuri, Edwin B. Willis (Set Decoration)
Executive Suite (1954)
Max Ophüls (Art Direction)
Le Plaisir (1952)
Hal Pereira, Walter H. Tyler (Art Direction),
Sam Comer, Ray Moyer (Set Decoration)
Sabrina (1954)

Best Directing
↓ Elia Kazan ↓
On the Waterfront (1954)
Alfred Hitchcock
Rear Window (1954)
George Seaton
The Country Girl (1954)
William A. Wellman
The High and the Mighty (1954)
Billy Wilder
Sabrina (1954)

Best Documentary, Feature
↓ Walt Disney (Producer) ↓
The Vanishing Prairie (1954)
Guy Glover (Producer)
The Stratford Adventure (1954)

Best Documentary, Short Subject
↓ World Wide Pictures and Morse Films ↓
Thursday's Children (1954)
Otto Lang (Producer)
Jet Carrier (1954)
Morrie Roizman (Producer)
Rembrandt: A Self-Portrait (1954)

Best Cinematography, Black and White
↓ Boris Kaufman ↓
On the Waterfront (1954)
George J. Folsey
Executive Suite (1954)
Charles Lang Jr.
Sabrina (1954)
John F. Seitz
Rogue Cop (1954)
John F. Warren
The Country Girl (1954)

Best Cinematography, Color

�️ **Milton R. Krasner** �️
Three Coins in the Fountain (1954)

Robert Burks
Rear Window (1954)

George J. Folsey
Seven Brides for Seven Brothers (1954)

Leon Shamroy
The Egyptian (1954)

William V. Skall
The Silver Chalice (1954)

Best Costume Design, Black and White

�️ **Edith Head** �️
Sabrina (1954)

Georges Annenkov, Rosine Delamare
Madame de… (eng. The Earrings of Madame De…) (1953)

Christian Dior
Stazione Termini (eng. Indiscretion of an American Wife) (1953)

Jean Louis
It Should Happen to You (1954)

Helen Rose
Executive Suite (1954)

Best Costume Design, Color

�️ **Mitsuzô Wada** �️
Jigokumon (eng. Gate of Hell) (1953)

René Hubert, Charles Le Maire
Désirée (1954)

Jean Louis, Mary Ann Nyberg, Irene Sharaff
A Star Is Born (1954)

Charles Le Maire, Travilla, Miles White
There's No Business Like Show Business (1954)

Irene Sharaff
Brigadoon (1954)

Best Film Editing

�️ **Gene Milford** �️
On the Waterfront (1954)

Henry Batista, William A. Lyon
The Caine Mutiny (1954)

Ralph Dawson
The High and the Mighty (1954)

Elmo Williams
20,000 Leagues Under the Sea (1954)

Ralph E. Winters
Seven Brides for Seven Brothers (1954)

Honorary Foreign Language Film Award

�️ **Japan** �️
Jigokumon (eng. Gate of Hell) (1953)

Best Short Subject, One Reel

ꞁ **Robert Youngson (Producer)** ꞁ
This Mechanical Age (1954)

Johnny Green (Producer)
Strauss Fantasy (1954)

Otto Lang (Producer)
The First Piano Quartette (1954)

Best Short Subject, Two Reel

ꞁ **Denis Sanders, Terry Sanders (Producers)** ꞁ
A Time Out of War (1954)

Walt Disney (Producer)
Siam (1954)

Cedric Francis (Producer)
Beauty and the Bull (1954)

Otto Lang (Producer)
Jet Carrier (1954)

Best Motion Picture

ꞁ **Sam Spiegel (Producer)** ꞁ
On the Waterfront (1954)

Jack Cummings (Producer)
Seven Brides for Seven Brothers (1954)

Stanley Kramer (Producer)
The Caine Mutiny (1954)

William Perlberg (Producer)
The Country Girl (1954)

Sol C. Siegel (Producer)
Three Coins in the Fountain (1954)

Best Music, Music Score of a Dramatic or Comedy Picture

ꞁ **Dimitri Tiomkin** ꞁ
The High and the Mighty (1954)

Larry Adler
Genevieve (1953)

Leonard Bernstein
On the Waterfront (1954)

Max Steiner
The Caine Mutiny (1954)

Franz Waxman
The Silver Chalice (1954)

Best Music, Scoring of a Musical Picture

ꞁ **Saul Chaplin, Adolph Deutsch** ꞁ
Seven Brides for Seven Brothers (1954)

Joseph Gershenson, Henry Mancini
The Glenn Miller Story (1954)

Herschel Burke Gilbert
Carmen Jones (1954)

Ray Heindorf
A Star Is Born (1954)

Alfred Newman, Lionel Newman
There's No Business Like Show Business (1954)

Best Music, Song

Jule Styne (Music), Sammy Cahn (Lyrics)
for the song "Three Coins in the Fountain"
Three Coins in the Fountain (1954)

Harold Arlen (Music), Ira Gershwin (Lyrics)
for the song "The Man that Got Away"
A Star Is Born (1954)

Irving Berlin (Music & Lyrics)
for the song "Count Your Blessings Instead of Sheep"
White Christmas (1954)

Jack Lawrence, Richard Myers (Music & Lyrics) for the song "Hold My Hand"
Susan Slept Here (1954)

Dimitri Tiomkin (Music), Ned Washington (Lyrics)
for the song "The High and the Mighty"
The High and the Mighty (1954)

Best Sound Recording

Leslie I. Carey (Sound Director),
Universal-International Studio Sound Department
The Glenn Miller Story (1954)

John O. Aalberg (Sound Director), RKO Radio Studio Sound Department
Susan Slept Here (1954)

John P. Livadary (Sound Director), Columbia Studio Sound Department
The Caine Mutiny (1954)

Wesley C. Miller (Sound Director),
Metro-Goldwyn-Mayer Studio Sound Department
Brigadoon (1954)

Loren L. Ryder (Sound Director), Paramount Studio Sound Department
Rear Window (1954)

Best Special Effects

Walt Disney Studios
20,000 Leagues Under the Sea (1954)

20th Century-Fox Studio
Hell and High Water (1954)

Warner Bros. Studio
Them! (1954)

Best Writing, Motion Picture Story

Philip Yordan
Broken Lance (1954)

François Boyer
Jeux interdits (eng. Forbidden Games) (1952)

Jed Harris, Tom Reed
Night People (1954)

Ettore Maria Margadonna
Pane, amore e fantasia (eng. Bread, Love and Dreams) (1953)

Lamar Trotti
(posthumous)
There's No Business Like Show Business (1954)

Best Writing, Screenplay

⚑ George Seaton ⚑
The Country Girl (1954)

Frances Goodrich, Albert Hackett, Dorothy Kingsley
Seven Brides for Seven Brothers (1954)

John Michael Hayes
Rear Window (1954)

Ernest Lehman, Samuel A. Taylor, Billy Wilder
Sabrina (1954)

Stanley Roberts
The Caine Mutiny (1954)

Best Writing, Story and Screenplay

⚑ Budd Schulberg ⚑
On the Waterfront (1954)

Oscar Brodney, Valentine Davies
The Glenn Miller Story (1954)

Melvin Frank, Norman Panama
Knock on Wood (1954)

Joseph L. Mankiewicz
The Barefoot Contessa (1954)

William Rose
Genevieve (1953)

Best Short Subject, Cartoon

⚑ Stephen Bosustow (Producer) ⚑
When Magoo Flew (1954)

Walt Disney (Producer)
Pigs Is Pigs (1954)

Walter Lantz (Producer)
Crazy Mixed Up Pup (1954)

Fred Quimby (Producer)
Touché, Pussy Cat! (1954)

Edward Selzer (Producer)
Sandy Claws (1954)

Juvenile Award

⚑ Vincent Winter ⚑
For his outstanding juvenile performance in The Little Kidnappers (1953)

⚑ Jon Whiteley ⚑
For his outstanding juvenile performance in The Little Kidnappers (1953)

Honorary Award

⚑ Danny Kaye ⚑
For his unique talents, his service to the Academy, the motion picture industry,
and the American people.

⚑ Greta Garbo ⚑
For her unforgettable screen performances.

⚑ Kemp Niver ⚑
For the development of the Renovare Process which has made possible
the restoration of the Library of Congress Paper Film Collection.

⚑ Bausch & Lomb Optical Company ⚑
For their contributions to the advancement of the motion picture industry.

The 28th Academy Awards® - March 21, 1956

Hosts: Claudette Colbert, Jerry Lewis, Joseph L. Mankiewicz
Venue: RKO Pantages Theatre
Honoring movies released in 1955

Best Special Effects

↓ Paramount Studio ↓
The Bridges at Toko-Ri (1954)

20th Century-Fox Studio
The Rains of Ranchipur (1955)

Associated British Picture Corporation, Ltd.
The Dam Busters (1955)

Best Actor

↓ Ernest Borgnine ↓
Marty (1955) role "Marty Piletti"

James Cagney
Love Me or Leave Me (1955) role "Martin Snyder"

James Dean
(posthumous)
East of Eden (1955) role "Caleb Trask"

Frank Sinatra
The Man with the Golden Arm (1955) role "Frankie "Dealer" Machine"

Spencer Tracy
Bad Day at Black Rock (1955) role "John J. Macreedy"

Best Actor in a Supporting Role

↓ Jack Lemmon ↓
Mister Roberts (1955) role "Ensign Frank Thurlowe Pulver"

Arthur Kennedy
Trial (1955) role "Bernard Castle"

Joe Mantell
Marty (1955) role "Angie"

Sal Mineo
Rebel Without a Cause (1955) role "John "Plato" Crawford"

Arthur O'Connell
Picnic (1955) role "Howard Bevans"

Best Actress

↓ Anna Magnani ↓
The Rose Tattoo (1955) role "Serafina Delle Rose"

Susan Hayward
I'll Cry Tomorrow (1955) role "Lillian Roth"

Katharine Hepburn
Summertime (1955) role "Jane Hudson"

Jennifer Jones
Love Is a Many-Splendored Thing (1955) role "Dr. Han Suyin"

Eleanor Parker
Interrupted Melody (1955) role "Marjorie Lawrence"

Best Actress in a Supporting Role

⚐ Jo Van Fleet ⚐
East of Eden (1955) role "Cathy Ames / Kate Trask"

Betsy Blair
Marty (1955) role "Clara Snyder"

Peggy Lee
Pete Kelly's Blues (1955) role "Rose Hopkins"

Marisa Pavan
The Rose Tattoo (1955) role "Rosa Delle Rose"

Natalie Wood
Rebel Without a Cause (1955) role "Judy"

Best Art Direction, Black and White

**⚐ Tambi Larsen, Hal Pereira (Art Direction), ⚐
Sam Comer, Arthur Krams (Set Decoration)**
The Rose Tattoo (1955)

**Malcolm Brown, Cedric Gibbons (Art Direction),
Hugh B. Hunt, Edwin B. Willis (Set Decoration)**
I'll Cry Tomorrow (1955)

**Randall Duell, Cedric Gibbons (Art Direction),
Henry Grace, Edwin B. Willis (Set Decoration)**
Blackboard Jungle (1955)

**Ted Haworth, Walter M. Simonds (Art Direction),
Robert Priestley (Set Decoration)**
Marty (1955)

Joseph C. Wright (Art Direction), Darrell Silvera (Set Decoration)
The Man with the Golden Arm (1955)

Best Art Direction, Color

**⚐ William Flannery, Jo Mielziner (Art Direction), ⚐
Robert Priestley (Set Decoration)**
Picnic (1955)

**John DeCuir, Lyle R. Wheeler (Art Direction),
Paul S. Fox, Walter M. Scott (Set Decoration)**
Daddy Long Legs (1955)

**George W. Davis, Lyle R. Wheeler (Art Direction),
Walter M. Scott, Jack Stubbs (Set Decoration)**
Love Is a Many-Splendored Thing (1955)

**Joseph McMillan Johnson, Hal Pereira (Art Direction),
Sam Comer, Arthur Krams (Set Decoration)**
To Catch a Thief (1955)

**Oliver Smith, Joseph C. Wright (Art Direction),
Howard Bristol (Set Decoration)**
Guys and Dolls (1955)

Best Documentary, Short Subject

⚐ Walt Disney (Producer) ⚐
Men Against the Arctic (1955)

Wilbur T. Blume (Producer)
The Face of Lincoln (1956)

Dore Schary (Producer)
The Battle of Gettysburg (1955)

Best Documentary, Feature
⌁ Nancy Hamilton (Producer) ⌁
Helen Keller in Her Story (aka The Unconquered) (1954)
René Risacher (Producer)
Heartbreak Ridge (aka Crèvecoeur) (1955)

Best Cinematography, Black and White
⌁ James Wong Howe ⌁
The Rose Tattoo (1955)
Arthur E. Arling
I'll Cry Tomorrow (1955)
Russell Harlan
Blackboard Jungle (1955)
Charles Lang
Queen Bee (1955)
Joseph LaShelle
Marty (1955)

Best Cinematography, Color
⌁ Robert Burks ⌁
To Catch a Thief (1955)
Harold Lipstein
A Man Called Peter (1955)
Leon Shamroy
Love Is a Many-Splendored Thing (1955)
Harry Stradling Sr.
Guys and Dolls (1955)
Robert Surtees
Oklahoma! (1955)

Best Costume Design, Black and White
⌁ Helen Rose ⌁
I'll Cry Tomorrow (1955)
Beatrice Dawson
The Pickwick Papers (1952)
Edith Head
The Rose Tattoo (1955)
Tadaoto Kainoshô
Ugetsu monogatari (eng. Ugetsu) (1953)
Jean Louis
Queen Bee (1955)

Best Costume Design, Color
⌁ Charles Le Maire ⌁
Love Is a Many-Splendored Thing (1955)
Edith Head
To Catch a Thief (1955)
Charles Le Maire, Mary Wills
The Virgin Queen (1955)
Helen Rose
Interrupted Melody (1955)
Irene Sharaff
Guys and Dolls (1955)

Best Sound Recording
⚐ **Fred Hynes (Sound Director), Todd-AO Sound Department** ⚐
Oklahoma! (1955)
Carl W. Faulkner (Sound Director),
20th Century-Fox Studio Sound Department
Love Is a Many-Splendored Thing (1955)
Watson Jones (Sound Director),
Radio Corporation of America Sound Department
Not as a Stranger (1955)
Wesley C. Miller (Sound Director),
Metro-Goldwyn-Mayer Studio Sound Department
Love Me or Leave Me (1955)
William A. Mueller (Sound Director), Warner Bros. Studio Sound Department
Mister Roberts (1955)

Best Music, Music Score of a Dramatic or Comedy Picture
⚐ **Alfred Newman** ⚐
Love Is a Many-Splendored Thing (1955)
Elmer Bernstein
The Man with the Golden Arm (1955)
George Duning
Picnic (1955)
Alex North
The Rose Tattoo (1955)
Max Steiner
Battle Cry (1955)

Best Music, Song
⚐ **Sammy Fain (Music), Paul Francis Webster (Lyrics)**
for the song "Love Is a Many-Splendored Thing" ⚐
Love Is a Many-Splendored Thing (1955)
Nicholas Brodszky (Music), Sammy Cahn (Lyrics)
for the song "I'll Never Stop Loving You"
Love Me or Leave Me (1955)
Jimmy Van Heusen (Music), Sammy Cahn (Lyrics)
for the song "(Love Is) The Tender Trap"
The Tender Trap (1955)
Johnny Mercer (Music & Lyrics) for the song "Something's Gotta Give"
Daddy Long Legs (1955)
Alex North (Music), Hy Zaret (Lyrics) for the song "Unchained Melody"
Unchained (1955)

Best Music, Scoring of a Musical Picture
⚐ **Robert Russell Bennett, Jay Blackton, Adolph Deutsch** ⚐
Oklahoma! (1955)
Jay Blackton, Cyril J. Mockridge
Guys and Dolls (1955)
Percy Faith, George Stoll
Love Me or Leave Me (1955)
Alfred Newman
Daddy Long Legs (1955)
André Previn
It's Always Fair Weather (1955)

Best Motion Picture
⚰ **Harold Hecht (Producer)** ⚰
Marty (1955)
Buddy Adler (Producer)
Love Is a Many-Splendored Thing (1955)
Leland Hayward (Producer)
Mister Roberts (1955)
Fred Kohlmar (Producer)
Picnic (1955)
Hal B. Wallis (Producer)
The Rose Tattoo (1955)

Honorary Foreign Language Film Award
⚰ **Japan** ⚰
Miyamoto Musash (eng. Samurai, The Legend of Musashi) (1954)

Best Short Subject, Two Reel
⚰ **Wilbur T. Blume (Producer)** ⚰
The Face of Lincoln (1956)
George K. Arthur (Producer)
On the Twelfth Day... (1955)
Walt Disney (Producer)
Switzerland (1955)
Cedric Francis (Producer)
24 Hour Alert (1955)
Dore Schary (Producer)
The Battle of Gettysburg (1955)

Best Short Subject, One Reel
⚰ **Edmund Reek (Producer)** ⚰
Survival City (1955)
Carson Davidson (Producer)
3rd Ave. El (1955)
Justin Herman (Producer)
Three Kisses (1955)
Robert Youngson (Producer)
Gadgets Galore (1955)

Best Directing
⚰ **Delbert Mann** ⚰
Marty (1955)
Elia Kazan
East of Eden (1955)
David Lean
Summertime (1955)
Joshua Logan
Picnic (1955)
John Sturges
Bad Day at Black Rock (1955)

Best Film Editing

⚊ William A. Lyon, Charles Nelson ⚊
Picnic (1955)

George Boemler, Gene Ruggiero
Oklahoma! (1955)

Warren Low
The Rose Tattoo (1955)

Alma Macrorie
The Bridges at Toko-Ri (1954)

Ferris Webster
Blackboard Jungle (1955)

Best Writing, Motion Picture Story

⚊ Daniel Fuchs ⚊
Love Me or Leave Me (1955)

Joe Connelly, Bob Mosher
The Private War of Major Benson (1955)

Beirne Lay Jr.
Strategic Air Command (1955)

Jean Marsan, Jacques Perret, Raoul Ploquin, Henry Troyat, Henri Verneuil
Le mouton à cinq pattes (eng. The Sheep Has Five Legs) (1954)

Nicholas Ray
Rebel Without a Cause (1955)

Best Writing, Screenplay

⚊ Paddy Chayefsky ⚊
Marty (1955)

Richard Brooks
Blackboard Jungle (1955)

Daniel Fuchs, Isobel Lennart
Love Me or Leave Me (1955)

Millard Kaufman
Bad Day at Black Rock (1955)

Paul Osborn
East of Eden (1955)

Best Writing, Story and Screenplay

⚊ Sonya Levien, William Ludwig ⚊
Interrupted Melody (1955)

Betty Comden, Adolph Green
It's Always Fair Weather (1955)

Emmet Lavery, Milton Sperling
The Court-Martial of Billy Mitchell (1955)

Henri Marquet, Jacques Tati
Les vacances de Monsieur Hulot (eng. Monsieur Hulot's Holiday) (1953)

Jack Rose, Melville Shavelson
The Seven Little Foys (1955)

Best Short Subject, Cartoon
⚊ **Edward Selzer (Producer)** ⚊
Speedy Gonzales (1955)
Joseph Barbera, William Hanna, Fred Quimby (Producers)
Good Will to Men (1955)
Walt Disney (Producer)
No Hunting (1955)
Walter Lantz (Producer)
The Legend of Rockabye Point (1955)

The 29ᵗʰ Academy Awards® - March 27, 1957
Hosts: Celeste Holm, Jerry Lewis
Venue: RKO Pantages Theatre
Honoring movies released in 1956

Best Actor
⚊ **Yul Brynner** ⚊
The King and I (1956) role "King Mongkut of Siam"
James Dean
(posthumous)
Giant (1956) role "Jett Rink"
Kirk Douglas
Lust for Life (1956) role "Vincent van Gogh"
Rock Hudson
Giant (1956) role "Jordan "Bick" Benedict Jr."
Sir Laurence Olivier
Richard III (1955) role "King Richard III of England"

Best Actor in a Supporting Role
⚊ **Anthony Quinn** ⚊
Lust for Life (1956) role "Paul Gauguin"
Don Murray
Bus Stop (1956) role "Beauregard "Bo" Decker"
Anthony Perkins
Friendly Persuasion (1956) role "Josh Birdwell"
Mickey Rooney
The Bold and the Brave (1956) role "Willie Dooley"
Robert Stack
Written on the Wind (1956) role "Kyle Hadley"

Best Actress
⚊ **Ingrid Bergman** ⚊
Anastasia (1956) role "Anna Koreff / Anastasia"
Carroll Baker
Baby Doll (1956) role "Baby Doll Meighan"
Katharine Hepburn
The Rainmaker (1956) role "Lizzie Curry"
Nancy Kelly
The Bad Seed (1956) role "Christine Penmark"
Deborah Kerr
The King and I (1956) role "Anna Leonowens"

Best Actress in a Supporting Role

⚜ Dorothy Malone ⚜
Written on the Wind (1956) role "Marylee Hadley"

Mildred Dunnock
Baby Doll (1956) role "Aunt Rose Comfort"

Eileen Heckart
The Bad Seed (1956) role "Mrs. Hortense Daigle"

Mercedes McCambridge
Giant (1956) role "Luz Benedict"

Patty McCormack
The Bad Seed (1956) role "Rhoda Penmark"

Best Art Direction, Black and White

**⚜ Malcolm F. Brown, Cedric Gibbons (Art Direction), ⚜
F. Keogh Gleason, Edwin B. Willis (Set Decoration)**
Somebody Up There Likes Me (1956)

Ross Bellah (Art Direction), Louis Diage, William R. Kiernan (Set Decoration)
The Solid Gold Cadillac (1956)

**A. Earl Hedrick, Hal Pereira (Art Direction),
Samuel M. Comer, Frank R. McKelvy (Set Decoration)**
The Proud and Profane (1956)

Takashi Matsuyama (Art Direction)
Shichinin no samurai (eng. Seven Samurai aka The Magnificent Seven) (1954)

**Jack Martin Smith, Lyle R. Wheeler (Art Direction),
Stuart A. Reiss, Walter M. Scott (Set Decoration)**
Teenage Rebel (1956)

Best Art Direction, Color

**⚜ John DeCuir, Lyle R. Wheeler (Art Direction), ⚜
Paul S. Fox, Walter M. Scott (Set Decoration)**
The King and I (1956)

Ken Adam, James W. Sullivan (Art Direction), Ross J. Dowd (Set Decoration)
Around the World in 80 Days (1956)

**E. Preston Ames, Cedric Gibbons, Hans Peters (Art Direction),
F. Keogh Gleason, Edwin B. Willis (Set Decoration)**
Lust for Life (1956)

Boris Leven (Art Direction), Ralph S. Hurst (Set Decoration)
Giant (1956)

**Albert Nozaki, Hal Pereira, Walter H. Tyler (Art Direction),
Samuel M. Comer, Ray Moyer (Set Decoration)**
The Ten Commandments (1956)

Best Cinematography, Black and White

⚜ Joseph Ruttenberg ⚜
Somebody Up There Likes Me (1956)

Burnett Guffey
The Harder They Fall (1956)

Boris Kaufman
Baby Doll (1956)

Harold Rosson
The Bad Seed (1956)

Walter Strenge
Stagecoach to Fury (1956)

Best Cinematography, Color

⬇ **Lionel Lindon** ⬇
Around the World in 80 Days (1956)

Jack Cardiff
War and Peace (1956)

Loyal Griggs
The Ten Commandments (1956)

Leon Shamroy
The King and I (1956)

Harry Stradling Sr.
The Eddy Duchin Story (1956)

Best Special Effects

⬇ **John P. Fulton** ⬇
The Ten Commandments (1956)

A. Arnold Gillespie, Irving G. Ries, Wesley C. Miller
Forbidden Planet (1956)

Best Costume Design, Black and White

⬇ **Jean Louis** ⬇
The Solid Gold Cadillac (1956)

Kôhei Ezaki
Shichinin no samurai (eng. Seven Samurai aka The Magnificent Seven) (1954)

Edith Head
The Proud and Profane (1956)

Charles Le Maire, Mary Wills
Teenage Rebel (1956)

Helen Rose
The Power and the Prize (1956)

Best Costume Design, Color

⬇ **Irene Sharaff** ⬇
The King and I (1956)

Arnold Friberg, Edith Head, Dorothy Jeakins, John Jensen, Ralph Jester
The Ten Commandments (1956)

Moss Mabry, Marjorie Best
Giant (1956)

Marie De Matteis
War and Peace (1956)

Miles White
Around the World in 80 Days (1956)

Best Directing

⬇ **George Stevens** ⬇
Giant (1956)

Michael Anderson
Around the World in 80 Days (1956)

Walter Lang
The King and I (1956)

King Vidor
War and Peace (1956)

William Wyler
Friendly Persuasion (1956)

Best Documentary, Feature

⚐ **Jacques-Yves Cousteau (Producer)** ⚐
Le monde du silence (eng. The Silent World) (1956)

The Government Film Committee of Denmark
Hvor bjergene sejler (eng. Where Mountains Float) (1955)

Louis Clyde Stoumen (Producer)
The Naked Eye (1956)

Best Documentary, Short Subject

⚐ **Louis Clyde Stoumen (Producer)** ⚐
The True Story of the Civil War (1957)

Valentine Davies (Producer)
The House Without a Name (1956)

Charles Guggenheim & Associates, Inc.
A City Decides (1956)

John Healy (Producer)
The Dark Wave (1956)

Ward Kimball (Producer)
The Magical World of Disney - Season 1 episode 20 "Man in Space" (1955)

Irving G. Thalberg Memorial Award

⚐ **Buddy Adler** ⚐

Honorary Foreign Language Film Award

⚐ **Italy - Dino De Laurentiis, Carlo Ponti (Producers)** ⚐
La Strada (1954)

Denmark - O. Dalsgaard-Olsen (Producer)
Qivitoq (eng. The Mountain Hiker) (1956)

Federal Republic of Germany West -
Walter Koppel, Gyula Trebitsch (Producers)
Der Hauptmann von Köpenick (eng. The Captain from Köpenick) (1956)

France - Agnès Delahaie (Producer)
Gervaise (1956)

Japan - Masayuki Takagi (Producer)
Biruma no tategoto (eng. The Burmese Harp) (1956)

Best Music, Song

⚐ **Ray Evans, Jay Livingston (Music & Lyrics)**
for the song "Whatever Will Be, Will Be (Que Sera, Sera)" ⚐
The Man Who Knew Too Much (1956)

Cole Porter (Music & Lyrics) for the song "True Love"
High Society (1956)

Leith Stevens (Music), Tom Adair (Lyrics) for the song "Julie"
Julie (1956)

Dimitri Tiomkin (Music), Paul Francis Webster (Lyrics)
for the song "Friendly Persuasion (Thee I Love)"
Friendly Persuasion (1956)

Victor Young (Music), Sammy Cahn (Lyrics)
for the song "Written on the Wind"
(Victor Young - posthumous)
Written on the Wind (1956)

Best Music, Music Score of a Dramatic or Comedy Picture

⚰ Victor Young ⚰
(posthumous)
Around the World in 80 Days (1956)

Hugo Friedhofer
Between Heaven and Hell (1956)

Alfred Newman
Anastasia (1956)

Alex North
The Rainmaker (1956)

Dimitri Tiomkin
Giant (1956)

Best Music, Scoring of a Musical Picture

⚰ Ken Darby, Alfred Newman ⚰
The King and I (1956)

George Duning, Morris Stoloff
The Eddy Duchin Story (1956)

Saul Chaplin, Johnny Green
High Society (1956)

Johnny Green, George Stoll
Meet Me in Las Vegas (1956)

Lionel Newman
The Best Things in Life Are Free (1956)

Best Film Editing

⚰ Gene Ruggiero, Paul Weatherwax ⚰
Around the World in 80 Days (1956)

Albert Akst
Somebody Up There Likes Me (1956)

Philip W. Anderson, Fred Bohanan, William Hornbeck
Giant (1956)

Anne Bauchens
The Ten Commandments (1956)

Merrill G. White
The Brave One (1956)

Best Motion Picture

⚰ Michael Todd (Producer) ⚰
Around the World in 80 Days (1956)

Charles Brackett (Producer)
The King and I (1956)

Cecil B. DeMille (Producer)
The Ten Commandments (1956)

Henry Ginsberg, George Stevens (Producers)
Giant (1956)

William Wyler (Producer)
Friendly Persuasion (1956)

Honorary Award

⚰ Eddie Cantor ⚰
For distinguished service to the film industry.

Best Short Subject, One Reel

⬇ **Konstantin Kalser (Producer)** ⬇
Crashing the Water Barrier (1956)

Cedric Francis (Producer)
Time Stood Still (1956)

Robert Youngson (Producer)
I Never Forget a Face (1956)

Best Short Subject, Two Reel

⬇ **George K. Arthur (Producer), Romulus Films** ⬇
The Bespoke Overcoat (1955)

Walt Disney (Producer)
Samoa (1956)

John Healy (Producer)
The Dark Wave (1956)

Larry Lansburgh (Producer)
Cow Dog (1956)

Best Short Subject, Cartoon

⬇ **Stephen Bosustow (Producer)** ⬇
Magoo's Puddle Jumper (1956)

Stephen Bosustow (Producer)
Gerald McBoing! Boing! on Planet Moo (1956), The Jaywalker (1956)

Best Sound Recording

⬇ **Carlton W. Faulkner (Sound Director),
20th Century-Fox Studio Sound Department** ⬇
The King and I (1956)

**Gordon R. Glennan (Sound Director), Westrex Sound Services, Inc.,
Gordon Sawyer (Sound Director), Samuel Goldwyn Studio Sound Department**
Friendly Persuasion (1956)

John P. Livadary (Sound Director), Columbia Studio Sound Department
The Eddy Duchin Story (1956)

John Myers (Sound Director), King Bros. Productions, Inc., Sound Department
The Brave One (1956)

Loren L. Ryder (Sound Director), Paramount Studio Sound Department
The Ten Commandments (1956)

Best Writing, Motion Picture Story

⬇ **Dalton Trumbo** ⬇
The Brave One (1956)

Leo Katcher
The Eddy Duchin Story (1956)

Jean Paul Sartre
Les orgueilleux (eng. The Proud and the Beautiful) (1953)

Cesare Zavattini
Umberto D. (1952)

Edward Bernds, Elwood Ullman
(The screenwriters graciously and voluntarily declined the nomination.)
High Society (1956)

Best Writing, Screenplay Adapted
⚱ James Poe, John Farrow, S.J. Perelman ⚱
Around the World in 80 Days (1956)
Norman Corwin
Lust for Life (1956)
Fred Guiol, Ivan Moffat
Giant (1956)
Tennessee Williams
Baby Doll (1956)
Michael Wilson
Friendly Persuasion (1956)

Best Writing, Screenplay Original
⚱ Albert Lamorisse ⚱
Le ballon rouge (eng. The Red Balloon) (1956)
Federico Fellini, Tullio Pinelli
La Strada (1954)
Robert Lewin
The Bold and the Brave (1956)
William Rose
The Ladykillers (1955)
Andrew L. Stone
Julie (1956)

Jean Hersholt Humanitarian Award
⚱ Y. Frank Freeman ⚱

The 30th Academy Awards® - March 26, 1958
Hosts: Bob Hope, Jack Lemmon, David Niven, Rosalind Russell, James Stewart,
Donald Duck (voice of Clarence Nash)
Venue: RKO Pantages Theatre
Honoring movies released in 1957

Best Special Effects
⚱ Walter Rossi (Audible) ⚱
The Enemy Below (1957)
Louis Lichtenfield (Visual)
The Spirit of St. Louis (1957)

Best Actor
⚱ Alec Guinness ⚱
The Bridge on the River Kwai (1957) role "Lieutenant Colonel Nicholson"
Marlon Brando
Sayonara (1957) role "Major Lloyd "Ace" Gruver, USAF"
Anthony Franciosa
A Hatful of Rain (1957) role "Polo Pope"
Charles Laughton
Witness for the Prosecution (1957) role "Sir Wilfrid Robarts Q. C."
Anthony Quinn
Wild Is the Wind (1957) role "Gino"

Best Actor in a Supporting Role
⚑ Red Buttons ⚑
Sayonara (1957) role "Airman Joe Kelly"
Vittorio De Sica
A Farewell to Arms (1957) role "Major Alessandro Rinaldi"
Sessue Hayakawa
The Bridge on the River Kwai (1957) role "Colonel Saito"
Arthur Kennedy
Peyton Place (1957) role "Lucas Cross"
Russ Tamblyn
Peyton Place (1957) role "Norman Page"

Best Actress
⚑ Joanne Woodward ⚑
The Three Faces of Eve (1957) role "Eve White / Eve Black / Jane"
Deborah Kerr
Heaven Knows, Mr. Allison (1957) role "Sister Angela"
Anna Magnani
Wild Is the Wind (1957) role "Gioia"
Elizabeth Taylor
Raintree County (1957) role "Susanna Drake Shawnessy"
Lana Turner
Peyton Place (1957) role "Constance MacKenzie"

Best Actress in a Supporting Role
⚑ Miyoshi Umeki ⚑
Sayonara (1957) role "Katsumi Kelly"
Carolyn Jones
The Bachelor Party (1957) role "The Girl / The Existentialist"
Elsa Lanchester
Witness for the Prosecution (1957) role "Miss Plimsoll"
Hope Lange
Peyton Place (1957) role "Selena Cross"
Diane Varsi
Peyton Place (1957) role "Allison MacKenzie"

Best Art Direction
⚑ Ted Haworth (Art Direction), Robert Priestley (Set Decoration) ⚑
Sayonara (1957)
Gene Allen, William A. Horning (Art Direction),
Richard Pefferle, Edwin B. Willis (Set Decoration)
Les Girls (1957)
George W. Davis, Hal Pereira (Art Direction),
Sam Comer, Ray Moyer (Set Decoration)
Funny Face (1957)
Walter Holscher (Art Direction),
Louis Diage, William Kiernan (Set Decoration)
Pal Joey (1957)
William A. Horning, Urie McCleary (Art Direction),
Hugh Hunt, Edwin B. Willis (Set Decoration)
Raintree County (1957)

Best Directing
⚜ David Lean ⚜
The Bridge on the River Kwai (1957)

Joshua Logan
Sayonara (1957)

Sidney Lumet
12 Angry Men (1957)

Mark Robson
Peyton Place (1957)

Billy Wilder
Witness for the Prosecution (1957)

Best Cinematography
⚜ Jack Hildyard ⚜
The Bridge on the River Kwai (1957)

Ellsworth Fredricks
Sayonara (1957)

Ray June
Funny Face (1957)

Milton R. Krasner
An Affair to Remember (1957)

William C. Mellor
Peyton Place (1957)

Best Sound Recording
⚜ George Groves (Sound Director), Warner Bros. Studio Sound Department ⚜
Sayonara (1957)

George Dutton (Sound Director), Paramount Studio Sound Department
Gunfight at the O.K. Corral (1957)

John P. Livadary (Sound Director), Columbia Studio Sound Department
Pal Joey (1957)

Dr. Wesley C. Miller (Sound Director), Metro-Goldwyn-Mayer Studio Sound Department
Les Girls (1957)

Gordon E. Sawyer (Sound Director), Samuel Goldwyn Studio Sound Department
Witness for the Prosecution (1957)

Best Costume Design
⚜ Orry-Kelly ⚜
Les Girls (1957)

Charles Le Maire
An Affair to Remember (1957)

Hubert de Givenchy, Edith Head
Funny Face (1957)

Jean Louis
Pal Joey (1957)

Walter Plunkett
Raintree County (1957)

Best Film Editing
⏳ **Peter Taylor** ⏳
The Bridge on the River Kwai (1957)
Viola Lawrence, Jerome Thoms
Pal Joey (1957)
Warren Low
Gunfight at the O.K. Corral (1957)
Daniel Mandell
Witness for the Prosecution (1957)
Arthur P. Schmidt, Philip W. Anderson
Sayonara (1957)

Best Documentary, Feature
⏳ **Jerome Hill (Producer)** ⏳
Albert Schweitzer (1957)
Manuel Barbachano Ponce (Producer)
Torero! (1956)
Lionel Rogosin (Producer)
On the Bowery (1956)

Best Foreign Language Film
⏳ **Italy** ⏳
Le notti di Cabiria (eng. Nights of Cabiria) (1957)
France
Porte des Lilas (eng. The Gates of Paris) (1957)
India
Mother India (1957)
Norway
Ni liv (eng. Nine Lives) (1957)
West Germany
Nachts wenn der Teufel kam (eng. The Devil Strikes at Night) (1957)

Best Motion Picture
⏳ **Sam Spiegel (Producer)** ⏳
The Bridge on the River Kwai (1957)
Henry Fonda, Reginald Rose (Producers)
12 Angry Men (1957)
William Goetz (Producer)
Sayonara (1957)
Arthur Hornblow Jr. (Producer)
Witness for the Prosecution (1957)
Jerry Wald (Producer)
Peyton Place (1957)

Best Music, Scoring
⏳ **Malcolm Arnold** ⏳
The Bridge on the River Kwai (1957)
Hugo Friedhofer
An Affair to Remember (1957), Boy on a Dolphin (1957)
Johnny Green
Raintree County (1957)
Paul J. Smith
Perri (1957)

Best Music, Song

Jimmy Van Heusen (Music), Sammy Cahn (Lyrics)
for the song "All the Way"
The Joker Is Wild (1957)

Ray Evans, Jay Livingston (Music & Lyrics) for the song "Tammy"
Tammy and the Bachelor (1957)

Sammy Fain (Music), Paul Francis Webster (Lyrics) for the song "April Love"
April Love (1957)

Dimitri Tiomkin (Music), Ned Washington (Lyrics)
for the song "Wild Is the Wind"
Wild Is the Wind (1957)

Harry Warren (Music), Harold Adamson, Leo McCarey (Lyrics)
for the song "An Affair to Remember"
An Affair to Remember (1957)

Best Writing, Screenplay based on material from another medium

Pierre Boulle, Carl Foreman, Michael Wilson
The Bridge on the River Kwai (1957)

John Michael Hayes
Peyton Place (1957)

John Huston, John Lee Mahin
Heaven Knows, Mr. Allison (1957)

Paul Osborn
Sayonara (1957)

Reginald Rose
12 Angry Men (1957)

Best Writing, Story & Screenplay written directly for the screen

George Wells
Designing Woman (1957)

Federico Fellini, Ennio Flaiano, Tullio Pinelli (Story),
Federico Fellini, Ennio Flaiano (Screenplay)
I Vitelloni (1953)

Leonard Gershe
Funny Face (1957)

Joel Kane, Barney Slater (Story), Dudley Nichols (Screenplay)
The Tin Star (1957)

Ralph Wheelwright (Story),
R. Wright Campbell, Ivan Goff, Ben Roberts (Screenplay)
Man of a Thousand Faces (1957)

Best Short Subject, Cartoon

Edward Selzer (Producer)
Birds Anonymous (1957)

Joseph Barbera, William Hanna (Producers)
One Droopy Knight (1957)

Stephen Bosustow (Producer)
Trees and Jamaica Daddy (1957)

Walt Disney (Producer)
The Truth About Mother Goose (1957)

Edward Selzer (Producer)
Tabasco Road (1957)

Best Short Subject, Live Action
🏆 **Larry Lansburgh (Producer)** 🏆
The Wetback Hound (1957)

James Carr (Producer)
Foothold on Antarctica (1957)

Tom Daly (Producer)
City of Gold (1957)

Norman McLaren (Producer)
A Chairy Tale (1957)

Ben Sharpsteen (Producer)
Portugal (1957)

Honorary Award
🏆 **Gilbert M. 'Broncho Billy' Anderson** 🏆
Motion picture pioneer, for his contributions to the development of motion pictures as entertainment.

🏆 **Charles Brackett** 🏆
For outstanding service to the Academy.

🏆 **B. B. Kahane** 🏆
For distinguished service to the motion picture industry.

🏆 **The Society of Motion Picture and Television Engineers** 🏆
For their contributions to the advancement of the motion picture industry.

The 31ˢᵗ Academy Awards® - April 6, 1959
Hosts: Bob Hope, Jerry Lewis, David Niven, Laurence Olivier, Tony Randall, Mort Sahl
Venue: RKO Pantages Theatre
Honoring movies released in 1958

Best Actor
🏆 **David Niven** 🏆
Separate Tables (1958) role "Major David Angus Pollock"

Tony Curtis
The Defiant Ones (1958) role "John "Joker" Jackson"

Paul Newman
Cat on a Hot Tin Roof (1958) role "Brick Pollitt"

Sidney Poitier
The Defiant Ones (1958) role "Noah Cullen"

Spencer Tracy
The Old Man and the Sea (1958) role "The Old Man / Narrator"

Best Actor in a Supporting Role
🏆 **Burl Ives** 🏆
The Big Country (1958) role "Rufus Hannassey"

Theodore Bikel
The Defiant Ones (1958) role "Sheriff Max Muller"

Lee J. Cobb
The Brothers Karamazov (1958) role "Fyodor Karamazov"

Arthur Kennedy
Some Came Running (1958) role "Frank Hirsh"

Gig Young
Teacher's Pet (1958) role "Dr. Hugo Pine"

Best Actress

⚱ Susan Hayward ⚱
I Want to Live! (1958) role "Barbara Graham"

Deborah Kerr
Separate Tables (1958) role "Sibyl Railton-Bell"

Shirley MacLaine
Some Came Running (1958) role "Ginny Moorehead"

Rosalind Russell
Auntie Mame (1958) role "Mame Dennis"

Elizabeth Taylor
Cat on a Hot Tin Roof (1958) role "Margaret "Maggie the Cat" Pollitt"

Best Actress in a Supporting Role

⚱ Wendy Hiller ⚱
Separate Tables (1958) role "Pat Cooper"

Peggy Cass
Auntie Mame (1958) role "Agnes Gooch"

Martha Hyer
Some Came Running (1958) role "Gwen French"

Maureen Stapleton
Lonelyhearts (1958) role "Fay Doyle"

Cara Williams
The Defiant Ones (1958) role "Billy's mother"

Best Art Direction

**⚱ E. Preston Ames, William A. Horning (Art Direction),
F. Keogh Gleason, Henry Grace (Set Decoration) ⚱**
(William A. Horning - posthumous)
Gigi (1958)

Malcolm C. Bert (Art Direction), George James Hopkins (Set Decoration)
Auntie Mame (1958)

**Henry Bumstead, Hal Pereira (Art Direction),
Sam Comer, Frank R. McKelvy (Set Decoration)**
Vertigo (1958)

**John DeCuir, Lyle R. Wheeler (Art Direction),
Paul S. Fox, Walter M. Scott (Set Decoration)**
A Certain Smile (1958)

Cary Odell (Art Direction), Louis Diage (Set Decoration)
Bell Book and Candle (1958)

Best Cinematography, Black and White

⚱ Sam Leavitt ⚱
The Defiant Ones (1958)

Daniel L. Fapp
Desire Under the Elms (1958)

Charles Lang Jr.
Separate Tables (1958)

Lionel Lindon
I Want to Live! (1958)

Joe MacDonald
The Young Lions (1958)

Best Cinematography, Color

⚜ **Joseph Ruttenberg** ⚜
Gigi (1958)

William H. Daniels
Cat on a Hot Tin Roof (1958)

James Wong Howe
The Old Man and the Sea (1958)

Leon Shamroy
South Pacific (1958)

Harry Stradling Sr.
Auntie Mame (1958)

Best Special Effects

⚜ **Tom Howard (Visual)** ⚜
Tom Thumb (1958)

A. Arnold Gillespie (Visual), Harold Humbrock (Audible)
Torpedo Run (1958)

Best Costume Design

⚜ **Cecil Beaton** ⚜
Gigi (1958)

Edith Head, John Jensen, Ralph Jester
The Buccaneer (1958)

Jean Louis
Bell Book and Candle (1958)

Charles Le Maire, Mary Wills
A Certain Smile (1958)

Walter Plunkett
Some Came Running (1958)

Best Directing

⚜ **Vincente Minnelli** ⚜
Gigi (1958)

Richard Brooks
Cat on a Hot Tin Roof (1958)

Stanley Kramer
The Defiant Ones (1958)

Mark Robson
The Inn of the Sixth Happiness (1958)

Robert Wise
I Want to Live! (1958)

Best Documentary, Feature

⚜ **Ben Sharpsteen (Producer)** ⚜
White Wilderness (1958)

James Carr (Producer)
Antarctic Crossing (1959)

Robert Snyder (Producer)
The Hidden World (1958)

Nathan Zucker (Producer)
Psychiatric Nursing (1958)

Best Documentary, Short Subject
⚊ Ben Sharpsteen (Producer) ⚊
Ama Girls (1958)
Kenneth G. Brown (Producer)
Employees Only (1958)
Tom Daly (Producer)
The Living Stone (1959)
Thorold Dickinson (Producer)
Overture (1959)
Ian Ferguson (Producer)
Journey Into Spring (1958)

Best Film Editing
⚊ Adrienne Fazan ⚊
Gigi (1958)
Al Clark, William A. Lyon
Cowboy (1958)
William Hornbeck
I Want to Live! (1958)
Frederic Knudtson
The Defiant Ones (1958)
William H. Ziegler
Auntie Mame (1958)

Honorary Foreign Language Film Award
⚊ France ⚊
Mon oncle (eng. My Uncle) (1958)
Italy
I soliti ignoti (eng. Big Deal on Madonna Street) (1958)
Spain
La venganza (eng. Vengeance) (1958)
West Germany
Helden (eng. Arms and the Man) (1958)
Yugoslavia
La strada lunga un anno (eng. The Year Long Road) (1958)

Honorary Award
⚊ Maurice Chevalier ⚊
For his contributions to the world of entertainment for more than half a century.

Best Music, Music Score of a Dramatic or Comedy Picture
⚊ Dimitri Tiomkin ⚊
The Old Man and the Sea (1958)
Hugo Friedhofer
The Young Lions (1958)
Jerome Moross
The Big Country (1958)
David Raksin
Separate Tables (1958)
Oliver Wallace
White Wilderness (1958)

Best Music, Scoring of a Musical Picture

⚊ André Previn ⚊
Gigi (1958)

Ken Darby, Alfred Newman
South Pacific (1958)

Yuri Faier, Gennadi Rozhdestvensky
The Bolshoi Ballet (1957)

Ray Heindorf
Damn Yankees (1958)

Lionel Newman
Mardi Gras (1958)

Best Music, Song

⚊ Frederick Loewe (Music), Alan Jay Lerner (Lyrics) for the song "Gigi" ⚊
Gigi (1958)

Ray Evans, Jay Livingston (Music & Lyrics)
for the song "Almost in Your Arms (Love Song from Houseboat)"
Houseboat (1958)

Sammy Fain (Music), Paul Francis Webster (Lyrics)
for the song "A Certain Smile"
A Certain Smile (1958)

Sammy Fain (Music), Paul Francis Webster (Lyrics)
for the song "A Very Precious Love"
Marjorie Morningstar (1958)

Jimmy Van Heusen (Music), Sammy Cahn (Lyrics)
for the song "To Love and Be Loved"
Some Came Running (1958)

Irving G. Thalberg Memorial Award

⚊ Jack L. Warner ⚊

Best Motion Picture

⚊ Arthur Freed (Producer) ⚊
Gigi (1958)

Harold Hecht (Producer)
Separate Tables (1958)

Stanley Kramer (Producer)
The Defiant Ones (1958)

Jack L. Warner (Producer)
Auntie Mame (1958)

Lawrence Weingarten (Producer)
Cat on a Hot Tin Roof (1958)

Best Short Subject, Cartoon

⚊ John W. Burton (Producer) ⚊
Knighty Knight Bugs (1958)

Walt Disney (Producer)
Paul Bunyan (1958)

William M. Weiss (Producer)
Sidney's Family Tree (1958)

Best Short Subject, Live Action

⚊ **Walt Disney (Producer)** ⚊
Grand Canyon (1958)

Ian Ferguson (Producer)
Journey Into Spring (1958)

John Patrick Hayes (Producer)
The Kiss (1958)

James A. Lebenthal (Producer)
T Is for Tumbleweed (1958)

New Zealand Screen Board
Snows of Aorangi (1958)

Best Sound

⚊ **Fred Hynes (Sound Director), Todd-AO Sound Department** ⚊
South Pacific (1958)

Leslie I. Carey (Sound Director),
Universal-International Studio Sound Department
A Time to Love and a Time to Die (1958)

George Dutton (Sound Director), Paramount Studio Sound Department
Vertigo (1958)

Carlton W. Faulkner (Sound Director),
20th Century-Fox Studio Sound Department
The Young Lions (1958)

Gordon E. Sawyer (Sound Director),
Samuel Goldwyn Studio Sound Department
I Want to Live! (1958)

Best Writing, Screenplay based on material from another medium

⚊ **Alan Jay Lerner** ⚊
Gigi (1958)

Richard Brooks, James Poe
Cat on a Hot Tin Roof (1958)

John Gay, Terence Rattigan
Separate Tables (1958)

Nelson Gidding, Don Mankiewicz
I Want to Live! (1958)

Alec Guinness
The Horse's Mouth (1958)

Best Writing, Story & Screenplay written directly for the screen

⚊ **Nedrick Young, Harold Jacob Smith** ⚊
The Defiant Ones (1958)

Paddy Chayefsky
The Goddess (1958)

James Edward Grant (Story),
William Bowers, James Edward Grant (Screenplay)
The Sheepman (1958)

Fay Kanin, Michael Kanin
Teacher's Pet (1958)

Jack Rose, Melville Shavelson
Houseboat (1958)

The 32nd Academy Awards® - April 4, 1960

Host: Bob Hope
Venue: RKO Pantages Theatre
Honoring movies released in 1959

Honorary Award

⚐ **Lee De Forest** ⚐

For his pioneering inventions which brought sound to the motion picture.

⚐ **Buster Keaton** ⚐

For his unique talents which brought immortal comedies to the screen.

Jean Hersholt Humanitarian Award

⚐ **Bob Hope** ⚐

Best Actor

⚐ **Charlton Heston** ⚐
Ben-Hur (1959) role "Judah Ben-Hur"

Laurence Harvey
Room at the Top (1959) role "Joe Lampton"

Jack Lemmon
Some Like It Hot (1959) role "Jerry / Daphne"

Paul Muni
The Last Angry Man (1959) role "Dr. Samuel 'Sam' Abelman"

James Stewart
Anatomy of a Murder (1959) role "Paul Biegler"

Best Actor in a Supporting Role

⚐ **Hugh Griffith** ⚐
Ben-Hur (1959) role "Sheik Ilderim"

Arthur O'Connell
Anatomy of a Murder (1959) role "Parnell Emmett McCarthy"

George C. Scott
Anatomy of a Murder (1959) role "Assistant State Attorney General Claude Dancer"

Robert Vaughn
The Young Philadelphians (1959) role "Chester A. "Chet" Gwynn"

Ed Wynn
The Diary of Anne Frank (1959) role "Mr. Albert Dussell"

Best Actress

⚐ **Simone Signoret** ⚐
Room at the Top (1959) role "Alice Aisgill"

Doris Day
Pillow Talk (1959) role "Jan Morrow"

Audrey Hepburn
The Nun's Story (1959) role "Sister Luke / Gabrielle van der Mal"

Katharine Hepburn
Suddenly, Last Summer (1959) role "Violet Venable"

Elizabeth Taylor
Suddenly, Last Summer (1959) role "Catherine Holly"

Best Actress in a Supporting Role

⚑ Shelley Winters ⚑
The Diary of Anne Frank (1959) role "Mrs. Petronella van Daan"

Hermione Baddeley
Room at the Top (1959) role "Elspeth"

Susan Kohner
Imitation of Life (1959) role "Sarah Jane Johnson (18)"

Juanita Moore
Imitation of Life (1959) role "Annie Johnson"

Thelma Ritter
Pillow Talk (1959) role "Alma"

Best Special Effects

⚑ A. Arnold Gillespie, Robert A. MacDonald (Visual), ⚑ Milo B. Lory (Audible)
Ben-Hur (1959)

L. B. Abbott, James B. Gordon (Visual), Carlton W. Faulkner (Audible)
Journey to the Center of the Earth (1959)

Best Art Direction, Black and White

⚑ George W. Davis, Lyle R. Wheeler (Art Direction), ⚑ Stuart A. Reiss, Walter M. Scott (Set Decoration)
The Diary of Anne Frank (1959)

Carl Anderson (Art Direction), William Kiernan (Set Decoration)
The Last Angry Man (1959)

Ted Haworth (Art Direction), Edward G. Boyle (Set Decoration)
Some Like It Hot (1959)

William Kellner, Oliver Messel (Art Direction), Scot Slimon (Set Decoration)
Suddenly, Last Summer (1959)

Hal Pereira, Walter H. Tyler (Art Direction), Sam Comer, Arthur Krams (Set Decoration)
Career (1959)

Best Art Direction, Color

⚑ Edward C. Carfagno, William A. Horning (Art Direction), ⚑ Hugh Hunt (Set Decoration)
(William A. Horning - posthumous)
Ben-Hur (1959)

Franz Bachelin, Herman A. Blumenthal, Lyle R. Wheeler (Art Direction), Joseph Kish, Walter M. Scott (Set Decoration)
Journey to the Center of the Earth (1959)

Robert F. Boyle, William A. Horning, Merrill Pye (Art Direction), Henry Grace, Frank R. McKelvy (Set Decoration)
(William A. Horning - posthumous)
North by Northwest (1959)

John DeCuir (Art Direction), Julia Heron (Set Decoration)
The Big Fisherman (1959)

Richard H. Riedel (Art Direction), Russell A. Gausman, Ruby R. Levitt (Set Decoration)
(Richard H. Riedel - posthumous)
Pillow Talk (1959)

Best Cinematography, Black and White
⚲ **William C. Mellor** ⚲
The Diary of Anne Frank (1959)

Charles Lang Jr.
Some Like It Hot (1959)

Sam Leavitt
Anatomy of a Murder (1959)

Joseph LaShelle
Career (1959)

Harry Stradling Sr.
The Young Philadelphians (1959)

Best Cinematography, Color
⚲ **Robert L. Surtees** ⚲
Ben-Hur (1959)

Daniel L. Fapp
The Five Pennies (1959)

Lee Garmes
The Big Fisherman (1959)

Franz Planer
The Nun's Story (1959)

Leon Shamroy
Porgy and Bess (1959)

Best Costume Design, Black and White
⚲ **Orry-Kelly** ⚲
Some Like It Hot (1959)

Edith Head
Career (1959)

Charles Le Maire, Mary Wills
The Diary of Anne Frank (1959)

Helen Rose
The Gazebo (1959)

Howard Shoup
The Young Philadelphians (1959)

Best Costume Design, Color
⚲ **Elizabeth Haffenden** ⚲
Ben-Hur (1959)

Edith Head
The Five Pennies (1959)

Adele Palmer
The Best of Everything (1959)

Renié
The Big Fisherman (1959)

Irene Sharaff
Porgy and Bess (1959)

Best Documentary, Feature
⚲ **Bernhard Grzimek (Producer)** ⚲
Serengeti darf nicht sterben (eng. Serengeti Shall Not Die) (1959)

David L. Wolper (Producer)
The Race for Space (1959)

Best Documentary, Short Subject
⚐ Bert Haanstra (Producer) ⚐
Glas (eng. Glass) (1958)
Edward F. Cullen (Producer)
From Generation to Generation (1959)
Walt Disney (Producer)
Donald in Mathmagic Land (1959)

Best Directing
⚐ William Wyler ⚐
Ben-Hur (1959)
Jack Clayton
Room at the Top (1959)
George Stevens
The Diary of Anne Frank (1959)
Billy Wilder
Some Like It Hot (1959)
Fred Zinnemann
The Nun's Story (1959)

Best Film Editing
⚐ John D. Dunning, Ralph E. Winters ⚐
Ben-Hur (1959)
Frederic Knudtson
On the Beach (1959)
Louis R. Loeffler
Anatomy of a Murder (1959)
George Tomasini
North by Northwest (1959)
Walter Thompson
The Nun's Story (1959)

Best Foreign Language Film
⚐ France ⚐
Orfeu Negro (eng. Black Orpheus) (1959)
Denmark
Paw (eng. Boy of Two Worlds) (1959)
Italy
La grande guerra (eng. The Great War) (1959)
The Netherlands
Dorp aan de rivier (eng. Village on the River) (1958)
West Germany
Die Brücke (eng. The Bridge) (1959)

Best Short Subject, Cartoon
⚐ John Hubley (Producer) ⚐
Moonbird (1959)
John W. Burton (Producer)
Mexicali Shmoes (1959)
Walt Disney (Producer)
Noah's Ark (1959)
Ernest Pintoff (Producer)
The Violinist (1959)

Best Short Subject, Live Action

⚐ Jacques-Yves Cousteau (Producer) ⚐
Histoire d'un poisson rouge (eng. The Golden Fish) (1959)

Shirley Clarke, Willard Van Dyke, Irving Jacoby (Producers)
Skyscraper (1960)

Walt Disney (Producer)
Mysteries of the Deep (1959)

Ian Ferguson (Producer)
Between the Tides (1959)

Peter Sellers (Producer)
The Running Jumping & Standing Still Film (1959)

Best Music, Music Score of a Dramatic or Comedy Picture

⚐ Miklós Rózsa ⚐
Ben-Hur (1959)

Ernest Gold
On the Beach (1959)

Alfred Newman
The Diary of Anne Frank (1959)

Frank De Vol
Pillow Talk (1959)

Franz Waxman
The Nun's Story (1959)

Best Music, Song

⚐ Jimmy Van Heusen (Music), Sammy Cahn (Lyrics) ⚐
for the song "High Hopes"
A Hole in the Head (1959)

Sylvia Fine (Music & Lyrics) for the song "The Five Pennies"
The Five Pennies (1959)

Jerry Livingston (Music), Mack David (Lyrics)
for the song "The Hanging Tree"
The Hanging Tree (1959)

Alfred Newman (Music), Sammy Cahn (Lyrics)
for the song "The Best of Everything"
The Best of Everything (1959)

Dimitri Tiomkin (Music), Ned Washington (Lyrics)
for the song "Strange Are the Ways of Love"
The Young Land (1959)

Best Music, Scoring of a Musical Picture

⚐ Ken Darby, André Previn ⚐
Porgy and Bess (1959)

George Bruns
Sleeping Beauty (1959)

Joseph J. Lilley, Nelson Riddle
Li'l Abner (1959)

Lionel Newman
Say One for Me (1959)

Leith Stevens
The Five Pennies (1959)

Best Motion Picture

⚐ **Sam Zimbalist (Producer)** ⚐
(posthumous)
Ben-Hur (1959)

Henry Blanke (Producer)
The Nun's Story (1959)

Otto Preminger (Producer)
Anatomy of a Murder (1959)

George Stevens (Producer)
The Diary of Anne Frank (1959)

James Woolf, John Woolf (Producers)
Room at the Top (1959)

Best Sound

⚐ **Franklin E. Milton (Sound Director),**
Metro-Goldwyn-Mayer Studio Sound Department ⚐
Ben-Hur (1959)

Carlton W. Faulkner (Sound Director),
20th Century-Fox Studio Sound Department
Journey to the Center of the Earth (1959)

George R. Groves (Sound Director), Warner Bros. Studio Sound Department
The Nun's Story (1959)

Gordon E. Sawyer (Sound Director), Samuel Goldwyn Studio Sound
Department, Fred Hynes (Sound Director), Todd-AO Sound Department
Porgy and Bess (1959)

A. W. Watkins (Sound Director),
Metro-Goldwyn-Mayer London Studio Sound Department
Libel (1959)

Best Writing, Screenplay based on material from another medium

⚐ **Neil Paterson** ⚐
Room at the Top (1959)

Robert Anderson
The Nun's Story (1959)

I. A. L. Diamond, Billy Wilder
Some Like It Hot (1959)

Wendell Mayes
Anatomy of a Murder (1959)

Karl Tunberg
Ben-Hur (1959)

Best Writing, Story & Screenplay written directly for the screen

⚐ **Clarence Greene, Russell Rouse (Story),**
Maurice Richlin, Stanley Shapiro (Screenplay) ⚐
Pillow Talk (1959)

Ingmar Bergman
Smultronstället (eng. Wild Strawberries) (1957)

Paul King, Joseph Stone (Story),
Maurice Richlin, Stanley Shapiro (Screenplay)
Operation Petticoat (1959)

Ernest Lehman
North by Northwest (1959)

Marcel Moussy, François Truffaut
Les quatre cents coups (eng. The 400 Blows) (1959)

The 33rd Academy Awards® - April 17, 1961

Host: Bob Hope
Venue: Santa Monica Civic Auditorium
Honoring movies released in 1960

Honorary Award
Gary Cooper
For his many memorable screen performances and the international recognition,
as an individual, has gained for the motion picture industry.
Stan Laurel
For his creative pioneering in the field of cinema comedy.

Jean Hersholt Humanitarian Award
Sol Lesser

Best Actor
Burt Lancaster
Elmer Gantry (1960) role "Elmer Gantry"
Trevor Howard
Sons and Lovers (1960) role "Walter Morel"
Jack Lemmon
The Apartment (1960) role "Calvin Clifford "Bud" Baxter"
Laurence Olivier
The Entertainer (1960) role "Archie Rice"
Spencer Tracy
Inherit the Wind (1960) role "Henry Drummond"

Best Actor in a Supporting Role
Peter Ustinov
Spartacus (1960) role "Lentulus Batiatus"
Peter Falk
Murder, Inc. (1960) role "Abe "Kid Twist" Reles"
Jack Kruschen
The Apartment (1960) role "Dr. Dreyfuss"
Sal Mineo
Exodus (1960) role "Dov Landau"
Chill Wills
The Alamo (1960) role "Beekeeper"

Best Actress
Elizabeth Taylor
Butterfield 8 (1960) role "Gloria Wandrous"
Greer Garson
Sunrise at Campobello (1960) role "Eleanor Roosevelt"
Deborah Kerr
The Sundowners (1960) role "Ida Carmody"
Shirley MacLaine
The Apartment (1960) role "Fran Kubelik"
Melina Mercouri
Pote tin Kyriaki (eng. Never on Sunday) (1960) role "Ilya"

Best Actress in a Supporting Role

↨ Shirley Jones ↨
Elmer Gantry (1960) role "Lulu Bains"

Glynis Johns
The Sundowners (1960) role "Mrs. Firth"

Shirley Knight
The Dark at the Top of the Stairs (1960) role "Reenie Flood"

Janet Leigh
Psycho (1960) role "Marion Crane"

Mary Ure
Sons and Lovers (1960) role "Clara Dawes"

Best Cinematography, Black and White

↨ Freddie Francis ↨
Sons and Lovers (1960)

Charles B. Lang Jr.
The Facts of Life (1960)

Ernest Laszlo
Inherit the Wind (1960)

Joseph LaShelle
The Apartment (1960)

John L. Russell
Psycho (1960)

Best Cinematography, Color

↨ Russell Metty ↨
Spartacus (1960)

William H. Clothier
The Alamo (1960)

Charles Harten, Joseph Ruttenberg
Butterfield 8 (1960)

Sam Leavitt
Exodus (1960)

Joseph MacDonald
Pepe (1960)

Best Art Direction, Color

**↨ Alexander Golitzen, Eric Orbom (Art Direction),
Russell A. Gausman, Julia Heron (Set Decoration) ↨**
(Eric Orbom - posthumous)
Spartacus (1960)

**Roland Anderson, Hal Pereira (Art Direction),
Arrigo Breschi, Sam Comer (Set Decoration)**
It Started in Naples (1960)

Edward Carrere (Art Direction), George James Hopkins (Set Decoration)
Sunrise at Campobello (1960)

**George W. Davis, Addison Hehr (Art Direction),
Henry Grace, Hugh Hunt, Otto Siegel (Set Decoration)**
Cimarron (1960)

Ted Haworth (Art Direction), William Kiernanv (Set Decoration)
Pepe (1960)

Best Art Direction, Black and White
⚜ **Alexander Trauner (Art Direction), Edward G. Boyle (Set Decoration)** ⚜
The Apartment (1960)

**Robert Clatworthy, Joseph Hurley (Art Direction),
George Milo (Set Decoration)**
Psycho (1960)

**Joseph McMillan Johnson, Kenneth A. Reid (Art Direction),
Ross Dowd (Set Decoration)**
The Facts of Life (1960)

Tom N. Morahan (Art Direction), Lionel Couch (Set Decoration)
Sons and Lovers (1960)

**Hal Pereira, Walter H. Tyler (Art Direction),
Sam Comer, Arthur Krams (Set Decoration)**
Visit to a Small Planet (1960)

Best Costume Design, Black and White
⚜ **Edith Head, Edward Stevenson** ⚜
The Facts of Life (1960)

Howard Shoup
The Rise and Fall of Legs Diamond (1960)

Bill Thomas
Seven Thieves (1960)

Theoni V. Aldredge (as Deni Vachlioti)
Pote tin Kyriaki (eng. Never on Sunday) (1960)

Marik Vos-Lundh
Jungfrukällan (eng. The Virgin Spring) (1960)

Best Costume Design, Color
⚜ **Bill Thomas, Valles** ⚜
Spartacus (1960)

Marjorie Best
Sunrise at Campobello (1960)

Irene
Midnight Lace (1960)

Edith Head
Pepe (1960)

Irene Sharaff
Can-Can (1960)

Juvenile Award
⚜ **Hayley Mills** ⚜
For Pollyanna (1960), the most outstanding juvenile performance during 1960.

Best Short Subject, Cartoon
⚜ **William L. Snyder (Producer)** ⚜
Munro (1961)

Walt Disney (Producer)
Goliath II (1960)

Warner Bros.
High Note (1960), Mouse and Garden (1960)

Frantisek Vystrecil (Producer)
O místo na slunci (eng. A Place in the Sun) (1959)

Best Short Subject, Live Action
⬇ **Ezra R. Baker (Producer)** ⬇
Day of the Painter (1960)
Walt Disney (Producer)
Islands of the Sea (1960)
Ismail Merchant, Charles F. Schwep (Producers)
The Creation of Woman (1961)
Leslie Winik (Producer)
A Sport Is Born (1960)

Best Directing
⬇ **Billy Wilder** ⬇
The Apartment (1960)
Jack Cardiff
Sons and Lovers (1960)
Jules Dassin
Pote tin Kyriaki (eng. Never on Sunday) (1960)
Alfred Hitchcock
Psycho (1960)
Fred Zinnemann
The Sundowners (1960)

Best Documentary, Feature
⬇ **Larry Lansburgh (Producer)** ⬇
The Horse with the Flying Tail (1960)
Robert D. Fraser (Producer)
Rebel in Paradise (1960)

Best Documentary, Short Subject
⬇ **James Hill (Producer)** ⬇
Giuseppina (1960)
Altina Carey, Charles Carey (Producers)
George Grosz' Interregnum (1964)
Colin Low (Producer)
Universe (1960)
Statens Filmcentral, The Danish Government Film Office
En by ved navn København (eng. A City Called Copenhagen) (1960)
United States Information Agency
Beyond Silence (1960)

Best Film Editing
⬇ **Daniel Mandell** ⬇
The Apartment (1960)
Al Clark, Viola Lawrence
Pepe (1960)
Stuart Gilmore
The Alamo (1960)
Frederic Knudtson
Inherit the Wind (1960)
Robert Lawrence
Spartacus (1960)

Best Special Effects
⚱ **Tim Baar, Gene Warren (Visual)** ⚱
The Time Machine (1960)
Augie J. Lohman (Visual)
The Last Voyage (1960)

Best Foreign Language Film
⚱ **Sweden** ⚱
Jungfrukällan (eng. The Virgin Spring) (1960)
France
La Vérité (1960)
Italy
Kapò (eng. Kapo) (1960)
Mexico
Macario (1960)
Yugoslavia
Deveti krug (eng. The Ninth Circle) (1960)

Best Motion Picture
⚱ **Billy Wilder (Producer)** ⚱
The Apartment (1960)
Bernard Smith (Producer)
Elmer Gantry (1960)
Jerry Wald (Producer)
Sons and Lovers (1960)
John Wayne (Producer)
The Alamo (1960)
Fred Zinnemann (Producer)
The Sundowners (1960)

Best Music, Music Score of a Dramatic or Comedy Picture
⚱ **Ernest Gold** ⚱
Exodus (1960)
Elmer Bernstein
The Magnificent Seven (1960)
Alex North
Spartacus (1960)
André Previn
Elmer Gantry (1960)
Dimitri Tiomkin
The Alamo (1960)

Best Music, Scoring of a Musical Picture
⚱ **Morris Stoloff, Harry Sukman** ⚱
Song Without End (1960)
Johnny Green
Pepe (1960)
Earle H. Hagen, Lionel Newman
Let's Make Love (1960)
André Previn
Bells Are Ringing (1960)
Nelson Riddle
Can-Can (1960)

Best Music, Song

Manos Hadjidakis (Music & Lyrics)
ǂ for the song "Ta paidia tou Peiraia" ("Never on Sunday") ǂ
Pote tin Kyriaki (eng. Never on Sunday) (1960)

Jimmy Van Heusen (Music), Sammy Cahn (Lyrics)
for the song "The Second Time Around"
High Time (1960)

Johnny Mercer (Music & Lyrics) for the song "The Facts of Life"
The Facts of Life (1960)

André Previn (Music), Dory Previn (as Dory Langdon) (Lyrics)
for the song "Faraway Part of Town"
Pepe (1960)

Dimitri Tiomkin (Music), Paul Francis Webster (Lyrics)
for the song "The Green Leaves of Summer"
The Alamo (1960)

Best Sound

Fred Hynes (Sound Director), Todd-AO Sound Department,
ǂ **Gordon E. Sawyer (Sound Director),** ǂ
Samuel Goldwyn Studio Sound Department
The Alamo (1960)

George R. Groves (Sound Director), Warner Bros. Studio Sound Department
Sunrise at Campobello (1960)

Franklin E. Milton (Sound Director),
Metro-Goldwyn-Mayer Studio Sound Department
Cimarron (1960)

Charles J. Rice (Sound Director), Columbia Studio Sound Department
Pepe (1960)

Gordon E. Sawyer (Sound Director),
Samuel Goldwyn Studio Sound Department
The Apartment (1960)

Best Writing, Screenplay based on material from another medium

ǂ **Richard Brooks** ǂ
Elmer Gantry (1960)

T. E. B. Clarke, Gavin Lambert
Sons and Lovers (1960)

James Kennaway
Tunes of Glory (1960)

Isobel Lennart
The Sundowners (1960)

Harold Jacob Smith, Nedrick Young
Inherit the Wind (1960)

Best Writing, Story & Screenplay written directly for the screen

ǂ **I. A. L. Diamond, Billy Wilder** ǂ
The Apartment (1960)

Michael Craig, Richard Gregson (Story), Bryan Forbes (Screenplay)
The Angry Silence (1960)

Jules Dassin
Pote tin Kyriaki (eng. Never on Sunday) (1960)

Marguerite Duras
Hiroshima Mon Amour (1959)

Melvin Frank, Norman Panama
The Facts of Life (1960)

The 34ᵗʰ Academy Awards® - April 9, 1962

Host: Bob Hope
Venue: Santa Monica Civic Auditorium
Honoring movies released in 1961

Honorary Award

⚊ William L. Hendricks ⚊

For his outstanding patriotic service in the conception, writing and production of
the Marine Corps film, A Force in Readiness (1961),
which has brought honor to the Academy and the motion picture industry.

⚊ Fred L. Metzler ⚊

For his dedication and outstanding service to Academy of Motion Picture Arts & Sciences

⚊ Jerome Robbins ⚊

For his brilliant achievements in the art of choreography on film.

Best Actor

⚊ Maximilian Schell ⚊

Judgment at Nuremberg (1961) role "Hans Rolfe"

Charles Boyer
Fanny (1961) role "César"

Paul Newman
The Hustler (1961) role "Eddie Felson"

Spencer Tracy
Judgment at Nuremberg (1961) role "Chief Judge Dan Haywood"

Stuart Whitman
The Mark (1961) role "Jim Fuller"

Best Actor in a Supporting Role

⚊ George Chakiris ⚊

.West Side Story (1961) role "Bernardo Nuñez"

Montgomery Clift
Judgment at Nuremberg (1961) role "Rudolph Peterson"

Peter Falk
Pocketful of Miracles (1961) role "Joy Boy"

Jackie Gleason
The Hustler (1961) role "Minnesota Fats"

George C. Scott
The Hustler (1961) role "Bert Gordon"

Best Actress

⚊ Sophia Loren ⚊

La ciociara (eng. Two Women) (1960) role "Cesira"

Audrey Hepburn
Breakfast at Tiffany's (1961) role "Holly Golightly / Lula Mae Barnes"

Piper Laurie
The Hustler (1961) role "Sarah Packard"

Geraldine Page
Summer and Smoke (1961) role "Alma Winemiller"

Natalie Wood
Splendor in the Grass (1961) role "Wilma Dean "Deanie" Loomis"

Best Actress in a Supporting Role
⚡ Rita Moreno ⚡
West Side Story (1961) role "Anita del Carmen"
Fay Bainter
The Children's Hour (1961) role "Mrs. Amelia Tilford"
Judy Garland
Judgment at Nuremberg (1961) role "Irene Hoffmann-Wallner"
Lotte Lenya
The Roman Spring of Mrs. Stone (1961) role "Contessa Magda Terribili-Gonzales"
Una Merkel
Summer and Smoke (1961) role "Mrs. Winemiller"

Irving G. Thalberg Memorial Award
⚡ Stanley Kramer ⚡

Best Art Direction, Black and White
⚡ Harry Horner (Art Direction), Gene Callahan (Set Decoration) ⚡
The Hustler (1961)
Fernando Carrere (Art Direction), Edward G. Boyle (Set Decoration)
The Children's Hour (1961)
Carroll Clark (Art Direction), Hal Gausman, Emile Kuri (Set Decoration)
The Absent Minded Professor (1961)
Piero Gherardi (Art Direction)
La Dolce Vita (1960)
Rudolph Sternad (Art Direction), George Milo (Set Decoration)
Judgment at Nuremberg (1961)

Best Art Direction, Color
⚡ Boris Leven (Art Direction), Victor A. Gangelin (Set Decoration) ⚡
West Side Story (1961)
Roland Anderson, Hal Pereira (Art Direction),
Sam Comer, Ray Moyer (Set Decoration)
Breakfast at Tiffany's (1961)
Veniero Colasanti, John Moore (Art Direction)
El Cid (1961)
Alexander Golitzen, Joseph C. Wright (Art Direction),
Howard Bristol (Set Decoration)
Flower Drum Song (1961)
Hal Pereira, Walter H. Tyler (Art Direction),
Sam Comer, Arthur Krams (Set Decoration)
Summer and Smoke (1961)

Best Short Subject, Cartoon
⚡ Zagreb Film ⚡
Surogat (eng. The Substitute) (1961)
Walt Disney (Producer)
Aquamania (1961)
Friz Freleng (Producer)
The Pied Piper of Guadalupe (1961)
Chuck Jones (Producer)
Beep Prepared (1961), Nelly's Folly (1961)

Best Short Subject, Live Action
⚡ **Templar Film Studios** ⚡
Seawards the Great Ships (1961)
Cine Documents, Kingsley International
Ballon vole (1960)
Robert Gaffney (Producer)
Rooftops of New York (1961)
Dr. John D. Jennings (Producer)
The Face of Jesus (1961)
National Film Board of Canada
Very Nice, Very Nice (1961)

Best Cinematography, Black and White
⚡ **Eugen Schüfftan** ⚡
The Hustler (1961)
Edward Colman
The Absent Minded Professor (1961)
Daniel L. Fapp
One, Two, Three (1961)
Ernest Laszlo
Judgment at Nuremberg (1961)
Franz F. Planer
The Children's Hour (1961)

Best Cinematography, Color
⚡ **Daniel L. Fapp** ⚡
West Side Story (1961)
Jack Cardiff
Fanny (1961)
Charles Lang Jr.
One-Eyed Jacks (1961)
Russell Metty
Flower Drum Song (1961)
Harry Stradling Sr.
A Majority of One (1961)

Best Special Effects
⚡ **Bill Warrington (Visual), Vivian C. Greenham (Audible)** ⚡
The Guns of Navarone (1961)
Eustace Lycett, Robert A. Mattey (Visual)
The Absent Minded Professor (1961)

Best Costume Design, Black and White
⚡ **Piero Gherardi** ⚡
La Dolce Vita (1960)
Dorothy Jeakins
The Children's Hour (1961)
Jean Louis
Judgment at Nuremberg (1961)
Yoshirô Muraki
Yojimbo (1961)
Howard Shoup
Claudelle Inglish (1961)

Best Costume Design, Color

⚐ Irene Sharaff ⚐
West Side Story (1961)

Edith Head, Walter Plunkett
Pocketful of Miracles (1961)

Jean Louis
Back Street (1961)

Irene Sharaff
Flower Drum Song (1961)

Bill Thomas
Babes in Toyland (1961)

Best Directing

⚐ Jerome Robbins, Robert Wise ⚐
West Side Story (1961)

Federico Fellini
La Dolce Vita (1960)

Stanley Kramer
Judgment at Nuremberg (1961)

Robert Rossen
The Hustler (1961)

J. Lee Thompson
The Guns of Navarone (1961)

Best Film Editing

⚐ Thomas Stanford ⚐
West Side Story (1961)

Philip W. Anderson
The Parent Trap (1961)

Frederic Knudtson
Judgment at Nuremberg (1961)

Alan Osbiston
The Guns of Navarone (1961)

William H. Reynolds
Fanny (1961)

Best Foreign Language Film

⚐ Sweden ⚐
Såsom i en spegel (eng. Through a Glass Darkly) (1961)

Denmark
Harry og kammertjeneren (eng. Harry and the Butler) (1961)

Japan
Eien no hito (eng. Immortal Love) (1961)

Mexico
Ánimas Trujano (El hombre importante) (eng. The Important Man) (1961)

Spain
Plácido (eng. Placido) (1961)

Jean Hersholt Humanitarian Award

⚐ George Seaton ⚐

Best Music, Music Score of a Dramatic or Comedy Picture

🎵 **Henry Mancini** 🎵
Breakfast at Tiffany's (1961)

Elmer Bernstein
Summer and Smoke (1961)

Miklós Rózsa
El Cid (1961)

Morris Stoloff, Harry Sukman
Fanny (1961)

Dimitri Tiomkin
The Guns of Navarone (1961)

Best Music, Scoring of a Musical Picture

🎵 **Saul Chaplin, Johnny Green, Sid Ramin, Irwin Kostal** 🎵
West Side Story (1961)

George Bruns
Babes in Toyland (1961)

Ken Darby, Alfred Newman
Flower Drum Song (1961)

Duke Ellington
Paris Blues (1961)

Dimitri Shostakovich
Khovanschina (1959)

Best Music, Song

🎵 **Henry Mancini (Music), Johnny Mercer (Lyrics)** 🎵
for the song "Moon River"
Breakfast at Tiffany's (1961)

Jimmy Van Heusen (Music), Sammy Cahn (Lyrics)
for the song "Pocketful of Miracles"
Pocketful of Miracles (1961)

Henry Mancini (Music), Mack David (Lyrics)
for the song "Bachelor in Paradise"
Bachelor in Paradise (1961)

Miklós Rózsa (Music), Paul Francis Webster (Lyrics)
for the song "Love Theme from El Cid (The Falcon and the Dove)"
El Cid (1961)

Dimitri Tiomkin (Music), Ned Washington (Lyrics)
for the song "Town Without Pity"
Town Without Pity (1961)

Best Motion Picture

🎵 **Robert Wise (Producer)** 🎵
West Side Story (1961)

Carl Foreman (Producer)
The Guns of Navarone (1961)

Stanley Kramer (Producer)
Judgment at Nuremberg (1961)

Joshua Logan (Producer)
Fanny (1961)

Robert Rossen (Producer)
The Hustler (1961)

Best Writing, Screenplay based on material from another medium

⚟ Abby Mann ⚟
Judgment at Nuremberg (1961)

George Axelrod
Breakfast at Tiffany's (1961)

Sidney Carroll, Robert Rossen
The Hustler (1961)

Carl Foreman
The Guns of Navarone (1961)

Ernest Lehman
West Side Story (1961)

Best Writing, Story & Screenplay written directly for the screen

⚟ William Inge ⚟
Splendor in the Grass (1961)

Sergio Amidei, Diego Fabbri, Indro Montanelli
Il Generale Della Rovere (1959)

Grigori Chukhrai, Valentin Yoshov
Ballada o soldate (eng. Ballad of a Soldier) (1959)

Federico Fellini, Ennio Flaiano, Tullio Pinelli, Brunello Rondi
La Dolce Vita (1960)

Paul Henning, Stanley Shapiro
Lover Come Back (1961)

Best Sound

Fred Hynes (Sound Director), Todd-AO Sound Department,
Gordon E. Sawyer (Sound Director),
Samuel Goldwyn Studio Sound Department
West Side Story (1961)

Robert O. Cook (Sound Director), Walt Disney Studio Sound Department
The Parent Trap (1961)

John Cox (Sound Director), Shepperton Studio Sound Department
The Guns of Navarone (1961)

Gordon E. Sawyer (Sound Director),
Samuel Goldwyn Studio Sound Department
The Children's Hour (1961)

Waldon O. Watson (Sound Director), Revue Studio Sound Department
Flower Drum Song (1961)

Best Documentary, Short Subject

⚟ Frank P. Bibas (Producer) ⚟
Project Hope (1961)

Benedetto Benedetti (Producer)
L'uomo in grigio (eng. The Man in Gray) (1961)

Jim O'Connor, Tom Hayes (Producers)
Cradle of Genius (1961)

Dido-Film-GmbH
Kahl (1961)

United States Air Force
Breaking the Language Barrier (1961)

Best Documentary, Feature
⚐ Arthur Cohn, Rene Lafuite (Producers) ⚐
Le ciel et la boue (eng. The Sky Above, the Mud Below) (1961)
Dell Istituto Nazionale Luce, Comitato Organizzatore
Del Giochi Della XVII Olimpiade
La Grande Olimpiade (eng. The Grand Olympics) (1961)

The 35th Academy Awards® - April 8, 1963
Host: Frank Sinatra
Venue: Santa Monica Civic Auditorium
Honoring movies released in 1962

Jean Hersholt Humanitarian Award
⚐ Steve Broidy ⚐

Best Actor
⚐ Gregory Peck ⚐
To Kill a Mockingbird (1962) role "Atticus Finch"
Burt Lancaster
Birdman of Alcatraz (1962) role "Robert Franklin Stroud"
Jack Lemmon
Days of Wine and Roses (1962) role "Joe Clay"
Marcello Mastroianni
Divorzio all'italiana (eng. Divorce Italian Style) (1961) role "Ferdinando Cefalù"
Peter O'Toole
Lawrence of Arabia (1962) role "T. E. Lawrence"

Best Actor in a Supporting Role
⚐ Ed Begley ⚐
Sweet Bird of Youth (1962) role "Tom "Boss" Finley"
Victor Buono
What Ever Happened to Baby Jane? (1962) role "Edwin Flagg"
Telly Savalas
Birdman of Alcatraz (1962) role "Feto Gomez"
Omar Sharif
Lawrence of Arabia (1962) role "Sherif Ali ibn el Kharish"
Terence Stamp
Billy Budd (1962) role "Billy Budd - Merchant Seaman, Rights of Man"

Best Actress
⚐ Anne Bancroft ⚐
The Miracle Worker (1962) role "Anne Sullivan"
Bette Davis
What Ever Happened to Baby Jane? (1962) role "Baby Jane Hudson"
Katharine Hepburn
Long Day's Journey Into Night (1962) role "Mary Cavan Tyrone"
Geraldine Page
Sweet Bird of Youth (1962) role "Alexandra Del Lago"
Lee Remick
Days of Wine and Roses (1962) role "Kirsten Arnesen Clay"

Best Actress in a Supporting Role
⚊ **Patty Duke** ⚊
The Miracle Worker (1962) role "Helen Keller"

Mary Badham
To Kill a Mockingbird (1962) role "Jean Louise "Scout" Finch"

Shirley Knight
Sweet Bird of Youth (1962) role "Heavenly Finley"

Angela Lansbury
The Manchurian Candidate (1962) role "Mrs. Eleanor Shaw Iselin"

Thelma Ritter
Birdman of Alcatraz (1962) role "Elizabeth McCartney Stroud"

Best Art Direction, Black and White
Henry Bumstead, Alexander Golitzen (Art Direction), Oliver Emert (Set Decoration)
To Kill a Mockingbird (1962)

Roland Anderson, Hal Pereira (Art Direction), Sam Comer, Frank R. McKelvy (Set Decoration)
The Pigeon That Took Rome (1962)

Léon Barsacq, Ted Haworth, Vincent Korda (Art Direction), Gabriel Béchir (Set Decoration)
The Longest Day (1962)

Edward C. Carfagno, George W. Davis (Art Direction), Henry Grace, Dick Pefferle (Set Decoration)
Period of Adjustment (1962)

Joseph C. Wright (Art Direction), George James Hopkins (Set Decoration)
Days of Wine and Roses (1962)

Best Art Direction, Color
⚊ **John Box, John Stoll (Art Direction), Dario Simoni (Set Decoration)** ⚊
Lawrence of Arabia (1962)

Edward C. Carfagno, George W. Davis (Art Direction), Henry Grace, Dick Pefferle (Set Decoration)
The Wonderful World of the Brothers Grimm (1962)

Robert Clatworthy, Alexander Golitzen (Art Direction), George Milo (Set Decoration)
That Touch of Mink (1962)

George W. Davis, J. McMillan Johnson (Art Direction), Henry Grace, Hugh Hunt (Set Decoration)
Mutiny on the Bounty (1962)

Paul Groesse (Art Direction), George James Hopkins (Set Decoration)
Meredith Willson's The Music Man (1962)

Best Documentary, Short Subject
⚊ **Jack Howells (Producer)** ⚊
A Tribute to Dylan Thomas (1961)

William L. Hendricks (Producer)
The John Glenn Story (1962)

Robert Saudek (Producer)
The Road to the Wall (1962)

Best Documentary, Feature
⬇ **Louis Clyde Stoumen (Producer)** ⬇
Black Fox: The True Story of Adolf Hitler (1962)
Hugo Niebeling (Producer)
Alvorada - Brazil's Changing Face (1962)

Best Cinematography, Black and White
⬇ **Jean Bourgoin, Walter Wottitz** ⬇
The Longest Day (1962)
Burnett Guffey
Birdman of Alcatraz (1962)
Ernest Haller
What Ever Happened to Baby Jane? (1962)
Russell Harlan
To Kill a Mockingbird (1962)
Ted D. McCord
Two for the Seesaw (1962)

Best Cinematography, Color
⬇ **Fred A. Young** ⬇
Lawrence of Arabia (1962)
Russell Harlan
Hatari! (1962)
Harry Stradling Sr.
Gypsy (1962)
Robert L. Surtees
Mutiny on the Bounty (1962)
Paul C. Vogel
The Wonderful World of the Brothers Grimm (1962)

Best Costume Design, Black and White
⬇ **Norma Koch** ⬇
What Ever Happened to Baby Jane? (1962)
Don Feld
Days of Wine and Roses (1962)
Edith Head
The Man Who Shot Liberty Valance (1962)
Ruth Morley
The Miracle Worker (1962)
Theoni V. Aldredge (as Denny Vachlioti)
Phaedra (1962)

Best Costume Design, Color
⬇ **Mary Wills** ⬇
The Wonderful World of the Brothers Grimm (1962)
Edith Head
My Geisha (1962)
Dorothy Jeakins
Meredith Willson's The Music Man (1962)
Orry-Kelly
Gypsy (1962)
Bill Thomas
Bon Voyage! (1962)

Best Directing

⸸ David Lean ⸸
Lawrence of Arabia (1962)

Pietro Germi
Divorzio all'italiana (eng. Divorce Italian Style) (1961)

Robert Mulligan
To Kill a Mockingbird (1962)

Arthur Penn
The Miracle Worker (1962)

Frank Perry
David and Lisa (1962)

Best Special Effects

⸸ Robert MacDonald (Visual), Jacques Maumont (Audible) ⸸
The Longest Day (1962)

A. Arnold Gillespie (Visual), Milo Lory (Audible)
Mutiny on the Bounty (1962)

Best Film Editing

⸸ Anne V. Coates ⸸
Lawrence of Arabia (1962)

Samuel E. Beetley
The Longest Day (1962)

John McSweeney Jr.
Mutiny on the Bounty (1962)

Ferris Webster
The Manchurian Candidate (1962)

William H. Ziegler
Meredith Willson's The Music Man (1962)

Best Foreign Language Film

⸸ France ⸸
Les dimanches de Ville d'Avray (eng. Sundays and Cybèle) (1962)

Brazil
O Pagador de Promessas (eng. Keeper of Promises (The Given Word)) (1962)

Greece
Ilektra (eng. Electra) (1962)

Italy
Le quattro giornate di Napoli (eng. The Four Days of Naples) (1962)

Mexico
Tlayucan (eng. The Pearl of Tlayucan) (1962)

Best Music, Music Score substantially original

⸸ Maurice Jarre ⸸
Lawrence of Arabia (1962)

Elmer Bernstein
To Kill a Mockingbird (1962)

Jerry Goldsmith
Freud (1962)

Bronislau Kaper
Mutiny on the Bounty (1962)

Franz Waxman
Taras Bulba (1962)

Best Music, Scoring of Music adaptation or treatment

⟁ Ray Heindorf ⟁
Meredith Willson's The Music Man (1962)

Leigh Harline
The Wonderful World of the Brothers Grimm (1962)

Michel Magne
Gigot (1962)

Frank Perkins
Gypsy (1962)

George Stoll
Billy Rose's Jumbo (1962)

Best Music, Song

⟁ Henry Mancini (Music), Johnny Mercer (Lyrics)
for the song "Days of Wine and Roses"
Days of Wine and Roses (1962)

Elmer Bernstein (Music), Mack David (Lyrics)
for the song "Walk on the Wild Side"
Walk on the Wild Side (1962)

Sammy Fain (Music), Paul Francis Webster (Lyrics)
for the song "Tender Is the Night"
Tender Is the Night (1962)

Bronislau Kaper (Music), Paul Francis Webster (Lyrics)
for the song "Love Song from Mutiny on the Bounty (Follow Me)"
Mutiny on the Bounty (1962)

André Previn (Music), Dory Previn (as Dory Langdon) (Lyrics)
for the song "Song from Two for the Seesaw (Second Chance)"
Two for the Seesaw (1962)

Best Picture

⟁ Sam Spiegel (Producer) ⟁
Lawrence of Arabia (1962)

Morton Da Costa (Producer)
Meredith Willson's The Music Man (1962)

Alan J. Pakula (Producer)
To Kill a Mockingbird (1962)

Aaron Rosenberg (Producer)
Mutiny on the Bounty (1962)

Darryl F. Zanuck (Producer)
The Longest Day (1962)

Best Short Subject, Cartoon

⟁ Faith Hubley, John Hubley (Producers) ⟁
The Hole (1962)

Walt Disney (Producer)
A Symposium on Popular Songs (1962)

Jules Engel (Producer)
Icarus Montgolfier Wright (1962)

William L. Snyder (Producer)
Self Defense... for Cowards (1962)

Warner Bros.
Now Hear This (1962)

Best Short Subject, Live Action

⚑ **Jean-Claude Carrière, Pierre Étaix (Producers)** ⚑
Heureux Anniversaire (eng. Happy Anniversary) (1962)

Hayward Anderson (Producer)
The Cliff Dwellers (1962)

Robert Clouse (Producer)
The Cadillac (1962)

Herman van der Horst (Producer)
Pan (1962)

Charles Huguenot van der Linden,
Martina Huguenot van der Linden (Producers)
Big City Blues (1962)

Best Writing, Story & Screenplay written directly for the screen

⚑ **Ennio de Concini, Pietro Germi, Alfredo Giannetti** ⚑
Divorzio all'italiana (eng. Divorce Italian Style) (1961)

Ingmar Bergman
Såsom i en spegel (eng. Through a Glass Darkly) (1961)

Charles Kaufman (Story), Charles Kaufman, Wolfgang Reinhardt (Screenplay)
Freud (1962)

Nate Monaster, Stanley Shapiro
That Touch of Mink (1962)

Alain Robbe-Grillet
L'année dernière à Marienbad (eng. Last Year at Marienbad) (1961)

Best Writing, Screenplay based on material from another medium

⚑ **Horton Foote** ⚑
To Kill a Mockingbird (1962)

Robert Bolt, Michael Wilson
Lawrence of Arabia (1962)

William Gibson
The Miracle Worker (1962)

Vladimir Nabokov
Lolita (1962)

Eleanor Perry
David and Lisa (1962)

Best Sound

⚑ **John Cox (Sound Director), Shepperton Studio Sound Department** ⚑
Lawrence of Arabia (1962)

Robert O. Cook (Sound Director), Walt Disney Studio Sound Department
Bon Voyage! (1962)

George R. Groves (Sound Director), Warner Bros. Studio Sound Department
Meredith Willson's The Music Man (1962)

Joseph D. Kelly (Sound Director), Glen Glenn Sound Department
What Ever Happened to Baby Jane? (1962)

Waldon O. Watson (Sound Director), Universal City Studio Sound Department
That Touch of Mink (1962)

The 36ᵗʰ Academy Awards® - April 13, 1964

Host: Jack Lemmon
Venue: Santa Monica Civic Auditorium
Honoring movies released in 1963

Best Actor

⚰ Sidney Poitier ⚰
Lilies of the Field (1963) role "Homer Smith"

Albert Finney
Tom Jones (1963) role "Tom Jones"

Richard Harris
This Sporting Life (1963) role "Frank Machin"

Rex Harrison
Cleopatra (1963) role "Julius Caesar"

Paul Newman
Hud (1963) role "Hud Bannon"

Best Actor in a Supporting Role

⚰ Melvyn Douglas ⚰
Hud (1963) role "Homer Bannon"

Nick Adams
Twilight of Honor (1963) role "Ben Brown"

Bobby Darin
Captain Newman, M.D. (1963) role "Corporal Jim Tompkins, USAAF"

Hugh Griffith
Tom Jones (1963) role "Squire Western"

John Huston
The Cardinal (1963) role "Cardinal Glennon"

Best Actress

⚰ Patricia Neal ⚰
Hud (1963) role "Alma Brown"

Leslie Caron
The L-Shaped Room (1962) role "Jane Fosset"

Shirley MacLaine
Irma La Douce (1963) role "Irma La Douce"

Rachel Roberts
This Sporting Life (1963) role "Margaret Hammond"

Natalie Wood
Love with the Proper Stranger (1963) role "Angie Rossini"

Best Actress in a Supporting Role

⚰ Margaret Rutherford ⚰
The V.I.P.s (1963) role "The Duchess of Brighton"

Diane Cilento
Tom Jones (1963) role "Molly Seagrim"

Edith Evans
Tom Jones (1963) role "Miss Western"

Joyce Redman
Tom Jones (1963) role "Mrs. Waters / Jenny Jones"

Lilia Skala
Lilies of the Field (1963) role "Mother Maria Marthe"

Best Art Direction, Black and White
⚐ **Gene Callahan (Art Direction)** ⚐
America America (1963)

Roland Anderson, Hal Pereira (Art Direction),
Sam Comer, Grace Gregory (Set Decoration)
Love with the Proper Stranger (1963)

George W. Davis, Paul Groesse (Art Direction),
Henry Grace, Hugh Hunt (Set Decoration)
Twilight of Honor (1963)

Piero Gherardi (Art Direction)
8½ (1963)

Tambi Larsen, Hal Pereira (Art Direction),
Robert R. Benton, Sam Comer (Set Decoration)
Hud (1963)

Best Art Direction, Color
⚐ **Herman A. Blumenthal, Hilyard M. Brown, John DeCuir, Boris Juraga,**
Maurice Pelling, Jack Martin Smith, Elven Webb (Art Direction), ⚐
Paul S. Fox, Ray Moyer, Walter M. Scott (Set Decoration)
Cleopatra (1963)

Roland Anderson, Hal Pereira (Art Direction),
Sam Comer, James W. Payne (Set Decoration)
Come Blow Your Horn (1963)

Ralph W. Brinton, Jocelyn Herbert, Ted Marshall (Art Direction),
Josie MacAvin (Set Decoration)
Tom Jones (1963)

George W. Davis, William Ferrari, Addison Hehr (Art Direction),
Henry Grace, Don Greenwood Jr., Jack Mills (Set Decoration)
(William Ferrari - posthumous)
How the West Was Won (1962)

Lyle R. Wheeler (Art Direction), Gene Callahan (Set Decoration)
The Cardinal (1963)

Best Documentary, Feature
⚐ **Robert Hughes (Producer)** ⚐
Robert Frost: A Lover's Quarrel with the World (1963)

Marshall Flaum (Producer)
The Yanks Are Coming (1963)

Paul de Roubaix (Producer)
Le maillon et la chaîne (eng. The Link and the Chain) (1963)

Best Documentary, Short Subject
⚐ **Simon Schiffrin (Producer)** ⚐
Chagall (1963)

Edgar Anstey (Producer)
Thirty Million Letters (1963)

Mel London (Producer)
To Live Again (1963)

George Stevens Jr. (Producer)
The Five Cities of June (1963)

Algernon G. Walker (Producer)
The Spirit of America (1963)

Best Cinematography, Color

⌰ Leon Shamroy ⌰
Cleopatra (1963)

William H. Daniels, Milton R. Krasner, Charles Lang Jr., Joseph LaShelle
How the West Was Won (1962)

Joseph LaShelle
Irma La Douce (1963)

Ernest Laszlo
It's a Mad Mad Mad Mad World (1963)

Leon Shamroy
The Cardinal (1963)

Best Cinematography, Black and White

⌰ James Wong Howe ⌰
Hud (1963)

Lucien Ballard
The Caretakers (1963)

George J. Folsey
The Balcony (1963)

Ernest Haller
Lilies of the Field (1963)

Milton R. Krasner
Love with the Proper Stranger (1963)

Best Costume Design, Black and White

⌰ Piero Gherardi ⌰
8½ (1963)

Edith Head
Love with the Proper Stranger (1963), Wives and Lovers (1963)

Bill Thomas
Toys in the Attic (1963)

Travilla
The Stripper (1963)

Best Costume Design, Color

⌰ Vittorio Nino Novarese, Renié, Irene Sharaff ⌰
Cleopatra (1963)

Donald Brooks
The Cardinal (1963)

Edith Head
A New Kind of Love (1963)

Walter Plunkett
How the West Was Won (1962)

Piero Tosi
Il gattopardo (eng. The Leopard) (1963)

Best Special Effects

⌰ Emil Kosa Jr. ⌰
Cleopatra (1963)

Ub Iwerks
The Birds (1963)

Best Directing

↓ **Tony Richardson** ↓
Tom Jones (1963)

Federico Fellini
8½ (1963)

Elia Kazan
America America (1963)

Otto Preminger
The Cardinal (1963)

Martin Ritt
Hud (1963)

Best Film Editing

↓ **Harold F. Kress** ↓
How the West Was Won (1962)

Gene Fowler Jr., Frederic Knudtson, Robert C. Jones
(Frederic Knudtson - posthumous)
It's a Mad Mad Mad Mad World (1963)

Louis R. Loeffler
The Cardinal (1963)

Dorothy Spencer
Cleopatra (1963)

Ferris Webster
The Great Escape (1963)

Irving G. Thalberg Memorial Award

↓ **Sam Spiegel** ↓

Best Foreign Language Film

↓ **Italy** ↓
8½ (1963)

Greece
Ta kokkina fanaria (eng. The Red Lanterns) (1963)

Japan
Kyoto (eng. Twin Sisters of Kyoto) (1963)

Poland
Nóż w wodzie (eng. Knife in the Water) (1962)

Spain
Los Tarantos (1963)

Best Music, Music Score substantially original

↓ **John Addison** ↓
Tom Jones (1963)

Ken Darby, Alfred Newman
How the West Was Won (1962)

Ernest Gold
It's a Mad Mad Mad Mad World (1963)

Alex North
Cleopatra (1963)

Dimitri Tiomkin
55 Days at Peking (1963)

Best Music, Scoring of Music adaptation or treatment

🏆 **André Previn** 🏆
Irma La Douce (1963)

George Bruns
The Sword in the Stone (1963)

John Green
Bye Bye Birdie (1963)

Maurice Jarre
Les dimanches de Ville d'Avray (eng. Sundays and Cybèle) (1962)

Leith Stevens
A New Kind of Love (1963)

Best Music, Song

🏆 **Jimmy Van Heusen (Music), Sammy Cahn (Lyrics)** 🏆
for the song "Call Me Irresponsible"
Papa's Delicate Condition (1963)

Ernest Gold (Music), Mack David (Lyrics)
for the song "It's a Mad Mad Mad Mad World"
It's a Mad Mad Mad Mad World (1963)

Henry Mancini (Music), Johnny Mercer (Lyrics) for the song "Charade"
Charade (1963)

Nino Oliviero, Riz Ortolani (Music), Norman Newell (Lyrics)
for the song "More"
Mondo cane (eng. A Dog's Life) (1962)

Dimitri Tiomkin (Music), Paul Francis Webster (Lyrics)
for the song "So Little Time"
55 Days at Peking (1963)

Best Motion Picture

🏆 **Tony Richardson (Producer)** 🏆
Tom Jones (1963)

Elia Kazan (Producer)
America America (1963)

Ralph Nelson (Producer)
Lilies of the Field (1963)

Bernard Smith (Producer)
How the West Was Won (1962)

Walter Wanger (Producer)
Cleopatra (1963)

Best Short Subject, Cartoon

🏆 **Ernest Pintoff (Producer)** 🏆
The Critic (1963)

Tom Daly, Colin Low (Producers)
My Financial Career (1962)

Carmen D'Avino (Producer)
Pianissimo (1963)

John Halas (Producer)
Automania 2000 (1963)

Dusan Vukotic (Producer)
Igra (eng. The Game) (1962)

Best Short Subject, Live Action

↓ Marcel Ichac, Paul de Roubaix (Producers) ↓
La rivière du hibou (eng. Occurrence at Owl Creek Bridge) (1961)

Ezra R. Baker (Producer)
Koncert (eng. The Concert) (1962)

James Hill (Producer)
The Home-Made Car (1963)

Christopher Miles (Producer)
The Six-Sided Triangle (1963)

Walker Stuart (Producer)
That's Me (1963)

Best Writing, Screenplay based on material from another medium

↓ John Osborne ↓
Tom Jones (1963)

Richard L. Breen, Phoebe Ephron, Henry Ephron
Captain Newman, M.D. (1963)

Serge Bourguignon, Antoine Tudal
Les dimanches de Ville d'Avray (eng. Sundays and Cybèle) (1962)

Harriet Frank Jr., Irving Ravetch
Hud (1963)

James Poe
Lilies of the Field (1963)

Best Writing, Screenplay

↓ James R. Webb ↓
How the West Was Won (1962)

Pasquale Festa Campanile, Massimo Franciosa, Nanni Loy,
Vasco Pratolini (Story), Carlo Bernari, Pasquale Festa Campanile,
Massimo Franciosa, Nanni Loy (Screenplay)
Le quattro giornate di Napoli (eng. The Four Days of Naples) (1962)

Federico Fellini, Ennio Flaiano, Tullio Pinelli, Brunello Rondi
8½ (1963)

Elia Kazan
America America (1963)

Arnold Schulman
Love with the Proper Stranger (1963)

Best Sound

↓ Franklin E. Milton (Sound Director), ↓
Metro-Goldwyn-Mayer Studio Sound Department
How the West Was Won (1962)

Charles J. Rice (Sound Director), Columbia Studio Sound Department
Bye Bye Birdie (1963)

Waldon O. Watson (Sound Director), Universal City Studio Sound Department
Captain Newman, M.D. (1963)

James P. Corcoran (Sound Director), 20th Century-Fox Studio Sound
Department, Fred Hynes (Sound Director), Todd-AO Sound Department
Cleopatra (1963)

Gordon E. Sawyer (Sound Director),
Samuel Goldwyn Studio Sound Department
It's a Mad Mad Mad Mad World (1963)

Best Sound Effects
⚱ Walter G. Elliott ⚱
It's a Mad Mad Mad Mad World (1963)
Robert L. Bratton
A Gathering of Eagles (1963)

The 37ᵗʰ Academy Awards® - April 5, 1965
Host: Bob Hope
Venue: Santa Monica Civic Auditorium
Honoring movies released in 1964

Honorary Award
⚱ William Tuttle ⚱
For his outstanding make-up achievement for 7 Faces of Dr. Lao (1964).

Best Actor
⚱ Rex Harrison ⚱
My Fair Lady (1964) role "Professor Henry Higgins"
Richard Burton
Becket (1964) role "Thomas Becket"
Peter O'Toole
Becket (1964) role "King Henry II of England"
Anthony Quinn
Alexis Zorbas (eng. Zorba the Greek) (1964) role "Alexis Zorba"
Peter Sellers
Dr. Strangelove or: How I Learned to Stop Worrying and Love the Bomb (1964)
role "Group Captain Lionel Mandrake, President Merkin Muffley, Dr. Strangelove"

Best Actor in a Supporting Role
⚱ Peter Ustinov ⚱
Topkapi (1964) role "Arthur Simon Simpson"
John Gielgud
Becket (1964) role "King Louis VII of France"
Stanley Holloway
My Fair Lady (1964) role "Alfred P. Doolittle"
Edmond O'Brien
Seven Days in May (1964) role "Senator Raymond Clark"
Lee Tracy
The Best Man (1964) role "President Art Hockstader"

Best Actress
⚱ Julie Andrews ⚱
Mary Poppins (1964) role "Mary Poppins"
Anne Bancroft
The Pumpkin Eater (1964) role "Jo Armitage"
Sophia Loren
Matrimonio all'italiana (eng. Marriage Italian Style) (1964)
role "Filumena Marturano"
Debbie Reynolds
The Unsinkable Molly Brown (1964) role "Molly Brown"
Kim Stanley
Seance on a Wet Afternoon (1964) role "Myra Savage"

Best Actress in a Supporting Role
⚇ Lila Kedrova ⚇
Alexis Zorbas (eng. Zorba the Greek) (1964) role "Madame Hortense"
Gladys Cooper
My Fair Lady (1964) role "Mrs. Higgins"
Edith Evans
The Chalk Garden (1964) role "Mrs. St. Maugham"
Grayson Hall
The Night of the Iguana (1964) role "Judith Fellowes"
Agnes Moorehead
Hush...Hush, Sweet Charlotte (1964) role "Velma Cruther"

Best Art Direction, Black and White
⚇ Vassilis Fotopoulos (Art Direction) ⚇
Alexis Zorbas (eng. Zorba the Greek) (1964)
**George W. Davis, Hans Peters, Elliot Scott (Art Direction),
Robert R. Benton, Henry Grace (Set Decoration)**
The Americanization of Emily (1964)
William Glasgow (Art Direction), Raphael Bretton (Set Decoration)
Hush...Hush, Sweet Charlotte (1964)
Stephen B. Grimes (Art Direction)
The Night of the Iguana (1964)
Cary Odell (Art Direction), Edward G. Boyle (Set Decoration)
Seven Days in May (1964)

Best Art Direction, Color
**⚇ Gene Allen, Cecil Beaton (Art Direction),
George James Hopkins (Set Decoration) ⚇**
My Fair Lady (1964)
**E. Preston Ames, George W. Davis (Art Direction),
Henry Grace, Hugh Hunt (Art Direction)**
The Unsinkable Molly Brown (1964)
**John Bryan, Maurice Carter (Art Direction),
Robert Cartwright, Patrick McLoughlin (Set Decoration)**
Becket (1964)
**Carroll Clark, William H. Tuntke (Art Direction),
Hal Gausman, Emile Kuri (Set Decoration)**
Mary Poppins (1964)
**Ted Haworth, Jack Martin Smith (Art Direction),
Stuart A. Reiss, Walter M. Scott (Set Decoration)**
What a Way to Go! (1964)

Best Cinematography, Black and White
⚇ Walter Lassally ⚇
Alexis Zorbas (eng. Zorba the Greek) (1964)
Joseph F. Biroc
Hush...Hush, Sweet Charlotte (1964)
Gabriel Figueroa
The Night of the Iguana (1964)
Milton R. Krasner
Fate Is the Hunter (1964)
Philip H. Lathrop
The Americanization of Emily (1964)

Best Cinematography, Color

⚑ Harry Stradling Sr. ⚑
My Fair Lady (1964)

William H. Clothier
Cheyenne Autumn (1964)

Edward Colman
Mary Poppins (1964)

Daniel L. Fapp
The Unsinkable Molly Brown (1964)

Geoffrey Unsworth
Becket (1964)

Best Costume Design, Black and White

⚑ Dorothy Jeakins ⚑
The Night of the Iguana (1964)

Edith Head
A House Is Not a Home (1964)

René Hubert
The Visit (1964)

Norma Koch
Hush...Hush, Sweet Charlotte (1964)

Howard Shoup
Kisses for My President (1964)

Best Costume Design, Color

⚑ Cecil Beaton ⚑
My Fair Lady (1964)

Margaret Furse
Becket (1964)

Morton Haack
The Unsinkable Molly Brown (1964)

Edith Head, Moss Mabry
What a Way to Go! (1964)

Tony Walton
Mary Poppins (1964)

Best Directing

⚑ George Cukor ⚑
My Fair Lady (1964)

Michael Cacoyannis
Alexis Zorbas (eng. Zorba the Greek) (1964)

Peter Glenville
Becket (1964)

Stanley Kubrick
Dr. Strangelove or: How I Learned to Stop Worrying and Love the Bomb (1964)

Robert Stevenson
Mary Poppins (1964)

Best Special Visual Effects

⚑ Peter Ellenshaw, Hamilton Luske, Eustace Lycett ⚑
Mary Poppins (1964)

Jim Danforth
7 Faces of Dr. Lao (1964)

Best Sound Effects
↓ Norman Wanstall ↓
Goldfinger (1964)

Robert L. Bratton
The Lively Set (1964)

Best Documentary, Feature
↓ Jacques-Yves Cousteau (Producer) ↓
Le monde sans soleil (eng. World Without Sun) (1964)

Jean Aurel (Producer)
Over There, 1914-18 (1963)

Bert Haanstra (Producer)
Alleman (eng. The Human Dutch) (1963)

Jack Le Vien (Producer)
The Finest Hours (1964)

Mel Stuart (Producer)
Four Days in November (1964)

Best Documentary, Short Subject
↓ Charles Guggenheim (Producer) ↓
Nine from Little Rock (1964)

Charles Guggenheim (Producer)
Children Without (1965)

Oxley Hughan, Geoffrey Scott (Producers)
140 Days Under the World (1964)

Henry Jacobs, John Korty (Producers)
Breaking the Habit (1965)

National Film Board of Canada
Eskimo Artist: Kenojuak (1964)

Best Film Editing
↓ Cotton Warburton ↓
Mary Poppins (1964)

Anne V. Coates
Becket (1964)

Ted J. Kent
Father Goose (1964)

Michael Luciano
Hush...Hush, Sweet Charlotte (1964)

William H. Ziegler
My Fair Lady (1964)

Best Foreign Language Film
↓ Italy ↓
Ieri oggi domani (eng. Yesterday, Today and Tomorrow) (1963)

France
Les parapluies de Cherbourg (eng. The Umbrellas of Cherbourg) (1964)

Israel
Sallah Shabati (eng. Sallah) (1964)

Japan
Suna no onna (eng. Woman in the Dunes) (1964)

Sweden
Kvarteret Korpen (eng. Raven's End) (1963)

Best Picture

⚜ **Jack L. Warner (Producer)** ⚜
My Fair Lady (1964)

Michael Cacoyannis (Producer)
Alexis Zorbas (eng. Zorba the Greek) (1964)

Walt Disney, Bill Walsh (Producers)
Mary Poppins (1964)

Stanley Kubrick (Producer)
Dr. Strangelove or: How I Learned to Stop Worrying and Love the Bomb (1964)

Hal B. Wallis (Producer)
Becket (1964)

Best Music, Music Score substantially original

⚜ **Richard M. Sherman, Robert B. Sherman** ⚜
Mary Poppins (1964)

Frank De Vol
Hush...Hush, Sweet Charlotte (1964)

Henry Mancini
The Pink Panther (1963)

Laurence Rosenthal
Becket (1964)

Dimitri Tiomkin
The Fall of the Roman Empire (1964)

Best Music, Scoring of Music adaptation or treatment

⚜ **André Previn** ⚜
My Fair Lady (1964)

**Robert Armbruster, Leo Arnaud, Jack Elliott, Jack Hayes,
Calvin Jackson, Leo Shuken**
The Unsinkable Molly Brown (1964)

Irwin Kostal
Mary Poppins (1964)

George Martin
A Hard Day's Night (1964)

Nelson Riddle
Robin and the 7 Hoods (1964)

Best Music, Song

⚜ **Richard M. Sherman, Robert B. Sherman (Music & Lyrics)** ⚜
for the song "Chim Chim Cher-ee"
Mary Poppins (1964)

Frank De Vol (Music), Mack David (Lyrics)
for the song "Hush...Hush, Sweet Charlotte"
Hush...Hush, Sweet Charlotte (1964)

Henry Mancini (Music), Ray Evans, Jay Livingston (Lyrics)
for the song "Dear Heart"
Dear Heart (1964)

Jimmy Van Heusen (Music), Sammy Cahn (Lyrics)
for the song "My Kind of Town"
Robin and the 7 Hoods (1964)

Jimmy Van Heusen (Music), Sammy Cahn (Lyrics)
for the song "Where Love Has Gone"
Where Love Has Gone (1964)

Best Sound

George R. Groves (Sound Director),
Warner Bros. Studio Sound Department
My Fair Lady (1964)

Robert O. Cook (Sound Director), Walt Disney Studio Sound Department
Mary Poppins (1964)

John Cox (Sound Director), Shepperton Studio Sound Department
Becket (1964)

Franklin E. Milton (Sound Director),
Metro-Goldwyn-Mayer Studio Sound Department
The Unsinkable Molly Brown (1964)

Waldon O. Watson (Sound Director), Universal City Studio Sound Department
Father Goose (1964)

Best Short Subject, Cartoon

David H. DePatie, Friz Freleng (Producers)
The Pink Phink (1964)

National Film Board of Canada
Christmas Cracker (1963)

William L. Snyder (Producer)
How to Avoid Friendship (1964), Nudnik #2 (eng. Here's Nudnik) (1965)

Best Short Subject, Live Action

Edward Schreiber (Producer)
Casals Conducts: 1964 (1964)

Robert Clouse (Producer)
The Legend of Jimmy Blue Eyes (1965)

Carson Davidson (Producer)
Help! My Snowman's Burning Down (1965)

Best Writing, Screenplay based on material from another medium

Edward Anhalt
Becket (1964)

Michael Cacoyannis
Alexis Zorbas (eng. Zorba the Greek) (1964)

Don DaGradi, Bill Walsh
Mary Poppins (1964)

Peter George, Stanley Kubrick, Terry Southern
Dr. Strangelove or: How I Learned to Stop Worrying and Love the Bomb (1964)

Alan Jay Lerner
My Fair Lady (1964)

Best Writing, Story & Screenplay written directly for the screen

S. H. Barnett (Story), Peter Stone, Frank Tarloff (Screenplay)
Father Goose (1964)

Daniel Boulanger, Philippe De Broca, Ariane Mnouchkine,
Jean-Paul Rappeneau
L'homme de Rio (eng. That Man from Rio) (1964)

Orville H. Hampton (Story), Orville H. Hampton, Raphael Hayes (Screenplay)
One Potato, Two Potato (1964)

Agenore Incrocci, Mario Monicelli, Furio Scarpelli
I compagni (eng. The Organizer) (1963)

Alun Owen
A Hard Day's Night (1964)

The 38ᵗʰ Academy Awards® - April 18, 1966

Host: Bob Hope
Venue: Santa Monica Civic Auditorium
Honoring movies released in 1965

Honorary Award

Bob Hope

(gold medal) For unique and distinguished service to industry and the Academy.

Irving G. Thalberg Memorial Award

⚊ William Wyler ⚊

Jean Hersholt Humanitarian Award

⚊ Edmond L. DePatie ⚊

Best Actor

⚊ Lee Marvin ⚊
Cat Ballou (1965) role "Kid Shelleen / Tim Strawn"

Richard Burton
The Spy Who Came in from the Cold (1965) role "Alec Leamas"

Laurence Olivier
Othello (1965) role "Othello"

Rod Steiger
The Pawnbroker (1964) role "Sol Nazerman"

Oskar Werner
Ship of Fools (1965) role "Dr. Wilhelm "Willi" Schumann"

Best Actor in a Supporting Role

⚊ Martin Balsam ⚊
A Thousand Clowns (1965) role "Arnold Burns"

Ian Bannen
The Flight of the Phoenix (1965) role ""Ratbags" Crow"

Tom Courtenay
Doctor Zhivago (1965) role "Pavel "Pasha" Antipov / Strelnikov"

Michael Dunn
Ship of Fools (1965) role "Carl Glocken"

Frank Finlay
Othello (1965) role "Iago"

Best Actress

⚊ Julie Christie ⚊
Darling (1965) role "Diana Scott"

Julie Andrews
The Sound of Music (1965) role "Maria von Trapp"

Samantha Eggar
The Collector (1965) role "Miranda Grey"

Elizabeth Hartman
A Patch of Blue (1965) role "Selina D'Arcey"

Simone Signoret
Ship of Fools (1965) role "La Condesa"

Best Actress in a Supporting Role

⚲ Shelley Winters ⚲
A Patch of Blue (1965) role "Rose-Ann D'Arcey"

Ruth Gordon
Inside Daisy Clover (1965) role "Lucile Clover / The Dealer"

Joyce Redman
Othello (1965) role "Emilia"

Maggie Smith
Othello (1965) role "Desdemona"

Peggy Wood
The Sound of Music (1965) role "Mother Abbess"

Best Art Direction, Black and White

⚲ Robert Clatworthy (Art Direction), Joseph Kish (Set Decoration) ⚲
Doctor Zhivago (1965)

**George W. Davis, Urie McCleary (Art Direction),
Henry Grace, Charles S. Thompson (Set Decoration)**
A Patch of Blue (1965)

**Tambi Larsen, Edward Marshall, Hal Pereira (Art Direction),
Josie MacAvin (Set Decoration)**
The Spy Who Came in from the Cold (1965)

**Hal Pereira, Jack Poplin (Art Direction),
Robert R. Benton, Joseph Kish (Set Decoration)**
The Slender Thread (1965)

Robert Emmet Smith (Art Direction), Frank Tuttle (Set Decoration)
King Rat (1965)

Best Art Direction, Color

⚲ John Box, Terry Marsh (Art Direction), Dario Simoni (Set Decoration) ⚲
Doctor Zhivago (1965)

Robert Clatworthy (Art Direction), George James Hopkins (Set Decoration)
Inside Daisy Clover (1965)

**William J. Creber, Richard Day, David S. Hall (Art Direction),
Fred M. MacLean, Ray Moyer, Norman Rockett (Set Decoration)**
(David S. Hall - posthumous)
The Greatest Story Ever Told (1965)

John DeCuir, Jack Martin Smith (Art Direction), Dario Simoni (Set Decoration)
The Agony and the Ecstasy (1965)

Boris Leven (Art Direction), Ruby R. Levitt, Walter M. Scott (Set Decoration)
The Sound of Music (1965)

Best Cinematography, Black and White

⚲ Ernest Laszlo ⚲
Ship of Fools (1965)

Robert Burks
A Patch of Blue (1965)

Loyal Griggs
In Harm's Way (1965)

Burnett Guffey
King Rat (1965)

Conrad L. Hall
Morituri (1965)

Best Cinematography, Color

⚊ **Freddie Young** ⚊
Doctor Zhivago (1965)

Loyal Griggs, William C. Mellor
(William C. Mellor - posthumous)
The Greatest Story Ever Told (1965)

Russell Harlan
The Great Race (1965)

Ted D. McCord
The Sound of Music (1965)

Leon Shamroy
The Agony and the Ecstasy (1965)

Best Sound Effects

⚊ **Tregoweth Brown** ⚊
The Great Race (1965)

Walter A. Rossi
Von Ryan's Express (1965)

Best Costume Design, Black and White

⚊ **Julie Harris** ⚊
Darling (1965)

Edith Head
The Slender Thread (1965)

Jean Louis, Bill Thomas
Ship of Fools (1965)

Moss Mabry
Morituri (1965)

Howard Shoup
A Rage to Live (1965)

Best Costume Design, Color

⚊ **Phyllis Dalton** ⚊
Doctor Zhivago (1965)

Marjorie Best, Vittorio Nino Novarese
The Greatest Story Ever Told (1965)

Edith Head, Bill Thomas
Inside Daisy Clover (1965)

Dorothy Jeakins
The Sound of Music (1965)

Vittorio Nino Novarese
The Agony and the Ecstasy (1965)

Best Short Subject, Cartoon

⚊ **Les Goldman, Chuck Jones (Producers)** ⚊
The Dot and the Line: A Romance in Lower Mathematics (1965)

Emanuele Luzzati (Producer)
La gazza ladra (eng. The Thieving Magpie) (1964)

Eliot Noyes Jr. (Producer)
Clay or the Origin of Species (1967)

Best Short Subject, Live Action
⚱ Claude Berri (Producer) ⚱
Le poulet (eng. The Chicken) (1963)
Edgar Anstey (Producer)
Snow (1963)
Marshal Backlar, Noel Black (Producers)
Skaterdater (1966)
Jim Henson (Producer)
Time Piece (1965)
Lothar Wolff (Producer)
Fortress of Peace (1965)

Best Directing
⚱ Robert Wise ⚱
The Sound of Music (1965)
David Lean
Doctor Zhivago (1965)
John Schlesinger
Darling (1965)
Hiroshi Teshigahara
Suna no onna (eng. Woman in the Dunes) (1964)
William Wyler
The Collector (1965)

Best Documentary, Feature
⚱ Sidney Glazier (Producer) ⚱
The Eleanor Roosevelt Story (1965)
Marshall Flaum (Producer)
Let My People Go: The Story of Israel (1965)
Laurence E. Mascott (Producer)
The Battle of the Bulge... The Brave Rifles (1965)
Peter Mills (Producer)
The Forth Road Bridge (1965)
Frédéric Rossif
Mourir à Madrid (eng. To Die in Madrid) (1963)

Best Documentary, Short Subject
⚱ Francis Thompson (Producer) ⚱
To Be Alive! (1964)
Patrick Carey, Joe Mendoza (Producers)
Yeats Country (1965)
Mafilm Productions
Nyitány (eng. Ouverture) (1965)
Kirk Smallman (Producer)
Mural on Our Street (1965)
Vision Associates Productions
Point of View (1966)

Best Special Visual Effects
⚱ John Stears ⚱
Thunderball (1965)
J. McMillan Johnson
The Greatest Story Ever Told (1965)

Best Film Editing

⚱ William Reynolds ⚱
The Sound of Music (1965)

Michael Luciano
The Flight of the Phoenix (1965)

Charles Nelson
Cat Ballou (1965)

Norman Savage
Doctor Zhivago (1965)

Ralph E. Winters
The Great Race (1965)

Best Music, Music Score substantially original

⚱ Maurice Jarre ⚱
Doctor Zhivago (1965)

Jacques Demy, Michel Legrand
Les parapluies de Cherbourg (eng. The Umbrellas of Cherbourg) (1964)

Jerry Goldsmith
A Patch of Blue (1965)

Alfred Newman
The Greatest Story Ever Told (1965)

Alex North
The Agony and the Ecstasy (1965)

Best Music, Scoring of Music adaptation or treatment

⚱ Irwin Kostal ⚱
The Sound of Music (1965)

Alexander Courage, Lionel Newman
The Pleasure Seekers (1964)

Frank De Vol
Cat Ballou (1965)

Michel Legrand
Les parapluies de Cherbourg (eng. The Umbrellas of Cherbourg) (1964)

Don Walker
A Thousand Clowns (1965)

Best Music, Song

⚱ Johnny Mandel (Music), Paul Francis Webster (Lyrics) ⚱
for the song "The Shadow of Your Smile"
The Sandpiper (1965)

Burt Bacharach (Music), Hal David (Lyrics)
for the song "What's New, Pussycat?"
What's New Pussycat (1965)

Michel Legrand (Music), Jacques Demy (Lyrics)
Norman Gimbel (English Lyrics) for the song "I Will Wait for You"
Les parapluies de Cherbourg (eng. The Umbrellas of Cherbourg) (1964)

Jerry Livingston (Music), Mack David (Lyrics)
for the song "The Ballad of Cat Ballou"
Cat Ballou (1965)

Henry Mancini (Music), Johnny Mercer (Lyrics)
for the song "The Sweetheart Tree"
The Great Race (1965)

Best Motion Picture

⚱ Robert Wise (Producer) ⚱
The Sound of Music (1965)

Fred Coe (Producer)
A Thousand Clowns (1965)

Joseph Janni (Producer)
Darling (1965)

Stanley Kramer (Producer)
Ship of Fools (1965)

Carlo Ponti (Producer)
Doctor Zhivago (1965)

Best Foreign Language Film

⚱ Czechoslovakia ⚱
Obchod na korze (eng. The Shop on Main Street) (1965)

Greece
To homa vaftike kokkino (eng. Blood on the Land) (1965)

Italy
Matrimonio all'italiana (eng. Marriage Italian Style) (1964)

Japan
Kaidan (eng. Kwaidan) (1964)

Sweden
Käre John (eng. Dear John) (1964)

Best Writing, Screenplay based on material from another medium

⚱ Robert Bolt ⚱
Doctor Zhivago (1965)

Herb Gardner
A Thousand Clowns (1965)

John Kohn, Stanley Mann
The Collector (1965)

Walter Newman, Frank R. Pierson
Cat Ballou (1965)

Abby Mann
Ship of Fools (1965)

Best Writing, Story & Screenplay written directly for the screen

⚱ Frederic Raphael ⚱
Darling (1965)

Ken Annakin, Jack Davies
Those Magnificent Men in Their Flying Machines or
How I Flew from London to Paris in 25 hours 11 minutes (1965)

Franklin Coen, Frank Davis
The Train (1964)

**Suso Cecchi D'Amico, Tonino Guerra, Agenore Incrocci, Mario Monicelli,
Giorgio Salvioni, Furio Scarpelli**
Casanova 70 (1965)

Jacques Demy
Les parapluies de Cherbourg (eng. The Umbrellas of Cherbourg) (1964)

Best Sound

James P. Corcoran (Sound Director), 20th Century-Fox Studio Sound Department, Fred Hynes (Sound Director), Todd-AO Sound Department
The Sound of Music (1965)

James P. Corcoran (Sound Director),
20th Century-Fox Studio Sound Department
The Agony and the Ecstasy (1965)

George R. Groves (Sound Director), Warner Bros. Studio Sound Department
The Great Race (1965)

Franklin E. Milton (Sound Director), Metro-Goldwyn-Mayer Studio Sound Department, A. W. Watkins (Sound Director), Metro-Goldwyn-Mayer British Studio Sound Department
Doctor Zhivago (1965)

Waldon O. Watson (Sound Director), Universal City Studio Sound Department
Shenandoah (1965)

The 39th Academy Awards® - April 10, 1967

Host: Bob Hope
Venue: Santa Monica Civic Auditorium
Honoring movies released in 1966

Irving G. Thalberg Memorial Award

Robert Wise

Jean Hersholt Humanitarian Award

George Bagnall

Best Actor

Paul Scofield
A Man for All Seasons (1966) role "Sir Thomas More"

Alan Arkin
The Russians Are Coming the Russians Are Coming (1966) role "Lieutenant Yuri Rozanov"

Richard Burton
Who's Afraid of Virginia Woolf? (1966) role "George"

Michael Caine
Alfie (1966) role "Alfie Elkins"

Steve McQueen
The Sand Pebbles (1966) role "Jake Holman"

Best Actor in a Supporting Role

Walter Matthau
The Fortune Cookie (1966) role "Willie "Whiplash Willie" Gingrich"

Mako
The Sand Pebbles (1966) role "Po-han"

James Mason
Georgy Girl (1966) role "James Leamington"

George Segal
Who's Afraid of Virginia Woolf? (1966) role "Nick"

Robert Shaw
A Man for All Seasons (1966) role "King Henry VIII of England"

Best Actress

⟂ Elizabeth Taylor ⟂
Who's Afraid of Virginia Woolf? (1966) role "Martha"

Anouk Aimée
Un homme et une femme (eng. A Man and a Woman) (1966) role "Anne Gauthier"

Ida Kamińska
Obchod na korze (eng. The Shop on Main Street) (1965) role "Rozália Lautmannová"

Lynn Redgrave
Georgy Girl (1966) role "Georgina "Georgy" Parkin"

Vanessa Redgrave
Morgan: A Suitable Case for Treatment (1966) role "Leonie Delt"

Best Actress in a Supporting Role

⟂ Sandy Dennis ⟂
Who's Afraid of Virginia Woolf? (1966) role "Honey"

Wendy Hiller
A Man for All Seasons (1966) role "Alice More"

Jocelyne LaGarde
Hawaii (1966) role "Queen Malama Kanakoa / The Ali'i Nui"

Vivien Merchant
Alfie (1966) role "Lily Clamacraft"

Geraldine Page
You're a Big Boy Now (1966) role "Margery Chanticleer"

Best Cinematography, Black and White

⟂ Haskell Wexler ⟂
Who's Afraid of Virginia Woolf? (1966)

Marcel Grignon
Paris brûle-t-il? (eng. Is Paris Burning?) (1966)

Ken Higgins
Georgy Girl (1966)

Joseph LaShelle
The Fortune Cookie (1966)

James Wong Howe
Seconds (1966)

Best Cinematography, Color

⟂ Ted Moore ⟂
A Man for All Seasons (1966)

Conrad L. Hall
The Professionals (1966)

Russell Harlan
Hawaii (1966)

Ernest Laszlo
Fantastic Voyage (1966)

Joseph MacDonald
The Sand Pebbles (1966)

Best Special Visual Effects

⟂ Art Cruickshank ⟂
Fantastic Voyage (1966)

Linwood G. Dunn
Hawaii (1966)

Best Art Direction, Black and White

⚊ **Richard Sylbert (Art Direction), George James Hopkins (Set Decoration)** ⚊
Who's Afraid of Virginia Woolf? (1966)

**George W. Davis, Paul Groesse (Art Direction),
Henry Grace, Hugh Hunt (Set Decoration)**
Mister Buddwing (1966)

Willy Holt (Art Direction), Marc Frédérix, Pierre Guffroy (Set Decoration)
Paris brûle-t-il? (eng. Is Paris Burning?) (1966)

Robert Luthardt (Art Direction), Edward G. Boyle (Set Decoration)
The Fortune Cookie (1966)

Luigi Scaccianoce (Art Direction)
Il vangelo secondo Matteo (eng. The Gospel According to St. Matthew) (1964)

Best Art Direction, Color

⚊ **Dale Hennesy, Jack Martin Smith (Art Direction),
Stuart A. Reiss Walter M. Scott (Set Decoration)** ⚊
Fantastic Voyage (1966)

Piero Gherardi (Art Direction)
Giulietta degli spiriti (eng. Juliet of the Spirits) (1965)

**Alexander Golitzen, George C. Webb (Art Direction),
John P. Austin, John McCarthy Jr. (Set Decoration)**
Gambit (1966)

**Boris Leven (Art Direction),
William Kiernan, Walter M. Scott, John Sturtevant (Set Decoration)**
The Sand Pebbles (1966)

**Arthur Lonergan, Hal Pereira (Art Direction),
Robert R. Benton, James W. Payne (Set Decoration)**
The Oscar (1966)

Best Costume Design, Black and White

⚊ **Irene Sharaff** ⚊
Who's Afraid of Virginia Woolf? (1966)

Danilo Donati
Il vangelo secondo Matteo (eng. The Gospel According to St. Matthew) (1964),
La mandragola (eng. Mandragola) (1965)

Jocelyn Rickards
Morgan: A Suitable Case for Treatment (1966)

Helen Rose
Mister Buddwing (1966)

Best Costume Design, Color

⚊ **Joan Bridge, Elizabeth Haffenden** ⚊
A Man for All Seasons (1966)

Piero Gherardi
Giulietta degli spiriti (eng. Juliet of the Spirits) (1965)

Edith Head
The Oscar (1966)

Dorothy Jeakins
Hawaii (1966)

Jean Louis
Gambit (1966)

Best Directing

⚑ **Fred Zinnemann** ⚑
A Man for All Seasons (1966)

Michelangelo Antonioni
Blow-Up (1966)

Richard Brooks
The Professionals (1966)

Claude Lelouch
Un homme et une femme (eng. A Man and a Woman) (1966)

Mike Nichols
Who's Afraid of Virginia Woolf? (1966)

Best Documentary, Feature

⚑ **Peter Watkins (Producer)** ⚑
The War Game (1966)

Tom Daly, Peter Jones (Producers)
Helicopter Canada (1966)

Alexander Grasshoff (Producer)
The Really Big Family (1967)

Alfred R. Kelman (Producer)
The Face of a Genius (1966)

Haroun Tazieff (Producer)
Le volcan interdit (eng. The Forbidden Volcano) (1966)

Best Documentary, Short Subject

⚑ **Edmond A. Levy (Producer)** ⚑
A Year Toward Tomorrow (1966)

Michael Ahnemann, Gary Schlosser (Producers)
Cowboy (1966)

Lee R. Bobker, Helen Kristt Radin (Producers)
The Odds Against (1966)

Vladimir Forgency, Marin Karmitz (Producers)
Adolescence (1966)

Mafilm Studio
Részletek J.S. Bach Máté passiójából (eng. Saint Matthew Passion) (1966)

Best Film Editing

⚑ **Henry Berman, Stewart Linder, Frank Santillo, Fredric Steinkamp** ⚑
Grand Prix (1966)

Hal Ashby, J. Terry Williams
The Russians Are Coming the Russians Are Coming (1966)

William B. Murphy
Fantastic Voyage (1966)

William Reynolds
The Sand Pebbles (1966)

Sam O'Steen
Who's Afraid of Virginia Woolf? (1966)

Best Sound Effects

⚑ **Gordon Daniel** ⚑
Grand Prix (1966)

Walter Rossi
Fantastic Voyage (1966)

Best Foreign Language Film
⚰ France ⚰
Un homme et une femme (eng. A Man and a Woman) (1966)
Czechoslovakia
Lásky jedné plavovlásky (eng. Loves of a Blonde) (1965)
Italy
La battaglia di Algeri (eng. The Battle of Algiers) (1966)
Poland
Faraon (eng. Pharaoh) (1966)
Yugoslavia
Tri (eng. Three) (1965)

Best Music, Original Music Score
⚰ John Barry ⚰
Born Free (1966)
Elmer Bernstein
Hawaii (1966)
Jerry Goldsmith
The Sand Pebbles (1966)
Toshirô Mayuzumi
The Bible: In the Beginning... (1966)
Alex North
Who's Afraid of Virginia Woolf? (1966)

Best Music, Scoring of Music adaptation or treatment
⚰ Ken Thorne ⚰
A Funny Thing Happened on the Way to the Forum (1966)
Luis Enrique Bacalov
Il vangelo secondo Matteo (eng. The Gospel According to St. Matthew) (1964)
Elmer Bernstein
Return of the Seven (1966)
Al Ham
Stop the World: I Want to Get Off (1966)
Harry Sukman
The Singing Nun (1966)

Best Sound
⚰ Franklin E. Milton (Sound Director), Metro-Goldwyn-Mayer Studio Sound Department ⚰
Grand Prix (1966)
James P. Corcoran (Sound Director), 20th Century-Fox Studio Sound Department
The Sand Pebbles (1966)
George R. Groves (Sound Director), Warner Bros. Studio Sound Department
Who's Afraid of Virginia Woolf? (1966)
Gordon E. Sawyer (Sound Director), Samuel Goldwyn Studio Sound Department
Hawaii (1966)
Waldon O. Watson (Sound Director), Universal City Studio Sound Department
Gambit (1966)

Best Music, Song

⚐ **John Barry (Music), Don Black (Lyrics) for the song "Born Free"** ⚐
Born Free (1966)

Burt Bacharach (Music), Hal David (Lyrics) for the song "Alfie"
Alfie (1966)

Elmer Bernstein (Music), Mack David (Lyrics) for the song "My Wishing Doll"
Hawaii (1966)

**Johnny Mandel (Music), Paul Francis Webster (Lyrics)
for the song "A Time for Love"**
An American Dream (1966)

Tom Springfield (Music), Jim Dale (Lyrics) for the song "Georgy Girl"
Georgy Girl (1966)

Best Short Subject, Cartoon

⚐ **Faith Hubley, John Hubley (Producers)** ⚐
A Herb Alpert & the Tijuana Brass Double Feature (1966)

David H. DePatie, Friz Freleng (Producers)
The Pink Blueprint (1966)

Wolf Koenig, Robert Verrall (Producers)
The Drag (1966)

Best Short Subject, Live Action

⚐ **Edgar Anstey (Producer)** ⚐
Wild Wings (1965)

Derek Williams (Producer)
Turkey the Bridge (1966)

Leslie Winik (Producer)
The Winning Strain (1966)

Best Picture

⚐ **Fred Zinnemann (Producer)** ⚐
A Man for All Seasons (1966)

Lewis Gilbert (Producer)
Alfie (1966)

Norman Jewison (Producer)
The Russians Are Coming the Russians Are Coming (1966)

Ernest Lehman (Producer)
Who's Afraid of Virginia Woolf? (1966)

Robert Wise (Producer)
The Sand Pebbles (1966)

Best Writing, Screenplay based on material from another medium

⚐ **Robert Bolt** ⚐
A Man for All Seasons (1966)

Richard Brooks
The Professionals (1966)

Ernest Lehman
Who's Afraid of Virginia Woolf? (1966)

Bill Naughton
Alfie (1966)

William Rose
The Russians Are Coming the Russians Are Coming (1966)

Best Writing, Story & Screenplay written directly for the screen

Claude Lelouch (Story),
⚐ Claude Lelouch, Pierre Uytterhoeven (Screenplay) ⚐
Un homme et une femme (eng. A Man and a Woman) (1966)

Michelangelo Antonioni (Story),
Michelangelo Antonioni, Edward Bond, Tonino Guerra (Screenplay)
Blow-Up (1966)

Robert Ardrey
Khartoum (1966)

I. A. L. Diamond, Billy Wilder
The Fortune Cookie (1966)

Clint Johnston, Don Peters
The Naked Prey (1965)

Honorary Award

⚐ Yakima Canutt ⚐
For achievements as a stunt man and for developing safety devices to protect stunt men everywhere.

⚐ Y. Frank Freeman ⚐
For unusual and outstanding service to the Academy during his thirty years in Hollywood.

The 40th Academy Awards® - April 10, 1968

Host: Bob Hope
Venue: Santa Monica Civic Auditorium
Honoring movies released in 1967

Best Actor

⚐ Rod Steiger ⚐
In the Heat of the Night (1967) role "Police Chief Bill Gillespie"

Warren Beatty
Bonnie and Clyde (1967) role "Clyde Barrow"

Dustin Hoffman
The Graduate (1967) role "Benjamin Braddock"

Paul Newman
Cool Hand Luke (1967) role "Lucas "Cool Hand Luke" Jackson"

Spencer Tracy
(posthumous)
Guess Who's Coming to Dinner (1967) role "Matt Drayton"

Best Actor in a Supporting Role

⚐ George Kennedy ⚐
Cool Hand Luke (1967) role "Dragline"

John Cassavetes
The Dirty Dozen (1967) role "Victor R. Franko"

Gene Hackman
Bonnie and Clyde (1967) role "Buck Barrow"

Cecil Kellaway
Guess Who's Coming to Dinner (1967) role "Monsignor Mike Ryan"

Michael J. Pollard
Bonnie and Clyde (1967) role "C. W. Moss"

Best Actress
↓ Katharine Hepburn ↓
Guess Who's Coming to Dinner (1967) role "Christina Drayton"
Anne Bancroft
The Graduate (1967) role "Mrs. Robinson"
Faye Dunaway
Bonnie and Clyde (1967) role "Bonnie Parker"
Dame Edith Evans
The Whisperers (1967) role "Mrs. Maggie Ross"
Audrey Hepburn
Wait Until Dark (1967) role "Susy Hendrix"

Best Actress in a Supporting Role
↓ Estelle Parsons ↓
Bonnie and Clyde (1967) role "Blanche Barrow"
Carol Channing
Thoroughly Modern Millie (1967) role "Muzzy van Hossmere"
Mildred Natwick
Barefoot in the Park (1967) role "Ethel Banks"
Beah Richards
Guess Who's Coming to Dinner (1967) role "Mrs. Mary Prentice"
Katharine Ross
The Graduate (1967) role "Elaine Robinson"

Honorary Award
↓ Arthur Freed ↓
For distinguished service to Academy and the production of six top-rated Awards telecasts.

Best Cinematography
↓ Burnett Guffey ↓
Bonnie and Clyde (1967)
Conrad L. Hall
In Cold Blood (1967)
Richard H. Kline
Camelot (1967)
Robert Surtees
Doctor Dolittle (1967), The Graduate (1967)

Best Art Direction
↓ Edward Carrere, John Truscott (Art Direction), ↓ John W. Brown (Set Decoration)
Camelot (1967)
Mario Chiari, Ed Graves, Jack Martin Smith (Art Direction), Stuart A. Reiss, Walter M. Scott (Set Decoration)
Doctor Dolittle (1967)
Robert Clatworthy (Art Direction), Frank Tuttle (Set Decoration)
Guess Who's Coming to Dinner (1967)
John DeCuir, Giuseppe Mariani, Lorenzo "Renzo" Mongiardino, Elven Webb (Art Direction), Luigi Gervasi, Dario Simoni (Set Decoration)
The Taming of the Shrew (1967)
Alexander Golitzen, George C. Webb (Art Direction), Howard Bristol (Set Decoration)
Thoroughly Modern Millie (1967)

Best Costume Design
⚱ **John Truscott** ⚱
Camelot (1967)

Danilo Donati, Irene Sharaff
The Taming of the Shrew (1967)

Jean Louis
Thoroughly Modern Millie (1967)

Theadora Van Runkle
Bonnie and Clyde (1967)

Bill Thomas
The Happiest Millionaire (1967)

Jean Hersholt Humanitarian Award
⚱ **Gregory Peck** ⚱

Best Directing
⚱ **Mike Nichols** ⚱
The Graduate (1967)

Arthur Penn
Bonnie and Clyde (1967)

Stanley Kramer
Guess Who's Coming to Dinner (1967)

Richard Brooks
In Cold Blood (1967)

Norman Jewison
In the Heat of the Night (1967)

Best Sound Effects
⚱ **John Poyner** ⚱
The Dirty Dozen (1967)

James A. Richard
In the Heat of the Night (1967)

Best Special Visual Effects
⚱ **L. B. Abbott** ⚱
Doctor Dolittle (1967)

Howard A. Anderson Jr., Albert Whitlock
Tobruk (1967)

Best Documentary, Feature
⚱ **Pierre Schoendoerffer (Producer)** ⚱
La section Anderson (eng. The Anderson Platoon) (1967)

Carroll Ballard (Producer)
Harvest (1967)

William C. Jersey (Producer)
A Time for Burning (1967)

Murray Lerner (Producer)
Festival (1967)

Jack Le Vien (Producer)
A King's Story (1965)

Best Documentary, Short Subject

⌇ **Trevor Greenwood, Mark Jonathan Harris (Producers)** ⌇
The Redwoods (1967)

Christopher Chapman (Producer)
A Place to Stand (1967)

Robert Fitchet (Producer)
See You at the Pillar (1967)

Charles E. Guggenheim (Producer)
Monument to the Dream (1967)

Carl V. Ragsdale (Producer)
While I Run This Race (1967)

Irving G. Thalberg Memorial Award

⌇ **Alfred Hitchcock** ⌇

Best Film Editing

⌇ **Hal Ashby** ⌇
In the Heat of the Night (1967)

Samuel E. Beetley, Marjorie Fowler
Doctor Dolittle (1967)

Robert C. Jones
Guess Who's Coming to Dinner (1967)

Frank P. Keller
Beach Red (1967)

Michael Luciano
The Dirty Dozen (1967)

Best Foreign Language Film

⌇ **Czechoslovakia** ⌇
Ostre sledované vlaky (eng. Closely Watched Trains) (1966)

France
Vivre pour vivre (eng. Live for Life) (1967)

Japan
Chieko-sho (eng. Portrait of Chieko) (1967)

Spain
El amor brujo (eng. Bewitched Love) (1967)

Yugoslavia
Skupljaci perja (eng. I Even Met Happy Gypsies) (1967)

Best Picture

⌇ **Walter Mirisch (Producer)** ⌇
In the Heat of the Night (1967)

Warren Beatty (Producer)
Bonnie and Clyde (1967)

Arthur P. Jacobs (Producer)
Doctor Dolittle (1967)

Stanley Kramer (Producer)
Guess Who's Coming to Dinner (1967)

Lawrence Turman (Producer)
The Graduate (1967)

Best Short Subject, Cartoon
⚱ **Fred Wolf (Producer)** ⚱
The Box (1967)

Wolf Koenig, Robert Verrall (Producers)
What on Earth! (1967)

Jean-Charles Meunier (Producer)
Hypothèse Beta (1967)

Best Short Subject, Live Action
⚱ **Christopher Chapman (Producer)** ⚱
A Place to Stand (1967)

Julian Biggs (Producer)
Paddle to the Sea (1966)

John Fernhout (Producer)
Sky Over Holland (1967)

Len Janson, Chuck Menville (Producers)
Stop Look and Listen (1967)

Best Music, Original Music Score
⚱ **Elmer Bernstein** ⚱
Thoroughly Modern Millie (1967)

Richard Rodney Bennett
Far from the Madding Crowd (1967)

Leslie Bricusse
Doctor Dolittle (1967)

Quincy Jones
In Cold Blood (1967)

Lalo Schifrin
Cool Hand Luke (1967)

Best Music, Scoring of Music adaptation or treatment
⚱ **Ken Darby, Alfred Newman** ⚱
Camelot (1967)

Alexander Courage, Lionel Newman
Doctor Dolittle (1967)

Joseph Gershenson, André Previn
Thoroughly Modern Millie (1967)

Frank De Vol
Guess Who's Coming to Dinner (1967)

John Williams
Valley of the Dolls (1967)

Best Sound
⚱ **Samuel Goldwyn Studio Sound Department** ⚱
In the Heat of the Night (1967)

20th Century-Fox Studio Sound Department
Doctor Dolittle (1967)

Metro-Goldwyn-Mayer Studio Sound Department
The Dirty Dozen (1967)

Universal City Studio Sound Department
Thoroughly Modern Millie (1967)

Warner Bros.-Seven Arts Studio Sound Department
Camelot (1967)

Best Music, Song
⇂ **Leslie Bricusse (Music & Lyrics) for the song "Talk to the Animals"** ⇂
Doctor Dolittle (1967)

Burt Bacharach (Music), Hal David (Lyrics) for the song "The Look of Love"
Casino Royale (1967)

**Sammy Cahn, Jimmy Van Heusen (Music & Lyrics)
for the song "Thoroughly Modern Millie"**
Thoroughly Modern Millie (1967)

Terry Gilkyson (Music & Lyrics) for the song "The Bare Necessities"
The Jungle Book (1967)

Quincy Jones (Music), Bob Russell (Lyrics) for the song "The Eyes of Love"
Banning (1967)

Best Writing, Screenplay based on material from another medium
⇂ **Stirling Silliphant** ⇂
In the Heat of the Night (1967)

Richard Brooks
In Cold Blood (1967)

Fred Haines, Joseph Strick
Ulysses (1967)

Buck Henry, Calder Willingham
The Graduate (1967)

Donn Pearce, Frank R. Pierson
Cool Hand Luke (1967)

Best Writing, Story & Screenplay written directly for the screen
⇂ **William Rose** ⇂
Guess Who's Coming to Dinner (1967)

Robert Benton, David Newman
Bonnie and Clyde (1967)

Robert Kaufman (Story), Norman Lear (Screenplay)
Divorce American Style (1967)

Frederic Raphael
Two for the Road (1967)

Jorge Semprún
La guerre est finie (eng. The War Is Over) (1966)

The 41ˢᵗ Academy Awards® - April 14, 1969
Host: No official host
Venue: Dorothy Chandler Pavilion
Honoring movies released in 1968

Honorary Award
⇂ **John Chambers** ⇂
For his outstanding make-up achievement in the movie Planet of the Apes (1968)
⇂ **Onna White** ⇂
For her outstanding choreography achievement for Oliver! (1968)

Jean Hersholt Humanitarian Award
⇂ **Martha Raye** ⇂

Best Actor
♟ Cliff Robertson ♟
Charly (1968) role "Charlie Gordon"
Alan Arkin
The Heart Is a Lonely Hunter (1968) role "John Singer"
Alan Bates
The Fixer (1968) role "Yakov Bok"
Ron Moody
Oliver! (1968) role "Fagin"
Peter O'Toole
The Lion in Winter (1968) role "King Henry II of England"

Best Actor in a Supporting Role
♟ Jack Albertson ♟
The Subject Was Roses (1968) role "John Cleary"
Seymour Cassel
Faces (1968) role "Chet"
Daniel Massey
Star! (1968) role "Noël Coward"
Jack Wild
Oliver! (1968) role "Jack Dawkins ("The Artful Dodger")"
Gene Wilder
The Producers (1967) role "Leopold "Leo" Bloom"

Best Actress
♟ Katharine Hepburn ♟
The Lion in Winter (1968) role "Eleanor of Aquitaine"
♟ Barbra Streisand ♟
Funny Girl (1968) role "Fanny Brice"
Patricia Neal
The Subject Was Roses (1968) role "Nettie Cleary"
Vanessa Redgrave
Isadora (1968) role "Isadora Duncan"
Joanne Woodward
Rachel, Rachel (1968) role "Rachel Cameron"

Best Actress in a Supporting Role
♟ Ruth Gordon ♟
Rosemary's Baby (1968) role "Minnie Castevet"
Lynn Carlin
Faces (1968) role "Maria Frost"
Sondra Locke
The Heart Is a Lonely Hunter (1968) role "Mick Kelly"
Kay Medford
Funny Girl (1968) role "Rose Brice"
Estelle Parsons
Rachel, Rachel (1968) role "Calla Mackie"

Best Special Visual Effects
♟ Stanley Kubrick ♟
2001: A Space Odyssey (1968)
J. McMillan Johnson, Hal Millar
Ice Station Zebra (1968)

Best Cinematography

ɪ Pasqualino De Santis ɪ
Romeo and Juliet (1968)

Daniel L. Fapp
Ice Station Zebra (1968)

Ernest Laszlo
Star! (1968)

Oswald Morris
Oliver! (1968)

Harry Stradling Sr.
Funny Girl (1968)

Best Art Direction

**John Box, Terence Marsh (Art Direction),
Vernon Dixon, Ken Muggleston (Set Decoration)**
Oliver! (1968)

Ernie Archer, Harry Lange, Anthony Masters (Art Direction)
2001: A Space Odyssey (1968)

**Mikhail Bogdanov, Gennady Myasnikov (Art Direction),
G. Koshelev, V. Uvarov (Set Decoration)**
Voyna i mir (eng. War and Peace) (1965)

Edward C. Carfagno, George W. Davis (Art Direction)
The Shoes of the Fisherman (1968)

Boris Leven (Art Direction), Howard Bristol, Walter M. Scott (Set Decoration)
Star! (1968)

Best Music, Song Original for the Picture

**Michel Legrand (Music), Alan Bergman, Marilyn Bergman (Lyrics)
for the song "The Windmills of Your Mind"**
The Thomas Crown Affair (1968)

Jimmy Van Heusen (Music), Sammy Cahn (Lyrics) for the song "Star!"
Star! (1968)

Quincy Jones (Music), Bob Russell (Lyrics) for the song "For Love of Ivy"
For Love of Ivy (1968)

**Richard M. Sherman, Robert B. Sherman (Music & Lyrics)
for the song "Chitty Chitty Bang Bang"**
Chitty Chitty Bang Bang (1968)

Jule Styne (Music), Bob Merrill (Lyrics) for the song "Funny Girl"
Funny Girl (1968)

Best Costume Design

ɪ Danilo Donati ɪ
Romeo and Juliet (1968)

Donald Brooks
Star! (1968)

Phyllis Dalton
Oliver! (1968)

Margaret Furse
The Lion in Winter (1968)

Morton Haack
Planet of the Apes (1968)

Best Short Subject, Cartoon
⚐ Walt Disney (Producer) ⚐
(posthumous)
Winnie the Pooh and the Blustery Day (1968)
Faith Hubley, John Hubley (Producers)
Windy Day (1968)
Wolf Koenig, Jim MacKay (Producers)
La maison de Jean-Jacques (eng. The House That Jack Built) (1967)
Jimmy T. Murakami (Producer)
The Magic Pear Tree (1968)

Best Short Subject, Live Action
⚐ Charles Guggenheim (Producer) ⚐
Robert Kennedy Remembered (1968)
John Astin (Producer)
Prelude (1968)
George Coe, Sidney Davis, Anthony Lover (Producers)
De Düva: The Dove (1968)
National Film Board of Canada
Pas de deux (eng. Duo) (1968)

Best Sound
⚐ Shepperton Studio Sound Department ⚐
Oliver! (1968)
20th Century-Fox Studio Sound Department
Star! (1968)
Columbia Studio Sound Department
Funny Girl (1968)
Warner Bros.-Seven Arts Studio Sound Department
Bullitt (1968), Finian's Rainbow (1968)

Best Directing
⚐ Carol Reed ⚐
Oliver! (1968)
Anthony Harvey
The Lion in Winter (1968)
Stanley Kubrick
2001: A Space Odyssey (1968)
Gillo Pontecorvo
La battaglia di Algeri (eng. The Battle of Algiers) (1966)
Franco Zeffirelli
Romeo and Juliet (1968)

Best Documentary, Feature
⚐ Bill McGaw (Producer) ⚐
Journey Into Self (1969)
James Blue (Producer)
A Few Notes on Our Food Problem (1968)
William Cayton (Producer)
Legendary Champions (1968)
David H. Sawyer (Producer)
Other Voices (1970)

Best Documentary, Short Subject

⚑ **Saul Bass (Producer)** ⚑
Why Man Creates (1968)

Fali Bilimoria (Producer)
The House That Ananda Built (1968)

Lee R. Bobker (Producer)
The Revolving Door (1969)

Thomas P. Kelly Jr. (Producer)
A Space to Grow (1968)

Dan E. Weisburd (Producer)
A Way Out of the Wilderness (1968)

Best Film Editing

⚑ **Frank P. Keller** ⚑
Bullitt (1968)

Frank Bracht
The Odd Couple (1968)

Fred Feitshans, Eve Newman
Wild in the Streets (1968)

Ralph Kemplen
Oliver! (1968)

William Sands, Robert Swink, Maury Winetrobe
Funny Girl (1968)

Best Foreign Language Film

⚑ **Union of Soviet Socialist Republics** ⚑
Voyna i mir (eng. War and Peace) (1965)

Czechoslovakia
Horí, má panenko (eng. The Firemen's Ball) (1967)

France
Baisers volés (eng. Stolen Kisses) (1968)

Hungary
A Pál utcai fiúk (eng. The Boys of Paul Street) (1968)

Italy
La ragazza con la pistola (eng. The Girl with a Pistol) (1968)

Best Music, Original Score for a motion picture [not a musical]

⚑ **John Barry** ⚑
The Lion in Winter (1968)

Jerry Goldsmith
Planet of the Apes (1968)

Michel Legrand
The Thomas Crown Affair (1968)

Alex North
The Shoes of the Fisherman (1968)

Lalo Schifrin
The Fox (1967)

Best Music, Score of a Musical Picture original or adaptation

⇟ **John Green (Adaptation score)** ⇟
Oliver! (1968)

Lennie Hayton (Adaptation score)
Star! (1968)

Ray Heindorf (Adaptation score)
Finian's Rainbow (1968)

Michel Legrand (Music & Adaptation score), Jacques Demy (Lyrics)
Les demoiselles de Rochefort (eng. The Young Girls of Rochefort) (1967)

Walter Scharf (Adaptation score)
Funny Girl (1968)

Best Motion Picture

⇟ **John Woolf (Producer)** ⇟
Oliver! (1968)

John Brabourne, Anthony Havelock-Allan (Producers)
Romeo and Juliet (1968)

Paul Newman (Producer)
Rachel, Rachel (1968)

Martin Poll (Producer)
The Lion in Winter (1968)

Ray Stark (Producer)
Funny Girl (1968)

Best Writing, Screenplay based on material from another medium

⇟ **James Goldman** ⇟
The Lion in Winter (1968)

Vernon Harris
Oliver! (1968)

Roman Polanski
Rosemary's Baby (1968)

Neil Simon
The Odd Couple (1968)

Stewart Stern
Rachel, Rachel (1968)

Best Writing, Story & Screenplay written directly for the screen

⇟ **Mel Brooks** ⇟
The Producers (1967)

John Cassavetes
Faces (1968)

Arthur C. Clarke, Stanley Kubrick
2001: A Space Odyssey (1968)

Gillo Pontecorvo, Franco Solinas
La battaglia di Algeri (eng. The Battle of Algiers) (1966)

Peter Ustinov, Ira Wallach
Hot Millions (1968)

The 42ⁿᵈ Academy Awards® - April 7, 1970

Host: No official host
Venue: Dorothy Chandler Pavilion
Honoring movies released in 1969

Honorary Award

⚜ Cary Grant ⚜

For his unique mastery of the art of screen acting with the respect and affection of his colleagues.

Jean Hersholt Humanitarian Award

⚜ George Jessel ⚜

Best Actor

⚜ John Wayne ⚜
True Grit (1969) role "Reuben "Rooster" Cogburn"

Richard Burton
Anne of the Thousand Days (1969) role "King Henry VIII of England"

Dustin Hoffman
Midnight Cowboy (1969) role "Enrico Salvatore "Ratso" "Rico" Rizzo"

Peter O'Toole
Goodbye, Mr. Chips (1969) role "Arthur Chipping"

Jon Voight
Midnight Cowboy (1969) role "Joe Buck"

Best Actor in a Supporting Role

⚜ Gig Young ⚜
They Shoot Horses, Don't They? (1969) role "Rocky Graver"

Rupert Crosse
The Reivers (1969) role "Ned McCaslin"

Elliott Gould
Bob & Carol & Ted & Alice (1969) role "Ted Henderson"

Jack Nicholson
Easy Rider (1969) role "George Hanson"

Anthony Quayle
Anne of the Thousand Days (1969) role "Cardinal Thomas Wolsey"

Best Actress

⚜ Maggie Smith ⚜
The Prime of Miss Jean Brodie (1969) role "Jean Brodie"

Geneviève Bujold
Anne of the Thousand Days (1969) role "Anne Boleyn"

Jane Fonda
They Shoot Horses, Don't They? (1969) role "Gloria Beatty"

Liza Minnelli
The Sterile Cuckoo (1969) role "Mary Ann "Pookie" Adams"

Jean Simmons
The Happy Ending (1969) role "Mary Wilson"

Best Actress in a Supporting Role
⚑ Goldie Hawn ⚑
Cactus Flower (1969) role "Toni Simmons"
Catherine Burns
Last Summer (1969) role "Rhoda"
Dyan Cannon
Bob & Carol & Ted & Alice (1969) role "Alice Henderson"
Sylvia Miles
Midnight Cowboy (1969) role "Cass"
Susannah York
They Shoot Horses, Don't They? (1969) role "Alice LeBlanc"

Best Art Direction
Herman A. Blumenthal, John DeCuir, ⚑ Jack Martin Smith (Art Direction), Raphael Bretton, ⚑ George James Hopkins, Walter M. Scott (Set Decoration)
Hello, Dolly! (1969)
Robert F. Boyle, George B. Chan (Art Direction), Carl Biddiscombe, Edward G. Boyle (Set Decoration)
Gaily, Gaily (1969)
Maurice Carter, Lionel Couch (Art Direction), Patrick McLoughlin (Set Decoration)
Anne of the Thousand Days (1969)
Alexander Golitzen, George C. Webb (Art Direction), Jack D. Moore (Set Decoration)
Sweet Charity (1969)
Harry Horner (Art Direction), Frank R. McKelvy (Set Decoration)
They Shoot Horses, Don't They? (1969)

Best Cinematography
⚑ Conrad L. Hall ⚑
Butch Cassidy and the Sundance Kid (1969)
Daniel L. Fapp
Marooned (1969)
Arthur Ibbetson
Anne of the Thousand Days (1969)
Charles B. Lang
Bob & Carol & Ted & Alice (1969)
Harry Stradling Sr.
(posthumous)
Hello, Dolly! (1969)

Best Costume Design
⚑ Margaret Furse ⚑
Anne of the Thousand Days (1969)
Ray Aghayan
Gaily, Gaily (1969)
Donfeld
They Shoot Horses, Don't They? (1969)
Edith Head
Sweet Charity (1969)
Irene Sharaff
Hello, Dolly! (1969)

Best Directing

⚐ John Schlesinger ⚐
Midnight Cowboy (1969)

Costa-Gavras
Z (1969)

George Roy Hill
Butch Cassidy and the Sundance Kid (1969)

Arthur Penn
Alice's Restaurant (1969)

Sydney Pollack
They Shoot Horses, Don't They? (1969)

Best Documentary, Feature

⚐ Bernard Chevry (Producer) ⚐
L'amour de la vie - Artur Rubinstein (eng. Love of Life - Artur Rubinstein) (1969)

Emile de Antonio (Producer)
In the Year of the Pig (1968)

Comite Organizador de los Juegos de la XIX Olimpiada
The Olympics in Mexico (1969)

Irwin Rosten (Producer)
The Wolf Men (1969)

Robert K. Sharpe (Producer)
Before the Mountain Was Moved (1970)

Best Documentary, Short Subject

⚐ Robert M. Fresco, Denis Sanders (Producers) ⚐
Czechoslovakia 1968 (1969)

Joan Horvath (Producer)
Jenny Is a Good Thing (1969)

Russell A. Mosser, Arthur H. Wolf (Producers)
Leo Beuerman (1969)

Joan Keller Stern (Producer)
The Magic Machines (1969)

Donald Wrye (Producer)
An Impression of John Steinbeck: Writer (1969)

Best Film Editing

⚐ Françoise Bonnot ⚐
Z (1969)

Earle Herdan, William A. Lyon
The Secret of Santa Vittoria (1969)

William Reynolds
Hello, Dolly! (1969)

Hugh A. Robertson
Midnight Cowboy (1969)

Fredric Steinkamp
They Shoot Horses, Don't They? (1969)

Best Special Visual Effects

⚐ Robbie Robertson ⚐
Marooned (1969)

Eugène Lourié, Alex Weldon
Krakatoa: East of Java (1968)

Best Music, Original Score for a motion picture [not a musical]

⚜ Burt Bacharach ⚜
Butch Cassidy and the Sundance Kid (1969)

Georges Delerue
Anne of the Thousand Days (1969)

Jerry Fielding
The Wild Bunch (1969)

Ernest Gold
The Secret of Santa Vittoria (1969)

John Williams
The Reivers (1969)

Best Music, Score of a Musical Picture original or adaptation

⚜ Lennie Hayton, Lionel Newman (Adaptation score) ⚜
Hello, Dolly! (1969)

Cy Coleman (Adaptation score)
Sweet Charity (1969)

John Green, Albert Woodbury (Adaptation score)
They Shoot Horses, Don't They? (1969)

Nelson Riddle (Adaptation score)
Paint Your Wagon (1969)

John Williams, Leslie Bricusse (Adaptation score), (Music & Lyrics)
Goodbye, Mr. Chips (1969)

Best Music, Song Original for the Picture

⚜ Burt Bacharach (Music), Hal David (Lyrics)
for the song "Raindrops Keep Fallin' on My Head" ⚜
Butch Cassidy and the Sundance Kid (1969)

Elmer Bernstein (Music), Don Black (Lyrics) for the song "True Grit"
True Grit (1969)

Fred Karlin (Music), Dory Previn (Lyrics)
for the song "Come Saturday Morning"
The Sterile Cuckoo (1969)

Michel Legrand (Music), Alan Bergman, Marilyn Bergman (Lyrics)
for the song "What Are You Doing for the Rest of Your Life?"
The Happy Ending (1969)

Rod McKuen (Music & Lyrics) for the song "Jean"
The Prime of Miss Jean Brodie (1969)

Best Picture

⚜ Jerome Hellman (Producer) ⚜
Midnight Cowboy (1969)

John Foreman (Producer)
Butch Cassidy and the Sundance Kid (1969)

Ernest Lehman (Producer)
Hello, Dolly! (1969)

Jacques Perrin, Hamed Rachedi (Producers)
Z (1969)

Hal B. Wallis (Producer)
Anne of the Thousand Days (1969)

Best Short Subject, Cartoon

↓ **Ward Kimball (Producer)** ↓
It's Tough to Be a Bird (1969)

Faith Hubley, John Hubley (Producers)
Of Men and Demons (1969)

Ryan Larkin (Producer)
En marchant (eng. Walking) (1968)

Best Short Subject, Live Action

↓ **Joan Keller Stern (Producer)** ↓
The Magic Machines (1969)

Doug Jackson (Producer)
Blake (1969)

Marc Merson (Producer)
People Soup (1969)

Best Sound

↓ **Jack Solomon, Murray Spivack** ↓
Hello, Dolly! (1969)

John Aldred
Anne of the Thousand Days (1969)

William Edmondson, David Dockendorf
Butch Cassidy and the Sundance Kid (1969)

Les Fresholtz, Arthur Piantadosi
Marooned (1969)

Robert Martin, Clem Portman
Gaily, Gaily (1969)

Best Foreign Language Film

↓ **Algeria** ↓
Z (1969)

France
Ma nuit chez Maud (eng. My Night at Maud's) (1969)

Sweden
Ådalen 31 (eng. Adalen 31) (1969)

Union of Soviet Socialist Republics
Bratya Karamazovy (eng. The Brothers Karamazov) (1969)

Yugoslavia
Bitka na Neretvi (eng. The Battle of Neretva) (1969)

Best Writing, Screenplay based on material from another medium

↓ **Waldo Salt** ↓
Midnight Cowboy (1969)

Bridget Boland, John Hale (Screenplay), Richard Sokolove (Adaptation)
Anne of the Thousand Days (1969)

Costa-Gavras, Jorge Semprún
Z (1969)

James Poe, Robert E. Thompson
They Shoot Horses, Don't They? (1969)

Arnold Schulman
Goodbye, Columbus (1969)

Best Writing, Story and Screenplay based on material not previously published or produced

✠ **William Goldman** ✠
Butch Cassidy and the Sundance Kid (1969)

Nicola Badalucco (Story),
Nicola Badalucco, Enrico Medioli, Luchino Visconti (Screenplay)
La caduta degli dei (Götterdämmerung) (eng. The Damned) (1969)

Peter Fonda, Dennis Hopper, Terry Southern
Easy Rider (1969)

Walon Green, Roy N. Sickner (Story),
Walon Green, Sam Peckinpah (Screenplay)
The Wild Bunch (1969)

Paul Mazursky, Larry Tucker
Bob & Carol & Ted & Alice (1969)

The 43ʳᵈ Academy Awards® - April 15, 1971

Host: No official host
Venue: Dorothy Chandler Pavilion
Honoring movies released in 1970

Honorary Award

✠ **Lillian Gish** ✠
For superlative artistry and for distinguished contribution to the progress of motion pictures.

✠ **Orson Welles** ✠
For superlative artistry and versatility in the creation of motion pictures.

Best Actor

✠ **George C. Scott** ✠
(Refused to accept the nomination and the award)
Patton (1970) role "General George S. Patton Jr."

Melvyn Douglas
I Never Sang for My Father (1970) role "Tom Garrison"

James Earl Jones
The Great White Hope (1970) role "Jack Jefferson"

Jack Nicholson
Five Easy Pieces (1970) role "Robert Eroica Dupea"

Ryan O'Neal
Love Story (1970) role "Oliver Barrett IV"

Best Actor in a Supporting Role

✠ **John Mills** ✠
Ryan's Daughter (1970) role "Michael"

Richard S. Castellano
Lovers and Other Strangers (1970) role "Frank Vecchio"

Chief Dan George
Little Big Man (1970) role "Old Lodge Skins"

Gene Hackman
I Never Sang for My Father (1970) role "Gene Garrison"

John Marley
Love Story (1970) role "Phil Cavalleri"

Best Actress
⚊ Glenda Jackson ⚊
Women in Love (1969) role "Gundrun Brangwen"
Jane Alexander
The Great White Hope (1970) role "Eleanor Backman"
Ali MacGraw
Love Story (1970) role "Jennifer "Jenny" Cavalleri-Barrett"
Sarah Miles
Ryan's Daughter (1970) role "Rosy Ryan"
Carrie Snodgress
Diary of a Mad Housewife (1970) role "Bettina "Tina" Balser"

Best Actress in a Supporting Role
⚊ Helen Hayes ⚊
Airport (1970) role "Ada Quonsett"
Karen Black
Five Easy Pieces (1970) role "Rayette Dipesto"
Lee Grant
The Landlord (1970) role "Joyce Enders"
Sally Kellerman
M*A*S*H (1970) role "Major Margaret 'Hot Lips' O'Houlihan"
Maureen Stapleton
Airport (1970) role "Inez Guerrero"

Best Art Direction
⚊ Urie McCleary, Gil Parrondo (Art Direction), Antonio Mateos, Pierre-Louis Thévenet (Set Decoration) ⚊
Patton (1970)
E. Preston Ames, Alexander Golitzen (Art Direction), Mickey S. Michaels, Jack D. Moore (Set Decoration)
Airport (1970)
Bob Cartwright, Terry Marsh (Art Direction), Pamela Cornell (Set Decoration)
Scrooge (1970)
Richard Day, Taizô Kawashima, Yoshirô Muraki, Jack Martin Smith (Art Direction), Carl Biddiscombe, Norman Rockett, Walter M. Scott (Set Decoration)
Tora! Tora! Tora! (1970)
Tambi Larsen (Art Direction), Darrell Silvera (Set Decoration)
The Molly Maguires (1970)

Best Cinematography
⚊ Freddie Young ⚊
Ryan's Daughter (1970)
Osami Furuya, Sinsaku Himeda, Masamichi Satoh, Charles F. Wheeler
Tora! Tora! Tora! (1970)
Fred J. Koenekamp
Patton (1970)
Ernest Laszlo
Airport (1970)
Billy Williams
Women in Love (1969)

Best Costume Design

⚑ Vittorio Nino Novarese ⚑
Cromwell (1970)

Jack Bear, Donald Brooks
Darling Lili (1970)

Margaret Furse
Scrooge (1970)

Edith Head
Airport (1970)

Bill Thomas
The Hawaiians (1970)

Best Directing

⚑ Franklin J. Schaffner ⚑
Patton (1970)

Robert Altman
M*A*S*H (1970)

Federico Fellini
Fellini Satyricon (1969)

Arthur Hiller
Love Story (1970)

Ken Russell
Women in Love (1969)

Best Documentary, Feature

⚑ Bob Maurice (Producer) ⚑
Woodstock (1970)

Jim Jacobs (Producer)
Jack Johnson (1970)

Ely A. Landau (Producer)
King: A Filmed Record... Montgomery to Memphis (1970)

Dr. Harald Reinl (Producer)
Erinnerungen an die Zukunft (eng. Chariots of the Gods) (1970)

David H. Vowell (Producer)
Say Goodbye (1971)

Best Documentary, Short Subject

⚑ Joseph Strick (Producer) ⚑
Interviews with My Lai Veterans (1971)

Bob Aller (Producer)
A Long Way from Nowhere (1970)

Patrick Carey, Vivien Carey (Producers)
Oisin (1970)

Horst Dallmayr, Robert Ménégoz (Producers)
Time Is Running Out (1970)

Robert McBride (Producer)
The Gifts (1970)

Best Special Visual Effects

⚑ L. B. Abbott, A. D. Flowers ⚑
Tora! Tora! Tora! (1970)

Alex Weldon
Patton (1970)

Best Film Editing

↧ Hugh S. Fowler ↧
Patton (1970)

Inoue Chikaya, Pembroke J. Herring, James E. Newcom
Tora! Tora! Tora! (1970)

Stuart Gilmore
Airport (1970)

Danford B. Greene
M*A*S*H (1970)

Thelma Schoonmaker
Woodstock (1970)

Best Foreign Language Film

↧ Italy ↧
Indagine su un cittadino al di sopra di ogni sospetto
(eng. Investigation of a Citizen Above Suspicion) (1970)

Belgium
Paix sur les champs (eng. Peace Over the Fields) (1970)

France
Hoa Binh (1970)

Spain
Tristana (1970)

Switzerland
Erste Liebe (eng. First Love) (1970)

Best Music, Original Score

↧ Francis Lai ↧
Love Story (1970)

Frank Cordell
Cromwell (1970)

Jerry Goldsmith
Patton (1970)

Henry Mancini
I girasoli (eng. Sunflower) (1970)

Alfred Newman
(posthumous)
Airport (1970)

Best Music, Original Song Score

↧ The Beatles (Music & Lyrics) ↧
Let It Be (1969)

Leslie Bricusse (Music & Lyrics)
Ian Fraser, Herbert W. Spencer (Adaptation score)
Scrooge (1970)

Fred Karlin (Music), Tylwyth Kymry (Lyrics)
The Baby Maker (1970)

Henry Mancini (Music), Johnny Mercer (Lyrics)
Darling Lili (1970)

Rod McKuen, John Scott Trotter (Music), Rod McKuen, Bill Melendez,
Al Shean (Lyrics) Vince Guaraldi (Adaptation score)
A Boy Named Charlie Brown (1969)

Best Music, Song Original for the Picture

Fred Karlin (Music), Jimmy Griffin (aka Arthur James), Robb Royer (aka Robb Wilson) (Lyrics) for the song "For All We Know"
Lovers and Other Strangers (1970)

Leslie Bricusse (Music & Lyrics) for the song "Thank You Very Much"
Scrooge (1970)

Michel Legrand (Music), Alan Bergman, Marilyn Bergman (Lyrics) for the song "Pieces of Dreams"
Pieces of Dreams (1970)

Henry Mancini (Music), Johnny Mercer (Lyrics) for the song "Whistling Away the Dark"
Darling Lili (1970)

Riz Ortolani (Music), Arthur Hamilton (Lyrics) for the song "Till Love Touches Your Life"
Madron (eng. His Name Was Madron) (1970)

Best Picture

Frank McCarthy (Producer)
Patton (1970)

Ross Hunter (Producer)
Airport (1970)

Howard G. Minsky (Producer)
Love Story (1970)

Ingo Preminger (Producer)
M*A*S*H (1970)

Bob Rafelson, Richard Wechsler (Producers)
Five Easy Pieces (1970)

Best Sound

Don J. Bassman, Douglas O. Williams
Patton (1970)

John Bramall, Gordon K. McCallum
Ryan's Daughter (1970)

Larry A. Johnson, Dan Wallin
Woodstock (1970)

Herman Lewis, Murray Spivack
Tora! Tora! Tora! (1970)

David H. Moriarty, Ronald Pierce
Airport (1970)

Best Writing, Screenplay based on material from another medium

Ring Lardner Jr.
M*A*S*H (1970)

Robert Anderson
I Never Sang for My Father (1970)

Joseph Bologna, David Zelag Goodman, Renée Taylor
Lovers and Other Strangers (1970)

Larry Kramer
Women in Love (1969)

George Seaton
Airport (1970)

Best Writing, Story and Screenplay based on factual material or material not previously published or produced

⭷ Francis Ford Coppola, Edmund H. North ⭷
Patton (1970)

Carole Eastman (as Adrien Joyce), Bob Rafelson (Story), Carole Eastman (as Adrien Joyce) (Screenplay)
Five Easy Pieces (1970)

Éric Rohmer
Ma nuit chez Maud (eng. My Night at Maud's) (1969)

Erich Segal
Love Story (1970)

Norman Wexler
Joe (1970)

Jean Hersholt Humanitarian Award
⭷ Frank Sinatra ⭷

Irving G. Thalberg Memorial Award
⭷ Ingmar Bergman ⭷

Best Short Subject, Cartoon
⭷ Nick Bosustow (Producer) ⭷
Is It Always Right to Be Right? (1970)

Dale Case, Robert Mitchell (Producers)
The Further Adventures of Uncle Sam (1971)

Cameron Guess (Producer)
The Shepherd (1969)

Best Short Subject, Live Action
⭷ John Longenecker (Producer) ⭷
The Resurrection of Broncho Billy (1970)

John D. Hancock (Producer)
Sticky My Fingers... Fleet My Feet (1970)

Robert Siegler (Producer)
Shut Up... I'm Crying (1970)

The 44ᵗʰ Academy Awards® - April 10, 1972
Hosts: Sammy Davis Jr., Helen Hayes, Alan King, Jack Lemmon
Venue: Dorothy Chandler Pavilion
Honoring movies released in 1971

Best Cinematography
⭷ Oswald Morris ⭷
Fiddler on the Roof (1971)

Owen Roizman
The French Connection (1971)

Robert Surtees
The Last Picture Show (1971), Summer of '42 (1971)

Freddie Young
Nicholas and Alexandra (1971)

Best Actor
⚊ Gene Hackman ⚊
The French Connection (1971) role "Detective Jimmy "Popeye" Doyle"
Peter Finch
Sunday Bloody Sunday (1971) role "Dr. Daniel Hirsch"
Walter Matthau
Kotch (1971) role "Joseph P. Kotcher"
George C. Scott
The Hospital (1971) role "Dr. Herbert "Herb" Bock"
Chaim Topol
Fiddler on the Roof (1971) role "Tevye"

Best Actor in a Supporting Role
⚊ Ben Johnson ⚊
The Last Picture Show (1971) role "Sam the Lion"
Jeff Bridges
The Last Picture Show (1971) role "Duane Jackson"
Leonard Frey
Fiddler on the Roof (1971) role "Motel Kamzoil"
Richard Jaeckel
Sometimes a Great Notion (1971) role "Joe Ben Stamper"
Roy Scheider
The French Connection (1971) role "Detective Buddy "Cloudy" Russo"

Best Actress
⚊ Jane Fonda ⚊
Klute (1971) role "Bree Daniels"
Julie Christie
McCabe & Mrs. Miller (1971) role "Constance Miller"
Glenda Jackson
Sunday Bloody Sunday (1971) role "Alex Greville"
Vanessa Redgrave
Mary, Queen of Scots (1971) role "Mary, Queen of Scots"
Janet Suzman
Nicholas and Alexandra (1971) role "Empress Alexandra of Russia"

Best Actress in a Supporting Role
⚊ Cloris Leachman ⚊
The Last Picture Show (1971) role "Ruth Popper"
Ann-Margret
Carnal Knowledge (1971) role "Bobbie"
Ellen Burstyn
The Last Picture Show (1971) role "Lois Farrow"
Barbara Harris
Who Is Harry Kellerman and Why Is He Saying Those Terrible Things About Me?
(1971) role "Allison Densmore"
Margaret Leighton
The Go-Between (1971) role "Mrs. Maudsley"

Honorary Award
⚊ Charles Chaplin ⚊
For the incalculable effect he has had in making motion pictures the art form of
this century.

Best Art Direction

Ernest Archer, John Box, Jack Maxsted,
Gil Parrondo (Art Direction), Vernon Dixon (Set Decoration)
Nicholas and Alexandra (1971)

Robert F. Boyle, Michael Stringer (Art Direction),
Peter Lamont (Set Decoration)
Fiddler on the Roof (1971)

Robert Cartwright, Terence Marsh (Art Direction),
Peter Howitt (Set Decoration)
Mary, Queen of Scots (1971)

Peter Ellenshaw , John B. Mansbridge (Art Direction),
Hal Gausman, Emile Kuri (Set Decoration)
Bedknobs and Broomsticks (1971)

Boris Leven, William H. Tuntke (Art Direction),
Ruby R. Levitt (Set Decoration)
The Andromeda Strain (1971)

Best Costume Design

Yvonne Blake, Antonio Castillo
Nicholas and Alexandra (1971)

Margaret Furse
Mary, Queen of Scots (1971)

Morton Haack
What's the Matter with Helen? (1971)

Bill Thomas
Bedknobs and Broomsticks (1971)

Piero Tosi
Morte a Venezia (eng. Death in Venice) (1971)

Best Directing

William Friedkin
The French Connection (1971)

Peter Bogdanovich
The Last Picture Show (1971)

Norman Jewison
Fiddler on the Roof (1971)

Stanley Kubrick
A Clockwork Orange (1971)

John Schlesinger
Sunday Bloody Sunday (1971)

Best Documentary, Feature

Walon Green (Producer)
The Hellstrom Chronicle (1971)

Bruce Brown (Producer)
On Any Sunday (1971)

Lennart Ehrenborg, Thor Heyerdahl (Producers)
The Ra Expeditions (1971)

Alan Landsburg (Producer)
Alaska Wilderness Lake (1971)

Marcel Ophuls (Producer)
Le chagrin et la pitié (eng. The Sorrow and the Pity) (1969)

Best Documentary, Short Subject
⚐ **Robert Amram, Manuel Arango (Producers)** ⚐
Centinelas del silencio (eng. Sentinels of Silence) (1971)
Han van Gelder (Producer)
Met het oog op avontuur (eng. Adventures in Perception) (1972)
Julian Krainin, DeWitt L. Sage Jr. (Producers)
Art Is... (1972)
Sherwood Omens, Hal Riney, Dick Snider (Producers)
Somebody Waiting (1972)
Donald Wrye (Producer)
The Numbers Start with the River (1971)

Best Film Editing
⚐ **Gerald B. Greenberg (as Jerry Greenberg)** ⚐
The French Connection (1971)
Folmar Blangsted
Summer of '42 (1971)
Bill Butler
A Clockwork Orange (1971)
Stuart Gilmore, John W. Holmes
(Stuart Gilmore - posthumous)
The Andromeda Strain (1971)
Ralph E. Winters
Kotch (1971)

Best Foreign Language Film
⚐ **Italy** ⚐
Il giardino dei Finzi Contini (eng. The Garden of the Finzi-Continis) (1970)
Israel
Ha-Shoter Azulai (eng. The Policeman) (1971)
Japan
Dodesukaden (eng. Dodes'ka-den) (1970)
Sweden
Utvandrarna (eng. The Emigrants) (1971)
Union of Soviet Socialist Republics
Tchaikovsky (1970)

Best Music, Song Original for the Picture
⚐ **Isaac Hayes (Music & Lyrics) for the song "Theme from Shaft"** ⚐
Shaft (1971)
Perry Botkin Jr., Barry De Vorzon (Music & Lyrics) for the song "Bless the Beasts and the Children"
Bless the Beasts & Children (1971)
Marvin Hamlisch (Music), Johnny Mercer (Lyrics) for the song "Life Is What You Make It"
Kotch (1971)
Henry Mancini (Music), Alan Bergman, Marilyn Bergman (Lyrics) for the song "All His Children"
Sometimes a Great Notion (1971)
Richard M. Sherman, Robert B. Sherman (Music & Lyrics) for the song "The Age of Not Believing"
Bedknobs and Broomsticks (1971)

Best Music, Scoring: Adaptation and Original Song Score

⚐ **John Williams (Adaptation Score)** ⚐
Fiddler on the Roof (1971)

Leslie Bricusse, Anthony Newley (Song Score),
Walter Scharf (Adaptation Score)
Willy Wonka & the Chocolate Factory (1971)

Peter Maxwell Davies, Peter Greenwell (Adaptation Score)
The Boy Friend (1971)

Dimitri Tiomkin (Adaptation Score)
Tchaikovsky (1970)

Richard M. Sherman, Robert B. Sherman (Song Score),
Irwin Kostal (Adaptation Score)
Bedknobs and Broomsticks (1971)

Best Music, Original Dramatic Score

⚐ **Michel Legrand** ⚐
Summer of '42 (1971)

John Barry
Mary, Queen of Scots (1971)

Richard Rodney Bennett
Nicholas and Alexandra (1971)

Jerry Fielding
Straw Dogs (1971)

Isaac Hayes
Shaft (1971)

Best Special Visual Effects

⚐ **Danny Lee, Eustace Lycett, Alan Maley** ⚐
Bedknobs and Broomsticks (1971)

Jim Danforth, Roger Dicken
When Dinosaurs Ruled the Earth (1970)

Best Picture

⚐ **Philip D'Antoni (Producer)** ⚐
The French Connection (1971)

Stephen J. Friedman (Producer)
The Last Picture Show (1971)

Norman Jewison (Producer)
Fiddler on the Roof (1971)

Stanley Kubrick (Producer)
A Clockwork Orange (1971)

Sam Spiegel (Producer)
Nicholas and Alexandra (1971)

Best Short Subject, Animated

⚐ **Ted Petok (Producer)** ⚐
The Crunch Bird (1971)

Michael Mills (Producer)
Evolution (1971)

Peter Sander, Murray Shostak (Producers)
The Selfish Giant (1971)

Best Short Subject, Live Action

⚐ Robert Amram, Manuel Arango (Producers) ⚐
Centinelas del silencio (eng. Sentinels of Silence) (1971)

Denny Evans, Ken Greenwald (Producers)
Good Morning (1971)

Stephen F. Verona (Producer)
The Rehearsal (1969)

Best Sound

⚐ David Hildyard, Gordon K. McCallum ⚐
Fiddler on the Roof (1971)

John Aldred, Bob Jones
Mary, Queen of Scots (1971)

Gordon K. McCallum, John W. Mitchell, Alfred J. Overton
Diamonds Are Forever (1971)

Christopher Newman, Theodore Soderberg
The French Connection (1971)

Richard Portman, Jack Solomon
Kotch (1971)

Best Writing, Screenplay based on material from another medium

⚐ Ernest Tidyman ⚐
The French Connection (1971)

Bernardo Bertolucci
Il conformista (eng. The Conformist) (1970)

Peter Bogdanovich, Larry McMurtry
The Last Picture Show (1971)

Vittorio Bonicelli, Ugo Pirro
Il giardino dei Finzi Contini (eng. The Garden of the Finzi-Continis) (1970)

Stanley Kubrick
A Clockwork Orange (1971)

Best Writing, Story and Screenplay based on factual material or material not previously published or produced

⚐ Paddy Chayefsky ⚐
The Hospital (1971)

Penelope Gilliatt
Sunday Bloody Sunday (1971)

Andy Lewis, David E. Lewis
Klute (1971)

Elio Petri, Ugo Pirro
Indagine su un cittadino al di sopra di ogni sospetto
(eng. Investigation of a Citizen Above Suspicion) (1970)

Herman Raucher
Summer of '42 (1971)

The 45th Academy Awards® - March 27, 1973

Hosts: Carol Burnett, Michael Caine, Charlton Heston, Rock Hudson
Venue: Dorothy Chandler Pavilion
Honoring movies released in 1972

Best Actor
↓ Marlon Brando ↓
(Refused to accept the nomination and the award)
The Godfather (1972) role "Don Vito Corleone"
Michael Caine
Sleuth (1972) role "Milo Tindle"
Laurence Olivier
Sleuth (1972) role "Andrew Wyke"
Peter O'Toole
The Ruling Class (1972) role "Jack Gurney, 14th Earl of Gurney"
Paul Winfield
Sounder (1972) role "Nathan Lee Morgan"

Best Actor in a Supporting Role
↓ Joel Grey ↓
Cabaret (1972) role "Master of Ceremonies"
Eddie Albert
The Heartbreak Kid (1972) role "Mr. Corcoran"
James Caan
The Godfather (1972) role "Santino "Sonny" Corleone"
Robert Duvall
The Godfather (1972) role "Tom Hagen"
Al Pacino
The Godfather (1972) role "Michael Corleone"

Best Actress
↓ Liza Minnelli ↓
Cabaret (1972) role "Sally Bowles"
Diana Ross
Lady Sings the Blues (1972) role "Billie Holiday"
Maggie Smith
Travels with My Aunt (1972) role "Augusta Bertram"
Cicely Tyson
Sounder (1972) role "Rebecca Morgan"
Liv Ullmann
Utvandrarna (eng. The Emigrants) (1971) role "Kristina Nilsson"

Best Actress in a Supporting Role
↓ Eileen Heckart ↓
Butterflies Are Free (1972) role "Mrs. Baker"
Jeannie Berlin
The Heartbreak Kid (1972) role "Lila Kolodny"
Geraldine Page
Pete 'n' Tillie (1972) role "Gertrude Wilson"
Susan Tyrrell
Fat City (1972) role "Oma Lee Greer"
Shelley Winters
The Poseidon Adventure (1972) role "Belle Rosen"

Special Achievement Award (Visual Effects)
↓ L. B. Abbott, A. D. Flowers ↓
The Poseidon Adventure (1972)

Jean Hersholt Humanitarian Award
⚵ **Rosalind Russell** ⚵

Best Art Direction
⚵ **Hans Jürgen Kiebach, Rolf Zehetbauer (Art Direction),** ⚵
Herbert Strabel (Set Decoration)
Cabaret (1972)

Carl Anderson (Art Direction), Reg Allen (Set Decoration)
Lady Sings the Blues (1972)

Don M. Ashton, Geoffrey Drake, John Graysmark,
William Hutchinson (Art Direction), Peter James (Set Decoration)
Young Winston (1972)

John Box, Robert W. Laing, Gil Parrondo (Art Direction)
Travels with My Aunt (1972)

William J. Creber (Art Direction), Raphael Bretton (Set Decoration)
The Poseidon Adventure (1972)

Best Cinematography
⚵ **Geoffrey Unsworth** ⚵
Cabaret (1972)

Charles B. Lang
Butterflies Are Free (1972)

Harold E. Stine
The Poseidon Adventure (1972)

Douglas Slocombe
Travels with My Aunt (1972)

Harry Stradling Jr.
1776 (1972)

Best Costume Design
⚵ **Anthony Powell** ⚵
Travels with My Aunt (1972)

Ray Aghayan, Norma Koch, Bob Mackie
Lady Sings the Blues (1972)

Anna Hill Johnstone
The Godfather (1972)

Anthony Mendleson
Young Winston (1972)

Paul Zastupnevich
The Poseidon Adventure (1972)

Best Directing
⚵ **Bob Fosse** ⚵
Cabaret (1972)

John Boorman
Deliverance (1972)

Francis Ford Coppola
The Godfather (1972)

Joseph L. Mankiewicz
Sleuth (1972)

Jan Troell
Utvandrarna (eng. The Emigrants) (1971)

Best Documentary, Feature

⚊ **Sarah Kernochan, Howard Smith (Producers)** ⚊
Marjoe (1972)

Bert Haanstra (Producer)
Bij de beesten af (eng. Ape and Super-Ape) (1972)

Robert Hendrickson, Laurence Merrick (Producers)
Manson (1973)

Eckehard Munck (Producer)
The Silent Revolution (1972)

Arnold Perl, Marvin Worth (Producers)
(Arnold Perl - posthumous)
Malcolm X (1972)

Best Documentary, Short Subject

⚊ **Charles Huguenot van der Linden,**
Martina Huguenot van der Linden (Producers) ⚊
Deze kleine wereld (eng. This Tiny World) (1972)

Tadeusz Jaworski (Producer)
Selling Out (1972)

Peter Schamoni (Producer)
Hundertwassers Regentag (1971)

Humphrey Swingler (Producer)
The Tide of Traffic (1972)

Giorgio Treves (Producer)
K-Z (1972)

Best Music, Original Dramatic Score

⚊ **Charles Chaplin, Raymond Rasch, Larry Russell** ⚊
(Raymond Rasch, Larry Russell - posthumous)
Limelight (1952)

John Addison
Sleuth (1972)

Buddy Baker
Napoleon and Samantha (1972)

John Williams
Images (1972), The Poseidon Adventure (1972)

Best Music, Song Original for the Picture

⚊ **Joel Hirschhorn, Al Kasha (Music & Lyrics)**
for the song "The Morning After" ⚊
The Poseidon Adventure (1972)

Sammy Fain (Music), Paul Francis Webster (Lyrics)
for the song "Strange Are the Ways of Love"
The Stepmother (1972)

Maurice Jarre (Music), Alan Bergmanx, Marilyn Bergman (Lyrics)
for the song "Marmalade, Molasses & Honey"
The Life and Times of Judge Roy Bean (1972)

Fred Karlin (Music), Meg Karlin (Lyrics)
for the song "Come Follow, Follow Me"
The Little Ark (1972)

Walter Scharf (Music), Don Black (Lyrics) for the song "Ben"
Ben (1972)

Best Music, Scoring: Adaptation and Original Song Score
⚐ Ralph Burns (Adaptation Score) ⚐
Cabaret (1972)

Gil Askey (Adaptation Score)
Lady Sings the Blues (1972)

Laurence Rosenthal (Adaptation Score)
Man of La Mancha (1972)

Best Film Editing
⚐ David Bretherton ⚐
Cabaret (1972)

Fred W. Berger, Frank P. Keller
The Hot Rock (1972)

Harold F. Kress
The Poseidon Adventure (1972)

Tom Priestley
Deliverance (1972)

William Reynolds, Peter Zinner
The Godfather (1972)

Best Foreign Language Film
⚐ France ⚐
Le charme discret de la bourgeoisie (eng. The Discreet Charm of the Bourgeoisie) (1972)

Israel
Ani Ohev Otach Rosa (eng. I Love You Rosa) (1972)

Spain
Mi querida señorita (eng. My Dearest Senorita) (1972)

Sweden
Nybyggarna (eng. The New Land) (1972)

Union of Soviet Socialist Republics
A zori zdes tikhie (eng. The Dawns Here Are Quiet) (1972)

Best Picture
⚐ Albert S. Ruddy (Producer) ⚐
The Godfather (1972)

John Boorman (Producer)
Deliverance (1972)

Cy Feuer (Producer)
Cabaret (1972)

Bengt Forslund (Producer)
Utvandrarna (eng. The Emigrants) (1971)

Robert B. Radnitz (Producer)
Sounder (1972)

Best Short Subject, Animated
⚐ Richard Williams (Producer) ⚐
A Christmas Carol (1971)

Nedeljko Dragic (Producer)
Tup Tup (1972)

Bob Godfrey (Producer)
Kama Sutra Rides Again (1971)

Best Short Subject, Live Action
⚐ **Richard Barclay (Producer)** ⚐
Norman Rockwell's World... An American Dream (1972)

David Adams (Producer)
Solo (1972)

Ray Gideon, Ron Satlof (Producers)
Frog Story (1972)

Best Sound
⚐ **David Hildyard, Robert Knudson** ⚐
Cabaret (1972)

Gene S. Cantamessa, Richard Portman
The Candidate (1972)

Bud Grenzbach, Christopher Newman, Richard Portman
The Godfather (1972)

Charles T. Knight, Arthur Piantadosi
Butterflies Are Free (1972)

Herman Lewis, Theodore Soderberg
The Poseidon Adventure (1972)

Best Writing, Screenplay based on material from another medium
⚐ **Francis Ford Coppola, Mario Puzo** ⚐
The Godfather (1972)

Jay Presson Allen
Cabaret (1972)

Lonne Elder III
Sounder (1972)

Julius J. Epstein
Pete 'n' Tillie (1972)

Bengt Forslund, Jan Troell
Utvandrarna (eng. The Emigrants) (1971)

Best Writing, Story and Screenplay based on factual material or material not previously published or produced
⚐ **Jeremy Larner** ⚐
The Candidate (1972)

Luis Buñuel (Story & Screenplay), Jean-Claude Carrière (Collaboration)
Le charme discret de la bourgeoisie (eng. The Discreet Charm of the Bourgeoisie) (1972)

Carl Foreman
Young Winston (1972)

Louis Malle
Le souffle au coeur (eng. Murmur of the Heart) (1971)

Terence McCloy, Chris Clark, Suzanne de Passe
Lady Sings the Blues (1972)

Honorary Award
⚐ **Charles S. Boren** ⚐
Leader for 38 years of the industry's enlightened labor relations and architect of its policy of non-discrimination. With the respect and affection of all who work in films.

⚐ **Edward G. Robinson** ⚐
(posthumous)
Who achieved greatness as a player, a patron of the arts, and a dedicated citizen ... in sum, a Renaissance man. From his friends in the industry he loves.

The 46ᵗʰ Academy Awards® - April 2, 1974

Hosts: John Huston, David Niven, Burt Reynolds, Diana Ross
Venue: Dorothy Chandler Pavilion
Honoring movies released in 1973

Honorary Award

⚊ Groucho Marx ⚊

In recognition of his brilliant creativity and for the unequaled achievements of
the Marx Brothers in the art of motion picture comedy.

⚊ Henri Langlois ⚊

For his devotion to the art of film, his massive contributions in preserving its past
and his unswerving faith in its future.

Irving G. Thalberg Memorial Award

⚊ Lawrence Weingarten ⚊

Best Actor

⚊ Jack Lemmon ⚊
Save the Tiger (1973) role "Harry Stoner"

Marlon Brando
Ultimo tango a Parigi (eng. Last Tango in Paris) (1972) role "Paul"

Jack Nicholson
The Last Detail (1973) role "Signalman First Class Billy L. "Badass" Buddusky"

Al Pacino
Serpico (1973) role "Frank Serpico"

Robert Redford
The Sting (1973) role "Johnny "Kelly" Hooker"

Best Actor in a Supporting Role

⚊ John Houseman ⚊
The Paper Chase (1973) role "Professor Charles W. Kingsfield Jr."

Vincent Gardenia
Bang the Drum Slowly (1973) role "Dutch Schnell"

Jack Gilford
Save the Tiger (1973) role "Phil Greene"

Jason Miller
The Exorcist (1973) role "Father Damien Karras"

Randy Quaid
The Last Detail (1973) role "Larry Meadows"

Best Actress

⚊ Glenda Jackson ⚊
A Touch of Class (1973) role "Vicki Allessio"

Ellen Burstyn
The Exorcist (1973) role "Chris MacNeil"

Marsha Mason
Cinderella Liberty (1973) role "Maggie Paul"

Barbra Streisand
The Way We Were (1973) role "Katie Morosky"

Joanne Woodward
Summer Wishes, Winter Dreams (1973) role "Rita Pritchett-Walden"

Best Actress in a Supporting Role
⚐ Tatum O'Neal ⚐
Paper Moon (1973) role "Addie Loggins"
Linda Blair
The Exorcist (1973) role "Regan MacNeil"
Candy Clark
American Graffiti (1973) role "Debbie Dunham"
Madeline Kahn
Paper Moon (1973) role "Trixie Delight"
Sylvia Sidney
Summer Wishes, Winter Dreams (1973) role "Mrs. Pritchett"

Best Art Direction
⚐ Henry Bumstead (Art Direction), James W. Payne (Set Decoration) ⚐
The Sting (1973)
Stephen B. Grimes (Art Direction), William Kiernan (Set Decoration)
(William Kiernan - posthumous)
The Way We Were (1973)
Philip M. Jefferies (Art Direction), Robert de Vestel (Set Decoration)
Tom Sawyer (1973)
Bill Malley (Art Direction), Jerry Wunderlich (Set Decoration)
The Exorcist (1973)
**Lorenzo Mongiardino, Gianni Quaranta (Art Direction),
Carmelo Patrono (Set Decoration)**
Fratello sole, sorella luna (eng. Brother Sun, Sister Moon) (1972)

Best Cinematography
⚐ Sven Nykvist ⚐
Viskningar och rop (eng. Cries & Whispers) (1972)
Jack Couffer
Jonathan Livingston Seagull (1973)
Owen Roizman
The Exorcist (1973)
Harry Stradling Jr.
The Way We Were (1973)
Robert Surtees
The Sting (1973)

Best Short Subject, Animated
⚐ Frank Mouris (Producer) ⚐
Frank Film (1973)
David Adams, Nick Bosustow (Producers)
The Legend of John Henry (1974)
Giulio Gianini, Emanuele Luzzati (Producers)
Pulcinella (1973)

Best Short Subject, Live Action
⚐ William Fertik, Allan Miller (Producers) ⚐
The Bolero (1973)
Pen Densham, John Watson (Producers)
Life Times Nine (1973)
Richard Gayer (Producer)
Clockmaker (1971)

Best Costume Design

⊥ Edith Head ⊥
The Sting (1973)

Donfeld
Tom Sawyer (1973)

Dorothy Jeakins, Moss Mabry
The Way We Were (1973)

Piero Tosi
Ludwig (1973)

Marik Vos-Lundh
Viskningar och rop (eng. Cries & Whispers) (1972)

Best Directing

⊥ George Roy Hill ⊥
The Sting (1973)

Ingmar Bergman
Viskningar och rop (eng. Cries & Whispers) (1972)

Bernardo Bertolucci
Ultimo tango a Parigi (eng. Last Tango in Paris) (1972)

William Friedkin
The Exorcist (1973)

George Lucas
American Graffiti (1973)

Jean Hersholt Humanitarian Award

⊥ Lew Wasserman ⊥

Best Writing, Story and Screenplay based on factual material or material not previously published or produced

⊥ David S. Ward ⊥
The Sting (1973)

Ingmar Bergman
Viskningar och rop (eng. Cries & Whispers) (1972)

Melvin Frank, Jack Rose
A Touch of Class (1973)

Willard Huyck, Gloria Katz, George Lucas
American Graffiti (1973)

Steve Shagan
Save the Tiger (1973)

Best Writing, Screenplay based on material from another medium

⊥ William Peter Blatty ⊥
The Exorcist (1973)

James Bridges
The Paper Chase (1973)

Waldo Salt, Norman Wexler
Serpico (1973)

Alvin Sargent
Paper Moon (1973)

Robert Towne
The Last Detail (1973)

Best Documentary, Feature

⚑ **Kieth Merrill (Producer)** ⚑
The Great American Cowboy (1974)

John D. Goodell (Producer)
Always a New Beginning (1974)

Alex Grasshoff (Producer)
Journey to the Outer Limits (1973)

Gertrude Ross Marks, Edmund F. Penney (Producers)
Walls of Fire (1971)

Bengt von zur Mühlen (Producer)
Schlacht um Berlin (eng. Battle of Berlin) (1973)

Best Documentary, Short Subject

⚑ **Julian Krainin, DeWitt L. Sage Jr. (Producers)** ⚑
Princeton: A Search for Answers (1974)

Carmen D'Avino (Producer)
Background (1973)

Louis Marcus (Producer)
Paisti ag obair (eng. Children at Work) (1973)

Albert Maysles, David Maysles (Producers)
Christo's Valley Curtain (1974)

Terry Sanders, June Wayne (Producers)
Four Stones for Kanemitsu (1973)

Best Film Editing

⚑ **William Reynolds** ⚑
The Sting (1973)

Verna Fields, Marcia Lucas
American Graffiti (1973)

James Galloway, Frank P. Keller
Jonathan Livingston Seagull (1973)

Norman Gay, Jordan Leondopoulos, Evan A. Lottman, Bud S. Smith
The Exorcist (1973)

Ralph Kemplen
The Day of the Jackal (1973)

Best Music, Song

⚑ **Marvin Hamlisch (Music), Alan Bergman, Marilyn Bergman (Lyrics)** ⚑
for the song "The Way We Were"
The Way We Were (1973)

George Barrie (Music), Sammy Cahn (Lyrics)
for the song "All That Love Went to Waste"
A Touch of Class (1973)

George Bruns (Music), Floyd Huddleston (Lyrics) for the song "Love"
Robin Hood (1973)

Paul McCartney, Linda McCartney (Music & Lyrics)
for the song "Live and Let Die"
Live and Let Die (1973)

John Williams (Music), Paul Williams (Lyrics)
for the song "Nice to Be Around"
Cinderella Liberty (1973)

Best Foreign Language Film
⚰ France ⚰
La nuit américaine (eng. Day for Night) (1973)
Israel
Ha-Bayit Berechov Chelouche (eng. The House on Chelouche Street) (1973)
The Netherlands
Turks fruit (eng. Turkish Delight) (1973)
Switzerland
L'invitation (eng. The Invitation) (1973)
West Germany
Der Fußgänger (eng. The Pedestrian) (1973)

Best Music, Original Dramatic Score
⚰ Marvin Hamlisch ⚰
The Way We Were (1973)
John Cameron
A Touch of Class (1973)
Georges Delerue
The Day of the Dolphin (1973)
Jerry Goldsmith
Papillon (1973)
John Williams
Cinderella Liberty (1973)

Best Picture
⚰ Tony Bill, Michael Phillips, Julia Phillips (Producers) ⚰
The Sting (1973)
Ingmar Bergman (Producer)
Viskningar och rop (eng. Cries & Whispers) (1972)
William Peter Blatty (Producer)
The Exorcist (1973)
Francis Ford Coppola (Producer), Gary Kurtz (Co-Producer)
American Graffiti (1973)
Melvin Frank (Producer)
A Touch of Class (1973)

Best Sound
⚰ Robert Knudson, Chris Newman ⚰
The Exorcist (1973)
Robert R. Bertrand, Ronald K. Pierce
The Sting (1973)
Les Fresholtz, Richard Portman
Paper Moon (1973)
Lawrence O. Jost, Richard Portman
The Day of the Dolphin (1973)
Lawrence O. Jost, Donald O. Mitchell
The Paper Chase (1973)

Best Music, Scoring: Original Song Score and Adaptation or Scoring: Adaptation

⚑ **Marvin Hamlisch (Adaptation Score)** ⚑
The Sting (1973)

Andre Previn, Herbert Spencer, Andrew Lloyd Webber (Adaptation Score)
Jesus Christ Superstar (1973)

**Richard M. Sherman, Robert B. Sherman(Song Score),
John Williams (Adaptation Score)**
Tom Sawyer (1973)

The 47th Academy Awards® - April 8, 1975

Hosts: Sammy Davis Jr., Bob Hope, Shirley MacLaine, Frank Sinatra
Venue: Dorothy Chandler Pavilion
Honoring movies released in 1974

Best Actor

⚑ **Art Carney** ⚑
Harry and Tonto (1974) role "Harry Coombes"

Albert Finney
Murder on the Orient Express (1974) role "Hercule Poirot"

Dustin Hoffman
Lenny (1974) role "Lenny Bruce"

Jack Nicholson
Chinatown (1974) role "J. J. "Jake" Gittes"

Al Pacino
The Godfather: Part II (1974) role "Michael Corleone"

Best Actor in a Supporting Role

⚑ **Robert De Niro** ⚑
The Godfather: Part II (1974) role "Vito Corleone"

Fred Astaire
The Towering Inferno (1974) role "Harlee Claiborne"

Jeff Bridges
Thunderbolt and Lightfoot (1974) role "Lightfoot"

Michael V. Gazzo
The Godfather: Part II (1974) role "Frank Pentangeli"

Lee Strasberg
The Godfather: Part II (1974) role "Hyman Roth"

Best Actress

⚑ **Ellen Burstyn** ⚑
Alice Doesn't Live Here Anymore (1974) role "Alice Hyatt"

Diahann Carroll
Claudine (1974) role "Claudine Price"

Faye Dunaway
Chinatown (1974) role "Evelyn Cross Mulwray"

Valerie Perrine
Lenny (1974) role "Harriett Jolliff / Honey Bruce"

Gena Rowlands
A Woman Under the Influence (1974) role "Mabel Longhetti"

Best Actress in a Supporting Role

⚑ Ingrid Bergman ⚑
Murder on the Orient Express (1974) role "Greta Ohlsson"

Valentina Cortese
La nuit américaine (eng. Day for Night) (1973) role "Séverine"

Madeline Kahn
Blazing Saddles (1974) role "Lili von Shtüpp"

Diane Ladd
Alice Doesn't Live Here Anymore (1974) role "Florence "Flo" Castleberry"

Talia Shire
The Godfather: Part II (1974) role "Connie Corleone"

Best Art Direction

**⚑ Angelo P. Graham, Dean Tavoularis (Art Direction), ⚑
George R. Nelson (Set Decoration)**
The Godfather: Part II (1974)

**E. Preston Ames, Alexander Golitzen (Art Direction),
Frank R. McKelvy (Set Decoration)**
Earthquake (1974)

**W. Stewart Campbell, Richard Sylbert (Art Direction),
Ruby R. Levitt (Set Decoration)**
Chinatown (1974)

**William J. Creber, Ward Preston (Art Direction),
Raphael Bretton (Set Decoration)**
The Towering Inferno (1974)

**Peter Ellenshaw, John B. Mansbridge, Al Roelofs,
Walter H. Tyler (Art Direction), Hal Gausman (Set Decoration)**
The Island at the Top of the World (1974)

Best Cinematography

⚑ Joseph F. Biroc, Fred J. Koenekamp ⚑
The Towering Inferno (1974)

John A. Alonzo
Chinatown (1974)

Philip H. Lathrop
Earthquake (1974)

Bruce Surtees
Lenny (1974)

Geoffrey Unsworth
Murder on the Orient Express (1974)

Best Costume Design

⚑ Theoni V. Aldredge ⚑
The Great Gatsby (1974)

John Furness
Daisy Miller (1974)

Theadora Van Runkle
The Godfather: Part II (1974)

Anthea Sylbert
Chinatown (1974)

Tony Walton
Murder on the Orient Express (1974)

Best Directing

⚐ Francis Ford Coppola ⚐
The Godfather: Part II (1974)

John Cassavetes
A Woman Under the Influence (1974)

Bob Fosse
Lenny (1974)

Roman Polanski
Chinatown (1974)

François Truffaut
La nuit américaine (eng. Day for Night) (1973)

Best Documentary, Feature

⚐ Peter Davis, Bert Schneider (Producers) ⚐
Hearts and Minds (1974)

David Bergman, Jacquot Ehrlich, Haim Gouri (Producers)
Ha-Makah Hashmonim V'Echad (eng. The 81st Blow) (1974)

Judy Collins, Jill Godmilow (Producers)
Antonia: A Portrait of the Woman (1974)

Eugene S. Jones, Natalie R. Jones (Producers)
The Wild and the Brave (1974)

Herbert Kline (Producer)
The Challenge... A Tribute to Modern Art (1975)

Best Documentary, Short Subject

⚐ Robin Lehman (Producer) ⚐
Don't (1975)

Jon Boorstin (Producer)
Exploratorium (1974)

Lesley Foster, Dewitt Jones (Producers)
John Muir's High Sierra (1974)

Ronald S. Kass, Mervyn Lloyd (Producers)
Naked Yoga (1974)

Francis Thompson (Producer)
City Out of Wilderness (1974)

Best Film Editing

⚐ Carl Kress, Harold F. Kress ⚐
The Towering Inferno (1974)

Danford B. Greene, John C. Howard
Blazing Saddles (1974)

Michael Luciano
The Longest Yard (1974)

Sam O'Steen
Chinatown (1974)

Dorothy Spencer
Earthquake (1974)

Special Achievement Award, Visual Effects

⚐ Frank Brendel, Glen Robinson, Albert Whitlock ⚐
Earthquake (1974)

Best Foreign Language Film
ⵊ Italy ⵊ
Amarcord (1973)

Argentina
La tregua (eng. The Truce) (1974)

France
Lacombe, Lucien (1974)

Hungary
Macskajáték (eng. Cat's Play) (1974)

Poland
Potop (eng. The Deluge) (1974)

Jean Hersholt Humanitarian Award
ⵊ Arthur B. Krim ⵊ

Best Music, Original Dramatic Score
ⵊ **Carmine Coppola, Nino Rota** ⵊ
The Godfather: Part II (1974)

Richard Rodney Bennett
Murder on the Orient Express (1974)

Jerry Goldsmith
Chinatown (1974)

Alex North
Shanks (1974)

John Williams
The Towering Inferno (1974)

Best Music, Scoring: Original Song Score and Adaptation or Scoring: Adaptation
ⵊ **Nelson Riddle (Adaptation Score)** ⵊ
The Great Gatsby (1974)

**Alan Jay Lerner, Frederick Loewe (Song Score),
Douglas Gamley, Angela Morley (Adaptation Score)**
The Little Prince (1974)

**Paul Williams (Song Score),
George Aliceson Tipton, Paul Williams (Adaptation Score)**
Phantom of the Paradise (1974)

Best Music, Song
ⵊ **Joel Hirschhorn, Al Kasha (Music & Lyrics)
for the song "We May Never Love Like This Again"** ⵊ
The Towering Inferno (1974)

**Elmer Bernstein (Music), Don Black (Lyrics)
for the song "Wherever Love Takes Me"**
Gold (1974)

**Euel Box (Music), Betty E. Box (Lyrics)
for the song "Benji's Theme (I Feel Love)"**
Benji (1974)

Frederick Loewe (Music), Alan Jay Lerner (Lyrics) for the song "Little Prince"
The Little Prince (1974)

John Morris (Music), Mel Brooks (Lyrics) for the song "Blazing Saddles"
Blazing Saddles (1974)

Best Picture

**Francis Ford Coppola (Producer),
Gray Frederickson, Fred Roos (Co-Producers)**
The Godfather: Part II (1974)

Irwin Allen (Producer)
The Towering Inferno (1974)

Francis Ford Coppola (Producer), Fred Roos (Co-Producer)
The Conversation (1974)

Robert Evans (Producer)
Chinatown (1974)

Marvin Worth (Producer)
Lenny (1974)

Best Short Film, Animated

Bob Gardiner, Will Vinton (Producers)
Closed Mondays (1974)

Peter Foldes, René Jodoin (Producers)
Hunger (1974)

Faith Hubley, John Hubley (Producers)
Voyage to Next (1974)

Yvon Mallette, Robert Verrall (Producers)
The Family That Dwelt Apart (1973)

Wolfgang Reitherman (Producer)
Winnie the Pooh and Tigger Too (1974)

Best Short Film, Live Action

Paul Claudon, Edmond Séchan (Producers)
Les... borgnes sont rois (eng. One-Eyed Men Are Kings) (1974)

George V. Casey (Producer)
Planet Ocean (1974)

Claude Chagrin, Julian Chagrin (Producers)
The Concert (1974)

Dewitt Jones (Producer)
Climb (1974)

George Pastic, Andrew Welsh (Producers)
The Violin (1974)

Best Sound

Melvin M. Metcalfe Sr., Ronald Pierce
Earthquake (1974)

Gene S. Cantamessa, Richard Portman
Young Frankenstein (1974)

Bud Grenzbach, Larry Jost
Chinatown (1974)

Herman Lewis, Theodore Soderberg
The Towering Inferno (1974)

Walter Murch, Arthur Rochester
The Conversation (1974)

Best Writing, Original Screenplay

⚊ **Robert Towne** ⚊
Chinatown (1974)

Francis Ford Coppola
The Conversation (1974)

Robert Getchell
Alice Doesn't Live Here Anymore (1974)

Josh Greenfeld, Paul Mazursky
Harry and Tonto (1974)

Jean-Louis Richard, Suzanne Schiffman, François Truffaut
La nuit américaine (eng. Day for Night) (1973)

Best Writing, Screenplay Adapted from Other Material

⚊ **Francis Ford Coppola, Mario Puzo** ⚊
The Godfather: Part II (1974)

Julian Barry
Lenny (1974)

Mel Brooks, Gene Wilder
Young Frankenstein (1974)

Paul Dehn
Murder on the Orient Express (1974)

Mordecai Richler (Screenplay), Lionel Chetwynd (Adaptation)
The Apprenticeship of Duddy Kravitz (1974)

Honorary Award

⚊ **Howard Hawks** ⚊
A master American filmmaker whose creative efforts hold a distinguished place in world cinema.

⚊ **Jean Renoir** ⚊
A genius who, with grace, responsibility and enviable devotion through silent film, sound film, feature, documentary and television has won the world's admiration.

The 48ᵗʰ Academy Awards® - March 29, 1976

Hosts: Goldie Hawn, Gene Kelly, Walter Matthau, George Segal, Robert Shaw
Venue: Dorothy Chandler Pavilion
Honoring movies released in 1975

Best Actor

⚊ **Jack Nicholson** ⚊
One Flew Over the Cuckoo's Nest (1975) role "Randle Patrick "Mac" McMurphy"

Walter Matthau
The Sunshine Boys (1975) role "Willy Clark"

Al Pacino
Dog Day Afternoon (1975) role "Sonny Wortzik"

Maximilian Schell
The Man in the Glass Booth (1975) role "Arthur Goldman"

James Whitmore
Give 'em Hell, Harry! (1975) role "Harry S. Truman"

Irving G. Thalberg Memorial Award

⚊ **Mervyn LeRoy** ⚊

Best Actor in a Supporting Role
⚱ George Burns ⚱
The Sunshine Boys (1975) role "Al Lewis"
Brad Dourif
One Flew Over the Cuckoo's Nest (1975) role "Billy Bibbit"
Burgess Meredith
The Day of the Locust (1975) role "Harry Greener"
Chris Sarandon
Dog Day Afternoon (1975) role "Leon Shermer"
Jack Warden
Shampoo (1975) role "Lester Karpf"

Best Actress
⚱ Louise Fletcher ⚱
One Flew Over the Cuckoo's Nest (1975) role "Nurse Mildred Ratched"
Isabelle Adjani
L'histoire d'Adèle H. (eng. The Story of Adele H) (1975) role "Adèle Hugo / Adèle Lewry"
Ann-Margret
Tommy (1975) role "Nora Walker"
Glenda Jackson
Hedda (1975) role "Hedda Gabler"
Carol Kane
Hester Street (1975) role "Gitl"

Best Actress in a Supporting Role
⚱ Lee Grant ⚱
Shampoo (1975) role "Felicia Karpf"
Ronee Blakley
Nashville (1975) role "Barbara Jean"
Sylvia Miles
Farewell, My Lovely (1975) role "Jessie Halstead Florian"
Lily Tomlin
Nashville (1975) role "Linnea Reese"
Brenda Vaccaro
Once Is Not Enough (1975) role "Linda Riggs"

Best Art Direction
⚱ Ken Adam, Roy Walker (Art Direction), Vernon Dixon (Set Decoration) ⚱
Barry Lyndon (1975)
Albert Brenner (Art Direction), Marvin March (Set Decoration)
The Sunshine Boys (1975)
W. Stewart Campbell, Richard Sylbert (Art Direction), George Gaines (Set Decoration)
Shampoo (1975)
Edward C. Carfagno (Art Direction), Frank R. McKelvy (Set Decoration)
The Hindenburg (1975)
Tony Inglis, Alexander Trauner (Art Direction), Peter James (Set Decoration)
The Man Who Would Be King (1975)

Best Special Achievement Award, Sound Effects
⚱ Peter Berkos ⚱
The Hindenburg (1975)

Best Special Achievement Award, Visual Effects
⚐ **Glen Robinson, Albert Whitlock** ⚐
The Hindenburg (1975)

Best Cinematography
⚐ **John Alcott** ⚐
Barry Lyndon (1975)

Bill Butler, Haskell Wexler
One Flew Over the Cuckoo's Nest (1975)

Conrad L. Hall
The Day of the Locust (1975)

James Wong Howe
Funny Lady (1975)

Robert Surtees
The Hindenburg (1975)

Best Costume Design
⚐ **Milena Canonero, Ulla-Britt Söderlund** ⚐
Barry Lyndon (1975)

Ray Aghayan, Bob Mackie
Funny Lady (1975)

Yvonne Blake, Ron Talsky
The Four Musketeers: Milady's Revenge (1974)

Karin Erskine, Henny Noremark
Trollflöjten (eng. The Magic Flute) (1975)

Edith Head
The Man Who Would Be King (1975)

Best Directing
⚐ **Milos Forman** ⚐
One Flew Over the Cuckoo's Nest (1975)

Robert Altman
Nashville (1975)

Federico Fellini
Amarcord (1973)

Stanley Kubrick
Barry Lyndon (1975)

Sidney Lumet
Dog Day Afternoon (1975)

Best Documentary, Feature
⚐ **F. R. Crawley, James Hager, Dale Hartleben (Producers)** ⚐
The Man Who Skied Down Everest (1975)

Keith F. Critchlow, Walter F. Parkes (Producers)
The California Reich (1975)

Shirley MacLaine (Producer)
The Other Half of the Sky: A China Memoir (1975)

Glen Pearcy (Producer)
Fighting for Our Lives (1975)

Irwin Rosten (Producer)
The Incredible Machine (1975)

Best Documentary, Short Subject
⚐ Robin Lehman, Claire Wilbur (Producers) ⚐
The End of the Game (1976)
Manfred Baier (Producer)
Millions of Years Ahead of Man (1975)
George V. Casey (Producer)
Probes in Space (1975)
Jon Else, Steven Kovacs, Kristine Samuelson (Producers)
Arthur and Lillie (1975)
Barrie Howells, Michael J. F. Scott (Producers)
Whistling Smith (1975)

Best Film Editing
⚐ Verna Fields ⚐
Jaws (1975)
Dede Allen
Dog Day Afternoon (1975)
Richard Chew, Sheldon Kahn, Lynzee Klingman
One Flew Over the Cuckoo's Nest (1975)
Don Guidice, Fredric Steinkamp
Three Days of the Condor (1975)
Russell Lloyd
The Man Who Would Be King (1975)

Jean Hersholt Humanitarian Award
⚐ Dr. Jules C. Stein ⚐

Honorary Award
⚐ Mary Pickford ⚐
In recognition of her unique contributions to the film industry and the development of film as an artistic medium.

Best Foreign Language Film
⚐ Union of Soviet Socialist Republics ⚐
Dersu Uzala (1975)
Italy
Profumo di donna (eng. Scent of a Woman) (1974)
Japan
Sandakan hachibanshokan bohkyo (eng. Sandakan no. 8) (1974)
Mexico
Actas de Marusia (eng. Letters from Marusia) (1975)
Poland
Ziemia obiecana (eng. The Promised Land) (1975)

Best Music, Scoring: Original Song Score and Adaptation or Scoring: Adaptation
⚐ Leonard Rosenman (Adaptation Score) ⚐
Barry Lyndon (1975)
Peter Matz (Adaptation Score)
Funny Lady (1975)
Peter Townshend (Adaptation Score)
Tommy (1975)

Best Music, Original Score
⚊ John Williams ⚊
Jaws (1975)
Gerald Fried
Birds Do It, Bees Do It (1974)
Jerry Goldsmith
The Wind and the Lion (1975)
Jack Nitzsche
One Flew Over the Cuckoo's Nest (1975)
Alex North
Bite the Bullet (1975)

Best Music, Original Song
⚊ Keith Carradine (Music & Lyrics) for the song "I'm Easy" ⚊
Nashville (1975)
**George Barrie (Music), Sammy Cahn (Lyrics)
for the song "Now That We're In Love"**
Whiffs (1975)
Fred Ebb, John Kander (Music & Lyrics) for the song "How Lucky Can You Get"
Funny Lady (1975)
Charles Fox (Music), Norman Gimbel (Lyrics) for the song "Richard's Window"
The Other Side of the Mountain (1975)
**Michael Masser (Music), Gerry Goffin (Lyrics)
for the song "Theme from Mahogany (Do You Know Where You're Going To)"**
Mahogany (1975)

Best Sound
⚊ John R. Carter, Roger Heman Jr., Robert L. Hoyt, Earl Madery ⚊
Jaws (1975)
John A. Bolger Jr., John L. Mack, Leonard Peterson, Don K. Sharpless
The Hindenburg (1975)
Roy Charman, William L. McCaughey, Aaron Rochin, Harry W. Tetrick
The Wind and the Lion (1975)
Les Fresholtz, Al Overton Jr., Arthur Piantadosi, Richard Tyler
Bite the Bullet (1975)
Don MacDougall, Richard Portman, Jack Solomon, Curly Thirlwell
Funny Lady (1975)

Best Picture
⚊ Michael Douglas, Saul Zaentz (Producers) ⚊
One Flew Over the Cuckoo's Nest (1975)
Robert Altman (Producer)
Nashville (1975)
Martin Bregman, Martin Elfand (Producers)
Dog Day Afternoon (1975)
David Brown, Richard D. Zanuck (Producers)
Jaws (1975)
Stanley Kubrick (Producer)
Barry Lyndon (1975)

Best Short Film, Animated
⚐ **Bob Godfrey (Producer)** ⚐
Great (Isambard Kingdom Brunel) (1975)
Marcell Jankovics (Producer)
Sisyphus (1974)
André Leduc, Bernard Longpré (Producers)
Monsieur Pointu (1976)
Robert Swarthe (Producer)
Kick Me (1975)

Best Short Film, Live Action
⚐ **Bert Salzman (Producer)** ⚐
Angel and Big Joe (1976)
Alan Beattie (Producer)
Doubletalk (1975)
Brian Lansburgh, Lawrence M. Lansburgh (Producers)
Dawn Flight (1976)
Louis Marcus (Producer)
Conquest of Light (1975)
Barry Spinello (Producer)
A Day in the Life of Bonnie Consolo (1975)

Best Writing, Original Screenplay
⚐ **Frank Pierson** ⚐
Dog Day Afternoon (1975)
Ted Allan
Lies My Father Told Me (1975)
Warren Beatty, Robert Towne
Shampoo (1975)
Federico Fellini, Tonino Guerra
Amarcord (1973)
Claude Lelouch, Pierre Uytterhoeven
Toute une vie (eng. And Now My Love) (1974)

Best Writing, Screenplay Adapted from Other Material
⚐ **Bo Goldman, Lawrence Hauben** ⚐
One Flew Over the Cuckoo's Nest (1975)
Gladys Hill, John Huston
The Man Who Would Be King (1975)
Stanley Kubrick
Barry Lyndon (1975)
Ruggero Maccari, Dino Risi
Profumo di donna (eng. Scent of a Woman) (1974)
Neil Simon
The Sunshine Boys (1975)

The 49ᵗʰ Academy Awards® - March 28, 1977
Hosts: Ellen Burstyn, Warren Beatty, Jane Fonda, Richard Pryor
Venue: Dorothy Chandler Pavilion
Honoring movies released in 1976

Irving G. Thalberg Memorial Award
⚑ Pandro S. Berman ⚑

Best Actor in a Leading Role
⚑ Peter Finch ⚑
(posthumous)
Network (1976) role "Howard Beale"
Giancarlo Giannini
Pasqualino Settebellezze (eng. Seven Beauties) (1975) role "Pasqualino Frafuso"
William Holden
Network (1976) role "Max Schumacher"
Robert De Niro
Taxi Driver (1976) role "Travis Bickle"
Sylvester Stallone
Rocky (1976) role "Rocky Balboa"

Best Actor in a Supporting Role
⚑ Jason Robards ⚑
All the President's Men (1976) role "Ben Bradlee"
Ned Beatty
Network (1976) role "Arthur Jensen"
Burgess Meredith
Rocky (1976) role ""Mickey" Goldmill"
Laurence Olivier
Marathon Man (1976) role "Dr. Christian Szell"
Burt Young
Rocky (1976) role "Paulie Pennino"

Best Actress in a Leading Role
⚑ Faye Dunaway ⚑
Network (1976) role "Diana Christensen"
Marie-Christine Barrault
Cousin cousine (1975) role "Marthe"
Talia Shire
Rocky (1976) role "Adrian Pennino"
Sissy Spacek
Carrie (1976) role "Carrie White"
Liv Ullmann
Ansikte mot ansikte (eng. Face to Face) (1976) role "Jenny Isaksson"

Best Actress in a Supporting Role
⚑ Beatrice Straight ⚑
Network (1976) role "Louise Schumacher"
Jane Alexander
All the President's Men (1976) role "Judy Graham Hoback"
Jodie Foster
Taxi Driver (1976) role "Iris "Easy" Steensma"
Lee Grant
Voyage of the Damned (1976) role "Lillian Rosen"
Piper Laurie
Carrie (1976) role "Margaret White"

Best Art Direction

⚐ **George Jenkins (Art Direction), George Gaines (Set Decoration)** ⚐
All the President's Men (1976)

Robert F. Boyle (Art Direction), Arthur Jeph Parker (Set Decoration)
The Shootist (1976)

Gene Callahan, Jack T. Collis (Art Direction),
Jerry Wunderlich (Set Decoration)
The Last Tycoon (1976)

Dale Hennesy (Art Direction), Robert de Vestel (Set Decoration)
Logan's Run (1976)

Norman Reynolds, Elliot Scott (Art Direction), Peter Howitt (Set Decoration)
The Incredible Sarah (1976)

Best Cinematography

⚐ **Haskell Wexler** ⚐
Bound for Glory (1976)

Richard H. Kline
King Kong (1976)

Ernest Laszlo
Logan's Run (1976)

Owen Roizman
Network (1976)

Robert Surtees
A Star Is Born (1976)

Best Music, Original Score

⚐ **Jerry Goldsmith** ⚐
The Omen (1976)

Jerry Fielding
The Outlaw Josey Wales (1976)

Bernard Herrmann
(posthumous)
Obsession (1976), Taxi Driver (1976)

Lalo Schifrin
Voyage of the Damned (1976)

Best Costume Design

⚐ **Danilo Donati** ⚐
Il Casanova di Federico Fellini (eng. Fellini's Casanova) (1976)

Alan Barrett
The Passover Plot (1976)

Anthony Mendleson
The Incredible Sarah (1976)

William Ware Theiss
Bound for Glory (1976)

Mary Wills
The Seven-Per-Cent Solution (1976)

Special Achievement Award, Visual Effects

⚐ **L. B. Abbott, Glen Robinson, Matthew Yuricich** ⚐
Logan's Run (1976)

Carlo Rambaldi, Glen Robinson, Frank Van der Veer
King Kong (1976)

Best Directing

⚐ John G. Avildsen ⚐
Rocky (1976)

Ingmar Bergman
Ansikte mot ansikte (eng. Face to Face) (1976)

Sidney Lumet
Network (1976)

Alan J. Pakula
All the President's Men (1976)

Lina Wertmuller
Pasqualino Settebellezze (eng. Seven Beauties) (1975)

Best Documentary, Feature

⚐ Barbara Kopple (Producer) ⚐
Harlan County U.S.A. (1976)

Donald Brittain, Robert A. Duncan (Producers)
Volcano: An Inquiry Into the Life and Death of Malcolm Lowry (1976)

Michael Firth (Producer)
Off the Edge (1976)

James C. Gutman, David Helpern Jr. (Producers)
Hollywood on Trial (1976)

Anthony Howarth, David Koff (Producers)
People of the Wind (1976)

Best Documentary, Short Subject

⚐ Lynne Littman (Producer) ⚐
Number Our Days (1976)

John Armstrong (Producer)
The End of the Road (1976)

Sparky Greene (Producer)
American Shoeshine (1976)

Tony Ianzelo, Andy Thomson (Producers)
Blackwood (1976)

Lester Novros (Producer)
Universe (1976)

Best Sound

⚐ Dick Alexander, Les Fresholtz, Arthur Piantadosi, James E. Webb ⚐
All the President's Men (1976)

**Bud Alper, Lyle J. Burbridge, William L. McCaughey,
Harry Warren Tetrick**
(Harry Warren Tetrick - posthumous)
Rocky (1976)

**Harold M. Etherington, Donald O. Mitchell, Richard Tyler,
Douglas O. Williams**
Silver Streak (1976)

Robert Glass, Robert Knudson, Tom Overton, Dan Wallin
A Star Is Born (1976)

**William L. McCaughey, Aaron Rochin, Jack Solomon,
Harry Warren Tetrick**
(Harry Warren Tetrick - posthumous)
King Kong (1976)

Best Music, Original Song
Barbra Streisand (Music), Paul Williams (Lyrics)
for the song "Evergreen (Love Theme from A Star Is Born)"
A Star Is Born (1976)

Bill Conti (Music), Carol Connors, Ayn Robbins (Lyrics)
for the song "Gonna Fly Now"
Rocky (1976)

Sammy Fain (Music), Paul Francis Webster (Lyrics)
for the song "A World that Never Was"
Half a House (1975)

Jerry Goldsmith, for the song "Ave Satani"
The Omen (1976)

Henry Mancini (Music), Don Black (Lyrics) for the song "Come to Me"
The Pink Panther Strikes Again (1976)

Best Writing, Screenplay Written Directly for the Screen-based on factual material or on story material not previously published or produced
Paddy Chayefsky
Network (1976)

Walter Bernstein
The Front (1976)

Sylvester Stallone
Rocky (1976)

Jean-Charles Tacchella (Story and Screenplay),
Daniele Thompson (Adaptation)
Cousin cousine (1975)

Lina Wertmüller
Pasqualino Settebellezze (eng. Seven Beauties) (1975)

Best Writing, Screenplay-based on material from another medium
William Goldman
All the President's Men (1976)

David Butler, Steve Shagan
Voyage of the Damned (1976)

Federico Fellini, Bernardino Zapponi
Il Casanova di Federico Fellini (eng. Fellini's Casanova) (1976)

Robert Getchell
Bound for Glory (1976)

Nicholas Meyer
The Seven-Per-Cent Solution (1976)

Best Film Editing
Richard Halsey, Scott Conrad
Rocky (1976)

Walter Hannemann, Eve Newman
Two-Minute Warning (1976)

Alan Heim
Network (1976)

Pembroke J. Herring, Robert C. Jones
Bound for Glory (1976)

Robert L. Wolfe
All the President's Men (1976)

Best Foreign Language Film
⚱ Ivory Coast ⚱
La victoire en chantant (eng. Black and White in Color) (1976)

France
Cousin cousine (1975)

German Democratic Republic
Jakob, der Lügner (eng. Jacob the Liar) (1974)

Italy
Pasqualino Settebellezze (eng. Seven Beauties) (1975)

Poland
Noce i dnie (eng. Nights and Days) (1975)

Best Picture
⚱ Robert Chartoff, Irwin Winkler (Producers) ⚱
Rocky (1976)

Robert F. Blumofe, Harold Leventhal (Producers)
Bound for Glory (1976)

Walter Coblenz (Producer)
All the President's Men (1976)

Howard Gottfried (Producer)
Network (1976)

Julia Phillips, Michael Phillips (Producers)
Taxi Driver (1976)

Best Short Film, Animated
⚱ Suzanne Baker (Producer) ⚱
Leisure (1976)

Guy Glover, Caroline Leaf (Producers)
The Street (1976)

Manfredo Manfredi (Producer)
Dedalo (eng. Labyrinth) (1976)

Best Short Film, Live Action
⚱ Andre R. Guttfreund, Peter Werner (Producers) ⚱
In the Region of Ice (1976)

Dyan Cannon, Vince Cannon (Producers)
Number One (1976)

Claude Chagrin, Julian Chagrin (Producers)
The Morning Spider (1976)

Robin Lehman, Claire Wilbur (Producers)
Nightlife (1976)

Marjorie Anne Short (Producer)
Kudzu (1977)

Best Music, Original Song Score and Its Adaptation or Adaptation Score
⚱ Leonard Rosenman (Adaptation Score) ⚱
Bound for Glory (1976)

Roger Kellaway (Adaptation Score)
A Star Is Born (1976)

Paul Williams (Song Score and Adaptation Score)
Bugsy Malone (1976)

49th Ceremony 6/6

The 50ᵗʰ Academy Awards® – April 3, 1978

Host: Bob Hope
Venue: Dorothy Chandler Pavilion
Honoring movies released in 1977

Honorary Award
↓ Margaret Booth ↓

For her exceptional contribution to the art of film editing in the motion picture industry.

Jean Hersholt Humanitarian Award
↓ Charlton Heston ↓

Irving G. Thalberg Memorial Award
↓ Walter Mirisch ↓

Best Actor in a Leading Role
↓ Richard Dreyfuss ↓
The Goodbye Girl (1977) role "Elliot Garfield"

Woody Allen
Annie Hall (1977) role "Alvy "Max" Singer"

Richard Burton
Equus (1977) role "Doctor Martin Dysart"

Marcello Mastroianni
Una giornata particolare (eng. A Special Day) (1977) role "Gabriele"

John Travolta
Saturday Night Fever (1977) role "Anthony "Tony" Manero"

Best Actor in a Supporting Role
↓ Jason Robards ↓
Julia (1977) role "Dashiell Hammett"

Mikhail Baryshnikov
The Turning Point (1977) role "Yuri Kopeikine"

Peter Firth
Equus (1977) role "Alan Strang"

Alec Guinness
Star Wars: Episode IV - A New Hope (1977) role "Ben Obi-Wan Kenobi"

Maximilian Schell
Julia (1977) role "Johann"

Best Actress in a Leading Role
↓ Diane Keaton ↓
Annie Hall (1977) role "Annie Hall"

Anne Bancroft
The Turning Point (1977) role "Emma Jacklin"

Jane Fonda
Julia (1977) role "Lillian Hellman"

Shirley MacLaine
The Turning Point (1977) role "DeeDee Rodgers"

Marsha Mason
The Goodbye Girl (1977) role "Paula McFadden"

Best Actress in a Supporting Role

⚜ Vanessa Redgrave ⚜
Julia (1977) role "Julia"

Leslie Browne
The Turning Point (1977) role "Emilia Rodgers"

Quinn Cummings
The Goodbye Girl (1977) role "Lucy McFadden"

Melinda Dillon
Close Encounters of the Third Kind (1977) role "Jillian Guiler"

Tuesday Weld
Looking for Mr. Goodbar (1977) role "Katherine Dunn"

Best Art Direction

⚜ John Barry, Leslie Dilley, Norman Reynolds (Art Direction), ⚜
Roger Christian (Set Decoration)
Star Wars: Episode IV - A New Hope (1977)

Ken Adam, Peter Lamont (Art Direction), Hugh Scaife (Set Decoration)
The Spy Who Loved Me (1977)

Joe Alves, Daniel A. Lomino (Art Direction), Phil Abramson (Set Decoration)
Close Encounters of the Third Kind (1977)

Albert Brenner (Art Direction), Marvin March (Set Decoration)
The Turning Point (1977)

George C. Webb (Art Direction), Mickey S. Michaels (Set Decoration)
Airport '77 (1977)

Best Music, Original Song

⚜ Joseph Brooks (Music & Lyrics) for the song "You Light Up My Life" ⚜
You Light Up My Life (1977)

Sammy Fain (Music), Carol Connors, Ayn Robbins (Lyrics)
for the song "Someone's Waiting For You"
The Rescuers (1977)

Marvin Hamlisch (Music), Carole Bayer Sager (Lyrics)
for the song "Nobody Does It Better"
The Spy Who Loved Me (1977)

Joel Hirschhorn, Al Kasha (Music & Lyrics) for the song "Candle on the Water"
Pete's Dragon (1977)

Richard M. Sherman, Robert B. Sherman (Music & Lyrics) for the song
"The Slipper and the Rose Waltz (He Danced with Me/She Danced with Me)"
The Slipper and the Rose: The Story of Cinderella (1976)

Best Cinematography

⚜ Vilmos Zsigmond ⚜
Close Encounters of the Third Kind (1977)

William A. Fraker
Looking for Mr. Goodbar (1977)

Fred J. Koenekamp
Islands in the Stream (1977)

Douglas Slocombe
Julia (1977)

Robert Surtees
The Turning Point (1977)

Best Costume Design
⟂ John Mollo ⟂
Star Wars: Episode IV - A New Hope (1977)
Edith Head, Burton Miller
Airport '77 (1977)
Florence Klotz
A Little Night Music (1977)
Irene Sharaff
The Other Side of Midnight (1977)
Anthea Sylbert
Julia (1977)

Best Visual Effects
**⟂ Robert Blalack, John Dykstra, Richard Edlund, ⟂
Grant McCune, John Stears**
Star Wars: Episode IV - A New Hope (1977)
**Roy Arbogast, Gregory Jein, Douglas Trumbull, Matthew Yuricich,
Richard Yuricich**
Close Encounters of the Third Kind (1977)

Special Achievement Award
⟂ Benjamin Burtt Jr. ⟂
(For sound effects and for the creation of the alien, creature and robot voices)
Star Wars: Episode IV - A New Hope (1977)
Frank E. Warner
(For sound effects editing)
Close Encounters of the Third Kind (1977)

Best Directing
⟂ Woody Allen ⟂
Annie Hall (1977)
George Lucas
Star Wars: Episode IV - A New Hope (1977)
Herbert Ross
The Turning Point (1977)
Steven Spielberg
Close Encounters of the Third Kind (1977)
Fred Zinnemann
Julia (1977)

Best Documentary, Feature
⟂ John Korty, Warren L. Lockhart, Dan McCann (Producers) ⟂
Who Are the DeBolts? And Where Did They Get Nineteen Kids? (1977)
Bill Brind, Tony Ianzelo, Torben Schioler (Producers)
High Grass Circus (1977)
Robert Dornhelm, Earle Mack (Producers)
The Children of Theatre Street (1977)
James Klein, Miles Mogulescu, Julia Reichert (Producers)
Union Maids (1976)
Harry Rasky (Producer)
Homage to Chagall: The Colours of Love (1977)

Best Documentary, Short Subject
⚐ John C. Joseph, Jan Stussy (Producers) ⚐
Gravity Is My Enemy (1977)
Moctesuma Esparza (Producer)
Agueda Martinez: Our People, Our Country (1977)
Douglas Gordon (Producer)
The Shetland Experience (1977)
James R. Messenger,
Paul N. Raimondi (Producers)
Of Time, Tombs and Treasures (1977)
DeWitt L. Sage Jr., Helen Whitney (Producers)
First Edition (1977)

Best Film Editing
⚐ Richard Chew, Paul Hirsch, Marcia Lucas ⚐
Star Wars: Episode IV - A New Hope (1977)
Marcel Durham, Walter Murch
Julia (1977)
Walter Hannemann, Angelo Ross
Smokey and the Bandit (1977)
Michael Kahn
Close Encounters of the Third Kind (1977)
William Reynolds
The Turning Point (1977)

Best Foreign Language Film
⚐ France ⚐
La vie devant soi (eng. Madame Rosa) (1977)
Greece
Ifigeneia (eng. Iphigenia) (1977)
Israel
Mivtsa Yonatan (eng. Operation Thunderbolt) (1977)
Italy
Una giornata particolare (eng. A Special Day) (1977)
Spain
Cet obscur objet du désir (eng. That Obscure Object of Desire) (1977)

Best Writing, Screenplay Written Directly for the Screen-based on factual material or on story material not previously published or produced
⚐ Woody Allen, Marshall Brickman ⚐
Annie Hall (1977)
Robert Benton
The Late Show (1977)
Arthur Laurents
The Turning Point (1977)
George Lucas
Star Wars: Episode IV - A New Hope (1977)
Neil Simon
The Goodbye Girl (1977)

Best Writing, Screenplay-based on material from another medium

↓ **Alvin Sargent** ↓
Julia (1977)

Luis Buñuel, Jean-Claude Carrière
Cet obscur objet du désir (eng. That Obscure Object of Desire) (1977)

Lewis John Carlino, Gavin Lambert
I Never Promised You a Rose Garden (1977)

Larry Gelbart
Oh, God! (1977)

Peter Shaffer
Equus (1977)

Best Music, Original Score

↓ **John Williams** ↓
Star Wars: Episode IV - A New Hope (1977)

Georges Delerue
Julia (1977)

Marvin Hamlisch
The Spy Who Loved Me (1977)

Maurice Jarre
Mohammad: Messenger of God (1976)

John Williams
Close Encounters of the Third Kind (1977)

Best Picture

↓ **Charles H. Joffe (Producer)** ↓
Annie Hall (1977)

Gary Kurtz (Producer)
Star Wars: Episode IV - A New Hope (1977)

Arthur Laurents, Herbert Ross (Producers)
The Turning Point (1977)

Richard N. Roth (Producer)
Julia (1977)

Ray Stark (Producer)
The Goodbye Girl (1977)

Best Music, Original Song Score and Its Adaptation or Adaptation Score

↓ **Jonathan Tunick (Adaptation Score)** ↓
A Little Night Music (1977)

Joel Hirschhorn, Al Kasha (Song Score), Irwin Kostal (Adaptation Score)
Pete's Dragon (1977)

Richard M. Sherman, Robert B. Sherman (Song Score), Angela Morley (Adaptation Score)
The Slipper and the Rose: The Story of Cinderella (1976)

Best Short Film, Animated
⚐ Co Hoedeman (Producer) ⚐
Le château de sable (eng. The Sand Castle) (1977)
Robert Grossman, James Picker, Craig Whitaker (Producers)
Jimmy the C (1977)
Faith Hubley, John Hubley, Garry Trudeau (Producers)
(John Hubley - posthumous)
A Doonesbury Special (1977)
Ishu Patel (Producer)
The Bead Game (1977)

Best Short Film, Live Action
⚐ Beverly Shaffer, Yuki Yoshida (Producers) ⚐
I'll Find a Way (1977)
Saul Bass (Producer)
Notes on the Popular Arts (1978)
Jerry Butts (Producer)
Floating Free (1978)
Philip Dauber (Producer)
Spaceborne (1977)
William E. McEuen (Producer)
The Absent-Minded Waiter (1977)

Best Sound
⚐ Derek Ball, Don MacDougall, Bob Minkler, Ray West ⚐
Star Wars: Episode IV - A New Hope (1977)
Dick Alexander, Tom Beckert, Walter Goss, Robin Gregory
The Deep (1977)
Gene S. Cantamessa, Robert J. Glass, Robert Knudson, Don MacDougall
Close Encounters of the Third Kind (1977)
Jean-Louis Ducarme, Robert J. Glass, Robert Knudson, Richard Tyler
Sorcerer (1977)
Jerry Jost, Theodore Soderberg, Paul Wells, Douglas O. Williams
The Turning Point (1977)

The 51st Academy Awards® - April 9, 1979
Host: Johnny Carson
Venue: Dorothy Chandler Pavilion
Honoring movies released in 1978

Best Actor in a Leading Role
⚐ Jon Voight ⚐
Coming Home (1978) role "Luke Martin"
Warren Beatty
Heaven Can Wait (1978) role "Joe Pendleton/Leo Farnsworth/Tom Jarrett"
Gary Busey
The Buddy Holly Story (1978) role "Buddy Holly"
Robert De Niro
The Deer Hunter (1978) role "Sergeant Michael "Mike" Vronsky"
Laurence Olivier
The Boys from Brazil (1978) role "Ezra Lieberman"

Best Actor in a Supporting Role
⚐ Christopher Walken ⚐
The Deer Hunter (1978) role "Corporal Nikanor "Nick" Chevotarevich"
Bruce Dern
Coming Home (1978) role "Captain Bob Hyde"
Richard Farnsworth
Comes a Horseman (1978) role "Dodger"
John Hurt
Midnight Express (1978) role "Max"
Jack Warden
Heaven Can Wait (1978) role "Max Corkle"

Best Actress in a Leading Role
⚐ Jane Fonda ⚐
Coming Home (1978) role "Sally Hyde"
Ingrid Bergman
Höstsonaten (eng. Autumn Sonata) (1978) role "Charlotte Andergast"
Ellen Burstyn
Same Time, Next Year (1978) role "Doris"
Jill Clayburgh
An Unmarried Woman (1978) role "Erica Benton"
Geraldine Page
Interiors (1978) role "Eve"

Best Actress in a Supporting Role
⚐ Maggie Smith ⚐
California Suite (1978) role "Diana Barrie"
Dyan Cannon
Heaven Can Wait (1978) role "Julia Farnsworth"
Penelope Milford
Coming Home (1978) role "Vi Munson"
Maureen Stapleton
Interiors (1978) role "Pearl"
Meryl Streep
The Deer Hunter (1978) role "Linda"

Jean Hersholt Humanitarian Award
⚐ Leo Jaffe ⚐

Best Art Direction
⚐ Edwin O'Donovan, Paul Sylbert (Art Direction), George Gaines (Set Decoration) ⚐
Heaven Can Wait (1978)
Mel Bourne (Art Direction), Daniel Robert (Set Decoration)
Interiors (1978)
Albert Brenner(Art Direction), Marvin March (Set Decoration)
California Suite (1978)
Angelo P. Graham, Dean Tavoularis (Art Direction), Bruce Kay, George R. Nelson (Set Decoration)
The Brink's Job (1978)
Philip Rosenberg, Tony Walton (Art Direction), Robert Drumheller, Edward Stewart (Set Decoration)
The Wiz (1978)

Best Cinematography
⚲ Néstor Almendros ⚲
Days of Heaven (1978)
William A. Fraker
Heaven Can Wait (1978)
Oswald Morris
The Wiz (1978)
Robert Surtees
Same Time, Next Year (1978)
Vilmos Zsigmond
The Deer Hunter (1978)

Best Short Film, Animated
⚲ Eunice Macaulay, John Weldon (Producers) ⚲
Special Delivery (1978)
Nico Crama (Producer)
Oh My Darling ... (1978)
Will Vinton (Producer)
Rip Van Winkle (1978)

Best Short Film, Live Action
⚲ Taylor Hackford (Producer) ⚲
Teenage Father (1978)
Jim Belcher, Fern Field (Producers)
A Different Approach (1978)
Seth Pinsker (Producer)
Strange Fruit (1979)
Andrew Sugerman (Producer)
Mandy's Grandmother (1979)

Best Costume Design
⚲ Anthony Powell ⚲
Death on the Nile (1978)
Renié Conley
Caravans (1978)
Patricia Norris
Days of Heaven (1978)
Tony Walton
The Wiz (1978)
Paul Zastupnevich
The Swarm (1978)

Best Directing
⚲ Michael Cimino ⚲
The Deer Hunter (1978)
Woody Allen
Interiors (1978)
Hal Ashby
Coming Home (1978)
Warren Beatty, Buck Henry
Heaven Can Wait (1978)
Alan Parker
Midnight Express (1978)

Best Documentary, Feature

⚊ **Arnold Shapiro (Producer)** ⚊
Scared Straight! (1978)

Anne Bohlen, Lyn Goldfarb, Lorraine Gray (Producers)
With Babies and Banners: Story of the Women's Emergency Brigade (1979)

Jean-Pierre Dutilleux, Michel Gast, Barry Williams (Producers)
Raoni (1978)

Albert Lamorisse (Producer)
(posthumous)
Le vent des amoureux (eng. The Lovers' Wind) (1978)

Alan Root (Producer)
Mysterious Castles of Clay (1978)

Best Documentary, Short Subject

⚊ **Ben Shedd, Jacqueline Phillips Shedd (Producers)** ⚊
The Flight of the Gossamer Condor (1978)

Jerry Aronson (Producer)
The Divided Trail: A Native American Odyssey (1977)

August Cinquegrana (Producer)
Goodnight Miss Ann (1978)

K.K. Kapil (Producer)
An Encounter with Faces (1978)

J. Gary Mitchell (Producer)
Squires of San Quentin (1978)

Best Film Editing

⚊ **Peter Zinner** ⚊
The Deer Hunter (1978)

Stuart Baird
Superman (1978)

Gerry Hambling
Midnight Express (1978)

Robert E. Swink
The Boys from Brazil (1978)

Don Zimmerman
Coming Home (1978)

Best Foreign Language Film

⚊ **France** ⚊
Préparez vos mouchoirs (eng. Get Out Your Handkerchiefs) (1978)

German Federal Republic
Die gläserne Zelle (eng. The Glass Cell) (1978)

Hungary
Magyarok (eng. Hungarians) (1978)

Italy
I nuovi mostri (eng. Viva Italia!) (1977)

Union of Soviet Socialist Republics
Belyy Bim Chernoe ukho (eng. White Bim Black Ear) (1977)

Special Achievement Award, Visual Effects

⚊ **Les Bowie, Colin Chilvers, Denys N. Coop, Roy Field, Derek Meddings, Zoran Perisic** ⚊
Superman (1978)

Best Music, Original Song

⚊ **Paul Jabara (Music & Lyrics) for the song "Last Dance"** ⚊
Thank God It's Friday (1978)

John Farrar (Music & Lyrics) for the song "Hopelessly Devoted to You"
Grease (1978)

**Charles Fox (Music), Norman Gimbel (Lyrics)
for the song "Ready to Take a Chance Again"**
Foul Play (1978)

**Marvin Hamlisch (Music), Alan Bergman, Marilyn Bergman (Lyrics)
for the song "The Last Time I Felt Like This"**
Same Time, Next Year (1978)

**Richard M. Sherman, Robert B. Sherman (Music & Lyrics)
for the song "When You're Loved"**
The Magic of Lassie (1978)

Best Sound

⚊ **C. Darin Knight, William L. McCaughey, Richard Portman,
Aaron Rochin** ⚊
The Deer Hunter (1978)

Willie D. Burton , Joel Fein, Tex Rudloff, Curly Thirlwell
The Buddy Holly Story (1978)

**Roy Charman, Graham V. Hartstone, Gordon K. McCallum,
Nicolas Le Messurier**
Superman (1978)

Robert J. Glass, Robert Knudson, Don MacDougall, Jack Solomon
Hooper (1978)

Robert W. Glass Jr., John T. Reitz, Barry Thomas, John K. Wilkinson
Days of Heaven (1978)

Best Picture

⚊ **Michael Cimino, Michael Deeley, John Peverall,
Barry Spikings (Producers)** ⚊
The Deer Hunter (1978)

Warren Beatty (Producer)
Heaven Can Wait (1978)

Jerome Hellman (Producer)
Coming Home (1978)

Alan Marshall, David Puttnam (Producers)
Midnight Express (1978)

Paul Mazursky, Tony Ray (Producers)
An Unmarried Woman (1978)

Best Music, Original Score

⚊ **Giorgio Moroder** ⚊
Midnight Express (1978)

Jerry Goldsmith
The Boys from Brazil (1978)

Dave Grusin
Heaven Can Wait (1978)

Ennio Morricone
Days of Heaven (1978)

John Williams
Superman (1978)

Best Writing, Screenplay Based on Material from Another Medium

⬇ Oliver Stone ⬇
Midnight Express (1978)

Warren Beatty, Elaine May
Heaven Can Wait (1978)

Walter Newman
Bloodbrothers (1978)

Neil Simon
California Suite (1978)

Bernard Slade
Same Time, Next Year (1978)

Best Writing, Screenplay Written Directly for the Screen

⬇ Nancy Dowd (Story), Robert C. Jones, Waldo Salt (Screenplay) ⬇
Coming Home (1978)

Woody Allen
Interiors (1978)

Ingmar Bergman
Höstsonaten (eng. Autumn Sonata) (1978)

Michael Cimino, Louis Garfinkle, Quinn K. Redeker, Deric Washburn (Story), Deric Washburn (Screenplay)
The Deer Hunter (1978)

Paul Mazursky
An Unmarried Woman (1978)

Best Music, Adaptation Score

⬇ Joe Renzetti ⬇
The Buddy Holly Story (1978)

Quincy Jones
The Wiz (1978)

Jerry Wexler
Pretty Baby (1978)

Honorary Award

⬇ Walter Lantz ⬇
For bringing joy and laughter to every part of the world through his unique animated motion pictures.

⬇ Museum of Modern Art Department of Film ⬇
For the contribution it has made to the public's perception of movies as an art form.

⬇ Laurence Olivier ⬇
For the full body of his work, for the unique achievements of his entire career and his lifetime of contribution to the art of film.

⬇ King Vidor ⬇
For his incomparable achievements as a cinematic creator and innovator.

The 52ⁿᵈ Academy Awards® - April 14, 1980

Host: Johnny Carson

Venue: Dorothy Chandler Pavilion

Honoring movies released in 1979

Jean Hersholt Humanitarian Award
⚜ Robert Benjamin ⚜
(posthumous)

Best Actor in a Leading Role
⚜ Dustin Hoffman ⚜
Kramer vs. Kramer (1979) role "Ted Kramer"
Jack Lemmon
The China Syndrome (1979) role "Jack Godell"
Al Pacino
...And Justice for All (1979) role "Arthur Kirkland"
Roy Scheider
All That Jazz (1979) role "Joseph "Joe" Gideon"
Peter Sellers
Being There (1979) role "Chance the gardener (Chauncey Gardiner)"

Best Actor in a Supporting Role
⚜ Melvyn Douglas ⚜
Being There (1979) role "Benjamin Turnbull Rand"
Robert Duvall
Apocalypse Now (1979) role "Lieutenant Colonel William "Bill" Kilgore"
Frederic Forrest
The Rose (1979) role "Huston Dyer"
Justin Henry
Kramer vs. Kramer (1979) role "Billy Kramer"
Mickey Rooney
The Black Stallion (1979) role "Henry Dailey"

Best Actress in a Leading Role
⚜ Sally Field ⚜
Norma Rae (1979) role "Norma Rae Webster"
Jill Clayburgh
Starting Over (1979) role "Marilyn Holmberg"
Jane Fonda
The China Syndrome (1979) role "Kimberly Wells"
Marsha Mason
Chapter Two (1979) role "Jennie MacLaine"
Bette Midler
The Rose (1979) role "Mary Rose Foster"

Best Actress in a Supporting Role
⚜ Meryl Streep ⚜
Kramer vs. Kramer (1979) role "Joanna Kramer"
Jane Alexander
Kramer vs. Kramer (1979) role "Margaret Phelps"
Barbara Barrie
Breaking Away (1979) role "Evelyn Stoller"
Candice Bergen
Starting Over (1979) role "Jessica Potter"
Mariel Hemingway
Manhattan (1979) role "Tracy"

Best Art Direction

⚰ Philip Rosenberg, Tony Walton (Art Direction), ⚰
Gary J. Brink, Edward Stewart (Set Decoration)
All That Jazz (1979)

Roger Christian, Les Dilley, Michael Seymour (Art Direction),
Ian Whittaker (Set Decoration)
Alien (1979)

Angelo P. Graham, Dean Tavoularis (Art Direction),
George R. Nelson (Set Decoration)
Apocalypse Now (1979)

Leon Harris, Joseph R. Jennings, Harold Michelson,
John Vallone (Art Direction), Linda DeScenna (Set Decoration)
Star Trek: The Motion Picture (1979)

George Jenkins (Art Direction), Arthur Jeph Parker (Set Decoration)
The China Syndrome (1979)

Best Cinematography

⚰ Vittorio Storaro ⚰
Apocalypse Now (1979)

Néstor Almendros
Kramer vs. Kramer (1979)

William A. Fraker
1941 (1979)

Frank V. Phillips
The Black Hole (1979)

Giuseppe Rotunno
All That Jazz (1979)

Best Costume Design

⚰ Albert Wolsky ⚰
All That Jazz (1979)

Ambra Danon, Piero Tosi
La Cage aux Folles (1978)

Judy Moorcroft
The Europeans (1979)

Shirley Russell
Agatha (1979)

William Ware Theiss
Butch and Sundance: The Early Days (1979)

Best Directing

⚰ Robert Benton ⚰
Kramer vs. Kramer (1979)

Francis Ford Coppola
Apocalypse Now (1979)

Bob Fosse
All That Jazz (1979)

Édouard Molinaro
La Cage aux Folles (1978)

Peter Yates
Breaking Away (1979)

Best Documentary, Feature
⚱ Ira Wohl (Producer) ⚱
Best Boy (1979)

Jacques Bobet, Paul Cowan (Producers)
Going the Distance (1979)

Barry Alexander Brown, Glenn Silber (Producers)
The War at Home (1979)

Tom Priestley, Steve Singer (Producers)
The Killing Ground (1979)

David A. Vassar (Producer)
Generation on the Wind (1979)

Best Documentary, Short Subject
⚱ Saul J. Turell (Producer) ⚱
Paul Robeson: Tribute to an Artist (1979)

Phillip Borsos (Producer)
Nails (1979)

Donald A. Connolly, James R. Messenger (Producers)
Koryo Celadon (1979)

Risto Teofilovski (Producer)
Dae (1979)

Dick Young (Producer)
Remember Me (1979)

Best Film Editing
⚱ Alan Heim ⚱
All That Jazz (1979)

Robert Dalva
The Black Stallion (1979)

Lisa Fruchtman, Gerald Benjamin "Jerry" Greenberg, Richard Marks, Walter Murch, Gerald Benjamin "Jerry" Greenberg
Apocalypse Now (1979)

Gerald Benjamin "Jerry" Greenberg
Kramer vs. Kramer (1979)

Carroll Timothy O'Meara, Robert L. Wolfe
The Rose (1979)

Best Foreign Language Film
⚱ Federal Republic of Germany ⚱
Die Blechtrommel (eng. The Tin Drum) (1979)

France
Une histoire simple (eng. A Simple Story) (1978)

Italy
Dimenticare Venezia (eng. To Forget Venice) (1979)

Poland
Panny z Wilka (eng. The Maids of Wilko) (1979)

Spain
Mamá cumple 100 años (eng. Mama Turns 100) (1979)

Special Achievement Award, Sound Editing
⚱ Alan Splet ⚱
The Black Stallion (1979)

Best Music, Original Score

⚐ **Georges Delerue** ⚐
A Little Romance (1979)

Jerry Goldsmith
Star Trek: The Motion Picture (1979)

Dave Grusin
The Champ (1979)

Henry Mancini
10 (1979)

Lalo Schifrin
The Amityville Horror (1979)

Best Sound

⚐ **Richard Beggs, Mark Berger, Nathan Boxer, Walter Murch** ⚐
Apocalypse Now (1979)

Gene S. Cantamessa, Robert J. Glass, Robert Knudson, Don MacDougall
1941 (1979)

Les Fresholtz, Michael Minkler, Al Overton Jr., Arthur Piantadosi
The Electric Horseman (1979)

Michael J. Kohut, William L. McCaughey, Aaron Rochin, Jack Solomon
Meteor (1979)

Theodore Soderberg, Jim E. Webb, Paul Wells, Douglas O. Williams
The Rose (1979)

Best Music, Original Song Score and Its Adaptation or Adaptation Score

⚐ **Ralph Burns (Adaptation Score)** ⚐
All That Jazz (1979)

Kenny Ascher, Paul Williams (Song Score), Paul Williams (Adaptation Score)
The Muppet Movie (1979)

Patrick Williams (Adaptation Score)
Breaking Away (1979)

Best Music, Original Song

⚐ **David Shire (Music), Norman Gimbel (Lyrics)**
for the song "It Goes Like It Goes" ⚐
Norma Rae (1979)

Kenny Ascher, Paul Williams (Music & Lyrics)
for the song "The Rainbow Connection"
The Muppet Movie (1979)

Marvin Hamlisch (Music), Carole Bayer Sager (Lyrics)
for the song "Through the Eyes of Love"
Ice Castles (1978)

Henry Mancini (Music), Robert Wells (Lyrics) for the song "It's Easy to Say"
10 (1979)

David Shire (Music), Alan Bergman, Marilyn Bergman (Lyrics)
for the song "I'll Never Say 'Goodbye'"
The Promise (1979)

Irving G. Thalberg Memorial Award

⚐ **Ray Stark** ⚐

Best Picture
⚑ Stanley R. Jaffe (Producer) ⚑
Kramer vs. Kramer (1979)

Tamara Asseyev, Alex Rose (Producers)
Norma Rae (1979)

Robert Alan Aurthur (Producer)
(posthumous)
All That Jazz (1979)

Francis Ford Coppola (Producer),
Gray Frederickson, Fred Roos, Tom Sternberg (Co-Producers)
Apocalypse Now (1979)

Peter Yates (Producer)
Breaking Away (1979)

Best Short Film, Animated
⚑ Derek Lamb (Producer) ⚑
Every Child (1979)

Paul Fierlinger (Producer)
It's So Nice to Have a Wolf Around the House (1979)

Bob Godfrey, Zlatko Grgic (Producers)
Dream Doll (1979)

Best Short Film, Live Action
⚑ Ron Ellis, Sarah Pillsbury (Producers) ⚑
Board and Care (1980)

Saul Bass, Michael Britton (Producers)
The Solar Film (1980)

Larry Hankin, Harry Mathias, Jay Zukerman (Producers)
Solly's Diner (1980)

Roman Kroitor, Stefan Wodoslawsky (Producers)
Bravery in the Field (1979)

Carol Lowell, Ross Lowell (Producers)
Oh Brother, My Brother (1979)

Honorary Award
⚑ Hal Elias ⚑
For his dedication and distinguished service to the Academy of Motion Picture Arts and Sciences.

⚑ Alec Guinness ⚑
For advancing the art of screen acting through a host of memorable and distinguished performances.

Best Writing, Screenplay Based on Material from Another Medium
⚑ Robert Benton ⚑
Kramer vs. Kramer (1979)

Allan Burns
A Little Romance (1979)

Francis Ford Coppola, John Milius
Apocalypse Now (1979)

Marcello Danon, Édouard Molinaro, Jean Poiret, Francis Veber
La Cage aux Folles (1978)

Harriet Frank Jr., Irving Ravetch
Norma Rae (1979)

Best Writing, Screenplay Written Directly for the Screen

↓ Steve Tesich ↓
Breaking Away (1979)

Woody Allen, Marshall Brickman
Manhattan (1979)

Robert Alan Aurthur, Bob Fosse
(Robert Alan Aurthur - posthumous)
All That Jazz (1979)

James Bridges, T.S. Cook, Mike Gray
The China Syndrome (1979)

Valerie Curtin, Barry Levinson
...And Justice for All (1979)

Best Visual Effects

↓ Nick Allder, Denys Ayling, H.R. Giger, Brian Johnson, Carlo Rambaldi ↓
Alien (1979)

Art Cruickshank, Harrison Ellenshaw, Peter Ellenshaw, Joe Hale, Danny Lee, Eustace Lycett
The Black Hole (1979)

John Dykstra, Grant McCune, Dave K. Stewart, Robert Swarthe, Douglas Trumbull, Richard Yuricich
Star Trek: The Motion Picture (1979)

John Evans, Derek Meddings, Paul Wilson
Moonraker (1979)

A. D. Flowers, William A. Fraker, Gregory Jein
1941 (1979)

The 53rd Academy Awards® - March 31, 1981

Host: Johnny Carson
Venue: Dorothy Chandler Pavilion
Honoring movies released in 1980

Honorary Award

↓ Henry Fonda ↓

The consummate actor, in recognition of his brilliant accomplishments and enduring contribution to the art of motion pictures.

Best Actor in a Leading Role

↓ Robert De Niro ↓
Raging Bull (1980) role "Jake LaMotta"

Robert Duvall
The Great Santini (1979) role "Lieutenant Colonel Wilbur "Bull" Meechum"

John Hurt
The Elephant Man (1980) role "Joseph Merrick"

Jack Lemmon
Tribute (1980) role "Scottie Templeton"

Peter O'Toole
The Stunt Man (1980) role "Eli Cross"

Best Actor in a Supporting Role
⚑ Timothy Hutton ⚑
Ordinary People (1980) role "Conrad Jarrett"
Judd Hirsch
Ordinary People (1980) role "Doctor Tyrone C. Berger"
Michael O'Keefe
The Great Santini (1979) role "Ben Meechum"
Joe Pesci
Raging Bull (1980) role "Joey LaMotta"
Jason Robards
Melvin and Howard (1980) role "Howard Hughes"

Best Actress in a Leading Role
⚑ Sissy Spacek ⚑
Coal Miner's Daughter (1980) role "Loretta Lynn"
Ellen Burstyn
Resurrection (1980) role " Edna Mae Harper-McCauley"
Goldie Hawn
Private Benjamin (1980) role "Judy Benjamin"
Mary Tyler Moore
Ordinary People (1980) role "Beth Jarrett"
Gena Rowlands
Gloria (1980) role "Gloria Swenson"

Best Actress in a Supporting Role
⚑ Mary Steenburgen ⚑
Melvin and Howard (1980) role "Lynda West-Dummar"
Eileen Brennan
Private Benjamin (1980) role "Captain Doreen Lewis"
Eva Le Gallienne
Resurrection (1980) role "Grandma Pearl"
Cathy Moriarty
Raging Bull (1980) role "Vikki LaMotta"
Diana Scarwid
Inside Moves (1980) role "Louise"

Best Art Direction
⚑ Pierre Guffroy, Jack Stephens (Art Direction) ⚑
Tess (1979)
Stuart Craig, Bob Cartwright (Art Direction), Hugh Scaife (Set Decoration)
The Elephant Man (1980)
John W. Corso (Art Direction), John M. Dwyer (Set Decoration)
Coal Miner's Daughter (1980)
Leslie Dilley, Harry Lange, Norman Reynolds, Alan Tomkins (Art Direction), Michael Ford (Set Decoration)
Star Wars: Episode V - The Empire Strikes Back (1980)
Yoshirô Muraki (Art Direction)
Kagemusha (eng. The Shadow Warrior) (1980)

Special Achievement Award, Visual Effects
⚑ Richard Edlund, Brian Johnson, Dennis Muren, Bruce Nicholson ⚑
Star Wars: Episode V - The Empire Strikes Back (1980)

Best Cinematography

⚐ Ghislain Cloquet, Geoffrey Unsworth ⚐
(Geoffrey Unsworth - posthumous)
Tess (1979)

Néstor Almendros
The Blue Lagoon (1980)

Ralf D. Bode
Coal Miner's Daughter (1980)

Michael Chapman
Raging Bull (1980)

James Crabe
The Formula (1980)

Best Costume Design

⚐ Anthony Powell ⚐
Tess (1979)

Jean-Pierre Dorléac
Somewhere in Time (1980)

Patricia Norris
The Elephant Man (1980)

Anna Senior
My Brilliant Career (1979)

Paul Zastupnevich
When Time Ran Out... (1980)

Best Picture

⚐ Ronald L. Schwary (Producer) ⚐
Ordinary People (1980)

Claude Berri (Producer), Timothy Burrill (Co-Producer)
Tess (1979)

Robert Chartoff, Irwin Winkler (Producers)
Raging Bull (1980)

Jonathan Sanger (Producer)
The Elephant Man (1980)

Bernard Schwartz (Producer)
Coal Miner's Daughter (1980)

Best Short Film, Animated

⚐ Ferenc Rofusz (Producer) ⚐
A légy (eng. The Fly) (1980)

Frédéric Back (Producer)
Tout rien (eng. All Nothing) (1978)

Michael Mills (Producer)
History of the World in Three Minutes Flat (1980)

Best Short Film, Dramatic Live Action

⚐ Lloyd Phillips (Producer) ⚐
The Dollar Bottom (1981)

Bob Carmichael, Greg Lowe (Producers)
Fall Line (1981)

Sally Heckel (Producer)
A Jury of Her Peers (1980)

Best Directing

⚑ Robert Redford ⚑
Ordinary People (1980)

David Lynch
The Elephant Man (1980)

Roman Polanski
Tess (1979)

Richard Rush
The Stunt Man (1980)

Martin Scorsese
Raging Bull (1980)

Best Documentary, Feature

⚑ Murray Lerner (Producer) ⚑
From Mao to Mozart: Isaac Stern in China (1979)

David Bradbury (Producer)
Front Line (1979)

Arthur Cohn, Bengt von zur Mühlen (Producers)
Der gelbe Stern - Ein Film über die Judenverfolgung 1933-1945
(eng. The Yellow Star: The Persecution of the Jews in Europe - 1933-1945) (1981)

Jon Else (Producer)
The Day After Trinity (1981)

Ross Spears (Producer)
Agee (1980)

Best Documentary, Short Subject

⚑ Roland Hallé, Peter W. Ladue (Producers) ⚑
Karl Hess: Toward Liberty (1980)

George Casey (Producer)
The Eruption of Mount St. Helens! (1980)

Pen Densham, John Watson (Producers)
Don't Mess with Bill (1980)

Richard Hawkins, Jorge Preloran (Producers)
Luther Metke a los 94 (eng. Luther Metke at 94) (1980)

Dick Young (Producer)
It's the Same World (1981)

Best Music, Original Score

⚑ Michael Gore ⚑
Fame (1980)

John Corigliano
Altered States (1980)

John Morris
The Elephant Man (1980)

Philippe Sarde
Tess (1979)

John Williams
Star Wars: Episode V - The Empire Strikes Back (1980)

Best Sound

⚑ **Gregg Landaker, Steve Maslow, Peter Sutton, Bill Varney** ⚑
Star Wars: Episode V - The Empire Strikes Back (1980)

James R. Alexander, Roger Heman Jr., Richard Portman
Coal Miner's Daughter (1980)

Willie D. Burton, Les Fresholtz, Michael Minkler, Arthur Piantadosi
Altered States (1980)

David J. Kimball, Les Lazarowitz, Donald O. Mitchell, Bill Nicholson
Raging Bull (1980)

Jay M. Harding, Michael J. Kohut, Chris Newman, Aaron Rochin
Fame (1980)

Best Music, Original Song

⚑ **Michael Gore (Music), Dean Pitchford (Lyrics) for the song "Fame"** ⚑
Fame (1980)

Michael Gore (Music), Lesley Gore (Lyrics) for the song "Out Here on My Own"
Fame (1980)

Willie Nelson (Music & Lyrics) for the song "On the Road Again"
Honeysuckle Rose (1980)

Dolly Parton (Music & Lyrics) for the song "Nine to Five"
Nine to Five (1980)

Lalo Schifrin (Music), Will Jennings (Lyrics) for the song "People Alone"
The Competition (1980)

Best Film Editing

⚑ **Thelma Schoonmaker** ⚑
Raging Bull (1980)

David E. Blewitt
The Competition (1980)

Anne V. Coates
The Elephant Man (1980)

Gerry Hambling
Fame (1980)

Arthur Schmidt
Coal Miner's Daughter (1980)

Best Foreign Language Film

⚑ **Union of Soviet Socialist Republics** ⚑
Moskva slezam ne verit (eng. Moscow Does Not Believe in Tears) (1980)

France
Le dernier métro (eng. The Last Metro) (1980)

Hungary
Bizalom (eng. Confidence) (1980)

Japan
Kagemusha (eng. The Shadow Warrior) (1980)

Spain
El nido (eng. The Nest) (1980)

Best Writing, Screenplay Based on Material from Another Medium
⬇ **Alvin Sargent (Screenplay)** ⬇
Ordinary People (1980)

Eric Bergren, David Lynch, Christopher De Vore (Screenplay)
The Elephant Man (1980)

Bruce Beresford, Jonathan Hardy, David Stevens (Screenplay)
Breaker Morant (1980)

Lawrence B. Marcus (Screenplay), Richard Rush (Adaptation)
The Stunt Man (1980)

Tom Rickman (Screenplay)
Coal Miner's Daughter (1980)

Best Writing, Screenplay Written Directly for the Screen
⬇ **Bo Goldman (Screenplay)** ⬇
Melvin and Howard (1980)

Christopher Gore (Screenplay)
Fame (1980)

Jean Gruault (Screenplay)
Mon oncle d'Amérique (eng. My American Uncle) (1980)

Nancy Meyers, Harvey Miller , Charles Shyer (Screenplay)
Private Benjamin (1980)

W. D. Richter (Screenplay), W. D. Richter, Arthur A. Ross (Story)
Brubaker (1980)

The 54ᵗʰ Academy Awards® - March 29, 1982
Host: Johnny Carson
Venue: Dorothy Chandler Pavilion
Honoring movies released in 1981

Best Actor in a Leading Role
⬇ **Henry Fonda** ⬇
On Golden Pond (1981) role "Norman Thayer Jr."

Warren Beatty
Reds (1981) role "John Silas "Jack" Reed"

Burt Lancaster
Atlantic City (1980) role "Lou Pascal"

Dudley Moore
Arthur (1981) role "Arthur Bach"

Paul Newman
Absence of Malice (1981) role "Michael Colin Gallagher"

Best Actor in a Supporting Role
⬇ **John Gielgud** ⬇
Arthur (1981) role "Hobson"

James Coco
Only When I Laugh (1981) role "Jimmy Perrino"

Ian Holm
Chariots of Fire (1981) role "Sam Mussabini"

Jack Nicholson
Reds (1981) role "Eugene O'Neill"

Howard E. Rollins Jr.
Ragtime (1981) role "Coalhouse Walker Jr."

Best Actress in a Leading Role
⚊ **Katharine Hepburn** ⚊
On Golden Pond (1981) role "Ethel Thayer"
Diane Keaton
Reds (1981) role "Louise Bryant"
Marsha Mason
Only When I Laugh (1981) role "Georgia Hines"
Susan Sarandon
Atlantic City (1980) role "Sally Matthews"
Meryl Streep
The French Lieutenant's Woman (1981) role "Sarah Woodruff / Anna"

Best Actress in a Supporting Role
⚊ **Maureen Stapleton** ⚊
Reds (1981) role "Emma Goldman"
Melinda Dillon
Absence of Malice (1981) role "Teresa Perrone"
Jane Fonda
On Golden Pond (1981) role "Chelsea Thayer Wayne"
Joan Hackett
Only When I Laugh (1981) role "Toby Landau"
Elizabeth McGovern
Ragtime (1981) role "Evelyn Nesbit"

Irving G. Thalberg Memorial Award
⚊ **Albert R. Broccoli** ⚊

Best Cinematography
⚊ **Vittorio Storaro** ⚊
Reds (1981)
Miroslav Ondricek
Ragtime (1981)
Douglas Slocombe
Indiana Jones and the Raiders of the Lost Ark (1981)
Alex Thomson
Excalibur (1981)
Billy Williams
On Golden Pond (1981)

Best Art Direction
⚊ **Leslie Dilley, Norman Reynolds (Art Direction), Michael Ford (Set Decoration)** ⚊
Indiana Jones and the Raiders of the Lost Ark (1981)
Patrizia Von Brandenstein, John Graysmark, Anthony Reading (Art Direction), Peter Howitt, George de Titta Jr., George de Titta Sr. (Set Decoration)
Ragtime (1981)
Assheton Gorton (Art Direction), Ann Mollo (Set Decoration)
The French Lieutenant's Woman (1981)
Tambi Larsen (Art Direction), James L. Berkey (Set Decoration)
Heaven's Gate (1980)
Richard Sylbert (Art Direction), Michael Seirton (Set Decoration)
Reds (1981)

Best Costume Design

⏣ Milena Canonero ⏣
Chariots of Fire (1981)

Anna Hill Johnstone
Ragtime (1981)

Bob Mackie
Pennies from Heaven (1981)

Tom Rand
The French Lieutenant's Woman (1981)

Shirley Russell
Reds (1981)

Best Directing

⏣ Warren Beatty ⏣
Reds (1981)

Hugh Hudson
Chariots of Fire (1981)

Louis Malle
Atlantic City (1980)

Mark Rydell
On Golden Pond (1981)

Steven Spielberg
Indiana Jones and the Raiders of the Lost Ark (1981)

Best Short Film, Animated

⏣ Frédéric Back (Producer) ⏣
Crac (1980)

Janet Perlman (Producer)
The Tender Tale of Cinderella Penguin (1981)

Will Vinton (Producer)
The Creation (1981)

Best Short Film, Live Action

⏣ Paul Kemp, Shelley Levinson (Producers) ⏣
Violet (1982)

Christine Oestreicher (Producer)
Couples and Robbers (1981)

John N. Smith (Producer)
First Winter (1981)

Best Documentary, Feature

⏣ Rabbi Marvin Hier, Arnold Schwartzman (Producers) ⏣
Genocide (1982)

Suzanne Bauman, Jim Burroughs, Paul Neshamkin (Producers)
Against Wind and Tide: A Cuban Odyssey (1981)

Mary Benjamin, Boyd Estus, Susanne Simpson (Producers)
Eight Minutes to Midnight: A Portrait of Dr. Helen Caldicott (1981)

Ken Burns (Producer)
Brooklyn Bridge (1981)

Glenn Silber, Tete Vasconcellos (Producers)
El Salvador: Another Vietnam (1981)

Best Documentary, Short Subject
⌁ Nigel Noble (Producer) ⌁
Close Harmony (1981)
Obie Benz (Producer)
Americas in Transition (1982)
Linda Chapman, Pam LeBlanc, Freddi Stevens (Producers)
See What I Say (1981)
Roland Hallé, John Hoover (Producers)
Urge to Build (1981)
Dick Young (Producer)
Journey for Survival (1981)

Jean Hersholt Humanitarian Award
⌁ Danny Kaye ⌁

Best Film Editing
⌁ Michael Kahn ⌁
Indiana Jones and the Raiders of the Lost Ark (1981)
Dede Allen, Craig McKay
Reds (1981)
John Bloom
The French Lieutenant's Woman (1981)
Terry Rawlings
Chariots of Fire (1981)
Robert L. Wolfe
(posthumous)
On Golden Pond (1981)

Best Foreign Language Film
⌁ Hungary ⌁
Mephisto (1981)
Italy
Tre fratelli (eng. Three Brothers) (1981)
Japan
Doro no kawa (eng. Muddy River) (1981)
Poland
Człowiek z żelaza (eng. Man of Iron) (1981)
Switzerland
Das Boot ist voll (eng. The Boat Is Full) (1981)

Best Music, Original Score
⌁ Vangelis ⌁
Chariots of Fire (1981)
Dave Grusin
On Golden Pond (1981)
Randy Newman
Ragtime (1981)
Alex North
Dragonslayer (1981)
John Williams
Indiana Jones and the Raiders of the Lost Ark (1981)

Best Music, Original Song

**Peter Allen, Burt Bacharach, Christopher Cross, Carole Bayer Sager (Music & Lyric)
for the song "Arthur's Theme (Best That You Can Do)"**
Arthur (1981)

Bill Conti (Music), Mick Leeson (Lyrics) for the song "For Your Eyes Only"
For Your Eyes Only (1981)

Randy Newman (Music & Lyric) for the song "One More Hour"
Ragtime (1981)

Joe Raposo (Music & Lyric), for the song "The First Time It Happens"
The Great Muppet Caper (1981)

Lionel Richie (Music & Lyric) for the song "Endless Love"
Endless Love (1981)

Best Picture

David Puttnam (Producer)
Chariots of Fire (1981)

Warren Beatty (Producer)
Reds (1981)

Bruce Gilbert (Producer)
On Golden Pond (1981)

Denis Héroux, John Kemeny (Producers)
Atlantic City (1980)

Frank Marshall (Producer)
Indiana Jones and the Raiders of the Lost Ark (1981)

Best Sound

Roy Charman , Gregg Landaker, Steve Maslow, Bill Varney
Indiana Jones and the Raiders of the Lost Ark (1981)

Tom Fleischman, Simon Kaye, Dick Vorisek
Reds (1981)

Robert W. Glass Jr., Robin Gregory, Robert M. Thirlwell, John K. Wilkinson
Outland (1981)

Jay M. Harding, Michael J. Kohut, Al Overton Jr., Richard Tyler
Pennies from Heaven (1981)

Richard Portman, David Ronne
On Golden Pond (1981)

Special Achievement Award, Sound Effects Editing

Richard L. Anderson, Ben Burtt
Indiana Jones and the Raiders of the Lost Ark (1981)

Best Visual Effects

Richard Edlund, Joe Johnston, Bruce Nicholson, Kit West
Indiana Jones and the Raiders of the Lost Ark (1981)

Brian Johnson, Dennis Muren, Ken Ralston, Phil Tippett
Dragonslayer (1981)

Honorary Award

Barbara Stanwyck
For superlative creativity and unique contribution to the art of screen acting.

Best Writing, Screenplay Based on Material from Another Medium
Ernest Thompson
On Golden Pond (1981)
Jay Presson Allen, Sidney Lumet
Prince of the City (1981)
Harold Pinter
The French Lieutenant's Woman (1981)
Dennis Potter
Pennies from Heaven (1981)
Michael Weller
Ragtime (1981)

Best Writing, Screenplay Written Directly for the Screen
Colin Welland
Chariots of Fire (1981)
Warren Beatty, Trevor Griffiths
Reds (1981)
Steve Gordon
Arthur (1981)
John Guare
Atlantic City (1980)
Kurt Luedtke
Absence of Malice (1981)

Best Makeup
Rick Baker
An American Werewolf in London (1981)
Stan Winston
Heartbeeps (1981)

The 55th Academy Awards® - April 11, 1983
Hosts: Walter Matthau, Liza Minnelli, Dudley Moore, Richard Pryor
Venue: Dorothy Chandler Pavilion
Honoring movies released in 1982

Honorary Award
Mickey Rooney
In recognition of his 60 years of versatility in a variety of memorable film performances.

Best Actor in a Leading Role
Ben Kingsley
Gandhi (1982) role "Mahatma Gandhi"
Dustin Hoffman
Tootsie (1982) role "Michael Dorsey / Dorothy Michaels"
Jack Lemmon
Missing (1982) role "Edmund Horman"
Paul Newman
The Verdict (1982) role "Frank Galvin"
Peter O'Toole
My Favorite Year (1982) role "Alan Swann"

Best Actor in a Supporting Role
⇓ Louis Gossett Jr. ⇓
An Officer and a Gentleman (1982) role "Gunnery Sergeant Emil Foley"
Charles Durning
The Best Little Whorehouse in Texas (1982) role "The Governor"
John Lithgow
The World According to Garp (1982) role "Roberta Muldoon"
James Mason
The Verdict (1982) role "Ed Concannon"
Robert Preston
Victor Victoria (1982) role "Caroll "Toddy" Todd"

Best Actress in a Leading Role
⇓ Meryl Streep ⇓
Sophie's Choice (1982) role "Zofia "Sophie" Zawistowski"
Julie Andrews
Victor Victoria (1982) role "Victoria Grant / Count Victor Grazinski"
Jessica Lange
Frances (1982) role "Frances Farmer"
Sissy Spacek
Missing (1982) role "Beth Horman"
Debra Winger
An Officer and a Gentleman (1982) role "Paula Pokrifki"

Best Actress in a Supporting Role
⇓ Jessica Lange ⇓
Tootsie (1982) role "Julie Nichols"
Glenn Close
The World According to Garp (1982) role "Jenny Fields"
Teri Garr
Tootsie (1982) role "Sandra "Sandy" Lester"
Kim Stanley
Frances (1982) role "Lillian Van Ornum Farmer"
Lesley Ann Warren
Victor Victoria (1982) role "Norma Cassidy"

Best Art Direction
⇓ Stuart Craig, Robert W. Laing (as Bob Laing) (Art Direction), Michael Seirton (Set Decoration) ⇓
Gandhi (1982)
Dale Hennesy (Art Direction), Marvin March (Set Decoration)
(Dale Hennesy - posthumous)
Annie (1982)
Rodger Maus, William Craig Smith, Tim Hutchinson (Art Direction), Harry Cordwell (Set Decoration)
Victor Victoria (1982)
Lawrence G. Paull, David L. Snyder (Art Direction), Linda DeScenna (Set Decoration)
Blade Runner (1982)
Franco Zeffirelli (Art Direction), Gianni Quaranta (Set Decoration)
La traviata (1982)

Best Cinematography
⚐ **Ronnie Taylor, Billy Williams** ⚐
Gandhi (1982)

Néstor Almendros
Sophie's Choice (1982)

Allen Daviau
E.T. the Extra-Terrestrial (1982)

Owen Roizman
Tootsie (1982)

Jost Vacano
Das Boot (1981)

Best Costume Design
⚐ **Bhanu Athaiya, John Mollo** ⚐
Gandhi (1982)

Elois Jenssen, Rosanna Norton
TRON (1982)

Patricia Norris
Victor Victoria (1982)

Piero Tosi
La traviata (1982)

Albert Wolsky
Sophie's Choice (1982)

Best Makeup
⚐ **Michèle Burke, Sarah Monzani** ⚐
La guerre du feu (eng. Quest for Fire) (1981)

Tom Smith
Gandhi (1982)

Best Directing
⚐ **Richard Attenborough** ⚐
Gandhi (1982)

Sidney Lumet
The Verdict (1982)

Wolfgang Petersen
Das Boot (1981)

Sydney Pollack
Tootsie (1982)

Steven Spielberg
E.T. the Extra-Terrestrial (1982)

Best Documentary, Feature
⚐ **John Zaritsky (Producer)** ⚐
The Fifth Estate: For episode Just Another Missing Kid (1981)

Michel Chalufour, John Karol Producers
Ben's Mill (1982)

Sturla Gunnarsson, Steve Lucas (Producers)
After the Axe (1981)

Meg Switzgable (Producer)
In Our Water (1982)

Joseph Wishy (Producer)
A Portrait of Giselle (1982)

Best Sound Effects Editing
⚱ Ben Burtt, Charles L. Campbell ⚱
E.T. the Extra-Terrestrial (1982)
Richard L. Anderson, Stephen Hunter Flick
Poltergeist (1982)
Mike Le Mare
Das Boot (1981)

Best Visual Effects
⚱ Dennis Muren, Carlo Rambaldi, Kenneth F. Smith ⚱
E.T. the Extra-Terrestrial (1982)
David Dryer, Douglas Trumbull, Richard Yuricich
Blade Runner (1982)
Richard Edlund, Bruce Nicholson, Michael Wood
Poltergeist (1982)

Best Documentary, Short Subject
⚱ Edward Le Lorrain, Terri Nash (Producers) ⚱
If You Love This Planet (1982)
John G. Avildsen (Producer)
Traveling Hopefully (1982)
Charles Guggenheim, Werner Schumann (Producers)
The Klan: A Legacy of Hate in America (1982)
Freida Lee Mock (Producer)
To Live or Let Die (1982)
Robert Richter (Producer)
Gods of Metal (1982)

Best Film Editing
⚱ John Bloom ⚱
Gandhi (1982)
Carol Littleton
E.T. the Extra-Terrestrial (1982)
Hannes Nikel
Das Boot (1981)
Fredric Steinkamp, William Steinkamp
Tootsie (1982)
Peter Zinner
An Officer and a Gentleman (1982)

Best Foreign Language Film
⚱ Spain ⚱
Volver a empezar (eng. To Begin Again) (1982)
France
Coup de Torchon (1981)
Nicaragua
Alsino y el cóndor (eng. Alsino and the Condor) (1982)
Sweden
Ingenjör Andrées luftfärd (eng. The Flight of the Eagle) (1982)
Union of Soviet Socialist Republics
Chastnaya zhizn (eng. Private Life) (1982)

Best Music, Original Score
⚐ John Williams ⚐
E.T. the Extra-Terrestrial (1982)
George Fenton, Ravi Shankar
Gandhi (1982)
Jerry Goldsmith
Poltergeist (1982)
Marvin Hamlisch
Sophie's Choice (1982)
Jack Nitzsche
An Officer and a Gentleman (1982)

Best Music, Original Song Score and Its Adaptation or Adaptation Score
⚐ Leslie Bricusse, Henry Mancini (Song Score), Henry Mancini (Adaptation Score) ⚐
Victor Victoria (1982)
Ralph Burns (Adaptation Score)
Annie (1982)
Tom Waits (Song Score)
One from the Heart (1981)

Best Music, Original Song
⚐ Jack Nitzsche, Buffy Sainte-Marie (Music), Will Jennings (Lyrics) ⚐ for the song "Up Where We Belong"
An Officer and a Gentleman (1982)
Dave Grusin (Music), Alan Bergman, Marilyn Bergman (Lyrics) for the song "It Might Be You"
Tootsie (1982)
Michel Legrand (Music), Alan Bergman, Marilyn Bergman (Lyrics) for the song "How Do You Keep the Music Playing?"
Best Friends (1982)
Jim Peterik, Frankie Sullivan (Music & Lyrics) for the song "Eye of the Tiger"
Rocky III (1982)
John Williams (Music), Alan Bergman, Marilyn Bergman (Lyrics) for the song "If We Were In Love"
Yes, Giorgio (1982)

Best Sound
⚐ Gene S. Cantamessa, Don Digirolamo, Robert Glass, Robert Knudson ⚐
E.T. the Extra-Terrestrial (1982)
Rick Alexander (as Dick Alexander), Les Fresholtz, Les Lazarowitz, Arthur Piantadosi
Tootsie (1982)
Jonathan Bates, Gerry Humphreys, Simon Kaye, Robin O'Donoghue
Gandhi (1982)
Milan Bor, Mike Le Mare, Trevor Pyke
Das Boot (1981)
Bob Minkler, Lee Minkler, Michael Minkler, Jim La Rue
TRON (1982)

Jean Hersholt Humanitarian Award
⚐ Walter Mirisch ⚐

Best Short Film, Animated

⚐ **Zbigniew Rybczynski (Producer)** ⚐
Tango (1981)

John Coates (Producer)
The Snowman (1982)

Will Vinton (Producer)
The Great Cognito (1982)

Best Short Film, Live Action

⚐ **Christine Oestreicher (Producer)** ⚐
A Shocking Accident (1982)

Joseph Benson, Michael Toshiyuki Uno (Producers)
The Silence (1982)

Andrew Birkin (Producer)
Sredni Vashtar (1981)

Bob Rogers, (Producer)
Ballet Robotique (1982)

Jan Saunders (Producer)
Split Cherry Tree (1982)

Best Picture

⚐ **Richard Attenborough (Producer)** ⚐
Gandhi (1982)

David Brown, Richard D. Zanuck (Producers)
The Verdict (1982)

Kathleen Kennedy, Steven Spielberg (Producers)
E.T. the Extra-Terrestrial (1982)

Edward Lewis, Mildred Lewis (Producers)
Missing (1982)

Sydney Pollack, Dick Richards (Producers)
Tootsie (1982)

Best Writing, Screenplay Based on Material from Another Medium

⚐ **Costa-Gavras, Donald E. Stewart** ⚐
Missing (1982)

Blake Edwards
Victor Victoria (1982)

David Mamet
The Verdict (1982)

Alan J. Pakula
Sophie's Choice (1982)

Wolfgang Petersen
Das Boot (1981)

Best Writing, Screenplay Written Directly for the Screen

⚐ **John Briley (Screenplay)** ⚐
Gandhi (1982)

**Larry Gelbart, Murray Schisgal (Screenplay),
Larry Gelbart, Don McGuire (Story)**
Tootsie (1982)

Barry Levinson (Screenplay)
Diner (1982)

Melissa Mathison (Screenplay)
E.T. the Extra-Terrestrial (1982)

Douglas Day Stewart (Screenplay)
An Officer and a Gentleman (1982)

55th Ceremony 6/6

The 56ᵗʰ Academy Awards® - April 9, 1984

Host: Johnny Carson
Venue: Dorothy Chandler Pavilion
Honoring movies released in 1983

Best Actor in a Leading Role

↓ **Robert Duvall** ↓
Tender Mercies (1983) role "Mac Sledge"

Michael Caine
Educating Rita (1983) role "Dr. Frank Bryant"

Tom Conti
Reuben, Reuben (1983) role "Gowan McGland"

Tom Courtenay
The Dresser (1983) role "Norman"

Albert Finney
The Dresser (1983) role "Sir"

Best Actor in a Supporting Role

↓ **Jack Nicholson** ↓
Terms of Endearment (1983) role "Garrett Breedlove"

Charles Durning
To Be or Not to Be (1983) role "S. S. Colonel Erhardt"

John Lithgow
Terms of Endearment (1983) role "Sam Burns"

Sam Shepard
The Right Stuff (1983) role "Chuck Yeager"

Rip Torn
Cross Creek (1983) role "Marsh Turner"

Best Actress in a Leading Role

↓ **Shirley MacLaine** ↓
Terms of Endearment (1983) role "Aurora Greenway"

Jane Alexander
Testament (1983) role "Carol Wetherly"

Meryl Streep
Silkwood (1983) role "Karen Silkwood"

Julie Walters
Educating Rita (1983) role "Susan "Rita" White"

Debra Winger
Terms of Endearment (1983) role "Emma Greenway Horton"

Best Actress in a Supporting Role

↓ **Linda Hunt** ↓
The Year of Living Dangerously (1982) role "Billy Kwan"

Cher
Silkwood (1983) role "Dolly Pelliker"

Glenn Close
The Big Chill (1983) role "Sarah Cooper"

Amy Irving
Yentl (1983) role "Hadass Vishkower"

Alfre Woodard
Cross Creek (1983) role "Beatrice "Geechee""

Best Cinematography

⚱ Sven Nykvist ⚱
Fanny och Alexander (eng. Fanny and Alexander) (1982)

Caleb Deschanel
The Right Stuff (1983)

William A. Fraker
WarGames (1983)

Donald Peterman
Flashdance (1983)

Gordon Willis
Zelig (1983)

Best Costume Design

⚱ Marik Vos-Lundh ⚱
Fanny och Alexander (eng. Fanny and Alexander) (1982)

Santo Loquasto
Zelig (1983)

Anne-Marie Marchand
Le retour de Martin Guerre (eng. The Return of Martin Guerre) (1982)

William Ware Theiss
Heart Like a Wheel (1983)

Joe I. Tompkins
Cross Creek (1983)

Best Art Direction

⚱ Anna Asp (Art Direction), Susanne Lingheim (Set Decoration) ⚱
Fanny och Alexander (eng. Fanny and Alexander) (1982)

**W. Stewart Campbell, Geoffrey Kirkland, Richard J. Lawrence,
Peter R. Romero (Art Direction),
George R. Nelson, Pat Pending (Set Decoration)**
The Right Stuff (1983)

**Fred Hole, Norman Reynolds, James L. Schoppe (Art Direction),
Michael Ford (Set Decoration)**
Star Wars: Episode VI - Return of the Jedi (1983)

**Harold Michelson, Polly Platt (Art Direction),
Anthony Mondell, Tom Pedigo (Set Decoration)**
Terms of Endearment (1983)

Leslie Tomkins, Roy Walker (Art Direction), Tessa Davies (Set Decoration)
Yentl (1983)

Best Directing

⚱ James L. Brooks ⚱
Terms of Endearment (1983)

Bruce Beresford
Tender Mercies (1983)

Ingmar Bergman
Fanny och Alexander (eng. Fanny and Alexander) (1982)

Mike Nichols
Silkwood (1983)

Peter Yates
The Dresser (1983)

Best Sound Effects Editing

↓ Jay Boekelheide ↓
The Right Stuff (1983)

Ben Burtt
Star Wars: Episode VI - Return of the Jedi (1983)

Special Achievement Award, Visual Effects

↓ Richard Edlund, Dennis Muren, Ken Ralston, Phil Tippett ↓
Star Wars: Episode VI - Return of the Jedi (1983)

Best Documentary, Feature

↓ Emile Ardolino (Producer) ↓
He Makes Me Feel Like Dancin' (1983)

Robin Anderson, Bob Connolly (Producers)
First Contact (1982)

Michael Bryans, Tina Viljoen (Producers)
The Profession of Arms (1983)

Ara Chekmayan, Richard Kotuk (Producers)
Children of Darkness (1983)

James Klein, Julia Reichert (Producers)
Seeing Red (1983)

Best Documentary, Short Subject

↓ Cynthia Scott, Adam Symansky (Producers) ↓
Flamenco at 5:15 (1983)

Dea Brokman, Ilene Landis (Producers)
Ihr zent frei (eng. You Are Free) (1983)

Arthur Dong (Producer)
Sewing Woman (1982)

Robert Eisenhardt (Producer)
Spaces: The Architecture of Paul Rudolph (1983)

Vivienne Verdon-Roe, Eric Thiermann (Producers)
In the Nuclear Shadow: What Can the Children Tell Us? (1984)

Best Film Editing

↓ Glenn Farr, Lisa Fruchtman,Tom Rolf, Stephen A. Rotter, Douglas Stewart ↓
The Right Stuff (1983)

Edward M. Abroms, Frank Morriss
Blue Thunder (1983)

Richard Marks
Terms of Endearment (1983)

Walt Mulconery, Bud S. Smith
Flashdance (1983)

Sam O'Steen
Silkwood (1983)

Honorary Award

↓ Hal Roach ↓
In recognition of his unparalleled record of distinguished contributions to the motion picture art form.

Best Foreign Language Film

⚑ Sweden ⚑
Fanny och Alexander (eng. Fanny and Alexander) (1982)

Algeria
Le Bal (1983)

France
Coup de foudre (eng. Entre Nous) (1983)

Hungary
Jób lázadása (eng. The Revolt of Job) (1983)

Spain
Carmen (1983)

Best Music, Original Score

⚑ Bill Conti ⚑
The Right Stuff (1983)

Jerry Goldsmith
Under Fire (1983)

Michael Gore
Terms of Endearment (1983)

Leonard Rosenman
Cross Creek (1983)

John Williams
Star Wars: Episode VI - Return of the Jedi (1983)

Best Music, Original Song

Giorgio Moroder (Music), Irene Cara, Keith Forsey (Lyrics) for the song "Flashdance...What a Feeling"
Flashdance (1983)

Bobby Hart, Austin Roberts (Music & Lyrics) for the song "Over You"
Tender Mercies (1983)

Michel Legrand (Music), Alan Bergman, Marilyn Bergman (Lyrics) for the song "Papa, Can You Hear Me?"
Yentl (1983)

Michel Legrand (Music), Alan Bergman, Marilyn Bergman (Lyrics) for the song "The Way He Makes Me Feel"
Yentl (1983)

Dennis Matkosky, Michael Sembello (Music & Lyrics) for the song "Maniac"
Flashdance (1983)

Best Sound

⚑ Mark Berger, David MacMillan, Tom Scott, Randy Thom ⚑
The Right Stuff (1983)

James R. Alexander (as Jim Alexander), Rick Kline, Donald O. Mitchell, Kevin O'Connell
Terms of Endearment (1983)

Todd Boekelheide, David Parker, Alan R. Splet, Randy Thom
Never Cry Wolf (1983)

Carlos Delarios, Willie D. Burton, Michael J. Kohut, Aaron Rochin
WarGames (1983)

Ben Burtt, Tony Dawe, Gary Summers, Randy Thom
Star Wars: Episode VI - Return of the Jedi (1983)

Best Music, Original Song Score or Adaptation Score

⚐ **Alan Bergman, Marilyn Bergman, Michel Legrand (Song Score)** ⚐
Yentl (1983)

Elmer Bernstein (Adaptation Score)
Trading Places (1983)

Lalo Schifrin (Adaptation Score)
The Sting II (1983)

Best Picture

⚐ **James L. Brooks (Producer)** ⚐
Terms of Endearment (1983)

Robert Chartoff, Irwin Winkler (Producers)
The Right Stuff (1983)

Philip S. Hobel (Producer)
Tender Mercies (1983)

Michael Shamberg (Producer)
The Big Chill (1983)

Peter Yates (Producer)
The Dresser (1983)

Best Short Film, Animated

⚐ **Jimmy Picker (Producer)** ⚐
Sundae in New York (1983)

Eda Godel Hallinan (Producer)
Sound of Sunshine - Sound of Rain (1983)

Burny Mattinson (Producer)
Mickey's Christmas Carol (1983)

Best Short Film, Live Action

⚐ **Janice L. Platt (Producer)** ⚐
Boys and Girls (1983)

Jon N. Bloom (Producer)
Overnight Sensation (1984)

Ian Emes (Producer)
Goodie-Two-Shoes (1984)

Jean Hersholt Humanitarian Award

⚐ **M. J. Frankovich** ⚐

Best Writing, Screenplay Based on Material from Another Medium

⚐ **James L. Brooks** ⚐
Terms of Endearment (1983)

Julius J. Epstein
Reuben, Reuben (1983)

Ronald Harwood
The Dresser (1983)

Harold Pinter
Betrayal (1983)

Willy Russell
Educating Rita (1983)

Best Writing, Screenplay Written Directly for the Screen

⚊ Horton Foote ⚊
Tender Mercies (1983)

Alice Arlen, Nora Ephron
Silkwood (1983)

Barbara Benedek, Lawrence Kasdan
The Big Chill (1983)

Ingmar Bergman
Fanny och Alexander (eng. Fanny and Alexander) (1982)

Lawrence Lasker, Walter F. Parkes
WarGames (1983)

The 57th Academy Awards® - March 25, 1985

Host: Jack Lemmon
Venue: Dorothy Chandler Pavilion
Honoring movies released in 1984

Honorary Award

⚊ James Stewart ⚊
For his fifty years of memorable performances, for his high ideals both on and off the screen, with respect and affection of his colleagues.

⚊ The National Endowment for the Arts ⚊
In recognition of its 20th anniversary and its dedicated commitment to fostering artistic and creative activity and excellence in every area of the arts

Jean Hersholt Humanitarian Award

⚊ David L. Wolper ⚊

Best Actor in a Leading Role

⚊ F. Murray Abraham ⚊
Amadeus (1984) role "Antonio Salieri"

Jeff Bridges
Starman (1984) role "Starman / Scott Hayden"

Albert Finney
Under the Volcano (1984) role "Geoffrey Firmin"

Tom Hulce
Amadeus (1984) role "Wolfgang Amadeus Mozart"

Sam Waterston
The Killing Fields (1984) role "Sydney Schanberg"

Best Actor in a Supporting Role

⚊ Haing S. Ngor ⚊
The Killing Fields (1984) role "Dith Pran"

Adolph Caesar
A Soldier's Story (1984) role "Sergeant Waters"

John Malkovich
Places in the Heart (1984) role "Mr. Will"

Noriyuki 'Pat' Morita
The Karate Kid (1984) role "Kesuke Miyagi"

Ralph Richardson
(posthumous)
Greystoke: The Legend of Tarzan, Lord of the Apes (1984) role "The Sixth Earl of Greystoke"

Best Actress in a Leading Role
⚐ Sally Field ⚐
Places in the Heart (1984) role "Edna Spalding"
Judy Davis
A Passage to India (1984) role "Adela Quested"
Jessica Lange
Country (1984) role "Jewell Ivy"
Vanessa Redgrave
The Bostonians (1984) role "Olive Chancellor"
Sissy Spacek
The River (1984) role "Mae Garvey"

Best Actress in a Supporting Role
⚐ Peggy Ashcroft ⚐
A Passage to India (1984) role "Mrs. Moore"
Glenn Close
The Natural (1984) role "Iris Gaines"
Lindsay Crouse
Places in the Heart (1984) role "Margaret Lomax"
Christine Lahti
Swing Shift (1984) role "Hazel Zanussi"
Geraldine Page
The Pope of Greenwich Village (1984) role "Mrs. Ritter"

Best Art Direction
⚐ Patrizia Von Brandenstein (Art Direction), Karel Cerný (Set Decoration) ⚐
Amadeus (1984)
**Mel Bourne, Angelo P. Graham, Speed Hopkins,
James J. Murakami (Art Direction), Bruce Weintraub (Set Decoration)**
The Natural (1984)
John Box, Leslie Tomkins (Art Direction), Hugh Scaife (Set Decoration)
A Passage to India (1984)
Albert Brenner (Art Direction), Rick Simpson (Set Decoration)
2010: The Year We Make Contact (1984)
Richard Sylbert (Art Direction), Les Bloom, George Gaines (Set Decoration)
The Cotton Club (1984)

Best Cinematography
⚐ Chris Menges ⚐
The Killing Fields (1984)
Ernest Day
A Passage to India (1984)
Caleb Deschanel
The Natural (1984)
Miroslav Ondrícek
Amadeus (1984)
Vilmos Zsigmond
The River (1984)

Special Achievement Award, Sound Effects Editing
⚐ Kay Rose ⚐
The River (1984)

Best Makeup

⚱ Paul LeBlanc, Dick Smith ⚱
Amadeus (1984)

Rick Baker, Paul Engelen
Greystoke: The Legend of Tarzan, Lord of the Apes (1984)

Michael Westmore
2010: The Year We Make Contact (1984)

Best Costume Design

⚱ Theodor Pistek ⚱
Amadeus (1984)

Jenny Beavan, John Bright
The Bostonians (1984)

Judy Moorcroft
A Passage to India (1984)

Patricia Norris
2010: The Year We Make Contact (1984)

Ann Roth
Places in the Heart (1984)

Best Visual Effects

⚱ George Gibbs, Michael J. McAlister, Dennis Muren, Lorne Peterson ⚱
Indiana Jones and the Temple of Doom (1984)

John Bruno, Richard Edlund, Chuck Gaspar, Mark Vargo
Ghostbusters (1984)

Richard Edlund, George Jenson, Neil Krepela, Mark Stetson
2010: The Year We Make Contact (1984)

Best Directing

⚱ Milos Forman ⚱
Amadeus (1984)

Woody Allen
Broadway Danny Rose (1984)

Robert Benton
Places in the Heart (1984)

Roland Joffé
The Killing Fields (1984)

David Lean
A Passage to India (1984)

Best Documentary, Feature

⚱ Robert Epstein, Richard Schmiechen (Producers) ⚱
The Times of Harvey Milk (1984)

Zev Braun, Karel Dirka (Producers)
Marlene (1984)

Frank Christopher, Alex W. Drehsler (Producers)
In the Name of the People (1985)

Charles Guggenheim, Nancy Sloss (Producers)
High Schools (1983)

Cheryl McCall (Producer)
Streetwise (1984)

Best Documentary, Short Subject

⚐ Marjorie Hunt, Paul Wagner (Producers) ⚐
The Stone Carvers (1984)

Ben Achtenberg, Joan Sawyer (Producers)
Code Gray: Ethical Dilemmas in Nursing (1984)

Gary Bush, Paul T.K. Lin (Producers)
The Children of Soong Ching Ling (1985)

Lawrence R. Hott, Roger M. Sherman (Producers)
The Garden of Eden (1984)

Irina Kalinina (Producer)
Vospominaniye o Pavlovske (eng. Recollections of Pavlovsk) (1984)

Best Film Editing

⚐ Jim Clark ⚐
The Killing Fields (1984)

Donn Cambern, Frank Morriss
Romancing the Stone (1984)

Michael Chandler, Nena Danevic
Amadeus (1984)

David Lean
A Passage to India (1984)

Robert Q. Lovett, Barry Malkin
The Cotton Club (1984)

Best Foreign Language Film

⚐ Switzerland ⚐
La diagonale du fou (eng. Dangerous Moves) (1984)

Argentina
Camila (1984)

Israel
Me'Ahorei Hasoragim (eng. Beyond the Walls) (1984)

Spain
Sesión continua (eng. Double Feature) (1984)

Union of Soviet Socialist Republics
Voenno-polevoy roman (eng. War-Time Romance) (1983)

Best Music, Original Score

⚐ Maurice Jarre ⚐
A Passage to India (1984)

Randy Newman
The Natural (1984)

Alex North
Under the Volcano (1984)

John Williams
Indiana Jones and the Temple of Doom (1984), The River (1984)

Best Music, Original Song Score

⚐ Prince ⚐
Purple Rain (1984)

Kris Kristofferson
Songwriter (1984)

Jeff Moss
The Muppets Take Manhattan (1984)

Best Music, Original Song

Stevie Wonder (Music & Lyrics)
for the song "I Just Called to Say I Love You"
The Woman in Red (1984)

Phil Collins (Music & Lyrics)
for the song "Against All Odds (Take a Look at Me Now)"
Against All Odds (1984)

Kenny Loggins (Music), Dean Pitchford (Lyrics) for the song "Footloose"
Footloose (1984)

Ray Parker Jr. (Music & Lyrics) for the song "Ghostbusters"
Ghostbusters (1984)

Dean Pitchford, Tom Snow (Music & Lyrics)
for the song "Let's Hear It for the Boy"
Footloose (1984)

Best Sound

Mark Berger, Todd Boekelheide, Chris Newman, Thomas Scott
Amadeus (1984)

Nick Alphin, Richard Portman, David M. Ronne, Robert Thirlwell
The River (1984)

Gene S. Cantamessa, Carlos Delarios, Michael J. Kohut, Aaron Rochin
2010: The Year We Make Contact (1984)

Michael A. Carter, Graham V. Hartstone, Nicolas Le Messurier, John W. Mitchell
A Passage to India (1984)

Steve Maslow, Kevin O'Connell, Nelson Stoll, Bill Varney
Dune (1984)

Best Writing, Screenplay Based on Material from Another Medium

Peter Shaffer
Amadeus (1984)

Michael Austin, Robert Towne (as P.H. Vazak)
Greystoke: The Legend of Tarzan, Lord of the Apes (1984)

Charles Fuller
A Soldier's Story (1984)

David Lean
A Passage to India (1984)

Bruce Robinson
The Killing Fields (1984)

Best Writing, Screenplay Written Directly for the Screen

Robert Benton
Places in the Heart (1984)

Woody Allen
Broadway Danny Rose (1984)

Bruce Jay Friedman, Lowell Ganz, Babaloo Mandel (Screenplay), Bruce Jay Friedman (Screen Story), Brian Grazer (Story)
Splash (1984)

Gregory Nava, Anna Thomas
El Norte (1983)

Daniel Petrie Jr. (Screenplay), Danilo Bach, Daniel Petrie Jr. (Story)
Beverly Hills Cop (1984)

Best Picture
⚊ Saul Zaentz (Producer) ⚊
Amadeus (1984)

John Brabourne, Richard Goodwin (Producers)
A Passage to India (1984)

Arlene Donovan (Producer)
Places in the Heart (1984)

Norman Jewison, Patrick J. Palmer, Ronald L. Schwary (Producers)
A Soldier's Story (1984)

David Puttnam (Producer)
The Killing Fields (1984)

Best Short Film, Animated
⚊ Jon Minnis (Producer) ⚊
Charade (1984)

Ishu Patel (Producer)
Paradise (1984)

Morton Schindel, Michael Sporn (Producers)
Doctor DeSoto (1984)

Best Short Film, Live Action
⚊ Mike Hoover (Producer) ⚊
Up (1985)

Lesli Linka Glatter, Sharon Oreck (Producers)
Tales of Meeting and Parting (1985)

Michael MacMillan, Janice L. Platt (Producers)
The Painted Door (1984)

The 58ᵗʰ Academy Awards® - March 24, 1986
Hosts: Alan Alda, Jane Fonda, Robin Williams
Venue: Dorothy Chandler Pavilion
Honoring movies released in 1985

Honorary Award
⚊ Paul Newman ⚊
In recognition of his many and memorable and compelling screen performances and for his personal integrity and dedication to his craft.

⚊ Alex North ⚊
In recognition of his brilliant artistry in the creation of memorable music for a host of distinguished motion pictures.

Best Actor in a Leading Role
⚊ William Hurt ⚊
Kiss of the Spider Woman (1985) role "Luis Molina"

Harrison Ford
Witness (1985) role "Detective Captain John Book"

James Garner
Murphy's Romance (1985) role "Murphy Jones"

Jack Nicholson
Prizzi's Honor (1985) role "Charley Partanna"

Jon Voight
Runaway Train (1985) role "Oscar "Manny" Manheim"

Best Actor in a Supporting Role
⬇ Don Ameche ⬇
Cocoon (1985) role "Arthur Selwyn"
Klaus Maria Brandauer
Out of Africa (1985) role "Baron Bror von Blixen-Finecke / Baron Hans von Blixen-Finecke"
William Hickey
Prizzi's Honor (1985) role "Don Corrado Prizzi"
Robert Loggia
Jagged Edge (1985) role "Sam Ransom"
Eric Roberts
Runaway Train (1985) role "Buck McGeehy"

Best Actress in a Leading Role
⬇ Geraldine Page ⬇
The Trip to Bountiful (1985) role "Carrie Watts"
Anne Bancroft
Agnes of God (1985) role "Mother Miriam Ruth / Anna Maria Burchetti"
Whoopi Goldberg
The Color Purple (1985) role "Celie Harris Johnson"
Jessica Lange
Sweet Dreams (1985) role "Patsy Cline"
Meryl Streep
Out of Africa (1985) role "Karen Blixen"

Best Actress in a Supporting Role
⬇ Anjelica Huston ⬇
Prizzi's Honor (1985) role "Maerose Prizzi"
Margaret Avery
The Color Purple (1985) role "Shug Avery"
Amy Madigan
Twice in a Lifetime (1985) role "Sunny MacKenzie-Sobel"
Meg Tilly
Agnes of God (1985) role "Sister Agnes Devereaux"
Oprah Winfrey
The Color Purple (1985) role "Sofia Johnson"

Jean Hersholt Humanitarian Award
⬇ Charles "Buddy" Rogers ⬇

Best Art Direction
⬇ Stephen B. Grimes (Art Direction), Josie MacAvin (Set Decoration) ⬇
Out of Africa (1985)
Norman Garwood (Art Direction), Maggie Gray (Set Decoration)
Brazil (1985)
Stan Jolley (Art Direction), John H. Anderson (Set Decoration)
Witness (1985)
Shinobu Muraki, Yoshirô Muraki (Art Direction)
Ran (1985)
J. Michael Riva, Robert W. Welch (Art Direction), Linda DeScenna (Set Decoration)
The Color Purple (1985)

Best Cinematography

⌐ David Watkin ⌐
Out of Africa (1985)

Allen Daviau
The Color Purple (1985)

William A. Fraker
Murphy's Romance (1985)

Asakazu Nakai, Takao Saitô, Shôji Ueda
Ran (1985)

John Seale
Witness (1985)

Best Costume Design

⌐ Emi Wada ⌐
Ran (1985)

Milena Canonero
Out of Africa (1985)

Donfeld
Prizzi's Honor (1985)

Aggie Guerard Rodgers
The Color Purple (1985)

Albert Wolsky
The Journey of Natty Gann (1985)

Best Picture

⌐ Sydney Pollack (Producer) ⌐
Out of Africa (1985)

Edward S. Feldman (Producer)
Witness (1985)

John Foreman (Producer)
Prizzi's Honor (1985)

**Quincy Jones, Kathleen Kennedy, Frank Marshall,
Steven Spielberg (Producers)**
The Color Purple (1985)

David Weisman (Producer)
Kiss of the Spider Woman (1985)

Best Short Film, Animated

⌐ Cilia Van Dijk (Producer) ⌐
Anna & Bella (1984)

Richard Condie, Michael J. F. Scott (Producers)
The Big Snit (1985)

Alison Snowden (Producer)
Second Class Mail (1985)

Best Short Film, Live Action

⌐ Jeffrey D. Brown, Chris Pelzer (Producers) ⌐
Molly's Pilgrim (1985)

Dianna Costello (Producer)
Graffiti (1985)

Bob Rogers (Producer)
Rainbow War (1987)

Best Directing
⚑ Sydney Pollack ⚑
Out of Africa (1985)
Hector Babenco
Kiss of the Spider Woman (1985)
John Huston
Prizzi's Honor (1985)
Akira Kurosawa
Ran (1985)
Peter Weir
Witness (1985)

Best Documentary, Feature
⚑ Maria Florio, Victoria Mudd (Producers) ⚑
Broken Rainbow (1985)
Japhet Asher (Producer)
Soldiers in Hiding (1985)
Ken Burns, Buddy Squires (Producers)
The Statue of Liberty (1985)
Susana Blaustein Muñoz, Lourdes Portillo (Producers)
Las madres de la Plaza de Mayo (eng. The Mothers of the Plaza of Mayo) (1985)
Steven Okazaki (Producer)
Unfinished Business (1985)

Best Documentary, Short Subject
⚑ David Goodman (Producer) ⚑
Witness to War: Dr. Charlie Clements (1985)
Michael Crowley, James Wolpaw (Producers)
Keats and His Nightingale: A Blind Date (1985)
Alan Edelstein (Producer)
The Wizard of the Strings (1985)
Robert H. Gardner (Producer)
The Courage to Care (1985)
Barbara Willis Sweete (Producer)
Making Overtures: The Story of a Community Orchestra (1984)

Best Music, Original Song
⚑ Lionel Richie (Music & Lyrics) for the song "Say You, Say Me" ⚑
White Nights (1985)
Stephen Bishop (Music & Lyrics)
for the song "Separate Lives (Love Theme from "White Nights")"
White Nights (1985)
Johnny Colla, Chris Hayes (Music), Huey Lewis (Lyrics)
for the song "The Power of Love"
Back to the Future (1985)
Marvin Hamlisch (Music), Ed Kleban (Lyrics)
for the song "Surprise, Surprise"
A Chorus Line (1985)
Quincy Jones, Rod Temperton (Music), Quincy Jones, Lionel Richie, Rod Temperton (Lyrics) for the song "Miss Celie's Blues (Sister)"
The Color Purple (1985)

Best Film Editing

⚐ **Thom Noble** ⚐
Witness (1985)

John Bloom
A Chorus Line (1985)

Kaja Fehr, Rudi Fehr
Prizzi's Honor (1985)

Pembroke J. Herring, Sheldon Kahn, Fredric Steinkamp, William Steinkamp
Out of Africa (1985)

Henry Richardson
Runaway Train (1985)

Best Foreign Language Film

⚐ **Argentina** ⚐
La historia oficial (eng. The Official Story) (1985)

Federal Republic of Germany
Bittere Ernte (eng. Angry Harvest) (1985)

France
3 hommes et un couffin (eng. Three Men and a Cradle) (1985)

Hungary
Oberst Redl (eng. Colonel Redl) (1985)

Yugoslavia
Otac na sluzbenom putu (eng. When Father Was Away on Business) (1985)

Best Makeup

⚐ **Zoltan Elek, Michael Westmore** ⚐
Mask (1985)

Ken Chase
The Color Purple (1985)

Carl Fullerton
Remo Williams: The Adventure Begins (1985)

Best Music, Original Score

⚐ **John Barry** ⚐
Out of Africa (1985)

Chris Boardman, Jorge Calandrelli, Andraé Crouch, Jack Hayes, Jerry Hey, Quincy Jones, Randy Kerberm, Jeremy Lubbock, Joel Rosenbaum, Caiphus Semenya, Fred Steiner, Rod Temperton
The Color Purple (1985)

Bruce Broughton
Silverado (1985)

Georges Delerue
Agnes of God (1985)

Maurice Jarre
Witness (1985)

Best Sound Effects Editing

⚐ **Charles L. Campbell, Robert R. Rutledge** ⚐
Back to the Future (1985)

Frederick J. Brown
Rambo: First Blood Part II (1985)

Robert G. Henderson, Alan Robert Murray
Ladyhawke (1985)

Best Visual Effects

⚓ David Berry, Scott Farrar, Ralph McQuarrie, Ken Ralston ⚓
Cocoon (1985)

David Allen, John Ellis, Dennis Muren, Kit West
Young Sherlock Holmes (1985)

Michael Lloyd, Zoran Perisic, Will Vinton, Ian Wingrove
Return to Oz (1985)

Best Sound

⚓ Gary Alexander, Peter Handford, Chris Jenkins, Larry Stensvold ⚓
Out of Africa (1985)

Rick Alexander (as Dick Alexander), Bud Alper, Les Fresholtz, Vern Poore
Ladyhawke (1985)

**Gerry Humphreys, Michael Minkler,
Donald O. Mitchell, Christopher Newman**
Silverado (1985)

William B. Kaplan, B. Tennyson Sebastian II, Robert Thirlwell, Bill Varney
Back to the Future (1985)

Rick Kline, Donald O. Mitchell, Kevin O'Connell, David M. Ronne
A Chorus Line (1985)

Best Writing, Screenplay Based on Material from Another Medium

⚓ Kurt Luedtke ⚓
Out of Africa (1985)

Richard Condon, Janet Roach
Prizzi's Honor (1985)

Horton Foote
The Trip to Bountiful (1985)

Menno Meyjes
The Color Purple (1985)

Leonard Schrader
Kiss of the Spider Woman (1985)

Best Writing, Screenplay Written Directly for the Screen

William Kelley, Earl W. Wallace (Screenplay),
⚓ **William Kelley, Earl W. Wallace, Pamela Wallace (Story)** ⚓
Witness (1985)

Woody Allen
The Purple Rose of Cairo (1985)

Aída Bortnik, Luis Puenzo
La historia oficial (eng. The Official Story) (1985)

Bob Gale, Robert Zemeckis
Back to the Future (1985)

Terry Gilliam, Charles McKeown, Tom Stoppard
Brazil (1985)

The 59th Academy Awards® - March 30, 1987

Hosts: Chevy Chase, Goldie Hawn, Paul Hogan
Venue: Dorothy Chandler Pavilion
Honoring movies released in 1986

Irving G. Thalberg Memorial Award
↓ Steven Spielberg ↓

Best Actor in a Leading Role
↓ Paul Newman ↓
The Color of Money (1986) role "Eddie "Fast Eddie" Felson"

Dexter Gordon
'Round Midnight (1986) role "Dale Turner"

Bob Hoskins
Mona Lisa (1986) role "George"

William Hurt
Children of a Lesser God (1986) role "James Leeds"

James Woods
Salvador (1986) role "Richard Boyle"

Best Actor in a Supporting Role
↓ Michael Caine ↓
Hannah and Her Sisters (1986) role "Elliott Daniels"

Tom Berenger
Platoon (1986) role "Sergeant Bob Barnes"

Willem Dafoe
Platoon (1986) role "Sergeant Elias Grodin"

Denholm Elliott
A Room with a View (1985) role "Mr. Emerson"

Dennis Hopper
Hoosiers (1986) role "Wilbur "Shooter" Flatch"

Best Actress in a Leading Role
↓ Marlee Matlin ↓
Children of a Lesser God (1986) role "Sarah Norman"

Jane Fonda
The Morning After (1986) role "Alex Sternbergen / Viveca Van Loren"

Sissy Spacek
Crimes of the Heart (1986) role "Babe Botrelle / Rebecca MaGrath"

Kathleen Turner
Peggy Sue Got Married (1986) role "Peggy Sue Kelcher-Bodell"

Sigourney Weaver
Aliens (1986) role "Ellen Ripley"

Best Actress in a Supporting Role
↓ Dianne Wiest ↓
Hannah and Her Sisters (1986) role "Holly"

Tess Harper
Crimes of the Heart (1986) role "Chick Boyle"

Piper Laurie
Children of a Lesser God (1986) role "Mrs. Norman"

Mary Elizabeth Mastrantonio
The Color of Money (1986) role "Carmen"

Maggie Smith
A Room with a View (1985) role "Charlotte Bartlett"

Best Art Direction

Brian Ackland-Snow, Gianni Quaranta (Art Direction), Elio Altamura, Brian Savegar (Set Decoration)
A Room with a View (1985)

Stuart Craig (Art Direction), Jack Stephens (Set Decoration)
The Mission (1986)

Peter Lamont (Art Direction), Crispian Sallis (Set Decoration)
Aliens (1986)

Boris Leven (Art Direction), Karen A. O'Hara (Set Decoration)
(Boris Leven - posthumous)
The Color of Money (1986)

Stuart Wurtzel (Art Direction), Carol Joffe (Set Decoration)
Hannah and Her Sisters (1986)

Best Cinematography

Chris Menges
The Mission (1986)

Jordan Cronenweth
Peggy Sue Got Married (1986)

Don Peterman
Star Trek IV: The Voyage Home (1986)

Tony Pierce-Roberts
A Room with a View (1985)

Robert Richardson
Platoon (1986)

Best Makeup

Stephan Dupuis, Chris Walas
The Fly (1986)

Rob Bottin, Peter Robb-King
Legend (1985)

Michèle Burke, Michael G. Westmore
The Clan of the Cave Bear (1986)

Best Costume Design

Jenny Beavan, John Bright
A Room with a View (1985)

Anna Anni, Maurizio Millenotti
Otello (1986)

Anthony Powell
Pirates (1986)

Theadora Van Runkle
Peggy Sue Got Married (1986)

Enrico Sabbatini
The Mission (1986)

Best Visual Effects

Suzanne M. Benson, John Richardson, Robert Skotak, Stan Winston
Aliens (1986)

John Bruno, Richard Edlund, William Neil, Garry Waller
Poltergeist II: The Other Side (1986)

Lyle Conway, Bran Ferren, Martin Gutteridge
Little Shop of Horrors (1986)

Best Directing
⚑ Oliver Stone ⚑
Platoon (1986)
Woody Allen
Hannah and Her Sisters (1986)
James Ivory
A Room with a View (1985)
David Lynch
Blue Velvet (1986)
Roland Joffé
The Mission (1986)

Best Documentary, Feature
⚑ Brigitte Berman (Producer) ⚑
Artie Shaw: Time Is All You've Got (1985)
⚑ Joseph Feury, Milton Justice (Producers) ⚑
Down and Out in America (1986)
David Bradbury (Producer)
Chile: Hasta Cuando? (1986)
Amram Nowak, Kirk Simon (Producers)
Isaac in America: A Journey with Isaac Bashevis Singer (1987)
Sharon I. Sopher (Producer)
Witness to Apartheid (1986)

Best Documentary, Short Subject
⚑ Vivienne Verdon-Roe (Producer) ⚑
Women - for America, for the World (1986)
Madeline Bell, Thomas L. Neff (Producers)
Red Grooms: Sunflower in a Hothouse (1986)
Sonya Friedman (Producer)
The Masters of Disaster (1986)
Alison Nigh-Strelich (Producer)
Debonair Dancers (1986)
Aaron D. Weisblatt (Producer)
Sam (1986)

Best Film Editing
⚑ Claire Simpson ⚑
Platoon (1986)
Jim Clark
The Mission (1986)
Billy Weber, Chris Lebenzon
Top Gun (1986)
Ray Lovejoy
Aliens (1986)
Susan E. Morse
Hannah and Her Sisters (1986)

Honorary Award
⚑ Ralph Bellamy ⚑
For his unique artistry and his distinguished service to the profession of acting.

Best Foreign Language Film
⚱ The Netherlands ⚱
De aanslag (eng. The Assault) (1986)
Austria
38 (1986)
Canada
Le déclin de l'empire américain (eng. The Decline of the American Empire) (1986)
Czechoslovakia
Vesnicko má stredisková (eng. My Sweet Little Village) (1985)
France
37°2 le matin (eng. Betty Blue) (1986)

Best Picture
⚱ Arnold Kopelson (Producer) ⚱
Platoon (1986)
Fernando Ghia, David Puttnam (Producers)
The Mission (1986)
Robert Greenhut (Producer)
Hannah and Her Sisters (1986)
Ismail Merchant (Producer)
A Room with a View (1985)
Patrick J. Palmer, Burt Sugarman (Producers)
Children of a Lesser God (1986)

Best Music, Original Score
⚱ Herbie Hancock ⚱
'Round Midnight (1986)
Jerry Goldsmith
Hoosiers (1986)
James Horner
Aliens (1986)
Ennio Morricone
The Mission (1986)
Leonard Rosenman
Star Trek IV: The Voyage Home (1986)

Best Music, Original Song
⚱ Giorgio Moroder (Music), Tom Whitlock (Lyrics) ⚱
for the song "Take My Breath Away"
Top Gun (1986)
Peter Cetera, David Foster (Music), Peter Cetera, Diane Nini (Lyrics)
for the song "Glory of Love"
The Karate Kid Part II (1986)
James Horner, Barry Mann (Music), Cynthia Weil (Lyrics)
for the song "Somewhere Out There"
An American Tail (1986)
Henry Mancini (Music), Leslie Bricusse (Lyrics)
for the song "Life in a Looking Glass"
That's Life! (1986)
Alan Menken (Music), Howard Ashman (Lyrics)
for the song "Mean Green Mother from Outer Space"
Little Shop of Horrors (1986)

Best Short Film, Animated
↯ **Willem Thijssen, Linda Van Tulden (Producers)** ↯
Een griekse tragedie (eng. A Greek Tragedy) (1985)
John Lasseter, William Reeves (Producers)
Luxo Jr. (1986)
Hugh Macdonald, Martin Townsend (Producer)
The Frog, the Dog, and the Devil (1986)

Best Short Film, Live Action
↯ **Chuck Workman (Producer)** ↯
Precious Images (1986)
Pino Quartullo, Stefano Reali (Producers)
Exit (1985)
Fredda Weiss (Producer)
Love Struck (1986)

Best Sound
↯ **Charles "Bud" Grenzbach, Simon Kaye,** ↯
Richard D. Rogers, John K. Wilkinson
Platoon (1986)
Rick Alexander (as Dick Alexander), Les Fresholtz,
William Nelson, Vern Poore
Heartbreak Ridge (1986)
Gene S. Cantamessa, Dave J. Hudson, Mel Metcalfe, Terry Porter
Star Trek IV: The Voyage Home (1986)
Michael A. Carter, Roy Charman, Graham V. Hartstone, Nicolas Le Messurier
Aliens (1986)
William B. Kaplan, Rick Kline, Donald O. Mitchell, Kevin O'Connell
Top Gun (1986)

Best Writing, Screenplay Based on Material from Another Medium
↯ **Ruth Prawer Jhabvala** ↯
A Room with a View (1985)
Hesper Anderson, Mark Medoff
Children of a Lesser God (1986)
Raynold Gideon, Bruce A. Evans
Stand by Me (1986)
Beth Henley
Crimes of the Heart (1986)
Richard Price
The Color of Money (1986)

Best Writing, Screenplay Written Directly for the Screen
↯ **Woody Allen** ↯
Hannah and Her Sisters (1986)
Richard Boyle, Oliver Stone
Salvador (1986)
John Cornell, Paul Hogan, Ken Shadie (Screenplay), Paul Hogan (Story)
Crocodile Dundee (1986)
Hanif Kureishi
My Beautiful Laundrette (1985)
Oliver Stone
Platoon (1986)

Best Sound Effects Editing
⤓ Don Sharpe ⤓
Aliens (1986)
Cecelia Hall, George Watters II
Top Gun (1986)
Mark A. Mangini
Star Trek IV: The Voyage Home (1986)

The 60ᵗʰ Academy Awards® - April 11, 1988
Host: Chevy Chase
Venue: Shrine Civic Auditorium
Honoring movies released in 1987

Irving G. Thalberg Memorial Award
⤓ Billy Wilder ⤓

Best Actor in a Leading Role
⤓ Michael Douglas ⤓
Wall Street (1987) role "Gordon Gekko"
William Hurt
Broadcast News (1987) role "Tom Grunick"
Marcello Mastroianni
Oci ciornie (eng. Dark Eyes) (1987) role "Romano"
Jack Nicholson
Ironweed (1987) role "Francis Phelan"
Robin Williams
Good Morning, Vietnam (1987) role "Adrian Cronauer"

Best Actor in a Supporting Role
⤓ Sean Connery ⤓
The Untouchables (1987) role "Jim Malone"
Albert Brooks
Broadcast News (1987) role "Aaron Altman"
Morgan Freeman
Street Smart (1987) role "Leo "Fast Black" Smalls Jr."
Vincent Gardenia
Moonstruck (1987) role "Cosmo Castorini"
Denzel Washington
Cry Freedom (1987) role "Steve Biko"

Best Actress in a Leading Role
⤓ Cher ⤓
Moonstruck (1987) role "Loretta Castorini"
Glenn Close
Fatal Attraction (1987) role "Alex Forrest"
Holly Hunter
Broadcast News (1987) role "Jane Craig"
Sally Kirkland
Anna (1987) role "Anna"
Meryl Streep
Ironweed (1987) role "Helen Archer"

Best Actress in a Supporting Role

⬇ **Olympia Dukakis** ⬇
Moonstruck (1987) role "Rose Castorini"

Norma Aleandro
Gaby: A True Story (1987) role "Florencia Sánchez Morales"

Anne Archer
Fatal Attraction (1987) role "Beth Rogerson-Gallagher"

Anne Ramsey
Throw Momma from the Train (1987) role "Momma Lift"

Ann Sothern
The Whales of August (1987) role "Letitia "Tisha" Benson-Doughty"

Best Art Direction

⬇ **Ferdinando Scarfiotti (Art Direction),
Bruno Cesari, Osvaldo Desideri (Set Decoration)** ⬇
The Last Emperor (1987)

**Patrizia Von Brandenstein, William A. Elliott (Art Direction),
Hal Gausman (Set Decoration)**
The Untouchables (1987)

**Santo Loquasto (Art Direction),
Les Bloom, George DeTitta Jr., Carol Joffe (Set Decoration)**
Radio Days (1987)

Anthony Pratt (Art Direction), Joan Woollard (Set Decoration)
Hope and Glory (1987)

Norman Reynolds (Art Direction), Harry Cordwell (Set Decoration)
Empire of the Sun (1987)

Best Cinematography

⬇ **Vittorio Storaro** ⬇
The Last Emperor (1987)

Michael Ballhaus
Broadcast News (1987)

Allen Daviau
Empire of the Sun (1987)

Philippe Rousselot
Hope and Glory (1987)

Haskell Wexler
Matewan (1987)

Best Visual Effects

⬇ **William George, Harley Jessup, Dennis Muren, Kenneth Smith** ⬇
Innerspace (1987)

Richard Greenberg, Robert M. Greenberg, Joel Hynek, Stan Winston
Predator (1987)

Best Short Film, Animated

⬇ **Frédéric Back (Producer)** ⬇
L'homme qui plantait des arbres (eng. The Man Who Planted Trees) (1987)

Eunice Macaulay (Producer)
George and Rosemary (1987)

Bill Plympton (Producer)
Your Face (1987)

Best Short Film, Live Action
⚑ Jana Sue Memel, Jonathan Sanger (Producers) ⚑
Ray's Male Heterosexual Dance Hall (1987)

Robert A. Katz (Producer)
Shoeshine (1987)

Ann Wingate (Producer)
Making Waves (1987)

Best Costume Design
⚑ James Acheson ⚑
The Last Emperor (1987)

Jenny Beavan, John Bright
Maurice (1987)

Dorothy Jeakins
The Dead (1987)

Bob Ringwood
Empire of the Sun (1987)

Marilyn Vance-Straker
The Untouchables (1987)

Best Makeup
⚑ Rick Baker ⚑
Harry and the Hendersons (1987)

Bob Laden
Happy New Year (1987)

Best Directing
⚑ Bernardo Bertolucci ⚑
The Last Emperor (1987)

John Boorman
Hope and Glory (1987)

Lasse Hallström
Mitt liv som hund (eng. My Life as a Dog) (1985)

Norman Jewison
Moonstruck (1987)

Adrian Lyne
Fatal Attraction (1987)

Best Music, Original Song
⚑ Donald Markowitz, John DeNicola, Franke Previte (Music), Franke Previte (Lyrics) for the song "(I've Had) The Time of My Life" ⚑
Dirty Dancing (1987)

Willy DeVille (Music & Lyrics) for the song "Storybook Love"
The Princess Bride (1987)

Harold Faltermeyer, Keith Forsey (Music), Harold Faltermeyer, Keith Forsey, Bob Seger (Lyrics) for the song "Shakedown"
Beverly Hills Cop II (1987)

George Fenton, Jonas Gwangwa (Music & Lyrics) for the song "Cry Freedom"
Cry Freedom (1987)

Albert Hammond, Diane Warren (Music & Lyrics) for the song "Nothing's Gonna Stop Us Now"
Mannequin (1987)

Best Film Editing

⚐ Gabriella Cristiani ⚐
The Last Emperor (1987)

Peter E. Berger, Michael Kahn
Fatal Attraction (1987)

Michael Kahn
Empire of the Sun (1987)

Richard Marks
Broadcast News (1987)

Frank J. Urioste
RoboCop (1987)

Best Foreign Language Film

⚐ Denmark ⚐
Babettes gæstebud (eng. Babette's Feast) (1987)

France
Au Revoir les Enfants (eng. Goodbye, Children) (1987)

Italy
La famiglia (eng. The Family) (1987)

Norway
Ofelas (eng. Pathfinder) (1987)

Spain
Asignatura aprobada (eng. Course Completed) (1987)

Best Picture

⚐ Jeremy Thomas (Producer) ⚐
The Last Emperor (1987)

John Boorman (Producer)
Hope and Glory (1987)

James L. Brooks (Producer)
Broadcast News (1987)

Stanley R. Jaffe, Sherry Lansing (Producers)
Fatal Attraction (1987)

Norman Jewison, Patrick J. Palmer (Producers)
Moonstruck (1987)

Best Sound

⚐ Bill Rowe, Ivan Sharrock ⚐
The Last Emperor (1987)

Rick Alexander (as Dick Alexander), Les Fresholtz, Bill Nelson, Vern Poore
Lethal Weapon (1987)

Wayne Artman, Tom Beckert, Tom E. Dahl, Art Rochester
The Witches of Eastwick (1987)

John Boyd, Tony Dawe, Don Digirolamo, Robert Knudson
Empire of the Sun (1987)

Carlos Delarios, Michael J. Kohut, Aaron Rochin, Robert Wald
RoboCop (1987)

Special Achievement Award, Sound Effects Editing

⚐ Stephen Hunter Flick, John Pospisil ⚐
RoboCop (1987)

Best Music, Original Score
⚐ David Byrne, Ryuichi Sakamoto, Cong Su ⚐
The Last Emperor (1987)
George Fenton, Jonas Gwangwa
Cry Freedom (1987)
Ennio Morricone
The Untouchables (1987)
John Williams
Empire of the Sun (1987), The Witches of Eastwick (1987)

Best Documentary, Feature
⚐ Aviva Slesin (Producer) ⚐
The Ten-Year Lunch: The Wit and Legend of the Algonquin Round Table (1987)
Cyril Christo, Barbara Herbich (Producers)
A Stitch for Time (1987)
Callie Crossley, James A. DeVinney (Producers)
Eyes on the Prize: America's Civil Rights Years / Bridge to Freedom 1965 (1987)
John W. Dower, John Junkerman (Producers)
Hellfire: A Journey from Hiroshima (1986)
Robert Stone (Producer)
Radio Bikini (1988)

Best Documentary, Short Subject
⚐ Pamela Conn, Sue Marx (Producers) ⚐
Young at Heart (1987)
Dr. Frank Daniel, Izak Ben-Meir (Producers)
In the Wee Wee Hours... (1987)
Deborah Dickson (Producer)
Frances Steloff: Memoirs of a Bookseller (1987)
Lynn Mueller (Producer)
Silver Into Gold (1987)
Megan Williams (Producer)
Language Says It All (1987)

Best Writing, Screenplay Based on Material from Another Medium
⚐ Bernardo Bertolucci, Mark Peploe ⚐
The Last Emperor (1987)
Per Berglund, Brasse Brännström, Lasse Hallström, Reidar Jönsson
Mitt liv som hund (eng. My Life as a Dog) (1985)
James Dearden
Fatal Attraction (1987)
Gustav Hasford, Michael Herr, Stanley Kubrick
Full Metal Jacket (1987)
Tony Huston
The Dead (1987)

Best Writing, Screenplay Written Directly for the Screen
⚐ John Patrick Shanley ⚐
Moonstruck (1987)
Woody Allen
Radio Days (1987)
John Boorman
Hope and Glory (1987)
James L. Brooks
Broadcast News (1987)
Louis Malle
Au Revoir les Enfants (eng. Goodbye, Children) (1987)

The 61ˢᵗ Academy Awards® - March 29, 1989

Host: No official host
Venue: Shrine Civic Auditorium
Honoring movies released in 1988

Honorary Award

⚘ National Film Board of Canada ⚘

In recognition of its 50ᵗʰ anniversary and its dedicated commitment to originate artistic, creative and technological activity and excellence in every area of filmmaking.

⚘ Eastman Kodak Company ⚘

In recognition of the company's fundamental contributions to the art of motion pictures during the first century of film history.

Best Actor in a Leading Role

⚘ Dustin Hoffman ⚘
Rain Man (1988) role "Raymond Babbit"

Gene Hackman
Mississippi Burning (1988) role "Agent Rupert Anderson"

Tom Hanks
Big (1988) role "Josh Baskin"

Edward James Olmos
Stand and Deliver (1988) role "Jaime Escalante"

Max von Sydow
Pelle erobreren (eng. Pelle the Conqueror) (1987) role "Lassefar"

Best Actor in a Supporting Role

⚘ Kevin Kline ⚘
A Fish Called Wanda (1988) role "Otto West"

Alec Guinness
Little Dorrit (1987) role "William Dorrit"

Martin Landau
Tucker: The Man and His Dream (1988) role "Abe Karatz"

River Phoenix
Running on Empty (1988) role "Danny Pope"

Dean Stockwell
Married to the Mob (1988) role "Tony "The Tiger" Russo"

Best Actress in a Leading Role

⚘ Jodie Foster ⚘
The Accused (1988) role "Sarah Tobias"

Glenn Close
Dangerous Liaisons (1988) role "Marquise Isabelle de Merteuil"

Melanie Griffith
Working Girl (1988) role "Tess McGill"

Meryl Streep
A Cry in the Dark (1988) role "Lindy Chamberlain"

Sigourney Weaver
Gorillas in the Mist (1988) role "Dian Fossey"

Best Actress in a Supporting Role
⚊ Geena Davis ⚊
The Accidental Tourist (1988) role "Muriel Pritchett"
Joan Cusack
Working Girl (1988) role "Cyn"
Frances McDormand
Mississippi Burning (1988) role "Mrs. Pell"
Michelle Pfeiffer
Dangerous Liaisons (1988) role "Madame Marie de Tourvel"
Sigourney Weaver
Working Girl (1988) role "Katharine Parker"

Best Art Direction
⚊ Stuart Craig (Art Direction), Gérard James (Set Decoration) ⚊
Dangerous Liaisons (1988)
Albert Brenner (Art Direction), Garrett Lewis (Set Decoration)
Beaches (1988)
Ida Random (Art Direction), Linda DeScenna (Set Decoration)
Rain Man (1988)
Elliot Scott (Art Direction), Peter Howitt (Set Decoration)
Who Framed Roger Rabbit (1988)
Dean Tavoularis (Art Direction), Armin Ganz (Set Decoration)
Tucker: The Man and His Dream (1988)

Best Cinematography
⚊ Peter Biziou ⚊
Mississippi Burning (1988)
Dean Cundey
Who Framed Roger Rabbit (1988)
Conrad L. Hall
Tequila Sunrise (1988)
Sven Nykvist
The Unbearable Lightness of Being (1988)
John Seale
Rain Man (1988)

Best Costume Design
⚊ James Acheson ⚊
Dangerous Liaisons (1988)
Milena Canonero
Tucker: The Man and His Dream (1988)
Deborah Nadoolman
Coming to America (1988)
Patricia Norris
Sunset (1988)
Jane Robinson
A Handful of Dust (1988)

Special Achievement Award
⚊ Richard Williams ⚊
Who Framed Roger Rabbit (1988)

Best Directing

⚱ Barry Levinson ⚱
Rain Man (1988)

Charles Crichton
A Fish Called Wanda (1988)

Mike Nichols
Working Girl (1988)

Alan Parker
Mississippi Burning (1988)

Martin Scorsese
The Last Temptation of Christ (1988)

Best Documentary, Feature

⚱ Marcel Ophüls (Producer) ⚱
Hôtel Terminus: The Life and Times of Klaus Barbie (1988)

Robert Bilheimer, Ronald Mix (Producers)
The Cry of Reason: Beyers Naude - An Afrikaner Speaks Out (1988)

Nan Bush, Bruce Weber (Producers)
Let's Get Lost (1988)

Christine Choy, Renee Tajima-Pena (Producers)
Who Killed Vincent Chin? (1987)

Ginny Durrin (Producer)
Promises to Keep (1988)

Best Documentary, Short Subject

⚱ Malcolm Clarke, William Guttentag (Producers) ⚱
You Don't Have to Die (1988)

Thomas B. Fleming, Daniel J. Marks (Producers)
Gang Cops (1987)

Karen Goodman (Producer)
The Children's Storefront (1988)

Nancy Hale, Meg Partridge (Producers)
Portrait of Imogen (1988)

Ann Tegnell, Lise Yasui (Producers)
Family Gathering (1988)

Best Makeup

⚱ Ve Neill, Steve La Porte, Robert Short ⚱
Beetlejuice (1988)

Rick Baker
Coming to America (1988)

Thomas R. Burman, Bari Dreiband-Burman
Scrooged (1988)

Best Visual Effects

⚱ George Gibbs, Edward Jones, Ken Ralston, Richard Williams ⚱
Who Framed Roger Rabbit (1988)

Brent Boates, Richard Edlund, Al DiSarro, Thaine Morris
Die Hard (1988)

Christopher Evans, Michael J. McAlister, Dennis Muren, Phil Tippett
Willow (1988)

Best Film Editing
⇣ Arthur Schmidt ⇣
Who Framed Roger Rabbit (1988)
Stuart Baird
Gorillas in the Mist (1988)
Gerry Hambling
Mississippi Burning (1988)
Stu Linder
Rain Man (1988)
John F. Link, Frank J. Urioste
Die Hard (1988)

Best Sound
⇣ Rick Alexander (as Dick Alexander), Willie D. Burton, ⇣ Les Fresholtz, Vern Poore
Bird (1988)
Don J. Bassman, Kevin F. Cleary, Richard Overton, Al Overton Jr.
Die Hard (1988)
John Boyd, Tony Dawe, Don Digirolamo, Robert Knudson
Who Framed Roger Rabbit (1988)
Peter Handford, Andy Nelson, Brian Saunders
Gorillas in the Mist (1988)
Rick Kline, Robert J. Litt, Danny Michael, Elliot Tyson
Mississippi Burning (1988)

Best Sound Effects Editing
⇣ Charles L. Campbell, Louis L. Edemann ⇣
Who Framed Roger Rabbit (1988)
Ben Burtt, Richard Hymns
Willow (1988)
Stephen Hunter Flick, Richard Shorr
Die Hard (1988)

Best Music, Original Score
⇣ Dave Grusin ⇣
The Milagro Beanfield War (1988)
George Fenton
Dangerous Liaisons (1988)
Maurice Jarre
Gorillas in the Mist (1988)
John Williams
The Accidental Tourist (1988)
Hans Zimmer
Rain Man (1988)

Best Music, Original Song
⇣ Carly Simon (Music & Lyrics) for the song "Let the River Run" ⇣
Working Girl (1988)
Lamont Dozier (Music), Phil Collins (Lyrics) for the song "Two Hearts"
Buster (1988)
Bob Telson (Music & Lyrics) for the song "Calling You"
Bagdad Cafe (1987)

Best Foreign Language Film
⚜ Denmark ⚜
Pelle erobreren (eng. Pelle the Conqueror) (1987)
Belgium
Le maître de musique (eng. The Music Teacher) (1988)
Hungary
Hanussen (1988)
India
Salaam Bombay! (1988)
Spain
Mujeres al borde de un ataque de "nervios"
(eng. Women on the Verge of a Nervous Breakdown) (1988)

Best Picture
⚜ Mark Johnson (Producer) ⚜
Rain Man (1988)
Robert F. Colesberry, Frederick Zollo (Producers)
Mississippi Burning (1988)
Michael Grillo, Lawrence Kasdan, Charles Okun (Producers)
The Accidental Tourist (1988)
Norma Heyman, Hank Moonjean (Producers)
Dangerous Liaisons (1988)
Douglas Wick (Producer)
Working Girl (1988)

Best Short Film, Animated
⚜ John Lasseter, William Reeves ⚜
Tin Toy (1988)
Cordell Barker
The Cat Came Back (1988)
Brian Jennings, Bill Kroyer
Technological Threat (1988)

Best Short Film, Live Action
⚜ Dean Parisot, Steven Wright ⚜
The Appointments of Dennis Jennings (1988)
George deGolian, Gary Moss
Gullah Tales (1988)
Abbee Goldstein, Matia Karrell
Cadillac Dreams (1988)

Best Writing, Screenplay Based on Material from Another Medium
⚜ Christopher Hampton ⚜
Dangerous Liaisons (1988)
Jean-Claude Carrière, Philip Kaufman
The Unbearable Lightness of Being (1988)
Christine Edzard
Little Dorrit (1987)
Frank Galati, Lawrence Kasdan
The Accidental Tourist (1988)
**Anna Hamilton Phelan (Screenplay),
Tab Murphy, Anna Hamilton Phelan (Story)**
Gorillas in the Mist (1988)

Best Writing, Screenplay Written Directly for the Screen

⚊ **Barry Morrow, Ronald Bass (Screenplay), Barry Morrow (Story)** ⚊
Rain Man (1988)

John Cleese (Screenplay), John Cleese, Charles Crichton (Story)
A Fish Called Wanda (1988)

Naomi Foner
Running on Empty (1988)

Gary Ross, Anne Spielberg
Big (1988)

Ron Shelton
Bull Durham (1988)

The 62nd Academy Awards® - March 26, 1990

Host: Billy Crystal
Venue: Dorothy Chandler Pavilion
Honoring movies released in 1989

Best Actor in a Leading Role

⚊ **Daniel Day-Lewis** ⚊
My Left Foot (1989) role "Christy Brown"

Kenneth Branagh
Henry V (1989) role "King Henry V of England"

Tom Cruise
Born on the Fourth of July (1989) role "Ron Kovic"

Morgan Freeman
Driving Miss Daisy (1989) role "Hoke Colburn"

Robin Williams
Dead Poets Society (1989) role "John Charles "Keats" Keating"

Best Actor in a Supporting Role

⚊ **Denzel Washington** ⚊
Glory (1989) role "Private Silas Trip"

Danny Aiello
Do the Right Thing (1989) role "Sal Frangione"

Dan Aykroyd
Driving Miss Daisy (1989) role "Boolie Werthan"

Marlon Brando
A Dry White Season (1989) role "Ian Mackenzie"

Martin Landau
Crimes and Misdemeanors (1989) role "Judah Rosenthal"

Best Actress in a Leading Role

⚊ **Jessica Tandy** ⚊
Driving Miss Daisy (1989) role "Daisy Werthan"

Isabelle Adjani
Camille Claudel (1988) role "Camille Claudel"

Pauline Collins
Shirley Valentine (1989) role "Shirley Valentine-Bradshaw"

Jessica Lange
Music Box (1989) role "Ann Talbot"

Michelle Pfeiffer
The Fabulous Baker Boys (1989) role "Susie Diamond"

Best Actress in a Supporting Role
⚐ Brenda Fricker ⚐
My Left Foot (1989) role "Bridget Fagan Brown"
Anjelica Huston
Enemies, A Love Story (1989) role "Tamara Broder"
Lena Olin
Enemies, A Love Story (1989) role "Masha Bloch"
Julia Roberts
Steel Magnolias (1989) role "Shelby Eatenton Latcherie"
Dianne Wiest
Parenthood (1989) role "Helen Buckman"

Honorary Award
⚐ Akira Kurosawa ⚐
For cinematic accomplishments that have inspired, delighted, enriched and
entertained worldwide audiences and influenced filmmakers throughout the world.

Best Art Direction
⚐ Anton Furst (Art Direction), Peter Young (Set Decoration) ⚐
Batman (1989)
Leslie Dilley (Art Direction), Anne Kuljian (Set Decoration)
The Abyss (1989)
Dante Ferretti (Art Direction), Francesca Lo Schiavo (Set Decoration)
The Adventures of Baron Munchausen (1988)
Norman Garwood (Art Direction), Garrett Lewis (Set Decoration)
Glory (1989)
Bruno Rubeo (Art Direction), Crispian Sallis (Set Decoration)
Driving Miss Daisy (1989)

Best Cinematography
⚐ Freddie Francis ⚐
Glory (1989)
Michael Ballhaus
The Fabulous Baker Boys (1989)
Robert Richardson
Born on the Fourth of July (1989)
Mikael Salomon
The Abyss (1989)
Haskell Wexler
Blaze (1989)

Best Costume Design
⚐ Phyllis Dalton ⚐
Henry V (1989)
Elizabeth McBride
Driving Miss Daisy (1989)
Gabriella Pescucci
The Adventures of Baron Munchausen (1988)
Theodor Pistek
Valmont (1989)
Joe I. Tompkins
Harlem Nights (1989)

Best Directing
⚱ Oliver Stone ⚱
Born on the Fourth of July (1989)
Woody Allen
Crimes and Misdemeanors (1989)
Kenneth Branagh
Henry V (1989)
Jim Sheridan
My Left Foot (1989)
Peter Weir
Dead Poets Society (1989)

Best Documentary, Feature
⚱ Bill Couturié, Robert Epstein (Producers) ⚱
Common Threads: Stories from the Quilt (1989)
Betsy Broyles Breier, Al Reinert (Producers)
For All Mankind (1989)
Vince DiPersio, William Guttentag (Producers)
Crack USA: County Under Siege (1989)
Bill Jersey, Judith Leonard (Producers)
Super Chief: The Life and Legacy of Earl Warren (1989)
Richard Kilberg, Yvonne Smith (Producers)
Adam Clayton Powell (1989)

Best Documentary, Short Subject
⚱ Charles Guggenheim (Producer) ⚱
The Johnstown Flood (1989)
Ray Errol Fox (Producer)
Yad Vashem: Preserving the Past to Ensure the Future (1989)
David Petersen (Producer)
Fine Food, Fine Pastries, Open 6 to 9 (1989)

Best Film Editing
⚱ David Brenner, Joe Hutshing ⚱
Born on the Fourth of July (1989)
Noëlle Boisson
L'ours (eng. The Bear) (1988)
Steven Rosenblum
Glory (1989)
William Steinkamp
The Fabulous Baker Boys (1989)
Mark Warner
Driving Miss Daisy (1989)

Best Makeup
⚱ Lynn Barber, Kevin Haney, Manlio Rocchetti ⚱
Driving Miss Daisy (1989)
Ken Diaz, Greg Nelson, Dick Smith
Dad (1989)
Fabrizio Sforza, Maggie Weston
The Adventures of Baron Munchausen (1988)

Best Foreign Language Film
⬇ Italy ⬇
Nuovo Cinema Paradiso (eng. Cinema Paradiso) (1988)
Canada
Jésus de Montréal (eng. Jesus of Montreal) (1989)
Denmark
Dansen med Regitze (eng. Memories of a Marriage) (1989)
France
Camille Claudel (1988)
Puerto Rico
Lo que le pasó a Santiago (eng. What Happened to Santiago) (1989)

Best Short Film, Animated
⬇ Christoph Lauenstein, Wolfgang Lauenstein ⬇
Balance (1989)
Mark Baker
The Hill Farm (1989)
Alexander Petrov
Korova (eng. The Cow) (1989)

Best Short Film, Live Action
⬇ James Hendrie ⬇
Work Experience (1989)
Robert Nixon
Amazon Diary (1989)
Jonathan Tammuz
The Child Eater (1989)

Best Music, Original Score
⬇ Alan Menken ⬇
The Little Mermaid (1989)
David Grusin
The Fabulous Baker Boys (1989)
James Horner
Field of Dreams (1989)
John Williams
Born on the Fourth of July (1989), Indiana Jones and the Last Crusade (1989)

Best Music, Original Song
⬇ Alan Menken (Music), Howard Ashman (Lyrics) ⬇
for the song "Under the Sea"
The Little Mermaid (1989)
Marvin Hamlisch (Music), Alan Bergman, Marilyn Bergman (Lyrics)
for the song "The Girl Who Used to Be Me"
Shirley Valentine (1989)
Alan Menken (Music), Howard Ashman (Lyrics) for the song "Kiss the Girl"
The Little Mermaid (1989)
Randy Newman (Music & Lyrics) for the song "I Love to See You Smile"
Parenthood (1989)
Tom Snow (Music), Dean Pitchford (Lyrics) for the song "After All"
Chances Are (1989)

Best Picture

⚱ Lili Fini Zanuck, Richard D. Zanuck (Producers) ⚱
Driving Miss Daisy (1989)

Charles Gordon, Lawrence Gordon (Producers)
Field of Dreams (1989)

Steven Haft, Tony Thomas, Paul Junger Witt (Producers)
Dead Poets Society (1989)

A. Kitman Ho, Oliver Stone (Producers)
Born on the Fourth of July (1989)

Noel Pearson (Producer)
My Left Foot (1989)

Best Sound

⚱ Donald O. Mitchell, Gregg C. Rudloff, Elliot Tyson, Russell Williams II ⚱
Glory (1989)

Don J. Bassman, Kevin F. Cleary, Lee Orloff, Richard Overton
The Abyss (1989)

Ben Burtt, Tony Dawe, Shawn Murphy, Gary Summers
Indiana Jones and the Last Crusade (1989)

Tod A. Maitland, Michael Minkler, Wylie Stateman, Gregory H. Watkins
Born on the Fourth of July (1989)

Donald O. Mitchell, Kevin O'Connell, Greg P. Russell, Keith A. Wester
Black Rain (1989)

Best Sound Effects Editing

⚱ Ben Burtt, Richard Hymns ⚱
Indiana Jones and the Last Crusade (1989)

Milton C. Burrow, William L. Manger
Black Rain (1989)

Robert G. Henderson, Alan Robert Murray
Lethal Weapon 2 (1989)

Best Visual Effects

⚱ John Bruno, Dennis Muren, Dennis Skotak, Hoyt Yeatman ⚱
The Abyss (1989)

John Bell, Steve Gawley, Michael Lantieri, Ken Ralston
Back to the Future Part II (1989)

Richard Conway, Kent Houston
The Adventures of Baron Munchausen (1988)

Best Writing, Screenplay Based on Material from Another Medium

⚱ Alfred Uhry ⚱
Driving Miss Daisy (1989)

Shane Connaughton, Jim Sheridan
My Left Foot (1989)

Ron Kovic, Oliver Stone
Born on the Fourth of July (1989)

Paul Mazursky, Roger L. Simon
Enemies, A Love Story (1989)

Phil Alden Robinson
Field of Dreams (1989)

Best Writing, Screenplay Written Directly for the Screen
⚐ Tom Schulman ⚐
Dead Poets Society (1989)
Woody Allen
Crimes and Misdemeanors (1989)
Nora Ephron
When Harry Met Sally... (1989)
Spike Lee
Do the Right Thing (1989)
Steven Soderbergh
Sex, Lies, and Videotape (1989)

Jean Hersholt Humanitarian Award
⚐ Howard W. Koch ⚐

The 63rd Academy Awards® - March 25, 1991
Host: Billy Crystal
Venue: Shrine Civic Auditorium
Honoring movies released in 1990

Honorary Award
⚐ Sophia Loren ⚐
For a career rich with memorable performances that has added permanent luster to our art form.
⚐ Myrna Loy ⚐
In recognition of her extraordinary qualities both on screen and off, with appreciation for a lifetime's worth of indelible performances.

Best Actor in a Leading Role
⚐ Jeremy Irons ⚐
Reversal of Fortune (1990) role "Claus von Bülow"
Kevin Costner
Dances with Wolves (1990) role "Lieutenant John J. Dunbar"
Robert De Niro
Awakenings (1990) role "Leonard Lowe"
Gérard Depardieu
Cyrano de Bergerac (1990) role "Cyrano de Bergerac"
Richard Harris
The Field (1990) role ""Bull" McCabe"

Best Actor in a Supporting Role
⚐ Joe Pesci ⚐
Goodfellas (1990) role "Tommy DeVito"
Bruce Davison
Longtime Companion (1989) role "David"
Andy García
The Godfather: Part III (1990) role "Vincenzo Santino Corleone (Mancini)"
Graham Greene
Dances with Wolves (1990) role "Kicking Bird"
Al Pacino
Dick Tracy (1990) role "Alphonse "Big Boy" Caprice"

Best Actress in a Leading Role
⚱ Kathy Bates ⚱
Misery (1990) role "Annie Wilkes"
Anjelica Huston
The Grifters (1990) role "Lilly Dillon"
Julia Roberts
Pretty Woman (1990) role "Vivian Ward"
Meryl Streep
Postcards from the Edge (1990) role "Suzanne Vale"
Joanne Woodward
Mr. & Mrs. Bridge (1990) role "India Bridge"

Best Actress in a Supporting Role
⚱ Whoopi Goldberg ⚱
Ghost (1990) role "Oda Mae Brown"
Annette Bening
The Grifters (1990) role "Myra Langtry"
Lorraine Bracco
Goodfellas (1990) role "Karen Friedman Hill"
Diane Ladd
Wild at Heart (1990) role "Marietta Fortune"
Mary McDonnell
Dances with Wolves (1990) role "Stands With a Fist"

Irving G. Thalberg Memorial Award
⚱ David Brown ⚱
⚱ Richard D. Zanuck ⚱

Best Art Direction
⚱ Richard Sylbert (Art Direction), Rick Simpson (Set Decoration) ⚱
Dick Tracy (1990)
Jeffrey Beecroft (Art Direction), Lisa Dean (Set Decoration)
Dances with Wolves (1990)
Dante Ferretti (Art Direction), Francesca Lo Schiavo (Set Decoration)
Hamlet (1990)
Ezio Frigerio (Art Direction), Jacques Rouxel (Set Decoration)
Cyrano de Bergerac (1990)
Dean Tavoularis (Art Direction), Gary Fettis (Set Decoration)
The Godfather: Part III (1990)

Best Cinematography
⚱ Dean Semler ⚱
Dances with Wolves (1990)
Allen Daviau
Avalon (1990)
Philippe Rousselot
Henry & June (1990)
Vittorio Storaro
Dick Tracy (1990)
Gordon Willis
The Godfather: Part III (1990)

Best Costume Design

ↂ **Franca Squarciapino** ↂ
Cyrano de Bergerac (1990)

Milena Canonero
Dick Tracy (1990)

Gloria Gresham
Avalon (1990)

Maurizio Millenotti
Hamlet (1990)

Elsa Zamparelli
Dances with Wolves (1990)

Best Makeup

ↂ **John Caglione Jr., Doug Drexler** ↂ
Dick Tracy (1990)

Michèle Burke, Jean-Pierre Eychenne
Cyrano de Bergerac (1990)

Ve Neill, Stan Winston
Edward Scissorhands (1990)

Best Sound Effects Editing

ↂ **Cecelia Hall, George Watters II** ↂ
The Hunt for Red October (1990)

Charles L. Campbell, Richard C. Franklin
Flatliners (1990)

Stephen Hunter Flick
Total Recall (1990)

Best Music, Original Score

ↂ **John Barry** ↂ
Dances with Wolves (1990)

David Grusin
Havana (1990)

Maurice Jarre
Ghost (1990)

Randy Newman
Avalon (1990)

John Williams
Home Alone (1990)

Best Sound

ↂ **Bill W. Benton, Jeffrey Perkins, Gregory H. Watkins, Russell Williams II** ↂ
Dances with Wolves (1990)

Don J. Bassman, Kevin F. Cleary, Richard Bryce Goodman, Richard Overton
The Hunt for Red October (1990)

David E. Campbell, Thomas Causey, Doug M. Hemphill, Chris Jenkins
Dick Tracy (1990)

Carlos Delarios, Michael J. Kohut, Aaron Rochin, Nelson Stoll
Total Recall (1990)

Rick Kline, Donald O. Mitchell, Kevin O'Connell, Charles M. Wilborn
Days of Thunder (1990)

Best Music, Original Song

Stephen Sondheim (Music & Lyrics)
⚊ for the song "Sooner or Later (I Always Get My Man)" ⚊
Dick Tracy (1990)

Carmine Coppola (Music), John Bettis (Lyrics)
for the song "Promise Me You'll Remember"
The Godfather: Part III (1990)

Jon Bon Jovi (Music & Lyrics) for the song "Blaze of Glory"
Young Guns II (1990)

Shel Silverstein (Music & Lyrics) for the song "I'm Checkin' Out"
Postcards from the Edge (1990)

John Williams (Music), Leslie Bricusse (Lyrics)
for the song "Somewhere in My Memory"
Home Alone (1990)

Best Picture

⚊ **Kevin Costner, Jim Wilson (Producers)** ⚊
Dances with Wolves (1990)

Francis Ford Coppola (Producer)
The Godfather: Part III (1990)

Lawrence Lasker, Walter F. Parkes (Producers)
Awakenings (1990)

Lisa Weinstein (Producer)
Ghost (1990)

Irwin Winkler (Producer)
Goodfellas (1990)

Best Short Film, Animated

⚊ **Nick Park** ⚊
Creature Comforts (1989)

Bruno Bozzetto
Cavallette (eng. Grasshoppers) (1990)

Nick Park
A Grand Day Out (1989)

Best Short Film, Live Action

⚊ **Adam Davidson** ⚊
The Lunch Date (1989)

Peter Cattaneo, Barnaby Thompson
Dear Rosie (1990)

Raymond De Felitta, Matthew Gross
Bronx Cheers (1991)

Jonathan Heap, Hillary Anne Ripps
12:01 PM (1991)

Bernard Joffa, Anthony E. Nicholas
Senzeni Na? (eng. What Have We Done?) (1990)

Special Achievement Award, Visual Effects

⚊ **Rob Bottin, Eric Brevig, Alex Funke, Tim McGovern** ⚊
Total Recall (1990)

Best Directing
⚱ **Kevin Costner** ⚱
Dances with Wolves (1990)
Francis Ford Coppola
The Godfather: Part III (1990)
Stephen Frears
The Grifters (1990)
Barbet Schroeder
Reversal of Fortune (1990)
Martin Scorsese
Goodfellas (1990)

Best Documentary, Feature
⚱ **Arthur Cohn, Barbara Kopple (Producers)** ⚱
American Dream (1990)
Eugene Corr, Robert Hillmann (Producers)
Waldo Salt: A Screenwriter's Journey (1990)
Mark Kitchell (Producer)
Berkeley in the Sixties (1990)
Judith Montell (Producer)
Forever Activists: Stories from the Veterans of the Abraham Lincoln Brigade (1990)
Mark Mori, Susan Robinson (Producers)
Building Bombs (1989)

Best Documentary, Short Subject
⚱ **Steven Okazaki (Producer)** ⚱
Days of Waiting (1991)
Derek Bromhall (Producer)
Journey Into Life: The World of the Unborn (1990)
Karen Goodman, Kirk Simon (Producers)
Chimps: So Like Us (1990)
Freida Lee Mock, Terry Sanders (Producers)
Rose Kennedy: A Life to Remember (1990)
Kit Thomas (Producer)
Burning Down Tomorrow (1990)

Best Film Editing
⚱ **Neil Travis** ⚱
Dances with Wolves (1990)
Lisa Fruchtman, Barry Malkin, Walter Murch
The Godfather: Part III (1990)
Walter Murch
Ghost (1990)
Thelma Schoonmaker
Goodfellas (1990)
Dennis Virkler, John Wright
The Hunt for Red October (1990)

Best Foreign Language Film

⚐ Switzerland ⚐
Reise der Hoffnung (eng. Journey of Hope) (1990)

France
Cyrano de Bergerac (1990)

Germany
Das schreckliche Mädchen (eng. The Nasty Girl) (1990)

Italy
Porte aperte (eng. Open Doors) (1990)

People's Republic of China
Ju Dou (1990)

Best Writing, Screenplay Based on Material from Another Medium

⚐ Michael Blake ⚐
Dances with Wolves (1990)

Nicholas Kazan
Reversal of Fortune (1990)

Nicholas Pileggi, Martin Scorsese
Goodfellas (1990)

Donald E. Westlake
The Grifters (1990)

Steven Zaillian
Awakenings (1990)

Best Writing, Screenplay Written Directly for the Screen

⚐ Bruce Joel Rubin ⚐
Ghost (1990)

Woody Allen
Alice (1990)

Barry Levinson
Avalon (1990)

Whit Stillman
Metropolitan (1990)

Peter Weir
Green Card (1990)

The 64th Academy Awards® - March 30, 1992

Host: Billy Crystal
Venue: Dorothy Chandler Pavilion
Honoring movies released in 1991

Best Actor in a Leading Role

⚐ Anthony Hopkins ⚐
The Silence of the Lambs (1991) role "Dr. Hannibal Lecter"

Warren Beatty
Bugsy (1991) role "Benjamin "Bugsy" Siegel"

Robert De Niro
Cape Fear (1991) role "Maximilian "Max" Cady"

Nick Nolte
The Prince of Tides (1991) role "Tom Wingo"

Robin Williams
The Fisher King (1991) role "Henry "Parry" Sagan"

Best Actor in a Supporting Role
⚱ Jack Palance ⚱
City Slickers (1991) role "Curly Washburn"
Tommy Lee Jones
JFK (1991) role "Clay Shaw"
Harvey Keitel
Bugsy (1991) role "Mickey Cohen"
Ben Kingsley
Bugsy (1991) role "Meyer Lansky"
Michael Lerner
Barton Fink (1991) role "Jack Lipnick"

Best Actress in a Leading Role
⚱ Jodie Foster ⚱
The Silence of the Lambs (1991) role "Clarice Starling"
Geena Davis
Thelma & Louise (1991) role "Thelma Dickinson"
Laura Dern
Rambling Rose (1991) role "Rose"
Bette Midler
For the Boys (1991) role "Dixie Leonard"
Susan Sarandon
Thelma & Louise (1991) role "Louise Sawyer"

Best Actress in a Supporting Role
⚱ Mercedes Ruehl ⚱
The Fisher King (1991) role "Anne Napolitano"
Diane Ladd
Rambling Rose (1991) role "Mrs. Hillyer (Mother)"
Juliette Lewis
Cape Fear (1991) role "Danielle Bowden"
Kate Nelligan
The Prince of Tides (1991) role "Lila Wingo Newbury"
Jessica Tandy
Fried Green Tomatoes (1991) role "Virginia "Ninny" Threadgoode"

Honorary Award
⚱ Satyajit Ray ⚱
For rare mastery of the art of motion pictures and for his profound humanitarian outlook, which has had an indelible influence on filmmakers & audiences throughout the world.

Best Art Direction
⚱ Dennis Gassner (Art Direction), Nancy Haigh (Set Decoration) ⚱
Bugsy (1991)
Mel Bourne (Art Direction), Cindy Carr (Set Decoration)
The Fisher King (1991)
Norman Garwood (Art Direction), Garrett Lewis (Set Decoration)
Hook (1991)
Dennis Gassner (Art Direction), Nancy Haigh (Set Decoration)
Barton Fink (1991)
Paul Sylbert (Art Direction), Caryl Heller (Set Decoration)
The Prince of Tides (1991)

Best Cinematography

⚜ **Robert Richardson** ⚜
JFK (1991)

Adrian Biddle
Thelma & Louise (1991)

Allen Daviau
Bugsy (1991)

Stephen Goldblatt
The Prince of Tides (1991)

Adam Greenberg
Terminator 2: Judgment Day (1991)

Best Visual Effects

⚜ **Dennis Muren, Robert Skotak, Gene Warren Jr., Stan Winston** ⚜
Terminator 2: Judgment Day (1991)

Eric Brevig, Harley Jessup, Michael Lantieri, Mark Sullivan
Hook (1991)

Scott Farrar, Allen Hall, Clay Pinney, Mikael Salomon
Backdraft (1991)

Best Costume Design

⚜ **Albert Wolsky** ⚜
Bugsy (1991)

Richard Hornung
Barton Fink (1991)

Corinne Jorry
Madame Bovary (1991)

Ruth Myers
The Addams Family (1991)

Anthony Powell
Hook (1991)

Best Directing

⚜ **Jonathan Demme** ⚜
The Silence of the Lambs (1991)

Barry Levinson
Bugsy (1991)

Ridley Scott
Thelma & Louise (1991)

John Singleton
Boyz n the Hood (1991)

Oliver Stone
JFK (1991)

Best Makeup

⚜ **Jeff Dawn, Stan Winston** ⚜
Terminator 2: Judgment Day (1991)

Greg Cannom, Christina Smith, Monty Westmore
Hook (1991)

Edward French, Michael Mills, Richard Snell
Star Trek VI: The Undiscovered Country (1991)

Best Documentary, Feature

⚊ **Allie Light, Irving Saraf (Producers)** ⚊
In the Shadow of the Stars (1991)

Hava Kohav Beller (Producer)
The Restless Conscience: Resistance to Hitler Within Germany 1933-1945 (1992)

Vince DiPersio, William Guttentag (Producers)
Death on the Job (1991)

Diane Garey, Lawrence R. Hott (Producers)
Wild by Law (1991)

Alan Raymond, Susan Raymond (Producers)
Doing Time: Life Inside the Big House (1991)

Best Documentary, Short Subject

⚊ **Debra Chasnoff (Producer)** ⚊
Deadly Deception: General Electric, Nuclear Weapons and Our Environment (1991)

Bill Couturié, Bernard Edelman (Producers)
Memorial: Letters from American Soldiers (1991)

Immy Humes (Producer)
A Little Vicious (1991)

Alain Majani d'Inguimbert, Eric Valli (Producers)
Chasseurs des ténèbres (eng. Birdnesters of Thailand) (1991)

David McGowan (Producer)
The Mark of the Maker (1991)

Best Picture

⚊ **Ron Bozman, Edward Saxon, Kenneth Utt (Producers)** ⚊
The Silence of the Lambs (1991)

Warren Beatty, Mark Johnson, Barry Levinson (Producers)
Bugsy (1991)

Don Hahn (Producer)
Beauty and the Beast (1991)

A. Kitman Ho, Oliver Stone (Producers)
JFK (1991)

Andrew S. Karsch, Barbra Streisand (Producers)
The Prince of Tides (1991)

Best Short Film, Animated

⚊ **Daniel Greaves** ⚊
Manipulation (1991)

Christopher Hinton
Blackfly (1991)

Wendy Tilby
Strings (1991)

Best Short Film, Live Action

⚊ **Robert N. Fried, Seth Winston** ⚊
Session Man (1991)

Thomas R. Conroy, Stephen Kessler
Birch Street Gym (1991)

David M. Massey
Last Breeze of Summer (1991)

Best Film Editing
⚜ Joe Hutshing, Pietro Scalia ⚜
JFK (1991)
Conrad Buff IV, Mark Goldblatt, Richard A. Harris
Terminator 2: Judgment Day (1991)
Gerry Hambling
The Commitments (1991)
Craig McKay
The Silence of the Lambs (1991)
Thom Noble
Thelma & Louise (1991)

Best Foreign Language Film
⚜ Italy ⚜
Mediterraneo (1991)
Czechoslovakia
Obecná skola (eng. The Elementary School) (1991)
Hong Kong
Dà hóng denglong gaogao guà (eng. Raise the Red Lantern) (1991)
Iceland
Börn náttúrunnar (eng. Children of Nature) (1991)
Sweden
Oxen (eng. The Ox) (1991)

Best Music, Original Score
⚜ Alan Menken ⚜
Beauty and the Beast (1991)
George Fenton
The Fisher King (1991)
James Newton Howard
The Prince of Tides (1991)
Ennio Morricone
Bugsy (1991)
John Williams
JFK (1991)

Best Music, Original Song
⚜ Alan Menken (Music), Howard Ashman (Lyrics) ⚜
for the song "Beauty and the Beast"
(Howard Ashman - posthumous)
Beauty and the Beast (1991)
Michael Kamen (Music), Bryan Adams, Mutt Lange (as Robert John Lange) (Lyrics) for the song "(Everything I Do) I Do It for You"
Robin Hood: Prince of Thieves (1991)
Alan Menken (Music), Howard Ashman (Lyrics) for the songs "Be Our Guest", "Belle"
(Howard Ashman - posthumous)
Beauty and the Beast (1991)
John Williams (Music), Leslie Bricusse (Lyrics) for the song "When You're Alone"
Hook (1991)

Best Sound

⚊ **Tom Johnson, Lee Orloff, Gary Rydstrom, Gary Summers** ⚊
Terminator 2: Judgment Day (1991)

Tom Fleischman, Christopher Newman
The Silence of the Lambs (1991)

David J. Hudson, Doc Kane, Mel Metcalfe, Terry Porter
Beauty and the Beast (1991)

Gregg Landaker, Tod A. Maitland, Michael Minkler
JFK (1991)

Gary Rydstrom, Gary Summers, Randy Thom, Glenn Williams
Backdraft (1991)

Best Sound Effects Editing

⚊ **Gloria S. Borders, Gary Rydstrom** ⚊
Terminator 2: Judgment Day (1991)

Richard Hymns, Gary Rydstrom
Backdraft (1991)

F. Hudson Miller, George Watters II
Star Trek VI: The Undiscovered Country (1991)

Best Writing, Screenplay Based on Material Previously Produced or Published

⚊ **Ted Tally** ⚊
The Silence of the Lambs (1991)

Pat Conroy, Becky Johnston
The Prince of Tides (1991)

Fannie Flagg, Carol Sobieski
(Carol Sobieski - posthumous)
Fried Green Tomatoes (1991)

Agnieszka Holland
Europa Europa (1990)

Zachary Sklar, Oliver Stone
JFK (1991)

Best Writing, Screenplay Written Directly for the Screen

⚊ **Callie Khouri** ⚊
Thelma & Louise (1991)

Lawrence Kasdan, Meg Kasdan
Grand Canyon (1991)

Richard LaGravenese
The Fisher King (1991)

John Singleton
Boyz n the Hood (1991)

James Toback
Bugsy (1991)

Irving G. Thalberg Memorial Award

⚊ **George Lucas** ⚊

64th Ceremony 6/6

The 65ᵗʰ Academy Awards® - March 29, 1993

Host: Billy Crystal
Venue: Dorothy Chandler Pavilion
Honoring movies released in 1992

Best Actor in a Leading Role

⚡ Al Pacino ⚡
Scent of a Woman (1992) role "Lieutenant Colonel Frank Slade"

Robert Downey Jr.
Chaplin (1992) role "Charles Spencer Chaplin Jr."

Clint Eastwood
Unforgiven (1992) role "William "Will" Munny"

Stephen Rea
The Crying Game (1992) role "Fergus"

Denzel Washington
Malcolm X (1992) role "Malcolm X"

Best Actor in a Supporting Role

⚡ Gene Hackman ⚡
Unforgiven (1992) role "Little Bill Daggett"

Jaye Davidson
The Crying Game (1992) role "Dil"

Jack Nicholson
A Few Good Men (1992) role "Colonel Nathan R. Jessup"

Al Pacino
Glengarry Glen Ross (1992) role "Richard "Ricky" Roma"

David Paymer
Mr. Saturday Night (1992) role "Stan Young"

Best Actress in a Leading Role

⚡ Emma Thompson ⚡
Howards End (1992) role "Margaret Schlegel"

Catherine Deneuve
Indochine (1992) role "Éliane Devries"

Mary McDonnell
Passion Fish (1992) role "May-Alice Culhane"

Michelle Pfeiffer
Love Field (1992) role "Louise Irene "Lurene" Hallett"

Susan Sarandon
Lorenzo's Oil (1992) role "Michaela Murphy Odone"

Best Actress in a Supporting Role

⚡ Marisa Tomei ⚡
My Cousin Vinny (1992) role "Mona Lisa Vito"

Judy Davis
Husbands and Wives (1992) role "Sally Simmons"

Joan Plowright
Enchanted April (1991) role "Mrs. Fisher"

Vanessa Redgrave
Howards End (1992) role "Ruth Wilcox"

Miranda Richardson
Damage (1992) role "Ingrid Thompson-Fleming"

Jean Hersholt Humanitarian Award

⚐ **Audrey Hepburn** ⚐
(posthumous)

⚐ **Elizabeth Taylor** ⚐

Best Art Direction

⚐ **Luciana Arrighi (Art Direction), Ian Whittaker (Set Decoration)** ⚐
Howards End (1992)

Henry Bumstead (Art Direction), Janice Blackie-Goodine (Set Decoration)
Unforgiven (1992)

Stuart Craig (Art Direction), Chris A. Butler (Set Decoration)
Chaplin (1992)

Thomas E. Sanders (Art Direction), Garrett Lewis (Set Decoration)
Dracula (1992)

Ferdinando Scarfiotti (Art Direction), Linda DeScenna (Set Decoration)
Toys (1992)

Best Cinematography

⚐ **Philippe Rousselot** ⚐
A River Runs Through It (1992)

Stephen H. Burum
Hoffa (1992)

Robert Fraisse
L'amant (eng. The Lover) (1992)

Jack N. Green
Unforgiven (1992)

Tony Pierce-Roberts
Howards End (1992)

Best Costume Design

⚐ **Eiko Ishioka** ⚐
Dracula (1992)

Jenny Beavan, John Bright
Howards End (1992)

Ruth E. Carter
Malcolm X (1992)

Sheena Napier
Enchanted April (1991)

Albert Wolsky
Toys (1992)

Best Directing

⚐ **Clint Eastwood** ⚐
Unforgiven (1992)

Robert Altman
The Player (1992)

Martin Brest
Scent of a Woman (1992)

James Ivory
Howards End (1992)

Neil Jordan
The Crying Game (1992)

Best Documentary, Feature

⇣ David Kasper, Barbara Trent (Producers) ⇣
The Panama Deception (1992)

Roma Baran, Margaret Smilow (Producers)
Music for the Movies: Bernard Herrmann (1992)

Sally Dundas (Producer)
Fires of Kuwait (1992)

David Haugland (Producer)
Changing Our Minds: The Story of Dr. Evelyn Hooker (1992)

William Miles, Nina Rosenblum (Producers)
Liberators: Fighting on Two Fronts in World War II (1992)

Best Documentary, Short Subject

⇣ Thomas C. Goodwin, Gerardine Wurzburg (Producers) ⇣
(Thomas C. Goodwin - posthumous)
Educating Peter (1992)

Sally Bochner, Richard Elson (Producers)
The Colours of My Father: A Portrait of Sam Borenstein (1992)

Dorothy Fadiman (Producer)
When Abortion Was Illegal: Untold Stories (1992)

Geoffrey O'Connor (Producer)
At the Edge of Conquest: The Journey of Chief Wai-Wai (1992)

Wendy L. Weinberg (Producer)
Beyond Imagining: Margaret Anderson and the 'Little Review' (1994)

Best Visual Effects

⇣ Doug Chiang, Ken Ralston, Doug Smythe, Tom Woodruff Jr. ⇣
Death Becomes Her (1992)

Craig Barron, John Bruno, Michael L. Fink, Dennis Skotak
Batman Returns (1992)

Richard Edlund, George Gibbs, Alec Gillis, Tom Woodruff Jr.
Alien 3 (1992)

Best Makeup

⇣ Michèle Burke, Greg Cannom, Matthew W. Mungle ⇣
Dracula (1992)

John Blake, Greg Cannom, Ve Neill
Hoffa (1992)

Ve Neill, Ronnie Specter, Stan Winston
Batman Returns (1992)

Best Film Editing

⇣ Joel Cox ⇣
Unforgiven (1992)

Robert Leighton
A Few Good Men (1992)

Kant Pan
The Crying Game (1992)

Geraldine Peroni
The Player (1992)

Frank J. Urioste
Basic Instinct (1992)

Best Foreign Language Film

⚜ France ⚜
Indochine (1992)

Belgium
Daens (1992)

Germany
Schtonk (1992)

Russia
Urga (eng. Close to Eden) (1991)

Uruguay
(withdrawn)
Un lugar en el mundo (eng. A Place in the World) (1992)

Best Music, Original Score

⚜ Alan Menken ⚜
Aladdin (1992)

John Barry
Chaplin (1992)

Jerry Goldsmith
Basic Instinct (1992)

Mark Isham
A River Runs Through It (1992)

Richard Robbins
Howards End (1992)

Best Music, Original Song

**⚜ Alan Menken (Music), Tim Rice (Lyrics) ⚜
for the song "A Whole New World"**
Aladdin (1992)

David Foster (Music), Linda Thompson (Lyrics) for the song "I Have Nothing"
The Bodyguard (1992)

Jud Friedman (Music), Allan Rich (Lyrics) for the song "Run to You"
The Bodyguard (1992)

**Robert Kraft (Music), Arne Glimcher (Lyrics)
for the song "Beautiful Maria of My Soul"**
The Mambo Kings (1992)

Alan Menken (Music), Howard Ashman (Lyrics) for the song "Friend Like Me"
(Howard Ashman - posthumous)
Aladdin (1992)

Best Picture

⚜ Clint Eastwood (Producer) ⚜
Unforgiven (1992)

Martin Brest (Producer)
Scent of a Woman (1992)

David Brown, Rob Reiner and Andrew Scheinman (Producers)
A Few Good Men (1992)

Ismail Merchant (Producer)
Howards End (1992)

Stephen Woolley (Producer)
The Crying Game (1992)

Best Short Film, Animated

⟐ Joan C. Gratz ⟐
Mona Lisa Descending a Staircase (1992)

Paul Berry
The Sandman (1991)

Peter Lord
Adam (1992)

Michaela Pavlátová
Reci, reci, reci... (eng. Words, Words, Words) (1991)

Barry J.C. Purves
Screen Play (1993)

Best Short Film, Live Action

⟐ Sam Karmann ⟐
Omnibus (1992)

Kenneth Branagh, David Parfitt
Swan Song (1992)

Jonathan Darby, Jana Sue Memel
Contact (1993)

Matt Palmieri
Cruise Control (1992)

Christian M. Taylor
The Lady in Waiting (1992)

Best Sound

⟐ Doug Hemphill, Chris Jenkins, Simon Kaye, Mark Smith ⟐
The Last of the Mohicans (1992)

Rick Alexander (as Dick Alexander), Les Fresholtz, Vern Poore, Rob Young
Unforgiven (1992)

Bob Eber, Rick Kline, Kevin O'Connell
A Few Good Men (1992)

Rick Hart, Donald O. Mitchell, Frank A. Montaño, Scott D. Smith
Under Siege (1992)

David J. Hudson, Doc Kane, Mel Metcalfe, Terry Porter
Aladdin (1992)

Honorary Award

⟐ Federico Fellini ⟐
In recognition of his cinematic accomplishments that have thrilled and entertained worldwide audiences.

Best Writing, Screenplay Based on Material Previously Produced or Published

⟐ Ruth Prawer Jhabvala ⟐
Howards End (1992)

Peter Barnes
Enchanted April (1991)

Richard Friedenberg
A River Runs Through It (1992)

Bo Goldman
Scent of a Woman (1992)

Michael Tolkin
The Player (1992)

Best Writing, Screenplay Written Directly for the Screen

⚐ **Neil Jordan** ⚐
The Crying Game (1992)

Woody Allen
Husbands and Wives (1992)

Nick Enright, George Miller
Lorenzo's Oil (1992)

David Webb Peoples
Unforgiven (1992)

John Sayles
Passion Fish (1992)

Best Sound Effects Editing

⚐ **Tom C. McCarthy, David E. Stone** ⚐
Dracula (1992)

John Leveque, Bruce Stambler
Under Siege (1992)

Mark A. Mangini
Aladdin (1992)

The 66ᵗʰ Academy Awards® - March 21, 1994

Host: Whoopi Goldberg
Venue: Dorothy Chandler Pavilion
Honoring movies released in 1993

Jean Hersholt Humanitarian Award

⚐ **Paul Newman** ⚐

Best Actor in a Leading Role

⚐ **Tom Hanks** ⚐
Philadelphia (1993) role "Andrew "Andy" Beckett"

Daniel Day-Lewis
In the Name of the Father (1993) role "Gerry Conlon"

Laurence Fishburne
What's Love Got to Do with It (1993) role "Ike Turner"

Anthony Hopkins
The Remains of the Day (1993) role "James Stevens"

Liam Neeson
Schindler's List (1993) role "Oskar Schindler"

Best Actor in a Supporting Role

⚐ **Tommy Lee Jones** ⚐
The Fugitive (1993) role "U.S. Marshal Samuel Gerard"

Leonardo DiCaprio
What's Eating Gilbert Grape (1993) role "Arnie Grape"

Ralph Fiennes
Schindler's List (1993) role "Amon Göth"

John Malkovich
In the Line of Fire (1993) role "Mitch Leary"

Pete Postlethwaite
In the Name of the Father (1993) role "Giuseppe Conlon"

Best Actress in a Leading Role
⚐ Holly Hunter ⚐
The Piano (1993) role "Ada McGrath"
Angela Bassett
What's Love Got to Do with It (1993) role "Anna Mae Bullock / Tina Turner"
Stockard Channing
Six Degrees of Separation (1993) role "Louisa "Ouisa" Kittredge"
Emma Thompson
The Remains of the Day (1993) role "Sarah "Sally" Kenton"
Debra Winger
Shadowlands (1993) role "Joy Davidman-Gresham"

Best Actress in a Supporting Role
⚐ Anna Paquin ⚐
The Piano (1993) role "Flora McGrath"
Holly Hunter
The Firm (1993) role "Tamara "Tammy" Hemphill"
Rosie Perez
Fearless (1993) role "Carla Rodrigo"
Winona Ryder
The Age of Innocence (1993) role "May Welland"
Emma Thompson
In the Name of the Father (1993) role "Gareth Peirce"

Honorary Award
⚐ Deborah Kerr ⚐
An artist of impeccable grace and beauty, a dedicated actress whose motion picture career has always stood for perfection, discipline and elegance.

Best Art Direction
⚐ Allan Starski (Art Direction), Ewa Braun (Set Decoration) ⚐
Schindler's List (1993)
Ken Adam (Art Direction), Marvin March (Set Decoration)
Addams Family Values (1993)
Luciana Arrighi (Art Direction), Ian Whittaker (Set Decoration)
The Remains of the Day (1993)
Dante Ferretti (Art Direction), Robert J. Franco (Set Decoration)
The Age of Innocence (1993)
Ben Van Os, Jan Roelfs (Art Direction)
Orlando (1992)

Best Cinematography
⚐ Janusz Kaminski ⚐
Schindler's List (1993)
Gu Changwei
Ba wang bie ji (eng. Farewell My Concubine) (1993)
Michael Chapman
The Fugitive (1993)
Stuart Dryburgh
The Piano (1993)
Conrad L. Hall
Searching for Bobby Fischer (1993)

Best Costume Design
⊥ Gabriella Pescucci ⊥
The Age of Innocence (1993)
Jenny Beavan, John Bright
The Remains of the Day (1993)
Anna Biedrzycka-Sheppard
Schindler's List (1993)
Janet Patterson
The Piano (1993)
Sandy Powell
Orlando (1992)

Best Makeup
⊥ Greg Cannom, Ve Neill, Yolanda Toussieng ⊥
Mrs. Doubtfire (1993)
Judy Alexander Cory, Matthew W. Mungle, Christina Smith
Schindler's List (1993)
Alan D'Angerio, Carl Fullerton
Philadelphia (1993)

Best Directing
⊥ Steven Spielberg ⊥
Schindler's List (1993)
Robert Altman
Short Cuts (1993)
Jane Campion
The Piano (1993)
James Ivory
The Remains of the Day (1993)
Jim Sheridan
In the Name of the Father (1993)

Best Documentary, Feature
⊥ Alan Raymond, Susan Raymond ⊥
I Am a Promise: The Children of Stanton Elementary School (1993)
David Collier, Betsy Thompson
For Better or for Worse (1993)
Arthur Ginsberg, David Paperny
The Broadcast Tapes of Dr. Peter (1993)
Chris Hegedus, D. A. Pennebaker
The War Room (1993)
Susan Todd, Andrew Young
Children of Fate: Life and Death in a Sicilian Family (1993)

Best Documentary, Short Subject
⊥ Margaret Lazarus, Renner Wunderlich ⊥
Defending Our Lives (1994)
Steven Cantor, Peter Spirer
Blood Ties: The Life and Work of Sally Mann (1994)
Elaine Holliman, Jason Schneider
Chicks in White Satin (1993)

Best Film Editing

⚱ **Michael Kahn** ⚱
Schindler's List (1993)

**Don Brochu, David Finfer, Dean Goodhill, Richard Nord,
Dov Hoenig, Dennis Virkler**
The Fugitive (1993)

Anne V. Coates
In the Line of Fire (1993)

Gerry Hambling
In the Name of the Father (1993)

Veronika Jenet
The Piano (1993)

Best Foreign Language Film

⚱ **Spain** ⚱
Belle Epoque (1992)

Hong Kong
Ba wang bie ji (eng. Farewell My Concubine) (1993)

Taiwan
Xi yan (eng. The Wedding Banquet) (1993)

United Kingdom
Hedd Wyn (1992)

Vietnam
Mùi du du xanh (eng. The Scent of Green Papaya) (1993)

Best Music, Original Song

⚱ **Bruce Springsteen (Music & Lyrics) for the song "Streets of Philadelphia"** ⚱
Philadelphia (1993)

**James Ingram, Clif Magness, Carole Bayer Sager (Music & Lyrics)
for the song "The Day I Fall in Love"**
Beethoven's 2nd (1993)

**James Samuel Harris III, Janet Jackson, Terry Steven Lewis (Music & Lyrics)
for the song "Again"**
Poetic Justice (1993)

**Marc Shaiman (Music), Ramsay McLean (Lyrics)
for the song "A Wink and a Smile"**
Sleepless in Seattle (1993)

Neil Young (Music & Lyrics) for the song "Philadelphia"
Philadelphia (1993)

Best Sound

⚱ **Ron Judkins, Shawn Murphy, Gary Rydstrom, Gary Summers** ⚱
Jurassic Park (1993)

Bob Beemer, Tim Cooney, Michael Minkler
Cliffhanger (1993)

Bill W. Benton, Chris Carpenter, Doug M. Hemphill, Lee Orloff
Geronimo: An American Legend (1993)

Michael Herbick, Donald O. Mitchell, Frank A. Montaño, Scott D. Smith
The Fugitive (1993)

Ron Judkins, Scott Millan, Andy Nelson, Steve Pederson
Schindler's List (1993)

Best Music, Original Score

⚰ **John Williams** ⚰
Schindler's List (1993)

Elmer Bernstein
The Age of Innocence (1993)

Dave Grusin
The Firm (1993)

James Newton Howard
The Fugitive (1993)

Richard Robbins
The Remains of the Day (1993)

Best Sound Effects Editing

⚰ **Richard Hymns, Gary Rydstrom** ⚰
Jurassic Park (1993)

Gregg Baxter, Wylie Stateman
Cliffhanger (1993)

John Leveque, Bruce Stambler
The Fugitive (1993)

Best Visual Effects

⚰ **Michael Lantieri, Dennis Muren, Phil Tippett, Stan Winston** ⚰
Jurassic Park (1993)

Gordon Baker, Pete Kozachik, Eric Leighton, Ariel Velasco Shaw
The Nightmare Before Christmas (1993)

John Bruno, Pamela Easley, Neil Krepela, John Richardson
Cliffhanger (1993)

Best Picture

⚰ **Branko Lustig, Gerald R. Molen, Steven Spielberg (Producers)** ⚰
Schindler's List (1993)

John Calley, Ismail Merchant, Mike Nichols (Producers)
The Remains of the Day (1993)

Jan Chapman (Producer)
The Piano (1993)

Arnold Kopelson (Producer)
The Fugitive (1993)

Jim Sheridan (Producer)
In the Name of the Father (1993)

Best Short Film, Animated

⚰ **Nick Park** ⚰
The Wrong Trousers (1993)

Frédéric Back, Hubert Tison
Le fleuve aux grandes eaux (eng. The Mighty River) (1993)

Mark Baker
The Village (1993)

Kevin Baldwin, Bob Godfrey
Small Talk (1994)

Stephen Palmer
Blindscape (1993)

Best Short Film, Live Action
ⵊ Pepe Danquart ⵊ
Schwarzfahrer (eng. Black Rider) (1993)
Jonathan Brett, Susan Seidelman
The Dutch Master (1993)
Didier Flamand
La vis (eng. The Screw) (1993)
Jana Sue Memel, Peter Weller
Partners (1993)
Jonathan Penner, Stacy Title
Down on the Waterfront (1993)

Best Writing, Screenplay Based on Material Previously Produced or Published
ⵊ Steven Zaillian ⵊ
Schindler's List (1993)
Jay Cocks, Martin Scorsese
The Age of Innocence (1993)
Terry George, Jim Sheridan
In the Name of the Father (1993)
Ruth Prawer Jhabvala
The Remains of the Day (1993)
William Nicholson
Shadowlands (1993)

Best Writing, Screenplay Written Directly for the Screen
ⵊ Jane Campion ⵊ
The Piano (1993)
Jeff Arch, Nora Ephron, David S. Ward (Screenplay), Jeff Arch (Story)
Sleepless in Seattle (1993)
Jeff Maguire
In the Line of Fire (1993)
Ron Nyswaner
Philadelphia (1993)
Gary Ross
Dave (1993)

The 67th Academy Awards® - March 27, 1995
Host: David Letterman
Venue: Shrine Auditorium & Expo Center
Honoring movies released in 1994

Honorary Award
ⵊ Michelangelo Antonioni ⵊ
In recognition of his place as one of the cinema's master visual stylists.

Irving G. Thalberg Memorial Award
ⵊ Clint Eastwood ⵊ

Jean Hersholt Humanitarian Award
ⵊ Quincy Jones ⵊ

Best Actor in a Leading Role

↓ Tom Hanks ↓

Forrest Gump (1994) role "Forrest Gump"

Morgan Freeman

The Shawshank Redemption (1994) role "Ellis Boyd "Red" Redding"

Nigel Hawthorne

The Madness of King George (1994) role "King George III"

Paul Newman

Nobody's Fool (1994) role "Donald "Sully" Sullivan"

John Travolta

Pulp Fiction (1994) role "Vincent Vega"

Best Actor in a Supporting Role

↓ Martin Landau ↓

Ed Wood (1994) role "Bela Lugosi"

Samuel L. Jackson

Pulp Fiction (1994) role "Jules Winnfield"

Chazz Palminteri

Bullets Over Broadway (1994) role "Cheech"

Paul Scofield

Quiz Show (1994) role "Mark Van Doren"

Gary Sinise

Forrest Gump (1994) role "Lieutenant Dan Taylor"

Best Actress in a Leading Role

↓ Jessica Lange ↓

Blue Sky (1994) role "Carly Marshall"

Jodie Foster

Nell (1994) role "Nell Kellty"

Miranda Richardson

Tom & Viv (1994) role "Vivienne Haigh-Wood"

Winona Ryder

Little Women (1994) role "Josephine "Jo" March"

Susan Sarandon

The Client (1994) role "Regina "Reggie" Love"

Best Actress in a Supporting Role

↓ Dianne Wiest ↓

Bullets Over Broadway (1994) role "Helen Sinclair"

Rosemary Harris

Tom & Viv (1994) role "Rose Robinson Haigh-Wood"

Helen Mirren

The Madness of King George (1994) role "Queen Charlotte"

Uma Thurman

Pulp Fiction (1994) role "Mia Wallace"

Jennifer Tilly

Bullets Over Broadway (1994) role "Olive Neal"

Best Art Direction

⌊ Ken Adam (Art Direction), Carolyn Scott (Set Decoration) ⌋
The Madness of King George (1994)

Rick Carter (Art Direction), Nancy Haigh (Set Decoration)
Forrest Gump (1994)

Dante Ferretti (Art Direction), Francesca Lo Schiavo (Set Decoration)
Interview with the Vampire: The Vampire Chronicles (1994)

Lilly Kilvert (Art Direction), Dorree Cooper (Set Decoration)
Legends of the Fall (1994)

Santo Loquasto (Art Direction), Susan Bode (Set Decoration)
Bullets Over Broadway (1994)

Best Cinematography

⌊ John Toll ⌋
Legends of the Fall (1994)

Don Burgess
Forrest Gump (1994)

Roger Deakins
The Shawshank Redemption (1994)

Owen Roizman
Wyatt Earp (1994)

Piotr Sobocinski
Trois couleurs: Rouge (eng. Three Colors: Red) (1994)

Best Costume Design

⌊ Tim Chappel, Lizzy Gardiner ⌋
The Adventures of Priscilla, Queen of the Desert (1994)

Colleen Atwood
Little Women (1994)

Moidele Bickel
La reine Margot (eng. Queen Margot) (1994)

April Ferry
Maverick (1994)

Jeffrey Kurland
Bullets Over Broadway (1994)

Best Makeup

⌊ Rick Baker, Ve Neill, Yolanda Toussieng ⌋
Ed Wood (1994)

Judith A. Cory, Hallie D'Amore, Daniel C. Striepeke
Forrest Gump (1994)

Paul Engelen, Carol Hemming, Daniel Parker
Mary Shelley's Frankenstein (1994)

Best Visual Effects

⌊ Allen Hall, George Murphy, Ken Ralston, Stephen Rosenbaum ⌋
Forrest Gump (1994)

Tom Bertino, Jon Farhat, Scott Squires, Steve 'Spaz' Williams
The Mask (1994)

John Bruno, Thomas L. Fisher, Patrick McClung, Jacques Stroweis
True Lies (1994)

Best Film Editing

⚰ **Arthur Schmidt** ⚰
Forrest Gump (1994)

Richard Francis-Bruce
The Shawshank Redemption (1994)

William Haugse (as Bill Haugse), Steve James, Frederick Marx
Hoop Dreams (1994)

Sally Menke
Pulp Fiction (1994)

John Wright
Speed (1994)

Best Writing, Screenplay Based on Material Previously Produced or Published

⚰ **Eric Roth** ⚰
Forrest Gump (1994)

Paul Attanasio
Quiz Show (1994)

Alan Bennett
The Madness of King George (1994)

Robert Benton
Nobody's Fool (1994)

Frank Darabont
The Shawshank Redemption (1994)

Best Writing, Screenplay Written Directly for the Screen

⚰ **Quentin Tarantino (Screenplay), Roger Avary, Quentin Tarantino (Stories)** ⚰
Pulp Fiction (1994)

Woody Allen, Douglas McGrath
Bullets Over Broadway (1994)

Richard Curtis
Four Weddings and a Funeral (1994)

Peter Jackson, Frances Walsh
Heavenly Creatures (1994)

Krzysztof Kieslowski, Krzysztof Piesiewicz
Trois couleurs: Rouge (eng. Three Colors: Red) (1994)

Best Music, Original Song

⚰ **Elton John (Music), Tim Rice (Lyrics) for the song "Can You Feel the Love Tonight"** ⚰
The Lion King (1994)

James Newton Howard, James Ingram, Carole Bayer Sager, Patty Smyth (Music & Lyrics) for the song "Look What Love Has Done"
Junior (1994)

Elton John (Music), Tim Rice (Lyrics) for the songs "Circle of Life", "Hakuna Matata"
The Lion King (1994)

Randy Newman (Music & Lyrics) for the song "Make Up Your Mind"
The Paper (1994)

Best Sound

↧ Bob Beemer, Gregg Landaker, Steve Maslow, David R. B. MacMillan ↧
Speed (1994)

Willie D. Burton, Michael Herbick, Robert J. Litt, Elliot Tyson
The Shawshank Redemption (1994)

David E. Campbell, Christopher David, Douglas Ganton, Paul Massey
Legends of the Fall (1994)

Michael Herbick, Donald O. Mitchell, Frank A. Montaño, Art Rochester
Clear and Present Danger (1994)

Tom Johnson, William B. Kaplan, Dennis S. Sands, Randy Thom
Forrest Gump (1994)

Best Sound Effects Editing

↧ Stephen Hunter Flick ↧
Speed (1994)

Gloria S. Borders, Randy Thom
Forrest Gump (1994)

John Leveque, Bruce Stambler
Clear and Present Danger (1994)

Best Music, Original Score

↧ Hans Zimmer ↧
The Lion King (1994)

Elliot Goldenthal
Interview with the Vampire: The Vampire Chronicles (1994)

Thomas Newman
Little Women (1994), The Shawshank Redemption (1994)

Alan Silvestri
Forrest Gump (1994)

Best Directing

↧ Robert Zemeckis ↧
Forrest Gump (1994)

Woody Allen
Bullets Over Broadway (1994)

Krzysztof Kieslowski
Trois couleurs: Rouge (eng. Three Colors: Red) (1994)

Robert Redford
Quiz Show (1994)

Quentin Tarantino
Pulp Fiction (1994)

Best Documentary, Feature

↧ Freida Lee Mock, Terry Sanders ↧
Maya Lin: A Strong Clear Vision (1994)

Jean Bach
A Great Day in Harlem (1994)

Connie Field, Marilyn Mulford
Freedom on My Mind (1994)

Charles Guggenheim
D-Day Remembered (1994)

Deborah Hoffmann
Complaints of a Dutiful Daughter (1994)

Best Documentary, Short Subject
⌶ Charles Guggenheim ⌶
A Time for Justice (1994)
Vince DiPersio, Bill Guttentag
Blues Highway (1994)
Marcel Lozinski
89 mm od Europy (eng. 89mm from Europe) (1993)
Dee Mosbacher, Frances Reid
Straight from the Heart (1994)
Robert Richter
School of the Americas Assassins (1994)

Best Foreign Language Film
⌶ Russia ⌶
Utomlennye solntsem (eng. Burnt by the Sun) (1994)
Belgium
Farinelli (1994)
Cuba
Fresa y chocolate (eng. Strawberry & Chocolate) (1993)
The Former Yugoslav Republic of Macedonia
Pred dozhdot (eng. Before the Rain) (1994)
Taiwan
Yin shi nan nu (eng. Eat Drink Man Woman) (1994)

Best Picture
⌶ Wendy Finerman, Steve Starkey, Steve Tisch (Producers) ⌶
Forrest Gump (1994)
Lawrence Bender (Producer)
Pulp Fiction (1994)
Michael Jacobs, Julian Krainin, Michael Nozik, Robert Redford (Producers)
Quiz Show (1994)
Duncan Kenworthy (Producer)
Four Weddings and a Funeral (1994)
Niki Marvin (Producer)
The Shawshank Redemption (1994)

Best Short Film, Animated
⌶ David Fine, Alison Snowden ⌶
Bob's Birthday (1993)
Michael Dudok de Wit
Le moine et le poisson (eng. The Monk and the Fish) (1994)
Erica Russell
Triangle (1994)
Vanessa Schwartz
The Janitor (1995)
David Stoten, Tim Watts
The Big Story (1994)

Best Short Film, Live Action
⚐ **Peter Capaldi, Ruth Kenley-Letts** ⚐
Franz Kafka's It's a Wonderful Life (1993)
⚐ **Peggy Rajski, Randy Stone** ⚐
Trevor (1994)
Christine Astin, Sean Astin
Kangaroo Court (1994)
Michele McGuire, JoBeth Williams
On Hope (1994)
Paul Unwin, Nick Vivian
Syrup (1994)

The 68ᵗʰ Academy Awards® - March 25, 1996
Host: Whoopi Goldberg
Venue: Dorothy Chandler Pavilion
Honoring movies released in 1995

Honorary Award
⚐ **Kirk Douglas** ⚐
For 50 years as a creative and moral force in the motion picture community.
⚐ **Chuck Jones** ⚐
For the creation of classic cartoons and cartoon characters whose animated lives have brought joy to our real ones for more than a half century.

Best Actor in a Leading Role
⚐ **Nicolas Cage** ⚐
Leaving Las Vegas (1995) role "Ben Sanderson"
Richard Dreyfuss
Mr. Holland's Opus (1995) role "Glenn Holland"
Anthony Hopkins
Nixon (1995) role "Richard M. Nixon"
Sean Penn
Dead Man Walking (1995) role "Matthew Poncelet"
Massimo Troisi
(posthumous)
Il postino (eng. The Postman) (1994) role "Mario Ruoppolo"

Best Actor in a Supporting Role
⚐ **Kevin Spacey** ⚐
The Usual Suspects (1995) role "Roger "Verbal" Kint"
James Cromwell
Babe (1995) role "Farmer Arthur Hoggett"
Ed Harris
Apollo 13 (1995) role "Gene Kranz"
Brad Pitt
12 Monkeys (1995) role "Jeffrey Goines"
Tim Roth
Rob Roy (1995) role "Archibald Cunningham"

Best Actress in a Leading Role
⚐ Susan Sarandon ⚐
Dead Man Walking (1995) role "Sister Helen Prejean"
Elisabeth Shue
Leaving Las Vegas (1995) role "Sera"
Sharon Stone
Casino (1995) role "Ginger McKenna"
Meryl Streep
The Bridges of Madison County (1995) role "Francesca Johnson"
Emma Thompson
Sense and Sensibility (1995) role "Elinor Dashwood"

Best Actress in a Supporting Role
⚐ Mira Sorvino ⚐
Mighty Aphrodite (1995) role "Linda Ash"
Joan Allen
Nixon (1995) role "Pat Nixon"
Kathleen Quinlan
Apollo 13 (1995) role "Marilyn Gerlach Lovell"
Mare Winningham
Georgia (1995) role "Georgia Flood"
Kate Winslet
Sense and Sensibility (1995) role "Marianne Dashwood"

Special Achievement Award
⚐ John Lasseter ⚐
(For the development and inspired application of techniques that have made possible the first feature-length computer-animated film)

Toy Story (1995)

Best Art Direction
⚐ Eugenio Zanetti (Art Direction) ⚐
Restoration (1995)
Tony Burrough (Art Direction)
Richard III (1995)
Michael Corenblith (Art Direction), Merideth Boswell (Set Decoration)
Apollo 13 (1995)
Roger Ford (Art Direction), Kerrie Brown (Set Decoration)
Babe (1995)
Bo Welch (Art Direction), Cheryl Carasik (Set Decoration)
A Little Princess (1995)

Best Cinematography
⚐ John Toll ⚐
Braveheart (1995)
Michael Coulter
Sense and Sensibility (1995)
Stephen Goldblatt
Batman Forever (1995)
Emmanuel Lubezki
A Little Princess (1995)
Lu Yue
Yao a yao, yao dao wai po qiao (eng. Shanghai Triad) (1995)

Best Costume Design
⚓ **James Acheson** ⚓
Restoration (1995)

Jenny Beavan, John Bright
Sense and Sensibility (1995)

Shuna Harwood
Richard III (1995)

Charles Knode
Braveheart (1995)

Julie Weiss
12 Monkeys (1995)

Best Directing
⚓ **Mel Gibson** ⚓
Braveheart (1995)

Mike Figgis
Leaving Las Vegas (1995)

Chris Noonan
Babe (1995)

Michael Radford
Il postino (eng. The Postman) (1994)

Tim Robbins
Dead Man Walking (1995)

Best Visual Effects
⚓ **Scott E. Anderson, John Cox, Charles Gibson, Neal Scanlan** ⚓
Babe (1995)

Leslie Ekker, Michael Kanfer, Robert Legato, Matt Sweeney
Apollo 13 (1995)

Best Music, Original Dramatic Score
⚓ **Luis Enrique Bacalov** ⚓
Il postino (eng. The Postman) (1994)

Patrick Doyle
Sense and Sensibility (1995)

James Horner
Apollo 13 (1995), Braveheart (1995)

John Williams
Nixon (1995)

Best Music, Original Musical or Comedy Score
⚓ **Alan Menken (Music & Orchestral Score), Stephen Schwartz (Lyrics)** ⚓
Pocahontas (1995)

Randy Newman
Toy Story (1995)

Thomas Newman
Unstrung Heroes (1995)

Marc Shaiman
The American President (1995)

John Williams
Sabrina (1995)

Best Music, Original Song
Alan Menken (Music), Stephen Schwartz (Lyrics)
for the song "Colors of the Wind"
Pocahontas (1995)

Bryan Adams, Michael Kamen, Robert John "Mutt" Lange (Music & Lyrics)
for the song "Have You Ever Really Loved a Woman"
Don Juan DeMarco (1994)

Randy Newman (Music & Lyrics) for the song "You've Got a Friend in Me"
Toy Story (1995)

Bruce Springsteen (Music & Lyrics) for the song "Dead Man Walking"
Dead Man Walking (1995)

John Williams (Music), Alan Bergman, Marilyn Bergman (Lyrics)
for the song "Moonlight"
Sabrina (1995)

Best Documentary, Feature
Jon Blair
Anne Frank Remembered (1995)

Steven Ascher, Jeanne Jordan
Troublesome Creek: A Midwestern (1995)

Michael Epstein, Thomas Lennon
The Battle Over Citizen Kane (1996)

Fredric Golding, Mike Tollin
Hank Aaron: Chasing the Dream (1995)

Allan Miller, Walter Scheuer
Small Wonders
(aka Fiddlefest—Roberta Tzavaras and Her East Harlem Violin Program) (1995)

Best Documentary, Short Subject
Kary Antholis
One Survivor Remembers (1995)

Nancy Dine, Richard Stilwell
Jim Dine: A Self-Portrait on the Walls (1995)

Charles Guggenheim
The Shadow of Hate (1995)

Alec Lorimore, Greg MacGillivray
The Living Sea (1995)

Freida Lee Mock, Terry Sanders
Never Give Up: The 20th Century Odyssey of Herbert Zipper (1995)

Best Film Editing
Daniel P. Hanley, Mike Hill
Apollo 13 (1995)

Marcus D'Arcy, Jay Friedkin
Babe (1995)

Richard Francis-Bruce
Seven (1995)

Chris Lebenzon
Crimson Tide (1995)

Steven Rosenblum
Braveheart (1995)

Best Foreign Language Film
♟ The Netherlands ♟
Antonia (eng. Antonia's Line) (1995)
Algeria
Poussières de vie (eng. Dust of Life) (1995)
Brazil
O Quatrilho (eng. The Quartet) (1995)
Italy
L'uomo delle stelle (eng. The Star Maker) (1995)
Sweden
Lust och fägring stor (eng. All Things Fair) (1995)

Best Makeup
♟ Lois Burwell, Peter Frampton, Paul Pattison ♟
Braveheart (1995)
Colleen Callaghan, Greg Cannom, Bob Laden
Roommates (1995)
Ken Diaz, Mark Sanchez
My Family (1995)

Best Sound Effects Editing
♟ Lon Bender, Per Hallberg ♟
Braveheart (1995)
John Leveque, Bruce Stambler
Batman Forever (1995)
George Watters II
Crimson Tide (1995)

Best Sound
♟ Rick Dior, David MacMillan, Scott Millan, Steve Pederson ♟
Apollo 13 (1995)
Anna Behlmer, Scott Millan, Andy Nelson, Brian Simmons
Braveheart (1995)
Michael Herbick, Petur Hliddal, Donald O. Mitchell, Frank A. Montaño
Batman Forever (1995)
William B. Kaplan, Rick Kline, Kevin O'Connell, Gregory H. Watkins
Crimson Tide (1995)
Gregg Landaker, Steve Maslow, Keith A. Wester
Waterworld (1995)

Best Picture
♟ Bruce Davey, Mel Gibson, Alan Ladd Jr. (Producers) ♟
Braveheart (1995)
Gaetano Daniele, Mario Cecchi Gori, Vittorio Cecchi Gori (Producers)
(Mario Cecchi Gori - posthumous)
Il postino (eng. The Postman) (1994)
Lindsay Doran (Producer)
Sense and Sensibility (1995)
Brian Grazer (Producer)
Apollo 13 (1995)
Bill Miller, George Miller, Doug Mitchell (Producers)
Babe (1995)

Best Short Film, Animated

⚝ **Nick Park** ⚝
A Close Shave (1995)

Chris Bailey
Runaway Brain (1995)

Robin Bargar, Chris Landreth
The End (1995)

John R. Dilworth
The Chicken from Outer Space (1996)

Alexij Kharitidi
Gagarin (1994)

Best Short Film, Live Action

⚝ **Christine Lahti, Jana Sue Memel** ⚝
Lieberman in Love (1995)

Thom Colwell, Griffin Dunne
Duke of Groove (1995)

Luke Cresswell, Steve McNicholas
Brooms (1996)

Tikki Goldberg, Jeff Goldblum
Little Surprises (1996)

Dianne Houston, Joy Ryan
Tuesday Morning Ride (1995)

Best Writing, Screenplay Based on Material Previously Produced or Published

⚝ **Emma Thompson** ⚝
Sense and Sensibility (1995)

William Broyles Jr., Al Reinert
Apollo 13 (1995)

Mike Figgis
Leaving Las Vegas (1995)

George Miller, Chris Noonan
Babe (1995)

Anna Pavignano, Michael Radford, Furio Scarpelli, Giacomo Scarpelli, Massimo Troisi
(Massimo Troisi - posthumous)
Il postino (eng. The Postman) (1994)

Best Writing, Screenplay Written Directly for the Screen

⚝ **Christopher McQuarrie** ⚝
The Usual Suspects (1995)

Woody Allen
Mighty Aphrodite (1995)

Joel Cohen, Alec Sokolow, Andrew Stanton, Joss Whedon (Screenplay), Peter Docter, John Lasseter, Joe Ranft, Andrew Stanton (Story)
Toy Story (1995)

Stephen J. Rivele, Oliver Stone, Christopher Wilkinson
Nixon (1995)

Randall Wallace
Braveheart (1995)

68th Ceremony 6/6

The 69th Academy Awards® - March 24, 1997

Host: Billy Crystal
Venue: Shrine Auditorium & Expo Center
Honoring movies released in 1996

Best Actor in a Leading Role

⚐ **Geoffrey Rush** ⚐
Shine (1996) role "David Helfgott"

Tom Cruise
Jerry Maguire (1996) role "Jerry Maguire"

Ralph Fiennes
The English Patient (1996) role "Count László de Almásy"

Woody Harrelson
The People vs. Larry Flynt (1996) role "Larry Flynt"

Billy Bob Thornton
Sling Blade (1996) role "Karl Childers"

Best Actor in a Supporting Role

⚐ **Cuba Gooding Jr.** ⚐
Jerry Maguire (1996) role "Rod Tidwell"

William H. Macy
Fargo (1996) role "Jerry Lundegaard"

Armin Mueller-Stahl
Shine (1996) role "Peter Helfgott"

Edward Norton
Primal Fear (1996) role "Aaron Stampler / Roy"

James Woods
Ghosts of Mississippi (1996) role "Byron De La Beckwith"

Best Actress in a Leading Role

⚐ **Frances McDormand** ⚐
Fargo (1996) role "Marge Gunderson"

Brenda Blethyn
Secrets & Lies (1996) role "Cynthia Rose Purley"

Diane Keaton
Marvin's Room (1996) role "Bessie Wakefield"

Kristin Scott Thomas
The English Patient (1996) role "Katharine Clifton"

Emily Watson
Breaking the Waves (1996) role "Bess McNeill"

Best Actress in a Supporting Role

⚐ **Juliette Binoche** ⚐
The English Patient (1996) role "Hana"

Joan Allen
The Crucible (1996) role "Elizabeth Proctor"

Lauren Bacall
The Mirror Has Two Faces (1996) role "Hannah Morgan"

Barbara Hershey
The Portrait of a Lady (1996) role "Madame Serena Merle"

Marianne Jean-Baptiste
Secrets & Lies (1996) role "Hortense Cumberbatch"

Honorary Award
⚑ **Michael Kidd** ⚑
In recognition of his services to the art of the dance in the art of the screen.

Best Art Direction
⚑ **Stuart Craig (Art Direction), Stephenie McMillan (Set Decoration)** ⚑
The English Patient (1996)

Tim Harvey (Art Direction)
Hamlet (1996)

Catherine Martin (Art Direction), Brigitte Broch (Set Decoration)
William Shakespeare's Romeo & Juliet (1996)

Brian Morris (Art Direction), Philippe Turlure (Set Decoration)
Evita (1996)

Bo Welch (Art Direction), Cheryl Carasik (Set Decoration)
The Birdcage (1996)

Best Cinematography
⚑ **John Seale** ⚑
The English Patient (1996)

Roger Deakins
Fargo (1996)

Caleb Deschanel
Fly Away Home (1996)

Darius Khondji
Evita (1996)

Chris Menges
Michael Collins (1996)

Best Costume Design
⚑ **Ann Roth** ⚑
The English Patient (1996)

Paul Brown
Angels and Insects (1995)

Alex Byrne
Hamlet (1996)

Ruth Myers
Emma (1996)

Janet Patterson
The Portrait of a Lady (1996)

Best Directing
⚑ **Anthony Minghella** ⚑
The English Patient (1996)

Joel Coen
Fargo (1996)

Milos Forman
The People vs. Larry Flynt (1996)

Scott Hicks
Shine (1996)

Mike Leigh
Secrets & Lies (1996)

Best Documentary, Feature
⚐ Leon Gast, David Sonenberg ⚐
When We Were Kings (1996)
Anne Belle, Deborah Dickson
Suzanne Farrell: Elusive Muse (1996)
Susan Warms Dryfoos
The Line King: The Al Hirschfeld Story (1996)
Angus Gibson, Jo Menell
Mandela (1996)
Rick Goldsmith
Tell the Truth and Run: George Seldes and the American Press (1996)

Best Documentary, Short Subject
⚐ Jessica Yu ⚐
Breathing Lessons: The Life and Work of Mark O'Brien (1996)
Ben Burtt, Susanne Simpson
Special Effects: Anything Can Happen (1996)
Jeffrey Marvin, Bayley Silleck
Cosmic Voyage (1996)
Nick Redman, Paul Seydor
The Wild Bunch: An Album in Montage (1996)
Perry Wolff
An Essay on Matisse (1996)

Best Film Editing
⚐ Walter Murch ⚐
The English Patient (1996)
Gerry Hambling
Evita (1996)
Joe Hutshing
Jerry Maguire (1996)
Ethan Coen (as Roderick Jaynes), Joel Coen (as Roderick Jaynes)
Fargo (1996)
Pip Karmel
Shine (1996)

Irving G. Thalberg Memorial Award
⚐ Saul Zaentz ⚐

Best Music, Original Song
⚐ Andrew Lloyd Webber (Music), Tim Rice (Lyrics) ⚐
for the song "You Must Love Me"
Evita (1996)
Bryan Adams, Marvin Hamlisch, Robert John "Mutt" Lange,
Barbra Streisand (Music & Lyrics) for the song "I've Finally Found Someone"
The Mirror Has Two Faces (1996)
Jud Friedman, James Newton Howard, Allan Rich (Music & Lyrics)
for the song "For the First Timc"
One Fine Day (1996)
Adam Schlesinger (Music & Lyrics) for the song "That Thing You Do!"
That Thing You Do! (1996)
Diane Warren (Music & Lyrics) for the song "Because You Loved Me"
Up Close & Personal (1996)

Best Music, Original Dramatic Score

⚑ Gabriel Yared ⚑
The English Patient (1996)

Patrick Doyle
Hamlet (1996)

Elliot Goldenthal
Michael Collins (1996)

David Hirschfelder
Shine (1996)

John Williams
Sleepers (1996)

Best Music, Original Musical or Comedy Score

⚑ Rachel Portman ⚑
Emma (1996)

Alan Menken (Music & Orchestral Score), Stephen Schwartz (Lyrics)
The Hunchback of Notre Dame (1996)

Randy Newman
James and the Giant Peach (1996)

Marc Shaiman
The First Wives Club (1996)

Hans Zimmer
The Preacher's Wife (1996)

Best Sound Effects Editing

⚑ Bruce Stambler ⚑
The Ghost and the Darkness (1996)

Richard L. Anderson, David A. Whittaker
Daylight (1996)

Bub Asman, Alan Robert Murray
Eraser (1996)

Best Foreign Language Film

⚑ Czech Republic ⚑
Kolja (eng. Kolya) (1996)

France
Ridicule (1996)

Georgia
Shekvarebuli kulinaris ataserti retsepti (eng. A Chef in Love) (1996)

Norway
Søndagsengler (eng. The Other Side of Sunday) (1996)

Russia
Kavkazskiy plennik (eng. Prisoner of the Mountains) (1996)

Best Makeup

⚑ David LeRoy Anderson, Rick Baker ⚑
The Nutty Professor (1996)

Deborah La Mia Denaver, Matthew W. Mungle
Ghosts of Mississippi (1996)

Jake Garber, Michael Westmore, Scott Wheeler
Star Trek: First Contact (1996)

Best Picture

⚔ **Saul Zaentz (Producer)** ⚔
The English Patient (1996)

James L. Brooks, Cameron Crowe, Laurence Mark, Richard Sakai (Producers)
Jerry Maguire (1996)

Simon Channing Williams (Producer)
Secrets & Lies (1996)

Ethan Coen (Producer)
Fargo (1996)

Jane Scott (Producer)
Shine (1996)

Best Short Film, Animated

⚔ **Tyron Montgomery, Thomas Stellmach** ⚔
Quest (1996)

Richard Condie
La Salla (1996)

Timothy Hittle, Chris Peterson
Canhead (1996)

Peter Lord
Wat's Pig (1996)

Best Short Film, Live Action

⚔ **David Frankel, Barry Jossen** ⚔
Dear Diary (1996)

Bernadette Carranza, Antonello De Leo
Senza parole (eng. Wordless) (1996)

Juan Carlos Fresnadillo
Esposados (eng. Linked) (1996)

Anders Thomas Jensen, Kim Magnusson
Ernst & lyset (1996)

Antonio Urrutia
De tripas, corazón (1996)

Best Sound

⚔ **Mark Berger, Walter Murch, Christopher Newman, David Parker** ⚔
The English Patient (1996)

Bob Beemer, Bill W. Benton, Chris Carpenter, Jeff Wexler
Independence Day (1996)

Anna Behlmer, Andy Nelson, Ken Weston
Evita (1996)

Gregg Landaker, Steve Maslow, Kevin O'Connell, Geoffrey Patterson
Twister (1996)

Kevin O'Connell, Greg P. Russell, Keith A. Wester
The Rock (1996)

Best Visual Effects

⚔ **Volker Engel, Clay Pinney, Douglas Smith, Joseph Viskocil** ⚔
Independence Day (1996)

Henry La Bounta, Stefen Fangmeier, John Frazier, Habib Zargarpour
Twister (1996)

Scott Squires, James Straus, Phil Tippett, Kit West
DragonHeart (1996)

Best Writing, Screenplay Written Directly for the Screen
⚡ Ethan Coen, Joel Coen ⚡
Fargo (1996)
Cameron Crowe
Jerry Maguire (1996)
Mike Leigh
Secrets & Lies (1996)
Jan Sardi (Screenplay), Scott Hicks (Story)
Shine (1996)
John Sayles
Lone Star (1996)

Best Writing, Screenplay Based on Material Previously Produced or Published
⚡ Billy Bob Thornton ⚡
Sling Blade (1996)
Kenneth Branagh
Hamlet (1996)
John Hodge
Trainspotting (1996)
Arthur Miller
The Crucible (1996)
Anthony Minghella
The English Patient (1996)

The 70ᵗʰ Academy Awards® - March 23, 1998
Host: Billy Crystal
Venue: Shrine Auditorium & Expo Center
Honoring movies released in 1997

Best Actor in a Leading Role
⚡ Jack Nicholson ⚡
As Good as It Gets (1997) role "Melvin Udall"
Matt Damon
Good Will Hunting (1997) role "Will Hunting"
Robert Duvall
The Apostle (1997) role "Euliss "Sonny" Dewey aka The Apostle E. F."
Peter Fonda
Ulee's Gold (1997) role "Ulysses "Ulee" Jackson"
Dustin Hoffman
Wag the Dog (1997) role "Stanley Motss"

Best Actor in a Supporting Role
⚡ Robin Williams ⚡
Good Will Hunting (1997) role "Dr. Sean Maguire"
Robert Forster
Jackie Brown (1997) role "Max Cherry"
Anthony Hopkins
Amistad (1997) role "John Quincy Adams"
Greg Kinnear
As Good as It Gets (1997) role "Simon Bishop"
Burt Reynolds
Boogie Nights (1997) role "Jack Horner"

Best Actress in a Leading Role
⚊ Helen Hunt ⚊
As Good as It Gets (1997) role "Carol Connelly"
Helena Bonham Carter
The Wings of the Dove (1997) role "Kate Croy"
Julie Christie
Afterglow (1997) role "Phyllis Mann"
Judi Dench
Mrs. Brown (1997) role "Queen Victoria"
Kate Winslet
Titanic (1997) role "Rose DeWitt Bukater"

Best Actress in a Supporting Role
⚊ Kim Basinger ⚊
L.A. Confidential (1997) role "Lynn Bracken"
Joan Cusack
In & Out (1997) role "Emily Montgomery"
Minnie Driver
Good Will Hunting (1997) role "Skylar Satenstein"
Julianne Moore
Boogie Nights (1997) role "Amber Waves / Maggie"
Gloria Stuart
Titanic (1997) role "Rose Dawson Calvert"

Best Art Direction
⚊ Peter Lamont (Art Direction), Michael Ford (Set Decoration) ⚊
Titanic (1997)
Dante Ferretti (Art Direction), Francesca Lo Schiavo (Set Decoration)
Kundun (1997)
Jeannine Oppewall (Art Direction), Jay R. Hart (Set Decoration)
L.A. Confidential (1997)
Jan Roelfs (Art Direction), Nancy Nye (Set Decoration)
Gattaca (1997)
Bo Welch (Art Direction), Cheryl Carasik (Set Decoration)
Men in Black (1997)

Best Sound Effects Editing
⚊ Tom Bellfort, Christopher Boyes ⚊
Titanic (1997)
Per Hallberg, Mark P. Stoeckinger
Face/Off (1997)
Mark A. Mangini
The Fifth Element (1997)

Best Visual Effects
⚊ Thomas L. Fisher, Michael Kanfer, Mark A. Lasoff, Robert Legato ⚊
Titanic (1997)
Scott E. Anderson, Alec Gillis, John Richardson, Phil Tippett
Starship Troopers (1997)
Randal M. Dutra, Michael Lantieri, Dennis Muren, Stan Winston
The Lost World: Jurassic Park (1997)

Honorary Award
⍟ Stanley Donen ⍟
In appreciation of a body of work marked by grace, elegance, wit and visual innovation.

Best Cinematography
⍟ Russell Carpenter ⍟
Titanic (1997)

Roger Deakins
Kundun (1997)

Janusz Kaminski
Amistad (1997)

Eduardo Serra
The Wings of the Dove (1997)

Dante Spinotti
L.A. Confidential (1997)

Best Costume Design
⍟ Deborah Lynn Scott ⍟
Titanic (1997)

Ruth E. Carter
Amistad (1997)

Dante Ferretti
Kundun (1997)

Janet Patterson
Oscar and Lucinda (1997)

Sandy Powell
The Wings of the Dove (1997)

Best Directing
⍟ James Cameron ⍟
Titanic (1997)

Peter Cattaneo
The Full Monty (1997)

Atom Egoyan
The Sweet Hereafter (1997)

Curtis Hanson
L.A. Confidential (1997)

Gus Van Sant
Good Will Hunting (1997)

Best Documentary, Feature
⍟ Rabbi Marvin Hier, Richard Trank ⍟
The Long Way Home (1997)

William Gazecki, Dan Gifford
Waco: The Rules of Engagement (1997)

Spike Lee, Sam Pollard
4 Little Girls (1997)

Michèle Ohayon, Julia Schachter
Colors Straight Up (1997)

Michael Paxton
Ayn Rand: A Sense of Life (1997)

Best Documentary, Short Subject

⚱ **Donna Dewey, Carol Pasternak** ⚱
A Story of Healing (1997)

Andrea Blaugrund Nevins, Mel Damski
Still Kicking: The Fabulous Palm Springs Follies (1997)

George Casey, Paul Novros
Alaska: Spirit of the Wild (1998)

Kieth Merrill, Jonathan Stern
Amazon (1997)

Terri Randall
Family Video Diaries: Daughter of the Bride (1997)

Best Writing, Screenplay Based on Material Previously Produced or Published

⚱ **Curtis Hanson, Brian Helgeland** ⚱
L.A. Confidential (1997)

Hossein Amini
The Wings of the Dove (1997)

Paul Attanasio
Donnie Brasco (1997)

Atom Egoyan
The Sweet Hereafter (1997)

Hilary Henkin, David Mamet
Wag the Dog (1997)

Best Writing, Screenplay Written Directly for the Screen

⚱ **Ben Affleck, Matt Damon** ⚱
Good Will Hunting (1997)

Woody Allen
Deconstructing Harry (1997)

Paul Thomas Anderson
Boogie Nights (1997)

Mark Andrus, James L. Brooks (Screenplay), Mark Andrus (Story)
As Good as It Gets (1997)

Simon Beaufoy
The Full Monty (1997)

Best Music, Original Song

⚱ **James Horner (Music), Will Jennings (Lyrics)**
for the song "My Heart Will Go On" ⚱
Titanic (1997)

Stephen Flaherty (Music), Lynn Ahrens (Lyrics)
for the song "Journey To The Past"
Anastasia (1997)

Alan Menken (Music), David Zippel (Lyrics) for the song "Go The Distance"
Hercules (1997)

Elliott Smith (Music & Lyrics) for the song "Miss Misery"
Good Will Hunting (1997)

Diane Warren (Music & Lyrics) for the song "How Do I Live"
Con Air (1997)

Best Music, Original Dramatic Score

⚊ **James Horner** ⚊
Titanic (1997)

Danny Elfman
Good Will Hunting (1997)

Philip Glass
Kundun (1997)

Jerry Goldsmith
L.A. Confidential (1997)

John Williams
Amistad (1997)

Best Film Editing

⚊ **Conrad Buff IV, James Cameron, Richard A. Harris** ⚊
Titanic (1997)

Richard Francis-Bruce
Air Force One (1997)

Peter Honess
L.A. Confidential (1997)

Richard Marks
As Good as It Gets (1997)

Pietro Scalia
Good Will Hunting (1997)

Best Foreign Language Film

⚊ **The Netherlands** ⚊
Karakter (eng. Character) (1997)

Brazil
O Que é Isso, Companheiro? (eng. Four Days in September) (1997)

Germany
Jenseits der Stille (eng. Beyond Silence) (1996)

Russia
Vor (eng. The Thief) (1997)

Spain
Secretos del corazón (eng. Secrets of the Heart) (1997)

Best Picture

⚊ **James Cameron, Jon Landau (Producers)** ⚊
Titanic (1997)

Lawrence Bender (Producer)
Good Will Hunting (1997)

James L. Brooks, Bridget Johnson, Kristi Zea (Producers)
As Good as It Gets (1997)

Curtis Hanson, Arnon Milchan, Michael G. Nathanson (Producers)
L.A. Confidential (1997)

Uberto Pasolini (Producer)
The Full Monty (1997)

Best Short Film, Animated
⚑ Jan Pinkava ⚑
Geri's Game (1997)
Sylvain Chomet
La vieille dame et les pigeons (eng. The Old Lady and the Pigeons) (1997)
Steve Moore, Dan O'Shannon
Redux Riding Hood (1997)
Alexander Petrov
Rusalka (eng. Mermaid) (1997)
Joanna Quinn
Famous Fred (1996)

Best Short Film, Live Action
⚑ Chris Donahue, Chris Tashima ⚑
Visas and Virtue (1997)
Roger Goldby, Barney Reisz
It's Good to Talk (1997)
Anders Thomas Jensen, Kim Magnusson
Wolfgang (1997)
Birger Larsen, Thomas Lydholm
Skal vi være kærester? (eng. Sweethearts?) (1997)
Tim Loane, Pearse Moore
Dance Lexie Dance (1996)

Best Sound
⚑ Tom Johnson, Gary Rydstrom, Gary Summers, Mark Ulano ⚑
Titanic (1997)
Anna Behlmer, Kirk Francis, Andy Nelson
L.A. Confidential (1997)
Doug M. Hemphill, Rick Kline, Paul Massey, Keith A. Wester
Air Force One (1997)
Tom Johnson, William B. Kaplan, Dennis S. Sands, Randy Thom
Contact (1997)
Kevin O'Connell, Arthur Rochester, Greg P. Russell
Con Air (1997)

Best Music, Original Musical or Comedy Score
⚑ Anne Dudley ⚑
The Full Monty (1997)
Danny Elfman
Men in Black (1997)
Stephen Flaherty (Music), Lynn Ahrens (Lyrics)
David Newman (Orchestral Score)
Anastasia (1997)
James Newton Howard
My Best Friend's Wedding (1997)
Hans Zimmer
As Good as It Gets (1997)

Best Makeup
⚑ David LeRoy Anderson, Rick Baker ⚑
Men in Black (1997)
Beverley Binda, Veronica McAleer (as Veronica Brebner), Lisa Westcott
Mrs. Brown (1997)
Greg Cannom, Tina Earnshaw, Simon Thompson
Titanic (1997)

The 71ˢᵗ Academy Awards® - March 21, 1999

Host: Whoopi Goldberg
Venue: Dorothy Chandler Pavilion
Honoring movies released in 1998

Best Actor in a Leading Role

⚊ Roberto Benigni ⚊
La vita è bella (eng. Life Is Beautiful) (1997) role "Guido Orefice"

Tom Hanks
Saving Private Ryan (1998) role "Captain John H. Miller"

Ian McKellen
Gods and Monsters (1998) role "James Whale"

Nick Nolte
Affliction (1997) role "Wade Whitehouse"

Edward Norton
American History X (1998) role "Derek Vinyard"

Best Actor in a Supporting Role

⚊ James Coburn ⚊
Affliction (1997) role "Glen Whitehouse"

Robert Duvall
A Civil Action (1998) role "Jerome Facher"

Ed Harris
The Truman Show (1998) role "Christof"

Geoffrey Rush
Shakespeare in Love (1998) role "Philip Henslowe"

Billy Bob Thornton
A Simple Plan (1998) role "Jacob Mitchell"

Best Actress in a Leading Role

⚊ Gwyneth Paltrow ⚊
Shakespeare in Love (1998) role "Viola de Lesseps / Thomas Kent"

Cate Blanchett
Elizabeth (1998) role "Queen Elizabeth I of England"

Fernanda Montenegro
Central do Brasil (eng. Central Station) (1998) role "Isadora "Dora" Teixeira"

Meryl Streep
One True Thing (1998) role "Kate Gulden"

Emily Watson
Hilary and Jackie (1998) role "Jacqueline du Pré"

Best Actress in a Supporting Role

⚊ Judi Dench ⚊
Shakespeare in Love (1998) role "Queen Elizabeth I of England"

Kathy Bates
Primary Colors (1998) role "Libby Holden"

Brenda Blethyn
Little Voice (1998) role "Mari Hoff"

Rachel Griffiths
Hilary and Jackie (1998) role "Hilary du Pré"

Lynn Redgrave
Gods and Monsters (1998) role "Hanna"

Honorary Award
⚊ **Elia Kazan** ⚊
In recognition of his indelible contributions to the art of motion picture direction.

Best Art Direction
⚊ **Martin Childs (Art Direction), Jill Quertier (Set Decoration)** ⚊
Shakespeare in Love (1998)

John Myhre (Art Direction), Peter Howitt (Set Decoration)
Elizabeth (1998)

Jeannine Oppewall (Art Direction), Jay Hart (Set Decoration)
Pleasantville (1998)

Thomas E. Sanders (Art Direction), Lisa Dean Kavanaugh (Set Decoration)
Saving Private Ryan (1998)

Eugenio Zanetti (Art Direction), Cindy Carr (Set Decoration)
What Dreams May Come (1998)

Best Cinematography
⚊ **Janusz Kaminski** ⚊
Saving Private Ryan (1998)

Remi Adefarasin
Elizabeth (1998)

Richard Greatrex
Shakespeare in Love (1998)

Conrad L. Hall
A Civil Action (1998)

John Toll
The Thin Red Line (1998)

Best Costume Design
⚊ **Sandy Powell** ⚊
Shakespeare in Love (1998)

Colleen Atwood
Beloved (1998)

Alexandra Byrne
Elizabeth (1998)

Judianna Makovsky
Pleasantville (1998)

Sandy Powell
Velvet Goldmine (1998)

Best Directing
⚊ **Steven Spielberg** ⚊
Saving Private Ryan (1998)

Roberto Benigni
La vita è bella (eng. Life Is Beautiful) (1997)

John Madden
Shakespeare in Love (1998)

Terrence Malick
The Thin Red Line (1998)

Peter Weir
The Truman Show (1998)

Irving G. Thalberg Memorial Award
⚱ Norman Jewison ⚱

Best Film Editing
⚱ Michael Kahn ⚱
Saving Private Ryan (1998)

Anne V. Coates
Out of Sight (1998)

David Gamble
Shakespeare in Love (1998)

Leslie Jones, Saar Klein, Billy Weber
The Thin Red Line (1998)

Simona Paggi
La vita è bella (eng. Life Is Beautiful) (1997)

Best Foreign Language Film
⚱ Italy ⚱
La vita è bella (eng. Life Is Beautiful) (1997)

Argentina
Tango (1998)

Brazil
Central do Brasil (eng. Central Station) (1998)

Iran
Bacheha-Ye aseman (eng. Children of Heaven) (1997)

Spain
El abuelo (eng. The Grandfather) (1998)

Best Music, Original Dramatic Score
⚱ Nicola Piovani ⚱
La vita è bella (eng. Life Is Beautiful) (1997)

David Hirschfelder
Elizabeth (1998)

Randy Newman
Pleasantville (1998)

John Williams
Saving Private Ryan (1998)

Hans Zimmer
The Thin Red Line (1998)

Best Music, Original Musical or Comedy Score
⚱ Stephen Warbeck ⚱
Shakespeare in Love (1998)

Randy Newman
A Bug's Life (1998)

Stephen Schwartz (Music & Lyrics) Hans Zimmer (Orchestral Score)
The Prince of Egypt (1998)

Marc Shaiman
Patch Adams (1998)

Matthew Wilder (Music), David Zippel (Lyrics)
Jerry Goldsmith (Orchestral Score)
Mulan (1998)

Best Music, Original Song

⊥ **Stephen Schwartz (Music & Lyrics) for the song "When You Believe"** ⊥
The Prince of Egypt (1998)

David Foster, Carole Bayer Sager (Music & Lyrics)
Tony Renis, Alberto Testa (Lyrics) for the song "The Prayer"
Quest for Camelot (1998)

Allison Moorer, Gwil Owen (Music & Lyrics) for the song "A Soft Place To Fall"
The Horse Whisperer (1998)

Randy Newman (Music & Lyrics) for the song "That'll Do"
Babe: Pig in the City (1998)

Diane Warren (Music & Lyrics) for the song "I Don't Want To Miss A Thing"
Armageddon (1998)

Best Makeup

⊥ **Jenny Shircore** ⊥
Elizabeth (1998)

Veronica McAleer (as Veronica Brebner), Lisa Westcott
Shakespeare in Love (1998)

Lois Burwell, Conor O'Sullivan, Daniel C. Striepeke
Saving Private Ryan (1998)

Best Picture

⊥ **Donna Gigliotti, Marc Norman, David Parfitt,** ⊥
Harvey Weinstein, Edward Zwick (Producers)
Shakespeare in Love (1998)

Tim Bevan, Eric Fellner, Alison Owen (Producers)
Elizabeth (1998)

Gianluigi Braschi, Elda Ferri (Producers)
La vita è bella (eng. Life Is Beautiful) (1997)

Ian Bryce, Mark Gordon, Gary Levinsohn, Steven Spielberg (Producers)
Saving Private Ryan (1998)

Robert Michael Geisler, Grant Hill, John Roberdeau (Producers)
The Thin Red Line (1998)

Best Documentary, Feature

⊥ **Ken Lipper, James Moll** ⊥
The Last Days (1998)

Janet Cole, Barbara Sonneborn
Regret to Inform (1998)

Matthew Diamond, Jerry Kupfer
Dancemaker (1998)

Liz Garbus, Jonathan Stack
The Farm: Angola, USA (1998)

Robert B. Weide
Lenny Bruce: Swear to Tell the Truth (1998)

Best Documentary, Short Subject

⊥ **Keiko Ibi** ⊥
The Personals: Improvisations on Romance in the Golden Years (1999)

Charles Guggenheim
A Place in the Land (1998)

Donald McWilliams, Shui-Bo Wang
Sunrise Over Tiananmen Square (1998)

Best Short Film, Animated

ᛚ **Chris Wedge** ᛚ
Bunny (1998)

Mark Baker
Jolly Roger (1999)

Stefan Fjeldmark, Karsten Kiilerich
Når livet går sin vej (eng. When Life Departs) (1997)

Christopher Grace, Jonathan Myerson
The Canterbury Tales (1998–2000)

Steve Kalafer, Mark Osborne
More (1998)

Best Short Film, Live Action

ᛚ **Anders Thomas Jensen, Kim Magnusson** ᛚ
Valgaften (eng. Election Night) (1998)

Joel Bergvall, Simon Sandquist
Victor (1998)

Vivian Goffette
La carte postale (eng. The Postcard) (1998)

Josh Gordon, Will Speck
Culture (1997)

Alexander Jovy, J. J. Keith
Holiday Romance (1998)

Best Sound

ᛚ **Ronald Judkins, Andy Nelson, Gary Rydstrom, Gary Summers** ᛚ
Saving Private Ryan (1998)

Anna Behlmer, Paul 'Salty' Brincat, Andy Nelson
The Thin Red Line (1998)

Pud Cusack, Kevin O'Connell, Greg P. Russell
The Mask of Zorro (1998)

Peter Glossop, Dominic Lester, Robin O'Donoghue
Shakespeare in Love (1998)

Kevin O'Connell, Greg P. Russell, Keith A. Wester
Armageddon (1998)

Best Sound Effects Editing

ᛚ **Richard Hymns, Gary Rydstrom** ᛚ
Saving Private Ryan (1998)

David McMoyler
The Mask of Zorro (1998)

George Watters II
Armageddon (1998)

Best Visual Effects

ᛚ **Nicholas Brooks, Joel Hynek, Kevin Scott Mack, Stuart Robertson** ᛚ
What Dreams May Come (1998)

Rick Baker, Allen Hall, Jim Mitchell, Hoyt Yeatman
Mighty Joe Young (1998)

John Frazier, Richard R. Hoover, Pat McClung
Armageddon (1998)

Best Writing, Screenplay Based on Material Previously Produced or Published

⚔ **Bill Condon** ⚔
Gods and Monsters (1998)

Scott Frank
Out of Sight (1998)

Terrence Malick
The Thin Red Line (1998)

Elaine May
Primary Colors (1998)

Scott B. Smith
A Simple Plan (1998)

Best Writing, Screenplay Written Directly for the Screen

⚔ **Marc Norman, Tom Stoppard** ⚔
Shakespeare in Love (1998)

Warren Beatty, Jeremy Pikser (Screenplay), Warren Beatty (Story)
Bulworth (1998)

Roberto Benigni, Vincenzo Cerami
La vita è bella (eng. Life Is Beautiful) (1997)

Andrew Niccol
The Truman Show (1998)

Robert Rodat
Saving Private Ryan (1998)

The 72nd Academy Awards® - March 26, 2000

Host: Billy Crystal
Venue: Shrine Auditorium & Expo Center
Honoring movies released in 1999

Irving G. Thalberg Memorial Award

⚔ **Warren Beatty** ⚔

Honorary Award

⚔ **Andrzej Wajda** ⚔
For five decades of extraordinary film direction.

Best Actor in a Leading Role

⚔ **Kevin Spacey** ⚔
American Beauty (1999) role "Lester Burnham"

Russell Crowe
The Insider (1999) role "Jeffrey Wigand"

Richard Farnsworth
The Straight Story (1999) role "Alvin Straight"

Sean Penn
Sweet and Lowdown (1999) role "Emmet Ray"

Denzel Washington
The Hurricane (1999) role "Rubin "The Hurricane" Carter"

Best Actor in a Supporting Role
↓ Michael Caine ↓
The Cider House Rules (1999) role "Dr. Wilbur Larch"
Tom Cruise
Magnolia (1999) role "Frank T. J. Mackey"
Michael Clarke Duncan
The Green Mile (1999) role "John Coffey"
Jude Law
The Talented Mr. Ripley (1999) role "Dickie Greenleaf"
Haley Joel Osment
The Sixth Sense (1999) role "Cole Sear"

Best Actress in a Leading Role
↓ Hilary Swank ↓
Boys Don't Cry (1999) role "Brandon Teena"
Annette Bening
American Beauty (1999) role "Carolyn Burnham"
Janet McTeer
Tumbleweeds (1999) role "Mary Jo Walker"
Julianne Moore
The End of the Affair (1999) role "Sarah Miles"
Meryl Streep
Music of the Heart (1999) role "Roberta Guaspari"

Best Actress in a Supporting Role
↓ Angelina Jolie ↓
Girl, Interrupted (1999) role "Lisa Rowe"
Toni Collette
The Sixth Sense (1999) role "Lynn Sear"
Catherine Keener
Being John Malkovich (1999) role "Maxine Lund"
Samantha Morton
Sweet and Lowdown (1999) role "Hattie"
Chloë Sevigny
Boys Don't Cry (1999) role "Lana Tisdel"

Best Makeup
↓ Christine Blundell, Trefor Proud ↓
Topsy-Turvy (1999)
Rick Baker
Life (1999)
Michèle Burke, Mike Smithson
Austin Powers: The Spy Who Shagged Me (1999)
Greg Cannom
Bicentennial Man (1999)

Best Visual Effects
↓ Steve Courtley, John Gaeta, Janek Sirrs, Jon Thum ↓
The Matrix (1999)
Eric Allard, Henry F. Anderson III, Jerome Chen, John Dykstra
Stuart Little (1999)
Rob Coleman, John Knoll, Dennis Muren, Scott Squires
Star Wars: Episode I - The Phantom Menace (1999)

Best Art Direction
⚜ Rick Heinrichs (Art Direction), Peter Young (Set Decoration) ⚜
Sleepy Hollow (1999)

Luciana Arrighi (Art Direction), Ian Whittaker (Set Decoration)
Anna and the King (1999)

David Gropman (Art Direction), Beth A. Rubino (Set Decoration)
The Cider House Rules (1999)

Eve Stewart (Art Direction), John Bush, Eve Stewart (Set Decoration)
Topsy-Turvy (1999)

Roy Walker (Art Direction), Bruno Cesari (Set Decoration)
The Talented Mr. Ripley (1999)

Best Cinematography
⚜ Conrad L. Hall ⚜
American Beauty (1999)

Emmanuel Lubezki
Sleepy Hollow (1999)

Roger Pratt
The End of the Affair (1999)

Robert Richardson
Snow Falling on Cedars (1999)

Dante Spinotti
The Insider (1999)

Best Documentary, Feature
⚜ Arthur Cohn, Kevin Macdonald ⚜
One Day in September (1999)

Adrian Belic, Roko Belic
Genghis Blues (1999)

Nanette Burstein, Brett Morgen
On the Ropes (1999)

Ulrich Felsberg, Wim Wenders
Buena Vista Social Club (1999)

Paola di Florio, Lilibet Foster
Speaking in Strings (1999)

Best Documentary, Short Subject
⚜ Susan Hannah Hadary, William A. Whiteford ⚜
King Gimp (1999)

Bert Van Bork
Eyewitness (2000)

Simeon Soffer, Jonathan Stack
The Wildest Show in the South: The Angola Prison Rodeo (1999)

Best Sound Effects Editing
⚜ Dane A. Davis ⚜
The Matrix (1999)

Tom Bellfort, Ben Burtt
Star Wars: Episode I - The Phantom Menace (1999)

Richard Hymns, Ren Klyce
Fight Club (1999)

Best Costume Design

⚱ Lindy Hemming ⚱
Topsy-Turvy (1999)

Colleen Atwood
Sleepy Hollow (1999)

Jenny Beavan
Anna and the King (1999)

Milena Canonero
Titus (1999)

Gary Jones, Ann Roth
The Talented Mr. Ripley (1999)

Best Directing

⚱ Sam Mendes ⚱
American Beauty (1999)

Lasse Hallström
The Cider House Rules (1999)

Spike Jonze
Being John Malkovich (1999)

Michael Mann
The Insider (1999)

M. Night Shyamalan
The Sixth Sense (1999)

Best Film Editing

⚱ Zach Staenberg ⚱
The Matrix (1999)

Tariq Anwar, Christopher Greenbury
American Beauty (1999)

Lisa Zeno Churgin
The Cider House Rules (1999)

William Goldenberg, David Rosenbloom, Paul Rubell
The Insider (1999)

Andrew Mondshein
The Sixth Sense (1999)

Best Writing, Screenplay Based on Material Previously Produced or Published

⚱ John Irving ⚱
The Cider House Rules (1999)

Frank Darabont
The Green Mile (1999)

Eric Roth, Michael Mann
The Insider (1999)

Anthony Minghella
The Talented Mr. Ripley (1999)

Alexander Payne, Jim Taylor
Election (1999)

Best Writing, Screenplay Written Directly for the Screen

⚜ Alan Ball ⚜
American Beauty (1999)

Paul Thomas Anderson
Magnolia (1999)

Charlie Kaufman
Being John Malkovich (1999)

Mike Leigh
Topsy-Turvy (1999)

M. Night Shyamalan
The Sixth Sense (1999)

Best Foreign Language Film

⚜ Spain ⚜
Todo sobre mi madre (eng. All About My Mother) (1999)

France
Est - Ouest (eng. East/West) (1999)

Nepal
Himalaya - l'enfance d'un chef (eng. Himalaya aka Caravan [festival title]) (1999)

Sweden
Under solen (eng. Under the Sun) (1998)

United Kingdom
Solomon and Gaenor (1999)

Best Music, Original Song

⚜ Phil Collins (Music & Lyrics) for the song "You'll Be In My Heart" ⚜
Tarzan (1999)

Aimee Mann (Music & Lyrics) for the song "Save Me"
Magnolia (1999)

Randy Newman (Music & Lyrics) for the song "When She Loved Me"
Toy Story 2 (1999)

Trey Parker, Marc Shaiman (Music & Lyrics) for the song "Blame Canada"
South Park: Bigger, Longer & Uncut (1999)

Diane Warren (Music & Lyrics) for the song "Music Of My Heart"
Music of the Heart (1999)

Best Music, Original Score

⚜ John Corigliano ⚜
Le violon rouge (eng. The Red Violin) (1998)

Thomas Newman
American Beauty (1999)

Rachel Portman
The Cider House Rules (1999)

John Williams
Angela's Ashes (1999)

Gabriel Yared
The Talented Mr. Ripley (1999)

Best Sound
⚐ **David E. Campbell, David Lee, John T. Reitz, Gregg Rudloff** ⚐
The Matrix (1999)

Willie D. Burton, Michael Herbick, Robert J. Litt, Elliot Tyson
The Green Mile (1999)

Chris Carpenter, Rick Kline, Chris Munro, Leslie Shatz
The Mummy (1999)

Doug Hemphill, Andy Nelson, Lee Orloff
The Insider (1999)

Tom Johnson, John Midgley, Shawn Murphy, Gary Rydstrom
Star Wars: Episode I - The Phantom Menace (1999)

Best Picture
⚐ **Bruce Cohen, Dan Jinks (Producers)** ⚐
American Beauty (1999)

Pieter Jan Brugge, Michael Mann (Producers)
The Insider (1999)

Frank Darabont, David Valdes (Producers)
The Green Mile (1999)

Richard N. Gladstein (Producer)
The Cider House Rules (1999)

Kathleen Kennedy, Frank Marshall, Barry Mendel (Producers)
The Sixth Sense (1999)

Best Short Film, Animated
⚐ **Alexander Petrov** ⚐
The Old Man and the Sea (1999)

Paul Driessen
3 Misses (1998)

Amanda Forbis, Wendy Tilby
When the Day Breaks (1999)

Torill Kove
My Grandmother Ironed the King's Shirts (1999)

Peter Peake
Humdrum (1999)

Best Short Film, Live Action
⚐ **Barbara Schock, Tammy Tiehel** ⚐
My Mother Dreams the Satan's Disciples in New York (1998)

Marc-Andreas Bochert, Gabriele Lins
Kleingeld (eng. Small Change) (1999)

Henrik Ruben Genz, Michael W. Horsten
Bror, min bror (eng. Theis and Nico) (1999)

Mehdi Norowzian, Steve Wax
Killing Joe (1999)

Marcus Olsson
Stora & små mirakel (eng. Major and Minor Miracles) (1999)

The 73rd Academy Awards® - March 25, 2001
Host: Steve Martin
Venue: Shrine Auditorium & Expo Center
Honoring movies released in 2000

Honorary Award
⚐ Jack Cardiff ⚐
Master of light and color.
⚐ Ernest Lehman ⚐
In appreciation of a body of varied and enduring work.

Best Actor in a Leading Role
⚐ Russell Crowe ⚐
Gladiator (2000) role "General Maximus Decimus Meridius"
Javier Bardem
Before Night Falls (2000) role "Reinaldo Arenas"
Tom Hanks
Cast Away (2000) role "Chuck Noland"
Ed Harris
Pollock (2000) role "Jackson Pollock"
Geoffrey Rush
Quills (2000) role "Marquis de Sade"

Best Actor in a Supporting Role
⚐ Benicio del Toro ⚐
Traffic (2000) role "Javier Rodriguez"
Jeff Bridges
The Contender (2000) role "President Jackson Evans"
Willem Dafoe
Shadow of the Vampire (2000) role "Max Schreck"
Albert Finney
Erin Brockovich (2000) role "Edward L. Masry"
Joaquin Phoenix
Gladiator (2000) role "Commodus"

Best Actress in a Leading Role
⚐ Julia Roberts ⚐
Erin Brockovich (2000) role "Erin Brockovich"
Joan Allen
The Contender (2000) role "Laine Hanson"
Juliette Binoche
Chocolat (2000) role "Vianne Rocher"
Ellen Burstyn
Requiem for a Dream (2000) role "Sara Goldfarb"
Laura Linney
You Can Count on Me (2000) role "Samantha "Sammy" Prescott"

Best Actress in a Supporting Role
⚐ Marcia Gay Harden ⚐
Pollock (2000) role "Lee Krasner"
Judi Dench
Chocolat (2000) role "Armande Voizin"
Kate Hudson
Almost Famous (2000) role "Penny Lane"
Frances McDormand
Almost Famous (2000) role "Elaine Miller"
Julie Walters
Billy Elliot (2000) role "Georgia Wilkinson"

Best Art Direction

⚑ Tim Yip (Art Direction, Set Decoration) ⚑
Wo hu cang long (eng. Crouching Tiger, Hidden Dragon) (2000)

Martin Childs (Art Direction), Jill Quertier (Set Decoration)
Quills (2000)

Michael Corenblith (Art Direction), Merideth Boswell (Set Decoration)
Dr. Seuss' How the Grinch Stole Christmas (2000)

Arthur Max (Art Direction), Crispian Sallis (Set Decoration)
Gladiator (2000)

Jean Rabasse (Art Direction), Françoise Benoît-Fresco (Set Decoration)
Vatel (2000)

Best Cinematography

⚑ Peter Pau ⚑
Wo hu cang long (eng. Crouching Tiger, Hidden Dragon) (2000)

Roger Deakins
O Brother, Where Art Thou? (2000)

Caleb Deschanel
The Patriot (2000)

Lajos Koltai
Malèna (eng. Malena) (2000)

John Mathieson
Gladiator (2000)

Best Costume Design

⚑ Janty Yates ⚑
Gladiator (2000)

Anthony Powell
102 Dalmatians (2000)

Rita Ryack
Dr. Seuss' How the Grinch Stole Christmas (2000)

Jacqueline West
Quills (2000)

Tim Yip
Wo hu cang long (eng. Crouching Tiger, Hidden Dragon) (2000)

Best Directing

⚑ Steven Soderbergh ⚑
Traffic (2000)

Stephen Daldry
Billy Elliot (2000)

Ang Lee
Wo hu cang long (eng. Crouching Tiger, Hidden Dragon) (2000)

Ridley Scott
Gladiator (2000)

Steven Soderbergh
Erin Brockovich (2000)

Best Sound Editing

⚑ Jon Johnson ⚑
U-571 (2000)

Bub Asman, Alan Robert Murray
Space Cowboys (2000)

Best Documentary, Feature
⚑ Mark Jonathan Harris, Deborah Oppenheimer ⚑
Into the Arms of Strangers: Stories of the Kindertransport (2000)
Daniel Anker, Barak Goodman
Scottsboro: An American Tragedy (2000)
Josh Aronson, Roger Weisberg
Sound and Fury (2000)
Deborah Hoffmann, Frances Reid
Long Night's Journey Into Day (2000)
Tod Lending
Legacy (2000)

Best Documentary, Short Subject
⚑ Tracy Seretean ⚑
Big Mama (2000)
Chuck Braverman, Steve Kalafer
Curtain Call (2000)
Leelai Demoz, Eric Simonson
On Tiptoe: Gentle Steps to Freedom (2000)
Alec Lorimore, Greg MacGillivray
Dolphins (2000)
Daniel Raim
The Man on Lincoln's Nose (2000)

Best Film Editing
⚑ Stephen Mirrione ⚑
Traffic (2000)
Dede Allen
Wonder Boys (2000)
Joe Hutshing, Saar Klein
Almost Famous (2000)
Pietro Scalia
Gladiator (2000)
Tim Squyres
Wo hu cang long (eng. Crouching Tiger, Hidden Dragon) (2000)

Best Foreign Language Film
⚑ Taiwan ⚑
Wo hu cang long (eng. Crouching Tiger, Hidden Dragon) (2000)
Belgium
Iedereen beroemd! (eng. Everybody's Famous!) (2000)
Czech Republic
Musíme si pomáhat (eng. Divided We Fall) (2000)
France
Le goût des autres (eng. The Taste of Others) (2000)
Mexico
Amores perros (2000)

Irving G. Thalberg Memorial Award
⚑ Dino De Laurentiis ⚑

Best Music, Original Score
🎬 **Tan Dun** 🎬
Wo hu cang long (eng. Crouching Tiger, Hidden Dragon) (2000)
Ennio Morricone
Malèna (eng. Malena) (2000)
Rachel Portman
Chocolat (2000)
John Williams
The Patriot (2000)
Hans Zimmer
Gladiator (2000)

Best Music, Original Song
🎬 **Bob Dylan (Music & Lyrics) for the song "Things Have Changed"** 🎬
Wonder Boys (2000)
**Björk (Music), Sjón Sigurdsson, Lars von Trier (Lyrics)
for the song "I've Seen It All"**
Dancer in the Dark (2000)
**Jorge Calandrelli, Dun Tan (Music), James Schamus (Lyrics)
for the song "A Love Before Time"**
Wo hu cang long (eng. Crouching Tiger, Hidden Dragon) (2000)
**Dave Hartley, Sting (Music), Sting (Lyrics)
for the song "My Funny Friend and Me"**
The Emperor's New Groove (2000)
Randy Newman (Music & Lyrics) for the song "A Fool In Love"
Meet the Parents (2000)

Best Sound
🎬 **Bob Beemer, Scott Millan, Ken Weston** 🎬
Gladiator (2000)
David E. Campbell, John T. Reitz, Gregg Rudloff, Keith A. Wester
The Perfect Storm (2000)
Tom Johnson, William B. Kaplan, Dennis S. Sands, Randy Thom
Cast Away (2000)
Rick Kline, Gregg Landaker, Steve Maslow, Ivan Sharrock
U-571 (2000)
Kevin O'Connell, Lee Orloff, Greg P. Russell
The Patriot (2000)

Best Picture
🎬 **David Franzoni, Branko Lustig, Douglas Wick (Producers)** 🎬
Gladiator (2000)
Laura Bickford, Marshall Herskovitz, Edward Zwick (Producers)
Traffic (2000)
David Brown, Kit Golden, Leslie Holleran (Producers)
Chocolat (2000)
Danny DeVito, Michael Shamberg, Stacey Sher (Producers)
Erin Brockovich (2000)
Li-Kong Hsu, William Kong, Ang Lee (Producers)
Wo hu cang long (eng. Crouching Tiger, Hidden Dragon) (2000)

Best Short Film, Animated

⚜ **Michael Dudok de Wit** ⚜
Father and Daughter (2000)

Don Hertzfeldt
Rejected (2000)

Annette Schäffler, Steffen Schäffler
The Periwig-Maker (1999)

Best Short Film, Live Action

⚜ **Florian Gallenberger** ⚜
Quiero ser (I want to be...) (2000)

Colin Campbell, Gail Lerner
Seraglio (2000)

Ericka Frederick, Peter Riegert
By Courier (2001)

Christina Lazaridi, Joan Stein Schimke
One Day Crossing (2001)

Paulo Machline
Uma História de Futebol (eng. A Soccer Story) (1998)

Best Visual Effects

⚜ **Tim Burke, Neil Corbould, Rob Harvey, John Nelson** ⚜
Gladiator (2000)

Scott E. Anderson, Craig Hayes, Stan Parks, Scott Stokdyk
Hollow Man (2000)

Walt Conti, Stefen Fangmeier, John Frazier, Habib Zargarpour
The Perfect Storm (2000)

Best Writing, Screenplay Based on Material Previously Produced or Published

⚜ **Stephen Gaghan (Screenplay)** ⚜
Traffic (2000)

Ethan Coen, Joel Coen (Screenplay)
O Brother, Where Art Thou? (2000)

Robert Nelson Jacobs (Screenplay)
Chocolat (2000)

Steve Kloves (Screenplay)
Wonder Boys (2000)

Wang Hui Ling, Tsai Kuo Jung, James Schamus (Screenplay)
Wo hu cang long (eng. Crouching Tiger, Hidden Dragon) (2000)

Best Writing, Screenplay Written Directly for the Screen

⚜ **Cameron Crowe (Screenplay)** ⚜
Almost Famous (2000)

David Franzoni, John Logan, William Nicholson (Screenplay), David Franzoni (Story)
Gladiator (2000)

Susannah Grant (Screenplay)
Erin Brockovich (2000)

Lee Hall (Screenplay)
Billy Elliot (2000)

Kenneth Lonergan (Screenplay)
You Can Count on Me (2000)

Best Makeup

⚑ **Rick Baker, Gail Rowell-Ryan** ⚑
Dr. Seuss' How the Grinch Stole Christmas (2000)

Ann Buchanan, Amber Sibley
Shadow of the Vampire (2000)

Michèle Burke, Edouard F. Henriques
The Cell (2000)

The 74th Academy Awards® - March 24, 2002

Host: Whoopi Goldberg
Venue: Kodak Theatre at Hollywood & Highland Center
Honoring movies released in 2001

Jean Hersholt Humanitarian Award

⚑ Arthur Hiller ⚑

Best Actor in a Leading Role

⚑ **Denzel Washington** ⚑
Training Day (2001) role "Detective Sergeant Alonzo Harris"

Russell Crowe
A Beautiful Mind (2001) role "John Forbes Nash Jr."

Sean Penn
I Am Sam (2001) role "Sam Dawson"

Will Smith
Ali (2001) role "Cassius Marcellus Clay Jr. / Muhammad Ali"

Tom Wilkinson
In the Bedroom (2001) role "Dr. Matthew Fowler"

Best Actor in a Supporting Role

⚑ **Jim Broadbent** ⚑
Iris (2001) role "John Bayley"

Ethan Hawke
Training Day (2001) role "Officer Jake Hoyt"

Ben Kingsley
Sexy Beast (2000) role "Don Logan"

Ian McKellen
The Lord of the Rings: The Fellowship of the Ring (2001) role "Gandalf the Grey"

Jon Voight
Ali (2001) role "Howard Cosell"

Best Actress in a Leading Role

⚑ **Halle Berry** ⚑
Monster's Ball (2001) role "Leticia Musgrove"

Judi Dench
Iris (2001) role "Iris Murdoch"

Nicole Kidman
Moulin Rouge! (2001) role "Satine"

Sissy Spacek
In the Bedroom (2001) role "Ruth Fowler"

Renée Zellweger
Bridget Jones's Diary (2001) role "Bridget Jones"

Best Actress in a Supporting Role
ⓘ **Jennifer Connelly** ⓘ
A Beautiful Mind (2001) role "Alicia Nash"
Helen Mirren
Gosford Park (2001) role "Mrs. Wilson"
Maggie Smith
Gosford Park (2001) role "Constance Trentham"
Marisa Tomei
In the Bedroom (2001) role "Natalie Strout"
Kate Winslet
Iris (2001) role "Iris Murdoch"

Best Art Direction
ⓘ **Catherine Martin (Art Direction), Brigitte Broch (Set Decoration)** ⓘ
Moulin Rouge! (2001)
Stephen Altman (Art Direction), Anna Pinnock (Set Decoration)
Gosford Park (2001)
Aline Bonetto (Art Direction), Marie-Laure Valla (Set Decoration)
Le fabuleux destin d'Amélie Poulain (eng. Amélie) (2001)
Stuart Craig (Art Direction), Stephenie McMillan (Set Decoration)
Harry Potter and the Sorcerer's Stone (2001)
Grant Major (Art Direction), Dan Hennah (Set Decoration)
The Lord of the Rings: The Fellowship of the Ring (2001)

Best Cinematography
ⓘ **Andrew Lesnie** ⓘ
The Lord of the Rings: The Fellowship of the Ring (2001)
Roger Deakins
The Man Who Wasn't There (2001)
Bruno Delbonnel
Le fabuleux destin d'Amélie Poulain (eng. Amélie) (2001)
Slawomir Idziak
Black Hawk Down (2001)
Donald M. McAlpine
Moulin Rouge! (2001)

Best Costume Design
ⓘ **Catherine Martin, Angus Strathie** ⓘ
Moulin Rouge! (2001)
Jenny Beavan
Gosford Park (2001)
Milena Canonero
The Affair of the Necklace (2001)
Ngila Dickson, Richard Taylor
The Lord of the Rings: The Fellowship of the Ring (2001)
Judianna Makovsky
Harry Potter and the Sorcerer's Stone (2001)

Best Sound Editing
ⓘ **Christopher Boyes, George Watters II** ⓘ
Pearl Harbor (2001)
Gary Rydstrom, Michael Silvers
Monsters, Inc. (2001)

Best Animated Feature Film

⚐ Aron Warner ⚐
Shrek (2001)

John A. Davis, Steve Oedekerk
Jimmy Neutron: Boy Genius (2001)

Pete Docter, John Lasseter
Monsters, Inc. (2001)

Best Directing

⚐ Ron Howard ⚐
A Beautiful Mind (2001)

Robert Altman
Gosford Park (2001)

Peter Jackson
The Lord of the Rings: The Fellowship of the Ring (2001)

David Lynch
Mulholland Drive (2001)

Ridley Scott
Black Hawk Down (2001)

Best Documentary, Feature

⚐ Jean-Xavier de Lestrade, Denis Poncet ⚐
Un coupable idéal (eng. Murder on a Sunday Morning) (2001)

Edet Belzberg
Children Underground (2001)

Deborah Dickson, Susan Froemke
LaLee's Kin: The Legacy of Cotton (2001)

Christian Frei
War Photographer (2001)

B. Z. Goldberg, Justine Shapiro
Promises (2001)

Best Documentary, Short Subject

⚐ Lynn Appelle, Sarah Kernochan ⚐
Thoth (2002)

Lianne Klapper McNally
Artists and Orphans: A True Drama (2001)

Freida Lee Mock, Jessica Sanders
Sing! (2001)

Best Film Editing

⚐ Pietro Scalia ⚐
Black Hawk Down (2001)

Jill Bilcock
Moulin Rouge! (2001)

Dody Dorn
Memento (2000)

John Gilbert
The Lord of the Rings: The Fellowship of the Ring (2001)

Daniel P. Hanley, Mike Hill
A Beautiful Mind (2001)

Best Foreign Language Film
⚰ Bosnia & Herzegovina ⚰
No Man's Land (2001)
Argentina
El hijo de la novia (eng. Son of the Bride) (2001)
France
Le fabuleux destin d'Amélie Poulain (eng. Amélie) (2001)
India
Lagaan: Once Upon a Time in India (2001)
Norway
Elling (2001)

Best Visual Effects
⚰ Randall William Cook, Jim Rygiel, Mark Stetson, Richard Taylor ⚰
The Lord of the Rings: The Fellowship of the Ring (2001)
Eric Brevig, John Frazier, Edward Hirsh, Ben Snow
Pearl Harbor (2001)
Scott Farrar, Michael Lantieri, Dennis Muren, Stan Winston
A.I. Artificial Intelligence (2001)

Best Music, Original Score
⚰ Howard Shore ⚰
The Lord of the Rings: The Fellowship of the Ring (2001)
James Horner
A Beautiful Mind (2001)
Randy Newman
Monsters, Inc. (2001)
John Williams
A.I. Artificial Intelligence (2001), Harry Potter and the Sorcerer's Stone (2001)

Best Music, Original Song
⚰ Randy Newman (Music & Lyrics) for the song "If I Didn't Have You" ⚰
Monsters, Inc. (2001)
Enya, Nicky Ryan, Roma Ryan (Music & Lyrics) for the song "May It Be"
The Lord of the Rings: The Fellowship of the Ring (2001)
Paul McCartney (Music & Lyrics) for the song "Vanilla Sky"
Vanilla Sky (2001)
Sting (Music & Lyrics) for the song "Until"
Kate & Leopold (2001)
Diane Warren (Music & Lyrics) for the song "There You'll Be"
Pearl Harbor (2001)

Best Picture
⚰ Brian Grazer, Ron Howard (Producers) ⚰
A Beautiful Mind (2001)
Robert Altman, Bob Balaban, David Levy (Producers)
Gosford Park (2001)
Fred Baron, Martin Brown, Baz Luhrmann (Producers)
Moulin Rouge! (2001)
Todd Field, Ross Katz, Graham Leader (Producers)
In the Bedroom (2001)
Peter Jackson, Barrie M. Osborne, Fran Walsh (Producers)
The Lord of the Rings: The Fellowship of the Ring (2001)

Best Short Film, Animated
⇣ Ralph Eggleston ⇣
For the Birds (2000)
Cordell Barker
Strange Invaders (2001)
Ruairi Robinson, Seamus Byrne
Fifty Percent Grey (2001)
Cathal Gaffney, Darragh O'Connell
Give Up Yer Aul Sins (2001)
Joseph E. Merideth
Stubble Trouble (2000)

Best Short Film, Live Action
⇣ Lisa Blount, Ray McKinnon ⇣
The Accountant (2001)
Kalman Apple, Shameela Bakhsh
Speed for Thespians (2000)
Slawomir Fabicki, Bogumil Godfrejów
Męska sprawa (eng. A Man Thing) (2001)
Johannes Kiefer
Gregors größte Erfindung (eng. Gregor's Greatest Invention) (2001)
Virgil Widrich
Copy Shop (2001)

Best Sound
⇣ Michael Minkler, Chris Munro, Myron Nettinga ⇣
Black Hawk Down (2001)
Vincent Arnardi, Guillaume Leriche, Jean Umansky
Le fabuleux destin d'Amélie Poulain (eng. Amélie) (2001)
Anna Behlmer, Andy Nelson, Roger Savage, Guntis Sics
Moulin Rouge! (2001)
Christopher Boyes, Gethin Creagh, Hammond Peek, Michael Semanick
The Lord of the Rings: The Fellowship of the Ring (2001)
Peter J. Devlin, Kevin O'Connell, Greg P. Russell
Pearl Harbor (2001)

Best Writing, Screenplay Based on Material Previously Produced or Published
⇣ Akiva Goldsman ⇣
A Beautiful Mind (2001)
Philippa Boyens, Peter Jackson, Fran Walsh
The Lord of the Rings: The Fellowship of the Ring (2001)
Daniel Clowes, Terry Zwigoff
Ghost World (2001)
Ted Elliott, Terry Rossio, Roger S.H. Schulman, Joe Stillman
Shrek (2001)
Rob Festinger, Todd Field
In the Bedroom (2001)

Best Writing, Screenplay Written Directly for the Screen

⚐ Julian Fellowes ⚐
Gosford Park (2001)

Milo Addica, Will Rokos
Monster's Ball (2001)

Wes Anderson, Owen Wilson
The Royal Tenenbaums (2001)

Jean-Pierre Jeunet, Guillaume Laurant
Le fabuleux destin d'Amélie Poulain (eng. Amélie) (2001)

Christopher Nolan, Jonathan Nolan (Story)
Memento (2000)

Honorary Award

⚐ Sidney Poitier ⚐
For his extraordinary performances and unique presence on the screen and for representing the industry with dignity, style and intelligence.

⚐ Robert Redford ⚐
Actor, director, producer, creator of Sundance, inspiration to independent and innovative filmmakers everywhere.

The 75ᵗʰ Academy Awards® - March 23, 2003

Host: Steve Martin
Venue: Kodak Theatre at Hollywood & Highland Center
Honoring movies released in 2002

Best Actor in a Leading Role

⚐ Adrien Brody ⚐
The Pianist (2002) role "Władysław Szpilman"

Nicolas Cage
Adaptation. (2002) role "Charlie Kaufman / Donald Kaufman"

Michael Caine
The Quiet American (2002) role "Thomas Fowler"

Daniel Day-Lewis
Gangs of New York (2002) role "William "Bill the Butcher" Cutting"

Jack Nicholson
About Schmidt (2002) role "Warren R. Schmidt"

Best Actor in a Supporting Role

⚐ Chris Cooper ⚐
Adaptation. (2002) role "John Laroche"

Ed Harris
The Hours (2002) role "Richard "Richie" Brown"

Paul Newman
Road to Perdition (2002) role "John Rooney"

John C. Reilly
Chicago (2002) role "Amos Hart"

Christopher Walken
Catch Me If You Can (2002) role "Frank Abagnale Sr."

Best Actress in a Leading Role
⚑ Nicole Kidman ⚑
The Hours (2002) role "Virginia Woolf"
Salma Hayek
Frida (2002) role "Frida Kahlo"
Diane Lane
Unfaithful (2002) role "Constance "Connie" Sumner"
Julianne Moore
Far from Heaven (2002) role "Cathy Whitaker"
Renée Zellweger
Chicago (2002) role "Roxie Hart"

Best Actress in a Supporting Role
⚑ Catherine Zeta-Jones ⚑
Chicago (2002) role "Velma Kelly"
Kathy Bates
About Schmidt (2002) role "Roberta Hertzel"
Queen Latifah
Chicago (2002) role "Matron "Mama" Morton"
Julianne Moore
The Hours (2002) role "Laura McGrath Brown"
Meryl Streep
Adaptation. (2002) role "Susan Orlean"

Best Animated Feature Film
⚑ Hayao Miyazaki ⚑
Sen to Chihiro no kamikakushi (eng. Spirited Away) (2001)
Ron Clements
Treasure Planet (2002)
Jeffrey Katzenberg
Spirit: Stallion of the Cimarron (2002)
Chris Sanders
Lilo & Stitch (2002)
Chris Wedge
Ice Age (2002)

Best Art Direction
⚑ John Myhre (Art Direction), Gordon Sim (Set Decoration) ⚑
Chicago (2002)
Dante Ferretti (Art Direction), Francesca Lo Schiavo (Set Decoration)
Gangs of New York (2002)
Dennis Gassner (Art Direction), Nancy Haigh (Set Decoration)
Road to Perdition (2002)
Grant Major (Art Direction), Dan Hennah, Alan Lee (Set Decoration)
The Lord of the Rings: The Two Towers (2002)
Felipe Fernández del Paso (Art Direction), Hania Robledo (Set Decoration)
Frida (2002)

Best Makeup
⚑ Beatrice De Alba, John E. Jackson ⚑
Frida (2002)
John M. Elliott Jr., Barbara Lorenz
The Time Machine (2002)

Best Costume Design
⚱ Colleen Atwood ⚱
Chicago (2002)
Sandy Powell
Gangs of New York (2002)
Ann Roth
The Hours (2002)
Anna B. Sheppard
The Pianist (2002)
Julie Weiss
Frida (2002)

Best Cinematography
⚱ Conrad L. Hall ⚱
(posthumous)
Road to Perdition (2002)
Michael Ballhaus
Gangs of New York (2002)
Dion Beebe
Chicago (2002)
Pawel Edelman
The Pianist (2002)
Edward Lachman
Far from Heaven (2002)

Honorary Award
⚱ Peter O'Toole ⚱
Whose remarkable talents have provided cinema history with some of its most memorable characters.

Best Directing
⚱ Roman Polanski ⚱
The Pianist (2002)
Pedro Almodóvar
Hable con ella (eng. Talk to Her) (2002)
Stephen Daldry
The Hours (2002)
Rob Marshall
Chicago (2002)
Martin Scorsese
Gangs of New York (2002)

Best Documentary, Feature
⚱ Michael Donovan, Michael Moore ⚱
Bowling for Columbine (2002)
Jeffrey Blitz, Sean Welch
Spellbound (2002)
Malcolm Clarke, Stuart Sender
Prisoner of Paradise (2002)
Gail Dolgin, Vicente Franco
Daughter from Danang (2002)
Jacques Perrin
Le peuple migrateur (eng. Winged Migration) (2001)

Best Documentary, Short Subject

⚜ **Bill Guttentag, Robert David Port** ⚜
Twin Towers (2003)

Alice Elliott
The Collector of Bedford Street (2002)

Bobby Houston, Robert Hudson
Mighty Times: The Legacy of Rosa Parks (2002)

Murray Nossel, Roger Weisberg
Why Can't We Be a Family Again? (2002)

Best Music, Original Song

⚜ **Jeff Bass, Eminem, Luis Resto (Music), Eminem (Lyrics)** ⚜
for the song "Lose Yourself"
8 Mile (2002)

Bono, Adam Clayton, The Edge, Larry Mullen Jr. (Music & Lyrics)
for the song "The Hands That Built America"
Gangs of New York (2002)

Elliot Goldenthal (Music), Julie Taymor (Lyrics) for the song "Burn It Blue"
Frida (2002)

John Kander (Music), Fred Ebb (Lyrics) for the song "I Move On"
Chicago (2002)

Paul Simon (Music & Lyrics) for the song "Father and Daughter"
The Wild Thornberrys (2002)

Best Sound

⚜ **David Lee, Michael Minkler, Dominick Tavella** ⚜
Chicago (2002)

Bob Beemer, Scott Millan, John Patrick Pritchett
Road to Perdition (2002)

Christopher Boyes, Michael Hedges, Hammond Peek, Michael Semanick
The Lord of the Rings: The Two Towers (2002)

Tom Fleischman, Eugene Gearty, Ivan Sharrock
Gangs of New York (2002)

Ed Novick, Kevin O'Connell, Greg P. Russell
Spider-Man (2002)

Best Sound Editing

⚜ **Michael Hopkins, Ethan Van der Ryn** ⚜
The Lord of the Rings: The Two Towers (2002)

Scott A. Hecker
Road to Perdition (2002)

Richard Hymns, Gary Rydstrom
Minority Report (2002)

Best Visual Effects

⚜ **Randall William Cook, Alex Funke, Joe Letteri, Jim Rygiel** ⚜
The Lord of the Rings: The Two Towers (2002)

Rob Coleman, Pablo Helman, John Knoll, Ben Snow
Star Wars: Episode II - Attack of the Clones (2002)

John Dykstra, John Frazier, Anthony LaMolinara, Scott Stokdyk
Spider-Man (2002)

Best Music, Original Score
⚱ Elliot Goldenthal ⚱
Frida (2002)
Elmer Bernstein
Far from Heaven (2002)
Philip Glass
The Hours (2002)
Thomas Newman
Road to Perdition (2002)
John Williams
Catch Me If You Can (2002)

Best Film Editing
⚱ Martin Walsh ⚱
Chicago (2002)
Peter Boyle
The Hours (2002)
Michael Horton
The Lord of the Rings: The Two Towers (2002)
Hervé de Luze
The Pianist (2002)
Thelma Schoonmaker
Gangs of New York (2002)

Best Foreign Language Film
⚱ Germany ⚱
Nirgendwo in Afrika (eng. Nowhere in Africa) (2001)
Finland
Mies vailla menneisyyttä (eng. The Man Without a Past) (2002)
Mexico
El crimen del Padre Amaro (eng. The Crime of Padre Amaro) (2002)
People's Republic of China
Ying xiong (eng. Hero) (2002)
The Netherlands
Zus & Zo (2001)

Best Writing, Adapted Screenplay
⚱ Ronald Harwood ⚱
The Pianist (2002)
Bill Condon
Chicago (2002)
David Hare
The Hours (2002)
Peter Hedges, Chris Weitz, Paul Weitz
About a Boy (2002)
Charlie Kaufman, Donald Kaufman
(Donald Kaufman was the fictitious twin brother of Charlie Kaufman)
Adaptation. (2002)

Best Writing, Original Screenplay
⚐ Pedro Almodóvar ⚐
Hable con ella (eng. Talk to Her) (2002)
Alfonso Cuarón, Carlos Cuarón
Y tu mamá también (eng. And Your Mother Too) (2001)
Jay Cocks, Kenneth Lonergan, Steve Zaillian, Jay Cocks (Story)
Gangs of New York (2002)
Todd Haynes
Far from Heaven (2002)
Nia Vardalos
My Big Fat Greek Wedding (2002)

Best Picture
⚐ Martin Richards (Producer) ⚐
Chicago (2002)
Robert Benmussa, Roman Polanski, Alain Sarde (Producers)
The Pianist (2002)
Robert Fox, Scott Rudin (Producers)
The Hours (2002)
Alberto Grimaldi, Harvey Weinstein (Producers)
Gangs of New York (2002)
Peter Jackson, Barrie M. Osborne, Fran Walsh (Producers)
The Lord of the Rings: The Two Towers (2002)

Best Short Film, Animated
⚐ Eric Armstrong ⚐
The Chubbchubbs! (2002)
Tomasz Baginski
Katedra (eng. The Cathedral) (2002)
Pete Docter, Roger Gould
Mike's New Car (2002)
Chris Stenner, Heidi Wittlinger
Das Rad (eng. Rocks) (2001)
Koji Yamamura
Atama-yama (eng. Mount Head) (2002)

Best Short Film, Live Action
⚐ Mie Andreasen, Martin Strange-Hansen ⚐
Der er en yndig mand (eng. This Charming Man) (2002)
Lexi Alexander, Alexander Buono
Johnny Flynton (2002)
Dirk Beliën, Anja Daelemans
Fait d'hiver (eng. Gridlock) (2001)
Thomas Gaudin, Philippe Orreindy
J'attendrai le suivant... (eng. I'll Wait for the Next One...) (2002)
Steven Pasvolsky, Joe Weatherstone
Inja (eng. Dog) (2002)

The 76ᵗʰ Academy Awards® - February 29, 2004
Host: Billy Crystal
Venue: Kodak Theatre at Hollywood & Highland Center
Honoring movies released in 2003

Honorary Award
⚜ Blake Edwards ⚜

In recognition of his writing, directing and producing an extraordinary body of work for the screen.

Best Actor in a Leading Role
⚜ Sean Penn ⚜
Mystic River (2003) role "Jimmy Markum"

Johnny Depp
Pirates of the Caribbean: The Curse of the Black Pearl (2003) role "Captain Jack Sparrow"

Ben Kingsley
House of Sand and Fog (2003) role "Colonel Massoud Amir Behrani"

Jude Law
Cold Mountain (2003) role "W. P. Inman"

Bill Murray
Lost in Translation (2003) role "Bob Harris"

Best Actor in a Supporting Role
⚜ Tim Robbins ⚜
Mystic River (2003) role "Dave Boyle"

Alec Baldwin
The Cooler (2003) role "Shelley Kaplow"

Benicio del Toro
21 Grams (2003) role "Jack Jordan"

Djimon Hounsou
In America (2002) role "Mateo Kuamey"

Ken Watanabe
The Last Samurai (2003) role "Lord Moritsugu Katsumoto"

Best Actress in a Leading Role
⚜ Charlize Theron ⚜
Monster (2003) role "Aileen "Lee" Wuornos"

Keisha Castle-Hughes
Whale Rider (2002) role "Paikea Apirana"

Diane Keaton
Something's Gotta Give (2003) role "Erica Jane Berry"

Samantha Morton
In America (2002) role "Sarah Sullivan"

Naomi Watts
21 Grams (2003) role "Cristina "Cris" Williams-Peck"

Best Actress in a Supporting Role
⚜ Renée Zellweger ⚜
Cold Mountain (2003) role "Ruby Thewes"

Shohreh Aghdashloo
House of Sand and Fog (2003) role "Nadereh Behrani"

Patricia Clarkson
Pieces of April (2003) role "Joy Burns"

Marcia Gay Harden
Mystic River (2003) role "Celeste Boyle"

Holly Hunter
Thirteen (2003) role "Melanie Freeland"

Best Art Direction

⚑ Grant Major (Art Direction), Dan Hennah, Alan Lee (Set Decoration) ⚑
The Lord of the Rings: The Return of the King (2003)

Lilly Kilvert (Art Direction), Gretchen Rau (Set Decoration)
The Last Samurai (2003)

Jeannine Oppewall (Art Direction), Leslie Pope (Set Decoration)
Seabiscuit (2003)

Ben Van Os (Art Direction), Cecile Heideman (Set Decoration)
Girl with a Pearl Earring (2003)

William Sandell (Art Direction), Robert Gould (Set Decoration)
Master and Commander: The Far Side of the World (2003)

Best Cinematography

⚑ Russell Boyd ⚑
Master and Commander: The Far Side of the World (2003)

César Charlone
Cidade de Deus (eng. City of God) (2002)

John Schwartzman
Seabiscuit (2003)

John Seale
Cold Mountain (2003)

Eduardo Serra
Girl with a Pearl Earring (2003)

Best Animated Feature Film

⚑ Andrew Stanton ⚑
Finding Nemo (2003)

Aaron Blaise, Robert Walker
Brother Bear (2003)

Sylvain Chomet
Les triplettes de Belleville (eng. The Triplets of Belleville) (2003)

Best Costume Design

⚑ Ngila Dickson, Richard Taylor ⚑
The Lord of the Rings: The Return of the King (2003)

Ngila Dickson
The Last Samurai (2003)

Judianna Makovsky
Seabiscuit (2003)

Wendy Stites
Master and Commander: The Far Side of the World (2003)

Dien van Straalen
Girl with a Pearl Earring (2003)

Best Makeup

⚑ Peter Swords King, Richard Taylor ⚑
The Lord of the Rings: The Return of the King (2003)

Edouard F. Henriques III, Yolanda Toussieng
Master and Commander: The Far Side of the World (2003)

Ve Neill, Martin Samuel
Pirates of the Caribbean: The Curse of the Black Pearl (2003)

Best Directing

⚱ Peter Jackson ⚱
The Lord of the Rings: The Return of the King (2003)

Sofia Coppola
Lost in Translation (2003)

Clint Eastwood
Mystic River (2003)

Fernando Meirelles
Cidade de Deus (eng. City of God) (2002)

Peter Weir
Master and Commander: The Far Side of the World (2003)

Best Film Editing

⚱ Jamie Selkirk ⚱
The Lord of the Rings: The Return of the King (2003)

William Goldenberg
Seabiscuit (2003)

Walter Murch
Cold Mountain (2003)

Daniel Rezende
Cidade de Deus (eng. City of God) (2002)

Lee Smith
Master and Commander: The Far Side of the World (2003)

Best Music, Original Song

**⚱ Annie Lennox, Howard Shore, Fran Walsh (Music & Lyrics) ⚱
for the song "Into the West"**
The Lord of the Rings: The Return of the King (2003)

T Bone Burnett, Elvis Costello (Music & Lyrics) for the song "Scarlet Tide"
Cold Mountain (2003)

**Benoît Charest (Music), Sylvain Chomet (Lyrics)
for the song "Belleville Rendez-Vous"**
Les triplettes de Belleville (eng. The Triplets of Belleville) (2003)

**Michael McKean, Annette O'Toole (Music & Lyrics)
for the song "A Kiss at the End of the Rainbow"**
A Mighty Wind (2003)

Sting (Music & Lyrics) for the song "You Will Be My Ain True Love"
Cold Mountain (2003)

Best Documentary, Feature

⚱ Errol Morris, Michael Williams ⚱
The Fog of War (2003)

Susan Rose Behr, Nathaniel Kahn
My Architect (2003)

Carlos Bosch, Josep Maria Domènech
Balseros (eng. Cuban Rafters) (2002)

Sam Green, Bill Siegel
The Weather Underground (2002)

Andrew Jarecki, Marc Smerling
Capturing the Friedmans (2003)

Best Documentary, Short Subject
⚊ **Maryann DeLeo** ⚊
Chernobyl Heart (2003)
Katja Esson
Ferry Tales (2003)
Sandy McLeod, Gini Reticker
Asylum (2003)

Best Sound Mixing
⚊ **Christopher Boyes, Michael Hedges, Hammond Peek, Michael Semanick** ⚊
The Lord of the Rings: The Return of the King (2003)
Anna Behlmer, Tod A. Maitland, Andy Nelson
Seabiscuit (2003)
Anna Behlmer, Andy Nelson, Jeff Wexler
The Last Samurai (2003)
Christopher Boyes, David E. Campbell, Lee Orloff, David Parker
Pirates of the Caribbean: The Curse of the Black Pearl (2003)
Doug M. Hemphill, Paul Massey, Arthur Rochester
Master and Commander: The Far Side of the World (2003)

Best Foreign Language Film
⚊ **Canada** ⚊
Les invasions barbares (eng. The Barbarian Invasions) (2003)
Czech Republic
Zelary (2003)
Japan
Tasogare Seibei (eng. The Twilight Samurai) (2002)
Sweden
Ondskan (eng. Evil) (2003)
The Netherlands
De Tweeling (eng. Twin Sisters) (2002)

Best Music, Original Score
⚊ **Howard Shore** ⚊
The Lord of the Rings: The Return of the King (2003)
Danny Elfman
Big Fish (2003)
James Horner
House of Sand and Fog (2003)
Thomas Newman
Finding Nemo (2003)
Gabriel Yared
Cold Mountain (2003)

Best Visual Effects
⚊ **Randall William Cook, Alex Funke, Joe Letteri, Jim Rygiel** ⚊
The Lord of the Rings: The Return of the King (2003)
Stefen Fangmeier, Nathan McGuinness, Robert Stromberg, Dan Sudick
Master and Commander: The Far Side of the World (2003)
Terry D. Frazee, Charles Gibson, Hal T. Hickel, John Knoll
Pirates of the Caribbean: The Curse of the Black Pearl (2003)

Best Picture

I Peter Jackson, Barrie M. Osborne, Fran Walsh (Producers) I
The Lord of the Rings: The Return of the King (2003)

Sofia Coppola, Ross Katz (Producers)
Lost in Translation (2003)

Clint Eastwood, Judie G. Hoyt, Robert Lorenz (Producers)
Mystic River (2003)

Samuel Goldwyn Jr., Duncan Henderson, Peter Weir (Producers)
Master and Commander: The Far Side of the World (2003)

Kathleen Kennedy, Frank Marshall, Gary Ross (Producers)
Seabiscuit (2003)

Best Short Film, Animated

I Adam Elliot I
Harvie Krumpet (2003)

Roy Edward Disney, Dominique Monfery
Destino (2003)

John C. Donkin, Carlos Saldanha
Gone Nutty (2002)

Chris Hinton
Nibbles (2003)

Bud Luckey
Boundin' (2003)

Best Short Film, Live Action

I Andrew J. Sacks, Aaron Schneider I
Two Soldiers (2003)

Stefan Arsenijevic
(A)Torzija (eng. (A)Torsion) (2003)

Lionel Bailliu
Squash (2002)

Florian Baxmeyer
Die rote Jacke (eng. The Red Jacket) (2002)

Bobby Garabedian, William Zabka
Most (eng. The Bridge) (2003)

Best Writing, Adapted Screenplay

I Philippa Boyens, Peter Jackson, Fran Walsh I
The Lord of the Rings: The Return of the King (2003)

Shari Springer Berman, Robert Pulcini
American Splendor (2003)

Brian Helgeland
Mystic River (2003)

Bráulio Mantovani
Cidade de Deus (eng. City of God) (2002)

Gary Ross
Seabiscuit (2003)

Best Writing, Original Screenplay
⚊ Sofia Coppola ⚊
Lost in Translation (2003)
Denys Arcand
Les invasions barbares (eng. The Barbarian Invasions) (2003)
Steven Knight
Dirty Pretty Things (2002)
Bob Peterson, David Reynolds, Andrew Stanton (Screenplay & Story)
Finding Nemo (2003)
Jim Sheridan, Kirsten Sheridan, Naomi Sheridan
In America (2002)

Best Sound Editing
⚊ Richard King ⚊
Master and Commander: The Far Side of the World (2003)
Christopher Boyes, George Watters II
Pirates of the Caribbean: The Curse of the Black Pearl (2003)
Gary Rydstrom, Michael Silvers
Finding Nemo (2003)

The 77ᵗʰ Academy Awards® - February 27, 2005
Host: Chris Rock
Venue: Kodak Theatre at Hollywood & Highland Center
Honoring movies released in 2004

Jean Hersholt Humanitarian Award
⚊ Roger Mayer ⚊

Best Actor in a Leading Role
⚊ Jamie Foxx ⚊
Ray (2004) role "Ray Charles"
Don Cheadle
Hotel Rwanda (2004) role "Paul Rusesabagina"
Johnny Depp
Finding Neverland (2004) role "Sir James Matthew Barrie"
Leonardo DiCaprio
The Aviator (2004) role "Howard Hughes"
Clint Eastwood
Million Dollar Baby (2004) role "Frankie Dunn"

Best Actor in a Supporting Role
⚊ Morgan Freeman ⚊
Million Dollar Baby (2004) role "Eddie "Scrap-Iron" Dupris"
Alan Alda
The Aviator (2004) role "Senator Ralph Owen Brewster"
Thomas Haden Church
Sideways (2004) role "Jack Cole"
Jamie Foxx
Collateral (2004) role "Max Durocher"
Clive Owen
Closer (2004) role "Larry Gray"

Best Actress in a Leading Role
⚑ Hilary Swank ⚑
Million Dollar Baby (2004) role "Margaret "Maggie" Fitzgerald"
Annette Bening
Being Julia (2004) role "Julia Lambert"
Catalina Sandino Moreno
Maria Full of Grace (2004) role "María Álvarez"
Imelda Staunton
Vera Drake (2004) role "Vera Rose Drake"
Kate Winslet
Eternal Sunshine of the Spotless Mind (2004) role "Clementine Kruczynski"

Best Actress in a Supporting Role
⚑ Cate Blanchett ⚑
The Aviator (2004) role "Katharine Hepburn"
Laura Linney
Kinsey (2004) role "Clara McMillen"
Virginia Madsen
Sideways (2004) role "Maya Randall"
Sophie Okonedo
Hotel Rwanda (2004) role "Tatiana Rusesabagina"
Natalie Portman
Closer (2004) role "Alice Ayres / Jane Jones"

Honorary Award
⚑ Sidney Lumet ⚑
In recognition of his brilliant services to screenwriters, performers and the art of the motion picture.

Best Art Direction
⚑ Dante Ferretti (Art Direction), Francesca Lo Schiavo (Set Decoration) ⚑
The Aviator (2004)
Aline Bonetto (Art Direction)
Un long dimanche de fiançailles (eng. A Very Long Engagement) (2004)
Rick Heinrichs (Art Direction), Cheryl Carasik (Set Decoration)
Lemony Snicket's A Series of Unfortunate Events (2004)
Gemma Jackson (Art Direction), Trisha Edwards (Set Decoration)
Finding Neverland (2004)
Anthony Pratt (Art Direction), Celia Bobak (Set Decoration)
The Phantom of the Opera (2004)

Best Cinematography
⚑ Robert Richardson ⚑
The Aviator (2004)
Bruno Delbonnel
Un long dimanche de fiançailles (eng. A Very Long Engagement) (2004)
Caleb Deschanel
The Passion of the Christ (2004)
John Mathieson
The Phantom of the Opera (2004)
Zhao Xiaoding
Shi mian mai fu (eng. House of Flying Daggers) (2004)

Best Animated Feature Film

⚱ Brad Bird ⚱
The Incredibles (2004)

Andrew Adamson
Shrek 2 (2004)

Bill Damaschke
Shark Tale (2004)

Best Costume Design

⚱ Sandy Powell ⚱
The Aviator (2004)

Colleen Atwood
Lemony Snicket's A Series of Unfortunate Events (2004)

Alexandra Byrne
Finding Neverland (2004)

Sharen Davis
Ray (2004)

Bob Ringwood
Troy (2004)

Best Makeup

⚱ Bill Corso, Valli O'Reilly ⚱
Lemony Snicket's A Series of Unfortunate Events (2004)

Jo Allen, Manolo García
Mar adentro (eng. The Sea Inside) (2004)

Christien Tinsley, Keith Vanderlaan
The Passion of the Christ (2004)

Best Directing

⚱ Clint Eastwood ⚱
Million Dollar Baby (2004)

Taylor Hackford
Ray (2004)

Mike Leigh
Vera Drake (2004)

Alexander Payne
Sideways (2004)

Martin Scorsese
The Aviator (2004)

Best Documentary, Feature

⚱ Zana Briski, Ross Kauffman ⚱
Born Into Brothels: Calcutta's Red Light Kids (2004)

Karolyn Ali, Lauren Lazin
Tupac: Resurrection (2003)

Byambasuren Davaa, Luigi Falorni
Die Geschichte vom weinenden Kamel (eng. The Story of the Weeping Camel) (2003)

Kirby Dick, Eddie Schmidt
Twist of Faith (2004)

Morgan Spurlock
Super Size Me (2004)

Best Documentary, Short Subject
⚐ Bobby Houston, Robert Hudson ⚐
Mighty Times: The Children's March (2004)
Andrzej Celinski, Hanna Polak
Dzieci z Leningradzkiego (eng. The Children of Leningradsky) (2005)
Hubert Davis, Erin Faith Young
Hardwood (2005)
Oren Jacoby, Steve Kalafer
Sister Rose's Passion (2004)
Gerardine Wurzburg
Autism Is a World (2004)

Best Film Editing
⚐ Thelma Schoonmaker ⚐
The Aviator (2004)
Matt Chesse
Finding Neverland (2004)
Joel Cox
Million Dollar Baby (2004)
Paul Hirsch
Ray (2004)
Jim Miller, Paul Rubell
Collateral (2004)

Best Foreign Language Film
⚐ Spain ⚐
Mar adentro (eng. The Sea Inside) (2004)
France
Les choristes (eng. The Chorus) (2004)
Germany
Der Untergang (eng. Downfall) (2004)
South Africa
Yesterday (2004)
Sweden
Så som i himmelen (eng. As It Is in Heaven) (2004)

Best Sound Editing
⚐ Michael Silvers, Randy Thom ⚐
The Incredibles (2004)
Dennis Leonard, Randy Thom
The Polar Express (2004)
Paul N.J. Ottosson
Spider-Man 2 (2004)

Best Visual Effects
⚐ John Dykstra, John Frazier, Anthony LaMolinara, Scott Stokdyk ⚐
Spider-Man 2 (2004)
Tim Burke, Bill George, Roger Guyett, John Richardson
Harry Potter and the Prisoner of Azkaban (2004)
Andrew R. Jones, Joe Letteri, Erik Nash, John Nelson
I, Robot (2004)

Best Music, Original Score

⚐ **Jan A.P. Kaczmarek** ⚐
Finding Neverland (2004)

John Debney
The Passion of the Christ (2004)

James Newton Howard
The Village (2004)

Thomas Newman
Lemony Snicket's A Series of Unfortunate Events (2004)

John Williams
Harry Potter and the Prisoner of Azkaban (2004)

Best Music, Original Song

⚐ **Jorge Drexler (Music & Lyrics) for the song "Al Otro Lado Del Río"** ⚐
Diarios de motocicleta (eng. The Motorcycle Diaries) (2004)

Glen Ballard, Alan Silvestri (Music & Lyrics) for the song "Believe"
The Polar Express (2004)

**Jim Bogios, David Bryson, Adam Duritz, Charles Gillingham,
David Immerglück, Matthew Malley (Music),
Adam Duritz, Dan Vickrey (Lyrics) for the song "Accidentally In Love"**
Shrek 2 (2004)

**Bruno Coulais (Music), Christophe Barratier (Lyrics)
for the song "Look To Your Path (Vois Sur Ton Chemin)"**
Les choristes (eng. The Chorus) (2004)

**Andrew Lloyd Webber (Music), Charles Hart (Lyrics)
for the song "Learn To Be Lonely"**
The Phantom of the Opera (2004)

Best Picture

⚐ **Clint Eastwood, Tom Rosenberg, Albert S. Ruddy (Producers)** ⚐
Million Dollar Baby (2004)

Howard Baldwin, Stuart Benjamin, Taylor Hackford (Producers)
Ray (2004)

Nellie Bellflower, Richard N. Gladstein (Producers)
Finding Neverland (2004)

Graham King, Michael Mann (Producers)
The Aviator (2004)

Michael London (Producer)
Sideways (2004)

Best Short Film, Animated

⚐ **Chris Landreth** ⚐
Ryan (2004)

Baker Bloodworth, Mike Gabriel
Lorenzo (2004)

Jeff Fowler, Tim Miller
Gopher Broke (2004)

Andrew Gregory, Sejong Park
Birthday Boy (2004)

Bill Plympton
Guard Dog (2004)

Best Short Film, Live Action
ℑ **Andrea Arnold** ℑ
Wasp (2003)
Ainsley Gardiner, Taika Waititi
Two Cars, One Night (2003)
Ashvin Kumar
Little Terrorist (2004)
Gary McKendry
Everything in This Country Must (2004)
Nacho Vigalondo
7:35 de la mañana (eng. 7:35 in the Morning) (2003)

Best Sound Mixing
ℑ **Bob Beemer, Steve Cantamessa, Scott Millan, Greg Orloff** ℑ
Ray (2004)
Tom Fleischman, Petur Hliddal
The Aviator (2004)
Joseph Geisinger, Jeffrey J. Haboush, Kevin O'Connell, Greg P. Russell
Spider-Man 2 (2004)
Tom Johnson, William B. Kaplan, Dennis S. Sands, Randy Thom
The Polar Express (2004)
Doc Kane, Gary A. Rizzo, Randy Thom
The Incredibles (2004)

Best Writing, Adapted Screenplay
ℑ **Alexander Payne, Jim Taylor** ℑ
Sideways (2004)
Julie Delpy, Ethan Hawke, Richard Linklater (Screenplay),
Kim Krizan, Richard Linklater (Story)
Before Sunset (2004)
Paul Haggis
Million Dollar Baby (2004)
David Magee
Finding Neverland (2004)
José Rivera
Diarios de motocicleta (eng. The Motorcycle Diaries) (2004)

Best Writing, Original Screenplay
Charlie Kaufman (Screenplay),
ℑ **Pierre Bismuth, Michel Gondry, Charlie Kaufman (Story)** ℑ
Eternal Sunshine of the Spotless Mind (2004)
Brad Bird
The Incredibles (2004)
Terry George, Keir Pearson
Hotel Rwanda (2004)
Mike Leigh
Vera Drake (2004)
John Logan
The Aviator (2004)

The 78ᵗʰ Academy Awards® - March 5, 2006

Host: Jon Stewart
Venue: Kodak Theatre at Hollywood & Highland Center
Honoring movies released in 2005

Best Actor in a Leading Role

↓ **Philip Seymour Hoffman** ↓
Capote (2005) role "Truman Capote"

Terrence Howard
Hustle & Flow (2005) role "DJay"

Heath Ledger
Brokeback Mountain (2005) role "Ennis Del Mar"

Joaquin Phoenix
Walk the Line (2005) role "Johnny R. Cash"

David Strathairn
Good Night, and Good Luck. (2005) role "Edward R. Murrow"

Best Actor in a Supporting Role

↓ **George Clooney** ↓
Syriana (2005) role "Bob Barnes"

Matt Dillon
Crash (2004) role "Officer John Ryan"

Paul Giamatti
Cinderella Man (2005) role "Joe Gould"

Jake Gyllenhaal
Brokeback Mountain (2005) role "Jack Twist"

William Hurt
A History of Violence (2005) role "Richie Cusack"

Best Actress in a Leading Role

↓ **Reese Witherspoon** ↓
Walk the Line (2005) role "June Carter Cash"

Judi Dench
Mrs. Henderson Presents (2005) role "Laura Forster-Henderson"

Felicity Huffman
Transamerica (2005) role "Sabrina "Bree" Osbourne / Stanley Schupak"

Keira Knightley
Pride & Prejudice (2005) role "Elizabeth Bennet"

Charlize Theron
North Country (2005) role "Josey Aimes"

Best Actress in a Supporting Role

↓ **Rachel Weisz** ↓
The Constant Gardener (2005) role "Tessa Quayle"

Amy Adams
Junebug (2005) role "Ashley Johnsten"

Catherine Keener
Capote (2005) role "Nelle Harper Lee"

Frances McDormand
North Country (2005) role "Glory Dodge"

Michelle Williams
Brokeback Mountain (2005) role "Alma Beers Del Mar"

Best Animated Feature Film
⚑ Steve Box, Nick Park ⚑
Wallace & Gromit: The Curse of the Were-Rabbit (2005)
Tim Burton, Mike Johnson
Corpse Bride (2005)
Hayao Miyazaki
Hauru no ugoku shiro (eng. Howl's Moving Castle) (2004)

Best Art Direction
⚑ John Myhre (Art Direction), Gretchen Rau (Set Decoration) ⚑
Memoirs of a Geisha (2005)
Jim Bissell (Art Direction), Jan Pascale (Set Decoration)
Good Night, and Good Luck. (2005)
Stuart Craig (Art Direction), Stephenie McMillan (Set Decoration)
Harry Potter and the Goblet of Fire (2005)
Sarah Greenwood (Art Direction), Katie Spencer (Set Decoration)
Pride & Prejudice (2005)
Grant Major (Art Direction), Simon Bright, Dan Hennah (Set Decoration)
King Kong (2005)

Best Cinematography
⚑ Dion Beebe ⚑
Memoirs of a Geisha (2005)
Robert Elswit
Good Night, and Good Luck. (2005)
Emmanuel Lubezki
The New World (2005)
Wally Pfister
Batman Begins (2005)
Rodrigo Prieto
Brokeback Mountain (2005)

Best Documentary, Feature
⚑ Yves Darondeau, Luc Jacquet ⚑
La marche de l'empereur (eng. March of the Penguins) (2005)
Marshall Curry
Street Fight (2005)
Alex Gibney, Jason Kliot
Enron: The Smartest Guys in the Room (2005)
Henry Alex Rubin, Dana Adam Shapiro
Murderball (2005)
Hubert Sauper
Darwin's Nightmare (2004)

Best Documentary, Short Subject
⚑ Corinne Marrinan, Eric Simonson ⚑
A Note of Triumph: The Golden Age of Norman Corwin (2005)
Kimberlee Acquaro, Stacy Sherman
God Sleeps in Rwanda (2005)
Dan Krauss
The Death of Kevin Carter: Casualty of the Bang Bang Club (2004)
Steven Okazaki
The Mushroom Club (2005)

Honorary Award
⚊ Robert Altman ⚊
In recognition of a career that has repeatedly reinvented the art form and inspired filmmakers and audiences alike.

Best Costume Design
⚊ Colleen Atwood ⚊
Memoirs of a Geisha (2005)
Jacqueline Durran
Pride & Prejudice (2005)
Gabriella Pescucci
Charlie and the Chocolate Factory (2005)
Arianne Phillips
Walk the Line (2005)
Sandy Powell
Mrs. Henderson Presents (2005)

Best Directing
⚊ Ang Lee ⚊
Brokeback Mountain (2005)
George Clooney
Good Night, and Good Luck. (2005)
Paul Haggis
Crash (2004)
Bennett Miller
Capote (2005)
Steven Spielberg
Munich (2005)

Best Film Editing
⚊ Hughes Winborne ⚊
Crash (2004)
Daniel P. Hanley, Mike Hill
Cinderella Man (2005)
Michael Kahn
Munich (2005)
Michael McCusker
Walk the Line (2005)
Claire Simpson
The Constant Gardener (2005)

Best Foreign Language Film
⚊ South Africa ⚊
Tsotsi (2005)
France
Joyeux Noël (eng. Merry Christmas) (2005)
Germany
Sophie Scholl - Die letzten Tage (eng. Sophie Scholl: The Final Days) (2005)
Italy
La bestia nel cuore (eng. Don't Tell) (2005)
The Palestinian Territories
Paradise Now (2005)

Best Music, Original Song

Cedric Coleman, Juicy J (as Jordan Michael Houston),
⚑ **D.J. Paul (as Paul Duane Beauregard) (Music & Lyrics)** ⚑
for the song "It's Hard Out Here for a Pimp"
Hustle & Flow (2005)

Michael Becker, Kathleen "Bird" York (Music), Kathleen "Bird" York (Lyrics)
for the song "In the Deep"
Crash (2004)

Dolly Parton (Music & Lyrics) for the song "Travelin' Thru"
Transamerica (2005)

Best Music, Original Score

⚑ **Gustavo Santaolalla** ⚑
Brokeback Mountain (2005)

Alberto Iglesias
The Constant Gardener (2005)

Dario Marianelli
Pride & Prejudice (2005)

John Williams
Memoirs of a Geisha (2005), Munich (2005)

Best Sound Editing

⚑ **Mike Hopkins, Ethan Van der Ryn** ⚑
King Kong (2005)

Richard King
War of the Worlds (2005)

Wylie Stateman
Memoirs of a Geisha (2005)

Best Picture

⚑ **Paul Haggis, Cathy Schulman (Producers)** ⚑
Crash (2004)

Caroline Baron, Michael Ohoven, William Vince (Producers)
Capote (2005)

Grant Heslov (Producer)
Good Night, and Good Luck. (2005)

Kathleen Kennedy, Barry Mendel, Steven Spielberg (Producers)
Munich (2005)

Diana Ossana, James Schamus (Producers)
Brokeback Mountain (2005)

Best Short Film, Animated

⚑ **John Canemaker, Peggy Stern** ⚑
The Moon and the Son: An Imagined Conversation (2005)

Shane Acker
9 (2005)

Mark Andrews, Andrew Jimenez
One Man Band (2005)

Sharon Colman
Badgered (2005)

Anthony Lucas
The Mysterious Geographic Explorations of Jasper Morello (2005)

Best Short Film, Live Action
ᛏ **Martin McDonagh** ᛏ
Six Shooter (2004)

Lene Bausager, Sean Ellis
Cashback (2004)

Pia Clemente, Rob Pearlstein
Our Time Is Up (2004)

Ulrike Grote
Ausreisser (eng. The Runaway) (2004)

Rúnar Rúnarsson, Thor Sigurjonsson
Síðasti bærinn (eng. The Last Farm) (2004)

Best Sound Mixing
ᛏ **Christopher Boyes, Michael Hedges, Hammond Peek, Michael Semanick** ᛏ
King Kong (2005)

Anna Behlmer, Ronald Judkins, Andy Nelson
War of the Worlds (2005)

Doug M. Hemphill, Peter F. Kurland, Paul Massey
Walk the Line (2005)

Tony Johnson, Terry Porter, Dean A. Zupancic
The Chronicles of Narnia: The Lion, the Witch and the Wardrobe (2005)

Rick Kline, John Pritchett, Kevin O'Connell, Greg P. Russell
Memoirs of a Geisha (2005)

Best Visual Effects
ᛏ **Brian Van't Hul, Joe Letteri, Christian Rivers, Richard Taylor** ᛏ
King Kong (2005)

Jim Berney, Scott Farrar, Bill Westenhofer, Dean Wright
The Chronicles of Narnia: The Lion, the Witch and the Wardrobe (2005)

Randal M. Dutra, Pablo Helman, Dennis Muren, Daniel Sudick
War of the Worlds (2005)

Best Makeup
ᛏ **Howard Berger, Tami Lane** ᛏ
The Chronicles of Narnia: The Lion, the Witch and the Wardrobe (2005)

David LeRoy Anderson, Lance Anderson
Cinderella Man (2005)

Dave Elsey, Nikki Gooley
Star Wars: Episode III - Revenge of the Sith (2005)

Best Writing, Adapted Screenplay
ᛏ **Larry McMurtry, Diana Ossana** ᛏ
Brokeback Mountain (2005)

Jeffrey Caine
The Constant Gardener (2005)

Dan Futterman
Capote (2005)

Tony Kushner, Eric Roth
Munich (2005)

Josh Olson
A History of Violence (2005)

Best Writing, Original Screenplay
⚑ **Paul Haggis, Bobby Moresco (Screenplay), Paul Haggis (Story)** ⚑
Crash (2004)
Woody Allen
Match Point (2005)
Noah Baumbach
The Squid and the Whale (2005)
George Clooney, Grant Heslov
Good Night, and Good Luck. (2005)
Stephen Gaghan
Syriana (2005)

The 79ᵗʰ Academy Awards® - February 25, 2007
Host: Ellen DeGeneres
Venue: Kodak Theatre at Hollywood & Highland Center
Honoring movies released in 2006

Best Actor in a Leading Role
⚑ **Forest Whitaker** ⚑
The Last King of Scotland (2006) role "Idi Amin"
Leonardo DiCaprio
Blood Diamond (2006) role "Danny Archer"
Ryan Gosling
Half Nelson (2006) role "Dan Dunne"
Peter O'Toole
Venus (2006) role "Maurice Russell"
Will Smith
The Pursuit of Happyness (2006) role "Chris Gardner"

Best Actor in a Supporting Role
⚑ **Alan Arkin** ⚑
Little Miss Sunshine (2006) role "Edwin Hoover"
Jackie Earle Haley
Little Children (2006) role "Ronald James McGorvey"
Djimon Hounsou
Blood Diamond (2006) role "Solomon Vandy"
Eddie Murphy
Dreamgirls (2006) role "James "Thunder" Early"
Mark Wahlberg
The Departed (2006) role "Staff Sergeant Sean Dignam"

Best Actress in a Leading Role
⚑ **Helen Mirren** ⚑
The Queen (2006) role "Queen Elizabeth II"
Penélope Cruz
Volver (2006) role "Raimunda"
Judi Dench
Notes on a Scandal (2006) role "Barbara Covett"
Meryl Streep
The Devil Wears Prada (2006) role "Miranda Priestly"
Kate Winslet
Little Children (2006) role "Sarah Pierce"

Best Actress in a Supporting Role
⚐ Jennifer Hudson ⚐
Dreamgirls (2006) role "Effie White"
Adriana Barraza
Babel (2006) role "Amelia Hernández"
Cate Blanchett
Notes on a Scandal (2006) role "Bathsheba "Sheba" Hart"
Abigail Breslin
Little Miss Sunshine (2006) role "Olive Hoover"
Rinko Kikuchi
Babel (2006) role "Chieko Wataya"

Best Animated Feature Film
⚐ George Miller ⚐
Happy Feet (2006)
Gil Kenan
Monster House (2006)
John Lasseter
Cars (2006)

Best Art Direction
⚐ Eugenio Caballero (Art Direction), Pilar Revuelta (Set Decoration) ⚐
El laberinto del fauno (eng. Pan's Labyrinth) (2006)
Nathan Crowley (Art Direction), Julie Ochipinti (Set Decoration)
The Prestige (2006)
Rick Heinrichs (Art Direction), Cheryl Carasik (Set Decoration)
Pirates of the Caribbean: Dead Man's Chest (2006)
John Myhre (Art Direction), Nancy Haigh (Set Decoration)
Dreamgirls (2006)
**Jeannine Oppewall (Art Direction),
Gretchen Rau, Leslie E. Rollins (Set Decoration)**
(Gretchen Rau - posthumous)
The Good Shepherd (2006)

Best Cinematography
⚐ Guillermo Navarro ⚐
El laberinto del fauno (eng. Pan's Labyrinth) (2006)
Emmanuel Lubezki
Children of Men (2006)
Wally Pfister
The Prestige (2006)
Dick Pope
The Illusionist (2006)
Vilmos Zsigmond
The Black Dahlia (2006)

Best Makeup
⚐ David Martí, Montse Ribé ⚐
El laberinto del fauno (eng. Pan's Labyrinth) (2006)
Bill Corso, Kazuhiro Tsuji
Click (2006)
Aldo Signoretti, Vittorio Sodano
Apocalypto (2006)

Best Costume Design

⚊ Milena Canonero ⚊
Marie Antoinette (2006)

Consolata Boyle
The Queen (2006)

Sharen Davis
Dreamgirls (2006)

Patricia Field
The Devil Wears Prada (2006)

Yee Chung Man
Man cheng jin dai huang jin jia (eng. Curse of the Golden Flower) (2006)

Best Directing

⚊ Martin Scorsese ⚊
The Departed (2006)

Clint Eastwood
Letters from Iwo Jima (2006)

Stephen Frears
The Queen (2006)

Paul Greengrass
United 93 (2006)

Alejandro González Iñárritu
Babel (2006)

Best Documentary, Feature

⚊ Davis Guggenheim ⚊
An Inconvenient Truth (2006)

Amy Berg, Frank Donner
Deliver Us from Evil (2006)

Heidi Ewing, Rachel Grady
Jesus Camp (2006)

Jocelyn Glatzer, Laura Poitras
My Country, My Country (2006)

James Longley, John Sinno
Iraq in Fragments (2006)

Best Documentary, Short Subject

⚊ Thomas Lennon, Ruby Yang ⚊
The Blood of Yingzhou District (2006)

Susan Rose Behr, Nathaniel Kahn
Two Hands: The Leon Fleisher Story (2006)

Mike Glad, Leslie Iwerks
Recycled Life (2006)

Karen Goodman, Kirk Simon
Rehearsing a Dream (2006)

Best Visual Effects

⚊ Charles Gibson, Allen Hall, Hal T. Hickel, John Knoll ⚊
Pirates of the Caribbean: Dead Man's Chest (2006)

Neil Corbould, Richard R. Hoover, Mark Stetson, Jon Thum
Superman Returns (2006)

John Frazier, Chas Jarrett, Kim Libreri, Boyd Shermis
Poseidon (2006)

Best Film Editing
⚱ **Thelma Schoonmaker** ⚱
The Departed (2006)

Douglas Crise, Stephen Mirrione
Babel (2006)

Alfonso Cuarón, Alex Rodríguez
Children of Men (2006)

Clare Douglas, Richard Pearson, Christopher Rouse
United 93 (2006)

Steven Rosenblum
Blood Diamond (2006)

Best Foreign Language Film
⚱ **Germany** ⚱
Das Leben der Anderen (eng. The Lives of Others) (2006)

Algeria
Indigènes (eng. Days of Glory) (2006)

Canada
Water (2005)

Denmark
Efter brylluppet (eng. After the Wedding) (2006)

Mexico
El laberinto del fauno (eng. Pan's Labyrinth) (2006)

Jean Hersholt Humanitarian Award
⚱ **Sherry Lansing** ⚱

Best Music, Original Score
⚱ **Gustavo Santaolalla** ⚱
Babel (2006)

Alexandre Desplat
The Queen (2006)

Philip Glass
Notes on a Scandal (2006)

Javier Navarrete
El laberinto del fauno (eng. Pan's Labyrinth) (2006)

Thomas Newman
The Good German (2006)

Best Music, Original Song
⚱ **Melissa Etheridge (Music & Lyrics) for the song "I Need To Wake Up"** ⚱
An Inconvenient Truth (2006)

Scott Cutler, Henry Krieger (Music), Anne Preven (Lyrics) for the song "Listen"
Dreamgirls (2006)

Henry Krieger (Music), Siedah Garrett (Lyrics) for the song "Love You I Do"
Dreamgirls (2006)

Henry Krieger (Music), Willie Reale (Lyrics) for the song "Patience"
Dreamgirls (2006)

Randy Newman (Music & Lyrics) for the song "Our Town"
Cars (2006)

Honorary Award
⚊ Ennio Morricone ⚊
For his magnificent and multifaceted contributions to the art of film music.

Best Picture
⚊ Graham King (Producer) ⚊
The Departed (2006)
Clint Eastwood, Robert Lorenz, Steven Spielberg (Producers)
Letters from Iwo Jima (2006)
David T. Friendly, Peter Saraf, Marc Turtletaub (Producers)
Little Miss Sunshine (2006)
Steve Golin, Alejandro G. Iñárritu, Jon Kilik (Producers)
Babel (2006)
Andy Harries, Christine Langan, Tracey Seaward (Producers)
The Queen (2006)

Best Short Film, Animated
⚊ Torill Kove ⚊
The Danish Poet (2006)
Roger Allers, Don Hahn
The Little Matchgirl (2006)
Chris Renaud, Michael Thurmeier
No Time for Nuts (2006)
Gary Rydstrom
Lifted (2006)
Géza M. Tóth
Maestro (2005)

Best Short Film, Live Action
⚊ Ari Sandel ⚊
West Bank Story (2005)
Borja Cobeaga
Éramos pocos (eng. One Too Many) (2005)
Javier Fesser, Luis Manso
Binta y la gran idea (eng. Binta and the Great Idea) (2004)
Søren Pilmark, Kim Magnusson
Helmer & søn (eng. Helmer & Son) (2006)
Stuart Parkyn, Peter Templeman
The Saviour (2005)

Best Sound Editing
⚊ Bub Asman, Alan Robert Murray ⚊
Letters from Iwo Jima (2006)
Kami Asgar, Sean McCormack
Apocalypto (2006)
Bub Asman, Alan Robert Murray
Flags of Our Fathers (2006)
Lon Bender
Blood Diamond (2006)
Christopher Boyes, George Watters II
Pirates of the Caribbean: Dead Man's Chest (2006)

Best Sound Mixing

⚐ Bob Beemer, Willie D. Burton, Michael Minkler ⚐
Dreamgirls (2006)

Anna Behlmer, Andy Nelson, Ivan Sharrock
Blood Diamond (2006)

Christopher Boyes, Paul Massey, Lee Orloff
Pirates of the Caribbean: Dead Man's Chest (2006)

Fernando Cámara, Kevin O'Connell, Greg P. Russell
Apocalypto (2006)

Dave E. Campbell, Walt Martin, John T. Reitz, Gregg Rudloff
Flags of Our Fathers (2006)

Best Writing, Adapted Screenplay

⚐ William Monahan ⚐
The Departed (2006)

David Arata, Alfonso Cuarón, Mark Fergus, Hawk Ostby, Timothy J. Sexton
Children of Men (2006)

**Peter Baynham, Sacha Baron Cohen, Anthony Hines,
Dan Mazer (Screenplay), Peter Baynham, Sacha Baron Cohen, Anthony Hines,
Todd Phillips (Story)**
Borat:Cultural Learnings of America
for Make Benefit Glorious Nation of Kazakhstan (2006)

Todd Field, Tom Perrotta
Little Children (2006)

Patrick Marber
Notes on a Scandal (2006)

Best Writing, Original Screenplay

⚐ Michael Arndt ⚐
Little Miss Sunshine (2006)

Guillermo Arriaga
Babel (2006)

Peter Morgan
The Queen (2006)

Guillermo del Toro
El laberinto del fauno (eng. Pan's Labyrinth) (2006)

Iris Yamashita (Screenplay), Paul Haggis, Iris Yamashita (Story)
Letters from Iwo Jima (2006)

The 80ᵗʰ Academy Awards® - February 24, 2008

Host: Jon Stewart
Venue: Kodak Theatre at Hollywood & Highland Center
Honoring movies released in 2007

Best Makeup

⚐ Jan Archibald, Didier Lavergne ⚐
La Môme (eng. La Vie En Rose) (2007)

Rick Baker, Kazuhiro Tsuji
Norbit (2007)

Ve Neill, Martin Samuel
Pirates of the Caribbean: At World's End (2007)

Honorary Award
⚐ Robert F. Boyle ⚐
In recognition of one of cinema's great careers in art direction.

Best Actor in a Leading Role
⚐ Daniel Day-Lewis ⚐
There Will Be Blood (2007) role "Daniel Plainview"
George Clooney
Michael Clayton (2007) role "Michael Clayton"
Johnny Depp
Sweeney Todd: The Demon Barber of Fleet Street (2007)
role "Benjamin Barker / Sweeney Todd"
Tommy Lee Jones
In the Valley of Elah (2007) role "Hank Deerfield"
Viggo Mortensen
Eastern Promises (2007) role "Nikolai Luzhin"

Best Actor in a Supporting Role
⚐ Javier Bardem ⚐
No Country for Old Men (2007) role "Anton Chigurh"
Casey Affleck
The Assassination of Jesse James by the Coward Robert Ford (2007) role "Robert "Bob" Ford"
Philip Seymour Hoffman
Charlie Wilson's War (2007) role "Gustav "Gust" Avrakotos"
Hal Holbrook
Into the Wild (2007) role "Ron Franz"
Tom Wilkinson
Michael Clayton (2007) role "Arthur Edens"

Best Actress in a Leading Role
⚐ Marion Cotillard ⚐
La Môme (eng. La Vie En Rose) (2007) role "Édith Piaf"
Cate Blanchett
Elizabeth: The Golden Age (2007) role "Queen Elizabeth I"
Julie Christie
Away from Her (2006) role "Fiona Anderson"
Laura Linney
The Savages (2007) role "Wendy Savage"
Elliot Page
(Nominated - as Ellen Page)
Juno (2007) role "Juno MacGuff"

Best Actress in a Supporting Role
⚐ Tilda Swinton ⚐
Michael Clayton (2007) role "Karen Crowder"
Cate Blanchett
I'm Not There (2007) role "Jude Quinn"
Ruby Dee
American Gangster (2007) role "Mahalee Lucas"
Saoirse Ronan
Atonement (2007) role "Briony Tallis (aged 13)"
Amy Ryan
Gone Baby Gone (2007) role "Helene McCready"

Best Animated Feature Film

⸸ Brad Bird ⸸
Ratatouille (2007)

Ash Brannon, Chris Buck
Surf's Up (2007)

Vincent Paronnaud, Marjane Satrapi
Persepolis (2007)

Best Art Direction

⸸ Dante Ferretti (Art Direction), Francesca Lo Schiavo (Set Decoration) ⸸
Sweeney Todd: The Demon Barber of Fleet Street (2007)

Jack Fisk (Art Direction), Jim Erickson (Set Decoration)
There Will Be Blood (2007)

Dennis Gassner (Art Direction), Anna Pinnock (Set Decoration)
The Golden Compass (2007)

Sarah Greenwood (Art Direction), Katie Spencer (Set Decoration)
Atonement (2007)

Arthur Max (Art Direction), Beth A. Rubino (Set Decoration)
American Gangster (2007)

Best Cinematography

⸸ Robert Elswit ⸸
There Will Be Blood (2007)

Roger Deakins
No Country for Old Men (2007)

Roger Deakins
The Assassination of Jesse James by the Coward Robert Ford (2007)

Janusz Kaminski
Le scaphandre et le papillon (eng. The Diving Bell and the Butterfly) (2007)

Seamus McGarvey
Atonement (2007)

Best Visual Effects

⸸ Michael L. Fink, Ben Morris, Bill Westenhofer, Trevor Wood ⸸
The Golden Compass (2007)

Scott Benza, Russell Earl, Scott Farrar, John Frazier
Transformers (2007)

John Frazier, Charles Gibson, Hal T. Hickel, John Knoll
Pirates of the Caribbean: At World's End (2007)

Best Costume Design

⸸ Alexandra Byrne ⸸
Elizabeth: The Golden Age (2007)

Marit Allen
(posthumous)
La Môme (eng. La Vie En Rose) (2007)

Colleen Atwood
Sweeney Todd: The Demon Barber of Fleet Street (2007)

Jacqueline Durran
Atonement (2007)

Albert Wolsky
Across the Universe (2007)

Best Directing
⚐ Ethan Coen, Joel Coen ⚐
No Country for Old Men (2007)
Paul Thomas Anderson
There Will Be Blood (2007)
Tony Gilroy
Michael Clayton (2007)
Jason Reitman
Juno (2007)
Julian Schnabel
Le scaphandre et le papillon (eng. The Diving Bell and the Butterfly) (2007)

Best Film Editing
⚐ Christopher Rouse ⚐
The Bourne Ultimatum (2007)
Jay Cassidy
Into the Wild (2007)
Ethan Coen (as Roderick Jaynes), Joel Coen (as Roderick Jaynes)
No Country for Old Men (2007)
Dylan Tichenor
There Will Be Blood (2007)
Juliette Welfling
Le scaphandre et le papillon (eng. The Diving Bell and the Butterfly) (2007)

Best Picture
⚐ Ethan Coen, Joel Coen, Scott Rudin (Producers) ⚐
No Country for Old Men (2007)
Paul Thomas Anderson, Daniel Lupi, JoAnne Sellar (Producers)
There Will Be Blood (2007)
Tim Bevan, Eric Fellner, Paul Webster (Producers)
Atonement (2007)
Jennifer Fox, Kerry Orent, Sydney Pollack (Producers)
Michael Clayton (2007)
Lianne Halfon, Mason Novick, Russell Smith (Producers)
Juno (2007)

Best Music, Original Score
⚐ Dario Marianelli ⚐
Atonement (2007)
Marco Beltrami
3:10 to Yuma (2007)
Michael Giacchino
Ratatouille (2007)
James Newton Howard
Michael Clayton (2007)
Alberto Iglesias
The Kite Runner (2007)

Best Foreign Language Film

⚐ Austria ⚐
Die Fälscher (eng. The Counterfeiters) (2007)

Israel
Beaufort (2007)

Kazakhstan
Mongol (eng. Mongol: The Rise of Genghis Khan) (2007)

Poland
Katyń (eng. Katyn) (2007)

Russia
12 (2007)

Best Short Film, Animated

⚐ Suzie Templeton, Hugh Welchman ⚐
Peter and The Wolf (2006)

Chris Lavis, Maciek Szczerbowski
Madame Tutli-Putli (2007)

Alexander Petrov
Moya lyubov (eng. My Love) (2006)

Josh Raskin
I Met the Walrus (2007)

Samuel Tourneux, Simon Vanesse
Même les pigeons vont au paradis (eng. Even Pigeons Go to Heaven) (2007)

Best Short Film, Live Action

⚐ Philippe Pollet-Villard ⚐
Le Mozart des pickpockets (eng. The Mozart of Pickpockets) (2006)

Daniel Barber, Matthew Brown
The Tonto Woman (2008)

Christian E. Christiansen, Louise Vesth
Om natten (eng. At Night) (2007)

Anja Daelemans, Guido Thys
Tanghi argentini (2006)

Andrea Jublin
Il supplente (eng. The Substitute) (2007)

Best Sound Editing

⚐ Per Hallberg, Karen Baker Landers ⚐
The Bourne Ultimatum (2007)

Mike Hopkins, Ethan Van der Ryn
Transformers (2007)

Skip Lievsay
No Country for Old Men (2007)

Christopher Scarabosio, Matthew Wood
There Will Be Blood (2007)

Michael Silvers, Randy Thom
Ratatouille (2007)

Best Writing, Adapted Screenplay

⚔ Ethan Coen, Joel Coen ⚔
No Country for Old Men (2007)

Paul Thomas Anderson
There Will Be Blood (2007)

Christopher Hampton
Atonement (2007)

Ronald Harwood
Le scaphandre et le papillon (eng. The Diving Bell and the Butterfly) (2007)

Sarah Polley
Away from Her (2006)

Best Writing, Original Screenplay

⚔ Diablo Cody ⚔
Juno (2007)

Brad Bird (Screenplay), Brad Bird, Jim Capobianco, Jan Pinkava (Story)
Ratatouille (2007)

Tony Gilroy
Michael Clayton (2007)

Tamara Jenkins
The Savages (2007)

Nancy Oliver
Lars and the Real Girl (2007)

Best Sound Mixing

⚔ Kirk Francis, Scott Millan, David Parker ⚔
The Bourne Ultimatum (2007)

Craig Berkey, Peter F. Kurland, Skip Lievsay, Greg Orloff
No Country for Old Men (2007)

Peter J. Devlin, Kevin O'Connell, Greg P. Russell
Transformers (2007)

David Giammarco, Paul Massey, Jim Stuebe
3:10 to Yuma (2007)

Doc Kane, Michael Semanick, Randy Thom
Ratatouille (2007)

Best Documentary, Feature

⚔ Alex Gibney, Eva Orner ⚔
Taxi to the Dark Side (2007)

Charles Ferguson, Audrey Marrs
No End in Sight (2007)

Andrea Nix Fine, Sean Fine
War Dance (2007)

Michael Moore, Meghan O'Hara
Sicko (2007)

Richard E. Robbins
Operation Homecoming: Writing the Wartime Experience (2007)

Best Documentary, Short Subject
⚊ Vanessa Roth, Cynthia Wade ⚊
Freeheld (2007)

Francisco Bello, Tim Sternberg
Salim Baba (2007)

James Longley
Sari's Mother (2006)

Amanda Micheli, Isabel Vega
La corona (eng. The Crown) (2008)

Best Music, Original Song
⚊ Glen Hansard, Markéta Irglová (Music & Lyrics) ⚊
for the song "Falling Slowly"
Once (2007)

Jamal Joseph, Charles Ray Mack, Tevin Thomas (Music & Lyrics)
for the song "Raise It Up"
August Rush (2007)

Alan Menken (Music), Stephen Schwartz (Lyrics)
for songs "Happy Working Song", "So Close", "That's How You Know"
Enchanted (2007)

The 81ˢᵗ Academy Awards® - February 22, 2009
Host: Hugh Jackman
Venue: Kodak Theatre at Hollywood & Highland Center
Honoring movies released in 2008

Best Actor in a Leading Role
⚊ Sean Penn ⚊
Milk (2008) role "Harvey Milk"

Richard Jenkins
The Visitor (2007) role "Walter Vale"

Frank Langella
Frost/Nixon (2008) role "Richard Nixon"

Brad Pitt
The Curious Case of Benjamin Button (2008) role "Benjamin Button"

Mickey Rourke
The Wrestler (2008) role "Randy "The Ram" Robinson"

Best Actor in a Supporting Role
⚊ Heath Ledger ⚊
(posthumous)
The Dark Knight (2008) role "The Joker"

Josh Brolin
Milk (2008) role "Dan White"

Robert Downey Jr.
Tropic Thunder (2008) role "Kirk Lazarus"

Philip Seymour Hoffman
Doubt (2008) role "Father Brendan Flynn"

Michael Shannon
Revolutionary Road (2008) role "John Givings Jr."

Best Actress in a Leading Role
⚑ Kate Winslet ⚑
The Reader (2008) role "Hanna Schmitz"
Anne Hathaway
Rachel Getting Married (2008) role "Kym Buchman"
Angelina Jolie
Changeling (2008) role "Christine Collins"
Melissa Leo
Frozen River (2008) role "Ray Eddy"
Meryl Streep
Doubt (2008) role "Sister Aloysius Beauvier"

Best Actress in a Supporting Role
⚑ Penélope Cruz ⚑
Vicky Cristina Barcelona (2008) role "María Elena"
Amy Adams
Doubt (2008) role "Sister James"
Viola Davis
Doubt (2008) role "Mrs. Miller"
Taraji P. Henson
The Curious Case of Benjamin Button (2008) role "Queenie"
Marisa Tomei
The Wrestler (2008) role "Cassidy / Pam"

Best Animated Feature Film
⚑ Andrew Stanton ⚑
WALL·E (2008)
Byron Howard, Chris Williams
Bolt (2008)
Mark Osborne, John Stevenson
Kung Fu Panda (2008)

Best Art Direction
⚑ Donald Graham Burt (Art Direction), Victor J. Zolfo (Set Decoration) ⚑
The Curious Case of Benjamin Button (2008)
Michael Carlin (Art Direction), Rebecca Alleway (Set Decoration)
The Duchess (2008)
Nathan Crowley (Art Direction), Peter Lando (Set Decoration)
The Dark Knight (2008)
James J. Murakami (Art Direction), Gary Fettis (Set Decoration)
Changeling (2008)
Kristi Zea (Art Direction), Debra Schutt (Set Decoration)
Revolutionary Road (2008)

Best Makeup
⚑ Greg Cannom ⚑
The Curious Case of Benjamin Button (2008)
John Caglione Jr., Conor O'Sullivan
The Dark Knight (2008)
Mike Elizalde, Thom Floutz
Hellboy II: The Golden Army (2008)

Best Cinematography

⬇ **Anthony Dod Mantle** ⬇
Slumdog Millionaire (2008)

Roger Deakins, Chris Menges
The Reader (2008)

Claudio Miranda
The Curious Case of Benjamin Button (2008)

Wally Pfister
The Dark Knight (2008)

Tom Stern
Changeling (2008)

Best Costume Design

⬇ **Michael O'Connor** ⬇
The Duchess (2008)

Danny Glicker
Milk (2008)

Catherine Martin
Australia (2008)

Jacqueline West
The Curious Case of Benjamin Button (2008)

Albert Wolsky
Revolutionary Road (2008)

Best Directing

⬇ **Danny Boyle** ⬇
Slumdog Millionaire (2008)

Stephen Daldry
The Reader (2008)

David Fincher
The Curious Case of Benjamin Button (2008)

Ron Howard
Frost/Nixon (2008)

Gus Van Sant
Milk (2008)

Best Picture

⬇ **Christian Colson (Producer)** ⬇
Slumdog Millionaire (2008)

Ceán Chaffin, Kathleen Kennedy, Frank Marshall (Producers)
The Curious Case of Benjamin Button (2008)

Bruce Cohen, Dan Jinks (Producers)
Milk (2008)

Eric Fellner, Brian Grazer, Ron Howard (Producers)
Frost/Nixon (2008)

**Donna Gigliotti, Anthony Minghella, Redmond Morris,
Sydney Pollack (Producers)**

(Anthony Minghella, Sydney Pollack - posthumous)
The Reader (2008)

Jean Hersholt Humanitarian Award

⬇ **Jerry Lewis** ⬇

Best Documentary, Feature
⚑ Simon Chinn, James Marsh ⚑
Man on Wire (2008)
Carl Deal, Tia Lessin
Trouble the Water (2008)
Werner Herzog, Henry Kaiser
Encounters at the End of the World (2007)
Scott Hamilton Kennedy
The Garden (2008)
Ellen Kuras, Thavisouk Phrasavath
Nerakhoon (eng. The Betrayal) (2008)

Best Documentary, Short Subject
⚑ Megan Mylan ⚑
Smile Pinki (2008)
Irene Taylor Brodsky, Tom Grant
The Final Inch (2009)
Margaret Hyde, Adam Pertofsky
The Witness from the Balcony of Room 306 (2008)
Steven Okazaki
The Conscience of Nhem En (2008)

Best Film Editing
⚑ Chris Dickens ⚑
Slumdog Millionaire (2008)
Kirk Baxter, Angus Wall
The Curious Case of Benjamin Button (2008)
Elliot Graham
Milk (2008)
Daniel P. Hanley, Mike Hill
Frost/Nixon (2008)
Lee Smith
The Dark Knight (2008)

Best Visual Effects
⚑ Eric Barba, Craig Barron, Burt Dalton, Steve Preeg ⚑
The Curious Case of Benjamin Button (2008)
Chris Corbould, Nick Davis, Paul J. Franklin, Tim Webber
The Dark Knight (2008)
Shane Mahan, John Nelson, Ben Snow, Daniel Sudick
Iron Man (2008)

Best Foreign Language Film
⚑ Japan ⚑
Okuribito (eng. Departures) (2008)
Austria
Revanche (2008)
France
Entre les murs (eng. The Class) (2008)
Germany
Der Baader Meinhof Komplex (eng. The Baader Meinhof Complex) (2008)
Israel
Vals Im Bashir (eng. Waltz with Bashir) (2008)

Best Writing, Adapted Screenplay

ↆ **Simon Beaufoy** ↆ
Slumdog Millionaire (2008)

David Hare
The Reader (2008)

Peter Morgan
Frost/Nixon (2008)

Eric Roth (Screenplay), Eric Roth, Robin Swicord (Story)
The Curious Case of Benjamin Button (2008)

John Patrick Shanley
Doubt (2008)

Best Writing, Original Screenplay

ↆ **Dustin Lance Black** ↆ
Milk (2008)

Courtney Hunt
Frozen River (2008)

Mike Leigh
Happy-Go-Lucky (2008)

Martin McDonagh
In Bruges (2008)

**Jim Reardon, Andrew Stanton (Screenplay),
Pete Docter, Andrew Stanton (Story)**
WALL·E (2008)

Best Music, Original Score

ↆ **A.R. Rahman** ↆ
Slumdog Millionaire (2008)

Alexandre Desplat
The Curious Case of Benjamin Button (2008)

Danny Elfman
Milk (2008)

James Newton Howard
Defiance (2008)

Thomas Newman
WALL·E (2008)

Best Short Film, Animated

ↆ **Kunio Kato** ↆ
Tsumiki no ie (eng. The House of Small Cubes) (2008)

Konstantin Bronzit
Ubornaya istoriya - lyubovnaya istoriya (eng. Lavatory Lovestory) (2007)

Adam Foulkes, Alan Smith
This Way Up (2008)

Thierry Marchand, Emud Mokhberi
Oktapodi (2007)

Doug Sweetland
Presto (2008)

Best Short Film, Live Action
⚜ **Jochen Alexander Freydank** ⚜
Spielzeugland (eng. Toyland) (2007)
Tamara Anghie, Steph Green
New Boy (2007)
Reto Caffi
Auf der Strecke (eng. On the Line) (2007)
Dorte Warnøe Høgh, Tivi Magnusson
Grisen (eng. The Pig) (2007)
Elizabeth Marre, Olivier Pont
Manon sur le bitume (eng. Manon on the Asphalt) (2007)

Best Sound Editing
⚜ **Richard King** ⚜
The Dark Knight (2008)
Christopher Boyes, Frank E. Eulner
Iron Man (2008)
Ben Burtt, Matthew Wood
WALL·E (2008)
Glenn Freemantle, Tom Sayers
Slumdog Millionaire (2008)
Wylie Stateman
Wanted (2008)

Best Sound Mixing
⚜ **Resul Pookutty, Richard Pryke, Ian Tapp** ⚜
Slumdog Millionaire (2008)
Ben Burtt, Tom Myers, Michael Semanick
WALL·E (2008)
Petr Forejt, Chris Jenkins, Frank A. Montaño
Wanted (2008)
Lora Hirschberg, Ed Novick, Gary A. Rizzo
The Dark Knight (2008)
Ren Klyce, David Parker, Michael Semanick, Mark Weingarten
The Curious Case of Benjamin Button (2008)

Best Music, Original Song
⚜ **A.R. Rahman (Music), Gulzar (Lyrics) for the song "Jai Ho"** ⚜
Slumdog Millionaire (2008)
**Peter Gabriel, Thomas Newman (Music), Peter Gabriel (Lyrics)
for the song "Down to Earth"**
WALL·E (2008)
**M.I.A. (as Maya Arulpragasam), A.R. Rahman (Music & Lyrics)
for the song "O Saya"**
Slumdog Millionaire (2008)

The 82ⁿᵈ Academy Awards® - March 7, 2010
Hosts: Alec Baldwin, Steve Martin
Venue: Kodak Theatre at Hollywood & Highland Center
Honoring movies released in 2009

Irving G. Thalberg Memorial Award
♦ John Calley ♦

Best Actor in a Leading Role
♦ Jeff Bridges ♦
Crazy Heart (2009) role "Otis "Bad" Blake"
George Clooney
Up in the Air (2009) role "Ryan Bingham"
Colin Firth
A Single Man (2009) role "George Falconer"
Morgan Freeman
Invictus (2009) role "Nelson Mandela"
Jeremy Renner
The Hurt Locker (2008) role "Sergeant First Class William James"

Best Actor in a Supporting Role
♦ Christoph Waltz ♦
Inglourious Basterds (2009) role "SS Colonel Hans Landa"
Matt Damon
Invictus (2009) role "Francois Pienaar"
Woody Harrelson
The Messenger (2009) role "Captain Tony Stone"
Christopher Plummer
The Last Station (2009) role "Leo Tolstoy"
Stanley Tucci
The Lovely Bones (2009) role "George Harvey"

Best Actress in a Leading Role
♦ Sandra Bullock ♦
The Blind Side (2009) role "Leigh Anne Tuohy"
Helen Mirren
The Last Station (2009) role "Sophia Tolstaya"
Carey Mulligan
An Education (2009) role "Jenny Mellor"
Gabourey Sidibe
Precious: Based on the Novel 'Push' by Sapphire (2009) role "Claireece "Precious" Jones"
Meryl Streep
Julie & Julia (2009) role "Julia Child"

Best Actress in a Supporting Role
♦ Mo'Nique ♦
Precious: Based on the Novel 'Push' by Sapphire (2009) role "Mary Lee Johnston"
Penélope Cruz
Nine (2009) role "Carla Albanese"
Vera Farmiga
Up in the Air (2009) role "Alex Goran"
Maggie Gyllenhaal
Crazy Heart (2009) role "Jean Craddock"
Anna Kendrick
Up in the Air (2009) role "Natalie Keener"

Best Animated Feature Film

⚜ Pete Docter ⚜
Up (2009)

Wes Anderson
Fantastic Mr. Fox (2009)

Ron Clements, John Musker
The Princess and the Frog (2009)

Tomm Moore
The Secret of Kells (2009)

Henry Selick
Coraline (2009)

Best Cinematography

⚜ Mauro Fiore ⚜
Avatar (2009)

Barry Ackroyd
The Hurt Locker (2008)

Christian Berger
Das weiße Band - Eine deutsche Kindergeschichte (eng. The White Ribbon) (2009)

Bruno Delbonnel
Harry Potter and the Half-Blood Prince (2009)

Robert Richardson
Inglourious Basterds (2009)

Best Visual Effects

⚜ Richard Baneham, Andrew R. Jones, Joe Letteri, Stephen Rosenbaum ⚜
Avatar (2009)

Matt Aitken, Robert Habros, Dan Kaufman, Peter Muyzers
District 9 (2009)

Burt Dalton, Russell Earl, Roger Guyett, Paul Kavanagh
Star Trek (2009)

Best Costume Design

⚜ Sandy Powell ⚜
The Young Victoria (2009)

Colleen Atwood
Nine (2009)

Catherine Leterrier
Coco avant Chanel (eng. Coco Before Chanel) (2009)

Janet Patterson
Bright Star (2009)

Monique Prudhomme
The Imaginarium of Doctor Parnassus (2009)

Best Makeup

⚜ Barney Burman, Mindy Hall, Joel Harlow ⚜
Star Trek (2009)

Jon Henry Gordon, Jenny Shircore
The Young Victoria (2009)

Aldo Signoretti, Vittorio Sodano
Il Divo (2008)

Best Directing
⇟ **Kathryn Bigelow** ⇟
The Hurt Locker (2008)

James Cameron
Avatar (2009)

Lee Daniels
Precious: Based on the Novel 'Push' by Sapphire (2009)

Jason Reitman
Up in the Air (2009)

Quentin Tarantino
Inglourious Basterds (2009)

Best Art Direction
⇟ **Rick Carter, Robert Stromberg (Production Design),** ⇟
Kim Sinclair (Set Decoration)
Avatar (2009)

Sarah Greenwood (Production Design), Katie Spencer (Set Decoration)
Sherlock Holmes (2009)

Anastasia Masaro, Dave Warren (Production Design),
Caroline Smith (Set Decoration)
The Imaginarium of Doctor Parnassus (2009)

John Myhre (Production Design), Gordon Sim (Set Decoration)
Nine (2009)

Patrice Vermette (Production Design), Maggie Gray (Set Decoration)
The Young Victoria (2009)

Best Music, Original Song
⇟ **Ryan Bingham, T Bone Burnett (Music & Lyrics)** ⇟
for the song "The Weary Kind"
Crazy Heart (2009)

Randy Newman (Music & Lyrics)
for the song "Almost There", "Down in New Orleans"
The Princess and the Frog (2009)

Reinhardt Wagner (Music), Frank Thomas (Lyrics)
for the song "Loin de Paname"
Faubourg 36 (eng. Paris 36) (2008)

Maury Yeston (Music & Lyrics) for the song "Take It All"
Nine (2009)

Best Documentary, Feature
⇟ **Louie Psihoyos, Fisher Stevens** ⇟
The Cove (2009)

Rebecca Cammisa
Which Way Home (2009)

Judith Ehrlich, Rick Goldsmith
The Most Dangerous Man in America: Daniel Ellsberg and the Pentagon Papers (2009)

Robert Kenner, Elise Pearlstein
Food, Inc. (2008)

Lise Lense-Møller, Anders Østergaard
Burma VJ: Reporter i et lukket land
(eng. Burma VJ: Reporting from a Closed Country) (2008)

Best Documentary, Short Subject

⇣ **Elinor Burkett, Roger Ross Williams** ⇣
Music by Prudence (2010)

Jon Alpert, Matthew O'Neill
China's Unnatural Disaster: The Tears of Sichuan Province (2009)

Henry Ansbacher, Daniel Junge
The Last Campaign of Governor Booth Gardner (2009)

Steven Bognar, Julia Reichert
The Last Truck: Closing of a GM Plant (2009)

Bartek Konopka, Anna Wydra
Królik po berlińsku (eng. Rabbit à la Berlin) (2009)

Best Film Editing

⇣ **Chris Innis, Bob Murawski** ⇣
The Hurt Locker (2008)

James Cameronm John Refoua, Stephen E. Rivkin
Avatar (2009)

Julian Clarke
District 9 (2009)

Joe Klotz
Precious: Based on the Novel 'Push' by Sapphire (2009)

Sally Menke
Inglourious Basterds (2009)

Honorary Award

⇣ **Lauren Bacall** ⇣
In recognition of her central place in the Golden Age of motion pictures.

⇣ **Roger Corman** ⇣
For his rich engendering of films and filmmakers.

⇣ **Gordon Willis** ⇣
For unsurpassed mastery of light, shadow, color and motion.

Best Picture

⇣ **Nicolas Chartier, Kathryn Bigelow, Mark Boal, Greg Shapiro (Producers)** ⇣
The Hurt Locker (2008)

Lawrence Bender (Producer)
Inglourious Basterds (2009)

James Cameron, Jon Landau (Producers)
Avatar (2009)

Ethan Coen, Joel Coen (Producers)
A Serious Man (2009)

Carolynne Cunningham, Peter Jackson (Producers)
District 9 (2009)

Lee Daniels, Gary Magness, Sarah Siegel-Magness (Producers)
Precious: Based on the Novel 'Push' by Sapphire (2009)

Daniel Dubiecki, Ivan Reitman, Jason Reitman (Producers)
Up in the Air (2009)

Finola Dwyer, Amanda Posey (Producers)
An Education (2009)

Broderick Johnson, Andrew A. Kosove, Gil Netter (Producers)
The Blind Side (2009)

Jonas Rivera (Producer)
Up (2009)

Best Short Film, Animated

ꙮ **Nicolas Schmerkin** ꙮ
Logorama (2009)

Javier Recio Gracia
La dama y la muerte (eng. The Lady and the Reaper) (2009)

Fabrice O. Joubert
French Roast (2008)

Nicky Phelan and Darragh O'Connell
Granny O'Grimm's Sleeping Beauty (2008)

Nick Park
A Matter of Loaf and Death (2008)

Best Short Film, Live Action

ꙮ **Joachim Back, Tivi Magnusson** ꙮ
The New Tenants (2009)

Drew Bailey, Luke Doolan
Miracle Fish (2009)

Patrik Eklund, Mathias Fjellström
Istället för abrakadabra (eng. Instead of Abracadabra) (2008)

James Flynn, Juanita Wilson
The Door (2008)

Gregg Helvey
Kavi (2009)

Best Foreign Language Film

ꙮ **Argentina** ꙮ
El secreto de sus ojos (eng. The Secret in Their Eyes) (2009)

France
Un prophète (eng. A Prophet) (2009)

Germany
Das weiße Band - Eine deutsche Kindergeschichte (eng. The White Ribbon) (2009)

Israel
Ajami (2009)

Peru
La teta asustada (eng. The Milk of Sorrow) (2009)

Best Writing, Original Screenplay

ꙮ **Mark Boal** ꙮ
The Hurt Locker (2008)

Alessandro Camon, Oren Moverman
The Messenger (2009)

Ethan Coen, Joel Coen
A Serious Man (2009)

**Pete Docter, Bob Peterson (Screenplay),
Pete Docter, Tom McCarthy, Bob Peterson (Story)**
Up (2009)

Quentin Tarantino
Inglourious Basterds (2009)

Best Writing, Adapted Screenplay
⚑ Geoffrey Fletcher ⚑
Precious: Based on the Novel 'Push' by Sapphire (2009)
Jesse Armstrong, Simon Blackwell, Armando Iannucci, Tony Roche
In the Loop (2009)
Neill Blomkamp, Terri Tatchell
District 9 (2009)
Nick Hornby
An Education (2009)
Jason Reitman, Sheldon Turner
Up in the Air (2009)

Best Music, Original Score
⚑ Michael Giacchino ⚑
Up (2009)
Marco Beltrami, Buck Sanders
The Hurt Locker (2008)
Alexandre Desplat
Fantastic Mr. Fox (2009)
James Horner
Avatar (2009)
Hans Zimmer
Sherlock Holmes (2009)

Best Sound Editing
⚑ Paul N. J. Ottosson ⚑
The Hurt Locker (2008)
Christopher Boyes, Gwendolyn Yates Whittle
Avatar (2009)
Tom Myers, Michael Silvers
Up (2009)
Alan Rankin, Mark P. Stoeckinger
Star Trek (2009)
Wylie Stateman
Inglourious Basterds (2009)

Best Sound Mixing
⚑ Ray Beckett, Paul N. J. Ottosson ⚑
The Hurt Locker (2008)
Anna Behlmer, Peter J. Devlin, Andy Nelson
Star Trek (2009)
Christopher Boyes, Tony Johnson, Andy Nelson, Gary Summers
Avatar (2009)
Tony Lamberti, Michael Minkler, Mark Ulano
Inglourious Basterds (2009)
Geoffrey Patterson, Greg P. Russell, Gary Summers
Transformers: Revenge of the Fallen (2009)

The 83rd Academy Awards® - February 27, 2011
Hosts: James Franco, Anne Hathaway
Venue: Kodak Theatre at Hollywood & Highland Center
Honoring movies released in 2010

Irving G. Thalberg Memorial Award
⚱ Francis Ford Coppola ⚱

Best Actor in a Leading Role
⚱ Colin Firth ⚱
The King's Speech (2010) role "King George VI"

Javier Bardem
Biutiful (2010) role "Uxbal"

Jeff Bridges
True Grit (2010) role "Deputy U.S. Marshal Reuben "Rooster" Cogburn"

Jesse Eisenberg
The Social Network (2010) role "Mark Zuckerberg"

James Franco
127 Hours (2010) role "Aron Ralston"

Best Actor in a Supporting Role
⚱ Christian Bale ⚱
The Fighter (2010) role "Dicky Eklund"

John Hawkes
Winter's Bone (2010) role "Teardrop Dolly"

Jeremy Renner
The Town (2010) role "James "Jem" Coughlin"

Mark Ruffalo
The Kids Are All Right (2010) role "Paul Hatfield"

Geoffrey Rush
The King's Speech (2010) role "Lionel Logue"

Best Actress in a Leading Role
⚱ Natalie Portman ⚱
Black Swan (2010) role "Nina Sayers / The Swan Queen"

Annette Bening
The Kids Are All Right (2010) role "Dr. Nicole "Nic" Allgood"

Nicole Kidman
Rabbit Hole (2010) role "Becca Corbett"

Jennifer Lawrence
Winter's Bone (2010) role "Ree Dolly"

Michelle Williams
Blue Valentine (2010) role "Cynthia "Cindy" Heller"

Best Actress in a Supporting Role
⚱ Melissa Leo ⚱
The Fighter (2010) role "Alice Eklund-Ward"

Amy Adams
The Fighter (2010) role "Charlene Fleming"

Helena Bonham Carter
The King's Speech (2010) role "Queen Elizabeth"

Hailee Steinfeld
True Grit (2010) role "Mattalyn "Mattie" Ross"

Jacki Weaver
Animal Kingdom (2010) role "Janine "Smurf" Cody"

Best Animated Feature Film
⚐ Lee Unkrich ⚐
Toy Story 3 (2010)
Sylvain Chomet
L'illusionniste (eng. The Illusionist) (2010)
Dean DeBlois, Chris Sanders
How to Train Your Dragon (2010)

Best Art Direction
⚐ Robert Stromberg (Production Design), Karen O'Hara (Set Decoration) ⚐
Alice in Wonderland (2010)
Stuart Craig (Production Design), Stephenie McMillan (Set Decoration)
Harry Potter and the Deathly Hallows: Part 1 (2010)
Guy Hendrix Dyas (Production Design),
Larry Dias, Douglas A. Mowat (Set Decoration)
Inception (2010)
Jess Gonchor (Production Design), Nancy Haigh (Set Decoration)
True Grit (2010)
Eve Stewart (Production Design), Judy Farr (Set Decoration)
The King's Speech (2010)

Best Cinematography
⚐ Wally Pfister ⚐
Inception (2010)
Danny Cohen
The King's Speech (2010)
Jeff Cronenweth
The Social Network (2010)
Roger Deakins
True Grit (2010)
Matthew Libatique
Black Swan (2010)

Best Costume Design
⚐ Colleen Atwood ⚐
Alice in Wonderland (2010)
Jenny Beavan
The King's Speech (2010)
Antonella Cannarozzi
Io sono l'amore (eng. I Am Love) (2009)
Sandy Powell
The Tempest (2010)
Mary Zophres
True Grit (2010)

Best Makeup
⚐ Rick Baker, Dave Elsey ⚐
The Wolfman (2010)
Gregory Funk, Edouard F. Henriques, Yolanda Toussieng
The Way Back (2010)
Adrien Morot
Barney's Version (2010)

Honorary Award
⚜ Kevin Brownlow ⚜
For the wise and devoted chronicling of the cinematic parade.
⚜ Jean-Luc Godard ⚜
For passion. For confrontation. For a new kind of cinema.
⚜ Eli Wallach ⚜
AMPAS® Governors Awards:
Given 'For a lifetime's worth of indelible screen characters'.

Best Documentary, Feature
⚜ Charles Ferguson, Audrey Marrs ⚜
Inside Job (2010)
Trish Adlesic, Josh Fox
GasLand (2010)
Angus Aynsley, Lucy Walker
Waste Land (2010)
Banksy, Jaimie D'Cruz
Exit Through the Gift Shop (2010)
Tim Hetherington, Sebastian Junger
Restrepo (2010)

Best Documentary, Short Subject
⚜ Karen Goodman, Kirk Simon ⚜
Strangers No More (2010)
Mitchell W. Block, Sara Nesson
Poster Girl (2010)
Thomas Lennon, Ruby Yang
The Warriors of Qiugang (2010)
Tim Metzger, Jennifer Redfearn
Sun Come Up (2011)
Jed Rothstein
Killing in the Name (2010)

Best Film Editing
⚜ Kirk Baxter, Angus Wall ⚜
The Social Network (2010)
Tariq Anwar
The King's Speech (2010)
Jon Harris
127 Hours (2010)
Pamela Martin
The Fighter (2010)
Andrew Weisblum
Black Swan (2010)

Best Directing

⚑ Tom Hooper ⚑
The King's Speech (2010)
Darren Aronofsky
Black Swan (2010)
Ethan Coen, Joel Coen
True Grit (2010)
David Fincher
The Social Network (2010)
David O. Russell
The Fighter (2010)

Best Writing, Original Screenplay

⚑ David Seidler ⚑
The King's Speech (2010)
Stuart Blumberg, Lisa Cholodenko
The Kids Are All Right (2010)
Eric Johnson, Scott Silver, Paul Tamasy (Screenplay),
Keith Dorrington, Eric Johnson, Paul Tamasy (Story)
The Fighter (2010)
Mike Leigh
Another Year (2010)
Christopher Nolan
Inception (2010)

Best Writing, Adapted Screenplay

⚑ Aaron Sorkin ⚑
The Social Network (2010)
Michael Arndt (Screenplay),
John Lasseter, Andrew Stanton, Lee Unkrich (Story)
Toy Story 3 (2010)
Simon Beaufoy, Danny Boyle
127 Hours (2010)
Ethan Coen, Joel Coen
True Grit (2010)
Debra Granik, Anne Rosellini
Winter's Bone (2010)

Best Music, Original Song

⚑ Randy Newman (Music & Lyrics) for the song "We Belong Together" ⚑
Toy Story 3 (2010)
Tom Douglas, Hillary Lindsey, Troy Verges (Music & Lyrics)
for the song "Coming Home"
Country Strong (2010)
Alan Menken (Music), Glenn Slater (Lyrics) for the song "I See the Light"
Tangled (2010)
A. R. Rahman (Music), Roland 'Rollo' Armstrong, Dido (Lyrics)
for the song "If I Rise"
127 Hours (2010)

Best Foreign Language Film

⚟ Denmark ⚟

Hævnen (eng. In a Better World) (2010)

Algeria

Hors la loi (eng. Outside the Law) (2010)

Canada

Incendies (2010)

Greece

Kynodontas (eng. Dogtooth) (2009)

Mexico

Biutiful (2010)

Best Music, Original Score

⚟ Trent Reznor, Atticus Ross ⚟

The Social Network (2010)

Alexandre Desplat

The King's Speech (2010)

John Powell

How to Train Your Dragon (2010)

A. R. Rahman

127 Hours (2010)

Hans Zimmer

Inception (2010)

Best Short Film, Animated

⚟ Andrew Ruhemann, Shaun Tan ⚟

The Lost Thing (2010)

Geefwee Boedoe

Let's Pollute (2009)

Bastien Dubois

Madagascar, carnet de voyage (eng. Madagascar, a Journey Diary) (2010)

Max Lang, Jakob Schuh

The Gruffalo (2009)

Teddy Newton

Day & Night (2010)

Best Short Film, Live Action

⚟ Luke Matheny ⚟

God of Love (2010)

Ian Barnes, Samantha Waite

Wish 143 (2009)

Michael Creagh

The Crush (2010)

Ivan Goldschmidt

Na Wewe (2010)

Tanel Toom

The Confession (2010)

Best Picture

⚱ **Iain Canning, Emile Sherman, Gareth Unwin (Producers)** ⚱
The King's Speech (2010)

Darla K. Anderson (Producer)
Toy Story 3 (2010)

Danny Boyle, Christian Colson, John Smithson (Producers)
127 Hours (2010)

**Dana Brunetti, Ceán Chaffin, Michael De Luca,
Scott Rudin (Producers)**
The Social Network (2010)

Ethan Coen, Joel Coen, Scott Rudin (Producers)
True Grit (2010)

Scott Franklin, Mike Medavoy, Brian Oliver (Producers)
Black Swan (2010)

**Gary Gilbert, Jeffrey Kusama-Hinte (as Jeffrey Levy-Hinte),
Celine Rattray (Producers)**
The Kids Are All Right (2010)

David Hoberman, Todd Lieberman, Mark Wahlberg (Producers)
The Fighter (2010)

Alix Madigan-Yorkin, Anne Rosellini (Producers)
Winter's Bone (2010)

Christopher Nolan, Emma Thomas (Producers)
Inception (2010)

Best Sound Editing

⚱ **Richard King** ⚱
Inception (2010)

Craig Berkey, Skip Lievsay
True Grit (2010)

Tom Myers, Michael Silvers
Toy Story 3 (2010)

Mark P. Stoeckinger
Unstoppable (2010)

Addison Teague, Gwendolyn Yates Whittle
TRON: Legacy (2010)

Best Sound Mixing

⚱ **Lora Hirschberg, Ed Novick, Gary A. Rizzo** ⚱
Inception (2010)

Craig Berkey, Peter F. Kurland, Skip Lievsay, Greg Orloff
True Grit (2010)

**Jeffrey J. Haboush, Scott Millan, Greg P. Russell,
William Sarokin**
Salt (2010)

Paul Hamblin, Martin Jensen, John Midgley
The King's Speech (2010)

Ren Klyce, David Parker, Michael Semanick, Mark Weingarten
The Social Network (2010)

Best Visual Effects
↓ **Peter Bebb, Chris Corbould, Paul J. Franklin, Andrew Lockley** ↓
Inception (2010)
Nicolas Aithadi, Tim Burke, Christian Manz, John Richardson
Harry Potter and the Deathly Hallows: Part 1 (2010)
Joe Farrell, Bryan Grill, Michael Owens, Stephan Trojansky
Hereafter (2010)
Sean Phillips, Ken Ralston, David Schaub, Carey Villegas
Alice in Wonderland (2010)
Janek Sirrs, Ben Snow, Daniel Sudick, Ged Wright
Iron Man 2 (2010)

The 84ᵗʰ Academy Awards® - February 26, 2012
Host: Billy Crystal
Venue: Hollywood & Highland Center
Honoring movies released in 2011

Best Actor in a Leading Role
↓ **Jean Dujardin** ↓
The Artist (2011) role "George Valentin"
Demián Bichir
A Better Life (2011) role "Carlos Galindo"
George Clooney
The Descendants (2011) role "Matthew "Matt" King"
Gary Oldman
Tinker Tailor Soldier Spy (2011) role "George Smiley"
Brad Pitt
Moneyball (2011) role "Billy Beane"

Best Actor in a Supporting Role
↓ **Christopher Plummer** ↓
Beginners (2010) role "Hal Fields"
Kenneth Branagh
My Week with Marilyn (2011) role "Sir Laurence Olivier"
Jonah Hill
Moneyball (2011) role "Peter Brand"
Nick Nolte
Warrior (2011) role "Paddy Conlon"
Max von Sydow
Extremely Loud & Incredibly Close (2011) role "The Renter"

Best Actress in a Leading Role
↓ **Meryl Streep** ↓
The Iron Lady (2011) role "Margaret Thatcher"
Glenn Close
Albert Nobbs (2011) role "Albert Nobbs"
Viola Davis
The Help (2011) role "Aibileen Clark"
Rooney Mara
The Girl with the Dragon Tattoo (2011) role "Lisbeth Salander"
Michelle Williams
My Week with Marilyn (2011) role "Marilyn Monroe"

Best Actress in a Supporting Role
⚐ Octavia Spencer ⚐
The Help (2011) role "Minny Jackson"
Bérénice Bejo
The Artist (2011) role "Peppy Miller"
Jessica Chastain
The Help (2011) role "Celia Foote"
Melissa McCarthy
Bridesmaids (2011) role "Megan Price"
Janet McTeer
Albert Nobbs (2011) role "Hubert Page"

Honorary Award
⚐ James Earl Jones ⚐
For his legacy of consistent excellence and uncommon versatility.
⚐ Dick Smith ⚐
For his unparalleled mastery of texture, shade, form, and illusion.

Best Animated Feature Film
⚐ Gore Verbinski ⚐
Rango (2011)
Jean-Loup Felicioli, Alain Gagnol
Une vie de chat (eng. A Cat in Paris) (2010)
Javier Mariscal, Fernando Trueba
Chico & Rita (2010)
Chris Miller
Puss in Boots (2011)
Jennifer Yuh Nelson
Kung Fu Panda 2 (2011)

Best Art Direction
⚐ Dante Ferretti (Production Design), Francesca Lo Schiavo (Set Decoration) ⚐
Hugo (2011)
Laurence Bennett (Production Design), Robert Gould (Set Decoration)
The Artist (2011)
Rick Carter (Production Design), Lee Sandales (Set Decoration)
War Horse (2011)
Stuart Craig (Production Design), Stephenie McMillan (Set Decoration)
Harry Potter and the Deathly Hallows: Part 2 (2011)
Anne Seibel (Production Design), Hélène Dubreuil (Set Decoration)
Midnight in Paris (2011)

Best Cinematography
⚐ Robert Richardson ⚐
Hugo (2011)
Jeff Cronenweth
The Girl with the Dragon Tattoo (2011)
Janusz Kaminski
War Horse (2011)
Emmanuel Lubezki
The Tree of Life (2011)
Guillaume Schiffman
The Artist (2011)

Best Costume Design
ꔸ **Mark Bridges** ꔸ
The Artist (2011)

Lisy Christl
Anonymous (2011)

Michael O'Connor
Jane Eyre (2011)

Arianne Phillips
W.E. (2011)

Sandy Powell
Hugo (2011)

Jean Hersholt Humanitarian Award
ꔸ **Oprah Winfrey** ꔸ

Best Directing
ꔸ **Michel Hazanavicius** ꔸ
The Artist (2011)

Woody Allen
Midnight in Paris (2011)

Terrence Malick
The Tree of Life (2011)

Alexander Payne
The Descendants (2011)

Martin Scorsese
Hugo (2011)

Best Documentary, Feature
ꔸ **Daniel Lindsay, T. J. Martin, Rich Middlemas** ꔸ
Undefeated (2011)

Joe Berlinger, Bruce Sinofsky
Paradise Lost 3: Purgatory (2011)

Sam Cullman, Marshall Curry
If a Tree Falls: A Story of the Earth Liberation Front (2011)

Danfung Dennis, Mike Lerner
Hell and Back Again (2011)

Gian-Piero Ringel, Wim Wenders
Pina (2011)

Best Documentary, Short Subject
ꔸ **Daniel Junge, Sharmeen Obaid-Chinoy** ꔸ
Saving Face (2012)

Julie Anderson, Rebecca Cammisa
God Is the Bigger Elvis (2012)

Kira Carstensen, Lucy Walker
The Tsunami and the Cherry Blossom (2011)

Gail Dolgin, Robin Fryday
(Gail Dolgin - posthumous)
The Barber of Birmingham: Foot Soldier of the Civil Rights Movement (2011)

James Spione
Incident in New Baghdad (2011)

Best Film Editing

⚐ Kirk Baxter, Angus Wall ⚐
The Girl with the Dragon Tattoo (2011)

Anne-Sophie Bion, Michel Hazanavicius
The Artist (2011)

Thelma Schoonmaker
Hugo (2011)

Christopher Tellefsen
Moneyball (2011)

Kevin Tent
The Descendants (2011)

Best Foreign Language Film

⚐ Iran ⚐
Jodaeiye Nader az Simin (eng. A Separation) (2011)

Belgium
Rundskop (eng. Bullhead) (2011)

Canada
Monsieur Lazhar (2011)

Israel
Hearat Shulayim (eng. Footnote) (2011)

Poland
W ciemności (eng. In Darkness) (2011)

Best Music, Original Score

⚐ Ludovic Bource ⚐
The Artist (2011)

Alberto Iglesias
Tinker Tailor Soldier Spy (2011)

Howard Shore
Hugo (2011)

John Williams
The Adventures of Tintin (2011), War Horse (2011)

Best Picture

⚐ Thomas Langmann (Producer) ⚐
The Artist (2011)

Letty Aronson, Stephen Tenenbaum (Producers)
Midnight in Paris (2011)

Michael Barnathan, Chris Columbus, Brunson Green (Producers)
The Help (2011)

Jim Burke, Alexander Payne, Jim Taylor (Producers)
The Descendants (2011)

Dede Gardner, Sarah Green, Grant Hill, Bill Pohlad (Producers)
The Tree of Life (2011)

Rachael Horovitz, Michael De Luca, Brad Pitt (Producers)
Moneyball (2011)

Kathleen Kennedy, Steven Spielberg (Producers)
War Horse (2011)

Graham King, Martin Scorsese (Producers)
Hugo (2011)

Scott Rudin (Producer)
Extremely Loud & Incredibly Close (2011)

Best Short Film, Animated

⸸ **William Joyce, Brandon Oldenburg** ⸸
The Fantastic Flying Books of Mr. Morris Lessmore (2011)

Enrico Casarosa
La Luna (2011)

Patrick Doyon
Dimanche (eng. Sunday) (2011)

Amanda Forbis, Wendy Tilby
Wild Life (2011)

Sue Goffe, Grant Orchard
A Morning Stroll (2011)

Best Short Film, Live Action

⸸ **Oorlagh George, Terry George** ⸸
The Shore (2011)

Andrew Bowler, Gigi Causey
Time Freak (2011)

Stefan Gieren, Max Zähle
Raju (2011)

Peter McDonald, Eimear O'Kane
Pentecost (2011)

Hallvar Witzø
(nomination withdrawn)
Tuba Atlantic (2010)

Best Makeup

⸸ **Mark Coulier, J. Roy Helland** ⸸
The Iron Lady (2011)

Martial Corneville, Lynn Johnston, Matthew W. Mungle
Albert Nobbs (2011)

Nick Dudman, Amanda Knight, Lisa Tomblin
Harry Potter and the Deathly Hallows: Part 2 (2011)

Best Music, Original Song

⸸ **Bret McKenzie (Music & Lyrics) for the song "Man or Muppet"** ⸸
The Muppets (2011)

**Carlinhos Brown, Sergio Mendes (Music), Siedah Garrett (Lyrics)
for the song "Real in Rio"**
Rio (2011)

Best Sound Editing

⸸ **Eugene Gearty, Philip Stockton** ⸸
Hugo (2011)

Erik Aadahl, Ethan Van der Ryn
Transformers: Dark of the Moon (2011)

Lon Bender, Victor Ray Ennis
Drive (2011)

Richard Hymns, Gary Rydstrom
War Horse (2011)

Ren Klyce
The Girl with the Dragon Tattoo (2011)

Best Sound Mixing

⚐ **Tom Fleischman, John Midgley** ⚐
Hugo (2011)

Deb Adair, Ron Bochar, David Giammarco, Ed Novick
Moneyball (2011)

Peter J. Devlin, Jeffrey J. Haboush,
Greg P. Russell, Gary Summers
Transformers: Dark of the Moon (2011)

Tom Johnson, Andy Nelson, Gary Rydstrom, Stuart Wilson
War Horse (2011)

Ren Klyce, David Parker, Bo Persson, Michael Semanick
The Girl with the Dragon Tattoo (2011)

Best Visual Effects

⚐ **Ben Grossmann, Alex Henning, Rob Legato, Joss Williams** ⚐
Hugo (2011)

Daniel Barrett, Dan Lemmon, Joe Letteri,
R. Christopher White
Rise of the Planet of the Apes (2011)

Scott Benza, Matthew E. Butler, Scott Farrar, John Frazier
Transformers: Dark of the Moon (2011)

Tim Burke, Greg Butler, John Richardson, David Vickery
Harry Potter and the Deathly Hallows: Part 2 (2011)

Swen Gillberg, Erik Nash, John Rosengrant, Danny Taylor
Real Steel (2011)

Best Writing, Adapted Screenplay

⚐ **Nat Faxon, Alexander Payne, Jim Rash** ⚐
The Descendants (2011)

George Clooney, Grant Heslov, Beau Willimon
The Ides of March (2011)

John Logan
Hugo (2011)

Bridget O'Connor, Peter Straughan
(Bridget O'Connor - posthumous)
Tinker Tailor Soldier Spy (2011)

Aaron Sorkin, Steven Zaillian (Screenplay),
Stan Chervin (Story)
Moneyball (2011)

Best Writing, Original Screenplay

⚐ **Woody Allen** ⚐
Midnight in Paris (2011)

J. C. Chandor
Margin Call (2011)

Asghar Farhadi
Jodaeiye Nader az Simin (eng. A Separation) (2011)

Michel Hazanavicius
The Artist (2011)

Annie Mumolo, Kristen Wiig
Bridesmaids (2011)

The 85th Academy Awards® - February 24, 2013

Host: Seth MacFarlane
Venue: Dolby Theatre at the Hollywood & Highland Center
Honoring movies released in 2012

Honorary Award

↓ Hal Needham ↓

An innovator, mentor, and master technician who elevated his craft to an art and made the impossible look easy.

↓ D. A. Pennebaker ↓

Who redefined the language of film and taught a generation of filmmakers to look to reality for inspiration.

↓ George Stevens Jr. ↓

A tireless champion of the arts in America and especially that most American of arts: the Hollywood film.

Best Actor in a Leading Role

↓ Daniel Day-Lewis ↓

Lincoln (2012) role "Abraham Lincoln"

Bradley Cooper

Silver Linings Playbook (2012) role "Patrizio "Pat" Solitano Jr."

Hugh Jackman

Les Misérables (2012) role "Jean Valjean"

Joaquin Phoenix

The Master (2012) role "Freddie Quell"

Denzel Washington

Flight (2012) role "William "Whip" Whitaker Sr."

Best Actor in a Supporting Role

↓ Christoph Waltz ↓

Django Unchained (2012) role "Dr. King Schultz"

Alan Arkin

Argo (2012) role "Lester Siegel"

Robert De Niro

Silver Linings Playbook (2012) role "Patrizio "Pat" Solitano Sr."

Philip Seymour Hoffman

The Master (2012) role "Lancaster Dodd"

Tommy Lee Jones

Lincoln (2012) role "Thaddeus Stevens"

Best Actress in a Leading Role

↓ Jennifer Lawrence ↓

Silver Linings Playbook (2012) role "Tiffany Maxwell"

Jessica Chastain

Zero Dark Thirty (2012) role "Maya Harris"

Emmanuelle Riva

Amour (2012) role "Anne Laurent"

Quvenzhané Wallis

Beasts of the Southern Wild (2012) role "Hushpuppy"

Naomi Watts

The Impossible (2012) role "Maria Bennett"

Best Actress in a Supporting Role
⚊ **Anne Hathaway** ⚊
Les Misérables (2012) role "Fantine"
Amy Adams
The Master (2012) role "Peggy Dodd"
Sally Field
Lincoln (2012) role "Mary Todd Lincoln"
Helen Hunt
The Sessions (2012) role "Cheryl Cohen-Greene"
Jacki Weaver
Silver Linings Playbook (2012) role "Dolores Solitano"

Best Animated Feature Film
⚊ **Mark Andrews, Brenda Chapman** ⚊
Brave (2012)
Chris Butler, Sam Fell
ParaNorman (2012)
Tim Burton
Frankenweenie (2012)
Peter Lord
The Pirates! Band of Misfits (2012)
Rich Moore
Wreck-It Ralph (2012)

Best Cinematography
⚊ **Claudio Miranda** ⚊
Life of Pi (2012)
Roger Deakins
Skyfall (2012)
Janusz Kaminski
Lincoln (2012)
Seamus McGarvey
Anna Karenina (2012)
Robert Richardson
Django Unchained (2012)

Best Production Design
⚊ **Rick Carter (Production Design), Jim Erickson (Set Decoration)** ⚊
Lincoln (2012)
Sarah Greenwood (Production Design), Katie Spencer (Set Decoration)
Anna Karenina (2012)
David Gropman (Production Design), Anna Pinnock (Set Decoration)
Life of Pi (2012)
Dan Hennah (Production Design), Simon Bright, Ra Vincent (Set Decoration)
The Hobbit: An Unexpected Journey (2012)
Eve Stewart (Production Design), Anna Lynch-Robinson (Set Decoration)
Les Misérables (2012)

Jean Hersholt Humanitarian Award
⚊ **Jeffrey Katzenberg** ⚊

Best Costume Design

⚐ Jacqueline Durran ⚐
Anna Karenina (2012)

Colleen Atwood
Snow White and the Huntsman (2012)

Paco Delgado
Les Misérables (2012)

Eiko Ishioka
(posthumous)
Mirror Mirror (2012)

Joanna Johnston
Lincoln (2012)

Best Visual Effects

Erik-Jan De Boer, Donald R. Elliott, Guillaume Rocheron, Bill Westenhofer
Life of Pi (2012)

David Clayton, Joe Letteri, Eric Saindon, R. Christopher White
The Hobbit: An Unexpected Journey (2012)

Philip Brennan, Neil Corbould, Michael Dawson, Cedric Nicolas-Troyan
Snow White and the Huntsman (2012)

Charley Henley, Martin Hill, Richard Stammers, Trevor Wood
Prometheus (2012)

Janek Sirrs, Dan Sudick, Jeff White, Guy Williams
The Avengers (2012)

Best Directing

⚐ Ang Lee ⚐
Life of Pi (2012)

Michael Haneke
Amour (2012)

David O. Russell
Silver Linings Playbook (2012)

Steven Spielberg
Lincoln (2012)

Benh Zeitlin
Beasts of the Southern Wild (2012)

Best Music, Original Song

⚐ Adele Adkins, Paul Epworth (Music & Lyrics) for the song "Skyfall" ⚐
Skyfall (2012)

Mychael Danna (Music), Bombay Jayashri (Lyrics) for the song "Pi's Lullaby"
Life of Pi (2012)

Walter Murphy (Music), Seth MacFarlane (Lyrics) for the song "Everybody Needs A Best Friend"
Ted (2012)

J. Ralph (Music & Lyrics) for the song "Before My Time"
Chasing Ice (2012)

Claude-Michel Schönberg (Music), Alain Boublil, Herbert Kretzmer (Lyrics) for the song "Suddenly"
Les Misérables (2012)

Best Film Editing

⚱ **William Goldenberg** ⚱
Argo (2012)

Jay Cassidy, Crispin Struthers
Silver Linings Playbook (2012)

William Goldenberg, Dylan Tichenor
Zero Dark Thirty (2012)

Michael Kahn
Lincoln (2012)

Tim Squyres
Life of Pi (2012)

Best Music, Original Score

⚱ **Mychael Danna** ⚱
Life of Pi (2012)

Alexandre Desplat
Argo (2012)

Dario Marianelli
Anna Karenina (2012)

Thomas Newman
Skyfall (2012)

John Williams
Lincoln (2012)

Best Makeup and Hairstyling

⚱ **Julie Dartnell, Lisa Westcott** ⚱
Les Misérables (2012)

Howard Berger, Peter Montagna, Martin Samuel
Hitchcock (2012)

Rick Findlater, Peter Swords King, Tami Lane
The Hobbit: An Unexpected Journey (2012)

Best Picture

⚱ **Ben Affleck, George Clooney, Grant Heslov (Producers)** ⚱
Argo (2012)

Stefan Arndt, Veit Heiduschka, Michael Katz, Margaret Ménégoz (Producers)
Amour (2012)

Tim Bevan, Eric Fellner, Debra Hayward, Cameron Mackintosh (Producers)
Les Misérables (2012)

Kathryn Bigelow, Mark Boal, Megan Ellison (Producers)
Zero Dark Thirty (2012)

Bruce Cohen, Donna Gigliotti, Jonathan Gordon (Producers)
Silver Linings Playbook (2012)

Michael Gottwald, Dan Janvey, Josh Penn (Producers)
Beasts of the Southern Wild (2012)

Reginald Hudlin, Pilar Savone, Stacey Sher (Producers)
Django Unchained (2012)

Kathleen Kennedy, Steven Spielberg (Producers)
Lincoln (2012)

Ang Lee, Gil Netter, David Womark (Producers)
Life of Pi (2012)

Best Documentary, Feature

⚐ **Malik Bendjelloul, Simon Chinn** ⚐
Searching for Sugar Man (2012)

Emad Burnat, Guy Davidi
5 Broken Cameras (2011)

Kirby Dick, Amy Ziering
The Invisible War (2012)

Philippa Kowarsky, Estelle Fialon, Dror Moreh
The Gatekeepers (2012)

David France, Howard Gertler
How to Survive a Plague (2012)

Best Documentary, Short Subject

⚐ **Andrea Nix Fine, Sean Fine** ⚐
Inocente (2012)

Jon Alpert, Matthew O'Neill
Redemption (2013)

Kief Davidson, Cori Shepherd Stern
Open Heart (2013)

Sari Gilman, Jedd Wider
Kings Point (2012)

Robin Honan, Cynthia Wade
Mondays at Racine (2012)

Best Sound Mixing

⚐ **Simon Hayes, Andy Nelson, Mark Paterson** ⚐
Les Misérables (2012)

Ron Bartlett, Doug M. Hemphill, Drew Kunin
Life of Pi (2012)

José Antonio García, John T. Reitz, Gregg Rudloff
Argo (2012)

Ronald Judkins, Andy Nelson, Gary Rydstrom
Lincoln (2012)

Scott Millan, Greg P. Russell, Stuart Wilson
Skyfall (2012)

Best Foreign Language Film

⚐ **Austria** ⚐
Amour (2012)

Canada
Rebelle (eng. War Witch) (2012)

Chile
No (2012)

Denmark
En kongelig affære (eng. A Royal Affair) (2012)

Norway
Kon-Tiki (2012)

Best Short Film, Animated
↨ John Kahrs ↨
Paperman (2012)
Minkyu Lee
Adam and Dog (2012)
Fodhla Cronin O'Reilly, Timothy Reckart
Head Over Heels (2012)
PES
Fresh Guacamole (2012)
David Silverman
The Longest Daycare (2012)

Best Short Film, Live Action
↨ Shawn Christensen ↨
Curfew (2012)
Tom Van Avermaet, Ellen De Waele
Dood van een Schaduw (eng. Death of a Shadow) (2012)
Bryan Buckley, Mino Jarjoura
Asad (2012)
Yan England
Henry (2011)
Sam French, Ariel Nasr
Buzkashi Boys (2012)

Best Writing, Adapted Screenplay
↨ Chris Terrio ↨
Argo (2012)
Lucy Alibar, Benh Zeitlin
Beasts of the Southern Wild (2012)
Tony Kushner
Lincoln (2012)
David Magee
Life of Pi (2012)
David O. Russell
Silver Linings Playbook (2012)

Best Writing, Original Screenplay
↨ Quentin Tarantino ↨
Django Unchained (2012)
Wes Anderson, Roman Coppola
Moonrise Kingdom (2012)
Mark Boal
Zero Dark Thirty (2012)
John Gatins
Flight (2012)
Michael Haneke
Amour (2012)

Best Sound Editing
⚐ **Per Hallberg, Karen Baker Landers** ⚐
Skyfall (2012)
⚐ **Paul N. J. Ottosson** ⚐
Zero Dark Thirty (2012)
Erik Aadahl, Ethan Van der Ryn
Argo (2012)
Eugene Gearty, Philip Stockton
Life of Pi (2012)
Wylie Stateman
Django Unchained (2012)

The 86ᵗʰ Academy Awards® - March 2, 2014
Host: Ellen DeGeneres
Venue: Dolby Theatre at the Hollywood & Highland Center
Honoring movies released in 2013

Best Actor in a Leading Role
⚐ **Matthew McConaughey** ⚐
Dallas Buyers Club (2013) role "Ron Woodroof"
Christian Bale
American Hustle (2013) role "Irving Rosenfeld"
Bruce Dern
Nebraska (2013) role "Woodrow "Woody" Grant"
Leonardo DiCaprio
The Wolf of Wall Street (2013) role "Jordan Belfort"
Chiwetel Ejiofor
12 Years a Slave (2013) role "Solomon Northup"

Best Actor in a Supporting Role
⚐ **Jared Leto** ⚐
Dallas Buyers Club (2013) role "Rayon"
Barkhad Abdi
Captain Phillips (2013) role "Abduwali Muse"
Bradley Cooper
American Hustle (2013) role "Richard "Richie" DiMaso"
Michael Fassbender
12 Years a Slave (2013) role "Edwin Epps"
Jonah Hill
The Wolf of Wall Street (2013) role "Donnie Azoff"

Best Actress in a Leading Role
⚐ **Cate Blanchett** ⚐
Blue Jasmine (2013) role "Jeanette "Jasmine" Francis"
Amy Adams
American Hustle (2013) role "Lady Edith Greensly / Sydney Prosser"
Sandra Bullock
Gravity (2013) role "Dr. Ryan Stone"
Judi Dench
Philomena (2013) role "Philomena Lee"
Meryl Streep
August: Osage County (2013) role "Violet Weston"

Best Actress in a Supporting Role
⚔ **Lupita Nyong'o** ⚔
12 Years a Slave (2013) role "Patsey"
Sally Hawkins
Blue Jasmine (2013) role "Ginger"
Jennifer Lawrence
American Hustle (2013) role "Rosalyn Rosenfeld"
Julia Roberts
August: Osage County (2013) role "Barbara Weston-Fordham"
June Squibb
Nebraska (2013) role "Kate Grant"

Jean Hersholt Humanitarian Award
⚔ **Angelina Jolie** ⚔

Best Animated Feature Film
⚔ **Chris Buck, Jennifer Lee, Peter Del Vecho** ⚔
Frozen (2013)
Kristine Belson, Kirk DeMicco, Chris Sanders
The Croods (2013)
Didier Brunner, Benjamin Renner
Ernest et Célestine (eng. Ernest & Celestine) (2012)
Pierre Coffin, Chris Meledandri, Chris Renaud
Despicable Me 2 (2013)
Hayao Miyazaki, Toshio Suzuki
Kaze tachinu (eng. The Wind Rises) (2013)

Best Cinematography
⚔ **Emmanuel Lubezki** ⚔
Gravity (2013)
Roger A. Deakins
Prisoners (2013)
Bruno Delbonnel
Inside Llewyn Davis (2013)
Phedon Papamichael
Nebraska (2013)
Philippe Le Sourd
Yi dai zong shi (eng. The Grandmaster) (2013)

Best Costume Design
⚔ **Catherine Martin** ⚔
The Great Gatsby (2013)
Patricia Norris
12 Years a Slave (2013)
Michael O'Connor
The Invisible Woman (2013)
William Chang Suk Ping
Yi dai zong shi (eng. The Grandmaster) (2013)
Michael Wilkinson
American Hustle (2013)

Best Production Design

⚱ **Catherine Martin (Production Design), Beverley Dunn (Set Decoration)** ⚱
The Great Gatsby (2013)

Judy Becker (Production Design), Heather Loeffler (Set Decoration)
American Hustle (2013)

K. K. Barrett (Production Design), Gene Serdena (Set Decoration)
Her (2013)

Andy Nicholson (Production Design),
Rosie Goodwin, Joanne Woollard (Set Decoration)
Gravity (2013)

Adam Stockhausen (Production Design), Alice Baker (Set Decoration)
12 Years a Slave (2013)

Best Directing

⚱ **Alfonso Cuarón** ⚱
Gravity (2013)

Steve McQueen
12 Years a Slave (2013)

Alexander Payne
Nebraska (2013)

David O. Russell
American Hustle (2013)

Martin Scorsese
The Wolf of Wall Street (2013)

Best Music, Original Song

⚱ **Kristen Anderson-Lopez, Robert Lopez (Music & Lyrics)** ⚱
for the song "Let It Go"
Frozen (2013)

Bono, Adam Clayton, The Edge, Larry Mullen Jr. (Music), Bono (Lyrics)
for the song "Ordinary Love"
Mandela: Long Walk to Freedom (2013)

Karen O (Music), Spike Jonze, Karen O (Lyrics) for the song "The Moon Song"
Her (2013)

Pharrell Williams (Music & Lyrics) for the song "Happy"
Despicable Me 2 (2013)

Bruce Broughton (Music), Dennis Spiegel (Lyrics)
for the song "Alone Yet Not Alone"
(nomination withdrawn)
Alone Yet Not Alone (2013)

Best Documentary, Feature

⚱ **Gil Friesen, Morgan Neville, Caitrin Rogers** ⚱
(Gil Friesen - posthumous)
20 Feet from Stardom (2013)

Karim Amer, Jehane Noujaim
Al midan (eng. The Square) (2013)

Zachary Heinzerling, Lydia Dean Pilcher
Cutie and the Boxer (2013)

Joshua Oppenheimer, Signe Byrge Sørensen
The Act of Killing (2012)

Richard Rowley, Jeremy Scahill
Dirty Wars (2013)

Best Documentary, Short Subject
⚱ **Malcolm Clarke, Nicholas Reed** ⚱
The Lady in Number 6: Music Saved My Life (2013)
Edgar Barens
Prison Terminal: The Last Days of Private Jack Hall (2013)
Jason Cohen
Facing Fear (2013)
Sara Ishaq
Karama Has No Walls (2012)
Jeffrey Karoff
Cavedigger (2013)

Best Film Editing
⚱ **Alfonso Cuarón, Mark Sanger** ⚱
Gravity (2013)
Alan Baumgarten, Jay Cassidy, Crispin Struthers
American Hustle (2013)
Jean-Marc Vallée (as John Mac McMurphy), Martin Pensa
Dallas Buyers Club (2013)
Christopher Rouse
Captain Phillips (2013)
Joe Walker
12 Years a Slave (2013)

Best Picture
⚱ **Dede Gardner, Anthony Katagas, Jeremy Kleiner, Steve McQueen, Brad Pitt (Producers)** ⚱
12 Years a Slave (2013)
Albert Berger, Ron Yerxa (Producers)
Nebraska (2013)
Robbie Brenner, Rachel Winter (Producers)
Dallas Buyers Club (2013)
Dana Brunetti, Michael De Luca, Scott Rudin (Producers)
Captain Phillips (2013)
Steve Coogan, Tracey Seaward, Gabrielle Tana (Producers)
Philomena (2013)
Alfonso Cuarón, David Heyman (Producers)
Gravity (2013)
Leonardo DiCaprio, Emma Tillinger Koskoff, Joey McFarland, Martin Scorsese (Producers)
The Wolf of Wall Street (2013)
Megan Ellison, Spike Jonze, Vincent Landay (Producers)
Her (2013)
Megan Ellison, Jonathan Gordon, Charles Roven, Richard Suckle (Producers)
American Hustle (2013)

Best Makeup and Hairstyling
⚱ **Adruitha Lee, Robin Mathews** ⚱
Dallas Buyers Club (2013)
Joel Harlow, Gloria Pasqua Casny
The Lone Ranger (2013)
Stephen Prouty
Bad Grandpa (2013)

Best Short Film, Animated

⚑ **Alexandre Espigares, Laurent Witz** ⚑
Mr. Hublot (2013)

Dan Golden, Daniel Sousa
Feral (2012)

Jan Lachauer, Max Lang
Room on the Broom (2012)

Dorothy McKim, Lauren MacMullan
Get a Horse! (2013)

Shuhei Morita
Tsukumo (eng. Possessions) (2012)

Best Short Film, Live Action

⚑ **Kim Magnusson, Anders Walter** ⚑
Helium (2013)

Esteban Crespo
Aquel no era yo (eng. That Wasn't Me) (2012)

Alexandre Gavras, Xavier Legrand
Avant que de tout perdre (eng. Just Before Losing Everything) (2013)

Mark Gill, Baldwin Li
The Voorman Problem (2011)

Kirsikka Saari, Selma Vilhunen
Pitääkö mun kaikki hoitaa? (eng. Do I Have to Take Care of Everything?) (2012)

Best Sound Mixing

⚑ **Niv Adiri, Christopher Benstead, Skip Lievsay, Chris Munro** ⚑
Gravity (2013)

Beau Borders, David Brownlow, Andy Koyama
Lone Survivor (2013)

**Christopher Boyes, Michael Hedges,
Tony Johnson, Michael Semanick**
The Hobbit: The Desolation of Smaug (2013)

**Chris Burdon, Chris Munro,
Mike Prestwood Smith, Mark Taylor**
Captain Phillips (2013)

Peter F. Kurland, Skip Lievsay, Greg Orloff
Inside Llewyn Davis (2013)

Best Visual Effects

⚑ **Neil Corbould , Chris Lawrence, David Shirk, Tim Webber** ⚑
Gravity (2013)

**Tim Alexander, Gary Brozenich,
John Frazier, Edson Williams**
The Lone Ranger (2013)

**David Clayton, Joe Letteri,
Eric Reynolds, Eric Saindon**
The Hobbit: The Desolation of Smaug (2013)

Burt Dalton, Ben Grossmann, Roger Guyett, Patrick Tubach
Star Trek Into Darkness (2013)

Erik Nash, Daniel Sudick, Christopher Townsend, Guy Williams
Iron Man 3 (2013)

Honorary Award
⚜ Angela Lansbury ⚜
An entertainment icon who has created some of cinema's most memorable characters, inspiring generations of actors.

⚜ Steve Martin ⚜
In recognition of his extraordinary talents and the unique inspiration he has brought to the art of motion pictures.

⚜ Piero Tosi ⚜
A visionary whose incomparable costume designs shaped timeless, living art in motion pictures.

Best Foreign Language Film
⚜ Italy ⚜
La grande bellezza (eng. The Great Beauty) (2013)

Belgium
The Broken Circle Breakdown (2012)

Cambodia
L'image manquante (eng. The Missing Picture) (2013)

Denmark
Jagten (eng. The Hunt) (2012)

Palestine
Omar (2013)

Best Music, Original Score
⚜ Steven Price ⚜
Gravity (2013)

William Butler, Owen Pallett
Her (2013)

Alexandre Desplat
Philomena (2013)

Thomas Newman
Saving Mr. Banks (2013)

John Williams
The Book Thief (2013)

Best Sound Editing
⚜ Glenn Freemantle ⚜
Gravity (2013)

Steve Boeddeker, Richard Hymns
All Is Lost (2013)

Brent Burge, Chris Ward
The Hobbit: The Desolation of Smaug (2013)

Wylie Stateman
Lone Survivor (2013)

Oliver Tarney
Captain Phillips (2013)

Best Writing, Adapted Screenplay

⬇ **John Ridley** ⬇
12 Years a Slave (2013)

Steve Coogan, Jeff Pope
Philomena (2013)

Julie Delpy, Ethan Hawke, Richard Linklater
Before Midnight (2013)

Billy Ray
Captain Phillips (2013)

Terence Winter
The Wolf of Wall Street (2013)

Best Writing, Original Screenplay

⬇ **Spike Jonze** ⬇
Her (2013)

Woody Allen
Blue Jasmine (2013)

Craig Borten, Melisa Wallack
Dallas Buyers Club (2013)

Bob Nelson
Nebraska (2013)

David O. Russell, Eric Warren Singer
American Hustle (2013)

The 87ᵗʰ Academy Awards® - February 22, 2015

Host: Neil Patrick Harris
Venue: Dolby Theatre at the Hollywood & Highland Center
Honoring movies released in 2014

Best Actor in a Leading Role

⬇ **Eddie Redmayne** ⬇
The Theory of Everything (2014) role "Stephen Hawking"

Steve Carell
Foxcatcher (2014) role "John Eleuthère du Pont"

Bradley Cooper
American Sniper (2014) role "Chris Kyle"

Benedict Cumberbatch
The Imitation Game (2014) role "Alan Turing"

Michael Keaton
Birdman or (The Unexpected Virtue of Ignorance) (2014) role "Riggan Thomson"

Best Actor in a Supporting Role

⬇ **J. K. Simmons** ⬇
Whiplash (2014) role "Terence Fletcher"

Robert Duvall
The Judge (2014) role "Judge Joseph Palmer"

Ethan Hawke
Boyhood (2014) role "Mason Evans Sr."

Edward Norton
Birdman or (The Unexpected Virtue of Ignorance) (2014) role "Mike Shiner"

Mark Ruffalo
Foxcatcher (2014) role "David Schultz"

Best Actress in a Leading Role
⚐ Julianne Moore ⚐
Still Alice (2014) role "Alice Howland"
Marion Cotillard
Deux jours, une nuit (eng. Two Days, One Night) (2014) role "Sandra Bya"
Felicity Jones
The Theory of Everything (2014) role "Jane Wilde Hawking"
Rosamund Pike
Gone Girl (2014) role "Amy Elliott-Dunne / Nancy"
Reese Witherspoon
Wild (2014) role "Cheryl Strayed"

Best Actress in a Supporting Role
⚐ Patricia Arquette ⚐
Boyhood (2014) role "Olivia Evans"
Laura Dern
Wild (2014) role "Bobbi Grey"
Keira Knightley
The Imitation Game (2014) role "Joan Clarke"
Emma Stone
Birdman or (The Unexpected Virtue of Ignorance) (2014) role "Sam Thomson"
Meryl Streep
Into the Woods (2014) role "The Witch"

Jean Hersholt Humanitarian Award
⚐ Harry Belafonte ⚐

Best Animated Feature Film
⚐ Roy Conli, Don Hall, Chris Williams ⚐
Big Hero 6 (2014)
Graham Annable, Travis Knight, Anthony Stacchi
The Boxtrolls (2014)
Bonnie Arnold, Dean DeBlois
How to Train Your Dragon 2 (2014)
Tomm Moore, Paul Young
Song of the Sea (2014)
Yoshiaki Nishimura, Isao Takahata
Kaguya-hime no monogatari (eng. The Tale of The Princess Kaguya) (2013)

Best Production Design
⚐ Adam Stockhausen (Production Design), Anna Pinnock (Set Decoration) ⚐
The Grand Budapest Hotel (2014)
Nathan Crowley (Production Design), Gary Fettis (Set Decoration)
Interstellar (2014)
Suzie Davies (Production Design),
Charlotte Dirickx (as Charlotte Watts) (Set Decoration)
Mr. Turner (2014)
Maria Djurkovic (Production Design), Tatiana Macdonald (Set Decoration)
The Imitation Game (2014)
Dennis Gassner (Production Design), Anna Pinnock (Set Decoration)
Into the Woods (2014)

Best Cinematography
ⵏ Emmanuel Lubezki ⵏ
Birdman or (The Unexpected Virtue of Ignorance) (2014)
Roger Deakins
Unbroken (2014)
Ryszard Lenczewski, Łukasz Żal
Ida (2013)
Dick Pope
Mr. Turner (2014)
Robert D. Yeoman
The Grand Budapest Hotel (2014)

Best Visual Effects
ⵏ Scott R. Fisher, Paul J. Franklin, Ian Hunter, Andrew Lockley ⵏ
Interstellar (2014)
Nicolas Aithadi, Stephane Ceretti, Paul Corbould, Jonathan Fawkner
Guardians of the Galaxy (2014)
Daniel Barrett, Dan Lemmon, Joe Letteri, Erik Winquist
Dawn of the Planet of the Apes (2014)
Tim Crosbie, Lou Pecora, Richard Stammers, Cameron Waldbauer
X-Men: Days of Future Past (2014)
Dan DeLeeuw, Russell Earl, Bryan Grill, Daniel Sudick
Captain America: The Winter Soldier (2014)

Best Costume Design
ⵏ Milena Canonero ⵏ
The Grand Budapest Hotel (2014)
Colleen Atwood
Into the Woods (2014)
Mark Bridges
Inherent Vice (2014)
Jacqueline Durran
Mr. Turner (2014)
Anna B. Sheppard
Maleficent (2014)

Best Music, Original Song
Common (as Lonnie Lynn),
ⵏ John Legend (as John Stephens) (Music & Lyrics) for the song "Glory" ⵏ
Selma (2014)
Gregg Alexander, Danielle Brisebois (Music & Lyrics)
for the song "Lost Stars"
Begin Again (2013)
Glen Campbell, Julian Raymond (Music & Lyrics)
for the song "I'm Not Gonna Miss You"
Glen Campbell: I'll Be Me (2014)
Shawn Patterson (Music & Lyrics)
for the song "Everything is Awesome"
The Lego Movie (2014)
Diane Warren (Music & Lyrics) for the song "Grateful"
Beyond the Lights (2014)

Best Picture

Alejandro G. Iñárritu, John Lesher, James W. Skotchdopole (Producers)
Birdman or (The Unexpected Virtue of Ignorance) (2014)

Wes Anderson, Jeremy Dawson, Steven Rales, Scott Rudin (Producers)
The Grand Budapest Hotel (2014)

Tim Bevan, Lisa Bruce, Eric Fellner, Anthony McCarten (Producers)
The Theory of Everything (2014)

Jason Blum, Helen Estabrook, David Lancaster (Producers)
Whiplash (2014)

Christian Colson, Dede Gardner, Jeremy Kleiner, Oprah Winfrey (Producers)
Selma (2014)

Bradley Cooper, Clint Eastwood, Andrew Lazar, Robert Lorenz, Peter Morgan (Producers)
American Sniper (2014)

Nora Grossman, Ido Ostrowsky, Teddy Schwarzman (Producers)
The Imitation Game (2014)

Richard Linklater, Cathleen Sutherland (Producers)
Boyhood (2014)

Best Short Film, Animated

Patrick Osborne, Kristina Reed
Feast (2014)

Christopher Hees, Daisy Jacobs
The Bigger Picture (2014)

Robert Kondo, Daisuke 'Dice' Tsutsumi
The Dam Keeper (2014)

Torill Kove
Me and My Moulton (2014)

Joris Oprins
A Single Life (2014)

Best Short Film, Live Action

Mat Kirkby, James Lucas
The Phone Call (2013)

Oded Binnun, Mihal Brezis
Aya (2012)

Ronan Blaney, Michael Lennox
Boogaloo and Graham (2014)

Stefan Eichenberger, Talkhon Hamzavi
Parvaneh (2012)

Julien Féret, Hu Wei
La lampe au beurre de yak (eng. Butter Lamp) (2013)

Honorary Award

Jean-Claude Carrière
Whose elegantly crafted screenplays elevate the art of screenwriting to the level of literature

Hayao Miyazaki
A master storyteller whose animated artistry has inspired filmmakers and audiences around the world

Maureen O'Hara
One of Hollywood's brightest stars, whose inspiring performances glowed with passion, warmth and strength

Best Documentary, Feature

⚔ **Mathilde Bonnefoy, Laura Poitras, Dirk Wilutzky** ⚔
Citizenfour (2014)

Orlando von Einsiedel, Joanna Natasegara
Virunga (2014)

Rory Kennedy, Keven McAlester
Last Days in Vietnam (2014)

John Maloof, Charlie Siskel
Finding Vivian Maier (2013)

**David Rosier, Juliano Ribeiro Salgado,
Wim Wenders**
The Salt of the Earth (2014)

Best Documentary, Short Subject

⚔ **Ellen Goosenberg Kent, Dana Perry** ⚔
Crisis Hotline: Veterans Press 1 (2013)

Gabriel Serra Arguello
La parka (eng. The Reaper) (2013)

J. Christian Jensen
White Earth (2014)

Aneta Kopacz
Joanna (2013)

Maciej Ślesicki, Tomasz Śliwiński
Nasza klątwa (eng. Our Curse) (2013)

Best Writing, Adapted Screenplay

⚔ **Graham Moore** ⚔
The Imitation Game (2014)

Paul Thomas Anderson
Inherent Vice (2014)

Damien Chazelle
Whiplash (2014)

Jason Hall
American Sniper (2014)

Anthony McCarten
The Theory of Everything (2014)

Best Writing, Original Screenplay

⚔ **Armando Bo, Alexander Dinelaris Jr.,
Nicolás Giacobone, Alejandro G. Iñárritu** ⚔
Birdman or (The Unexpected Virtue of Ignorance) (2014)

**Wes Anderson (Screenplay),
Wes Anderson, Hugo Guinness (Story)**
The Grand Budapest Hotel (2014)

E. Max Frye, Dan Futterman
Foxcatcher (2014)

Dan Gilroy
Nightcrawler (2014)

Richard Linklater
Boyhood (2014)

Best Sound Editing

ꜜ **Bub Asman, Alan Robert Murray** ꜜ
American Sniper (2014)

Brent Burge, Jason Canovas
The Hobbit: The Battle of the Five Armies (2014)

Andrew DeCristofaro, Becky Sullivan
Unbroken (2014)

Aaron Glascock, Martín Hernández
Birdman or (The Unexpected Virtue of Ignorance) (2014)

Richard King
Interstellar (2014)

Best Sound Mixing

ꜜ **Thomas Curley, Craig Mann, Ben Wilkins** ꜜ
Whiplash (2014)

**Gregg Landaker, Gary A. Rizzo,
Mark Weingarten**
Interstellar (2014)

David Lee, Frank A. Montaño, Jon Taylor
Unbroken (2014)

**Walt Martin, John T. Reitz,
Gregg Rudloff**
(Walt Martin - posthumous)
American Sniper (2014)

**Frank A. Montaño, Jon Taylor,
Thomas Varga**
Birdman or (The Unexpected Virtue of Ignorance) (2014)

Best Music, Original Score

ꜜ **Alexandre Desplat** ꜜ
The Grand Budapest Hotel (2014)

Alexandre Desplat
The Imitation Game (2014)

Jóhann Jóhannsson
The Theory of Everything (2014)

Gary Yershon
Mr. Turner (2014)

Hans Zimmer
Interstellar (2014)

Best Film Editing

ꜜ **Tom Cross** ꜜ
Whiplash (2014)

Sandra Adair
Boyhood (2014)

Joel Cox, Gary D. Roach
American Sniper (2014)

William Goldenberg
The Imitation Game (2014)

Barney Pilling
The Grand Budapest Hotel (2014)

Best Directing
⚐ Alejandro G. Iñárritu ⚐
Birdman or (The Unexpected Virtue of Ignorance) (2014)
Wes Anderson
The Grand Budapest Hotel (2014)
Richard Linklater
Boyhood (2014)
Bennett Miller
Foxcatcher (2014)
Morten Tyldum
The Imitation Game (2014)

Best Foreign Language Film
⚐ Poland ⚐
Ida (2013)
Argentina
Relatos salvajes (eng. Wild Tales) (2014)
Estonia
Mandariinid (eng. Tangerines) (2013)
Mauritania
Timbuktu (2014)
Russia
Leviafan (eng. Leviathan) (2014)

Best Makeup and Hairstyling
⚐ Mark Coulier, Frances Hannon ⚐
The Grand Budapest Hotel (2014)
Bill Corso, Dennis Liddiard
Foxcatcher (2014)
David White, Elizabeth Yianni-Georgiou
Guardians of the Galaxy (2014)

The 88th Academy Awards® - February 28, 2016
Host: Chris Rock
Venue: Dolby Theatre at the Hollywood & Highland Center
Honoring movies released in 2015

Jean Hersholt Humanitarian Award
⚐ Debbie Reynolds ⚐

Best Actor in a Leading Role
⚐ Leonardo DiCaprio ⚐
The Revenant (2015) role "Hugh Glass"
Bryan Cranston
Trumbo (2015) role "Dalton Trumbo"
Matt Damon
The Martian (2015) role "Mark Watney"
Michael Fassbender
Steve Jobs (2015) role "Steve Jobs"
Eddie Redmayne
The Danish Girl (2015) role "Lili Elbe"

Best Actor in a Supporting Role
⚜ **Mark Rylance** ⚜
Bridge of Spies (2015) role "Rudolf Abel"
Christian Bale
The Big Short (2015) role "Michael Burry"
Tom Hardy
The Revenant (2015) role "John Fitzgerald"
Mark Ruffalo
Spotlight (2015) role "Michael Rezendes"
Sylvester Stallone
Creed (2015) role "Rocky Balboa"

Best Actress in a Leading Role
⚜ **Brie Larson** ⚜
Room (2015) role "Joy "Ma" Newsome"
Cate Blanchett
Carol (2015) role "Carol Aird"
Jennifer Lawrence
Joy (2015) role "Joy Mangano"
Charlotte Rampling
45 Years (2015) role "Kate Mercer"
Saoirse Ronan
Brooklyn (2015) role "Eilis Lacey"

Best Actress in a Supporting Role
⚜ **Alicia Vikander** ⚜
The Danish Girl (2015) role "Gerda Wegener"
Jennifer Jason Leigh
The Hateful Eight (2015) role "Daisy Domergue"
Rooney Mara
Carol (2015) role "Therese Belivet"
Rachel McAdams
Spotlight (2015) role "Sacha Pfeiffer"
Kate Winslet
Steve Jobs (2015) role "Joanna Hoffman"

Best Production Design
⚜ **Colin Gibson (Production Design), Lisa Thompson (Set Decoration)** ⚜
Mad Max: Fury Road (2015)
**Jack Fisk (Production Design),
Hamish Purdy (Set Decoration)**
The Revenant (2015)
**Arthur Max (Production Design),
Celia Bobak (Set Decoration)**
The Martian (2015)
**Eve Stewart (Production Design),
Michael Standish (Set Decoration)**
The Danish Girl (2015)
**Adam Stockhausen (Production Design),
Rena DeAngelo, Bernhard Henrich (Set Decoration)**
Bridge of Spies (2015)

Best Writing, Adapted Screenplay

⚷ Adam McKay, Charles Randolph ⚷
The Big Short (2015)

Emma Donoghue
Room (2015)

Drew Goddard
The Martian (2015)

Nick Hornby
Brooklyn (2015)

Phyllis Nagy
Carol (2015)

Best Writing, Original Screenplay

⚷ Tom McCarthy, Josh Singer ⚷
Spotlight (2015)

**Andrea Berloff, Jonathan Herman (Screenplay),
Andrea Berloff, S. Leigh Savidge, Alan Wenkus (Story)**
Straight Outta Compton (2015)

Matt Charman, Ethan Coen, Joel Coen
Bridge of Spies (2015)

**Josh Cooley, Pete Docter, Meg LeFauve (Screenplay),
Ronnie del Carmen, Pete Docter (Original story)**
Inside Out (2015)

Alex Garland
Ex Machina (2014)

Honorary Award

⚷ Spike Lee ⚷
A champion of independent film and an inspiration to young filmmakers.

⚷ Gena Rowlands ⚷
An original talent whose devotion to her craft has earned her worldwide recognition as an independent film icon.

Best Cinematography

⚷ Emmanuel Lubezki ⚷
The Revenant (2015)

Roger Deakins
Sicario (2015)

Edward Lachman
Carol (2015)

Robert Richardson
The Hateful Eight (2015)

John Seale
Mad Max: Fury Road (2015)

Best Makeup and Hairstyling

⚷ Damian Martin, Lesley Vanderwalt, Elka Wardega ⚷
Mad Max: Fury Road (2015)

Eva von Bahr, Love Larson
Hundraåringen som klev ut genom fönstret och försvann
(eng. The 100 Year-Old Man Who Climbed Out the Window and Disappeared) (2013)

Siân Grigg, Duncan Jarman, Robert A. Pandini
The Revenant (2015)

Best Costume Design
⚊ Jenny Beavan ⚊
Mad Max: Fury Road (2015)
Paco Delgado
The Danish Girl (2015)
Sandy Powell
Carol (2015), Cinderella (2015)
Jacqueline West
The Revenant (2015)

Best Directing
⚊ Alejandro G. Iñárritu ⚊
The Revenant (2015)
Lenny Abrahamson
Room (2015)
Tom McCarthy
Spotlight (2015)
Adam McKay
The Big Short (2015)
George Miller
Mad Max: Fury Road (2015)

Best Animated Feature Film
⚊ Pete Docter, Jonas Rivera ⚊
Inside Out (2015)
Alê Abreu
O Menino e o Mundo (eng. The Boy and the World) (2013)
Mark Burton, Richard Starzak
Shaun the Sheep Movie (2015)
Duke Johnson, Charlie Kaufman, Rosa Tran
Anomalisa (2015)
Yoshiaki Nishimura, Hiromasa Yonebayashi
Omoide no Mânî (eng. When Marnie Was There) (2014)

Best Picture
⚊ Blye Pagon Faust, Steve Golin, Nicole Rocklin, Michael Sugar (Producers) ⚊
Spotlight (2015)
Finola Dwyer, Amanda Posey (Producers)
Brooklyn (2015)
Dede Gardner, Jeremy Kleiner, Brad Pitt (Producers)
The Big Short (2015)
**Steve Golin, Alejandro G. Iñárritu, Arnon Milchan, Mary Parent,
Keith Redmon (Producers)**
The Revenant (2015)
Ed Guiney (Producer)
Room (2015)
Mark Huffam, Simon Kinberg, Michael Schaefer, Ridley Scott (Producers)
The Martian (2015)
Kristie Macosko Krieger, Marc Platt, Steven Spielberg (Producers)
Bridge of Spies (2015)
George Miller, Doug Mitchell (Producers)
Mad Max: Fury Road (2015)

Best Documentary, Feature

⚱ **James Gay-Rees, Asif Kapadia** ⚱
Amy (2015)

Evgeny Afineevsky, Den Tolmor
Winter on Fire: Ukraine's Fight for Freedom (2015)

Liz Garbus, Amy Hobby, Justin Wilkes
What Happened, Miss Simone? (2015)

Matthew Heineman, Tom Yellin
Cartel Land (2015)

Joshua Oppenheimer, Signe Byrge Sørensen
The Look of Silence (2014)

Best Documentary, Short Subject

⚱ **Sharmeen Obaid-Chinoy** ⚱
A Girl in the River: The Price of Forgiveness (2015)

Adam Benzine
Claude Lanzmann: Spectres of the Shoah (2015)

David Darg, Bryn Mooser
Body Team 12 (2015)

Jerry Franck, Courtney Marsh
Chau, Beyond the Lines (2015)

Dee Hibbert-Jones, Nomi Talisman
Last Day of Freedom (2015)

Best Film Editing

⚱ **Margaret Sixel** ⚱
Mad Max: Fury Road (2015)

Maryann Brandon, Mary Jo Markey
Star Wars: Episode VII - The Force Awakens (2015)

Hank Corwin
The Big Short (2015)

Tom McArdle
Spotlight (2015)

Stephen Mirrione
The Revenant (2015)

Best Music, Original Song

⚱ **Jimmy Napes, Sam Smith (Music & Lyrics)** ⚱
for the song "Writing's On The Wall"
Spectre (2015)

**Belly (as Ahmad Balshe), DaHeala (as Jason Quenneville), Stephan Moccio,
The Weeknd (as Abel Tesfaye) (Music & Lyrics)**
for the song "Earned It"
Fifty Shades of Grey (2015)

Lady Gaga, Diane Warren (Music & Lyrics)
for the song "Til It Happens to You"
The Hunting Ground (2015)

David Lang (Music & Lyrics) for the song "Simple Song #3"
Youth (2015)

J. Ralph (Music), Anohni (Lyrics) for the song "Manta Ray"
Racing Extinction (2015)

Best Foreign Language Film
⬥ Hungary ⬥
Saul fia (eng. Son of Saul) (2015)
Colombia
El abrazo de la serpiente (eng. Embrace of the Serpent) (2015)
Denmark
Krigen (eng. A War) (2015)
France
Mustang (2015)
Jordan
Theeb (2014)

Best Music, Original Score
⬥ Ennio Morricone ⬥
The Hateful Eight (2015)
Carter Burwell
Carol (2015)
Jóhann Jóhannsson
Sicario (2015)
Thomas Newman
Bridge of Spies (2015)
John Williams
Star Wars: Episode VII - The Force Awakens (2015)

Best Visual Effects
⬥ Mark Williams Ardington, Sara Bennett, Paul Norris, Andrew Whitehurst ⬥
Ex Machina (2014)
Chris Corbould, Roger Guyett, Neal Scanlan, Patrick Tubach
Star Wars: Episode VII - The Force Awakens (2015)
Andrew Jackson, Dan Oliver, Andy Williams, Tom Wood
Mad Max: Fury Road (2015)
Anders Langlands, Chris Lawrence, Richard Stammers, Steven Warner
The Martian (2015)
Rich McBride, Matthew Shumway, Jason Smith, Cameron Waldbauer
The Revenant (2015)

Best Short Film, Animated
⬥ Pato Escala, Gabriel Osorio Vargas ⬥
Historia de un oso (eng. Bear Story) (2014)
Konstantin Bronzit
My ne mozhem zhit bez kosmosa (eng. We Can't Live Without Cosmos) (2014)
Nicole Paradis Grindle, Sanjay Patel
Sanjay's Super Team (2015)
Don Hertzfeldt
World of Tomorrow (2015)
Imogen Sutton, Richard Williams
Prologue (2015)

Best Short Film, Live Action

⚐ **Serena Armitage, Benjamin Cleary** ⚐
Stutterer (2015)

Jamie Donoughue
Shok (2015)

Eric Dupont, Basil Khalil
Ave Maria (2015)

Henry Hughes
Day One (2015)

Patrick Vollrath
Alles wird gut (eng. Everything Will Be Okay) (2015)

Best Sound Editing

⚐ **Mark A. Mangini, David White** ⚐
Mad Max: Fury Road (2015)

David Acord, Matthew Wood
Star Wars: Episode VII - The Force Awakens (2015)

Lon Bender, Martín Hernández
The Revenant (2015)

Alan Robert Murray
Sicario (2015)

Oliver Tarney
The Martian (2015)

Best Sound Mixing

⚐ **Chris Jenkins, Ben Osmo, Gregg Rudloff** ⚐
Mad Max: Fury Road (2015)

Chris Duesterdiek, Frank A. Montaño, Jon Taylor, Randy Thom
The Revenant (2015)

Drew Kunin, Andy Nelson, Gary Rydstrom
Bridge of Spies (2015)

Paul Massey, Mac Ruth, Mark Taylor
The Martian (2015)

Andy Nelson, Christopher Scarabosio, Stuart Wilson
Star Wars: Episode VII - The Force Awakens (2015)

The 89th Academy Awards® - February 26, 2017

Host: Jimmy Kimmel
Venue: Dolby Theatre at the Hollywood & Highland Center
Honoring movies released in 2016

Best Actor in a Leading Role

⚐ **Casey Affleck** ⚐
Manchester by the Sea (2016) role "Lee Chandler"

Andrew Garfield
Hacksaw Ridge (2016) role "Desmond Doss"

Ryan Gosling
La La Land (2016) role "Sebastian Wilder"

Viggo Mortensen
Captain Fantastic (2016) role "Ben Cash"

Denzel Washington
Fences (2016) role "Troy Maxson"

Best Actor in a Supporting Role

⚊ Mahershala Ali ⚊
Moonlight (2016) role "Juan"

Jeff Bridges
Hell or High Water (2016) role "Marcus Hamilton"

Lucas Hedges
Manchester by the Sea (2016) role "Patrick Chandler"

Dev Patel
Lion (2016) role "Saroo Brierley"

Michael Shannon
Nocturnal Animals (2016) role "Detective Lieutenant Bobby Andes"

Best Actress in a Leading Role

⚊ Emma Stone ⚊
La La Land (2016) role "Mia Dolan"

Isabelle Huppert
Elle (2016) role "Michèle Leblanc"

Ruth Negga
Loving (2016) role "Mildred Loving"

Natalie Portman
Jackie (2016) role "Jacqueline "Jackie" Kennedy"

Meryl Streep
Florence Foster Jenkins (2016) role "Florence Foster Jenkins"

Best Actress in a Supporting Role

⚊ Viola Davis ⚊
Fences (2016) role "Rose Lee Maxson"

Naomie Harris
Moonlight (2016) role "Paula Harris"

Nicole Kidman
Lion (2016) role "Sue Brierley"

Octavia Spencer
Hidden Figures (2016) role "Dorothy Vaughan"

Michelle Williams
Manchester by the Sea (2016) role "Randi Chandler"

Best Music, Original Song

Justin Hurwitz (Music), Benj Pasek, Justin Paul (Lyrics)
for the song "City of Stars"
La La Land (2016)

Justin Hurwitz (Music), Benj Pasek, Justin Paul (Lyrics)
for the song "Audition (The Fools Who Dream)"
La La Land (2016)

Max Martin, Karl Johan Schuster, Justin Timberlake (Music & Lyrics)
for the song "Can't Stop the Feeling"
Trolls (2016)

Lin-Manuel Miranda (Music & Lyrics)
for the song "How Far I'll Go"
Moana (2016)

J. Ralph, Sting (Music & Lyrics) for the song "The Empty Chair"
Jim: The James Foley Story (2016)

Best Animated Feature Film

⚊ Byron Howard, Rich Moore, Clark Spencer ⚊
Zootopia (2016)

Claude Barras, Max Karli
Ma vie de Courgette (eng. My Life as a Zucchini) (2016)

Ron Clements, John Musker, Osnat Shurer
Moana (2016)

Michael Dudok de Wit, Toshio Suzuki
La tortue rouge (eng. The Red Turtle) (2016)

Travis Knight, Arianne Sutner
Kubo and the Two Strings (2016)

Best Production Design

**⚊ David Wasco (Production Design),
Sandy Reynolds-Wasco (Set Decoration) ⚊**
La La Land (2016)

Stuart Craig (Production Design), Anna Pinnock (Set Decoration)
Fantastic Beasts and Where to Find Them (2016)

**Guy Hendrix Dyas (Production Design),
Gene Serdena (Set Decoration)**
Passengers (2016)

**Jess Gonchor (Production Design),
Nancy Haigh (Set Decoration)**
Hail, Caesar! (2016)

**Patrice Vermette (Production Design),
Paul Hotte (Set Decoration)**
Arrival (2016)

Best Cinematography

⚊ Linus Sandgren ⚊
La La,Land (2016)

Greig Fraser
Lion (2016)

James Laxton
Moonlight (2016)

Rodrigo Prieto
Silence (2016)

Bradford Young
Arrival (2016)

Best Costume Design

⚊ Colleen Atwood ⚊
Fantastic Beasts and Where to Find Them (2016)

Consolata Boyle
Florence Foster Jenkins (2016)

Madeline Fontaine
Jackie (2016)

Joanna Johnston
Allied (2016)

Mary Zophres
La La Land (2016)

Best Directing
⚑ Damien Chazelle ⚑
La La Land (2016)
Mel Gibson
Hacksaw Ridge (2016)
Barry Jenkins
Moonlight (2016)
Kenneth Lonergan
Manchester by the Sea (2016)
Denis Villeneuve
Arrival (2016)

Best Documentary, Feature
⚑ Ezra Edelman, Caroline Waterlow ⚑
O.J.: Made in America (2016)
Spencer Averick, Howard Barish, Ava DuVernay
13th (2016)
Julie Goldman, Roger Ross Williams
Life, Animated (2016)
Rémi Grellety, Hébert Peck, Raoul Peck
I Am Not Your Negro (2016)
Donatella Palermo, Gianfranco Rosi
Fuocoammare (eng. Fire at Sea) (2016)

Best Documentary, Short Subject
⚑ Orlando von Einsiedel, Joanna Natasegara ⚑
The White Helmets (2016)
Kahane Cooperman, Raphaela Neihausen
Joe's Violin (2016)
Stephen Ellis, Marcel Mettelsiefen
Watani: My Homeland (2016)
Dan Krauss
Extremis (2016)
Daphne Matziaraki
4.1 Miles (2016)

Honorary Award
⚑ Jackie Chan ⚑
Chan starred in – and sometimes wrote, directed and produced – more than 30 martial arts features in his native Hong Kong, charming audiences with his dazzling athleticism, inventive stunt work and boundless charisma.
⚑ Anne V. Coates ⚑
In her more than 60 years as a film editor, she has worked side by side with many leading directors on an impressive range of films.
⚑ Lynn Stalmaster ⚑
Over five decades, he applied his talents to more than 200 feature films and has been instrumental in the careers of celebrated actors.
⚑ Frederick Wiseman ⚑
Wiseman has made one film almost every year since 1967, illuminating lives in the context of social, cultural and government institutions.

Best Film Editing
↓ John Gilbert ↓
Hacksaw Ridge (2016)
Tom Cross
La La Land (2016)
Joi McMillon, Nat Sanders
Moonlight (2016)
Jake Roberts
Hell or High Water (2016)
Joe Walker
Arrival (2016)

Best Foreign Language Film
↓ Iran ↓
Forushande (eng. The Salesman) (2016)
Australia
Tanna (2015)
Denmark
Under sandet (eng. Land of Mine) (2015)
Germany
Toni Erdmann (2016)
Sweden
En man som heter Ove (eng. A Man Called Ove) (2015)

Best Music, Original Score
↓ Justin Hurwitz ↓
La La Land (2016)
Volker Bertelmann (as Hauschka), Dustin O'Halloran
Lion (2016)
Nicholas Britell
Moonlight (2016)
Mica Levi
Jackie (2016)
Thomas Newman
Passengers (2016)

Best Sound Mixing
↓ Peter Grace, Robert Mackenzie, Kevin O'Connell, Andy Wright ↓
Hacksaw Ridge (2016)
Jeffrey J. Haboush, Greg P. Russell, Mac Ruth, Gary Summers
(Greg P. Russell - 25.02.2017 rescinded for violation of Academy campaign regulations)
13 Hours (2016)
Claude La Haye, Bernard Gariépy Strobl
Arrival (2016)
Ai-Ling Lee, Steve A. Morrow, Andy Nelson
La La Land (2016)
David Parker, Christopher Scarabosio, Stuart Wilson
Rogue One: A Star Wars Story (2016)

Best Sound Editing

♟ Sylvain Bellemare ♟
Arrival (2016)

Bub Asman, Alan Robert Murray
Sully (2016)

Ai-Ling Lee, Mildred Iatrou Morgan
La La Land (2016)

Robert Mackenzie, Andy Wright
Hacksaw Ridge (2016)

Wylie Stateman, Renée Tondelli
Deepwater Horizon (2016)

Best Makeup and Hairstyling

♟ Alessandro Bertolazzi, Giorgio Gregorini, Christopher Allen Nelson ♟
Suicide Squad (2016)

Richard Alonzo, Joel Harlow
Star Trek Beyond (2016)

Eva von Bahr, Love Larson
En man som heter Ove (eng. A Man Called Ove) (2015)

Best Picture

♟ Dede Gardner, Jeremy Kleiner, Adele Romanski (Producers) ♟
Moonlight (2016)

Lauren Beck, Matt Damon, Chris Moore, Kimberly Steward, Kevin J. Walsh (Producers)
Manchester by the Sea (2016)

Fred Berger, Jordan Horowitz, Marc Platt (Producers)
La La Land (2016)

Todd Black, Scott Rudin, Denzel Washington (Producers)
Fences (2016)

Iain Canning, Angie Fielder, Emile Sherman (Producers)
Lion (2016)

Peter Chernin, Donna Gigliotti, Theodore Melfi, Jenno Topping, Pharrell Williams (Producers)
Hidden Figures (2016)

Carla Hacken, Julie Yorn (Producers)
Hell or High Water (2016)

Dan Levine, Shawn Levy, David Linde, Aaron Ryder (Producers)
Arrival (2016)

Bill Mechanic, David Permut (Producers)
Hacksaw Ridge (2016)

Best Short Film, Animated

♟ Alan Barillaro, Marc Sondheimer ♟
Piper (2016)

Andrew Coats, Lou Hamou-Lhadj
Borrowed Time (2015)

Patrick Osborne
Pearl (2016)

Cara Speller, Robert Valley
Pear Cider and Cigarettes (2016)

Theodore Ushev
Blind Vaysha (2016)

Best Short Film, Live Action
⚊ Kristóf Deák, Anna Udvardy ⚊
Mindenki (eng. Sing) (2016)
Sélim Azzazi
Ennemis intérieurs (2016)
Aske Bang, Kim Magnusson
Silent Nights (2016)
Giacun Caduff, Timo von Gunten
La femme et le TGV (2016)
Juanjo Giménez Peña (as Juanjo Giménez)
Timecode (2016)

Best Visual Effects
⚊ Andrew R. Jones, Robert Legato, Dan Lemmon, Adam Valdez ⚊
The Jungle Book (2016)
**Jason Billington, Burt Dalton,
Craig Hammack, Jason H. Snell**
Deepwater Horizon (2016)
**Richard Bluff, Stephane Ceretti,
Vincent Cirelli, Paul Corbould**
Doctor Strange (2016)
**Neil Corbould, Hal T. Hickel,
John Knoll, Mohen Leo**
Rogue One: A Star Wars Story (2016)
**Steve Emerson, Oliver Jones,
Brian McLean, Brad Schiff**
Kubo and the Two Strings (2016)

Best Writing, Adapted Screenplay
⚊ Barry Jenkins (Screenplay), Tarell Alvin McCraney (Story) ⚊
Moonlight (2016)
Luke Davies
Lion (2016)
Eric Heisserer
Arrival (2016)
Theodore Melfi, Allison Schroeder
Hidden Figures (2016)
August Wilson
(posthumous)
Fences (2016)

Best Writing, Original Screenplay
⚊ Kenneth Lonergan ⚊
Manchester by the Sea (2016)
Damien Chazelle
La La Land (2016)
Efthimis Filippou, Yorgos Lanthimos
The Lobster (2015)
Mike Mills
20th Century Women (2016)
Taylor Sheridan
Hell or High Water (2016)
89th Ceremony 7/7

The 90ᵗʰ Academy Awards® - March 4, 2018

Host: Jimmy Kimmel
Venue: Dolby Theatre at the Hollywood & Highland Center
Honoring movies released in 2017

Best Makeup and Hairstyling

⚰ Kazu Hiro (as Kazuhiro Tsuji), David Malinowski, Lucy Sibbick ⚰
Darkest Hour (2017)

Daniel Phillips, Loulia Sheppard
Victoria & Abdul (2017)

Arjen Tuiten
Wonder (2017)

Best Actor in a Leading Role

⚰ Gary Oldman ⚰
Darkest Hour (2017) role "Winston Churchill"

Timothée Chalamet
Call Me by Your Name (2017) role "Elio Perlman"

Daniel Day-Lewis
Phantom Thread (2017) role "Reynolds Woodcock"

Daniel Kaluuya
Get Out (2017) role "Chris Washington"

Denzel Washington
Roman J. Israel, Esq. (2017) role "Roman J. Israel"

Best Actor in a Supporting Role

⚰ Sam Rockwell ⚰
Three Billboards Outside Ebbing, Missouri (2017) role "Officer Jason Dixon"

Willem Dafoe
The Florida Project (2017) role "Bobby Hicks"

Woody Harrelson
Three Billboards Outside Ebbing, Missouri (2017)
role "Chief William "Bill" Willoughby"

Richard Jenkins
The Shape of Water (2017) role "Giles"

Christopher Plummer
All the Money in the World (2017) role "J. Paul Getty"

Best Actress in a Leading Role

⚰ Frances McDormand ⚰
Three Billboards Outside Ebbing, Missouri (2017) role "Mildred Hayes"

Sally Hawkins
The Shape of Water (2017) role "Elisa Esposito"

Margot Robbie
I, Tonya (2017) role "Tonya Harding"

Saoirse Ronan
Lady Bird (2017) role "Christine "Lady Bird" McPherson"

Meryl Streep
The Post (2017) role "Katharine Graham"

Best Actress in a Supporting Role
⚊ Allison Janney ⚊
I, Tonya (2017) role "LaVona Golden"
Mary J. Blige
Mudbound (2017) role "Florence Jackson"
Lesley Manville
Phantom Thread (2017) role "Cyril Woodcock"
Laurie Metcalf
Lady Bird (2017) role "Marion McPherson"
Octavia Spencer
The Shape of Water (2017) role "Zelda Delilah Fuller"

Honorary Award
⚊ Charles Burnett ⚊
A resolutely independent and influential film pioneer who has chronicled the lives of black Americans with eloquence and insight.
⚊ Owen Roizman ⚊
Whose expansive visual style and technical innovation have advanced the art of cinematography.
⚊ Donald Sutherland ⚊
For a lifetime of indelible characters, rendered with unwavering truthfulness.
⚊ Agnès Varda ⚊
Whose compassion and curiosity inform a uniquely personal cinema.

Best Animated Feature Film
⚊ Darla K. Anderson, Lee Unkrich ⚊
Coco (2017)
Lori Forte, Carlos Saldanha
Ferdinand (2017)
Dorota Kobiela, Ivan Mactaggart, Hugh Welchman
Loving Vincent (2017)
Anthony Leo, Nora Twomey
The Breadwinner (2017)
Tom McGrath, Ramsey Naito
The Boss Baby (2017)

Best Production Design
⚊ Paul Denham Austerberry (Production Design), Jeffrey A. Melvin, Shane Vieau (Set Decoration) ⚊
The Shape of Water (2017)
Nathan Crowley (Production Design), Gary Fettis (Set Decoration)
Dunkirk (2017)
Dennis Gassner (Production Design), Alessandra Querzola (Set Decoration)
Blade Runner 2049 (2017)
Sarah Greenwood (Production Design), Katie Spencer (Set Decoration)
Beauty and the Beast (2017), Darkest Hour (2017)

Best Cinematography

⚐ Roger A. Deakins ⚐
Blade Runner 2049 (2017)

Bruno Delbonnel
Darkest Hour (2017)

Hoyte van Hoytema
Dunkirk (2017)

Dan Laustsen
The Shape of Water (2017)

Rachel Morrison
Mudbound (2017)

Best Writing, Adapted Screenplay

⚐ James Ivory ⚐
Call Me by Your Name (2017)

Scott Frank, Michael Green, James Mangold (Screenplay), James Mangold (Story)
Logan (2017)

Scott Neustadter, Michael H. Weber
The Disaster Artist (2017)

Dee Rees, Virgil Williams
Mudbound (2017)

Aaron Sorkin
Molly's Game (2017)

Best Writing, Original Screenplay

⚐ Jordan Peele ⚐
Get Out (2017)

Emily V. Gordon, Kumail Nanjiani
The Big Sick (2017)

Greta Gerwig
Lady Bird (2017)

Vanessa Taylor, Guillermo del Toro (Screenplay), Guillermo del Toro (Story)
The Shape of Water (2017)

Martin McDonagh
Three Billboards Outside Ebbing, Missouri (2017)

Best Directing

⚐ Guillermo del Toro ⚐
The Shape of Water (2017)

Paul Thomas Anderson
Phantom Thread (2017)

Greta Gerwig
Lady Bird (2017)

Christopher Nolan
Dunkirk (2017)

Jordan Peele
Get Out (2017)

Best Music, Original Song

⚱ Kristen Anderson-Lopez, Robert Lopez (Music & Lyrics) ⚱
for the song "Remember Me"
Coco (2017)

Mary J. Blige, Raphael Saadiq, Taura Stinson (Music & Lyrics)
for the song "Mighty River"
Mudbound (2017)

Common (as Lonnie R. Lynn), Diane Warren (Music & Lyrics)
for the song "Stand Up for Something"
Marshall (2017)

Benj Pasek, Justin Paul (Music & Lyrics) for the song "This is Me"
The Greatest Showman (2017)

Sufjan Stevens (Music & Lyrics) for the song "Mystery of Love"
Call Me by Your Name (2017)

Best Picture

⚱ J. Miles Dale, Guillermo del Toro (Producers) ⚱
The Shape of Water (2017)

Paul Thomas Anderson, Megan Ellison, Daniel Lupi,
JoAnne Sellar (Producers)
Phantom Thread (2017)

Tim Bevan, Lisa Bruce, Eric Fellner, Anthony McCarten,
Douglas Urbanski (Producers)
Darkest Hour (2017)

Jason Blum, Edward H. Hamm Jr.,
Sean McKittrick, Jordan Peele (Producers)
Get Out (2017)

Graham Broadbent, Pete Czernin, Martin McDonagh (Producers)
Three Billboards Outside Ebbing, Missouri (2017)

Eli Bush, Evelyn O'Neill, Scott Rudin (Producers)
Lady Bird (2017)

Emilie Georges, Luca Guadagnino,
Marco Morabito, Peter Spears (Producers)
Call Me by Your Name (2017)

Kristie Macosko Krieger, Amy Pascal, Steven Spielberg (Producers)
The Post (2017)

Christopher Nolan, Emma Thomas (Producers)
Dunkirk (2017)

Best Short Film, Animated

⚱ Kobe Bryant, Glen Keane ⚱
Dear Basketball (2017)

Victor Caire, Gabriel Grapperon
Garden Party (2017)

Ru Kuwahata, Max Porter
Negative Space (2017)

Jan Lachauer, Jakob Schuh
Revolting Rhymes (2016)

Dave Mullins, Dana Murray
Lou (2017)

Best Short Film, Live Action

⚊ **Chris Overton, Rachel Shenton** ⚊
The Silent Child (2017)

Katja Benrath, Tobias Rosen
Watu Wote: All of us (2017)

Reed Van Dyk
DeKalb Elementary (2017)

Josh Lawson, Derin Seale
The Eleven O'Clock (2016)

Kevin Wilson Jr.
My Nephew Emmett (2017)

Best Visual Effects

⚊ **Richard R. Hoover, Paul Lambert, Gerd Nefzer, John Nelson** ⚊
Blade Runner 2049 (2017)

**Daniel Barrett, Dan Lemmon,
Joe Letteri, Joel Whist**
War for the Planet of the Apes (2017)

**Scott Benza, Mike Meinardus,
Stephen Rosenbaum, Jeff White**
Kong: Skull Island (2017)

**Chris Corbould, Ben Morris,
Mike Mulholland, Neal Scanlan**
Star Wars: Episode VIII - The Last Jedi (2017)

**Jonathan Fawkner, Dan Sudick,
Christopher Townsend, Guy Williams**
Guardians of the Galaxy Vol. 2 (2017)

Best Documentary, Feature

⚊ **Dan Cogan, Bryan Fogel** ⚊
Icarus (2017)

Kareem Abeed, Feras Fayyad, Søren Steen Jespersen
De sidste mænd i Aleppo (eng. Last Men in Aleppo) (2017)

Joslyn Barnes, Yance Ford
Strong Island (2017)

Julie Goldman, Steve James, Mark Mitten
Abacus: Small Enough to Jail (2016)

JR, Agnès Varda, Rosalie Varda
Visages villages (eng. Faces Places) (2017)

Best Documentary, Short Subject

⚊ **Frank Stiefel** ⚊
Heaven is a Traffic Jam on the 405 (2016)

Laura Checkoway, Thomas Lee Wright
Edith+Eddie (2017)

Kate Davis, David Heilbroner
Traffic Stop (2017)

Thomas Lennon
Knife Skills (2017)

Elaine McMillion Sheldon, Kerrin Sheldon
Heroin(e) (2017)

Best Film Editing
⌊ Lee Smith ⌋
Dunkirk (2017)
Jonathan Amos, Paul Machliss
Baby Driver (2017)
Jon Gregory
Three Billboards Outside Ebbing, Missouri (2017)
Tatiana S. Riegel
I, Tonya (2017)
Sidney Wolinsky
The Shape of Water (2017)

Best Foreign Language Film
⌊ Chile ⌋
Una mujer fantástica (eng. A Fantastic Woman) (2017)
Hungary
Teströl és lélekröl (eng. On Body and Soul) (2017)
Lebanon
L'insulte (eng. The Insult) (2017)
Russia
Nelyubov (eng. Loveless) (2017)
Sweden
The Square (2017)

Best Sound Mixing
⌊ Gregg Landaker, Gary A. Rizzo, Mark Weingarten ⌋
Dunkirk (2017)
Ron Bartlett, Doug Hemphill, Mac Ruth
Blade Runner 2049 (2017)
Tim Cavagin, Mary H. Ellis, Julian Slater
Baby Driver (2017)
Christian T. Cooke, Glen Gauthier, Brad Zoern
The Shape of Water (2017)
Ren Klyce, David Parker, Michael Semanick, Stuart Wilson
Star Wars: Episode VIII - The Last Jedi (2017)

Best Music, Original Score
⌊ Alexandre Desplat ⌋
The Shape of Water (2017)
Carter Burwell
Three Billboards Outside Ebbing, Missouri (2017)
Jonny Greenwood
Phantom Thread (2017)
John Williams
Star Wars: Episode VIII - The Last Jedi (2017)
Hans Zimmer
Dunkirk (2017)

Best Sound Editing

🎞 **Alex Gibson, Richard King** 🎞
Dunkirk (2017)

Nelson Ferreira, Nathan Robitaille
The Shape of Water (2017)

Theo Green, Mark A. Mangini
Blade Runner 2049 (2017)

Ren Klyce, Matthew Wood
Star Wars: Episode VIII - The Last Jedi (2017)

Julian Slater
Baby Driver (2017)

Best Costume Design

🎞 **Mark Bridges** 🎞
Phantom Thread (2017)

Consolata Boyle
Victoria & Abdul (2017)

Jacqueline Durran
Beauty and the Beast (2017), Darkest Hour (2017)

Luis Sequeira
The Shape of Water (2017)

The 91st Academy Awards® - February 24, 2019

Host: No official host
Venue: Dolby Theatre at the Hollywood & Highland Center
Honoring movies released in 2018

Best Actor in a Leading Role

🎞 **Rami Malek** 🎞
Bohemian Rhapsody (2018) role "Freddie Mercury"

Christian Bale
Vice (2018) role "Dick Cheney"

Bradley Cooper
A Star Is Born (2018) role "Jackson "Jack" Maine"

Willem Dafoe
At Eternity's Gate (2018) role "Vincent van Gogh"

Viggo Mortensen
Green Book (2018) role "Tony "Lip" Vallelonga"

Best Actor in a Supporting Role

🎞 **Mahershala Ali** 🎞
Green Book (2018) role "Dr. Donald Shirley"

Adam Driver
BlacKkKlansman (2018) role "Detective Philip "Flip" Zimmerman"

Sam Elliott
A Star Is Born (2018) role "Bobby Maine"

Richard E. Grant
Can You Ever Forgive Me? (2018) role "Jack Hock"

Sam Rockwell
Vice (2018) role "George W. Bush"

Best Actress in a Leading Role
⚊ Olivia Colman ⚊
The Favourite (2018) role "Queen Anne"
Yalitza Aparicio
Roma (2018) role "Cleodegaria "Cleo" Gutierrez"
Glenn Close
The Wife (2017) role "Joan Castleman"
Lady Gaga
A Star Is Born (2018) role "Ally Maine"
Melissa McCarthy
Can You Ever Forgive Me? (2018) role "Lee Israel"

Best Actress in a Supporting Role
⚊ Regina King ⚊
If Beale Street Could Talk (2018) role "Sharon Rivers"
Amy Adams
Vice (2018) role "Lynne Cheney"
Marina de Tavira
Roma (2018) role "Sofía"
Emma Stone
The Favourite (2018) role "Abigail Masham"
Rachel Weisz
The Favourite (2018) role "Lady Sarah Churchill"

Irving G. Thalberg Memorial Award
⚊ Kathleen Kennedy ⚊
⚊ Frank Marshall ⚊

Best Animated Feature Film
⚊ Phil Lord, Christopher Miller, Bob Persichetti, Peter Ramsey, Rodney Rothman ⚊
Spider-Man: Into the Spider-Verse (2018)
Wes Anderson, Jeremy Dawson, Steven Rales, Scott Rudin
Isle of Dogs (2018)
Brad Bird, Nicole Paradis Grindle, John Walker
Incredibles 2 (2018)
Mamoru Hosoda, Yûichirô Saitô
Mirai no Mirai (eng. Mirai) (2018)
Phil Johnston, Rich Moore, Clark Spencer
Ralph Breaks the Internet (2018)

Best Production Design
⚊ Hannah Beachler (Production Design), Jay Hart (Set Decoration) ⚊
Black Panther (2018)
Eugenio Caballero (Production Design), Bárbara Enríquez (Set Decoration)
Roma (2018)
Fiona Crombie (Production Design), Alice Felton (Set Decoration)
The Favourite (2018)
Nathan Crowley (Production Design), Kathy Lucas (Set Decoration)
First Man (2018)
John Myhre (Production Design), Gordon Sim (Set Decoration)
Mary Poppins Returns (2018)

Best Cinematography

⚑ Alfonso Cuarón ⚑
Roma (2018)

Caleb Deschanel
Werk ohne Autor (eng. Never Look Away) (2018)

Matthew Libatique
A Star Is Born (2018)

Robbie Ryan
The Favourite (2018)

Łukasz Żal
Zimna wojna (eng. Cold War) (2018)

Best Costume Design

⚑ Ruth E. Carter ⚑
Black Panther (2018)

Alexandra Byrne
Mary Queen of Scots (2018)

Sandy Powell
Mary Poppins Returns (2018), The Favourite (2018)

Mary Zophres
The Ballad of Buster Scruggs (2018)

Best Makeup and Hairstyling

⚑ Greg Cannom, Kate Biscoe, Patricia Dehaney ⚑
Vice (2018)

Jenny Shircore, Marc Pilcher, Jessica Brooks
Mary Queen of Scots (2018)

Göran Lundström, Pamela Goldammer
Gräns (eng. Border) (2018)

Best Directing

⚑ Alfonso Cuarón ⚑
Roma (2018)

Yorgos Lanthimos
The Favourite (2018)

Spike Lee
BlacKkKlansman (2018)

Adam McKay
Vice (2018)

Paweł Pawlikowski
Zimna wojna (eng. Cold War) (2018)

Best Documentary, Feature

⚑ Jimmy Chin, Shannon Dill, Evan Hayes, Elizabeth Chai Vasarhelyi ⚑
Free Solo (2018)

Joslyn Barnes, Su Kim, RaMell Ross
Hale County This Morning, This Evening (2018)

Julie Cohen, Betsy West
RBG (2018)

Talal Derki, Ansgar Frerich, Eva Kemme, Tobias N. Siebert
Kinder des Kalifats (eng. Of Fathers and Sons) (2017)

Bing Liu, Diane Moy Quon
Minding the Gap (2018)

Best Documentary, Short Subject

ᛁ **Melissa Berton, Rayka Zehtabchi** ᛁ
Period. End of Sentence. (2018)

Jonathan Chinn, Ed Perkins
Black Sheep (2018)

Marshall Curry
A Night at the Garden (2017)

Rob Epstein, Jeffrey Friedman
End Game (2018)

Skye Fitzgerald, Bryn Mooser
Lifeboat (2018)

Best Music, Original Song

ᛁ **Lady Gaga, Mark Ronson, Anthony Rossomando,** ᛁ
Andrew Wyatt (Music & Lyrics) for the song "Shallow"
A Star Is Born (2018)

Kendrick Lamar, Mark "Sounwave" Spears,
Anthony "Top Dawg" Tiffith (Music), Kendrick Lamar, SZA,
Anthony "Top Dawg" Tiffith (Lyrics) for the song "All the Stars"
Black Panther (2018)

David Rawlings, Gillian Welch (Music & Lyrics)
for the song "When a Cowboy Trades His Spurs for Wings"
The Ballad of Buster Scruggs (2018)

Marc Shaiman (Music), Marc Shaiman, Scott Wittman (Lyrics)
for the song "The Place Where Lost Things Go"
Mary Poppins Returns (2018)

Diane Warren (Music & Lyrics) for the song "I'll Fight"
RBG (2018)

Honorary Award

ᛁ **Marvin Levy** ᛁ
For an exemplary career in publicity that has brought films to the minds, hearts and souls
of audiences all over the world

ᛁ **Lalo Schifrin** ᛁ
In recognition of his unique musical style, compositional integrity and influential
contributions to the art of film scoring

ᛁ **Cicely Tyson** ᛁ
Whose unforgettable performances and personal integrity have inspired generations of
filmmakers, actors and audiences

Best Film Editing

ᛁ **John Ottman** ᛁ
Bohemian Rhapsody (2018)

Barry Alexander Brown
BlacKkKlansman (2018)

Hank Corwin
Vice (2018)

Patrick J. Don Vito
Green Book (2018)

Yorgos Mavropsaridis
The Favourite (2018)

Best Foreign Language Film
ǂ **Mexico** ǂ
Roma (2018)
Germany
Werk ohne Autor (eng. Never Look Away) (2018)
Japan
Manbiki kazoku (eng. Shoplifters) (2018)
Lebanon
Capharnaüm (eng. Capernaum) (2018)
Poland
Zimna wojna (eng. Cold War) (2018)

Best Music, Original Score
ǂ **Ludwig Göransson** ǂ
Black Panther (2018)
Terence Blanchard
BlacKkKlansman (2018)
Nicholas Britell
If Beale Street Could Talk (2018)
Alexandre Desplat
Isle of Dogs (2018)
Marc Shaiman
Mary Poppins Returns (2018)

Best Sound Editing
ǂ **Nina Hartstone, John Warhurst** ǂ
Bohemian Rhapsody (2018)
Erik Aadahl, Ethan Van der Ryn
A Quiet Place (2018)
Steve Boeddeker, Benjamin A. Burtt
Black Panther (2018)
Sergio Díaz, Skip Lievsay
Roma (2018)
Ai-Ling Lee, Mildred Iatrou Morgan
First Man (2018)

Best Sound Mixing
ǂ **John Casali, Tim Cavagin, Paul Massey** ǂ
Bohemian Rhapsody (2018)
Steve Boeddeker, Peter J. Devlin. Brandon Proctor
Black Panther (2018)
Mary H. Ellis, Ai-Ling Lee, Frank A. Montaño, Jon Taylor
First Man (2018)
José Antonio García, Craig Henighan, Skip Lievsay
Roma (2018)
Steve Morrow, Tom Ozanich, Jason Ruder, Dean A. Zupancic
A Star Is Born (2018)

Best Visual Effects

⚞ **Ian Hunter, Paul Lambert, Tristan Myles, J. D. Schwalm** ⚟
First Man (2018)

Rob Bredow, Neal Scanlan,
Dominic Tuohy, Patrick Tubach
Solo: A Star Wars Story (2018)

Matthew E. Butler, Grady Cofer,
Roger Guyett, David Shirk
Ready Player One (2018)

Chris Corbould, Michael Eames,
Theo Jones, Christopher Lawrence
Christopher Robin (2018)

Dan DeLeeuw, Russell Earl, Kelly Port, Dan Sudick
Avengers: Infinity War (2018)

Best Picture

⚞ **Jim Burke, Brian Hayes Currie, Peter Farrelly,**
Charles B. Wessler, Nick Vallelonga (Producers) ⚟
Green Book (2018)

Kevin Feige (Producer)
Black Panther (2018)

Jason Blum, Spike Lee, Raymond Mansfield,
Sean McKittrick, Jordan Peele (Producers)
BlacKkKlansman (2018)

Graham King (Producer)
Bohemian Rhapsody (2018)

Ceci Dempsey, Ed Guiney, Yorgos Lanthimos,
Lee Magiday (Producers)
The Favourite (2018)

Alfonso Cuarón, Gabriela Rodríguez (Producers)
Roma (2018)

Bradley Cooper, Bill Gerber,
Lynette Howell Taylor (Producers)
A Star Is Born (2018)

Dede Gardner, Jeremy Kleiner,
Adam McKay, Kevin J. Messick (Producers)
Vice (2018)

Best Short Film, Animated

⚞ **Becky Neiman-Cobb, Domee Shi** ⚟
Bao (2018)

Louise Bagnall, Nuria González Blanco
Late Afternoon (2017)

Andrew Chesworth, Bobby Pontillas
One Small Step (2018)

David Fine, Alison Snowden
Animal Behaviour (2018)

Trevor Jimenez
Weekends (2017)

Best Short Film, Live Action
⍭ **Guy Nattiv, Jaime Ray Newman** ⍭
Skin (2018)
Jeremy Comte, Maria Gracia Turgeon
Fauve (2018)
Marianne Farley, Marie-Hélène Panisset
Marguerite (2017)
Vincent Lambe, Darren Mahon
Detainment (2018)
María del Puy Alvarado, Rodrigo Sorogoyen
Madre (eng. Mother) (2017)

Best Writing, Adapted Screenplay
⍭ **Spike Lee, David Rabinowitz, Charlie Wachtel, Kevin Willmott** ⍭
BlacKkKlansman (2018)
Ethan Coen, Joel Coen
The Ballad of Buster Scruggs (2018)
Bradley Cooper, Will Fetters, Eric Roth
A Star Is Born (2018)
Nicole Holofcener, Jeff Whitty
Can You Ever Forgive Me? (2018)
Barry Jenkins
If Beale Street Could Talk (2018)

Best Writing, Original Screenplay
⍭ **Brian Hayes Currie, Peter Farrelly, Nick Vallelonga** ⍭
Green Book (2018)
Alfonso Cuarón
Roma (2018)
Deborah Davis, Tony McNamara
The Favourite (2018)
Adam McKay
Vice (2018)
Paul Schrader
First Reformed (2017)

The 92nd Academy Awards® - February 9, 2020
Host: No official host
Venue: Dolby Theatre at the Hollywood & Highland Center
Honoring movies released in 2019

Honorary Award
⍭ **David Lynch** ⍭
For fearlessly breaking boundaries in pursuit of his singular cinematic vision.
⍭ **Wes Studi** ⍭
In recognition of the power and craft he brings to his indelible film portrayals and for his
steadfast support of the Native American community.
⍭ **Lina Wertmüller** ⍭
For her provocative disruption of political and social norms delivered with bravery through
her weapon of choice: the camera lens.

Best Actor in a Leading Role
↨ Joaquin Phoenix ↨
Joker (2019) role "Arthur Fleck / Joker"
Antonio Banderas
Dolor y gloria (eng. Pain and Glory) (2019) role "Salvador Mallo"
Leonardo DiCaprio
Once Upon a Time... In Hollywood (2019) role "Rick Dalton"
Adam Driver
Marriage Story (2019) role "Charlie Barber"
Jonathan Pryce
The Two Popes (2019) role "Cardinal Jorge Mario Bergoglio / Pope Francis"

Best Actor in a Supporting Role
↨ Brad Pitt ↨
Once Upon a Time... In Hollywood (2019) role "Cliff Booth"
Tom Hanks
A Beautiful Day in the Neighborhood (2019) role "Fred Rogers"
Anthony Hopkins
The Two Popes (2019) role "Cardinal Ratzinger / Pope Benedict XVI"
Al Pacino
The Irishman (2019) role "Jimmy Hoffa"
Joe Pesci
The Irishman (2019) role "Russell Bufalino"

Best Actress in a Leading Role
↨ Renée Zellweger ↨
Judy (2019) role "Judy Garland"
Cynthia Erivo
Harriet (2019) role "Araminta "Minty" Ross / Harriet Tubman"
Scarlett Johansson
Marriage Story (2019) role "Nicole Barber"
Saoirse Ronan
Little Women (2019) role "Josephine "Jo" March"
Charlize Theron
Bombshell (2019) role "Megyn Kelly"

Best Actress in a Supporting Role
↨ Laura Dern ↨
Marriage Story (2019) role "Nora Fanshaw"
Kathy Bates
Richard Jewell (2019) role "Barbara "Bobi" Jewell"
Scarlett Johansson
Jojo Rabbit (2019) role "Rosie Betzler"
Florence Pugh
Little Women (2019) role "Amy March"
Margot Robbie
Bombshell (2019) role "Kayla Pospisil"

Jean Hersholt Humanitarian Award
↨ Geena Davis ↨

Best Animated Feature Film

⚱ Josh Cooley, Mark Nielsen, Jonas Rivera ⚱
Toy Story 4 (2019)

Bonnie Arnold, Dean DeBlois, Bradford Lewis
How to Train Your Dragon: The Hidden World (2019)

Chris Butler, Travis Knight, Arianne Sutner
Missing Link (2019)

Jérémy Clapin, Marc du Pontavice
J'ai perdu mon corps (eng. I Lost My Body) (2019)

Jinko Gotoh, Sergio Pablos, Marisa Román
Klaus (2019)

Best Production Design

⚱ Barbara Ling (Production Design), Nancy Haigh (Set Decoration) ⚱
Once Upon a Time... In Hollywood (2019)

Dennis Gassner (Production Design),
Lee Sandales (Set Decoration)
1917 (2019)

Lee Ha Jun (Production Design),
Cho Won Woo (Set Decoration)
Gisaengchung (eng. Parasite) (2019)

Bob Shaw (Production Design),
Regina Graves (Set Decoration)
The Irishman (2019)

Ra Vincent (Production Design),
Nora Sopková (Set Decoration)
Jojo Rabbit (2019)

Best Cinematography

⚱ Roger Deakins ⚱
1917 (2019)

Jarin Blaschke
The Lighthouse (2019)

Rodrigo Prieto
The Irishman (2019)

Robert Richardson
Once Upon a Time... In Hollywood (2019)

Lawrence Sher
Joker (2019)

Best Costume Design

⚱ Jacqueline Durran ⚱
Little Women (2019)

Mark Bridges
Joker (2019)

Christopher Peterson, Sandy Powell
The Irishman (2019)

Arianne Phillips
Once Upon a Time... In Hollywood (2019)

Mayes C. Rubeo
Jojo Rabbit (2019)

Best Directing
↧ Bong Joon Ho ↧
Gisaengchung (eng. Parasite) (2019)
Sam Mendes
1917 (2019)
Todd Phillips
Joker (2019)
Martin Scorsese
The Irishman (2019)
Quentin Tarantino
Once Upon a Time... In Hollywood (2019)

Best Music, Original Song
↧ Elton John (Music), Bernie Taupin (Lyrics) ↧
for the song "I'm Gonna Love Me Again"
Rocketman (2019)
Kristen Anderson-Lopez, Robert Lopez (Music & Lyrics)
for the song "Into the Unknown"
Frozen II (2019)
Joshuah Brian Campbell, Cynthia Erivo (Music & Lyrics)
for the song "Stand Up"
Harriet (2019)
Randy Newman (Music & Lyrics)
for the song "I Can't Let You Throw Yourself Away"
Toy Story 4 (2019)
Diane Warren (Music & Lyrics)
for the song "I'm Standing With You"
Breakthrough (2019)

Best Picture
↧ Bong Joon Ho, Kwak Sin Ae (Producers) ↧
Gisaengchung (eng. Parasite) (2019)
Noah Baumbach, David Heyman (Producers)
Marriage Story (2019)
Peter Chernin, James Mangold, Jenno Topping (Producers)
Ford v Ferrari (2019)
Bradley Cooper, Todd Phillips, Emma Tillinger Koskoff (Producers)
Joker (2019)
Robert De Niro, Jane Rosenthal, Martin Scorsese, Emma Tillinger Koskoff (Producers)
The Irishman (2019)
Pippa Harris, Callum McDougall, Sam Mendes, Jayne-Ann Tenggren (Producers)
1917 (2019)
David Heyman, Shannon McIntosh, Quentin Tarantino (Producers)
Once Upon a Time... In Hollywood (2019)
Carthew Neal, Taika Waititi, Chelsea Winstanley (Producers)
Jojo Rabbit (2019)
Amy Pascal (Producer)
Little Women (2019)

Best Short Film, Animated

ⵊ **Matthew A. Cherry, Karen Rupert Toliver** ⵊ
Hair Love (2019)

Bruno Collet, Jean-François Le Corre
Mémorable (eng. Memorable) (2019)

Kathryn Hendrickson, Rosana Sullivan
Kitbull (2019)

Daria Kashcheeva
Dcera (eng. Daughter) (2019)

Siqi Song
Sister (2018)

Best Short Film, Live Action

ⵊ **Marshall Curry** ⵊ
The Neighbors' Window (2019)

Bryan Buckley, Matt Lefebvre
Saria (2019)

Delphine Girard
Une soeur (eng. A Sister) (2018)

Meryam Joobeur, Maria Gracia Turgeon
Ikhwène (eng. Brotherhood) (2018)

Damien Megherbi, Yves Piat
Nefta Football Club (2018)

Best Visual Effects

ⵊ **Greg Butler, Guillaume Rocheron, Dominic Tuohy** ⵊ
1917 (2019)

Matt Aitken, Dan DeLeeuw, Russell Earl, Dan Sudick
Avengers: Endgame (2019)

Leandro Estebecorena, Stephane Grabli, Pablo Helman, Nelson Sepulveda-Fauser
The Irishman (2019)

Roger Guyett, Neal Scanlan, Patrick Tubach, Dominic Tuohy
Star Wars: Episode IX - The Rise of Skywalker (2019)

Robert Legato, Andrew R. Jones, Elliot Newman, Adam Valdez
The Lion King (2019)

Best Documentary, Feature

ⵊ **Steven Bognar, Jeff Reichert, Julia Reichert** ⵊ
American Factory (2019)

Waad al-Kateab, Edward Watts
For Sama (2019)

Kirstine Barfod, Sigrid Dyekjær, Feras Fayyad
The Cave (2019)

Shane Boris, Petra Costa, Joanna Natasegara, Tiago Pavan
The Edge of Democracy (2019)

Atanas Georgiev, Tamara Kotevska, Ljubo Stefanov
Honeyland (2019)

Best Documentary, Short Subject

⸸ Elena Andreicheva, Carol Dysinger ⸸
Learning to Skateboard in a Warzone (If You're a Girl) (2019)

John Haptas, Kristine Samuelson
Life Overtakes Me (2019)

Yi Seung-Jun, Gary Byung-Seok Kam
In the Absence (2018)

Sami Khan, Smriti Mundhra
St. Louis Superman (2019)

Laura Nix, Colette Sandstedt
Walk Run Cha-Cha (2019)

Best Film Editing

⸸ Andrew Buckland, Michael McCusker ⸸
Ford v Ferrari (2019)

Tom Eagles
Jojo Rabbit (2019)

Jeff Groth
Joker (2019)

Yang Jinmo
Gisaengchung (eng. Parasite) (2019)

Thelma Schoonmaker
The Irishman (2019)

Best International Feature Film

⸸ South Korea ⸸
Gisaengchung (eng. Parasite) (2019)

France
Les Misérables (2019)

North Macedonia
Honeyland (2019)

Poland
Boże Ciało (eng. Corpus Christi) (2019)

Spain
Dolor y gloria (eng. Pain and Glory) (2019)

Best Writing, Original Screenplay

**⸸ Bong Joon Ho, Han Jin Won (Screenplay),
Bong Joon Ho (Story) ⸸**
Gisaengchung (eng. Parasite) (2019)

Noah Baumbach
Marriage Story (2019)

Rian Johnson
Knives Out (2019)

Sam Mendes, Krysty Wilson-Cairns
1917 (2019)

Quentin Tarantino
Once Upon a Time... In Hollywood (2019)

Best Writing, Adapted Screenplay

ℹ **Taika Waititi** ℹ
Jojo Rabbit (2019)

Greta Gerwig
Little Women (2019)

Anthony McCarten
The Two Popes (2019)

Todd Phillips, Scott Silver
Joker (2019)

Steven Zaillian
The Irishman (2019)

Best Makeup and Hairstyling

ℹ **Vivian Baker, Kazu Hiro, Anne Morgan** ℹ
Bombshell (2019)

Rebecca Cole, Naomi Donne, Tristan Versluis
1917 (2019)

Kay Georgiou, Nicki Ledermann
Joker (2019)

Paul Gooch, Arjen Tuiten, David White
Maleficent: Mistress of Evil (2019)

Jeremy Woodhead
Judy (2019)

Best Sound Mixing

ℹ **Mark Taylor, Stuart Wilson** ℹ
1917 (2019)

**David Giammarco, Paul Massey,
Steven A. Morrow**
Ford v Ferrari (2019)

Tom Johnson, Gary Rydstrom, Mark Ulano
Ad Astra (2019)

**Tod A. Maitland, Tom Ozanich,
Dean A. Zupancic**
Joker (2019)

Christian P. Minkler, Michael Minkler, Mark Ulano
Once Upon a Time... In Hollywood (2019)

Best Music, Original Score

ℹ **Hildur Guðnadóttir** ℹ
Joker (2019)

Alexandre Desplat
Little Women (2019)

Randy Newman
Marriage Story (2019)

Thomas Newman
1917 (2019)

John Williams
Star Wars: Episode IX - The Rise of Skywalker (2019)

Best Sound Editing
⚐ Donald Sylvester ⚐
Ford v Ferrari (2019)
David Acord, Matthew Wood
Star Wars: Episode IX - The Rise of Skywalker (2019)
Alan Robert Murray
Joker (2019)
Wylie Stateman
Once Upon a Time... In Hollywood (2019)
Oliver Tarney, Rachael Tate
1917 (2019)

The 93rd Academy Awards® - April 25, 2021
Host: No official host
Venue: Union Station Los Angeles and the Dolby Theatre at
the Hollywood & Highland Center
Honoring movies released in 2020

Best Picture
⚐ Mollye Asher, Dan Janvey, Frances McDormand, Peter Spears, Chloé Zhao (Producers)
Nomadland (2020)
Philippe Carcassonne, Jean-Louis Livi, David Parfitt (Producers)
The Father (2020)
Ryan Coogler, Charles D. King, Shaka King (Producers)
Judas and the Black Messiah (2021)
Ceán Chaffin, Eric Roth, Douglas Urbanski (Producers)
Mank (2020)
Christina Oh (Producer)
Minari (2020)
Ben Browning, Emerald Fennell, Ashley Fox, Josey McNamara (Producers)
Promising Young Woman (2020)
Bert Hamelinck, Sacha Ben Harroche (Producers)
Sound of Metal (2019)
Stuart M. Besser, Marc Platt (Producers)
The Trial of the Chicago 7 (2020)

Best Actor in a Leading Role
⚐ Anthony Hopkins ⚐
The Father (2020) role "Anthony"
Riz Ahmed
Sound of Metal (2019) role "Ruben Stone"
Chadwick Boseman
(posthumous)
Ma Rainey's Black Bottom (2020) role "Levee Green"
Gary Oldman
Mank (2020) role "Herman J. Mankiewicz"
Steven Yeun
Minari (2020) role "Jacob Yi"

Best Actor in a Supporting Role
⚐ Daniel Kaluuya ⚐
Judas and the Black Messiah (2021) role "Fred Hampton"
Sacha Baron Cohen
The Trial of the Chicago 7 (2020) role "Abbie Hoffman"
Leslie Odom Jr.
One Night in Miami... (2020) role "Sam Cooke"
Paul Raci
Sound of Metal (2019) role "Joe"
Lakeith Stanfield
Judas and the Black Messiah (2021) role "William "Bill" O'Neal"

Best Actress in a Leading Role
⚐ Frances McDormand ⚐
Nomadland (2020) role "Fern"
Viola Davis
Ma Rainey's Black Bottom (2020) role "Ma Rainey"
Andra Day
The United States vs. Billie Holiday (2021) role "Billie Holiday"
Vanessa Kirby
Pieces of a Woman (2020) role "Martha Weiss"
Carey Mulligan
Promising Young Woman (2020) role "Cassandra "Cassie" Thomas"

Best Actress in a Supporting Role
⚐ Youn Yuh-jung ⚐
Minari (2020) role "Soon-ja"
Maria Bakalova
Borat Subsequent Moviefilm: Delivery of Prodigious Bribe to American Regime for Make Benefit Once Glorious Nation of Kazakhstan (2020) role "Tutar Sagdiyev"
Glenn Close
Hillbilly Elegy (2020) role "Bonnie "Mamaw" Vance"
Olivia Colman
The Father (2020) role "Anne"
Amanda Seyfried
Mank (2020) role "Marion Davies"

Best Animated Feature Film
⚐ Pete Docter, Dana Murray ⚐
Soul (2020)
Will Becher, Paul Kewley, Richard Phelan
A Shaun the Sheep Movie: Farmageddon (2019)
Peilin Chou, Glen Keane, Gennie Rim
Over the Moon (2020)
Tomm Moore, Stéphan Roelants, Ross Stewart, Paul Young
Wolfwalkers (2020)
Kori Rae, Dan Scanlon
Onward (2020)

Best Cinematography

⚐ **Erik Messerschmidt** ⚐
Mank (2020)

Sean Bobbitt
Judas and the Black Messiah (2021)

Phedon Papamichael
The Trial of the Chicago 7 (2020)

Joshua James Richards
Nomadland (2020)

Dariusz Wolski
News of the World (2020)

Best Costume Design

⚐ **Ann Roth** ⚐
Ma Rainey's Black Bottom (2020)

Alexandra Byrne
Emma. (2020)

Bina Daigeler
Mulan (2020)

Massimo Cantini Parrini
Pinocchio (2019)

Trish Summerville
Mank (2020)

Best Production Design

⚐ **Donald Graham Burt (Production Design), Jan Pascale (Set Decoration)** ⚐
Mank (2020)

**David Crank (Production Design),
Elizabeth Keenan (Set Decoration)**
News of the World (2020)

**Nathan Crowley (Production Design),
Kathy Lucas (Set Decoration)**
Tenet (2020)

**Peter Francis (Production Design),
Cathy Featherstone (Set Decoration)**
The Father (2020)

**Mark Ricker (Production Design),
Karen O'Hara, Diana Stoughton (Set Decoration)**
Ma Rainey's Black Bottom (2020)

Best Directing

⚐ **Chloé Zhao** ⚐
Nomadland (2020)

Lee Isaac Chung
Minari (2020)

Emerald Fennell
Promising Young Woman (2020)

David Fincher
Mank (2020)

Thomas Vinterberg
Druk (eng. Another Round) (2020)

Best Documentary, Feature

⚝ Pippa Ehrlich, Craig Foster, James Reed ⚝
My Octopus Teacher (2020)

Maite Alberdi, Marcela Santibáñez
El Agente Topo (eng. The Mole Agent) (2020)

Sara Bolder, Jim LeBrecht, Nicole Newnham
Crip Camp (2020)

Garrett Bradley, Lauren Domino, Kellen Quinn
Time (2020)

Alexander Nanau, Bianca Oana
Colectiv (eng. Collective) (2019)

Best Documentary, Short Subject

⚝ Alice Doyard, Anthony Giacchino ⚝
Colette (2020)

Sophia Nahli Allison, Janice Duncan
A Love Song for Latasha (2019)

Kris Bowers, Ben Proudfoot
A Concerto Is a Conversation (2020)

Charlotte Cook, Anders Sømme Hammer
Do Not Split (2020)

Skye Fitzgerald, Michael Scheuerman
Hunger Ward (2020)

Best Film Editing

⚝ Mikkel E. G. Nielsen ⚝
Sound of Metal (2019)

Alan Baumgarten
The Trial of the Chicago 7 (2020)

Yorgos Lamprinos
The Father (2020)

Frédéric Thoraval
Promising Young Woman (2020)

Chloé Zhao
Nomadland (2020)

Best Music, Original Song

**⚝ H.E.R., D'Mile (as Dernst Emile II) (Music),
H.E.R., Tiara Thomas (Lyrics) for the song "Fight for You" ⚝**
Judas and the Black Messiah (2021)

Sam Ashworth, Leslie Odom Jr. (Music & Lyrics) for the song "Speak Now"
One Night in Miami... (2020)

**Max Grahn (as Fat Max Gsus), Rickard Göransson,
Savan Kotecha (Music & Lyrics) for the song "Husavik"**
Eurovision Song Contest: The Story of Fire Saga (2020)

**Daniel Pemberton (Music), Celeste (as Celeste Waite),
Daniel Pemberton (Lyrics) for the song "Hear My Voice"**
The Trial of the Chicago 7 (2020)

**Diane Warren (Music), Laura Pausini, Diane Warren (Lyrics)
for the song "Io Si (Seen)"**
La vita davanti a sé (eng. The Life Ahead) (2020)

Best International Feature Film
⏷ Denmark ⏷
Druk (eng. Another Round) (2020)
Bosnia and Herzegovina
Quo Vadis, Aida? (2020)
Hong Kong
Shaonian de ni (eng. Better Days) (2019)
Romania
Colectiv (eng. Collective) (2019)
Tunisia
The Man Who Sold His Skin (2020)

Best Writing, Adapted Screenplay
⏷ Christopher Hampton, Florian Zeller ⏷
The Father (2020)
Ramin Bahrani
The White Tiger (2021)
Peter Baynham, Sacha Baron Cohen, Jena Friedman, Anthony Hines, Lee Kern, Dan Mazer, Erica Rivinoja, Dan Swimer (Screenplay), Sacha Baron Cohen, Anthony Hines, Nina Pedrad, Dan Swimer (Story)
Borat Subsequent Moviefilm: Delivery of Prodigious Bribe to American Regime for Make Benefit Once Glorious Nation of Kazakhstan (2020)
Kemp Powers
One Night in Miami... (2020)
Chloé Zhao
Nomadland (2020)

Best Writing, Original Screenplay
⏷ Emerald Fennell ⏷
Promising Young Woman (2020)
Will Berson, Shaka King (Screenplay), Will Berson, Shaka King, Keith Lucas, Kenny Lucas (Story)
Judas and the Black Messiah (2021)
Lee Isaac Chung
Minari (2020)
Abraham Marder, Darius Marder (Screenplay), Derek Cianfrance, Darius Marder (Story)
Sound of Metal (2019)
Aaron Sorkin
The Trial of the Chicago 7 (2020)

Best Makeup and Hairstyling
⏷ Sergio Lopez-Rivera, Mia Neal, Jamika Wilson ⏷
Ma Rainey's Black Bottom (2020)
Laura Allen, Marese Langan, Claudia Stolze
Emma. (2020)
Dalia Colli, Mark Coulier, Francesco Pegoretti
Pinocchio (2019)
Patricia Dehaney, Eryn Krueger Mekash, Matthew W. Mungle
Hillbilly Elegy (2020)
Colleen LaBaff, Kimberley Spiteri, Gigi Williams
Mank (2020)

Best Short Film, Animated
ꗣ **Michael Govier, Will McCormack** ꗣ
If Anything Happens I Love You (2020)
Michael Capbarat, Madeline Sharafian
Burrow (2020)
Arnar Gunnarsson, Gísli Darri Halldórsson
Já-Fólkið (eng. Yes-People) (2020)
Adrien Mérigeau, Amaury Ovise
Genius Loci (2020)
Erick Oh
Opera (2020)

Best Short Film, Live Action
ꗣ **Travon Free, Martin Desmond Roe** ꗣ
Two Distant Strangers (2020)
Ossama Bawardi, Farah Nabulsi
The Present (2020)
Shira Hochman, Tomer Shushan
White Eye (2019)
Elvira Lind, Sofia Sondervan
The Letter Room (2020)
Doug Roland, Susan Ruzenski
Feeling Through (2020)

Jean Hersholt Humanitarian Award
ꗣ **Motion Picture & Television Fund** ꗣ
ꗣ **Tyler Perry** ꗣ

Best Music, Original Score
ꗣ **Jon Batiste, Trent Reznor, Atticus Ross** ꗣ
Soul (2020)
Terence Blanchard
Da 5 Bloods (2020)
Emile Mosseri
Minari (2020)
James Newton Howard
News of the World (2020)
Trent Reznor, Atticus Ross
Mank (2020)

Best Sound
ꗣ **Jaime Baksht, Nicolas Becker, Phillip Bladh,**
Carlos Cortés Navarrete (as Carlos Cortés), Michellee Couttolenc ꗣ
Sound of Metal (2019)
Beau Borders, Michael Minkler, Warren Shaw, David Wyman
Greyhound (2020)
Coya Elliott, Ren Klyce, David Parker
Soul (2020)
Ren Klyce, Drew Kunin, Jeremy Molod, Nathan Nance, David Parker
Mank (2020)
William Miller, Mike Prestwood Smith, John Pritchett, Oliver Tarney
News of the World (2020)

Best Visual Effects

⚰ **Scott R. Fisher, Andrew Jackson, David Lee, Andrew Lockley** ⚰
Tenet (2020)

Genevieve Camilleri, Brian Cox, Matt Everitt, Matt Sloan
Love and Monsters (2020)

Santiago Colomo (as Santiago Colomo Martinez), Nick Davis, Greg Fisher, Ben Jones
The One and Only Ivan (2020)

Sean Andrew Faden (as Sean Faden), Steve Ingram, Anders Langlands, Seth Maury
Mulan (2020)

Matthew Kasmir, Christopher Lawrence, Max Solomon, David Watkins
The Midnight Sky (2020)

The 94ᵗʰ Academy Awards® - March 27, 2022

Hosts: Regina Hall, Amy Schumer, Wanda Sykes
Venue: Dolby Theatre at Ovation Hollywood
Honoring movies released in 2021

Honorary Award

⚰ **Samuel L. Jackson** ⚰
He is a cultural icon whose dynamic work has resonated across decades and generations and audiences worldwide.

⚰ **Elaine May** ⚰
For bold, uncompromising approach to filmmaking, as a writer, director and actress.

⚰ **Liv Ullmann** ⚰
For bravery and emotional transparency which she has gifted audiences with deeply affecting screen portrayals.

Best Actor in a Leading Role

⚰ **Will Smith** ⚰
King Richard (2021) role "Richard Williams"

Javier Bardem
Being the Ricardos (2021) role "Desi Arnaz"

Benedict Cumberbatch
The Power of the Dog (2021) role "Phil Burbank"

Andrew Garfield
tick, tick...BOOM! (2021) role "Jonathan Larson"

Denzel Washington
The Tragedy of Macbeth (2021) role "Lord Macbeth"

Best Actor in a Supporting Role

⚰ **Troy Kotsur** ⚰
CODA (2021) role "Frank Rossi"

Ciarán Hinds
Belfast (2021) role "Pop"

Jesse Plemons
The Power of the Dog (2021) role "George Burbank"

J. K. Simmons
Being the Ricardos (2021) role "William Frawley"

Kodi Smit-McPhee
The Power of the Dog (2021) role "Peter Gordon"

Best Actress in a Leading Role
⚊ **Jessica Chastain** ⚊
The Eyes of Tammy Faye (2021) role "Tammy Faye Bakker"
Olivia Colman
The Lost Daughter (2021) role "Leda Caruso"
Penélope Cruz
Madres paralelas (eng. Parallel Mothers) (2021) role "Janis Martínez Moreno"
Nicole Kidman
Being the Ricardos (2021) role "Lucille Ball"
Kristen Stewart
Spencer (2021) role "Diana, Princess of Wales"

Best Actress in a Supporting Role
⚊ **Ariana DeBose** ⚊
West Side Story (2021) role "Anita"
Jessie Buckley
The Lost Daughter (2021) role "Young Leda Caruso"
Judi Dench
Belfast (2021) role "Granny"
Kirsten Dunst
The Power of the Dog (2021) role "Rose Gordon-Burbank"
Aunjanue Ellis
King Richard (2021) role "Oracene "Brandy" Price"

Jean Hersholt Humanitarian Award
⚊ **Danny Glover** ⚊

Best Animated Feature Film
⚊ **Jared Bush, Byron Howard, Yvett Merino, Clark Spencer** ⚊
Encanto (2021)
Kurt Albrecht, Phil Lord, Christopher Miller, Mike Rianda
The Mitchells vs the Machines (2021)
Enrico Casarosa, Andrea Warren
Luca (2021)
Carlos López Estrada, Don Hall, Osnat Shurer, Peter Del Vecho
Raya and the Last Dragon (2021)
Charlotte De La Gournerie, Monica Hellström, Jonas Poher Rasmussen, Signe Byrge Sørensen
Flugt (eng. Flee) (2021)

Best Production Design
⚊ **Patrice Vermette (Production Design), Zsuzsanna Sipos (Set Decoration)** ⚊
Dune (2021)
Stefan Dechant (Production Design), Nancy Haigh (Set Decoration)
The Tragedy of Macbeth (2021)
Tamara Deverell (Production Design), Shane Vieau (Set Decoration)
Nightmare Alley (2021)
Grant Major (Production Design), Amber Richards (Set Decoration)
The Power of the Dog (2021)
Adam Stockhausen (Production Design), Rena DeAngelo (Set Decoration)
West Side Story (2021)

Best Cinematography
⚑ Greig Fraser ⚑
Dune (2021)
Bruno Delbonnel
The Tragedy of Macbeth (2021)
Janusz Kaminski
West Side Story (2021)
Dan Laustsen
Nightmare Alley (2021)
Ari Wegner
The Power of the Dog (2021)

Best Costume Design
⚑ Jenny Beavan ⚑
Cruella (2021)
Jacqueline Durran, Massimo Cantini Parrini
Cyrano (2021)
Robert Morgan, Jacqueline West
Dune (2021)
Luis Sequeira
Nightmare Alley (2021)
Paul Tazewell
West Side Story (2021)

Best Directing
⚑ Jane Campion ⚑
The Power of the Dog (2021)
Paul Thomas Anderson
Licorice Pizza (2021)
Kenneth Branagh
Belfast (2021)
Ryûsuke Hamaguchi
Doraibu mai kâ (eng. Drive My Car) (2021)
Steven Spielberg
West Side Story (2021)

Best Documentary, Feature
**⚑ David Dinerstein, Robert Fyvolent, Joseph Patel, ⚑
Ahmir "Questlove" Thompson**
Summer of Soul (...Or, When the Revolution Could Not Be Televised) (2021)
**Charlotte De La Gournerie, Monica Hellström, Jonas Poher Rasmussen,
Signe Byrge Sørensen**
Flugt (eng. Flee) (2021)
Traci A. Curry, Stanley Nelson
Attica (2021)
Sushmit Ghosh, Rintu Thomas
Writing with Fire (2021)
Jessica Kingdon, Kira Simon-Kennedy, Nathan Truesdell
Ascension (2021)

Best Documentary, Short Subject

⚐ **Ben Proudfoot** ⚐
The Queen of Basketball (2021)

Pedro Kos, Jon Shenk
Lead Me Home (2021)

Geoff McLean, Matthew Ogens
Audible (2021)

Elizabeth Mirzaei, Gulistan Mirzaei
Three Songs for Benazir (2021)

Jay Rosenblatt
When We Were Bullies (2021)

Best Film Editing

⚐ **Joe Walker** ⚐
Dune (2021)

Hank Corwin
Don't Look Up (2021)

Myron Kerstein, Andrew Weisblum
tick, tick...BOOM! (2021)

Pamela Martin
King Richard (2021)

Peter Sciberras
The Power of the Dog (2021)

Best International Feature Film

⚐ **Japan** ⚐
Doraibu mai kâ (eng. Drive My Car) (2021)

Bhutan
Lunana: A Yak in the Classroom (2019)

Denmark
Flugt (eng. Flee) (2021)

Italy
È stata la mano di Dio (eng. The Hand of God) (2021)

Norway
Verdens verste menneske (eng. The Worst Person in the World) (2021)

Best Music, Original Song

⚐ **Billie Eilish, Finneas O'Connell (Music & Lyrics)** ⚐
for the song "No Time to Die"
No Time to Die (2021)

Dixson, Beyoncé Knowles-Carter (Music & Lyrics)
for the song "Be Alive"
King Richard (2021)

Lin-Manuel Miranda (Music & Lyrics)
for the song "Dos Oruguitas"
Encanto (2021)

Van Morrison (Music & Lyrics)
for the song "Down to Joy"
Belfast (2021)

Diane Warren (Music & Lyrics) for the song "Somehow You Do"
Four Good Days (2020)

Best Sound

Ron Bartlett, Theo Green, Doug Hemphill, Mark A. Mangini, Mac Ruth
Dune (2021)

Niv Adiri, Simon Chase, James Mather, Denise Yarde
Belfast (2021)

Brian Chumney, Tod A. Maitland, Shawn Murphy, Andy Nelson, Gary Rydstrom
West Side Story (2021)

Richard Flynn, Robert Mackenzie, Tara Webb
The Power of the Dog (2021)

James Harrison, Simon Hayes, Paul Massey, Oliver Tarney, Mark Taylor
No Time to Die (2021)

Best Music, Original Score

Hans Zimmer
Dune (2021)

Nicholas Britell
Don't Look Up (2021)

Germaine Franco
Encanto (2021)

Jonny Greenwood
The Power of the Dog (2021)

Alberto Iglesias
Madres paralelas (eng. Parallel Mothers) (2021)

Best Picture

Fabrice Gianfermi, Philippe Rousselet, Patrick Wachsberger (Producers)
CODA (2021)

Paul Thomas Anderson, Sara Murphy, Adam Somner (Producers)
Licorice Pizza (2021)

Laura Berwick, Kenneth Branagh, Becca Kovacik, Tamar Thomas (Producers)
Belfast (2021)

Cale Boyter, Mary Parent, Denis Villeneuve (Producers)
Dune (2021)

Jane Campion, Iain Canning, Roger Frappier, Tanya Seghatchian, Emile Sherman (Producers)
The Power of the Dog (2021)

Bradley Cooper, J. Miles Dale, Guillermo del Toro (Producers)
Nightmare Alley (2021)

Kristie Macosko Krieger, Steven Spielberg (Producers)
West Side Story (2021)

Adam McKay, Kevin J. Messick (Producers)
Don't Look Up (2021)

Will Smith, Tim White, Trevor White (Producers)
King Richard (2021)

Teruhisa Yamamoto (Producer)
Doraibu mai kâ (eng. Drive My Car) (2021)

Best Short Film, Animated

⚐ **Alberto Mielgo, Leo Sanchez Barbosa (as Leo Sanchez)** ⚐
The Windshield Wiper (2021)

Hugo Covarrubias, Tevo Díaz
Bestia (eng. Beast) (2021)

Anton Dyakov
Boxballet (2020)

Les Mills, Joanna Quinn
Affairs of the Art (2021)

Dan Ojari, Mikey Please
Robin Robin (2021)

Best Short Film, Live Action

⚐ **Riz Ahmed, Aneil Karia** ⚐
The Long Goodbye (2020)

Maria Brendle, Nadine Lüchinger
Ala Kachuu - Take and Run (2020)

K.D. Dávila, Omer Levin Menekse
Please Hold (2020)

Tadeusz Łysiak, Maciej Ślesicki
Sukienka (eng. The Dress) (2020)

Kim Magnusson, Martin Strange-Hansen
On My Mind (2021)

Best Makeup and Hairstyling

⚐ **Linda Dowds, Stephanie Ingram, Justin Raleigh** ⚐
The Eyes of Tammy Faye (2021)

Frederic Aspiras, Anna Carin Lock, Göran Lundström
House of Gucci (2021)

Eva von Bahr, Love Larson, Donald Mowat
Dune (2021)

Naomi Donne, Nadia Stacey, Julia Vernon
Cruella (2021)

Carla Farmer, Michael Marino, Stacey Morris
Coming 2 America (2021)

Best Visual Effects

⚐ **Brian Connor, Paul Lambert, Tristan Myles, Gerd Nefzer** ⚐
Dune (2021)

Chris Corbould, Jonathan Fawkner, Joel Green, Charlie Noble
No Time to Die (2021)

Scott Edelstein, Kelly Port, Dan Sudick, Chris Waegner
Spider-Man: No Way Home (2021)

Joe Farrell, Dan Oliver, Christopher Townsend, Sean Noel Walker
Shang-Chi and the Legend of the Ten Rings (2021)

Swen Gillberg, Bryan Grill, Nikos Kalaitzidis, Dan Sudick
Free Guy (2021)

Best Writing, Adapted Screenplay
↓ **Siân Heder** ↓
CODA (2021)

Jane Campion
The Power of the Dog (2021)

Maggie Gyllenhaal
The Lost Daughter (2021)

Ryusuke Hamaguchi, Takamasa Oe
Doraibu mai kâ (eng. Drive My Car) (2021)

Eric Roth, Jon Spaihts, Denis Villeneuve
Dune (2021)

Best Writing, Original Screenplay
↓ **Kenneth Branagh** ↓
Belfast (2021)

Paul Thomas Anderson
Licorice Pizza (2021)

Zach Baylin
King Richard (2021)

Adam McKay (Screenplay), Adam McKay, David Sirota (Story)
Don't Look Up (2021)

Joachim Trier, Eskil Vogt
Verdens verste menneske (eng. The Worst Person in the World) (2021)

To Be Continued...

Most nominated films

Film	Nominations	Wins	Ceremony
Titanic (1997)	14	11	70th
All About Eve (1950)	14	6	23rd
La La Land (2016)	14	6	89th
From Here to Eternity (1953)	13	8	26th
Gone with the Wind (1939)	13	8	12th
Shakespeare in Love (1998)	13	7	71st
Chicago (2002)	13	6	75th
Forrest Gump (1994)	13	6	67th
Mary Poppins (1964)	13	5	37th
Who's Afraid of Virginia Woolf? (1966)	13	5	39th
The Lord of the Rings: The Fellowship of the Ring (2001)	13	4	74th
The Shape of Water (2017)	13	4	90th
The Curious Case of Benjamin Button (2008)	13	3	81st
Ben-Hur (1959)	12	11	32nd
The English Patient (1996)	12	9	69th
My Fair Lady (1964)	12	8	37th
On the Waterfront (1954)	12	8	27th
Dances with Wolves (1990)	12	7	63rd
Schindler's List (1993)	12	7	66th
Mrs. Miniver (1942)	12	6	15th
Oliver! (1968)	12	6	41st
Gladiator (2000)	12	5	73rd
A Streetcar Named Desire (1951)	12	4	24th
The King's Speech (2010)	12	4	83rd
The Song of Bernadette (1943)	12	4	16th
Reds (1981)	12	3	54th
The Revenant (2015)	12	3	88th
Lincoln (2012)	12	2	85th
Becket (1964)	12	1	37th
Johnny Belinda (1948)	12	1	21st
The Power of the Dog (2021)	12	1	94th

Most awarded films

Film	Nominations	Wins	Ceremony
Ben-Hur (1959)	12	**11**	32nd
The Lord of the Rings: The Return of the King (2003)	11	**11**	76th
Titanic (1997)	14	**11**	70th
West Side Story (1961)	11	**10**	34th
Gigi (1958)	9	9	31st
The English Patient (1996)	12	9	69th
The Last Emperor (1987)	9	9	60th
Amadeus (1984)	11	8	57th
Cabaret (1972)	10	8	45th
From Here to Eternity (1953)	13	8	26th
Gandhi (1982)	11	8	55th
Gone with the Wind (1939)	13	8	12th
My Fair Lady (1964)	12	8	37th
On the Waterfront (1954)	12	8	27th
Slumdog Millionaire (2008)	10	8	81st
The Best Years of Our Lives (1946)	9	8	19th
Dances with Wolves (1990)	12	7	63rd
Going My Way (1944)	10	7	17th
Gravity (2013)	10	7	86th
Lawrence of Arabia (1962)	10	7	35th
Out of Africa (1985)	11	7	58th
Patton (1970)	10	7	43rd
Schindler's List (1993)	12	7	66th
Shakespeare in Love (1998)	13	7	71st
Star Wars: Episode IV - A New Hope (1977)	11	7	50th
The Bridge on the River Kwai (1957)	8	7	30th
The Sting (1973)	10	7	46th

Printed in Great Britain
by Amazon

86122674R00298